S0-BCR-801

Risk Management and Insurance

Risk Management and Insurance

SEVENTH EDITION

C. Arthur Williams, Jr.
University of Minnesota

Michael L. Smith
Ohio State University

Peter C. Young
University of St. Thomas

McGraw-Hill, Inc.

*New York   St. Louis   San Francisco   Auckland   Bogotá   Caracas
Lisbon   London   Madrid   Mexico City   Milan   Montreal   New Delhi
San Juan   Singapore   Sydney   Tokyo   Toronto*

This book was set in Palatino by Ruttle, Shaw & Wetherill, Inc.
The editor was Theresa Varveris;
the production supervisor was Richard A. Ausburn.
The cover was designed by Joan Greenfield.
Project supervision was done by Ruttle, Shaw & Wetherill, Inc.
R. R. Donnelley & Sons Company was printer and binder.

RISK MANAGEMENT AND INSURANCE

Copyright ©1995, 1989, 1985, 1981, 1976, 1971, 1964 by McGraw-Hill, Inc. All
rights reserved. Printed in the United States of America. Except as permitted
under the United States Copyright Act of 1976, no part of this publication may be
reproduced or distributed in any form or by any means, or stored in a data base
or retrieval system, without the prior written permission of the publisher.

 This book is printed on recycled, acid-free
paper containing 10% postconsumer waste.

1 2 3 4 5 6 7 8 9 0   DOH   DOH   9 0 9 8 7 6 5

ISBN 0-07-070584-4

Library of Congress Cataloging-in-Publication Data
Williams, C. Arthur (Chester Arthur), (date).
   Risk management and insurance / C. Arthur Williams, Michael L.
Smith, Peter C. Young.
     p.   cm.
   Includes bibliographical references and index.
   ISBN 0-07-070584-4
   1. Risk management.   2. Insurance, Business.   3. Insurance.
I. Smith, Michael L.   II. Young, Peter C.   III. Title.
HG8051.W5   1995
658—dc20   94-40588

About the Authors

C. ARTHUR WILLIAMS, Jr., (Ph.D., Graduate School of Business, Columbia University) is Professor Emeritus of the Carlson School of Management at the University of Minnesota. While at the University of Minnesota, Dr. Williams held the Minnesota Industry Chair in Insurance, a chair which, since his retirement, has been renamed the C. Arthur Williams Insurance Industry Chair.

Dr. Williams is widely acclaimed as one of the leading scholars in the field of risk management and insurance. Over his 45 years of academic service, Dr. Williams produced well over 100 publications including textbooks, technical articles, treatises, and research studies. He was especially productive in the field of workers' compensation, and his 1991 publication *An International Comparison of Workers' Compensation* earned Dr. Williams the 1993 Elizur Wright Award.

MICHAEL L. SMITH (Ph.D., Graduate School of Business, University of Minnesota), is an Associate Professor in Risk Management and Insurance in the Max M. Fisher College of Business at The Ohio State University, Columbus. Dr. Smith is treasurer of the Risk Theory Society and trustee of the Griffith Foundation for Insurance Education. He served as a member of the Editorial Board of *The Journal of Risk and Insurance* from 1977 to 1992 and as a member of the Board of Directors of the American Risk and Insurance Association from 1984 to 1987.

Dr. Smith's areas of research include risk management and insurance economics, and he has published extensively in both areas. On two occasions Dr. Smith's published work won the *Journal of Risk and Insurance* research award for a feature article and on one occasion it won the Alpha Kappi Psi Foundation Spangler Award.

PETER C. YOUNG (Ph.D., Graduate School of Business, University of Minnesota), is the E. W. Blanch, Sr. Chair in Insurance at the University of St. Thomas Graduate School of Business in Minneapolis. Dr. Young also holds a Master's degree in Public Administration from the University of Nebraska,

Omaha. Prior to joining the faculty at the University of St. Thomas, he was active in the University of Nebraska's Center for Applied Urban Research, and from 1987 to 1994 he was responsible for the Risk Management and Insurance program at St. Cloud State University.

Dr. Young's research interests lie in the areas of public sector and non-profit risk management. He has written extensively on public sector risk financing pools, and is responsible for a continuing survey of pools underwritten by the Public Risk Management Association (PRIMA). Dr. Young is an academic advisor to PRIMA and a member of the State of Minnesota Risk Management Advisory Board.

To Roberta
C. A. W.

To Ann, Jim, and Julia
M. L. S.

To Sian, Hannah, and Mallory
P. C. Y.

Contents

Part Two
ASSESSING RISK

Part Three
RISK MANAGEMENT METHODS AND TECHNIQUES

Part Four
INSURANCE INSTITUTIONS AND COVERAGES

Part Five
TOPICS IN RISK MANAGEMENT
ADMINISTRATION

20. An Overview of Risk Management Administration   509

Preface

Like the first six editions of *Risk Management and Insurance,* this seventh edition is designed primarily for introductory one-semester or one-quarter courses in risk management and insurance. The content and structure of this text are based on the twin beliefs that (1) the study of insurance, a major tool of risk management, should be preceded by an understanding of procedures and concepts of risk management; and (2) most students will take only one course in the area. For students who plan further study in the area, the balanced treatment of both subjects provides a comprehensive introduction to the field, which can be followed by case courses or more intensive study of specific topics. The authors are pleased to count among readers of earlier editions many persons either professionally engaged as risk managers or holding prominent positions in the insurance industry.

BACKGROUND COURSES AND LEARNING AIDS

The material in the book presumes a background typically found in a junior- or senior-level student majoring in a university program in business administration. Knowledge of accounting, business law or legal environment, economics, finance, management, and statistics are all helpful but not essential to mastering the material in the book. In general, a student whose background includes all six of these areas will find the material in the book relatively straightforward. A student whose background does not include one or more of the six areas is likely to find the material more challenging.

Each chapter begins with an outline of objectives and closes with a list of terms and concepts introduced in the chapter. Important terms and concepts appear in italics when they are introduced. Review questions appear at the end of each chapter. Suggested answers to the review questions appear in an instructor's manual available to teachers who use the book. The instructor's manual also includes suggested course outlines and multiple-choice questions for each chapter.

ORGANIZATION AND DESIGN OF THE TEXT

The seventh edition of the text is divided into five parts. Part One acquaints the student with the concept of risk and with the management of risk in organizations. Part Two discusses the assessment of an organization's exposures to risk. Part Three offers an overview of risk management resources and methods, followed by a discussion of objectives and analysis for the risk management function. Part Four discusses the structure of the insurance industry, the analysis of insurance coverage, and functions related to insurance institutions. Part Five discusses topics in risk management administration, including the management of property and liability insurance coverage and employee benefit programs.

The text is designed to be adaptable within a range of student levels. Certain chapters have been written at a level appropriate for graduate-level introductory course offerings. In particular, the chapter on quantitative methods in risk assessment (Chapter 4) and the chapters on risk management decision methods (Chapters 11 and 12), could prove too challenging for undergraduate courses other than honors sections or advanced offerings. The text is designed to allow the instructor to omit these chapters or to include only selected portions without affecting the continuity of a course. Other surrounding chapters are designed to have little of their material depend critically on chapters 4, 11 and 12.

The text also is designed to offer flexibility with respect to features of the subject that an instructor wishes to emphasize. A course that emphasizes institutional aspects of risk management could be designed around the chapters whose primary purposes are to describe and to develop vocabulary: 1, 2, 3, 5–9, 13–19, and possibly 20–23. A more analytical course would incorporate chapters 4, 10, 11 and 12. The design and administration of employee benefit programs appears in separate chapters (24 and 25) to allow an instructor the option of deferring these subjects to other course offerings.

CHANGES FROM PREVIOUS EDITIONS

When the first edition of this text appeared in 1964, Professors Williams and Heins stated their intent that the book represent a substantial departure from existing texts on insurance principles. All chapters were written from the viewpoint of a risk manager. Business risk management received special emphasis, with management of risks in households treated separately. Although the discussion of insurance principles and institutions was an important part of the book, non-insurance methods of managing risk were prominent. The book added rigor to instruction in the risk management process by adapting statistical and economic analysis to the assessment of risk and to measuring the effectiveness of risk treatment methods.

These themes were maintained in the second through sixth editions. The seventh edition continues in this tradition, with four changes that are outlined below. We believe that fundamental principles identified by Professors Williams and Heins over 30 years ago still govern the risk management process. The four changes merely extend trends that were evident in the first six editions.

First, the book focuses almost exclusively on the management of risks in organizations. Our decision to reduce the discussion of household risk management in no way reflects a belief that the subject is unimportant. Rather, we believe that students who understand the management of risk in organizations can adapt this knowledge to a number of different environments including household risk management as well as financial planning, risk management consultation, brokerage, and so on. Where risks confronted by households are discussed in the seventh edition, they appear in the context of their effect on risk management in organizations.

Second, the statistical and economic analysis has been updated to reflect developments in finance and economics. Much of the updated material appears in Chapters 11 and 12, which present conceptual and analytical methods for handling problems likely to confront risk managers in organizations.

Third, the discussion of public sector risk management has been expanded. Management of risk in the private sector cannot ignore risk management in the public sector, and vice versa. However, we believe that risk management in the public sector has much in common with private sector risk management. Some of the common areas arise from similar issues and similar activities. Other common areas arise from fading boundaries between the public and private sectors. Where differences between the public and private sectors are present, the seventh edition incorporates sections noting the differences.

Fourth, we begin to explore the idea of risk management as a general management function. The key word in the preceding sentence is "begin." While the seventh edition acknowledges the possibility of unified management for all an organization's risks and offers illustrations extending traditional risk management principles into new areas, the text's primary orientation is towards traditional concerns of risk managers, such as: possible damage to the organization's assets, exposure to legal liability, or loss to human resources. The task of shifting towards a more balanced treatment of all an organizations' risks is left to future editions.

CONCEPTUAL APPROACH

Much of the sixth edition's structure survives intact in the seventh edition. The four changes identified earlier in this preface merely extend trends that were evident in the first six editions. Also, the sequence of topics explaining the risk management process (Chapters 1–12) is virtually identical to the pattern followed in the first six editions. Readers who are familiar with previous editions may notice few if any changes in this sequence compared with earlier editions. In planning for the seventh edition, we considered and in a few cases attempted to execute changes in the basic pattern developed by Professors Williams and Heins. Eventually we were drawn back to the strong framework developed by Professors Williams and Heins for explaining the logic of risk management.

The chapters on insurance institutions and coverage (Chapters 13–19) follow a pattern of organization that is different from the sixth edition. The seventh edition's approach is less encyclopedic, oriented towards presenting what the risk manager needs to know about insurance for the effective practice of risk management. The discussion of insurance institutions and types of coverage now focuses on the structure of insurance markets, the functions performed by insurers and insurance regulators, the financial assessment of insurers, and the analysis of insurance coverage. As has been the case with preceding editions, the seventh edition organizes the analysis of insurance coverage into three parts: property and liability insurance, life insurance, and health insurance. The analysis of life and health insurance coverage has been revised to focus on the issues and features that distinguish these lines of coverage from property and liability lines.

When we began writing the seventh edition, we had hoped to avoid much of the detailed description of insurance institutions and practices typically found in texts on risk management, including previous editions of this text. Our belief that risk management is a business function, which is articulated in chapter 2, led us to question the need for an extensive discussion of insurance institutions and types of coverage. Eventually our questions helped us realize that even in the absence of insurance, risk managers think about risks as insurance companies do. For example, they "underwrite" and "price" risks when they establish accounting systems for allocating risk management costs across a corporation's divisions. When insurance is used, the risk manager provides liaison between the organization and the insurance industry on matters such as providing evidence on loss control programs and in negotiating terms of coverage and reimbursement for claims. The seventh edition's discussion of insurance institutions and types of coverage recognizes the close connection between the risk management profession and the insurance industry.

The chapters on topics in risk management administration (Chapters 20–25) also follow a pattern of organization that is different from the sixth edition. In the sixth edition, the discussion of these topics appeared alongside other chapters on risk management resources and methods. We drew these topics together when we recognized two elements they have in common: they extend material presented in earlier chapters and they discuss issues likely to appear in the day-to-day administration of a risk management program. Again, the approach is to present what the risk manager needs to know for the effective practice of risk management.

SIGNIFICANT NEW ADDITIONS

1 In Chapter 2 we anchor the seventh edition's definition of risk management into an expanded view of organizational management: the strategic, operations, and risk management model.
2 Chapter 4 includes new sections on data requirements for risk management and on claim development methods.
3 The discussion of risks related to poor health in Chapter 7 has been expanded significantly, in line with its growing importance as a public policy

issue. Appendix 7.1 at the end of Chapter 7 offers a cultural and historical perspective on government and private methods for alleviating risks involving human resources.

4 The discussion of insurance as a risk financing technique appearing in Chapter 9 incorporates recent developments on the effect of the "law of large numbers" on insurance.

5 Chapter 10 presents new material on pooling and nontraditional risk financing techniques.

6 Chapters 11 and 12 are new chapters on the economic analysis of the risk management function in organizations.

7 Chapter 13 is a new chapter on the structure of the insurance industry. Previous editions discussed the structure of the insurance industry as an issue affecting the implementation of an insurance decision.

8 Chapter 15 now includes appendices 15.1 and 15.2, which offer a brief introduction to principles of accounting for insurance organizations.

9 Chapter 18 extends the concept of life insurance as a two-part contract comprised of term insurance and an investment. The two-part concept is extended to consider analysis of coverage features.

10 Chapter 19 is a new chapter on health insurance. The discussion of coverage features now focuses on efforts to control the behavior of health care providers and consumers.

11 Chapter 20 in a new chapter on day-to-day administrative issues faced by risk managers. Some of the information presented consolidates material previously appearing in other chapters.

12 Chapter 25 is a new chapter on issues affecting the design of employee benefit programs.

ACKNOWLEDGMENTS

A number of individuals contributed to the development of the seventh edition. Students at St. Cloud State University and Ohio State University offered helpful suggestions during classroom testing of chapters. The fact that many of them now enjoy careers in risk management and insurance professions suggests that they, as well as the text, benefited from the experience.

One danger in thanking individuals by name is that those named are likely to expect it, while those not named are not likely to forget it. With advance apology to individuals whose names we forgot to include, we can identify a number of persons who directly affected the final manuscript. Ken MacLeod was editor during nearly all of the development effort. He and the staff of McGraw-Hill provided invaluable advice during the two years the manuscript was being prepared. Fifteen reviewers offered constructive criticism while the manuscript was being written: Stephen Avila, Ball State University; Mark Cross, Louisiana Technical University; Louis Drapeau, Wayne State University, Donald Fehrs, University of Notre Dame; Elizabeth Grace, San Jose State University; Mike McNamara, University of Rhode Island; Joseph Meador, Northeastern University; Gregory Niehaus, University of South Carolina; Bernard Ross, American University; Barry Smith, New Mexico State University; Wayne Snider, Temple

University; Emilio Venezian, Rutgers University; Mary Wald, Temple University; David Ward, University of Wisconsin at Oshkosh; and Rudy Yaksick, Clark University. Ralph Walkling of The Ohio State University provided an insightful review of Chapters 11 and 12. The large number of reviews did not allow us to accept all comments, but reviewers' criticism signficiantly affected both the form and content of the final manuscript. The authors accept full responsibility for any remaining errors.

A number of persons in risk management and insurance professions and in our universities contributed insight or provided support that was important in preparing the seventh edition. Many are cited in references appearing in the text. In addition, we are grateful to the following persons for their contributions: Mike Anderson, Risk Manager of Northern States Power; Jayce Beckstrand and Todd Carlisle, Sedgwick James of Minnesota; Greg Berg of Tillinghast; Mark Blackburn of General Reinsurance Corp.; David Christopherson and Dwaine Tallent of St. Cloud State University; Jim Cicchetti, formerly risk manager at Borden, Inc.; Pat Doyle of Nationwide Insurance Co.; Russ Drake of The Ohio Companies; Mike Evers and Jim Mock, University of St. Thomas; Ron Guilfoile, Risk Manager for the City of St. Paul, Minnesota; Brad Johnson and David Randall of the Public Entities Division of Sedgwick; Fred Johnson, Risk Manager for the State of Minnesota; Felix Kloman of Tillinghast; Logic Associates, Inc.; Pat Mayer of the North Dakota Workers' Compensation Bureau; John Meder, Risk Manager at John W. Galbreath & Co.; members of the Public Risk Management Association; B. J. Reed of the University of Nebraska-Omaha; Ed Rice and Dan Monson of the St. Paul Companies; Steve Stoffel, Larry Lewellen, and Nick Maul, The Ohio State University; members of the Minnesota and Central Ohio chapters of RIMS; Roberta Williams; and Susan Witcraft of Milliman and Robertson.

The dedication of the text reflects our gratitude for the patient support we received from our families during the writing effort. Failing to acknowledge the grace with which they bore the indirect effects of our writing efforts would be gross negligence on our part.

Each edition of this text has been directed towards the goal of improving on its predecessors. Readers can judge whether the seventh edition meets this standard.

C. Arthur Williams, Jr.

Michael L. Smith

Peter C. Young

When life strips off all her finery, what remains is fortune.
Everything that happens is a constant collision of tossed dice.
Roberto Calasso
The Marriage of Cadmus and Harmony

PART ONE

An Overview of Risk and Risk Management

Risk and uncertainty exist whenever the future is unknown. Humankind has struggled through the ages to cope with and address risks and uncertainties, as well as the consequences of risks and uncertainties, and has achieved a modest level of success in doing so. Indeed, one could argue that humanity's struggle to manage or cope with risk is a critical theme in social, economic, and political history.

This textbook examines the formal process of risk management as it is practiced by organizations in the public, private, and nonprofit sectors. Historically, risk management has focused on the adverse consequences of risk. However, risk management is evolving to a position where the management of all risks and all consequences of risk is being done in a more inte-

grated and coordinated fashion. As such, risk management is defined in this textbook to include managing risks with possibly favorable outcomes, in addition to its more obvious role of preventing or controlling risks with only adverse outcomes.

Part 1 introduces the subjects of risk and risk management through a discussion of the concepts and theory of risk as well as through a discussion of the institutional practices of risk management. Chapter 1 covers the subjects of risk and uncertainty. What are they? What is their influence on organizations? Why do we choose to "manage" them? Chapter 2 addresses risk management. What is it, conceptually and in practice, and how did it evolve into its present structure?

An Introduction to Risk and Uncertainty

Learning Objectives

After you have completed this chapter, you should be able to:

1. Differentiate between "risk" and "uncertainty."
2. Explain risk aversion.
3. Distinguish between pure and speculative risk.
4. Distinguish between diversifiable and nondiversifiable risk.
5. Identify the three levels of uncertainty.
6. Explain the relationship between uncertainty and information.
7. Briefly describe how moral issues may relate to the concepts of risk and uncertainty.

INTRODUCTION

On Friday, February 26, 1993, a bomb blast rocked the World Trade Center complex in New York City. The event, apparently the work of a terrorist group protesting American policy in the Middle East, astonished a nation used to witnessing terrorism from a comfortable distance. Over the following days, the tangible and intangible effects of the explosion began to emerge. Early estimates placed the damage to the complex at $100 to $200 million, while the indirect costs to the Port Authority of New York and New Jersey (which owns the complex), the city of New York, and the tenants of the World Trade Center were estimated to exceed $1 billion. Those indirect costs included such things as lost work time, inventory damage/disruption, loss of records, temporary relocation expenses, traffic and transit disruption, and legal and accounting costs. Last, but most certainly not least, six people were killed and over 1000 people were injured as a result of the explosion.

At almost the same time that New York City was reeling from that event, Russian President Boris Yeltsin was locked in a major political struggle with the

Russian Parliament. At stake was the locus of political power in the new republic, and consequently, the future direction of one of the world's largest nations. Meanwhile, in Waco, Texas, local and federal law enforcement officials were mired in a standoff with a heavily armed religious cult. The confrontation, occurring at considerable expense to the public, was at least partially the consequence of an assault on the religious complex that had resulted in numerous casualties to both sides. Finally, two weeks after the New York bombing incident, one of the largest winter storms in one hundred years hammered the eastern coast of the United States, from Florida to Maine, causing losses on a massive scale and over 100 weather-related deaths.

Perhaps the most remarkable aspect of this two-week period is its unremarkability. At any given time in this world, unexpected death, destruction, disruption, and dislocation are occurring on a large scale. Indeed, these four stories overlaid several ongoing stories of equal, if not greater, importance: Florida's continuing struggle to recover from Hurricane Andrew, the conflict in the former Yugoslavian republic; the uneasy peace in Somalia; political negotiations in Cambodia; the worldwide recession; the United States' efforts to control its federal deficit.

Risk and uncertainty also affect life on a less grand scale. A shelter for the homeless wrestles with the uncertainty of obtaining sufficient resources to continue operations. A state legislature encounters risk and uncertainty when considering the economic impact of changes in fiscal policy. A pharmaceutical manufacturer anticipates difficult risks when evaluating the effectiveness of an experimental treatment for Parkinson's disease. A recently unemployed family head contemplates serious economic and human risks when deciding to forego increasingly expensive health insurance.

Noted management scholar Peter F. Drucker recently observed to a conference of risk managers that insurance and risk management may have been as important as entrepreneurship and business acumen in propelling the economic growth of the Western world in the eighteenth, nineteenth, and twentieth centuries. He argues that a society's ability to "manage" fortuity—the unexpected fire, the sudden shipwreck—mainly through insurance and loss control, is probably one of the characteristics that most distinguishes the developed world from the developing world. Disasters befall rich and poor nations alike (earthquakes in Japan, floods in Bangladesh), but a society that is able to control for and cushion against such events, Drucker reasons, is better able to deploy its resources toward economic and social advancement. This textbook is based upon the premise that Drucker's general argument can be extended to organizations. The management of risk provides important economic and organizational benefits to firms, nonprofit organizations, and governmental entities.

Although much in life is beyond the control and understanding of individuals and organizations, much can be done to control and manage uncertainty and risk. Everyday activities have a role in managing risk and uncertainty; wearing seatbelts, salting icy sidewalks, and monitoring and treating high blood pressure can dramatically control certain risks. However, it is the formal process of "risk management" that is this textbook's focus. As will be seen, the benefits of managing risk and uncertainty in a rational and carefully planned manner are significant in their own right, but are particularly important because the impact of uncertainty and risk on life is so pervasive and profound.

Chapter 1 introduces the concepts of risk and uncertainty. The chapter begins with a discussion of terminology, but then moves to the meaning and import of risk and uncertainty as they affect organizations. The chapter concludes with a brief discussion of the motivation to "manage" risks.

ESSENTIAL CONCEPTS: CERTAINTY, UNCERTAINTY, AND RISK

Certainty is lack of doubt. In *Webster's New Collegiate Dictionary,* one meaning of the term "certainty" is "a state of being free from doubt," a definition well-suited to the study of risk management. The antonym of certainty is *uncertainty,* which is "doubt about our ability to predict the future outcome of current actions." Clearly, the term "uncertainty" describes a state of mind. Uncertainty arises when an individual perceives that outcomes cannot be known with certainty.

Risk is potential variation in outcomes. Risk is present in almost everything humans do. When risk is present, the outcome cannot be forecasted precisely. The presence of risk gives rise to uncertainty. *Exposure to risk* is created whenever an act gives rise to possible gain or loss that cannot be predicted. The terms "risk" and "exposure to risk (or loss)" often are used interchangeably and may be used in the sense of an object, a situation, or a category of activities giving rise to outcomes that cannot be predicted. For example, one may hear of dwellings located near a river being exposed to a flood risk. One also may hear of the risk of passing a difficult college course, or the risk of falling in love. This book focuses primarily on risks faced by organizations, which tend to have outcomes that can be expressed in dollars. It should be noted, however, that there will be discussions touching upon many risks that may not have easily identifiable or measurable monetary outcomes, such as loss of political support, poor public image, or outcomes with significant moral or ethical components.

Risk is an objective concept, so it can be measured. Later in the text, formal methods for measuring risk are discussed. For the purpose of introducing the concept of risk informally, an example is shown in Table 1.1, which depicts the outcomes of two bets: One in which the amount at risk is $1, the other in which the amount at risk is $100. The decision to participate in either bet creates exposure to risk. Most individuals, when asked about their willingness to participate in either bet, indicate that the "$100 coin toss" is less desirable, and

TABLE 1.1. Outcomes of $1 and $100 Coin Tosses

	$1 Coin Toss		$100 Coin Toss	
	Outcome	Probability	Outcome	Probability
	+$1	0.5	+$100	0.5
	−$1	0.5	−$100	0.5
Probability of loss	0.5		0.5	
Expected value	$0.0		$0.0	
	(+$1)(0.5) + (−$1)(0.5)		(+$100)(0.5) + (−$100)(0.5)	

many individuals prefer not to bet at all. Their reluctance to bet is explained mainly as a consequence of *risk aversion*. A risk-averse individual prefers predictable outcomes to unpredictability, and tends to be more averse to "high stakes" risks than "low stakes" risks.

In Table 1.1, the notion of risk is captured by observing that the dispersion—or range—of possible outcomes is larger for the $100 coin toss than it is for the $1 coin toss. The bets are identical in all other respects. For both bets, the *probability of loss* (the proportion of outcomes resulting in loss) is 50 percent, or 0.5. Also, the *expected outcome* or *expected value* (the sum of the outcomes weighted by their respective probabilities) for both bets is zero. The expected value is the average gain or loss that would result from participating in the bet a large number of times.

In the example illustrated in Table 1.1, neither expected value nor probability of loss provides a rationale for an individual believing that the $100 coin toss is less desirable. The probability of loss and the expected loss for both bets are identical. However, if we think about what makes the $100 coin toss less desirable (or at least different from the $1 coin toss), we can see that the deviation of the outcomes from what we expect to occur (zero) is greater in the $100 coin toss. Because the variation is greater with the $100 coin toss, risk-averse individuals find it less desirable than the $1 coin toss.

Although a risk-averse individual finds the "$100 coin toss" less attractive, he or she may be willing to accept this risk if provided compensation. For example, some (but not all) risk-averse individuals are willing to participate in the $100 coin toss if paid $10 for participating. The level of necessary compensation is called the *risk premium*, which is the minimum amount over and above the expected value required to induce the individual to participate in the bet. We noted in Table 1.1 that the expected value of the "$100 coin toss" is zero in the absence of compensation. With a $10 risk premium, participating in the bet causes the individual's expected wealth to increase by $10.

The effect of the $10 compensation on the outcomes is shown in Table 1.2. The effect of the $10 inducement illustrates a consequence of risk aversion: In the absence of compensation, a risk-averse individual is unwilling to accept a risk whose expected value is zero. Instead, the risk-averse individual requires compensation over and above the expected value of the bet (i.e., a positive risk premium). Conversely, a risk-averse individual who faces risk is willing to compensate someone else for bearing this risk. In other words, risk aversion causes the individual to be willing to pay more than the expected value of losses for an insurance policy to cover the losses.

An individual's willingness to participate in a risky activity whose out-

TABLE 1.2. Effect of $10 Compensation on the $100 Coin Tosses

	Outcome	Probability
	+$110	0.5
	−$90	0.5
Probability of loss	0.5	
Expected value	$10.0	
	(+$110)(0.5) + (−$90)(0.5)	

comes and probabilities are known depends partly upon the degree of risk aversion. Even though two individuals may agree on the possible outcomes and their likelihood of occurrence, they may take different actions—and this behavior largely can be explained by differing aversions to risk.

What causes one person to be more risk averse than another? This is a question best answered by psychologists, sociologists, or anthropologists. However, it is safe to say that family and societal influences, genetics, and religious/philosophical beliefs all play an important role. Somewhat less clear is the relationship between a person's risk aversion and his or her uncertainty; a problem that is influenced by the imprecise way the terms "aversion" and "uncertainty" commonly are used. In some respects, uncertainty could be affected by aversion. For example, an individual might be so wary of risk in general that she/he would tend to discount her/his own judgment regarding a particular risk. In that respect, her/his level of uncertainty regarding a particular risk might be driven higher by her/his aversion to risk. In other situations, it is possible to say that uncertainty influences aversion, in that a person consistently exposed to an environment of seemingly random and unpredictable events (say, a citizen of Sarajevo) might eventually develop a high level of aversion to risk.

Some scholars have taken a different approach to relating risk, risk aversion, and uncertainty to one another. For instance, Williams and Heins (Williams and Heins, 1989) discuss risk as consisting of objective and subjective components. Objective risk refers to the measurable component of risk, while subjective risk reflects an individual's reaction to (attitude toward) risk. In this approach, uncertainty becomes an aspect of subjective risk. Other views are possible and perhaps the best that can be said is that risk aversion and uncertainty are distinct concepts that are not fully independent of one another.

Later in this textbook (Chapter 8), readers are exposed to the importance of information in reducing uncertainty. As a general proposition, information lessens the doubt a person has about the predictability of outcomes, thus reducing uncertainty. For instance, statistical information on the safety of nuclear power plants can reduce the level of uncertainty regarding potential outcomes. This is not to say that such information either reduces the risk itself or changes a person's aversion to risk. Indeed, information might heighten a person's aversion to risk if the statistical information reveals the risk to be much worse than expected. However, if readers can imagine uncertainty as a fog that obscures a hiker's view of a dangerous mountain path, they are likely to conclude that it is preferable to have the fog lift—revealing as it would the terrifying images of the dangerous path—rather than to grope blindly with great uncertainty. Is the basic "risk" (the hazardous path) reduced in this situation? No. Is the hiker's risk aversion lessened? No, but the hiker's decisions are more likely to be responsive and proportional to the risk, and this usually is a desirable result.

SOME FURTHER CONCEPTS RELATED TO RISK

Pure and Speculative Risks

Traditionally, textbooks on risk management and insurance have distinguished between pure and speculative risks (see, for instance, Mowbray, Blanchard, and

Williams, 1969). A *pure risk* exists when there is a chance of loss but no chance of gain. For example, the owner of an automobile faces the risk associated with a potential collision loss. If a collision occurs, the owner will suffer a financial loss. If no collision occurs, the owner does not gain, so the owner's financial position remains unchanged. A *speculative risk* exists when there is a chance of gain as well as a chance of loss. For instance, investment in a capital project might be profitable or it might prove to be a failure. Pure risks are always distasteful, but speculative risks possess some attractive features.

To a large extent, the distinction between pure and speculative risks is semantic. Typically, a given risk has both pure and speculative elements. For example, the owner of a dwelling faces the risk that the value of the dwelling at the end of a year may be greater or smaller than its current value. The potential variation in the value of the dwelling arises from a number of sources, including possible fire damage and possible changes in the market value of dwellings generally. Customarily the fire risk is considered a pure risk, while possible loss in market value is not. However, the fire risk and the market value risk are both elements of the total risk faced by the dwelling owner. Though the line between pure and speculative risks may be weak, this text will continue to make the distinction between pure and speculative risk because there is evidence that people react differently to each type of risk, and—perhaps most importantly—very few functions within an organization (or courses that study those functions) tend to focus on pure risks and their effect on the organization.

The differing reactions to pure and speculative risks can be illustrated in a number of ways. For instance, it is possible that the skills required for successful management of pure risks may not be identical to the skills required for successful management of speculative risks. Several experiments suggest that individuals may react differently in pure risk and speculative risk situations (Hammond, 1968). In one experiment, most subjects were unwilling to participate in a speculative venture that presented the possible gain of $100 and a possible loss of $4,900 unless the probability of winning was at least 99 percent, that is, the probability of losing was 1 percent or less. In the same experiment, however, most subjects were unwilling to pay a fee of $100 to avoid a loss of $5,000 in a situation in which the only possible outcomes were either the $5,000 loss or no loss—unless the probability of loss was 10 percent or more. For lower probabilities of loss they preferred to retain the risk associated with a possible gain of $100 (the "premium" saving) or a net loss of $4,900 (the $5,000 loss less the premium saving). One possible explanation for this difference in risk attitudes is that in the speculative risk situation the subjects had to take action to assume the risk. In the pure risk situation the subjects had to take action to rid themselves of the risk. Another possible explanation is that in the pure risk situation the subjects did not fully appreciate the risk they were retaining.

The essence of the differences in attitudes regarding pure and speculative risk also can be grasped with a simple real world illustration. An individual may sit down one morning to pay bills, including the payment of premiums for life, disability, health, automobile, and liability insurance. The buying of insurance is demonstrably the action of a risk-averse person. That afternoon, the same person may board a plane for a vacation of gambling and recreation in Las Vegas; risk-taking behavior, to say the least. How do we explain risk aversion and risk taking within a single individual? One way that is relevant to this discussion may be to note that pure and speculative risks offer distinctly different arrays of possible outcomes. The presence of an opportunity for gain may lead to risk taking under speculative risk conditions, whereas the absence of gain may eliminate motivation for risk taking. In any event, risk-taking and risk-averting behaviors may be viewed as consistent if we recognize that pure and speculative risks are fundamentally different.

Diversifiable and Nondiversifiable Risks

Some risks affect nearly all humans at the same time; the risk of worldwide economic depression is an example. Other risks are faced almost in isolation; the risk of automobile accident or theft of property are examples. Unless the manifestation of a risk affects organizations or individuals in the same way and at the same time, it is possible for the affected entities to reduce their risk through pooling or sharing agreements.

A risk is *diversifiable* if it is possible to reduce risk through pooling or risk-sharing agreements. A risk is *nondiversifiable* if pooling agreements are ineffective in reducing risk for the participants in the pool. For example, pooling agreements would be ineffective with respect to the risk of worldwide depression, as the risk affects all participants in much the same way and at the same time.

The distinction is best developed in the finance literature on pricing of marketable securities. Returns on individual securities tend to be correlated, but not perfectly. Hence, it is possible for an investor to reduce the risk by holding a diversified portfolio of securities rather than individual securities comprising the portfolio. The risk of holding a diversified portfolio of securities is not zero, however; the risk that remains in a well-diversified portfolio cannot be reduced through further diversification. This remaining risk, which is called *systematic risk*, involves movement in a group average over time. In contrast, *nonsystematic risk* involves deviation of individual security returns from the group average. Systematic risk cannot be reduced by pooling or diversification, while nonsystematic risk can.

The distinction between diversifiable and nondiversifiable risk is important in risk management because it affects the usefulness of pooling or risk-sharing agreements. To illustrate, the owner of a dwelling located in Miami, Florida, faces the risk of windstorm loss to the dwelling. The risk could be reduced through a loss-sharing agreement with other dwelling owners in Miami, but the effectiveness of the pooling agreement would be limited by the possibility of windstorm damaging a large number of dwellings in the pool at the same time—the aftermath of Hurricane Andrew is a powerful illustration of this point. A pooling agreement with owners of dwellings situated in other cities such as New York or St. Louis would be more effective in reducing their risk. However, even if the pooling agreement were extended worldwide, the participants in the pool would still face risk; the remaining risk after the pooling agreement is nondiversifiable. Presumably, this nondiversifiable risk would be the risk associated with not being able to predict the *number* of serious windstorms and the resulting damage worldwide in a given year.

From a slightly different perspective the distinction between diversifiable and nondiversifiable risk has another important effect. Risks that are "diversifiable" within a particular organization are more amenable to internal treatment than others. For instance, an organization might seek to pay directly for all costs arising from injuries incurred by employees while on the job. This risk may be manageable internally because, for the most part, worker injuries are independent of one another. As a consequence, the organization can spread the cost and the risk across its workforce. On the other hand, self-funding of the costs of unemployment for that same workforce (though sometimes done) is more problematic since the risk affects all employees in much the same way and arises from conditions external to the organization. That is, whereas individuals laboring in a common environment face a common risk of injury, the actual incidence is faced individually while unemployment comes to many in a single circumstance. The unemployment risk is not as diversifiable as the risk of work-related injury and is probably not as appropriate for internal pooling.

SOME FURTHER ISSUES RELATED TO UNCERTAINTY

Levels of Uncertainty

Uncertainty is doubt about our ability to predict outcomes. Uncertainty arises when an individual perceives risk. Uncertainty is a subjective concept, so it cannot be measured directly. Since uncertainty is a state of mind, it varies across individuals.

For complex activities, such as participating in a business venture, some persons are very cautious, while others are more aggressive. Although risk aversion explains some of the reluctance to participate, the level of risk perceived by individuals also plays a key role. The perceived level of risk depends on information that an individual can use to evaluate the likelihood of outcomes and, perhaps, on the individual's ability to evaluate this information. The level and type of information on the nature of a risky activity have an important effect on uncertainty. This type of uncertainty was not an issue in the coin tosses discussed in the previous section, in which the outcomes and their probabilities are known.

For the purposes of studying risk and risk management, a dictionary definition of the term "uncertainty" fails to make these distinctions, which can be important. Our ability to predict the future outcome of an action is strongly affected by the amount and type of information available to forecast the consequences of our actions. In other words, uncertainty is present in levels or degrees, which are illustrated in Table 1.3.

When no uncertainty is present, we are certain about our prediction; certainty is present when we can predict outcomes with no doubt. Examples of certainty are predictions from physical laws, such as the law of gravity or laws of motion in physics. The predictions from these laws closely correspond to the actual outcomes, often to the limits of our measuring instruments.

At level 1, the lowest level of uncertainty, possible outcomes have been identified and we know the likelihood of occurrence. Level 1 can be described as *objective uncertainty* (Machina and Schmeidler, 1992). Many games of chance,

TABLE 1.3. The Certainty–Uncertainty Continuum

Level of Uncertainty	Characteristics	Examples
None (certainty)	Outcomes can be predicted with precision	Physical laws, natural sciences
Level 1 (objective uncertainty)	Outcomes are identified and probabilities are known	Games of chance: cards, dice
Level 2 (subjective uncertainty	Outcomes are identified but probabilities are unknown	Fire, automobile accident, many investments
Level 3	Outcomes are not fully identified and probabilities are unknown	Space exploration, genetic research

such as cards, dice, or roulette, offer examples of the first level of uncertainty. In these games, the outcomes are fixed by the bets of the participants and the probabilities are known or can be calculated. The coin tosses illustrated earlier in Table 1.1 offer an example of the first level of uncertainty.

At level 2, we are uncertain about probabilities, although the possible outcomes have been identified. Uncertainty at level 2 could be present in a game of chance if the relative likelihood of outcomes is unknown (for example, predicting the color of a ball drawn at random from an urn containing 100 balls that are known to be either red or white, where the proportion colored red is unknown).

Level 2, which can be described as *subjective uncertainty,* characterizes many business ventures, investment projects, and insured risks. As an example, the owner of a vehicle that might be damaged in an accident can identify possible outcomes: The vehicle may or may not be involved in an accident. If an accident occurs, the amount of damage may range from minor amounts to the total loss of the vehicle. Most vehicle owners, however, will not have accurate estimates for the probability of the vehicle being involved in an accident, let alone for the likelihood of different amounts of damage. These estimates, if available, will depend on issues such as the terrain over which the vehicle is driven, the time of driving, the driving habits of the owner as well as of other drivers, the level of maintenance used on the vehicle, and repair costs.

At level 3, we are uncertain about the nature of the outcomes themselves, which have not been fully identified. Examples of uncertainty falling at this level are the early attempts at space exploration and the development of peacetime uses for atomic energy. In these projects, as well as in many types of scientific research, the nature of all possible outcomes may not be completely identified prior to undertaking the project. Presumably, the human desire for expanding the limits of knowledge and the quest for economic gains from exploiting new technology are inducements to undertake activities at this highest level of uncertainty.

The Response to Uncertainty

Uncertainty can have profound effects on human behavior. In extreme cases, uncertainty may lead to paralysis or inaction; more commonly, uncertainty affects levels of compensation required to undertake risky activities. Uncertainty also may cause individuals or entities to safeguard against outcomes they have identified as especially undesirable. For example, a research laboratory may be unwilling to develop a vaccine against a fatal communicable disease without a government promise to reimburse liability judgments against the laboratory for adverse effects of the vaccine. Clearly, the response to uncertainty will be partially influenced by the level of uncertainty.

The management of risks falling at level 1 is close to being a science. Gambling houses can forecast the profitability of their operations despite being unable to predict the outcome of individual plays of games of chance. Mortality (i.e., risk of loss of life) in large groups of individuals is another example of an uncertainty at level 1. Unfortunately, most important risks encountered by organizations involve uncertainty levels 2 and 3. The organization must rely on less-than-scientific methods to evaluate and control risks at these levels.

The level of uncertainty arising from a given type of risk can depend on the entity facing the risk; for example, an insurer or a governmental entity may regard the risk of earthquake as being at level 2, while the individual may regard the earthquake as being at level 3. This difference in perspective may be a consequence of an ability to estimate the likelihood of outcomes. An insurer or government entity has the resources to study the phenomenon of earthquake. If the insurer wishes to write earthquake insurance, it also has an economic incentive to develop reliable estimates. These estimates often are beyond the capacity of the individual.

Also, an entity facing a risk may take actions that move uncertainty to a lower level. Contractual limits may move uncertainty from level 3 to level 2. Many forms of liability insurance, for example, involve uncertainty at level 3. The outcome of the exposure to liability depends on the future evolution of the legal environment, which includes rules of law for determining whether an individual or entity is liable and if so, the amount of liability. However, insurers normally place limits on the amount of their liability, which allows at least two outcomes (the maximum and minimum loss) to become identified. This limitation tends to move the insurer's uncertainty from level 3 to level 2. Another example is the corporate form of organization, which limits an investor's possible loss to the amount invested.

In general, one would expect risk-averse individuals to prefer lower levels of uncertainty in the sense that they are willing to pay for information or for other acts that resolve uncertainty to a lower level. Insurance offers an obvious example: A driver who perceives the risk of automobile accident at level 2 is willing to pay an insurance premium exceeding the expected value of accidental damage for a policy to reimburse the damage. Because the insurer has expertise in evaluating this risk, its uncertainty is at level 1, while the uncertainty for the individual driver is at level 2 or 3.

Uncertainty, Information, and Communication

The reduction of uncertainty has economic value, and information can reduce uncertainty—as was noted earlier in this chapter. The level of uncertainty depends on the amount and type of information available to identify possible outcomes and estimate their likelihood. Communication can reduce levels of uncertainty in an organization's *stakeholders,* those whose well-being can be affected by the organization's activities. For a modern corporation, examples of stakeholders include investors, the corporation's employees, insurers writing policies to cover the corporation's losses, suppliers and customers, and creditors. For governments and nonprofit organizations, many of these stakeholders would also be present, but in these entities "the public," other governmental entities, volunteers, and contributors would have to be added to the list. Communication between the organization and these stakeholder groups is an important part of the manager's responsibility.

By communicating the organization's policies for managing risk, the organization may reduce levels of uncertainty in these stakeholders, which increases their willingness to deal with the organization on favorable terms. In the absence of this information, these stakeholders may be uncertain about the nature of the organization's actions with respect to matters affecting their interests. Their uncertainty leads them to charge a higher price for their goods and services or place restrictions on their activities that can be detrimental to other stakeholder groups, especially stockholders.

In other words, the organization can provide stakeholders with the assurance that it has not and will not take actions that are detrimental to their interests. The effect of the information is to reduce the level of uncertainty, which translates into an increased firm value, in the case of a for-profit organization. In the case of a governmental entity, the reduced uncertainty translates into favorable terms in financial markets (e.g., a lower rate of interest on bonds issued by a municipal hospital that institutes measures to protect itself from the consequences of legal liability). Ultimately, the taxpayer benefits when the reduced uncertainty translates into lower interest costs for the hospital.

The mere act of communication, however, does not necessarily reduce uncertainty unless the message is credible. In the short run, perhaps, stakeholders may be deceived by misleading signals concerning the organization's actions with regard to matters affecting their interests, but in the long run the true effects will become evident. Credibility is established if the context of the communication is factual and accurately reflects the intent of the organization's managers with regard to the issue of concern to a stakeholder group.

Two Specific Concepts Related to Uncertainty

Later in this textbook, insurance will be identified as an arrangement for reducing uncertainty. However, in the context of the present discussion, readers should be aware that insurance companies (or any risk assumers/retainers) encounter aspects of risk or uncertainty that are largely unique to the insurance arrangement. Though the reader's knowledge of insurance may be limited at present, the concepts of *adverse selection* and *moral hazard* are of such general importance to risk management that they are discussed here.

Adverse selection (occasionally, "antiselection") is the result of insurance having the greatest appeal to the individuals who are likely to have a loss. As a consequence, the demand for insurance is largest for individuals who are most likely to have a loss or, more generally, who expect their loss to be larger than average. The adverse selection problem is especially acute when buyers of insurance can conceal information that the insurer could use to evaluate the likelihood of loss or the amount of damage. For example, the demand for health insurance is likely to be high for an individual who feels in poor health, and the individual's feeling about his or her own health condition is not likely to be revealed to the health insurer.

Moral hazard describes the tendency of insurance to reduce incentives to prevent loss. Obviously, an individual's incentives to prevent loss are reduced when insurance is present to cover the loss. As an example, an individual who has health insurance covering routine visits to doctors' offices is more likely to use these medical services at the first sign of illness. More generally, the term *hazard* means a condition that increases the likelihood of loss or loss amount. A *physical hazard* refers to a physical condition or characteristic, such as flammable liquids stored near open flame, while a *moral hazard* describes an effect on an individual's behavior. Arson would be an extreme example of a moral hazard; here, the individual deliberately sets fire to collect insurance proceeds. A less extreme example (sometimes called a "morale hazard") is a person who, after leaving home for vacation, cannot recall whether all the doors on the house are locked. The existence of a theft insurance policy decreases the likelihood that the person will return home to check whether the doors are locked.

Moral hazard and adverse selection can pose significant problems for insurance companies, so much so that they choose to withdraw from providing a particular type of coverage. Moral hazard and adverse selection can also result from insurance-like arrangements in which no insurance company is present, and this is why the concepts are of general importance to the risk manager. The presence of any arrangement to pay for fortuitous losses may alter behaviors or provide unintended motivations. A good example would be an organization that directly pays benefits to employees who are injured on the job (i.e., they are self-insuring workers' compensation benefits). If care is not taken to monitor claims for benefits, fraudulent claims may be filed (moral hazard: the non-injured employee is seeking to "profit" from the financing arrangement). In the case of a self-insured group health insurance plan, slack supervision of employee enrollment practices could result in adverse selection problems (employees would only enroll when they believed they would require the benefits). In such situations, the risk manager's thought processes will be very similar to an insurance company's, in that the rules for "underwriting" the risks, for "pricing" the risks, and for controlling the cost of losses that occur will be of foremost importance.

RISK, UNCERTAINTY, AND MORALITY

Often, it is easy to focus upon risk and uncertainty as concepts devoid of emotional, or even ethical, content. In the abstract, risk could be seen as nothing more than a matter of probabilities, while uncertainty could be said to reflect our inability to know those probabilities. However, such a purely clinical view is troubling in a study of risk management. The impulse to manage risk and uncertainty, it may be argued, arises as much from morality as from science.

In an article on technological perspectives or risk management, Dr. Vernon

Leslie Grose describes his entry to the field of risk management as being motivated by "moral outrage" (Grose, 1992). Although he explains this outrage in the context of a personal story, his point can be generalized. Risk presents opportunity for gain or advancement, or for loss. Both of these outcomes may have profound moral implications: The probabilities of premature death are abstract, but the consequence of the risk is that a human being dies. Likewise, an organization might review its methods for disposing of hazardous waste with an eye toward the probabilities of legal liability, while ignoring its moral stewardship obligations to the environment. The consequences of risk and uncertainty are, commonly, visceral, and they often raise questions of right and wrong, good and evil.

What does this moral dimension of risk and uncertainty mean? Most importantly, it means that humans are motivated to deal with risk and uncertainty (to practice "risk management") for reasons beyond bottom-line considerations. Often, the management of risk and uncertainty may be understood to involve measures taken to fulfill the moral obligations owed to the world and to the human beings in the world.

An illustration is important here. An organization may be engaged in an activity that generates life-threatening risks for its employees and others, for example, working with hazardous materials or working in hazardous conditions. The organization has legal obligations to these workers in the form of legislated obligations (workers' compensation laws, right-to-know laws) and in the form of civil law (wrongful death cases, product liability cases). The organization also has moral obligations to safeguard those employees that transcend its narrower legal duties. In many ways, moral obligations are more exacting than legal duties, though defining the moral obligation may be very difficult. In any event, it would be improper for a textbook on risk management to ignore the moral implications of risk and uncertainty simply because measurement or quantification is difficult.

MANAGING RISK AND UNCERTAINTY

Risk and uncertainty have an important impact on organizations in that they exact a cost, commonly referred to as the *cost of risk*. The cost of risk is a widely-discussed concept in professional and academic circles, and though there are discrepancies in definition, the general thrust of the concept is that risk imposes costs on an organization that would not be incurred in a world of certainty. The most obvious cost is the *cost of losses;* that is, one of the consequences of risk and uncertainty is that a loss may occur—property is destroyed, a human is injured, a court rules against an organization. A second cost of risk is the *cost of uncertainty itself* (Willett, 1951). Even if no losses occur, the presence of risk and uncertainty may impose a cost. On its most basic level, the cost of uncertainty can be illustrated by "worry." Even if an individual never has an automobile accident, the risk of an accident takes a toll—fear, sleepless nights, and of course, the cost of insurance that is paid even when losses do not occur.

On an organizational level, the cost of uncertainty may appear in the form of worry or anxiety, but is probably most clearly seen in the misallocation of resources. This means that organizations do not deploy their resources in an optimal fashion because uncertainty clouds their judgment, or because the fear of loss discourages investment in certain activities. The reluctance of some pharmaceutical companies to invest in new product development (for fear of product liability suits) is often cited as an illustration of this cost of risk. Needless to say, the cost of uncertainty is very difficult to measure, though it may be the more damaging of the two costs of risk.

Risk and uncertainty also bestow benefits, however. Certainly life is more interesting when risk and uncertainty are present. Further, speculative risks can result in positive outcomes, in which the organization or individual is rewarded for facing the risk. Ideally, an organization would seek to manage its affairs to maximize both the possibility and value of such outcomes.

Undoubtedly, organizations have a motivation to address risk and uncertainty since the consequences are so important. This motivation gives rise to "risk management." At its most basic level, risk management is practiced because the negative and positive possibilities of risk (as well as moral considerations) provide incentives for an organization to take steps to minimize the costs of risk—in all their forms—and to maximize the benefits of risk. Chapter 2 introduces the formal practice of risk management, discusses its history, and explains its basic concepts and principles.

Key Concepts

risk The potential variation in outcomes.

uncertainty The doubt in our minds concerning our ability to predict the future.

exposure to risk A situation created whenever an act gives rise to possible gain or loss that cannot be predicted.

risk premium The amount over and above the expected value required to induce an individual to participate in a bet or risk.

pure risk A risk in which a gain is not possible. The best outcome is that no loss occurs.

speculative risk A risk in which either a gain or a loss may occur.

diversifiable/nondiversifiable risk Risk that may/may not be reduced through pooling or risk-sharing agreements.

adverse selection A potential effect of insurance whereby worse-than-average risks are likely to buy insurance.

moral hazard A potential cost of insurance in which the presence of insurance increases the tendency for losses to occur through careless, irresponsible, or perhaps illegal behavior. "Morale" hazard is a term sometimes used to distinguish between careless (morale) and illegal (moral) behavior.

cost of risk The cost imposed upon organizations because of the presence of risk. Its component parts are (1) the cost of losses that do occur and (2) the cost of uncertainty itself.

Review Questions

1. Uncertainty has a generally negative connotation. Are there positive aspects of uncertainty? What might they be?

2. Two students consider a vacation trip, when it is learned that a significant part of the trip must be taken in an 18-seat commuter plane. Based upon that fact, one of the students decides to stay home while the other goes. What might explain their differing decisions? What factors might explain why their decisions differ?

3. The text discusses levels of uncertainty at some length. Identify illustrations of level 1, 2, and 3 uncertainties in your life. Can you identify a situation in which a risk you face has moved from one level to another? How and why did that happen?

4. Attending college creates risks with both a pure and a speculative nature. Identify three pure and three speculative risks that you encounter by attending college.

5. Explain the difference between diversifiable and nondiversifiable risk.

6. Would you describe yourself as a risk-taker, as risk-averse, or as risk-neutral? How would you explain why you are risk taking, averse, or neutral? Is your attitude toward risk different when facing pure versus speculative risks? Why or why not?

7. Consider the situations below. Identify (1) possible pure and speculative risks present, (2) what kind of information might be useful to reduce the uncertainty you would have, and (3) any moral or ethical issues that might arise from the risk and uncertainty of each situation.

   Situation A: You are on a citizen advisory committee that is responsible for recommending a location for a new nuclear power facility.

   Situation B: You are a director of marketing for an industrial equipment manufacturer, and your company is considering marketing its commercial-grade drill press in Latin America.

   Situation C: You are President of the United States, and you must decide whether to send troops into a foreign country that is experiencing civil unrest, which could spill over into neighboring countries.

   Situation D: You are a superintendent of public schools in a large metropolitan area, and you are trying to decide whether to abandon school busing programs and replace them with "neighborhood schools."

References and Suggestions for Additional Reading

CARTER, R. L., and N. A. DOHERTY (EDS.): *Handbook of Risk Management* (London: Kluwer-Harrop Handbooks, 1974), pt. 1.

DOHERTY, N. A.: *Corporate Risk Management* (New York: McGraw-Hill Book Company, 1985), chaps. 1 and 2.

GROSE, VERNON LESLIE: "Risk Management from a Technological Perspective," *The Geneva Papers on Risk and Insurance* 12 (No. 64, July 1992), pp. 335–342.

HAMMOND, J. D. (ed.): *Essays in the Theory of Risk and Insurance* (Glenview, Ill.: Scott, Foresman, and Company, 1968).

MACHINA, MARK J. and DAVID SCHMEIDLER: "A More Robust Definition of Subjective Probability," *Econometrica* (Vol. 60, no. 4, 1992), pp. 745–780.

MEHR, R. I., and B. A. HEDGES: *Risk Management: Concepts and Applications* (Homewood, Ill.: Richard D. Irwin, Inc., 1974), chap. 1.

────── and ──────: *Risk Management in the Business Enterprise* (Homewood, Ill.: Richard D. Irwin, Inc., 1963), chap. 1.

MOWBRAY, A. H., R. H. BLANCHARD, and C. A. WILLIAMS, JR.: *Insurance* (6th ed., New York: McGraw-Hill Book Co., 1969).

PFEFFER, IRVING: *Insurance and Economic Theory* (Homewood, Ill.: Richard D. Irwin, Inc. 1956).

SCHOEMAKER, PAUL J. H.: *Experiments on Decisions Under Risk: The Expected Utility Hypothesis* (Boston: Kluwer-Nijhoff Publishing, 1980).

WILLETT, A. H.: *The Economic Theory of Risk and Insurance* (Philadelphia: The University of Pennsylvania Press, 1951).

WILLIAMS, C. A. Jr., and RICHARD M. HEINS: *Risk Management and Insurance, 6th ed.* (New York: McGraw-Hill Publishing Co., 1989).

CHAPTER 2

An Introduction to Risk Management

Learning Objectives

After you have completed this chapter, you should be able to:

1. Summarize the historical and current practices of risk management.
2. Discuss the relationship between risk management and insurance buying.
3. Identify the differences between the traditional view of risk management and this textbook's view of risk management.
4. Describe briefly the basic elements of risk management.
5. Identify the relationship between risk management, operations management, and strategic management.
6. Define risk management and briefly explain its purpose and value to organizations.

INTRODUCTION

Beginning with Chapter 3 and continuing to the concluding chapter, this textbook discusses risk management by introducing and analyzing its component parts. For newcomers to the subject, however, it is useful to begin with an initial bird's eye view of risk management and to provide a framework for analysis. This is the purpose of Chapter 2.

The chapter begins with a brief history of risk management. Of particular interest are the organizational functions that preceded and influenced risk management as well as the forces that affected its growth. The chapter then turns to a discussion of current risk management practices. Within this review of current practices, similarities and differences between public, private, and nonprofit risk management responsibilities and activities are noted. Following a discussion of current practices, the chapter provides a discussion of competing views of risk management. This discussion gives way to an introduction to this textbook's view of risk management; a view that is somewhat at variance with current practices and views. The authors believe, however, that this conceptual view is harmonious with the general direction of risk management's evolution, and that it allows the textbook to consider important questions concerning the logic and consistency of certain current practices and views.

HISTORICAL DEVELOPMENT OF THE RISK MANAGEMENT FUNCTION

Risk management has been practiced informally since the dawn of time. Prehistoric humans banded together in tribes to conserve resources, share responsibilities, and provide some protection against the uncertainties of life. Even today, *informal* risk management is practiced by almost everyone, whether they are conscious of it or not. We wear our seatbelts to reduce the likelihood of serious injury, we exercise and eat a proper diet to improve our prospects for good health. However, this textbook is focused on the *formal* practice of risk management as it is undertaken by organizations. The history of formal organizational risk management is of much shorter duration and much narrower scope.

Earlier editions of this textbook emphasized the recognition of "risk management–like" activities by early twentieth century management scholars—the work of Henri Fayol was particularly influential and is discussed in Chapter 20. While recognition of such foundations is important, risk management, as it is practiced today, essentially is a post–World War II phenomenon. Even within this limited time frame, risk management in most organizations prior to 1960 was fairly narrow in scope. Certainly, scholarly study of risk management does not extend much farther back than the mid-1950s.

Early Post–World War II

There is some controversy over whether scholars accelerated the development of risk management or whether business practice inspired scholars, but there is little doubt that the period from 1955 to 1964 gave birth to modern risk management, both academically and professionally (Snider, 1991). This is not to say that formal risk management did not exist prior to this time, but rather that risk management did not enjoy a widely agreed upon meaning to both practitioners and scholars until this period.

Like most managerial functions, risk management has predecessor functions. Perhaps the most influential of these is insurance buying. Most modern risk management positions evolved out of an insurance-buying function, and this historical artifact casts a very long shadow even today (as will be seen). The same can be said of the academic field of risk management; it is typically taught and researched within insurance departments, and the preeminent academic journal in the field, the *Journal of Risk and Insurance,* was known as the *Journal of Insurance* until 1964.

The evolutionary process that moved insurance buying to risk management is not easy to summarize, since it has not occurred uniformly nor sequentially in all cases. Indeed, a survey of organizations today would find widely varying levels of practice; many organizations have no one responsible for risk management or insurance buying, some only have a part-time insurance buyer, while others have highly sophisticated risk management programs. It is possible, however, to describe the direction of the evolutionary process.

In the early post–World War II era, most organizations that practiced any formal risk or insurance management had a part-time or full-time insurance buyer, whose duties essentially covered the placement and management of the insurance portfolio and some related duties. Within a number of these organizations, duties began to expand as the number of insurance coverages multiplied and the issues associated with insurance buying became more complex. Sometimes insurance market behavior influenced this expansion, sometimes it was a manager's initiative or ability, and sometimes the growth was due to risk characteristics of the organization. Nevertheless, the expansion of the function was sufficiently noticeable by the mid-1950s for both academicians and practitioners to begin the process of defining the function (usually the first stage in the development of any discipline). This period remains to this day the most fruitful period of academic research on the subject of risk management—the first edition of this textbook being but one example of that activity (Crockford, 1982).

Early studies reflect some of the tensions that were to influence the field from that day forward (for instance, see Snider, 1956). While risk management appeared to be evolving to a broader management function, organizations tended to persist in viewing risk management as a subfunction of finance—owing to the financial nature and purchasing processes of insurance buying. On a practitioner level, this tension was most obviously manifested in the placement of the risk manager within the organization. Insurance buyers mainly were located in either a finance department, a purchasing department, or, later (when employee benefit concerns became important) a human resources department. However, by the late 1950s, a number of risk managers (the term "risk manager" became more widely used during this period as well) began to express the view that their duties had moved beyond merely financial or purchasing concerns. Interestingly, most risk managers today remain placed within finance or purchasing departments, so the issue has not been resolved.

Post-1960

One of the important evolutionary stories in risk management is the movement away from the use of traditional insurance products (a phenomenon discussed thoroughly in Chapters 9 and 10). Although insurance is still used widely, larger organizations have reduced their reliance on more conventional arrangements as risk managers discovered that some risks were not insurable, or that insurance did not meet specific organizational needs, or that certain internal activities could control the impact of risk and uncertainty on the organization. For instance, some very large organizations found that they were able to forecast certain types of losses as well as the insurer, which led to decisions to "self-insure" risks. In other organizations, loss prevention activities were found to be an effective response to particularly challenging problems. Regardless of how this discovery process occurred within individual organizations, the cumulative effect was the expansion of the insurance buyer/risk manager function and an important shift away from insurance buying.

Though insurance buying is clearly the foundation for risk management today, other influences are important. Attorneys within organizations have had a major influence on the management of "liability" risks. Operations management experts have influenced the development of strategies for coping with risks arising from the organization's activities. Depending upon unique risk characteristics—marketing research, planning, public safety—others will have influenced risk management within particular organizations.

Ironically, one important influence, safety engineering, is only today being fully recognized and integrated into risk management. That is not to say that risk managers have not long acknowledged the relationship between their responsibilities and safety engineering. Rather, it is to say that the merging of the two into a cohesive whole has not occurred to any great extent. Part of the explanation for this fact derives from the organizational structure of most businesses and governments, which has permitted parallel but unrelated growth of the two functions. Part of the explanation must come from the fairly technical orientation of safety engineering. Since many early risk managers were "insurance people," there may have been some difficulty in interacting effectively with engineers.

As was implied above, however, that separation is slowly disappearing. In a 1992 article in *The Geneva Papers on Risk and Insurance,* Dr. Vernon Leslie Grose (Grose, 1992) discusses the historical development of "technological risk management." In this paper, Grose tracks the development of the engineering side of risk management through the "reliability" movement of the 1950s, and through the "system safety" movement of the 1960s and 1970s. He notes that safety engineering has created or promoted several concepts that have filtered into the insurance-buyer side of risk management (Grose refers to this side as the "financial" side of risk management). Among the many concepts he cites are totally integrated systems for ranking hazards, risk management direction from top management, organization-wide involvement in the risk management process, and the concept of spillover benefits from risk management practices.

Professor H. Wayne Snider of Temple University argues that risk management began to move into an international phase in the mid-1970s—what he refers to as a "globalization phase" (Snider, 1991). He observes that the Risk and Insurance Management Society (RIMS, the preeminent professional association in the field) began establishing contacts with European and Asian risk managers, which has led to the formation of various professional associations around the globe. In terms of the practice of risk management, the field began to gain wider acceptance in the 1970s and 1980s, and the practices began to increase in sophistication. RIMS began publishing a periodic "state of the profession" survey, which tracked the expanding responsibilities and increasing complexity of risk management practices. This period was characterized by a particular interest in risk financing activities—self-insurance plans, captive insurance companies, finite insurance plans, risk retention groups (all covered in this textbook), and so on. Further, two severe contractions in the commercial insurance market, the most severe occurring in the mid-1980s, resulted in an even more rapid movement away from the use of insurance as a means of financing the cost of losses.

In the 1990s, risk management practices continue to evolve. Risk management is not a mature field as is accounting or finance. Specific duties and functions vary widely among risk managers, largely because the significance of specific categories of risk varies substantially across organizations. For example, issues related to legal liability are likely to be paramount for the risk manager of a large hospital but are likely to be of smaller relative importance for a financial service organization, such as a lending institution. Regardless of variations among different organizations, it does seem to be clear that risk management has moved beyond its primary root; for though insurance buying continues to be a significant part of most risk manager's responsibilities, its relative importance is diminishing. Further, the insurance-buying side of the discipline is beginning to blend with other organizational risk management activities, such as safety engineering, legal risk management, information systems security, and so on.

Evidence of Current Risk Management Practices

Evidence of the adoption of risk management practices is mixed. In the private sector, surveys have found that the existence of a full-time risk manager is positively related to the size of the organization (for instance, see Logic Associates, Inc., 1983). Small businesses are less likely to have a full-time risk manager than large businesses. Further, these studies find that the risk manager's duties tend to expand with the size of the organization. Compared with the risk manager of a small- or medium-sized concern, a risk manager in a larger organization is more likely to have multiple responsibilities in areas such as insurance buying, loss control, other risk financing activities, and employee benefits.

These findings can be explained easily. Small businesses typically cannot afford to have a full-time position allocated to risk management, whereas larger entities can. This statement generalizes to other areas of management specialization as well. Further, larger organizations are more likely to undertake complex activities and have the resources to consider a greater variety of risk management options.

What is less clear from the studies is the quality of risk management practices within organizations. For instance, a small organization may not have a full-time risk manager, but may use advanced risk management methods. A sole proprietor may be knowledgeable about risk management and may introduce formal financing and loss control activities. Additionally, the growing availability of third-party risk management services now permits part-time risk managers to extend the risk management function far beyond the capabilities of a single manager. Conversely, a large corporation may have a full-time risk manager with limited management skills and technical knowledge. The point here is that the existence of a full-time risk manager does not necessarily reveal the quality of the risk management activities within an organization.

There is a competing view of risk management and its practice within organizations. Beginning in the mid-1970s, a number of individuals have seen a different relationship between the organization and the presence of a full-time risk manager. In this view, the presence of a full-time risk manager is positively related to the riskiness of the organization, that is, organizations operating in a high-risk environment are more likely to have a full-time risk manager. This relationship was first noted by Professor John O'Connell in a study conducted for RIMS (O'Connell, 1976). Like the findings cited previously, the correlation of risk manager to level of riskiness has an intuitive appeal. It would seem reasonable to assume that organizations that are high-risk (workers are very susceptible to physical harm, or the nature of the product poses significant hazards) would be more sensitive to the consequences of those risks.

There is very limited information regarding risk management in nonprofit organizations, and no studies have been devoted exclusively to the subject. Based upon rather indirect evidence (memberships in professional associations, for instance), it appears that the presence of a risk manager in a nonprofit organization possibly is related to the riskiness of the organization's activities. For example, hospitals and utility companies have long been visible participants in both the RIMS Inc. and the Public Risk Management Association (PRIMA, RIMS's public sector counterpart). As additional evidence of activity in this area, it could be noted that the proliferation of professional associations in recent years has been largely limited to nonprofit and public organizations: American Society of Healthcare Risk Management (ASHRM), State Risk and Insurance Management Association (STRIMA), University Risk Management and Insurance Association (URMIA), The National Center for Community Risk Management and Insurance (a center devoted mainly to nonprofit organizations), and so forth.

In the public sector, the development of risk management practices has lagged somewhat behind the private sector. Fully formed risk management programs in public entities are a relatively recent phenomena. As a formal practice, risk management was only rarely seen before the early 1970s. The slower development of risk management in the public sector may be explained in several different ways. Local governments have generally been somewhat more cautious in the adoption of management "innovations," which may have led to some reluctance to develop the risk management function (Young, 1988). Governmental entities have, in some cases, employed practices that masked the impact of risk on the organization. For instance, governmental accounting practices allowed (until recently) governments to ignore or defer the effect of some losses that occurred in a particular budgetary period. Finally, governments have historically enjoyed immunity from many types of legal liability, though this legal immunity has been shrinking since the early 1960s (Pine, 1992). Many observers note that this growing "exposure to risk" has a more than coincidental relationship with the rise of public sector risk management practices in the 1970s, 1980s, and 1990s.

One intriguing aspect of public sector risk management practice is that it seems to be most fully developed in medium-sized entities (cities, towns, counties, and other local government districts with populations between 250,000 and 1,000,000). Smaller entities are not as likely to have risk managers for the same reasons that small businesses do not, but large governmental entities do not appear to behave as do large businesses. The research that has been done to date finds that large entities are not likely to have centralized, coordinated risk management practices (PRIMA, 1992). It is true that most state governments, for instance, have a risk management department, but the duties are likely to be much more limited than they would be for a counterpart in a large private firm. For instance, a study of 38 state risk management departments recently found that only 19 had administrative responsibilities for workers' compensation (a program for employees who are injured on the job) (STRIMA, 1990). Conversely, risk managers in large businesses commonly identify workers' compensation as a central risk management responsibility.

The nature of government organizations—decentralized authority, democratic decision making, multiple and competing objectives—may make integrated and coordinated risk management impractical for large governmental entities. Also, the level at which the risk management authority would be vested is not always clear, which creates the possibility of conflict. One need only consider the New York City metropolitan area to recognize that overlapping jurisdictions, even within a single governmental entity, can create great administrative complexity. Further, the shear scope and size of such organizations make fully integrated risk management very difficult.

The Nature of Risk Management Activities

Since insurance buying is a historical foundation of risk management, one might expect that buying insurance would be a significant activity for most risk managers. The purchase of insurance continues to be a significant element of the risk manager's duties, even in large organizations for which the value of insurance might appear to be limited. The reasons for the continued importance of insurance are discussed later in this textbook.

Apart from buying insurance, risk managers' duties may include:

1. Assisting their organization in identifying risks
2. Implementing loss prevention and control programs
3. Reviewing contracts and documents for risk management purposes
4. Providing training and education on safety-related issues (CPR, workplace safety, right-to-know workshops)
5. Assuring compliance with governmental mandates, such as OSHA and the Americans with Disabilities Act
6. Arranging non-insurance financing schemes (e.g., self-insurance or captive insurance subsidiaries)
7. Claims management and working with legal representation to manage litigation
8. Designing and coordinating employee benefit programs.

Although some risk managers do not perform some of the duties listed above, the list does represent an itemization of activities that would be familiar to very many risk managers. Indeed, in the most progressive organizations, that list of duties might be expanded to include such things as:

1. Currency hedging
2. Capital budgeting
3. Public relations
4. Employee assistance and training

5. Government lobbying
6. Services marketing
7. Mergers and acquisitions.

Logic Associates, Inc., an executive/management recruiting and placement firm, has produced a report on the state of present private-sector risk management practices that seems to support this general summary (Logic Associates, Inc., 1993). Among many findings, the study found that for companies with a risk manager, the range of risk management responsibilities conforms to the generally understood scope of current practices. A majority of the respondents identified risk financing, insurance acquisition and management, claims handling, safety, security, benefits administration (to varying degrees), and contingency planning. Interestingly, up to one-quarter (depending on the size of the organization) of the respondents indicated that they have significant responsibilities for financial or treasury risk management—a nontraditional form of risk management activity that is discussed later in this chapter.

The Nature of the Risk Management Function

The fundamental nature of risk management in the 1990s is a subject of some debate. Scholars and practitioners generally agree that the practice of risk management is evolving, but there is wide disagreement over where the field is going. At one end of the spectrum, there are some who believe that risk management will completely disappear—though proponents of this view are a distinct minority. At the other end are a number of writers who believe that risk management is poised to move into an exciting new era of activity and responsibility. And, of course, there are observers who believe that the evolution is completely random and is not necessarily leading in any direction. The textbook will offer its own conceptual view of the risk management function shortly, but it is worthwhile to survey briefly some of the views of risk management that exist today.

The traditionalist or conventional view of risk management, as the name suggests, continues to hold sway among practitioners and many academicians. This view, perhaps best characterized by previous editions of this textbook (most recently, Williams and Heins, 1989), argues that risk management is an interdisciplinary discipline that manages the *pure* risks of an organization. It is an incrementalist view that is based upon the notion that risk management is evolving from, rather than radically shifting from, insurance buying (and to a lesser extent, safety engineering) and that it is fully appropriate that risk management should operate within the constraints history has placed upon the function. The traditionalists argue that factors beyond firm value maximization may influence risk management decision making.

H. Felix Kloman, a well-known risk management consultant, has the most fully developed public track record in advocating a distinctly nontraditional point of view. Since 1971, he has written in practitioner publications and some academic journals on the subject of risk management (for instance, see Kloman, 1992). Over this period, Kloman has argued that risk management's insurance-buying past was as much hindrance as help, mainly because it tended to focus the risk manager's attention on "insurable risks" while other risks were ignored. His view of risk management is largely based upon the idea that risk managers should manage "holistically" all organizational risks.

Yacov Y. Haimes, a professor of engineering and applied science at the University of Virginia, has written recently about "total risk management," a concept very similar to Kloman's (Haimes, 1989, 1991, 1992). He defines total risk management (TRM) as ". . . a systematic, statistically based, and holistic process that builds on formal risk assessment and management . . . and addresses . . . four sources of (system) failures within a hierarchical-multiobjective framework" (Haimes, 1992). Haimes' four sources of system failure are (1) hardware failure, (2) software failure, (3) organizational failure, and (4) human failure. He excludes external sources of failure, arguing that they are system dependent. This view is purposely harmonious with total quality management (TQM) principles, and relies heavily on the language and concepts of the engineering and operations management fields.

A third view has been argued by numerous individuals, but is represented in Neil Doherty's *Corporate Risk Management* (Doherty, 1985). This interpretation is based largely upon a modern finance theory view of the risk management function, that is, that risk management decisions are financial decisions and should be evaluated with respect to their effect on firm value. Because the financial view rests upon certain assumptions regarding markets, it most fully applies to large publicly held corporations, while its value to public and non-profit organizations, as well as smaller private organizations, is somewhat limited. Even within the large private-sector organization segment of the risk management community, the concepts have not been fully embraced, partly because many risk managers have not been exposed to modern finance theory. Nevertheless, the view has many academic adherents and has provided a useful analytical structure for investigating risk management issues.

One interesting trend that merits consideration here is the appropriation of the term "risk management" by other managers. "Appropriation" is, perhaps, too strong a term, but it is true that the activities described by traditionalists have some claim to the term because of the length of time it has applied to them. Nevertheless, as the concepts of risk become more general, we should expect that other approaches to risk management might develop. One of the most interesting developments in this regard is the emergence of "financial risk management" (not to be confused with the finance view of risk management). While the textbook's definition of risk management (proposed below) easily incorporates financial risk management into its structure, a brief—and separate—history of financial risk management is appropriate.

Financial risk management is a form of risk management that has arisen principally in the banking community as a systematic approach to dealing with specific financial risks, such as credit risks, currency exchange risks, transactional risks, as well as investment risk. Although banks have faced these risks for a long time, it is only recently that they have been motivated to aggressively address such risks, and it is only recently that they have had tools at their disposal for dealing with these financial risks.

Since the 1970s, banks have entered a new and riskier world. This is, in part, due to broad deregulation movements around the world, as well as economic trends that are creating new competitive pressures and global financial markets.

The perils of this new world are well documented; whether it is the reported $1 billion hit Salomon Brothers took as a consequence of scandal in its bond-trading operations, or Barclay Bank's 1992 provision of 2.6 billion pounds for bad loans, or Westpac's (an Australian bank) estimated A$1.5 billion in bad debt writeoffs in 1992. Whatever the root cause, the banking community has become aware of its exposure to risk (Freeman, 1993).

Awareness of risk has precipitated interest in various financial tools for managing banking risks. Most of these tools come from a set of financial instruments known as "derivatives." A derivative is essentially ". . . a financial contract whose value depends on the value of one or more underlying assets or indices of asset values" (Freeman, 1993). Examples of such instruments are *futures, options,* and *swaps.* In the context of financial risk management, each of these instruments is essentially a hedging arrangement that allows a bank to reduce financial volatility arising from foreign exchange, from interest rates, from commodities, and from equities (the concept of hedging is discussed fully in Chapter 9). For example, through swapping arrangements, banks may enjoy mutual enhancement of asset portfolios as well as a potential reduction of risk. Likewise, participation in futures markets can offset the risk inherent in an underlying asset.

ORGANIZATIONAL RISK MANAGEMENT

Risk management is defined in this textbook as "a general management function that seeks to identify, assess, and address the causes and effects of uncertainty and risk on an organization." The purpose of risk management is to enable an organization to progress toward its goals and objectives (its mission) in the most direct, efficient, and effective path. For purposes of clarity and simplification only, this definition will be referred to as the organizational risk management (ORM) view of risk management.

The ORM definition of risk management is somewhat at odds with the traditional view, while it shares many elements of Kloman's, Haimes', and Doherty's general views. In general, each of these views levels implicit or explicit criticisms of the traditional view. These criticisms are centered on three key points.

First, these critics note that risk management should not discriminate among risks. Although pure and speculative risks have different characteristics, there is no compelling reason why they should be managed separately. Second, risk management is not a specialized management function; it is a general management function. This is not to say that risk managers do not have specialized knowledge. It is to say, however, that risk management is broad and interdisciplinary and is not amenable to being narrowly described as an "insurance buying" function. Third, and to a much lesser extent, critics have noted that traditionalists have been somewhat oriented toward "loss management" as opposed to a "risk and uncertainty management" orientation. The costs of uncertainty can be quite profound (misallocated resources, poor organizational decisions, unnecessarily high costs of capital), yet risk managers have traditionally ignored this side of the cost of risk.

This textbook's definition of risk management incorporates the essence of these criticisms. Risk management is concerned with all risks. It is a general management function, as opposed to a narrow subfunction of finance (which might place this view somewhat at odds with the Doherty view) or some other managerial discipline. The definition also reflects a broader understanding of risk and uncertainty and their effects on an organization.

The Strategic, Operations, and Risk Management Model

Management scholars have proposed numerous ways of conceptualizing the structure and function of management within organizations, each with certain merits and limitations. In order to secure this textbook's definition of risk management into a larger view of organizational management, a somewhat different management model is proposed—the strategic, operations, and risk management model.

The management of organizations can differ in detail from organization to organization, but at a most fundamental level, organization management involves three core management functions: strategic management functions, operations management functions, and risk management functions. These three

FIGURE 2.1. The three core functions of an organization.

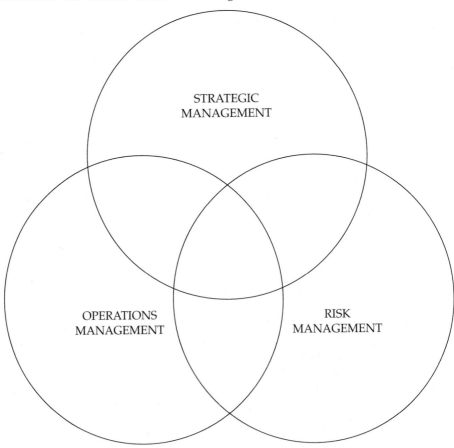

STRATEGIC
MANAGEMENT

OPERATIONS
MANAGEMENT

RISK
MANAGEMENT

functions are not mutually exclusive of one another, and may be visualized as shown in Figure 2.1.

The *strategic management function* consists of those activities that seek to identify the organization's mission, its goals and objectives, and its strategic plan, as well as the evaluative processes used to measure the organization's progress toward its mission. The *operations management function* is comprised of those activities that actually move the organization towards its mission. Operations management concerns itself with the process of providing the good or service, that is, with managing "how the organization does what it does." The *risk management function* consists of all those activities that facilitate the most direct achievement of the organization's mission.

In a world of complete certainty, only strategic management and operations management functions would be necessary. An organization would simply decide what it wanted to do, design a program to do it, and implement the program. Unfortunately, risk and uncertainty pervade our existence. Uncertainty affects our ability to fully identify the organization's true mission, our ability to measure the progress toward achieving the mission, and certainly, our ability to economically and efficiently move the organization to its mission. The same can be said of risk. Fires, unexpected accidents, poor business decisions, a surprise election result, a controversial piece of legislation, even unexpected good fortune intrude and cause deviation from the intended path. Risk management is the proactive management of risks and uncertainties that will move the organization toward its mission as expeditiously as possible—whatever that mission is.

The strategic, operations and risk management model should not be seen as a dismissal of the more traditional explanations of management structure and function. Budgeting, financial accounting, financial management, marketing, human resource management, and all other specializations fit into this model. As presented in Table 2.1, these specializations carry out the core functions, for instance, a marketing department's activities might be characterized as activities of a strategic, operational, and/or risk management nature.

It is essential to clearly elaborate on the overlap of the three core functions. There are many activities in which all three functions merge or closely interact. For example, a company might decide that its mission is to produce the highest quality lightbulb possible. It may further decide that one of the measures of mission fulfillment will be some minimum service life before the bulb fails. This target level of quality is essentially a strategic issue (as is general mission identification), but operations management will become involved in assessing actual levels of quality, and in the setting of the standard itself—to the extent that the assessment process involves statistical considerations. The risk management function will be involved here as well, particularly in identifying the potential consequences of failing to meet the standard of quality, and in understanding how goal failure might occur. Some of the risks here are pure, some are speculative, but the distinction is irrelevant, for risk management is concerned with all risks.

The strategic, operations and risk management model, which is produced for the first time in this textbook, is intended only to facilitate the discussion of risk management; and for that reason, a brief analogy may be helpful in rein-

TABLE 2.1.   The Strategic, Operations, and Risk Management Model from a Subfunctional Perspective

The Marketing Function

1. Market Research
   a. *Strategic:* How does our mission interact with the market demand for our products/services? What do we want to know?
   b. *Operations:* How are we assuring timely and accurate assessments of the market? How is research conducted?
   c. *Risk:* Is our research representative of reality? What are the risks of being wrong? What risks arise from aspiring to meet market demand?

2. Product Development
   a. *Strategic:* What must this product be to meet market demand? What must our product be to meet organizational objectives?
   b. *Operations:* How do we produce this product to meet market demand as well as organizational objectives?
   c. *Risk:* What risks arise in the development of this product? What potential risks arise from the creation of this product?

3. Pricing
   a. *Strategic:* How does pricing help accomplish the goals and objectives of the organization (market positioning, etc.)?
   b. *Operations:* Does pricing reflect the costs of production as well as appropriate overhead and profit charges?
   c. *Risk:* Does pricing recognize the risk inherent in the product: potential for liability suits, effects of competition, costs of contingencies?

4. Advertising/Promotion
   a. *Strategic:* How does product promotion relate to organization mission? What promotional strategy is appropriate?
   b. *Operations:* How do we work with wholesalers/retailers to present product to the market? What are the mechanics of producing advertising and promotional materials?
   c. *Risk:* What are the consequences and risks from adopting a particular promotional strategy? Do we have alternatives or fall-back positions? Does our advertising and promotion create potential liability problems for the organization?

forcing the basic idea. In the realm of philosophy and religion, belief systems seek to answer, essentially, three questions: (1) What is the meaning of life? (2) What is the path toward meaning? (3) How do we live in this world? Each of these questions is separate and distinct, yet each bears on and overlaps the other. As an example, Christians might say that the exhortation "to live as Jesus lived" could be seen as a reasonable answer to all three questions. Theologians would add, however, that each question also has elements and arguments that are separate and distinct.

So it is in management, that organizations seek answers to the core questions as well. What is our organization's purpose? How do we fulfill our purpose? What are the consequences of moving toward the fulfillment of our purpose? In asking that third question, readers arrive at the essence of this textbook's definition of risk management. How does the world in which we live, with all its risk and uncertainty, influence the fulfillment of our reason for being, and what do we do about it? Equally important, however, is the companion question. What is the responsibility of the organization to the world in which it exists?

Elements of Organizational Risk Management

Although the actual practice of risk management would be likely to vary among organizations, certain elements would be common to all risk management programs. Together, these elements comprise the risk management function. They are:

1. Mission identification
2. Risk and uncertainty assessment
3. Risk control
4. Risk financing
5. Program administration.

Despite the fact that the listing of these elements implies a sequence, risk management is not a sequential process. Certain elements logically appear to precede others (e.g., without risk assessment, it is difficult to consider the selection of risk control or risk financing methods). The issues confronting an established risk management program, however, can involve any one of the five elements. Also, some overlap among the five elements is almost inevitable. For example, a risk manager's review of insurance coverages proposed by a broker may reveal a type of risk that the risk manager failed to recognize during risk assessment. Normally, the review of coverages would be considered part of program administration, not risk assessment.

Other conceptualizations of the process or elements of risk management are possible. One notable alternative has been at least indirectly suggested by both Kloman and Haimes. This view of the elements of risk management is based upon a "systems" configuration, arguing that the risk management function may be seen as a kind of information system in which risk and uncertainty assessments are the core elements. In such a system, the risk manager exists at the center of a complex information system that is continuously sending information on risks and uncertainties to the risk manager, and that is continuously (more or less) sending information on the response to risk and uncertainty back out to the organization and to others. In such a model, the mission is taken as given, program administration is seen as the management of the system, and risk control and risk financing are the substance of communication *from* the risk manager. Even within the systems approach, however, the five elements are still present, so a brief explanation of each is appropriate as a vehicle for summarization of this chapter.

Mission Identification. The alignment of risk management goals and objectives with the mission of the organization is a fundamental task of the risk manager. This part of the risk management process identifies the relationship between risk management and the mission of the organization. Establishment of risk management goals and objectives is critical, for they serve as the foundation for all risk management activities. The goals and objectives provide the yardsticks against which the success or failure of the program is measured, and also determine the philosophy underlying risk management activities. This very important topic is a subject covered in Chapter 20.

Risk and Uncertainty Assessment. Risk and uncertainty assessment consists of three related activities. First, risks and uncertainties that affect the organization must be *identified.* Identification of risks usually is accompanied by both *hazard identification* and *exposure identification.* Hazards (or "risk factors" in the case of speculative risks) are activities or conditions that create or increase the likelihood of loss (gain) or the loss (gain) amount. An improperly maintained piece of heavy machinery is an example of a hazard. An exposure to loss or gain would be the object, individual, or situation subject to loss (gain), for example, the worker who could be injured operating the improperly maintained equipment.

Identification is followed by *analysis.* It is not sufficient to know that hazards, risk factors, and exposures to loss or gain exist. The risk manager must understand the nature of those hazards, risk factors, and exposures, how they come to exist, and how they interact to produce a loss or gain. Perceptions of risk, as well as uncertainty, are also analyzed, since they may be of profound importance. For instance, the hazards associated with the handling of a dangerous material may be well understood by the organization, but if employees perceive the risk to be extraordinary, that assessment of the risk may become a *de facto* management reality for the organization.

Analysis is related to the final assessment activity, *risk measurement.* Risk measurement evaluates the likelihood of loss or gain and the value of loss or gain along the dimensions of frequency and severity. The measurement process may take the form of a qualitative assessment—"this loss is pretty likely to occur"—or a numerical estimate.

Risk Control. Risk control activities are those that focus upon avoiding, preventing, reducing, or otherwise controlling risks and uncertainties. Risk control activities can take simple forms, such as making sure that a kitchen has functioning fire extinguishers. They also can be complex, such as developing a catastrophe contingency plan to use in a nuclear power plant emergency.

Risk Financing. Risk financing activities provide the means of reimbursing losses that occur and for funding other programs to reduce uncertainty and risk, or to enhance positive outcomes. Normally, some losses will occur despite risk control efforts. The financing of these losses can include measures such as the purchase of insurance coverages, the establishment of a captive insurance subsidiary, or the use of letters of credit. The funding of a highway safety program through earmarked taxes would be a less obvious, but valid, illustration of risk financing.

Readers will learn that risk control and risk financing activities are not always mutually exclusive. One might, for example, note that banks are actively involved in credit and interest rate risk management activities (such as interest rate swaps) that might reasonably be seen as both risk financing and risk control.

Program Administration. This element establishes procedures followed in the day-to-day operations of the risk management function. For example, procedures for buying insurance or the structuring of the program review and evaluation process fall into program administration. Procedures for communicating program efforts and results to intended target audiences is another example. Intricate knowledge of insurance coverages or sophisticated risk financing techniques is of limited use to a risk manager who has poor management or poor communication skills. Also, program administration is determined in the context of the organization and its resources. The task requires a firm knowledge of how the organization operates, its goals and objectives, its history, and its people.

The Placement of the Risk Management Function

The ORM view of risk management leads to an institutional scheme that departs from present practice—with but a few notable exceptions. Today, as has been noted, most risk managers and risk management departments are located within a finance department or some similar arrangement. In the Logic Associates, Inc. study, the vast majority of respondents reported to the Chief Financial Officer, the Treasurer or some similar supervisor, and the study found that these risk management departments ranged in size from three people (the average for companies with less than $200 million in annual sales) to just over nine (the average for companies with over $7 billion in annual sales) (Logic Associates, Inc. 1993). Further, since the risk management function is a staff function, it must operate within the constraints ordinarily seen in staff positions—degree of authority is based on distance to the executive, and scope of responsibilities is broad.

By contrast, the ORM view suggests, but does not require, that the risk manager be proximate to the executive. Overall direction for risk management should be provided by the executive level of the organization, particularly because the purpose of risk management is to address all organizational risks. Interestingly, the Logic Associates, Inc. study mentioned previously found that for companies with less than $200 million in annual sales, 14 percent of the respondents reported directly to their company's President or Chairman (for all other organizations, less than 5 percent responded that they reported directly to the CEO or President). Further, the ORM view of risk management is not highly conducive to a "departmental" approach to risk management. Rather, many or most of the activities that constitute the ORM approach to risk management would be practiced throughout the organization, so the ORM risk manager serves more as a "linking pin," coordinating and organizing the management of risk. Risk management responsibilities would be written into every employee's job description, and the risk manager (probably "departmentless" in such a circumstance) would coordinate these responsibilities, and facilitate their implementation. The operational issues arising from the textbook's view of risk management are discussed in Chapter 20.

Key Concepts

organizational risk management (ORM): A general management function that seeks to identify, assess and address the causes and effects of uncertainty and risk on an organization.

strategic, operations, and risk management model: A model of management functions that emphasizes the relationship between strategic management, operations management, and risk management.

risk and uncertainty assessment: All activities associated with identifying, analyzing, and measuring risk and uncertainty.

risk control: All activities associated with avoiding, preventing, reducing, or otherwise controlling risks and uncertainties.

risk financing: Those activities that provide the means of reimbursing losses that occur and that fund other programs to reduce risk and uncertainty.

program administration: All those activities and strategies associated with the long-term and day-to-day operation of the risk management function.

Review Questions

1. What is the relationship between risk management and insurance buying, and why do some argue that insurance buying exerts a negative influence on risk management today?
2. What are the differences between the "traditional" view and practice of risk management, and the ORM view of risk management?
3. Describe the general activities of risk management as it is practiced today.
4. Identify and briefly explain the elements of ORM.
5. What do we presently know about the differences between private-sector and public-sector risk management practices?
6. What is the strategic, operations and risk management model of management? How do the three management functions relate to one another?

References and Suggestions for Additional Reading

CROCKFORD, G. NEIL: "The Bibliography and History of Risk Management: Some Preliminary Observations," *The Geneva Papers on Risk and Insurance,* 7 (no. 23, April 1982) pp. 169–179.

DOHERTY, N. A.: Corporate Risk Management (New York: McGraw-Hill Book Company, 1985).

FINKEL, A. H.: *Confronting Uncertainty in Risk Management,* the Center for Risk Management, Washington, D.C., 1990.

FREEMAN, ANDREW: "New Tricks to Learn: A Survey of International Banking," *The Economist,* April 10, 1993, Insert pp. 1–38.

GROSE, VERNON LESLIE: "Risk Management from a Technological Perspective," *The Geneva Papers on Risk and Insurance,* 12 (no. 64, July 1992) pp. 335–342.

HAIMES, YACOV Y.: "Toward a Holistic Approach to Risk Assessment and Management, *Risk Analysis,* Vol. 9, no. 2, June 1989.

———: "Total Risk Management," *Risk Analysis,* Vol. 11, no. 2, June 1991.

———: "Toward a Holistic Approach to Total Risk Management," *The Geneva Papers on Risk and Insurance,* 17 (no. 64, July 1992) pp. 314–321.

KLOMAN, H. F.: "Rethinking Risk Management," *The Geneva Papers on Risk and Insurance,* 17 (no. 64, July 1992) pp. 299–313.

KRAJEWSKI, LEE J., and LARRY P. RITZMAN: *Operations Management: Strategy and Analysis,* 3rd edition (Reading, Mass.: Addison-Wesley), 1993.

Logic Associates, Inc., *1983 Risk Management Compensation Survey* (New York, 1984).

———: *1993 Risk Management Salary Survey* (New York, 1993).

MEHR, R. I., and B. A. HEDGES: *Risk Management: Concepts and Applications* (Homewood, Ill.: Richard D. Irwin, Inc. 1974).

———, and ———: *Risk Management in the Business Enterprise* (Homewood, Ill.: Richard D. Irwin, Inc., 1963).

O'CONNELL, J. J.: "Study Indicates Continuing Risk Management Movement,"*Risk Management* Vol. XXIII, no. 4 (April, 1976) pp. 54–56.

PINE, JOHN C.: *Tort Liability Today: A Guide for State and Local Governments, 1991 Update,* PRIMA, Arlington, Va., 1992.

PUBLIC RISK MANAGEMENT ASSOCIATION: *State of the Profession,* PRIMA, Arlington, Va., 1992.

SNIDER, H. W.: "Reaching professional status: A program for risk management," *Corporate Risk Management: Current Problems and Perspectives,* American Management Association, New York, 1956.

———: "Risk Management: A Retrospective View" *Risk Management,* April 1991, pp. 47–54.

STATE RISK AND INSURANCE MANAGEMENT ASSOCIATION: *Survey of State Risk Management Programs,* September, 1990.

THOMPSON, A. A., and A. J. STRICKLAND, III: *Strategic Management: Concepts and Cases,* 6th ed. (Irwin, Homewood, Ill.) 1992.

WILLIAMS, C. A. Jr., and RICHARD M. HEINS: *Risk Management and Insurance,* 6th ed. (New York: McGraw-Hill Publishing Co., 1989).

YOUNG, P. C.: *Local Government Pure Risk Management Pools: Theory and Practice,* unpublished doctoral dissertation, University of Minnesota, 1988.

PART TWO

Assessing Risk

Part 2 discusses a fundamental aspect of risk management: risk assessment. The five chapters of Part 2 present a process for identifying, analyzing, and measuring risk and uncertainty. These chapters have two objectives: to describe the process of risk assessment and to create an awareness of the variety of risks to which organizations are exposed.

Chapters 3 and 4 describe the tools and methods of risk assessment with no special reference to any particular category of risks confronting organizations. Chapter 3 is qualitative in nature, focusing on methods for identifying possible outcomes and for developing a qualitative assessment of their likelihood (e.g., "the chance of serious earthquake damage to this building is almost nil if frame construction is used"). Risk identification, hazard and risk factor analysis, and loss analysis are discussed in Chapter 3.

Chapter 4 develops applications of quantitative methods for risk assessment. The material in Chapter 4 presumes mastery of basic concepts in probability and statistics such as those

taught in a junior-level course required for business students. The authors recognize that many undergraduate instructors will find the material in Chapter 4 challenging for students and perhaps too time-consuming for the typical introductory course. Because the text is used in courses at both the undergraduate and graduate levels, the chapters are structured to allow the instructor to omit Chapter 4 without affecting the continuity of the course. The authors believe, however, that the material in Chapter 4 contributes substantially to students' grasp of risk management concepts.

Chapters 5, 6, and 7 apply principles of risk assessment to specific categories of risks often confronting organizations. Chapter 5 discusses risks related to property, such as, damage to or destruction of property and the inability to use property over a period of time. The inability to use property over a period of time, the "time element" loss, is identified as possibly a more significant type of loss than the direct damage itself. Chapter 6 presents an analysis of liability risks, that is, the risks imposed on organizations by the system of legal liability. Chapter 7, the final chapter, discusses risks related to human resources. Just as physical resources can be "at risk," so can human resources. These human resource exposures can be significant for the organization itself as well as for the affected individuals and their dependents, and the interests of both organizations and individuals are identified in Chapter 7.

CHAPTER 3

Risk Assessment I: Risk Assessment Fundamentals

Learning Objectives

After you have completed this chapter, you should be able to:

1. Understand the component parts of risk assessment.
2. Explain the process of risk identification.
3. Understand the distinction between hazard analysis and loss analysis.
4. Identify the general costs of losses.
5. Explain why a risk manager needs to measure these exposures to risk, what two dimensions must be measured, and why each of these two dimensions should be measured.
6. Understand the structure of a general organizational risk assessment.

INTRODUCTION

This chapter introduces and discusses risk assessment. *Risk assessment* consists of those activities that enable the risk manager to identify, evaluate, and measure risk and uncertainty and their potential impact on the organization. Risk assessment is the most fundamental activity undertaken by the risk manager. It involves the *identification of risks,* the *analysis of hazards and outcomes,* and the *measurement of risk.* While these assessment elements will be discussed sequentially, in practice they may be undertaken concurrently. For instance, at the same time the risk manager may have identified "fire" as a significant risk, the risk manager is likely to be evaluating the factors that produce losses (hazard analysis) and assessing the consequences of losses (loss analysis). Additionally, the risk manager is likely to attempt to gather statistical data on past loss experience to gain a better understanding of the risk and its potential impact (risk measurement).

Discussion begins with the subject of risk identification. A general framework for classifying organizational risks is offered, and a methodology for systematically identifying risks is provided. Although risk identification includes identification of positive or beneficial outcomes, the chapter focuses principally on identifying negative outcomes, that is, on hazard and loss analysis. Specific attention is given to the subject of accident causation and to the particularly challenging problem of ascertaining the costs of losses. Finally, this chapter provides an introductory discussion of risk measurement. Concepts and measurement fundamentals are discussed, with some basic statistical measures explained.

Presentation of specific risk categories is limited in this chapter. The main purpose is to present students with an exposure to the *process* of assessing risks. Chapters 5, 6, and 7 discuss and evaluate specific categories of risk, which rounds out the presentation of risk assessment.

RISK IDENTIFICATION

Risk identification is the process by which an organization systematically and continuously identifies risks and uncertainties. Identification activities are intended to develop information on sources of risk, hazards, risk factors, perils, and exposures to loss. The terminology is important here, so a brief explanation is necessary.

Sources of risk are the sources of factors or hazards that may contribute to positive or negative outcomes. As an example, the skilled labor market in Taiwan might be seen as an important factor in a speculative risk to build a new computer production facility in that country. Later, this factor will be identified as arising from certain "environmental" sources of risk. These same sources of risk also influence pure risks as well, for example, the nature of the labor force may produce higher/lower accident rates.

One might imagine risks as consisting of the component parts of *hazard* or *risk factors*, *peril*, and *exposure to loss or gain*. *Hazard* is a condition that creates or increases the chance of loss or its severity. *Risk factors* are the speculative risk corollary to "hazard." They are the conditions that influence the chance of loss or gain, and/or the magnitude of loss or gain.

Perils are causes of loss. *Exposures to loss or gain* are the objects or situations facing possible loss or gain. For instance, a hazard might be oily rags stored by a furnace. The fire that might arise from that hazard is the peril, and the warehouse that might burn as a result of that fire is the exposure to loss. The term "exposure" can also apply in speculative risk situations, as when an investment manager identifies fund assets as an exposure to market risks. However, the term "peril" cannot be extended to include "causes of gain"—if for no other reason than that "peril" has an overwhelmingly negative connotation in the minds of most people. Therefore, when discussing speculative risks, it is probably advisable to identify the elements of risk as (1) the risk factors, and (2) the exposures to risk factors. This structure does not allow for the subtlety of description permitted in the hazard-peril-exposure framework, but it will suit the purposes of this textbook.

Students are cautioned to keep a flexible view to the use of all these terms in any event, for although the textbook takes a disciplined approach to their usage, these terms may be used interchangeably in the risk management community. For example, a risk manager might refer to the oily rags as "the risk," or might refer to the warehouse as "a risk." For analytical purposes, however, it is useful to make these distinctions.

There are many different ways of classifying sources of risk. In Chapter 5, for instance, there will be some discussion about physical (fire), social (riot), and economic (inflation) sources of risk as important in dealing with risks to property. However, since the task at hand is the identification of all risk, the sources of risk must be specified somewhat differently. For instance, the following sources of risk represent one general categorization:

- Physical environment
- Social environment
- Political environment
- Legal environment
- Operational environment
- Economic environment
- Cognitive environment.

The Physical Environment.   Clearly, one of the most fundamental sources of risk arises from the physical environment. Earthquakes, drought, excessive rainfall can all lead to loss. Our inability to fully understand our environment, and the effects we have on it—as well as the effect it has on us—is a central aspect of this source of risk. The physical environment may be the source of speculative opportunity as well, for example, real estate as an investment, agribusiness, and weather as a contributing factor to tourism.

The Social Environment.   Changing mores and values, fundamental human behaviors, social structures, and institutions are a second source of risk. Many American business executives are frustrated when they move into the international domain. Differing social values and norms in, say, Japan, have proven to be a particular source of uncertainty for American and European business managers. Within the United States, possible civil unrest, as occurred in Los Angeles during 1992, further underscores the importance of this source of risk. Changing mores and values also create opportunities, as when changing values regarding women in the workforce opens a door to a significant talent pool.

The Political Environment.   Within a single country, the political environment can be an important source of risk. A new president can move the nation into a policy direction that might have dramatic effects on particular organizations (cuts in aid to local governments, new stringent regulations on toxic waste disposal). In the international realm, the political environment is even more complex. Not all nations are democratic in their form of government, and some have very different attitudes and policies toward business. Foreign assets might be confiscated by a host government or tax policies might change dramatically. The political environment can also promote positive opportunities through fiscal and monetary policy, enforcement of laws, and the education of the populace.

The Legal Environment.   Within the United States today, there is a great deal of uncertainty and risk that arises from the legal system. Not only are standards of conduct upheld and punishments enforced, but the system itself is evolutionary and these standards may not be fully anticipated. Of course, in the international domain, the complexity is much greater since legal standards may vary dramatically from country to country. The legal environment also produces positive outcomes in the sense that rights are protected and that the legal system provides a stabilizing influence on society.

The Operational Environment.   The processes and procedures of an organization generate risks and uncertainties. A formal procedure for promoting, hiring, or firing employees may generate a legal liability. The manufacturing process may put employees at risk of physical harm. The activities of an organization may result in harm to the environment. International businesses may suffer from risk or uncertainty due to unreliable transportation systems. In a more speculative vein, the operational environment ultimately yields the good or service by which the organization succeeds or fails.

The Economic Environment.   Although the economic environment often flows directly from the political realm, the dramatic expansion of the global marketplace has created an environment that is now supragovernmental. Although a particular government's actions may affect international capital markets, it is increasingly unlikely that a single nation can *control* capital markets. Inflation, recession, and depression are now elements of an economic system(s) that are considerably beyond the control of a single country. On a somewhat less macroeconomic level, such things as interest rates and credit can impose significant pure and speculative risk on an organization.

The Cognitive Environment.   In a management textbook such as this one, it is very easy to forget that the "observer" of trends, concepts, and practices is not all-knowing or objective. A risk manager's ability to understand, to see, to measure, and to assess is not a perfected ability. An important source of risk for most organizations is the risk that perceptions and reality are quite different. The cognitive environment is the most challenging source of risk to identify and analyze, since such an analysis must contemplate such questions as "how do we come to understand the effect of uncertainty on the organization," and "how do we know whether what we perceive is real?" Readers might consider an evaluation of the cognitive environment as partly addressing the issue of "uncertainty" as it was defined and discussed in Chapter 1.

The hazards and perils that arise from each of these environments are numerous. Some might be easily imagined, others much less so. Some perils could arise from more than one source of risk, "fire" being a good example, as it could arise from the physical environment (a lightning strike) or from the social environment (arson, civil unrest). Discussion of specific perils will be deferred to Chapters 5, 6, and 7.

Sources of risk are essentially of no concern to an organization unless that organization is exposed or vulnerable to the perils that arise from the hazards of those environments. Therefore, an important aspect of risk identification is exposure identification. Although in the broadest sense, an entire organization is an exposure to risk, it is useful to develop categorizations for analytical purposes. Three widely used categories of risk exposures are *property exposures, liability exposures,* and *human resource exposures.*

Property exposures to risk are exposures to gains or losses to physical or financial assets, as well as to intangible assets (goodwill, political support, intellectual property), that arise from exposures to the hazards or risk factors. Chapter 5 will provide a thorough discussion of these exposures, but it should be noted that property may be damaged, destroyed, lost, or suffer diminishment in value in many different ways. The inability to use property for a period of time, the so-called "time element" loss, provides an example of a type of loss often overlooked by individuals and organizations. Indeed, as will be seen, an event may transpire half a world away that can result in a catastrophic property loss for a business located in Omaha, Nebraska. Conversely, property exposures to risk may result in gain or enhancement. Investment in a successful entrepreneurial endeavor can enhance wealth; aggressive marketing and risk taking in the incipient Russian marketplace can result in dominant market share.

Liability exposures to risk are those losses that arise from legally imposed obligations. Civil and criminal law detail obligations that citizens carry; state and federal legislatures impose statutory limitations on certain activities; governmental agencies promulgate administrative rules and directives that establish standards of care. Legal obligations that differ from country to country are an increasingly important aspect of this area. One could argue that liability loss exposures are actually part of property loss exposures, in that a liability loss results in some diminishment of an organization's assets. However, the characteristics of liability loss exposures warrant separate study and treatment. Chapter 6 will be devoted to a discussion of these perils and the exposures to loss arising from the political and legal environments.

Readers should note that, unlike property exposures to risk, liability exposures do not technically have an "up side." That is, liability exposures are generally of the pure risk variety. It is true that the law establishes rights as well as obligations, and the enforcement of a right might have speculative elements. However, this textbook holds the position that rights enumerated by the law are better considered under the area of property exposures to risk, since a right may, in many respects, be considered an asset of the organization.

Human resource exposures to risk are exposures of the "human assets" of the organization. Risks can result in physical injury or death to managers and employees as well as significant other stakeholders (customers, secured creditors, stockholders, suppliers). In a speculative risk vein, employee productivity may be considered a "gain outcome" arising from a particular human resource risk. One might, for example, view a highly technical piece of machinery as source of loss (worker injury) and gain (increased productivity). In such a case, the risk management strategy is likely to incorporate elements that will reduce the potential for loss while maximizing the likelihood of gain (training the employee, for instance). As a final brief note, human resource exposures do not always translate into *physical* harm. Economic insecurity is a common resultant loss—unemployment and retirement being excellent examples. Therefore, human resource risk management is concerned with the physical and economic welfare of human beings, which Chapter 7 discusses in detail.

Methods of Risk Identification

Since a systematic method for risk identification is essential, a risk manager should use some type of formal procedure. Unless the risk manager identifies all the potential losses (and gains) confronting the organization, he or she will not have any opportunity to determine the best way to handle the undiscovered risks. The organization will unconsciously retain these risks, and this may not be the best or even a good thing to do. Conversely, failing to identify speculative risks that the organization *may want to seek out and assume* could be equally problematic.

Current risk managers seeking a comprehensive approach to risk identification will experience some frustration. To identify all the potential losses and gains, the risk manager needs first a framework for understanding all the losses and gains that could occur to any organization. Unfortunately, the development of such a framework—a framework usually provided in the form of a "risk checklist"—will require a good deal of work. This is because most existing risk checklists (and there are many) are oriented toward insurable risks and/or pure risks. A risk manager interested in identifying and understanding the realm of speculative risks will have to build upon such checklists, and this may be unfamiliar territory for some risk managers.

If a fairly comprehensive checklist can be developed, the next step is the creation of a systematic approach to discover which of the potential losses and gains included in the framework are faced by the organization. Implicit in this second step is the development of an identification "system" that will enable the risk manager to receive information on risks on a more or less continuous basis. Readers should note here that risk identification is not episodic and it most certainly is not a one-time thing. Identification involves a vigilant scanning of the organization environment in an effort to monitor existing risks, identify new risks, and detect changes in the organization's risk profile.

The following section is a discussion of a framework for risk identification. In an effort to reflect the process a typical risk manager may encounter in developing such a framework, the discussion is based upon building a checklist and identification methodology from an existing "pure risk" checklist. In this way the reader may see both the traditional form of risk identification and the relationship between pure and speculative risks.

A Framework for Identifying Potential Risks

Traditional risk assessment checklists commonly provide a framework for risk identification (Appendix 3.1 at the end of this chapter provides one example of such a checklist). A checklist of potential losses (that is, of pure risks) almost always appears as part of a questionnaire that is designed to serve a much broader purpose than merely providing such a checklist. Usually the questionnaire asks for information that will prove useful in dealing with the exposures as well as identifying them. For example, the questionnaire may ask whether the organization owns or rents a building, and the current cost of comparable buildings. Built into the questions, therefore, is a checklist of potential losses, but the answers also are useful in making and implementing risk control or risk financing decisions.

Both insurance survey and risk analysis questionnaires are available. Insurance survey questionnaires usually are limited to the types of exposures that can be insured; risk analysis questionnaires deal with all pure loss exposures. Questionnaires of both types have been developed by some insurers and risk management consulting firms. Three commonly cited risk analysis questionnaires are published by the American Management Association (AMA), by the Risk and Insurance Management Society (RIMS), and by the International Risk Management Institute. Some other questionnaires have been designed for specific industries.

To illustrate, Section 2 of the American Management Association's *Risk Analysis Guide to Insurance and Employee Benefits* is a risk analysis questionnaire that contains a list of questions designed to (1) remind the risk manager of possible loss exposures, (2) gather information that will describe in what way and to what extent the particular business is exposed to that potential loss, and (3) summarize the existing insurance program, including premiums paid and losses incurred (Pfaffle and Nicosia, 1977). Here are some sample (paraphrased) questions:

- If a building is leased from someone else, does the lease make the organization responsible for restoration of damage not resulting from its own negligence?
- Are organization-owned vehicles furnished to directors, executives, or employees for business and personal use? If so, to what extent?
- Are there any key service facilities or warehouses whose function must continue even though the structures and equipment may be damaged?
- Indicate the maximum amount of money, checks, and securities that may be on hand in any one office during and outside business hours.
- Indicate premiums and losses during the past four years for any excess workers' compensation insurance policies carried.

Part of this questionnaire asks the risk manager questions that summarize the eligibility requirements, benefits, and financial experience of employee benefit plans.

The AMA *Risk Analysis Guide* provides a checklist of (1) possible assets and (2) possible exposures. This checklist, though very useful, is limited to property and liability exposures. The exposures to loss are categorized as (1) direct, (2) indirect or consequential, or (3) third-party liabilities with numerous subcategories.

Such checklists are useful starting points for the development of an overall analytical framework, but there are two important limitations. First, standardized checklists will fail to list pure risks that are unusual or are unique to a particular organization. This is a natural limitation of standardization, but it will also arise because many checklists are oriented toward insurable risks. Therefore, the risk manager will have to recognize that his or her organization will be exposed to numerous pure risks that do not appear on a checklist.

Second, since traditional risk management practices have not focused on speculative risks, it is very unlikely that the checklist will provide any acknowledgment of such risks. While it is true that most current risk managers do not have managerial responsibility for many speculative risks, there is still great value in identifying such risks, primarily because speculative risks almost invariably generate pure risks and because speculative risks themselves have negative potential outcomes.

Over time, a risk manager is likely to modify a checklist to suit the needs of the organization, so it is almost impossible to discuss a "typical" comprehensive risk checklist. However, the framework used in this textbook for categorizing risks could serve as a structure for risk identification purposes. For instance, the outline of a comprehensive risk checklist might appear as follows:

I. Physical Environment
   A. Hazards/risk factors arising from source of risk
      1. Perils arising from hazards
         a. Exposures to risk
            (1) property exposures
            (2) liability exposures
            (3) human resource exposures
II. Social Environment
   B. Hazards/risk factors arising from source of risk
      1. Perils arising from hazards
         a. Exposures to risk
            (1) property exposures
            (2) liability exposures
            (3) human resource exposures

and so on, through the remaining sources of risk: political environment, legal environment, operational environment, economic environment, and cognitive environment.

Application of Checklist

Developing a comprehensive checklist and using it are not necessarily the same thing. The checklist becomes a framework for organizing the organization's risk profile, but the actual investigation of the organization's risks requires a methodology all its own.

The first step in applying the checklist is to focus upon the sources of risk. The seven sources of risk outlined earlier provide a good starting point for thinking about organizational risk. The goal of this first step is to develop a narrative detailing each source of risk. For instance, the physical environment could be summarized in a few short paragraphs, which would include a description of geographical, climatic, and other physical characteristics of the organization. The same could then be done for the other source areas. In developing these overview statements of the sources of risk, the risk manager is able to begin to develop a general sense of the scope of organizational risk, though little detail may be known at this point.

Others have proposed somewhat similar approaches. For instance, Professor John O'Connell has recommended a careful analysis of the external environment as well as internal exposures as an approach to identifying the exposures of a particular organization (O'Connell, 1976). Following a structure suggested by Dr. William Dill, Dr. O'Connell identifies four components of the "relevant" environment: (1) customers (or clients or constituents), (2) suppliers, (3) competitors, and (4) regulators. In analyzing each component, important considerations are the nature of the relationships, their heterogeneity, and their stability. For example, is the product distributed directly to one group of buyers or indirectly, through wholesalers and retailers, to many persons? Are the customers families, businesses, or government agencies? Are there single or multiple suppliers of important services? What contractual arrangements have been made with suppliers? Does competition with others require speedy advertising campaigns and possibly encourage improper product claims? What special obligations are imposed by outsiders, such as government regulators and legislators, consumers and consumer groups, and unions? How rapidly are these relationships changing? Courts, legislators, and economic and social forces are continuously affecting risk exposures. Workers' compensation benefits may be increased by a state legislature; a court may impose more responsibility upon firms for environmental pollution; a recession may cause theft rates to rise; and both economic and social inflation may cause a jury to award higher amounts to plaintiffs.

A second approach to analysis of environmental conditions that may be used derives from strategic management and is detailed by Edward R. Freeman in his book, *Strategic Management: A Stakeholder Approach* (Freeman, 1984). Dr. Freeman develops a stakeholder model for identifying interests that attach to the organization, from within and without. Although the purpose of this model is to identify and define the organization's mission and to develop strategic direction, its approach is helpful to a risk manager seeking to organize his or her thinking about environmental influences on the organization.

The next step, or set of steps, involves the identification of hazards/risk factors, perils, and exposures to risk. In some cases, it may be logical to identify the risk sequentially, for example, what are the hazards/risk factors, what are the perils that arise from those hazards, what are the exposures to risk. In other cases, the elements may be identified simultaneously. Whatever the case, several techniques or methods are available for identifying the risks. These methods include (1) the financial statement method, (2) the flow-chart method, (3) on-site inspections, (4) planned interactions with other departments, (5) interactions with external resources, (6) contract analysis, and (7) statistical analysis of loss records.

Before each of these methods is explored, three points should be emphasized. First, the risk manager should not rely upon any one method. Timely information from other departments, for example, may reveal an exposure that the financial statement method would miss. Each method supplements the others. Second, risk identification is a continuous process. The exposures may change from day to day. Third, applying the checklist of potential risks may suggest some gaps in the checklist itself that should be corrected.

The Financial Statement Method. The first procedure for determining which of the potential risks in the checklist apply to a particular organization and in what way is the financial statement method proposed by A. H. Criddle (Criddle, 1962). Although this approach was intended for private organizations, and although financial reporting practices vary from private to nonprofit to public organizations, the concepts of the financial statement approach are generalizable to all types of organizations.

By analyzing the balance sheet, operating statements, and supporting documents, Criddle maintained, the risk manager can identify all the existing property, liability, and personnel (what this text calls human resource) exposures of the organization. By coupling these statements with financial forecasts and budgets, the risk manager can discover future exposures. This follows because every organizational transaction ultimately involves either money or property.

Under this method each account title is studied in depth to determine what potential risks it creates. The results of the study are reported under the account titles. Criddle argued that this approach is reliable, objective, based upon readily available data, presentable in clear, concise terms, and applicable by either risk managers or professional consultants. Moreover, it translates risk identification into financial terminology that is more familiar, and consequently should be more acceptable, to other managers in the organization and to outsiders, such as accountants and bankers. Readers should also note that this approach does not preclude an identification of speculative risks, though this was not directly suggested by Criddle. Finally, in addition to aiding in risk identification, financial statements are useful in risk measurement and determining the best way to handle the exposure.

Criddle recognized that the risk manager must supplement the financial records with other sources of information, such as an inspection of the premises or legal documents. His thesis is that analyzing the financial statements will suggest these additional steps.

The analysis shown in Table 3.1 illustrates in abbreviated fashion how one account title, coupled with some appreciation of the various losses that could occur, can help to identify potential losses.

The Flow-Chart Method. A second systematic procedure for identifying the potential risks facing a particular organization is the flow-chart approach. First, a flow chart or series of flow charts is constructed, which shows all the operations of the organization, starting with raw materials, power, and other inputs at suppliers' locations and ending with finished products in the hands of customers. For example, Figure 3.1 shows the major operations of a hypothetical firm. Figure 3.2 is a more detailed picture of one part of those operations. More detailed pictures can and should be prepared. Second, the checklist of potential property, liability, and human resource risks is applied to each property and operation shown in the flow chart to determine which risks the organiza-

TABLE 3.1 Example of Identification of Potential Losses and Perils for a Specific Account Title

Account Title	Specific Property, Personnel, or Activity	Potential Loss	Peril

Inventory	Raw materials:
	  In supplier's hands
	  In transit to warehouses
	   in supplier's trucks
	  Warehouse
	  In transit to manufacturing
	   plant in firm's own trucks
	  Manufacturing plant
		Property losses
		  Direct
		  Indirect
		  Net Income
			Fire, wind-
			  storm, hail,
			  burglary,
			  and other
			  human perils

	Finished goods:
	  Manufacturing plant
	  In transit to warehouse
	   Firm's own trucks
	   Common carrier
	  Warehouse
	  In transit to retailers
	   Firm's own trucks
	   Common carrier
		Liability losses
		  arising out of
		  trucks, premises,
		  products,
		  injuries to
		  employees
			Negligence
			Breach of
			  warranty
			  and injuries
			  to employees

	In independent retailer's
	  hands
		Personnel
		  losses
			Death, poor
			  health, un-
			  employment,
			  retirement

tion faces. For example, Figure 3.1 suggests, among others, the following potential losses arising from risks:

Property Losses
    Replacement or repair of trucks, manufacturing plant, machinery and raw materials, goods in process, or finished goods, subject to physical and human perils on the manufacturing premises or in transit
    Shutdown or slowdown of manufacturing operations because of direct property losses

Liability Losses
    Liability for bodily injury or property damage to customers because of defective products, to visitors because of defects in the premises, and to others because of negligent operation of the firm's trucks
    Legal responsibility under (1) the workers' compensation law for bodily injury to employees and (2) automobile no-fault laws

Human Resource Losses
    Losses to firm because of death or disability of key employees
    Losses to families of employees because of death, poor health, retirement or unemployment of employees.

On-site Inspections. On-site inspections are a must for the risk manager. By observing firsthand the organization's facilities and the operations con-

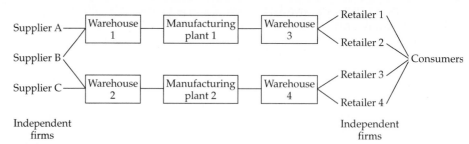

FIGURE 3.1. Flow chart—total operations. (The marketing, accounting, and other supporting management functions are not shown explicitly in this diagram, but their presence should be recognized.)

ducted therein, the risk manager can learn much about the exposures faced by the organization.

Interactions with Other Departments. A fourth way to identify the risks facing an organization is through systematic and continuous interactions with other departments in the organization. Included among these interactions are (1) extended visits with managers and employees of other departments during which the risk manager attempts to obtain a complete understanding of their activities and the potential losses created by these activities, and (2) oral or written reports from other departments on their own initiative or in response to a regular reporting system that keeps the risk manager informed of all relevant developments. The importance of such a communications network should not be underestimated. These departments are constantly creating or becoming aware of exposures that might otherwise escape the risk manager's attention. Indeed, the risk manager's success in risk identification is heavily dependent upon the cooperation he or she secures from other departments.

Unfortunately, risk managers often hear about new exposures long after they are created. For example, one risk manager was surprised to learn from his morning newspaper that his employer had purchased an expensive river barge two weeks earlier. As a result, for two weeks the firm was exposed to some serious property, liability, and human resource losses that were ignored in its risk management planning. Moreover, if these losses had been explicitly considered, the firm might have decided not to buy the barge.

In developing interactions with other managers and departments, the risk manager must overcome the natural reluctance of others to reveal unfavorable information. Most managers would not be expected to reveal activities that create the potential for unfavorable developments. A critical task for a risk manager is to persuade others that revealing possibly unfavorable information is in

FIGURE 3.2. Flow chart—manufacturing plant 1.

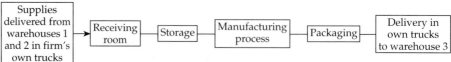

their own interest. Incentives for revealing this type of information are possible if the organization has a system for allocating the cost of losses. For example, when losses arise from unreported activities, a penalty could be imposed when the losses are charged against a manager's account or the losses could be charged at a higher rate than those arising from reported activities. To avoid confusion and possible ill will, the existence of such a penalty should be clearly communicated to managers at the same time they are asked for information on risk-creating activities.

Interactions with External Resources. In addition to communicating with other departments, the risk manager should interact with outsiders rendering related services to the organization. These outsiders, for example, might include accountants, lawyers, risk management consultants, actuaries, or loss control specialists. The objective would be to determine whether the outsiders have identified some exposures that otherwise would be missed or have themselves created some new exposures.

Contract Analysis. Because many exposures arise out of contractual relationships with others, the risk manager should study contracts to see whether the organization has increased or reduced its exposures under a contract. For example, under a lease, a landlord and a tenant can trade various kinds of exposures.

Statistical Records of Losses. A seventh approach, which will probably suggest fewer exposures than the others but which may identify some exposures not otherwise discovered, is to consult statistical records of losses or near losses that may be repeated in the future. Risk management information systems have been developed that analyze these losses according to cause, location, amount, and other variables.

Statistical records allow the risk manager to assess trends in the organization's loss experience and to compare the organization's loss experience with the experience of others. In addition, these records enable the risk manager to analyze issues such as the cause, time, and location of the accident, the identity of the injured individual and the supervisor, and any hazards or other special factors affecting the nature of the accident. Common patterns or frequently appearing sets of circumstances point toward issues requiring special attention. For example, if ladders appear frequently as a cause of accidents, the organization's risk manager is well advised to investigate ladders and their use and possibly set up a training program on safe practices.

When a significant amount of data on past losses is available, the risk manager may use this information to develop forecasts of loss costs. These forecasts may be developed through trending or loss development, a technique discussed in Chapter 4. Forecasts obtained using loss development are extremely useful in budgeting for programs in which an organization directly pays costs using its own funds (e.g., a self-insurance program). For example, an organization that uses its own funds to pay the cost of work-related injuries or to provide health benefits to its own employees has a vital interest in projecting costs of the program.

A comment on the seeking of new risk: Ordinarily, a risk manager takes the organization's risks as "given." Very rarely does the risk manager have the opportunity to pick and choose an organization's risks proactively, and when that opportunity occurs, it usually is given in the context of avoiding a risk with troubling potential. However, in the context of this textbook's view of risk management, risk identification must also include the identification of risks not currently faced, but which the organization may choose to assume. An example of this type of identification would be market research when an organization contemplates moving into a new line of business, or research and development of new products within an existing line.

The investigation of new risks is part of the risk identification process, and the fact that a "risk manager" is not actually conducting the investigation does not mean it is not risk management. Indeed, the idea that every employee practices elements of risk management flows naturally from the risk management model proposed in Chapter 2. The notion of integrating the identification of new risks into the overall effort of risk identification suggests that somewhere in the organization is a belief that the attempt to systematically identify *all* risks—present and future—is in the organization's best interest.

HAZARD AND LOSS ANALYSIS

The chapter now turns to a specific topic: the analysis of hazards and losses. Although this discussion does not address the analysis of positive outcomes arising from speculative risks, it is generally relevant to them. Further, as a practical matter, the typical risk manager is likely to spend a great deal more time addressing pure risks (and the negative consequence of speculative risks), so the emphasis on hazards and losses is entirely appropriate.

Risk assessment is not just the identification of risk. Knowing that a fire could destroy a grade school is useful in planning, but does not provide much insight into the nature of the risk manager's challenge. Identification must be coupled with an analysis of the hazards and perils as well as the losses themselves. How do losses occur? How does a particular sequence of events move a hazard to produce a loss? Before discussing hazard and loss analysis, a brief introduction to the subject of accident causation is helpful. The study of how and why accidents occur provides an important backdrop to an analysis of hazards and losses.

Accident Causation

Many schools of thought exist concerning causes of accidents. Two representative approaches are the "engineering" view and the "human relations" view. Other approaches may combine engineering and human relations simultaneously.

The person usually credited with the distinction between the engineering and human relations approaches is H. W. Heinrich, a pioneer in the human relations approach and many other safety concepts (Heinrich, 1959). According to

Heinrich's "domino theory," a preventable accident is one of five factors in a sequence that results in an injury.

1. Ancestry and social environment
2. Fault of the person (inherited or acquired fault of person constitutes proximate reasons for committing unsafe acts or for the existence of mechanical or physical hazards)
3. Unsafe act and/or mechanical or physical hazard
4. Accident
5. Injury

The engineering approach emphasizes mechanical or physical causes of accidents, such as defective wiring, improper disposal of waste products, poorly designed highway intersections or automobiles, and unguarded machinery. An examination of engineering hazards is supposed to be particularly pertinent to fire losses because tangible things, such as the construction of the building, the provisions for protection, the type of occupancy, and the external features, such as the quality of the surroundings, may contribute to fire hazard. Even so, personnel failures have been blamed for over one-third of the losses by fire. In his study, Heinrich claimed that unsafe acts of persons (operating or working at unsafe speed, using unsafe equipment or using any equipment unsafely, distracting or teasing workers, abusing equipment, making safety devices inoperative, etc.) are the major causes of 88 percent of the industrial accidents resulting in personal injury to workers.

The emphasis on human relations and, consequently, on the personal causes of risk became important during the 1930s when the engineering approach, despite its dramatic achievements, was seen to be an inconclusive answer. According to Somers and Somers, just as the development of scientific engineering around 1910 coincided with the development of scientific management by Frederick Taylor and others who argued that safety equals efficiency, so the development of the human relations approach to loss control, with its emphasis on safety education, safety contests, rest periods, and the like, coincided with the development of interest in the human relations field in industry (Somers and Somers, 1954).

Later, the emphasis on human relations was expanded to include special attention to the psychological problems of the accident-prone individual. Some trucking firms, for example, use psychological tests of driver attitudes in selecting personnel and in trying to locate trouble spots. This development also coincides with the general awakening of interest in mental health.

This increased attention to human errors has been criticized on several grounds. First, it is argued, the effect of mechanical causes has been underestimated. For example, using unsafe equipment probably should not be considered solely a human error; it might be possible to make this equipment nearly foolproof. Second, industry may devote so much of its resources to the more glamorous human relations preoccupations that engineering will be insufficiently considered. Third, blaming the worker for the industrial accident is not in accord with the principle of workers' compensation, which does not blame management or labor for industrial accidents.

Despite these criticisms, Heinrich's "domino theory" is still relevant and popular. One modern expert, Dan Petersen, agrees with Heinrich's emphasis on the unsafe acts of persons (Peterson, 1978). However, he emphasizes that behind every accident lie not one, but many contributing factors, causes and sub-causes. Root causes, he believes, are often related to the management system.

Dr. William Haddon, Jr., while president of the Insurance Institute for Highway Safety, suggested a more comprehensive way of classifying causes of accidents (Haddon, 1970). According to Haddon, accidents result from the transfer of energy in such ways and amounts and at such speeds that inanimate or animate structures are damaged. These accidents can be prevented either by controlling the energy involved or by changing the inanimate or animate structures it can damage. Unlike Heinrich, Haddon emphasizes the control of energy, a physical force, instead of human failings. Both approaches offer insight into causation, making them both worthy of study by risk managers.

Loss Analysis

To obtain information on possible losses the risk manager needs to develop (1) a network of information sources, and (2) forms for reporting accidents and near accidents. The major information sources are the line supervisors responsible for the operations where accidents occur. They can provide many details about accidents, and by completing the forms they should become more aware of what causes accidents and of the importance of controlling them. Line supervisors, however, are not safety specialists. They may not realize what information is needed for analysis, they may resent having to spend time completing the form, and their self-interest may cause them to provide incomplete or incorrect information. The forms therefore must be carefully designed. They must provide the information needed but be relatively easy to understand and complete. The final section of this textbook will focus on risk management program administration, which will include a discussion of the mechanics of managing and controlling the flow of information, so further discussion here will be brief.

According to Heinrich, ideally, one would study not only those accidents that caused injuries or property damage but also all those unplanned events that *might have* caused such losses. In other words, all *incidents*, the "near misses" as well as accidents causing losses, would be reported and studied. In his investigation of industrial accidents, he found that out of 330 accidents of a similar type, 300 will produce no injury, 29 will produce minor injuries, and 1 will produce a major injury. Too often, he claims, safety engineers ignore, in their record-keeping and loss control measures, accidents that do not cause injury. Moreover, they concentrate on those accidents that produce major injuries; but whether accidents result in injuries, and especially a major injury, is largely a matter of chance. Cost and the burden of reporting all such events have weighed against this approach in many cases. All organizations, however, tend to take special notice of events that did not cause any loss but in which it is clear they were extremely fortunate to escape a serious loss. They should also study property-damage-only accidents, which are commonly recorded, because the hazard that caused these accidents may cause injuries in the future. In one study based on an analysis of over 90,000 accidents over a 7-year period at a steel company, on the average 500 property damage accidents occurred for every 100 minor bodily injury accidents.

Various philosophies exist on the structure of the report forms. For example, one form may be used for reporting all accidents, or different forms might be used for different types of accidents (for instance, industrial accidents causing injuries and fire causing property damage). The forms also differ in the amount of detail they request concerning the accident and the persons and property involved. The form may specify several possible causes of accidents among which the supervisor may choose, or the question about possible causes may be open-ended. The form may permit the supervisor to identify only one possible cause of the accident or it may require the naming of more than one possible cause. The form may or may not require the supervisor to suggest measures that might be taken to prevent a similar accident in the future.

The information on losses provided through these reports can be used to (1) measure the performance of line managers, (2) determine which operations, if any, need to be corrected, (3) identify the hazards that have been responsible for the losses, and (4) provide information that can be used to motivate workers and managers to pay more attention to loss control.

Hazard Analysis

Loss analysis should reveal hazards that need to be investigated more carefully. Hazard analysis, however, cannot be limited to the hazards that have caused accidents. Instead, it is necessary to identify other hazards that the experience of other organizations, insurers, or government regulatory bodies suggests should be investigated. Increasingly, risk managers are made aware of new hazards that have not as yet caused a loss for anyone but that have been discovered through experimentation under controlled conditions. Hazards in new products, such as newly developed pharmaceuticals, have been uncovered in this way.

Hazards that have not caused losses may be discovered through inspections. Line supervisors are primarily responsible for these inspections, but risk managers may also become involved.

As an aid in making an inspection, the risk manager may design a checklist that reminds the inspector of the possible hazards and facilitates a comparison with existing conditions. These inspection forms, like the accident reporting forms, vary in the detail and nature of the information provided. For example, one form asks only for (1) an evaluation of the general conditions regarding housekeeping, equipment, hand tools, and so on, and (2) recommendations for improving these conditions. A more comprehensive form asks for (1) the unsafe conditions or acts noted, (2) whether each of these "symptoms" was discussed with the supervisor, (3) the causes found for each of these symptoms, and (4) suggestions as to future actions with respect to these causes.

One technique that has proved increasingly useful in analyzing the causes of accidents is *fault tree analysis*. This technique may be used in loss analysis to determine the causes of actual losses or in hazard analysis to determine the causes and effects of accidents. It shows the multiple causes of accidents and whether all or only some of these causes must be present to precipitate an accident. It thus provides a basis for preventing such accidents.

A second methodology, often referred to as the *risk chain*, provides an analytical structure for examining the relationship between hazards and losses—and because the methodology is viewed as both a loss and hazard analysis tool. This approach examines the hazard, the environment, the interaction between hazard and environment, the result of the interaction, and the long-term consequences of the interaction. For instance, the risk manager might break down the analysis of an industrial accident into an evaluation of the hazardous condition (an improperly ventilated work station, the harmful fumes and their source), the environment (the people working at the site and other exposures), the interaction of exposure to hazard (people breathing fumes), the results of the interaction (respiratory problems), and the long-term consequences (workers' compensation claims, worksite redesign costs, etc.). Because the risk chain idea serves as a useful method for assessing risk *and* for suggesting appropriate risk control tools and strategies, further discussion is deferred until Chapter 8.

RISK MEASUREMENT

The identification of risks and the possible outcomes is the initial step in risk assessment. This step, however, provides little information for ranking the importance of risks to the organization. Additional information is required for this ranking: estimates of possible financial consequences and estimates of the likelihood. The ranking is important because it influences the allocation of resources for managing and controlling risks. Risk measurement requires the risk manager to (1) develop yardsticks for measuring the importance of risks to the organization and (2) apply these yardsticks to the types of risk that have been identified.

The distinction between *direct* and *indirect* costs is fundamental in estimating possible financial consequences (direct and indirect benefits are also of concern). A *direct cost* is a direct consequence of a peril acting on an object or person. If a fire damages the roof of a retail store, for example, the direct loss is the cost to repair or replace the damage to the roof.

An *indirect cost* is related to the damage caused directly by the peril, but the financial consequences are not a direct consequence of the action of the peril on the object or person. For example, earnings lost by the owner of the retail store while the store is closed for roof repairs are an indirect loss. Indirect costs are often hidden, although their consequences can be greater than those of direct losses.

Hidden Costs of Accidents

A discussion of the "indirect" costs associated with an accident, and their relationship to the direct or more obvious costs, would be incomplete without some mention of Heinrich's investigation of industrial accident costs. According to Heinrich, the cost of industrial accidents is usually stated only in terms of workers' compensation paid the injured employee for lost time and his or her medical expenses. The actual costs, however, are much greater because he found the "incidental" or "hidden" costs to be four times as great as the compensation benefits.

If Heinrich's argument is accepted, the case for risk management is considerably strengthened. Some of the factors that Heinrich included among these hidden accident costs were as follows:

1. Cost of lost time of injured employee
2. Cost of time lost by other employees who stop work to help the injured worker
3. Cost of time lost by supervisors or other executives preparing reports on the accident and training a replacement
4. Cost due to damage to the machine, tools, or other property, or to the spoilage of material
5. Cost to employer of continuing the wages of the injured employee in full, after his return, even though the services of the employee (who is not yet fully recovered) may for a time be worth only about half of their normal value
6. Costs that occur in consequence of excitement or weakened morale due to the accident.

Heinrich did not contend that his 4-to-1 proportion applied to every accident or to every plant. He also acknowledged that the ratio may vary in nationwide application.

Heinrich's major point—that the "indirect" costs are substantial—holds true, but many writers have challenged the 4-to-1 ratio. Simonds and Grimaldi, using the terms "insured" and "uninsured" to correspond to Heinrich's "direct" and "indirect," believe that: (1) the ratio of uninsured costs to insured costs in industrial accidents is probably less than 4 to 1 because some of the uninsured costs included by Heinrich are not valid, and (2) because there is no direct correlation between uninsured costs and insured costs, applying a single ratio to total direct costs to determine the indirect costs produces inaccurate results (Simonds and Grimaldi, 1975).

As an alternative to expressing uninsured costs as a single multiple of insured costs, Simonds and Grimaldi suggest the following formula for the ordinary run of accidents:

Total cost = Insurance cost
+ A × the number of lost-time cases
+ B × the number of doctor's cases (no lost time)
+ C × the number of first-aid only cases
+ D × the number of accidents causing no injuries but causing property damage in excess of specified amounts

where A, B, C, and D are the average uninsured costs for each category of cases, and the number of cases refers to the actual count of each type during the period under consideration.

Bird and Germain claim, however, that this revised concept has also proved to be an ineffective tool in safety motivation (Bird and Germain, 1966). Obtaining and updating the necessary information, they believe, is a difficult, time-consuming task. Allocating uninsured costs among departments poses technical problems and is even more likely to meet opposition than the allocation of insured costs. They suggest, instead, a ledger-costs concept, so named because it involves only costs that appear on department ledgers. Government agencies call it the "elements of production-accident cost" concept. This method of accident cost accounting does not include all accident costs, but it does add some noninsured costs that could be many times the insured costs. The factors considered in this accounting are the following:

1. People power
   a. Total workers' compensation benefits
   b. Wages and medical costs paid during disability in addition to workers' compensation benefits
   c. Time lost on day of injury and on subsequent days
   d. Time spent on light work or reduced output
2. Machinery, material, equipment
   a. Cost of repairing damage, or cost of replacement
   b. Lost production time.

This method is applicable to all accidents, not only those that cause bodily injuries or that might have caused bodily injuries.

Despite their differences, Heinrich, Simonds and Grimaldi, and Bird and Germain all emphasize that accident costs tend to be underestimated.

A final point should be mentioned briefly. Although the preceding discussion was intentionally structured to discuss hazards and losses, the general points regarding direct and indirect costs of losses is translatable to the concept of direct and indirect benefits. That is, when considering speculative risks, the positive outcomes often generate direct benefits (increasing sales, for instance) and indirect benefits (enhanced public image, worker job satisfaction, and so on).

Dimensions of Exposure to Risk

Information is needed concerning two dimensions of each exposure. In the case of pure risks: (1) the loss frequency of the number of losses that will occur and (2) the severity of these losses. In the case of speculative risks: (1) the frequency of positive and negative outcomes and (2) the severity or magnitude of these outcomes. For each of these two dimensions, frequency and severity, it would be desirable to know at least the value in an average budget period and the possible variation in the values from one budget period to the next.

These data can be directly useful in determining the best methods for handling an exposure to risk. For example, multiplying expected loss frequency and average loss severity provides an estimate of the expected value of losses. This estimate can be compared with the amount an insurer charges for insurance protection, and estimates of possible variation allow the risk manager to estimate the likelihood that losses will exceed the cost of insurance.

Chapter 4 shows how techniques in probability and statistics can be used in

risk measurement. Normally, these techniques presume the existence of considerable information about the risk (i.e., uncertainty at level 2 as described in
Chapter 1). For purposes of the following discussion, the level of information required for these more sophisticated methods will not be presumed. Instead, the
present chapter tells why the risk manager needs information on each dimension and describes one approach to estimating loss frequency and loss severity.

Measurable dimensions of an exposure to risk are shown in Figure 3.3. This
matrix provides a conceptual structure to the risk measurement challenge. Cell
I represents risks that are low frequency/low severity; these risks only infrequently result in loss, and when loss occurs it is relatively inexpensive. Cell II
represents risks that are low frequency/high severity; losses occur infrequently,
but each loss is expensive. Cell III represents risks that are high frequency/low
severity; losses occur with great frequency, but each loss is relatively inexpensive. Cell IV represents risks that are high frequency/high severity; losses occur
with great frequency, and each of the losses is expensive. From a practical utility standpoint, this measurement matrix is not too helpful because "high" and
"low" are extremely relative terms, and the dividing lines between high and
low are difficult to discern. However, in a textbook, this frame of reference is extremely useful in assisting readers to think generally about the measurable aspects of risks.

The risk manager should recognize that the level of precision with which
these dimensions can be estimated depends on the level of information available to the risk manager. In general, the more frequently a loss occurs, the more
information is available to estimate its dimensions. Even with a great deal of information, however, estimates of loss frequency and loss severity are subject to
error. The risk manager may expect one loss to occur every five years (loss frequency of 1/5 per year), for example, but may be uncertain as to whether the
true frequency is as low as 1/20 or as high as 2/5. The uncertainty of the risk

FIGURE 3.3. Dimensions of Risk.

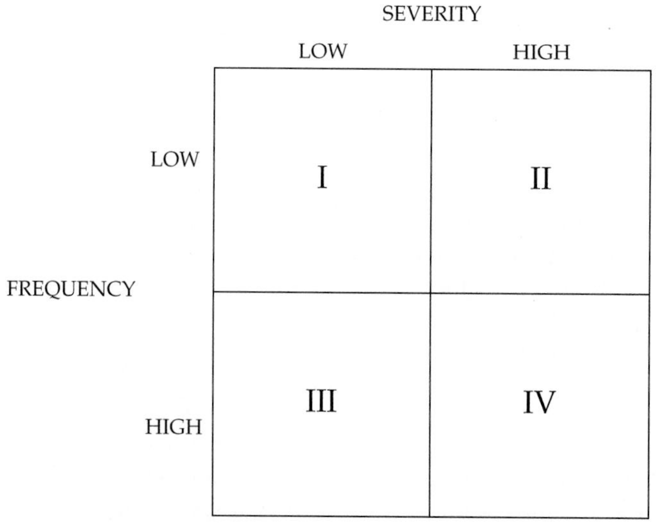

manager about the true value of loss frequency results from possible error; the true value may vary from the risk manager's estimate of the expected value.

For situations in which losses can vary as to amount, estimated loss frequency can depend on the size or severity category. For example, collision damage to automobiles can be divided into two categories: (1) collision damage costing $5,000 or less to repair and (2) damages exceeding $5,000. Damage in the second category is more severe, although less frequent.

Both loss-frequency and loss-severity data are needed to evaluate the relative importance of an exposure to potential loss. *Contrary to the views of many persons, however, the importance of an exposure to risk depends usually upon the potential loss severity, not the potential frequency.* A potential loss with catastrophic possibilities, although infrequent, is far more serious than one expected to produce frequent small losses and no large losses. An example may clarify the point. The chance of an automobile collision loss may be greater than the chance of being sued as a result of the collision, but the potential severity of the liability loss is so much greater than the damage to the owned automobile that the risk manager should not hesitate to rank the liability loss over the property loss. Another illustration would be the losses associated with relatively small medical expenses as contrasted with extremely large bills. Such a breakdown by size of loss shows clearly the desirability of assigning more weight to loss severity than to loss frequency.

In determining loss severity, the risk manager must be careful to include all the types of losses that might occur as a result of a given event as well as their ultimate financial impact upon the organization. Often, while the less important types of losses are obvious to the risk manager, the more important types are much more difficult to identify. Chapter 5, for example, will discuss the recognition and measurement of direct, indirect, and net income property losses. The potential direct property losses are rather generally appreciated in advance of any loss, but the potential indirect and net income losses (such as the interruption of business while the property is being repaired) that may result from the same event are often ignored until the loss occurs. This same event may also cause liability and human resource losses.

The risk manager should also consider whether a single event might involve two or more buildings, persons, or other exposure units. For example, a fire might spread through two blocks, causing two warehouses, not one, to be damaged or destroyed.

The ultimate financial impact of the loss may exceed the sum of all the losses discussed to this point. Relatively small losses, if retained, cause only minor problems because the organization can meet these losses fairly easily out of liquid assets. Somewhat larger losses may cause liquidity problems, which in turn may make it more difficult or more costly for the organization to borrow funds required for various purposes. Very large losses may have serious adverse effects upon the organization's financial planning, and their dollar impact may be much greater than it would be for an organization that could more easily absorb these losses. Ultimately, the loss could be the ruin of the organization. To illustrate, a fire could destroy a building and its contents valued at $600,000; the ensuing shutdown of the firm for six months might cause another $650,000 loss. This $1,250,000 loss might force the firm to shut its doors, an action that would result in an ultimate loss of the difference between the going-concern value of the business, say $4,800,000, and the value for which the remaining assets could be sold, say $3,000,000, causing a $1,800,000 loss.

Finally, in estimating loss severity, it is important to recognize the timing of any losses as well as their total dollar amount. For example, a loss of $20,000 a year for 20 years is not as severe as an immediate loss of $400,000 because of (1) the time value of money, which can be recognized by discounting future dollar losses at some assumed interest rate, and (2) the ability of the organization to spread the cash outlay over a longer period. For a second example, the destruction of a $1 million building that must be replaced immediately is more severe than a $1 million liability claim that need not be paid until four years later.

Loss-Frequency Measures

One method for estimating loss frequency is to consider the probability that a given exposure to a single peril will result in loss during a year. For example, a risk manager may estimate the probability that a single warehouse will be damaged by fire or the probability that a municipality will be sued for failing to provide proper police protection. If the risk manager assumes that more than one loss cannot occur during a year, the probability of loss is the same as annual loss frequency. When a loss occurs, on average, once every 10 years, the probability of loss during a year is 1/10 if at most one loss can occur during the year. Richard Prouty, the risk manager of a large business, suggested over 30 years ago that instead of using numerical estimates, the risk manager might classify these probabilities as (1) "almost nil" (meaning in the opinion of the risk manager the event will not happen), (2) "slight" (meaning that, though possible, the event has not happened to the present time and is unlikely to occur in the future), (3) "moderate" (meaning that it has happened once in a while and can be expected to occur some time in the future), or (4) "definite" (meaning that it has happened regularly and can be expected to occur regularly in the future) (Prouty, 1960). Though not as elaborate as the methods presented in Chapter 4, the Prouty method has the advantage of not presuming a high level of information about the risk.

Given time to think about the organization's exposures and to study records of past losses, many risk managers will find themselves able to classify their judgments into the categories needed for the Prouty method.

Most exposures to risk are more complex than single-peril or single-exposure estimates imply. For example, a given building can be damaged from windstorm, earthquake, or flood as well as from fire. In addition, a single peril, such as fire, may cause damage to several structures. The accuracy of loss-frequency estimates can depend on whether the relationships between perils and objects exposed to risk are considered. These considerations return us to the issue of the amount of information the risk manager has on the nature of the risk. Most risk management decisions are made on the basis of what the risk manager considers a reasonable subset of full information. Almost any decision can be improved by additional information allowing more precise estimates of possible outcomes and their likelihood. The risk manager's judgment is needed to integrate all available information and use it to develop estimates.

Loss-Severity Measures

Two measures commonly used to measure loss severity are the *maximum possible loss,* and the *maximum probable loss.* For the moment, we will concentrate on occurrences causing only one type of loss.

Risk managers often use the phrase "probable maximum loss" (PML) as synonymous with maximum probable loss. The maximum possible loss is the largest amount of damage that *possibly* can occur, the largest conceivable amount of damage. The maximum probable loss is the largest amount of damage that the risk manager believes *is likely* to occur. In other words, damage is *very unlikely* to exceed the maximum probable loss, while damages *cannot* exceed the maximum possible loss. Of the two measures, the maximum probable loss normally is the most difficult to estimate, but also the most useful. As in the case of loss frequency measures, the estimate of the maximum probable loss depends heavily on *all* the information the risk manager has about the nature of the risk.

The maximum probable loss depends on the nature of the peril causing the loss as well as the person or object exposed to loss; usually the maximum possible loss is not affected by the peril being considered. For example, a tenant in an apartment faces possible fire and theft losses to personal possessions. The maximum probable loss to the tenant's possessions may be the full value of these possessions for the peril of fire, but may be limited to the value of items that have high values relative to their weight and size for the peril of theft. In contrast, the maximum possible loss is the full value of all the possessions, regardless of which peril is considered.

As another example, most risk managers would agree that the maximum probable loss with respect to fire damage to a wood frame dwelling is the full value of the dwelling. For a large, modern concrete office building with fire-resistive measures, such as a sprinkler system, most risk managers also would agree that the likelihood of a total loss to the building is so remote that the maximum probable loss is less than the full value of the building. In this example, the estimate of the maximum probable loss is affected by features of the object exposed to possible loss.

However, risk managers may differ as to their estimates of the exact value of the maximum probable loss; some may believe that it is as high as 80 percent of the office building's value, while others may believe it as small as 10 percent of value. An estimated value does not imply that damage *cannot* exceed the maximum probable loss, only that it is *unlikely* to exceed the maximum probable loss. Presumably, the risk manager's willingness to tolerate a chance of being wrong influences the estimate; the lower the estimate, the higher the chance of the risk manager's estimate being too low. Occasionally, a large fire will remind us that even the most advanced construction methods and fire protection measures do not always produce the intended effects.

Alan Friedlander has suggested four measures of the severity of physical damage to a building caused by a single fire (Friedlander, 1977). The (1) "normal loss expectancy" is the dollar loss expected when both private and public protection systems are operative. The (2) "probable maximum loss" is the dollar loss expected when a critical part of the protection system, such as an automatic sprinkler, is out of service or ineffective. The (3) "maximum foreseeable loss" is the dollar loss expected when none of the private protection systems are functioning. The fire in this case would probably burn until stopped by a fire wall, until it burns all its fuel, or until the public fire department, summoned by an outsider, arrives. The (4) "maximum possible loss" is the dollar loss expected when all private and public protection systems are inoperative or ineffective. Generally, the probability of occurrence declines as we move from the normal loss expectancy to the maximum possible loss. The four values depend upon innumerable factors, such as construction, occupancy, private protecton, and public protection.

As explained in the discussion on costs of accidents, however, a single occurrence may involve more than one type of loss. In estimating the maximum possible loss and the maximum probable loss, the risk manager, ideally, would consider all types of losses that might result from a given peril. Fire loss potentials, for example, would include the possibility of direct, indirect, and net income losses, liability suits, and injuries to the organization's employees. The risk manager should also recognize that, though the probability may be low, more than one unit may be involved in a single occurrence, thus causing the loss potential to increase. The probability is high, for example, that a building and its contents will be damaged in the same occurrence.

Finally, in a series of articles directed to risk managers, Professors David Cummins and Leonard Freifelder emphasized the importance of the maximum probable yearly *aggregate* dollar loss—either from a single peril or from several perils (Cummins and Freifelder, 1978, 1979). The maximum probable yearly aggregate loss is the largest total loss amount that an exposure unit or group of exposure units is likely to suffer during a 1-year (or other budget) period. Like the maximum probable loss, this amount depends upon a probability level selected by the risk manager, but unlike the maximum probable loss, this measure does not refer just to severity of a single occurrence. Instead, it depends upon the number of occurrences as well as their severity. In the language of the next chapter, it depends upon the probability distribution of the total dollar losses per year, not upon the probability distribution of the dollar losses per occurrence. Like the maximum probable loss per occurrence, the losses can include all types of losses from the perils and exposure units included in the analysis.

Key Concepts

risk assessment Those activities that enable the risk manager to identify, evaluate, and measure risk and uncertainty and their potential impact on the organization.

risk identification The process of identifying the exposures to potential property, liability, and human resource losses, as well as the hazards and perils that lead to those losses.

loss and hazard analysis The processes by which the risk manager evaluates the conditions that create risks, the perils associated with these hazards, and the losses that occur as a result of perils.

hazard A condition that creates or increases the chance of loss or its severity.

peril A cause of loss.

risk factor A condition that creates or influences the positive or negative outcomes of a speculative risk.

risk measurement The process of determining the likelihood of a loss from an exposure and its probable severity.

maximum possible loss   The worst loss that could possibly occur because of a single event.

maximum probable loss   The worst loss that is likely to occur because of a single event.

Review Questions

1. "In a sense the most vital task in the performance of the risk management function is the establishment of a careful and systematic method of risk identification."
   a. Why is risk identification so important?
   b. Explain briefly the steps of risk identification.
2. Explain how the political environment and the legal environment affect the process of risk analysis, providing at least two examples of changes in these environments creating a risk that was not present previously and augmenting a previously existing type of risk.
3. How can a risk manager use financial statements to determine which of the potential losses in a checklist apply to his or her organization?
4. General managers might be reluctant to reveal situations in their operating units that ultimately could lead to accidental damage or to the organization being sued for injury. Explain how a risk manager might overcome this natural reluctance to reveal unfavorable information.
5. Explain the difference between engineering and human relations approaches to loss and hazard analysis.
6. Why might information on incidents that might have caused injury (but did not) be useful in risk assessment?
7. Distinguish between direct and indirect costs of accidents, giving an example of each type of cost.
8. In determining loss severity it is important to recognize (a) all types of losses, (b) their ultimate impact, (c) the number of units affected, and (d) their timing. Explain.
9. a. Instead of using precise probability estimates, Prouty suggested four probability categories. Explain.
   b. The probability of loss may differ according to the number of units, the types of loss, and the perils involved in the loss. Explain.
10. The risk manager of an organization maintains that the dollar value of the maximum probable loss to a building as a result of a steam-boiler explosion is $400,000, while his assistant estimates it to be $300,000. Both agree that the maximum possible loss is the complete destruction of the building.
    a. Why do their estimates of the dollar value of the maximum probable loss differ?
    b. Why might the maximum possible loss exceed their estimate?
11. Explain how Friedlander would assess fire loss potentials.
12. How does the risk manager's uncertainty affect the estimates of loss frequency and loss severity? What is likely to happen to this uncertainty as the loss frequency (e.g., the number of work-related injuries per year) increases?

References and Suggestions for Additional Reading

BIRD, F. E., and G. L. GERMAIN: *Damage Control* (New York: American Management Association, 1966).

CRIDDLE, A. HAWTHORNE: "The Use of Financial Statements in Corporate Risk Analysis,"

Identifying and Controlling the Risks of Accidental Loss, AMA Report no. 73 (New York: American Management Association, 1962).

CUMMINS, J. D., and L. R. FREIFELDER: "Statistical Analysis in Risk Management: Types of Probability Distributions—Parts I–V," *Risk Management,* Vols. XXV–XXVI, nos. 9–12, 1 (September, 1978–January, 1979).

FRIEDLANDER, ALAN W.: "Assessing Fire Loss Potentials," *Risk Management* (Vol. XXIV, no. 10, October, 1977).

FREEMAN, EDWARD R.: *Strategic Management: A Stakeholder Approach,* Boston: Pittman, 1984.

HADDON, WILLIAM, Jr.: "On Escape of Tigers: An Ecological Note," *Technology Review* (May, 1970), copyrighted by the Alumni Association of the Massachusetts Institute of Technology.

HEINRICH, H. W.: *Industrial Accident Prevention* (4th ed., New York: McGraw-Hill Book Company, 1959).

MEHR, R. I., and B. A. HEDGES: *Risk Management: Concepts and Applications* (Homewood, Ill.: Richard D. Irwin, Inc., 1974).

MERKHOFER, MILEY: *Decision Science and Social Risk Management* (Dordrecht, Holland: D. Reidel Publishing Co., 1987).

O'CONNELL, JOHN J.: "Systematic Risk Identification," *Risk Management* (Vol. XXIII, no. 3 March, 1976).

PETERSEN, DAN: *Techniques of Safety Management* (2d ed., New York: McGraw-Hill Book Company, 1978).

PFAFFLE, A. E., and SAL NICOSIA: *Risk Analysis Guide to Insurance and Employee Benefits* (New York: Amacom, 1977).

PROUTY, Richard: *Industrial Insurance: A Formal Approach to Risk Analysis and Evaluation* (Washington, D.C.: Machinery and Allied Products Institute, January 19, 1960).

SIMONDS, R. H., and J. W. GRIMALDI: *Safety Management* (3d ed., Homewood, Ill.: Richard D. Irwin, Inc., 1975).

SOMERS, H. M., and A. R. SOMERS: *Workmen's Compensation* (New York: John Wiley & Sons, Inc., 1954).

APPENDIX 3.1. ASSETS-EXPOSURES ANALYSIS

Assets

A. Physical Assets
   1. Real property
      (a) Buildings
         (1) Under construction
         (2) Owned or leased
         (3) Manufacturing
         (4) Offices
         (5) Warehouses
         (6) Garages and hangers
         (7) Dwellings and farms
         (8) Tanks, towers, and stacks
         (9) Wharfs and docks
         (10) Pipes and wires (aboveground)
      (b) Underground property
         (1) Cables and wires
         (2) Tanks
         (3) Shelters, caves, and tunnels
         (4) Mines and shafts
         (5) Wells, groundwater
         (6) Piping and pipelines
      (c) Land
         (1) Improved
         (2) Unimproved

A. Physical Assets *(continued)*
   2. Personal property (on and off premises and in transit)
      (a) Equipment and machinery
         (1) Machines and tools
         (2) Dies, jigs, molds, castings
         (3) Boilers and pressure vessels
            a. Fired vessels—steam and hot water boilers
            b. Unfired vessels
         (4) Mechanical electrical equipment—transformers, generators, motors, fans, pumps, compressors
         (5) Engines—diesel, gasoline, steam
         (6) Meters and gauges
         (7) Turbines—steam, gas, water
         (8) Conveyors and lifts, trams, elevators
      (b) Furniture and fixtures
      (c) Electronic data processing equipment
      (d) Improvements and betterments
      (e) Stock—supplies, raw materials, goods in process, finished goods
      (f) Fine arts—antiques, paintings, jewelry, libraries
      (g) Safety equipment—instruments, apparel, alarms, installations
      (h) Value papers

         (1) Blueprints
         (2) Formulas
         (3) Accounts receivable
         (4) Patents and copyrights
         (5) Titles and deeds
         (6) Tapes, cards, disks, programs
         (7) Own securities—negotiable and nonnegotiable
         (8) Other corporate securities
         (9) Cash (indicate currency)

   3. Miscellaneous property
      (a) Vehicles (including contents)
         (1) Commercial
         (2) Private passenger
         (3) Contractor's equipment (licensed)
         (4) Warehouse equipment
      (b) Aircraft
         (1) Missiles and satellites
         (2) Lighter-than-air
         (3) Aircraft—jet, piston, fixed-wing, rotary wing
      (c) Animals
      (d) Antennas
      (e) Crops, gardens, lawns
      (f) Fences
      (g) Firearms
      (h) Nuclear and radioactive property—isotopes, tracers, reactors, cyclotrons, accelerators, betatrons
      (i) Promotional displays—signs, models, plates, handbills, exhibits
      (j) Recreational facilities—parks, gyms, lakes, cafeterias
      (k) Watercraft (including contents)—boats, yachts, barges, ships, submersibles, buoys, drilling rigs

B. Intangible Assets
   (assets not necessarily shown on balance sheet or earnings statement)
   1. External assets
      (a) Markets
      (b) Resource availability

B. Intangible Assets *(continued)*
      (1) Supplies
      (2) Transportation
      (3) Employees (full-time and temporary)
      (4) Public utilities
      (5) Public protection
    (c) Communications—telephone, teletype, television, radio, newspaper
    (d) Locational—climate, political, economic and social stability, currency convertibility
    (e) Counsel and specialists—legal, architecture, accounting, insurance, real estate, general management, marketing, advertising, PR, banking
  2. Internal assets
    (a) Research and development
    (b) Goodwill and reputation
    (c) Financial
      (1) Credit cards
      (2) Credit lines (rec'd)
      (3) Insurance
      (4) Customer credit
      (5) Employee benefits program
      (6) Royalties and rents
      (7) Leasehold interest
      (8) Ownership of stock
      (9) Company foundations (nonprofit)
      (10) Tax loss carry-forward
    (d) Personnel (employees and executives)
      (1) Education and training
      (2) Experience
      (3) "Key" employees
    (e) Rights
      (1) Mineral and oil rights—aboveground, underground, and offshore
      (2) Air rights
      (3) Patents and copyrights
      (4) Royalty agreements
      (5) Distribution agreements
      (6) Manufacturing rights

Exposures to Loss

A. Direct Exposures
  1. Generally uncontrollable and unpredictable
    (a) Electrical disturbance—lightning, burnout, sunspots, power surge, demagnetization of tapes
    (b) Falling objects—aircraft, meteors, missiles, trees
    (c) Land movement—earthquake, volcano, landslide, avalanche
    (d) Sound and shock waves—sonic boom, vibration, water hammer
    (e) Subsidence—collapse, settlement, erosion
    (f) War, insurrection, rebellion, armed revolt, sabotage
    (g) Water damage—flood, rising waters, flash flood, mudslide, tidal waves (tsunami), geyser, groundwater, sprinkler leakage, sewer backup
    (h) Weight of ice, snow
    (i) Windstorm—typhoon, hurricane, cyclone, tornado, hailstorm, rain, dust, seche, sandstorm
  2. Generally controllable or predictable
    (a) Breakage of glass or other fragile items

A. Direct Exposures *(continued)*

    (b) Breakdown—malfunction of part, lubricant, etc.

    (c) Collision, on and off premises—watercraft, aircraft, vehicles

    (d) Contamination—liquid, solid, gaseous, radioactive, pollution

    (e) Corrosion—wear, tear, abuse, poor maintenance

    (f) Employee negligence

    (g) Explosion and implosion

    (h) Failure of environmental control—temperature, humidity, pressure

    (i) Fauna—animals, rodents, insects, pests

    (j) Fire

    (k) Installation and construction hazards—dropping, etc.

    (l) International destruction—jettison, backfiring, etc.

    (m) Perils of sea-pirates, rovers, barratry, etc.

    (n) Physical change—shrinkage, evaporation, color, mildew, expansion, contraction

    (o) Rupture or puncture of tank or vessel

    (p) Smoke damage, smudge

    (q) Spillage, leakage, paint spray

    (r) Structural defects, crane or elevator fall

    (s) Transportation—overturn, collision

    (t) Unintentional error—employee, computer, counsel

    (u) Vegetation

    (v) Vandalism, malicious mischief, defacing of property

    (w) Riots, civil disorders, strikes, boycotts, curfews

  3. Primarily financial in nature

    (a) Employee dishonesty—forgery, embezzlement, larceny

    (b) Expropriation—nationalization, seizure, exercise of eminent domain, confiscation

    (c) Fraud, forgery, theft, burglary, robbery

    (d) Invalidity of deed, title, patent, copyright

    (e) Inventory shortage—mysterious disappearance, lost or mislaid property

    (f) Obsolescence

B. Indirect or Consequential Exposures

  1. All direct exposures as they affect:

    (a) Suppliers

    (b) Customers

    (c) Utilities

    (d) Transportation—personnel and property

    (e) Employees

  2. Extra expense—rentals, communication, product, etc.

  3. Concentration of assets

  4. Change in style, taste, desire

  5. Bankruptcy—employee, executive, supplier, customer, counselor

  6. Disruption of education system—racial, political, economic

  7. Economic fluctuation—inflation, recession, depression

  8. Epidemic, disease, plague

  9. Increased replacement cost, depreciation

  10. Invasion of copyright, patent

  11. Loss of integral part of set, pair, group

  12. Loss of rights resulting from records destruction

B. Indirect or Consequential Exposures *(continued)*
   13. Managerial error in:
       (a) Pricing, marketing
       (b) Distribution
       (c) Production
       (d) Expansion
       (e) Economic predictions
       (f) Political predictions
       (g) Investments
       (h) Dividend declaration
       (i) Tax filing
   14. Recall of product
   15. Spoilage
C. Third-Party Liabilities (compensatory and punitive damages)
   1. Aviation liability
      (a) Owned and leased aircraft
      (b) Nonowned—officers and employees licensed
      (c) Grounding and sistership liability
   2. Athletic—sponsorship of teams, recreational facilities, etc.
   3. Advertiser's and publisher's liability
      (a) As agents
      (b) Libel, slander, defamation of character
      (c) Media use—radio, TV, newspaper, samples, exhibits
   4. Automobile liability
      (a) Operation of vehicles—owned and nonowned
      (b) Loading and unloading
      (c) Dangerous contents—flammables, explosives
   5. Contractual liability
      (a) Purchase agreements
      (b) Sales agreements
      (c) Lease agreements—real or personal property
      (d) Performance or service
      (e) Loans, mortgages, notes
      (f) Hold-harmless clauses
      (g) Surety agreements
   6. Directors' and officers' liability
   7. Easements
      (a) In gross
      (b) Appurtenant
      (c) Positive or negative under common law
      (d) Rights of access to light, water, drainage, support
   8. Employer's liability
      (a) Workers' Compensation or similar laws
      (b) Federal Employees Liability Act
      (c) Common law
      (d) U.S. Longshoremen and Harbor Workers Act
      (e) Jones Act
      (f) Defense Bases Act
      (g) Outer Continental Shelf Act
      (h) Unemployment compensation
      (i) Discrimination in employment
   9. Fiduciary and fringe benefits plans liability
      (a) Pensions, trusts, profit-sharing plans, investments
      (b) Insured—life, accident, health, etc.
      (c) Credit unions

C. Third-Party Liabilities (compensatory and punitive damages) *(continued)*
    10. Malpractice liability—errors and omissions
        (a) Medical—doctors, nurses, specialists
        (b) Lawyers
        (c) Engineers
        (d) Trustees of pension plans
        (e) Patent infringement
    11. Ordinary negligence
        (a) Of employees
        (b) Of agents
        (c) Of invited or uninvited guests
        (d) Of contractor or subcontractor
        (e) Failure to provide safety equipment, warnings, etc.
        (f) Inadequate enforcement of regulations
        (g) Improper preparation of food
    12. Nonownership liability
        (a) Leased real or personal property
        (b) Bailee's liability
        (c) Employee's use of vehicle, aircraft, watercraft
    13. Owner's liability
        (a) Attractive nuisance
        (b) Invited guests
        (c) Trespassers (false arrest)
        (d) Rights of others—riparian, mineral, light, air, view, lateral support, easements, part walls, licences, drainage, eminent domain
    14. Product liability (each product sold, distributed, made)
        (a) Implied warranty
        (b) Express warranty
            (1) By agents—sales, advertising, or general
            (2) By employees
            (3) Of merchantability
            (4) Of suitability or fitness for use
            (5) Of title
            (6) By sample
    15. Protective liability
        (a) Industrial contractors hired
        (b) Construction of demolition
    16. Railroad liability
        (a) Sidetrack agreements
        (b) Right of way
        (c) Grade crossings
    17. Director's and officer's liability (stockholder derivative suits)
    18. Watercraft liability
        (a) Ownership, leased, operation
        (b) Types—boats, yachts, ships, submersibles, rigs, platforms

Source: Reprinted, by permission of the publisher, from A. E. Pfaffle and Sal Nicosia, *Risk Analysis Guide to Insurance and Employee Benefits* (New York: Amacom, a Division of American Management Association, 1977), pp. 66–71. All rights reserved.

CHAPTER 4

Risk Assessment II: Quantitative Methods In Risk Assessment

Learning Objectives

After you have completed this chapter, you should be able to:

1. Give two reasons why numerical estimates are important in risk assessment.
2. Give examples of the types of data required by risk managers for risk assessment.
3. Use the incurred loss development method to project known claims into an estimate of future payments.
4. Use an exposure-based or tabular loss development method to estimate future claims from current activities.
5. Explain how the maximum probable cost is calculated if the probability distribution of costs is known.
6. Explain how the risk tolerance of the risk manager as reflected in his or her threshold probability affects estimated maximum probable cost.
7. Estimate the probability that the number of losses will exceed a stated threshold, using three different probability distributions.

INTRODUCTION

One objective of risk assessment is to substitute factual statements and numerical data for vague impressions. The attainment of this objective is limited by the extent and quality of information available to prepare estimates. Hardly ever will enough information be available to justify concrete predictions such as "exactly three losses will occur next year whose amount will total $76,327." In fact, one could argue that conditions leading to such concrete predictions do not constitute the management of risk. Instead, forecasts such as "with 95 percent certainty,[1] direct costs of work-related injuries next year should fall under $3

---

[1] The phrase "with 95 percent certainty" is used in the sense that the risk manager believes the chance of work-related injury costs totaling less than $3 million to be 95 percent.

million" are possible—when data of sufficient quality and reliability are available. The tools of risk assessment discussed in this chapter illustrate the thought process used by the risk manager to translate raw data into such forecasts.

Sophisticated statistical methods cannot overcome the handicap of poor or nonexistent data. As in any area of management, good data are essential to provide meaningful forecasts and to allocate resources efficiently. After first describing possible uses of risk assessment forecasts, this chapter briefly discusses a few essential characteristics of data required for risk assessment. Methods of developing estimates from less-than-complete data are described, along with other adjustments to reflect timing considerations. The final sections of the chapter examine issues related to accuracy and possible variation in forecasts.

All of the examples used in this chapter involve pure risks. To the extent that a risk manager is involved in the management of speculative risks or other financial risks, the assessment of these other-than-pure risks can become an issue of concern. The assessment of financial risks and other speculative risks requires an examination of issues beyond the intended scope of this chapter. Interested readers are directed to Part 2 of Brealey and Myers' (1991) finance text for an explanation of risk assessment in financial markets.

IMPORTANCE OF NUMERICAL ESTIMATES

Numerical estimates can be used in risk management for two purposes: (1) to set the budget for the risk management department and (2) to forecast future effects of current decisions.

Budget Setting

Although many risk management costs cannot be predicted with certainty, the risk management department usually operates within a budget. Quantitative methods are required to forecast the level of costs, particularly for programs in which the organization pays claims itself (a practice called "retention"). The task of budget setting can create a dilemma for the risk manager. On the one hand, if the budget for the risk management department is set too low, the risk manager faces possible disapproval from higher levels of management when costs that materialize during the year exceed the department's allocation. On the other hand, a low budget (without the need for supplementary allocations) reflects favorably on the cost-effectiveness of risk management methods. Competition between these possible outcomes leads to a need for a realistic assessment of risk management costs.

Estimation of Future Effects

The second use for quantitative estimates is to portray long-term effects of current decisions. Often the immediate effect of a decision to pay claims directly in lieu of purchasing insurance is a reduction in current costs. This immediate benefit creates a responsibility for the risk manager to consider long-run effects and communicate them to other managers, a responsibility that applies to either pure or speculative risks.

The estimation process may require the risk manager to recognize liabilities before they become evident, even if a long period is expected before actual payment occurs. A worker who is seriously injured may be entitled to compensation for the next 20 years. In determining whether to pay this compensation directly in lieu of purchasing insurance, information on the long-run consequences of the choice is desirable. Also, where costs are allocated within an organization, the full burden of providing benefits for the injury should be allocated to the activity or entity responsible. If only the current cost is allocated, incentives to prevent the injury are distorted in ways that may increase injury rates.

The successful use of methods for estimating future claim costs requires an extensive body of detailed, accurate records. Many of these records will need to be maintained for long periods if they are to be useful in estimating trends. Minimum requirements are outlined below, with the issue examined again in Chapter 20. At a minimum, the records need to include the date of the event giving rise to the claim and, if due to a product or service, the date the product was manufactured and sold or the date the service was delivered, the identity of the individuals involved, the cause of the event, the date of filing of any legal action together with the initial estimated amount of liability, and the date and amount of payment if the liability has been resolved, or if not resolved, an estimate of the future payment amount and its timing.

Estimation of future effects requires data on not only the number and type of claims that may occur, but also on the payment amounts and their timing. For many risks, uncertainty over the payment amount becomes resolved as the date of payment approaches, that is, we become more confident about predicting the amount of the payment as the time of the payment draws near. Uncertainty over the timing of payment tends to become resolved in the same way: when the timing of payment is uncertain, the uncertainty tends to decrease as the expected time remaining to payment shortens.

As a consequence, estimates of future effects are subject to revision over time as new data are revealed. Estimates can change over time as a result of several causes. The amount of an estimated payment can change over time, especially if the payment is indexed for inflation. Even when the original estimate considers inflation, costs may change due to changes in standards of compensation, changes in levels of knowledge (e.g., claims become revealed over time or scientific knowledge becomes more refined, as with asbestos), or changes in exposures to risk, such as scale and type of operation. In general, the overall change is the product of the separately considered changes.

CLAIM ESTIMATION

A *claim* is an assertion of a right to payment, as when a customer notifies a manufacturer of an injury from a defective product and expresses a belief that the injury justifies compensation. Usually, the payment is to occur at some future point in time. A *reported claim* is a claim for which the potentially responsible party has received notification; otherwise the claim is *unreported*. A *closed claim* is a claim for which the liability for payment has been resolved and full payment has been made. When liability for payment has not been resolved, the claim is an *open claim* and the estimated amount of payment is called a *"reserve."*

When payments and their timing is uncertain, an organization that requires estimates for budgeting purposes may rely on historical payment patterns. Techniques that rely on historical averages to estimate future payments are called *loss development* methods. These methods use historical averages to project known claims to an estimate of future payments. For example, the risk manager of a firm that manufactures artificial heart-valve replacements may find that, on average, one-third of the liability actions related to defective valves have been reported one year after the valve is sold. The remaining two-thirds are reported during the following 10 years. If the risk manager is willing to rely on historical experience, the ratio of unreported-to-reported claims (2:1) may be used to estimate the expected ultimate number of claims from valves sold during a year. This approach is called the *incurred loss development* method. If 10 claims have been reported within one year of sale on valves sold during 1993, the risk manager may rely on historical experience to estimate that another 20 claims are yet to be reported during the next 10 years from valves sold during 1993. The 20 claims are considered *incurred but not reported (IBNR)* claims. Claims are considered as incurred when a product is sold or a service is provided, even though the claims are not yet manifested in court action or reported in other ways. In other words, tangible evidence of the claims has not yet been provided to the manufacturer, but past history shows that they are likely to develop. The incurred loss development method uses historical averages to project unreported (and ultimate total) claims from experience to date.

The incurred loss development method is a general approach; it can be used to estimate the number of claims or the amount of payments. The examples appearing in Tables 4.1 and 4.2 are based on the number of claims. These data are based on the number of claims expected to arise from the firm's valves sold during a particular year. If 25 claims are reported by the end of the second year following the manufacture of a batch of valves, for example, the development factor in Table 4.1 suggests that the ultimate number of claims from this batch is expected to be (1.57)(25), or 39.25.

TABLE 4.1. Claim Development Factors Applicable to Number of Reported Claims

Number of Years Since Beginning of Experience Period	Development Factor— Ratio of Ultimate to Actual Reported Claims
1	3.33
2	1.57
3	1.19
4	1.08
5	1.05
6	1.04
7	1.03
8	1.02
9	1.01
10 or more	1.00

TABLE 4.2. Estimates of Ultimate Number of Claims Using Development Factors

Calendar Year of Experience	Number of Reported Claims	Development Factor	Expected Ultimate Number of Claims
1983	30	1.00	30.00
1984	21	1.00	21.00
1985	18	1.01	18.18
1986	42	1.02	42.84
1987	28	1.03	28.84
1988	25	1.04	26.00
1989	32	1.05	33.60
1990	27	1.08	29.16
1991	35	1.19	41.65
1992	33	1.57	51.81
1993	19	3.33	63.27
Totals	310		386.35

Table 4.2 shows how data in Table 4.1 can be used to estimate the ultimate number of claims that will be filed against the manufacturer for valves sold by the end of 1993. The estimate is prepared using claims data available at the end of 1993 covering the preceding 11 years, the length of time the manufacturer has been engaged in the manufacture of heart valves. Table 4.2 shows that 310 claims have been reported by the end of 1993, with 386.35 ultimately expected. As of the end of 1993, the expected number of incurred but unreported claims is 76.35. In Table 4.2, the largest development factors apply to the most recent years, and the development factor applying to a particular calendar year declines with the passage of time. The development factors decline with the passage of time because the reporting and settlement of claims becomes more certain as time elapses after the sale of a set of valves.

Sources and Types of Data

The data in Tables 4.1 and 4.2 are based on the number of claims rather than dollar amount of payments. Often insurance data in published sources are based on dollar amounts. The Reinsurance Association of America's *Loss Development Study* (1987 edition) and selected issues of *Best's Insurance Management Reports* are sources of loss development data based on dollar payments.

An organization also can estimate development factors using its own historical data on claims organized by calendar year of occurrence. The development factors shown in Tables 4.1 and 4.2 are estimated ratios of ultimate to reported claims, calculated for each year following the sale of the valve. If the process leading to development of claims is stable over time, data can be averaged across years to improve the accuracy of estimates.

To illustrate, consider claims arising from valves sold during 1983, the earliest time period shown in Table 4.2. As shown in Table 4.2, 30 claims have been reported by the end of 1993 from valves sold during 1983. Of these 30 claims, 9 may have been reported by the end of 1983 and 19 (including the 9 reported in 1983) reported by the end of 1984. The ratio of these two reported values, $19/9 = 2.11$, is an estimate of the one-to-two-year claim development factor. The same calculation can be repeated for each year in the sample period (i.e., 1985 reported claims to 1984 reported claims for valves manufactured in 1984, and so on) and the estimates averaged across years. If based on all the data available to the manufacturer, the ratio that could be calculated from Table 4.1 ($3.33/1.57 = 2.12$) is the average across the 10 years for which data allow the calculation.

In general, the largest and most reliable estimates will apply to data from calendar years long past, because the passage of time increases the likelihood that the claim will be reported and paid. By 1993, for example, the reported number of claims from products sold during 1983 has increased to 30, implying a development factor of $30/10 = 3.0$ for the 10-year ratio of ultimate claims to those reported at the end of the year of sale. When the above-described estimates are combined into a single table, the resulting array of claims data is called a *loss triangle* because of its triangular shape. For the most recent calendar year, data for only one year's development is available, while the largest number of observations apply to the most distant calendar years. However, the one-year development factor for the most recent year still provides useful information, because it can be compared with the one-year development factor for previous years. Such a comparison could be used to detect emerging trends.

The reader should recognize that an organization could not prepare Table 4.1 from its own payment history until 10 years have elapsed following the activity giving rise to possible payments. In general, many organizations will not have the resources or experience to develop data of the type shown in Table 4.1. Projections of this type often rely on consulting services, such as provided by actuaries, particularly if the consultant has access to data representing a broad range of experience. Data available from consultants often reflect a broader base of experience that a single organization could develop. The long time required for an organization to develop these data from its own payment records is another reason for consultants, such as actuaries, being used in the estimation process. Also, a consultant may be needed when estimates are needed for a new area of activity in which the organization lacks a history of exposure.

The changing nature of many exposures to risk often requires loss trending and other adjustments to accurately portray current exposure. As an example, the number of vehicles in a fleet may have doubled over a 10-year period and vehicle repair costs are certain to have increased over 10 years. The quality of roadways and driver education programs as well as changing legal trends are other factors possibly affecting costs. Trending techniques may be used to estimate the current costs of a standard unit of exposure such as a vehicle-mile or vehicle-year, possibly by employing regression methods.[2] Costs per unit of exposure are convenient for estimating levels of total cost, which are

---

[2] For example, if accident costs per vehicle-mile increase a constant percentage each year, the rate of increase can be estimated by regressing the logarithm of accident costs per vehicle-mile against a time variable ($1 = $ year 1, $2 = $ year 2, and so on). The estimated coefficient of the time variable is an estimate of the logarithm of $(1 + r)$, where $100r$ is the annual percentage rate of increase.

the product of the per-unit cost and the estimated number of units. Exposure-based loss development methods are discussed further in the next section.

Exposure-Based Loss Development Methods

Payments can be estimated using data on exposures or some other standard without reference to actual claims activity during the year using *exposure-based loss development methods*, sometimes referred to as *tabular loss development methods*. These methods assume that claims arise from identifiable activities, which are grouped by claim-producing potential into standard exposure units. A manufacturer of products, for example, may consider the sale of a product as creating an exposure to risk, with products grouped according to the likelihood of creating injury. As a second example, a hospital may consider the admission of a patient or the provision of outpatient services as creating exposure to risk, with each type of service weighted according to claim-producing potential estimated from past experience. A third example is workers' compensation, in which payroll in units of $100 often is considered the employer's exposure to the risk of work-related injury.

Table 4.3 illustrates a tabular method used to estimate the expected number of work-related injuries for a construction firm. The firm employs workers in several occupational categories in addition to direct involvement in construction: clerical, supervisory, managerial, and support activities such as transportation of materials. On average, a full-time construction worker experiences significant injury once every 1.5 years and earns $30,000 a year. In Table 4.3, the reference unit of exposure to work-related injury is a year of employment for a construction worker, or 300 units of $100 payroll. A reference unit of exposure is expected to result in 2/3 of a work-injury claim.

For other occupational categories, the estimates in Table 4.3 adjust the payroll in these categories according to the firm's own experience. For example, the average clerical worker may earn $20,000 in a year and, on average, be injured once every 30 years. For clerical workers, 20 years of employment, or 4,000 units

TABLE 4.3. Exposure-Based or Tabular Method for Estimating the Number of Work-Injury Claims

Occupational Category	Number Needed for One Unit of Exposure	Number of Units Expected for Next Year	Estimated Exposure Units
Construction	1.00	233.4	233.4
Clerical	13.33	63.5	4.8
Supervisory	4.27	27.6	6.5
Managerial	6.55	6.8	1.0
Support	2.13	55.2	25.9
		Total	271.6

Expected number of injury claims: $(2/3)(271.6) = 181.1$

Expected claim costs at $12,000 per claim: $(\$12,000)(181.1) = \$2,172,800$

of $100 payroll is required for an expected 2/3 of a claim (the illustration considers only the number of claims without regard to dollar amount). Hence 4,000/300, or 13.33 units of exposure for clerical workers result in the same exposure as one construction worker. If the firm expects 63.5 units to apply to clerical work next year ($1,905,000 of clerical payroll), the resulting exposure to work-related injury for this occupational category is 4.8 exposure units. As shown in Table 4.3, the firm's total number of exposure units is 271.6, with the expected number of injuries being 181.1. If the average cost per claim is $12,000, expected claim costs are $2,172,800.

Timing of Claim Payments

Estimates of the ultimate number of claims and their amounts are useful for accounting purposes, but these estimates do not consider the timing of payments. Timing considerations become important when setting budgets. For example, an employer may expect to pay an ultimate $50,000 in claims for work-related injuries arising out of employment during a particular calendar year, but these payments may be distributed over the next 10 years. This issue arises even after the claims become fully identified through the development process. In other words, information required to fully identify claims and estimate ultimate payment amounts becomes revealed over time. Even when claims become fully identified, however, actual payment may be subject to further delays.

A delay between the occurrence of a claim and its payment implies that investment income can be earned on funds held for payment of the claim. Payment lags are especially significant in liability claims. For example, work injury claims often are compensated through a series of payments over time known as a *structured settlement*. Also, large liability claims often are subject to substantial delays while issues are being litigated, resulting in the longest delays being associated with the largest claims. Estimates of payment lags may be based on an organization's own data (e.g., historical payment patterns or the terms of a court-ordered structured settlement) or on published data, such as the Reinsurance Association of America's *Loss Development Study* (1987 edition) or selected issues of *Best's Insurance Management Reports*.

The current amount required to fund the ultimate claim payment is known as the *present value* of the claim. The topic of present value estimation is discussed extensively in finance textbooks, so only a brief illustration is presented in Table 4.4. Interested readers are referred to these textbooks (e.g., Brealey and Myers [1991] chapter 2) for further information.

Table 4.4 illustrates present value estimation using a 6 percent interest rate for a series of claim payments distributed as shown in the second column. In Table 4.4, 10 percent (0.10) of the claim dollars are paid during the fourth year after occurrence. The present value of one dollar paid after four years at a 6 percent interest rate is 0.7921, as shown in the third column. The fourth column is obtained by multiplying the second column by the third column; the result for the fourth year is (0.10)(0.7921), or 0.0792. This result is the estimated amount, per dollar of claim, required to fund in the year of occurrence those claims that will be paid at the end of the fourth year. The total of column four, or 0.8264, represents the total required funding in the year of occurrence, per dollar of ul-

TABLE 4.4. Timing Distribution of Claim Payments and Present Values at 6 Percent Interest

Number of Years Elapsing Since Claim Occurrence	Proportion of Total Claim Amount Paid During Year	Present Value of One Dollar at 6 Percent Interest	Funding Required Per Dollar of Ultimate Claim
1	0.30	0.9434	0.2830
2	0.20	0.8900	0.1780
3	0.10	0.8396	0.0840
4	0.10	0.7921	0.0792
5	0.08	0.7473	0.0598
6	0.07	0.7050	0.0494
7	0.05	0.6651	0.0333
8	0.04	0.6274	0.0251
9	0.03	0.5919	0.0178
10	0.03	0.5584	0.0168
Totals	1.00		0.8264

timate claim payment. Using this result, the risk manager could set aside $41,320 in the year of occurrence to fund a group of claims whose ultimate amount is expected to be $50,000.

ESTIMATES OF PRECISION

The process illustrated in Tables 4.1 to 4.4 allows the risk manager to prepare *point estimates,* which are estimates of *expected values* of risk management costs. A second issue of vital concern is the level of precision or confidence the risk manager can place in the accuracy of the forecast. This second issue becomes important in estimating risk management budgets. The risk manager may esti-mate total costs for the next year at $5 million, for example, but how confident is the risk manager that they will not exceed $6 million, or even $10 million? This section discusses the process for estimating levels of precision and using the estimates.

For each of the organization's exposures to loss, the risk manager's concern is focused on not only the expected value, but also the *maximum probable loss* as defined near the end of the preceding chapter. The maximum probable loss is the largest amount of damage that the risk manager believes is likely to occur. When the risk management department is provided a fixed total budget apply-ing to all risk management activities, the level of total costs (e.g., costs of loss control programs as well as loss payments) should fall within the budget. When all the organization's loss exposures and the associated risk management activ-ities are considered relative to the department's budget, the risk manager's con-cern becomes focused on the expected value of these costs as well as the *maxi-mum probable cost (MPC):* the highest cost level the risk manager believes is likely to prevail during the year. More formally, the maximum probable cost is the dollar amount for which the risk manager is willing to tolerate the probability of costs exceeding the amount. If the risk manager is willing to tolerate a 10 percent chance of costs exceeding the estimated maximum, for example, the MPC is the level at which a 1-in-10 chance is present that costs will exceed the MPC. The MPC depends on two factors: (1) possible dispersion of actual costs around the expected value and (2) the chance that the risk manager is willing to tolerate that costs will exceed the estimated maximum, hereafter called "risk tolerance." The MPC is positively related to dispersion but negatively related to risk tolerance: greater levels of dispersion and lower levels of risk tolerance lead to higher estimates of MPC, and vice versa. In a sense, the risk manager is betting his or her career prospects when the MPC is estimated. If the estimate is set too low and supplemental allocations are requested during a budget period, these career prospects are diminished. Balanced against this unfavorable outcome is the generally favorable impression created by low risk management costs. The risk tolerance is chance that the risk manager is willing to tolerate of underestimating risk management costs and having career prospects diminished.

MPC Estimation in a Single Time Period

The process used to estimate MPC in the following sections of this chapter is set within a single time period. This context allows the conceptual framework to be described without becoming burdened with complexities that can arise in a multiperiod setting. The process described below assumes that the risk manager wishes to estimate MPC during the next year without reference to underestimates or overestimates that may have occurred in surrounding years.

A more realistic (and more complex) setting would lead us to consider two issues: (1) the current funding costs associated with claims arising during the next year, and (2) adjustments in estimated amounts required to maintain funding of claims from prior years. For example, the risk manager in an organization that uses self-funding for work injury claims could budget an amount at the beginning of the year for claims from injuries that occur during the year. In addition, the risk manager adjusts funding for claims that occurred during prior years to reflect errors made in the original funding estimates. These adjustments for already existing claims are not part of the discussion appearing below, although the risk manager could use the same procedure for estimating confidence levels on existing claims as is used for claims in a single time period.

Basic Probability Concepts

An understanding of the thought process used to estimate MPC requires a review of basic concepts related to probability distributions and risk measurement. Our description of the risk measurement process relies on measurement techniques applied to theoretical distributions used in probability and statistics. The discussion presumes a background in probability and statistics that would be expected for a management major. Since our purpose is to illustrate how these techniques would apply to risk measurement, our discussion of the assumptions underlying these methods and the restrictions that apply to the results is brief. Readers interested in these issues are encouraged to consult textbooks in probability and statistics, such as Neter, Wasserman and Whitmore

(1992), appearing as suggestions for additional reading at the end of this chapter.

A probability is an estimate of a proportion of outcomes in which a specified condition is expected to occur. As applied to risk measurement, the estimate of probability usually is set within a time period such as a year. For example, the probability that a driver in an urban area becomes involved in at least one automobile accident during the next year may be 0.25. In this example, one would expect 25 percent of a large group of drivers who operate vehicles in the urban area for one year to become involved in at least one accident, with the remaining 75 percent to be free of accidents for the year.

Mutually Exclusive Outcomes.   Two outcomes are mutually exclusive if they cannot occur together. A building cannot both burn and not burn during a time period; the events are mutually exclusive. If the only possible loss amounts are $0, $1000, $10,000, $50,000, and $100,000, the amounts are mutually exclusive in that the occurrence of one loss amount necessarily precludes the occurrence of some other amount. Under an important theorem, the probability that an outcome will be any one of a set of mutually exclusive outcomes is the sum of the probabilities of the separate outcomes. If the only possible loss amounts are $0, $1000, $10,000, $50,000, and $100,000, the probability of a loss of $50,000 or more is the probability of a $50,000 loss plus the probability of a $100,000 loss. If the probability of a $50,000 loss is 0.003 and the probability of a $100,000 loss is 0.001, the probability of a loss of $50,000 or more is $0.003 + 0.001 = 0.004$.

If one has identified all possible outcomes and they are mutually exclusive, the sum of their probabilities must total 1.0. The probabilities must sum to 1.0 because one of the outcomes is certain to occur. During a given year the probability that a building either will burn or not burn is 1.0. If the probability of fire is 0.01, the probability of no fire is 0.99.

Multiple Outcomes and Related Events.   When two or more events can happen during the same time period, the probability of combinations of outcomes becomes a matter of interest. Examples of outcomes combining events include fires at both of two buildings, a property loss and a liability loss arising out of the same accident, or injury to two or more workers. A person's first instinct may be to follow the rule for mutually exclusive events and add the probabilities, but straight addition is correct only if events are mutually exclusive. If two workers each face a 0.1 probability of being injured during the next year, for example, the probability of at least one injury is, in general, *not* $0.1 + 0.1 = 0.2$.

Unless the injuries are mutually exclusive, outcomes in which the first worker is injured include some situations in which the second worker also is injured, and vice versa. Straight addition of the two probabilities results in outcomes in which both workers are injured being "double counted." The correct procedure is to subtract the probability of injury to both workers. For example, if the probability of both workers being injured is 0.05 when each faces a 0.1 probability of being injured, the probability of at least one injury is $0.1 + 0.1 - 0.05 = 0.15$. However, if injuries to the two workers are perfectly dependent and injury to one worker always is accompanied by injury to the other worker, the probability of at least one injury is the same as the probability that either worker is injured: $0.1 + 0.1 - 0.1 = 0.1$.

The probability of an outcome combining events depends on whether the events are independent. Two events are *independent* if the occurrence of one event has no effect on the probability that the other event will occur. For example, the occurrence of a fire in a warehouse located in Los Angeles is not likely to affect the probability of fire damage to a warehouse located in New York City. Consequently, a risk manager may regard fire losses to the two warehouses as independent. However, a risk manager would be less likely to regard fire losses as independent if the warehouses are located next to each other. In the case of two adjacent warehouses, the occurrences of a fire in one is likely to increase the probability of fire in the other.

Independent Events. If two events are independent, the probability of an outcome combining events is the product of the associated probabilities. For example, if the probability of fire in the warehouse located in New York City is 0.005 and the probability of fire in the warehouse located in Los Angeles is 0.007, the probability of fire in both warehouses is $(0.005)(0.007) = 0.000035$ if fires in the warehouses are independent. The theorem for outcomes combining independent events can be combined with the theorem on mutually exclusive outcomes to calculate other possible outcomes. When the list of outcomes incorporates all possibilities, the probabilities sum to 1.0, for example:

Probability of:

Fire in both locations:	$(0.005)(0.007)$	$= 0.000035$
Fire in New York, none in Los Angeles:	$(0.005)(1.0 - 0.007)$	$= 0.004965$
No fire in New York, fire in Los Angeles:	$(1.0 - 0.005)(0.007)$	$= 0.006965$
No fire in either location:	$(1.0 - 0.005)(1.0 - 0.0007)$	$= \underline{0.988035}$
		1.000000

The probability of fire in at least one location also could be obtained using the rule for outcomes combining events: $0.005 + 0.007 - (0.005)(0.007) = 0.011965 = 1 - 0.988035$.

Dependent Events. If the events are not independent, *conditional probabilities* can be used to calculate the probability of a combination of events. The occurrence of events A and B during the same time period can be used as an example. The probability that both A and B occur is the product of two probabilities: (1) the probability of event A and (2) the conditional probability of event B, given that event A has occurred. The probability of event B, given the occurrence of event A, is called the *conditional probability of B given A.* In the case of independent events or exposures, in which the probability of B is not affected by the occurrence of A, the probability of an outcome combining events A and B is merely the product of the *unconditional probabilities,* as shown in the example above. When the events are not independent, however, the calculation requires conditional probabilities.

Two warehouses located next to each other can serve as an illustration. Considered as separate units, the probability of fire damage to either warehouse may be 0.008. However, the occurrence of fire in one warehouse may increase the probability of fire damage in the other warehouse to 0.05. The probability of fire damage to both warehouses is the product of (1) the probability of fire in one warehouse, times (2) the conditional probability of fire damage in the other, given fire in the first: $(0.008)(0.05) = 0.0004$.

The calculation may be reversed to obtain the conditional probability from the probability of the combination of events. If the probability of fire damage to both warehouses is 0.0004 and the probability of fire damage to a warehouse considered as a separate unit is 0.008, the conditional probability of damage to a second warehouse, given fire damage to the first is $0.0004/0.008 = 0.05$.

The probabilities of combinations of events can be calculated using conditional probabilities and separating the events into mutually exclusive outcomes, as in the case of independent exposures. When the list of outcomes incorporates all possibilities, the probabilities sum to 1.0, for example:

Probability of (assuming dependent exposures):

Fire in both warehouses:	$(0.008)(0.05) = 0.0004$
Fire in warehouse 1, no fire in warehouse 2:	$(0.008)(1.0 - 0.05) = 0.0076$
Fire in warehouse 2, no fire in warehouse 1:	$(0.008)(1.0 - 0.05) = 0.0076$
No fire in either location:	$1.0 - 0.0004 - 0.0076 - 0.0076 = 0.9844$
	$\overline{1.0000}$

The probability of fire in at least one location also could be obtained using the earlier rule for combinations of events: $0.008 + 0.008 - (0.008)(0.05) = 0.0156 = 1 - 0.9844$.

If the warehouses had been independently exposed to fire damage, the probability of fire damage to both warehouses would have been lower: $(0.008)(0.008) = 0.000064$; also, the probability of no fire in either location would have been lower: $(1.0 - 0.008)(1.0 - 0.008) = 0.984064$. As the degree of dependence increases, the probability of fire in one warehouse without fire in the other becomes smaller, so (1) the probability of fire in both locations increases and (2) the probability of no fire in either location increases. If the exposures are perfectly dependent, a fire in one warehouse implies a fire in the other. Holding the probability of fire at 0.008, with perfect dependence, the probability of fire in both warehouses becomes 0.008 and the probability of no fire in either warehouse becomes $1.0 - 0.008 = 0.992$.

Probability Distributions

A probability distribution shows, for each possible outcome, the probability of its occurrence. For example, a probability distribution of the number of accidents in a fleet of vehicles shows, for each number ($n = 0, 1, 2, \ldots,$), the probability of that number of accidents occurring. A distribution of the dollar amount of damage per accident shows, for each dollar amount, the probability of an accident that has occurred resulting in damage equal to or less than the given amount. A distribution of the dollar amount of damage per accident is a distribution of conditional probabilities: the probability of a given amount of damage given that an accident has occurred.

Ideally, risk assessment could examine the probability distribution of total dollar losses in a period such as a year. A hypothetical example of a probability distribution of vehicle accident repair costs in a fleet of three vehicles is shown in Table 4.5. In order to simplify the presentation, dollar loss amounts are collapsed into seven possible outcomes: $0 (no loss), and loss amounts of $1000, $2000, $4000, $10,000, $20,000, and $40,000. The probability of each loss amount is shown alongside the corresponding total in Table 4.5. For example, the probability of losses totaling $1000 is 0.273. Because the loss amounts are mutually exclusive events and cover all possible outcomes, the probabilities sum to 1.0.

Earlier in this chapter, the concept of maximum probable cost (MPC) was introduced. As an illustration, assume the risk manager is willing to tolerate at most a 0.002 probability of costs exceeding the estimated MPC. The data in Table 4.5 show a 0.001 probability of costs exceeding $20,000, a chance the risk manager is willing to tolerate. A risk manager applying this rule to Table 4.5 would estimate an MPC of $20,000. For any smaller amount, the chance of losses exceeding the amount is too high for this risk manager's threshold. For example, the probability of losses exceeding $10,000 is $0.002 + 0.001 = 0.003$, which exceeds 0.002.

Knowledge of the entire distribution of outcomes such as shown in Table 4.5 allows a variety of risk measurement techniques. For example, the data in Table 4.5 can be used to determine a distribution of total dollar costs, conditional on the occurrence of at least one accident. The procedure is to divide the probability associated with each dollar amount (except for $0) by the probability of loss: $1.0 - 0.606 = 0.394$. To illustrate: the probability of a $4000 loss, conditional on the occurrence of at least one accident, is $0.015/0.394 = 0.0380711$.

The logic behind the procedure for obtaining conditional probabilities is straightforward. The distribution of total dollar costs conditional on the occurrence of at least one accident is a set of mutually exclusive outcomes: costs of $1000, $2000, $4000, $10,000, $20,000, and $40,000. Because these outcomes are mutually exclusive and the condition "at least one loss has occurred" implies that one of these amounts is certain to occur, their probabilities must sum to 1.0. If each probability is divided by 0.394, which is the probability of loss, the new probabilities sum to 1.0.

Summary Statistics When Full Data Are Not Available

Table 4.5 provides data on the entire distribution of outcomes. This level of detailed information typically is not available to a risk manager. In most cases, data at best allow estimates of summary measures of a distribution. Two summary measures are discussed here, the *expected value* and *standard deviation*. The expected value is the average payment that would be expected if the exposure to possible damage were repeated a large number of times. More formally, the *expected value* is calculated by multiplying each outcome by the associated probability and summing the resulting terms. For the distribution shown in Table 4.5, the expected value is: ($0)(0.606) + ($1000)(0.273) + ($2000)(0.100) + ($4000)(0.015) + ($10,000)(0.003) + ($20,000)(0.002) + ($40,000)(0.001) = $643.

The *standard deviation* is a measure of dispersion. It measures the extent to which the outcomes tend to deviate from the expected value. More formally, the *standard deviation* is calculated by subtracting the expected value from each pos-

TABLE 4.5. Hypothetical Distribution of Vehicle Accident Repair Costs in a Fleet of Three Vehicles

Dollar Cost	Probability
$ 0	0.606
1,000	0.273
2,000	0.100
4,000	0.015
10,000	0.003
20,000	0.002
40,000	0.001
	1.000

sible outcome, squaring the result, multiplying by the associated probability, summing the resulting terms, and taking the square root of the total. For the distribution in Table 4.5, the standard deviation is: $[(\$0 - \$643)^2(0.606) + (\$1000 - \$643)^2(0.273) + (\$2000 - \$643)^2(0.100) + (\$4000 - \$643)^2(0.015) + (\$10,000 - \$643)^2(0.003) + (\$20,000 - \$643)^2(0.002) + (\$40,000 - \$643)^2(0.001)]^{1/2} = \$1,788.73$. The standard deviation is the square root of the *variance*, which is another measure of dispersion. The sum of the terms lying within the brackets in the expression immediately above (3,199,551) is the variance of the distribution in Table 4.5. The square root $[(3,199,551)^{1/2} = 1,788.73]$ is the standard deviation.

Probability Distributions and Measures of Risk

The techniques discussed in this section are based on three theoretical probability distributions, the *normal distribution*, the *binomial distribution* and the *Poisson distribution*. Although these distributions are related in a way that will be explained later, the assumptions underlying their derivations are not the same and, as a consequence, their usefulness depends on the type of problem the risk manager wishes to address. At this point, it is important to emphasize that these

TABLE 4.6. Selected Threshold Points from a Normal Distribution

Threshold Point	Threshold Value for Distribution with $500,000 Expected Value and $75,000 Standard Deviation	Probability of Exceeding Threshold
Expected value	$500,000	0.5000
Expected value plus 0.842 S.D.*	$563,150	0.2000
Expected value plus 1.182 S.D.	$588,650	0.1000
Expected value plus 1.645 S.D.	$623,375	0.0500
Expected value plus 1.960 S.D.	$647,000	0.0250
Expected value plus 2.327 S.D.	$674,525	0.0100
Expected value plus 2.575 S.D.	$693,125	0.0050
Expected value plus 3.719 S.D.	$778,925	0.0001

*S.D. denotes standard deviation.

distributions and the resulting estimates apply only approximately to observed occurrences. It is doubtful whether any of the risks typically addressed by risk managers are accurately described by *any* known theoretical probability distribution. Despite this reservation, the principles used to measure risk using these distributions apply generally to risk management and the results may apply approximately to risk measurement problems.

If the risk manager knows the probability distribution of costs, estimation of the MPC is a straightforward calculation. Unfortunately, little evidence exists that *costs* follow *any* known theoretical distribution. The best applications of the three distributions used in this chapter are as models of the *number* of accidents rather than dollar costs. However, a theorem in mathematics (the "central limit theorem"[3]) asserts that the average loss per unit in a large group tends to follow a *normal distribution* if three conditions are met: (1) the units are independently exposed to possible loss, (2) each unit faces an identical distribution of possible loss, and (3) the variance of the loss distribution is finite. Of these conditions, independence is the most crucial; independence also may be difficult to defend as an assumption for many risks. Independence requires that the occurrence of a loss to one unit does not affect losses to any other units. When risks are independent, however, the normal distribution holds approximately as a model for the average loss per unit in large groups.

The Normal Distribution. Most students using this text will be familiar with the normal distribution, which is the basis for many applications of statistics in management courses. The normal distribution is an example of a *two-parameter* distribution; that is, the entire distribution is determined completely by two numbers. The only information required to know the entire distribution is the expected value and the variance (or standard deviation). Once the expected value and the standard deviation are known for a normal distribution, the probability of any desired value can be calculated. Tables for the normal distribution appear in many textbooks on applied probability and statistics. A few selected threshold points from a normal distribution are shown in Table 4.6 along with values calculated for a normal distribution with expected value $500,000 and standard deviation $75,000. The threshold points shown in Table 4.6 are used in the examples later in this section.

The probabilities shown in Table 4.6 are the chance of exceeding a given threshold amount. For example, the probability of exceeding a threshold point lying 0.842 standard deviation unit above the expected value is 0.2, or 20 percent. For higher thresholds, the probability of exceeding the threshold declines. For a threshold lying 1.96 standard deviation units above the expected value, the probability of exceeding the threshold is only 0.025, or 2.5 percent.

---

[3] Some authors use the phrase "law of large numbers" to describe the result. Although the law of large numbers and the central limit theorems both focus on the predictability of outcomes in large groups of independent exposures to risk, their assumptions are not identical and their methods of proof are not the same. More important, the theorems often are misinterpreted as implying that the *absolute* level of losses becomes more predictable in large groups. Instead, the theorems show that losses become more predictable *relative* to the number of exposures or to a pool of resources. This distinction becomes important in the discussion of risk financing methods appearing later in Chapter 9.

Because the normal distribution is symmetrical about the expected value, the values shown in Table 4.6 can be used to calculate the probability of outcomes lying *between* two points. For example, the probability of an outcome *exceeding* $563,150 is 0.20, which is the probability of an outcome exceeding a threshold point lying 0.842 standard deviation unit *above* the expected value. By symmetry, the probability of an outcome being *less than* a threshold point lying 0.842 standard deviation unit *below* the expected value is 0.20. The dollar value of the threshold is $500,000 − 0.842($75,000) = $436,850. The probability of an outcome greater than $563,150 *or* less than $436,850 is the sum of the respective probabilities: 0.20 + 0.20 = 0.40. The outcome lies either outside these bounds or within them; hence, the probability of an outcome lying *between* $563,150 and $436,850 is 1.00 − 0.40 = 0.60. The values $436,850 and $563,150 are the bounds of a 60 percent "confidence interval" for outcomes.

Usually a risk manager's concerns are focused on costs exceeding a given amount. The thresholds shown in Table 4.6 apply directly to this type of issue. Statistical tests, however, often are tests of precision that consider possible variation in either direction. Many statistics texts explain the distinction using the terms "one-tailed" and "two-tailed" tests.

The Binomial Distribution. Like the normal distribution, the binomial distribution is a two-parameter distribution. The binomial distribution can be used to describe the distribution of the number of accidents when units within a group are independently exposed to the risk of accident and each unit can experience at most one accident. Two parameters determine the entire distribution: the number of units (n) and the probability that a randomly selected unit will be damaged (p). The formula for the binomial distribution is:

$$\text{Probability of r accidents} = \frac{n!}{r!(n - r)!} \, p^r(1 - p)^{n-r}$$

where $n! = n(n - 1)(n - 2) \cdots (2)(1)$; n! is called n factorial, and 0! is understood to equal 1.

For example, a firm that ships finished goods to customers faces the possibility of damage to the goods while in transit. If goods damaged while in shipment are considered totally lost and the probability of loss to a single item is 0.1, the binomial distribution can be used to describe the distribution of the number of lost items. When a group of two items is considered, n = 2 and p = 0.1. The possible number of losses are 0, 1, or 2 and their probabilities can be calculated directly using the formula:

$$\text{Probability of 0 losses} = \frac{2!}{(0!)(2!)} \, (0.1)^0(0.9)^2 = 0.81$$

$$\text{Probability of exactly 1 loss} = \frac{2!}{(1!)(1!)} (0.1)^1(0.9)^1 = 0.18$$

$$\text{Probability of exactly 2 losses} = \frac{2!}{(2!)(0!)} \, (0.1)^2(0.9)^0 = 0.01$$

For the binomial distribution, the expected number of losses is given by the formula np, while the standard deviation is given by $\sqrt{np(1-p)}$

For large n, the calculation of each probability would become a difficult task, even with modern computing equipment. The reason for the difficulty arises from the factorials, which quickly become very large. For example, 5! = 120 and 10! = 3,628,000. Fortunately, the central limit theorem applies when n becomes large, which allows us to approximate a binomial distribution using a normal distribution with expected value np and standard deviation $\sqrt{np(1-p)}$. The approximation is very close if both np > 50 and n(1 − p) > 50. In the above example involving items damaged in shipment, when 1000 items are shipped the distribution of damaged items is very closely described by a normal distribution with expected value (1000)(0.1) = 100 and standard deviation $\sqrt{(1000)(.01)(0.9)}$ = 9.487. Table 4.6 can be used to estimate the probability that a given threshold point will be exceeded. For example, with 1000 items shipped, a 1 percent chance is present (probability 0.01) that the number of damaged items will be greater than 100 + (2.327)(9.487), or approximately 122 items.

The Poisson Distribution. The Poisson distribution is named after a Frenchman who observed that "trouble comes in bunches." Like the binomial distribution, the Poisson distribution is a discrete distribution, making it useful for describing the possible number of accidents. Unlike the binomial distribution, however, the Poisson is a *single-parameter* distribution. The single parameter is the distribution's expected value. The formula for the Poisson distribution is:

$$\text{Probability of r accidents} = \frac{m^r e^{-m}}{r!}$$

where m = expected number of accidents

e = the base of natural logarithms (approximately 2.718)

r! = r(r − 1)(r − 2) ⋯ (2)(1), with 0! = 1.

The Poisson distribution is the limit of the binomial distribution as n becomes very large and p becomes very small, holding the expected value np constant. The Poisson distribution could apply to a very large number of units exposed to risk, each facing a very small chance of accident. For example, a vehicle-mile may be considered the unit of exposure for vehicle accidents, with a very small probability of accident in a single mile. This approach allows for the possibility of multiple accidents to the same vehicle, which the binomial distribution does not allow. Another possible use is to consider a worker-day (one worker for one day) as the unit of exposure to work-related injury.

Table 4.7 shows a Poisson distribution with an expected value of 2.0. In this example, m = 2 and e^{-2} is approximately 0.1353.

The standard deviation of a Poisson distribution is the square root of its expected value; the standard deviation of the Poisson distribution in Table 4.7 is $\sqrt{2}$. The single-parameter feature makes the Poisson distribution convenient to use, as only one parameter estimate is required for its use. This same feature also is a shortcoming; the Poisson distribution is not appropriate as a model unless the assumed relationship between the expected value and the standard deviation is reasonable.

TABLE 4.7. Poisson Distribution with Expected Value of 2.0

$$m = 2; e^{-2} \approx 0.1353$$

Probability of 0 accidents	=	$\dfrac{(2^0)(0.1353)}{0!}$	=	0.1353
Probability of exactly 1 accident	=	$\dfrac{(2^1)(0.1353)}{1!}$	=	0.2706
Probability of exactly 2 accidents	=	$\dfrac{(2^2)(0.1353)}{2!}$	=	0.2706
Probability of exactly 3 accidents	=	$\dfrac{(2^3)(0.1353)}{3!}$	=	0.1804
Probability of exactly 4 accidents	=	$\dfrac{(2^4)(0.1353)}{4!}$	=	0.0902
Probability of exactly 5 accidents	=	$\dfrac{(2^5)(0.1353)}{5!}$	=	0.0361
Probability of exactly 6 accidents	=	$\dfrac{(2^6)(0.1353)}{6!}$	=	0.0120
Probability of exactly 7 accidents	=	$\dfrac{(2^7)(0.1353)}{7!}$	=	0.0034
Probability of exactly 8 accidents	=	$\dfrac{(2^8)(0.1353)}{8!}$	=	0.0009
Probability of exactly 9 accidents	=	$\dfrac{(2^9)(0.1353)}{9!}$	=	0.0002
		Total		0.9997

As is true for the binomial distribution, the calculation of each probability becomes a difficult task when the possible number of accidents becomes larger than, say, 20. Fortunately, the central limit theorem applies when the expected number of accidents (m) becomes large, which allows us to approximate a Poisson distribution using a normal distribution with expected value m and standard deviation $\sqrt{m}$. The approximation is very close if m > 50, in which case the Poisson distribution becomes virtually indistinguishable from a normal distribution with a mean of 50 and a standard deviation of $\sqrt{50} = 7.07$.

The Accuracy of Estimates

If the probability distribution of costs is known or can be approximated reasonably, it is possible to estimate MPC or to determine conditions for predicting outcomes with a specified degree of accuracy. The procedure is based on two requirements: (1) a known probability distribution of costs; or a reasonable approximation, and parameters that can be estimated; and (2) a degree of risk tolerance or tolerance for the chance of an incorrect prediction. Assuming these requirements are met, the problem can be formally stated in the following word equation:

Probability threshold(s) = required accuracy.

For example, the risk manager may want to be 95 percent certain that costs will not exceed $1.5 million. In other words, the risk manager is willing to tolerate at most a 5 percent probability that costs will exceed $1.5 million. If costs follow a normal distribution with an expected value of $1.2 million and standard deviation of $182,371, the distribution of costs just meets the requirement. With reference to the threshold points for a normal distribution presented earlier in Table 4.6, a 5 percent chance is present that normally distributed costs will exceed a threshold lying 1.645 standard deviations above the expected value. For the assumed distribution of costs, $1.2 million + 1.645($182,371) = $1.5 million, rounded to the nearest dollar. Normally distributed costs with an expected value of $1.0 million and standard deviation of $400,000 do not meet the requirement, as $1.0 million + 1.645($400,000) = $1,658,000, which is greater than the $1.5 million level to which the risk manager wishes to hold costs.

The approach is illustrated by the three examples below, each using a slightly different set of assumptions.

Example 1. The number of units required for the probable range of outcomes to lie within 10 percent of the expected value. The example assumes that each unit can experience at most one loss, which is total. This assumption suggests the number of losses follows a binomial distribution.

If the probability of loss to a randomly chosen unit is p, and n units are held, the number of losses follows a binomial distribution with expected value np and standard deviation $\sqrt{np(1-p)}$. An initial step is to assume that the central limit theorem applies, in which case binomial distribution approximately follows a normal distribution with expected value np and standard deviation $\sqrt{np(1-p)}$. If the risk manager wants the number of losses to fall within 10 percent of the expected value with probability 0.95, the probability limits are the 95 percent points on the distribution and the required accuracy is 10 percent of expected value. The problem statement is:

Probability thresholds = required accuracy

or

95 Percent limits = 10 percent of expected value.

Because the problem specifies a *range* of outcomes rather than an upper limit, the chance of exceeding the *upper* limit should be at most 2.5 percent. Table 4.6 shows this point to be 1.960 standard deviations from the expected value. In symbolic form, the equation becomes:

$$np \pm 1.960 \sqrt{np(1-p)} = np \pm 0.10\,np.$$

The equation is solved using simple algebra, as follows:

$$(1.96)^2 np(1-p) = (0.10)^2 (np)^2$$

or

$$n = (1.96)^2(1-p)/(0.10)^2 p$$

If $p = 0.05$, for example,

$$n = (1.96)^2(0.95)/(0.10)^2(0.05) = 7299.$$

With this result, we can perform a final check to determine whether the assumption of normality is reasonable: $(7,299)(0.05) = 365$ and $(7,299)(0.95) = 6,934$, both of which exceed 50. Thus, 7,299 is enough units to make the normal distribution a reasonable approximation.

Example 2.   The number of units required for the probable maximum cost to be no greater than 120 percent of expected value. This problem statement assumes that the expected cost per unit and its standard deviation are known. Even if the actual distribution is not known, total costs divided by the number of exposures tends to follow a normal distribution when the exposures are independent and a large number of units are held. Expected costs are proportional to the number of units, while, if the units' exposures to possible damage are independent,   the standard deviation is proportional to the square root of the number of   units.

Assume that the expected cost per unit is $500 and the standard deviation is $5000. The risk manager is willing to tolerate a one-half of one percent chance that costs will exceed the MPC. The problem statement is:

Probability threshold = required accuracy

   or

99.5 Percent threshold = 120 percent of expected value.

Table 4.6 shows that the 99.5 percent threshold for a normal distribution lies 2.575 standard deviations above the expected value. In symbolic form, the equation becomes:

$$500n + 2.575(5000)\ \sqrt{n}\ = 1.20(500)n$$

The equation is solved using simple algebra, as follows:

$$2.575(5000)\ \sqrt{n}\ = 0.20(500)n$$

$$\sqrt{n}\ = (2.575)(5000)/0.20(500)$$

$$n = [(2.575)(5000)/0.20(500)]^2 = 16,577$$

Example 3.   The number of workers required to predict the number of injuries with a specified degree of accuracy. The risk manager determines that, on average, the number of injuries has been 80 percent of the number of employee-years (an employee-year is one employee working for one year, or about 2,000 hours of work time). The risk manager is willing to assume that the number of injuries follows a Poisson distribution. The risk manager is willing to self-insure these injuries if no more than a 5 percent chance is present that injuries will exceed 140 percent of the expected value. The problem statement is:

Probability threshold = required accuracy

   or

95 Percent limit = 140 percent of expected value.

The initial step is to assume that the normal approximation applies with a final check on the reasonableness of the assumption. Table 4.6 shows that the 95 percent threshold for a normal distribution lies 1.645 standard deviations above the expected value. In symbolic form, the equation becomes:

$$m + 1.645 \sqrt{m} = 1.4m$$

As in earlier examples, the equation is solved using simple algebra:

$$1.645 \sqrt{m} = 0.4m$$

$$\sqrt{m} = 1.645/0.4$$

$$m = (1.645/0.4)^2 = 16.91$$

16.91 is the expected number of injuries, which is 80 percent of the number of full-time equivalent employees. The required number of employees is 16.91/0.8 = 21.14. At this point, the use of the normal distribution as an approximation becomes questionable, because the expected number of injuries does not exceed 50. The result is a rough approximation.

A Word of Caution

The process for estimating precision illustrated in the above examples applies generally to the problem of risk assessment. The normal distribution is used in these examples as a convenient approximation; most students using this text have used the normal distribution in statistics courses. However, the use of the normal distribution does not imply an endorsement of its reasonableness. The normal approximation is unlikely to apply to many risks of concern to risk managers, especially if these risks are considered separately. A portfolio comprised of a large number of risks is more likely to permit the assumptions underlying the normal approximation.

Thus, while separate areas of risk will not be distributed normally, the distribution of the "cost of risk" as a percent of a firm's revenues or some other measure of risk-bearing capacity may be approximated by a normal distribution. However, the reasonableness of *any* assumption about the form of the distribution of costs needs to be considered before making financial commitments based on the assumption. Once the form of the distribution is known or estimated, the process of risk assessment can follow the thought process illustrated in the above examples.

Interdependence among risks held by the organization is a critical issue affecting the form of the distribution of total costs. The central limit theorem assumes independence among risks, an assumption that is unlikely to be supported by many sets of risks. Interdependence can be manifested in ways that are specific to the risks themselves (e.g., a fire may damage a business facility and also injure employees). Interdependence also may result from factors affecting assets or economic activity generally (i.e., factors related to systematic risk).

An employer's promise to pay a benefit to survivors of employees who die prior to retirement offers an illustration. Assume that the benefit amount is the employee's salary during the year preceding death. Two factors affect the total cost of the benefit program in predictable ways: (1) salary rates and (2) ages of employees. Without considering the effects of these factors, any convenient distribution including the normal distribution is likely to be a poor approximation to the distribution of total costs.

When ages and salary rates are taken into account, the normal distribution is likely to be a good approximation for the *deviation* of total costs around *predicted* levels. In this case, the expected cost for each employee is the employee's salary rate multiplied by the expected mortality rate for the employee's age. The predicted total cost is the sum of the per-employee expected costs. Although the normal distribution is likely to be a good approximation for the deviation of total costs around the predicted level, however, it still is only an approximation. One cause of a less-than-perfect fit could be a factor not considered in determining predicted costs (e.g., health condition). Another reason is the remaining dependence within the exposure (e.g., employees may be involved in the same accident or affected by the same fatal illness).

Sophisticated methods, such as computer simulation, may allow the use of distributions that conform more closely to results observed by analyzing the organization's own experience. Usually, such simulations require assistance from consultants who are experts in this line of work.

Key Concepts

claim   An assertion of a right to payment.

closed claim   A claim for which liability for payment has been resolved and the claim has been paid.

open claim   A claim for which liability for payment has not been fully resolved and hence full payment has not been made.

reserve   An estimate of a future payment.

loss development method   A technique that relies on historical averages to estimate future payments.

incurred but not reported (IBNR) claim   A claim that is believed to have occurred but has not yet been reported.

exposure-based loss development method   A technique for estimating future claims by relying on historical averages of claims arising from identifiable activities.

independence   As the concept would apply to losses, statistical independence is a condition under which the occurrence of loss to any one unit has no effect on the losses to other units.

structured settlement   A liability award in which compensation takes the form of a series of payments over time rather than a lump-sum payment.

present value   The dollar amount that will accumulate at an assumed rate of interest to an estimated future payment.

maximum probable cost (MPC)   The highest cost level the risk manager believes is likely to prevail during the year.

Review Questions

1. Give two uses for numerical estimates in risk management, explaining why these uses are important to the management of an organization.
2. List the types of loss data you would recommend collecting and storing for an organization that operates a fleet of heavy trucks to deliver its own manufactured goods and pays for losses arising from the operation of the fleet (both liability losses and damage to its own trucks), using its own funds. Explain why you would collect each type of data and how you would expect to use it.

3. After analyzing data on past losses, a risk manager for a service organization determines that one-third of liability claims are reported in the year that the service is provided to customers, with the remaining two-thirds split evenly across the following two years. For example, if five claims are reported in year 1, the risk manager would expect another five claims in year 2 and another five claims in year 3, all related to services provided in year 1. When claims are reported and become known, the settlement of the claims occurs evenly across the five years following the one in which the claims are reported. For example, if 10 claims are reported in year 5, an average of two of these claims are settled in each of the years 6 through 10.

During 1995, six claims are reported to the risk manager. Using a 7 percent interest rate and an assumed value of $15,000 per claim (paid at the end of the year in which the claim is settled), assume that claims continue to follow the above patterns of reporting and settlement to estimate (1) the ultimate number of claims paid in each year, (2) the dollar values paid each year, and (3) their present value.

4. Explain how you would use a hospital's historical data on the number of liability claims arising from categories of medical procedures and activities (e.g., emergency room, surgery, delivery of infants, and so on) and the level of these activities to estimate relative levels of liability exposure arising from these areas.

5. The questions below are based on the following distribution of fire damage to a warehouse:

Dollar Amount	Probability
0 (no loss)	0.9
500	0.06
1,000	0.03
10,000	0.008
50,000	0.001
100,000	0.001
	1.00

a. What is the probability that a loss whose dollar amount is positive will occur?
b. What is the probability that a loss of more than $1000 will occur?
c. What is the expected dollar loss?
d. What is the average value of losses that occur (i.e., the expected value of a loss conditional on a positive loss occurring)?
e. If a loss occurs, what is the probability that it will be $1000 or greater?
f. You are willing to ignore any event whose chance of occurrence is *less than* 0.002. What is the probable maximum loss if this "critical probability" is 0.002?
g. In part f, what is the maximum probable loss relative to the expected loss? Express your answer as a ratio.
h. Now place yourself in the position of an owner of 10,000 warehouses, each of which has a loss distribution as above. What is the expected loss? What is the standard deviation in losses, assuming the warehouses are independent of each other? The standard deviation in loss amounts for a single warehouse is about $3639.70.
i. What is the maximum probable loss to the 10,000 warehouses, assuming losses are normally distributed? Hint: 99.8 percent of the area under a normal distribution lies below a point 2.89 standard deviation units above the expected loss.
j. In part i, what is the maximum probable loss relative to the expected loss? Express your answer as a ratio. What does a comparison of your answer here with that to part g tell you?

6. A mail-order firm sells one item, a satellite dish for television signals. The dish sells for $1000, and is shipped by truck to the customer. Some of the dishes reach customers in a damaged condition. If they do, they cannot be repaired and are a total loss to the firm.

By examining past data on losses to truck shipments, you are able to establish that the average number of dishes damaged in shipment is about 1/10 of the total number shipped. You are also willing to assume that the binomial distribution adequately describes the distribution of the number of losses.

a. If the firm expects to ship 1000 dishes next year, what is its expected loss due to damaged shipments?

b. The actual number of losses may exceed or be less than the number in part a. Calculate the range around the expected loss in which you are 95% certain the actual dollar loss will fall if 1000 dishes are shipped. Use the normal approximation.

c. If 100,000 dishes are shipped, within what range are losses expected to occur 95% of the time? Use the normal approximation.

d. You are willing to self-insure the risk of dishes damaged in shipment if you are 95% certain that the actual loss will be within 10 percent of the expected loss. Will you self-insure with 1000 shipments? With 100,000? What is the minimum number required?

e. You are willing to self-insure the risk of dishes damaged in shipment if you are 95% certain that the actual number of losses will not vary from the expected number by more than 10 percent of the total number of shipments. Will you self-insure 1000 shipments? With 100,000? What is the minimum number required? What reservations would you have about basing a decision on these answers?

7. As a risk manager for a firm that specializes in construction of residential housing, you have reviewed records covering employee injuries during the last five years. You believe that losses resulting from injuries to employees are best summarized using the number of injuries per 2000 employee-hours (2000 hours represents about one year's labor). You discover that the loss rate for carpenters has averaged 1/2 injury per 2000 hours over the last five years. On average, an injury has cost the firm $3000. You also believe that the Poisson distribution reasonably well describes the distribution of the number of injuries in a particular year.

a. What is the probability of at least one injury during 2000 employee-hours of labor?

b. Explain how you would estimate the probability of five or more injuries given that the firm expects to use 6000 employee-hours of labor next year.

c. The firm is willing to self-insure if it can be 95% confident that the number of injuries will be within 50% of the expected number. How many employee-hours are required to self-insure? To how many full-time employees does this answer convert? Hint: Use the normal approximation.

d. The firm expects to use 12,000 employee-hours of labor next year. A safety consultant who specializes in running educational programs for construction employees offers to run a two-day program for a charge of $1000. Wage costs for employees attending the program are expected to run an additional $2000. If expected loss reduction is the only factor considered, how great a reduction in the employee injury rate is required to justify the program?

e. In the year following the one in which you ran the educational program described in d, three employees are injured. Your boss questions your wisdom in running the program. Justify your decision, being as specific as possible.

References and Suggestions for Additional Reading

Best's Insurance Management Reports (Oldwick, New Jersey: A. M. Best Company).

BILLINGSLEY, PATRICK: *Probability and Measure* (2nd ed. New York: John Wiley & Sons, 1986).

BLINN, J. D., and M. J. COLE (EDS.): *Pathways to RMIS* (New York: Risk Management Society Publishing, Inc., 1985).

BREALEY, RICHARD A., and STEWART C. MYERS: *Principles of Corporate Finance* (New York: McGraw-Hill Book Company, 1991).

CARTER, R. L., and N. A. DOHERTY (EDS.): *Handbook of Risk Management* (London: Kluwer-Harrop Handbooks, 1974), pt. 2.

CHOW, YUAN SHIH and HENRY TEICHER: *Probability Theory: Independence, Interchangeability, Martingales* (2nd ed., New York: Springer-Verlag, 1988).

CUMMINS, J. D., and L. R. FREIFELDER: "Statistical Analysis in Risk Management," an eight-part series appearing in the September, 1978, through April, 1979, issues of *Risk Management.*

DENENBERG, H. S., ET AL: *Risk and Insurance* (2nd ed., Englewood Cliffs, N.J.: Prentice-Hall, Inc., 1974), chap. 2.

DOHERTY, N. A.: *Corporate Risk Management* (New York: McGraw-Hill Book Company, 1985), chap. 4.

FELLER, WILLIAM: *An Introduction to Probability Theory and Its Applications* (New York: John Wiley & Sons, Inc., 1968).

Financial Applications for Risk Management Decisions (San Rafael, Calif.: Fireman's Fund Insurance Company and Risk Services Group, Inc., 1983), chaps. 1–4.

GREENE, MARK R.: *Decision Analysis for Risk Management—A Primer on Quantitative Methods* (New York: The Risk and Insurance Management Society, 1977).

———, and J. S. TRIESCHMANN: *Risk and Insurance* (8th ed., Cincinnati: South-Western Publishing Company, Inc., 1991).

———, and OSCAR N. SERBEIN: *Risk Management: Text and Cases* (2nd ed., Reston, Va.: Reston Publishing Company, 1983), chap. 3.

HEAD, G. L., and STEPHEN HORN, II: *Essentials of Risk Management* (Malvern, Pa.: Insurance Institute of America, 1991).

HOSSACK, I. B., J. H. POLLARD, and B. FEHNWIRTH: *Introductory Statistics with Applications in General Insurance* (Cambridge: Cambridge University Press, 1983).

Loss Development Study (Washington, D.C.: Reinsurance Association of America, 1987).

MEHR, R. I., and B. A. HEDGES: *Risk Management in the Business Enterprise* (Homewood, Ill.: Richard D. Irwin, Inc., 1963), appendix to chap. 4.

NETER, J., W. WASSERMAN, and G. A. WHITMORE: *Applied Statistics* (4th ed., Boston: Allyn and Bacon, Inc., 1992).

WILLIAMS, C. A., Jr., G. L. HEAD, R. C. HORN, and G. W. GLENDENNING: *Principles of Risk Management and Insurance* (2nd ed., Malvern, Pa.: American Institute for Property and Liability Underwriters, Inc., 1981), vol. 1, chaps. 4 and 5.

CHAPTER 5

Property Exposures to Risk

Learning Objectives

After you have completed this chapter, you should be able to:

1. Describe the types of property that are exposed to risk.
2. Explain why "economic" sources of risk are becoming more important to the risk manager.
3. Distinguish between direct and indirect property exposure outcomes.
4. Discuss the various interests that may attach to property.
5. Explain when an organization should decide to reinvest in damaged property and how to measure the loss to the organization in the case it intends to abandon the property.
6. Define a time element outcome (loss or gain).
7. Distinguish between a time element loss caused by a decrease in revenues and one caused by an increase in expenses.

INTRODUCTION

Discussion now turns to the "risks themselves" and the exposures to risk. Chapters 3 and 4 provided a discussion of assessment issues and techniques, but relatively little was said about the risks that were to be assessed. Chapters 5 through 7 expand on an exposure typology that was introduced in Chapter 3. Risk exposures are categorized as either "property," "liability," or "human resource" (sometimes, "personnel").

This chapter focuses on the general area of property exposures to risk. The discussion is directed toward an understanding of three different "types" of exposure outcomes (gains or losses) and their valuation: direct, indirect, and time element. Liability and human resource exposures are covered in Chapters 6 and 7, respectively.

Property exposures to risk can be classified in four ways, according to (1) the class of property affected, (2) the cause of the exposure outcome (gain or loss), (3) whether the outcome is direct, indirect, or time element in nature, and (4) the nature of the organization's interest in the property.

Property Class

Property may be divided into two broad classes: (1) real estate or land and its appurtenant structures or attachments and (2) personal property or property that is movable and not attached to land. Personal property is also commonly divided into two subclasses: (1) personal property in use and (2) personal property for sale.

Real estate is illustrated by vacant land, an office building, a manufacturing plant, a warehouse, a city hall, or some other structure. Personal property includes such items as machinery, patterns and dies, furniture and fixtures, raw materials, goods in process, finished goods, merchandise for sale, supplies, and money and securities. Except for the finished goods and the merchandise for sale, these examples usually illustrate property in use.

Cause of the Exposure Outcome

Chapter 3 introduced a framework for risk identification that identified sources of risk arising from various "environments" (physical, political, economic, and so on). Perils or causes of loss arising from those environments were identified, assessed and measured. In that chapter, causes of loss (gain) were not categorized, though that is certainly possible and is sometimes desirable. In the realm of property exposures to risk, the causes of loss or gain might be divided into three classes: (1) physical, (2) social, and (3) economic (Hardy, 1923). *Physical perils or causes* include such natural forces, such as fires, windstorms, and explosions that damage or destroy property, or—in the case of speculative risks— that in some sense enhance the value of the property (one might imagine a tropical locale, which presents the opportunity for hurricanes, but also enhances the property's value as a tourist destination). *Social perils or causes* are (a) deviations from expected individual conduct, such as theft, vandalism, embezzlement, or negligence, or (b) aberrations in group behavior, such as strikes or riots. Speculative gains may also occur, as when deviations in conduct (exceptional risk taking, for instance) results in economic or non-economic gain. *Economic perils or causes* may be due to external or internal forces. For example, a debtor may be unable to pay off an account receivable because of an economic recession or a contractor may not complete a project on schedule because of a management error. A speculative illustration would be a gain in asset value due to changes in interest rates. Two or more of these perils may be involved in one loss. For instance, a negligent act by an employee may lead to an explosion; an economic recession and a windstorm may together so severely cripple a debtor's department store that the debtor cannot pay the amount owed a wholesaler; strikers may set fire to a plant.

Readers may find the preceding terminology confusing, since the text now has discussed both physical, social, and economic *risk environments* and physical, social, and economic *causes of loss (gain)*. To make matters worse, each of the risk environments might produce physical, social, and economic causes of loss. For example, the social risk environment could produce social causes of loss (riot, vandalism), physical causes of loss (social preferences result in building homes in areas highly susceptible to mudslide), and economic causes of loss (currency exchange movement reduces the demand for a company's product). While the confusion is unfortunate, there is not likely to be any change in the use of such terms in the foreseeable future. The dual uses of the terms "physical," "social," and "economic" are widespread, so students of risk management should be alert to the possibility of ambiguity when the terms are employed.

Risk managers, for the most part, have concentrated their energies on physical and human (or social) causes of loss. This is partly due to the heritage of the profession—insurance buying and safety engineering. It is also due to the fact that economic risks have tended to be managed—if management were possible—by others within an organization. For instance, financial managers have had responsibilities for the management of interest rate–related risks. Top executives have dealt with risks arising from doing business in more than one economy: producing a good in Mexico, modifying it in the United States, and selling it in Japan.

In recent years, a number of risk managers have begun to absorb some responsibility for economic risks. This seems to be occurring because of organizational trends identified in the discussion of risk management in Chapter 2. Some organizations have found that a more coordinated management of all risks is desirable, and since risk managers deal with a great many organizational risks, they are likely candidates to assume greater responsibility.

Another factor has been the relatively recent shift from an international economy to a transnational or global economy. That is, rather than a world with several separate national economies that interact with one another, the world economy has shifted over the last 10 to 20 years into a single economy—an economy beyond the bounds of traditional national controls. This means that issues such as currency exchange rates, financial solvency of foreign insurers or banks, and effects of individual government policy on the flow of capital are fundamental issues for a great many organizations. For instance, it is not uncommon today for a local government in, say, Colorado to deal with international contractors and global capital markets to finance and construct a large wastewater treatment facility. Although a finance officer can assess interest rates and financial solvency as before, there is a set of "economic" risk-related issues that this finance officer may not be equipped to address, for example:

- Securing bid, performance, and completion bonds for international contractors raises a host of "underwriting" issues for the risk manager.
- Materials acquisition in a global market creates many economic issues related to monetary and fiscal policies of foreign governments, logistical and credit risks associated with raw material acquisition, and political risks associated with contracting for foreign services.
- Legal aspects of working in a global economy are present, such as gov-

ernment-mandated regulations, effects of trade agreements between nations and incongruities in legal systems—particularly with respect to contract law.

It might be argued that different existing managers within an organization might handle different elements of such an undertaking, but it is the coordination of the management of these various (and occasionally new and unusual) risks that has been limited or nonexistent in the past. In addressing this specific need, some risk managers have absorbed significant responsibilities for economic risks.

Before leaving this discussion of causes of exposure outcomes, readers should note that the globalization of the economy has yet another effect on risk management and that is that a business operating internationally is likely to encounter physical and social perils and causes with which it is not familiar. An auto parts manufacturer located in Michigan may suddenly find itself very concerned about the risk of monsoons when it relocates one of its facilities in the Pacific Rim. Earthquakes may become a looming problem for a major processed foods company that builds a production facility in central Mexico. Finally, widespread civil unrest in some areas of the former Soviet Union may pose perils for a private American University undertaking an international exchange program.

Direct, Indirect, and Time Element Outcomes

Property exposures can be classified as to whether direct, indirect, or time element outcomes can occur—terms first introduced in Chapter 3. A direct outcome occurs when a peril or cause acts on a physical object, resulting in a change in the value of the object. For example, when fire damages the interior of a building, the direct loss is the cost of repairing the damage. Further examples include the cost to repair an automobile damaged in a collision or the value of cash and securities stolen from a safe. Speculative risks, of course, have direct outcomes as well—and some of the outcomes could be positive. An insurance company can build a facility on undervalued property and experience a rapid increase in its value due to real estate speculation. However, the principal concern with speculative risk outcomes is "negative" outcomes. Banks, for example, face a number of financial risks that can result in a direct decrease in assets: credit risks, investment risks, and currency exchange risks being notable examples. These types of property losses are worthy of emphasis because while the loss is a direct loss (the asset diminishes or disappears), the factors precipitating the loss are often indirect, complex, and varied. Readers need only consider the various circumstances that might lead to a bank suffering excessive defaults on loans and mortgages to realize that direct property losses are not always simple to identify and comprehend.

An *indirect* outcome occurs as a consequence of a direct outcome, but does not involve the direct action of the peril or cause on the object. One example would be the spoilage of food or other perishable items stored under electric refrigeration when electric power is interrupted because of storm damage to electric power lines and transformers. In this example, the direct loss is the cost of repairing the damaged power lines and transformers, while the associated indirect loss does not involve the direct action of the peril (the storm) on the damaged property (the food). Another example of an indirect outcome occurs when a building is severely but not completely destroyed by fire but must be entirely rebuilt. This situation occurs when the fire damage is so severe (perhaps over 50 percent of the value of the structure) as to require the reconstruction of the entire building. Such a requirement may be part of local codes regulating building construction. In this example, the direct loss is the cost to repair the damaged portion of the structure, while the indirect loss is the cost of tearing down and rebuilding the undamaged portion.

A third example involves property consisting of two or more components. A matched set of jewelry such as a pair of earrings is a classic example. If one of the objects is lost or stolen, the other object loses value as a consequence of no longer being part of a set. Machinery that is unusable following damage to a critical component is another illustration, as is decreased collections resulting from the destruction of records of accounts receivable (the direct loss being the physical damage to the records themselves).

Finally, indirect outcomes could be positive. Investment in an employee training program may result in improved productivity (a direct gain), but also in increased worker job-satisfaction, which results in other gains (less employee turnover, for instance).

A *time element* exposure outcome is a special type of indirect outcome, one in which a time element is involved in the assessment of the outcome. In general, time element *losses* occur when property cannot be used following a direct loss. For example, a landlord may lose rental income when an apartment building cannot be occupied following fire damage. In this example, the lost rental income is a time element loss because the magnitude of the loss is directly related to the length of time that the apartments cannot be used. The relationship between the length of time and the ensuing loss is the feature that distinguishes time element from other indirect losses. It is instructive to note that the above example of the damaged apartment also may entail a time element loss for the tenants who are temporarily displaced following the fire. In their case, the time element loss is the "extra living expense," the difference between their living expenses in temporary accommodations, such as a hotel, and their ordinary living expenses in the undamaged apartment.

Sometimes the distinction between time element losses and other indirect losses appears to be semantic. For example, the profit that would have been earned if inventory had been sold (i.e., the difference between the sales price and the cost of the inventory) is *not* considered a time element loss because no time element is involved in the assessment. However, the earnings that are lost during the three weeks that a retail store is closed to repair fire damage *is* considered a time element loss, despite these earnings arising from the sale of inventory. The apparent contradiction arises from the basis against which the loss is assessed. When assessed against inventory, no time element is involved; the loss occurs at the same instant the fire damages the inventory. When assessed against a time period, the loss becomes a time element loss. An unexpected increase in the length of time the retail store is closed, for example, causes the magnitude of the time element loss to become larger but does not change the quantity of damaged inventory.

Time element *gains* are, perhaps, a little more obvious to the management student. A successful investment yields a return above the expected rate of return over some period of time. An investment in employee training results in a long-term increase in worker productivity.

Interest in Property

Property has a much broader meaning than mere physical or tangible assets. According to legal definitions, "property" refers to a bundle of rights that may flow from or be part of the tangible physical assets, but which independently possess economic values. In order to identify and measure the property exposures to which his or her business is exposed, the risk manager should be aware of the different kinds of interests that may exist and how they might be valued. The exposures that result from these interests may be property, including time element, or liability exposures. Only the direct and indirect property loss exposures are considered below.

Owners. The clearest property interest is sole ownership. An ownership interest may result from a purchase, a foreclosure on a mortgage or a conditional sales contract, a gift, or from some other event. If the property suffers a direct or indirect loss, the owner bears the amount of that loss. If an organization owns only part of the property, it bears only part of the loss.

The concept of property as a bundle of legal rights is illustrated by ownership of real estate. Legal ownership of real estate implies *title*; that is, the owner must possess the legal right to the property as evidenced by documents usually held at the county level. This ownership right may be restricted in ways that are not evident. For this reason, title transfers usually require an investigation of title history. Ownership of land does not entitle an individual to unrestricted use of land; usage is subject to restrictions, such as zoning ordinances or other laws related to public interest. Also, an owner may attach restrictions to the transfer of property that follow in subsequent transfers. If these restrictions are legal, subsequent transfers of ownership entail a bundle of rights subject to these restrictions even though the transfers have the outward appearance of being unrestricted. In an extreme case in which a transfer of ownership is invalid, the original owner or an heir may appear and assert title to the real estate despite apparently valid transfers occurring subsequently.

Another type of title restriction is a *lien*, which is a financial obligation attached to real estate. Usually, liens are imposed by municipal utilities or by construction contractors who work on the property. When a lien is known, its usual effect is to prevent the transfer of the property without satisfaction of the financial obligation. However, unknown liens can be present when the law allows a time period between the consumption of the service (e.g., the use of the utility services or the construction services) and the filing of the lien. In this case, the new owner may acquire title subject to a lien that becomes apparent after the transfer.

Secured Creditors. A secured creditor has an interest in property pledged as security for the loan, because the creditor's ability to collect from the debtor is diminished if the property is damaged or destroyed. The potential loss is the unpaid balance of the loan. The potential gain is the profit earned from extending credit. Examples of secured creditors are mortgagees for the amount of the mortgage, builders under a mechanic's lien for the value of the work performed on the property, transportations companies or warehouse companies for their transportation or storage charges, and, under a conditional sales contract, vendors for the unpaid balance of the purchase price. In each of these examples, multiple property interests exist. For example, the mortgagee has an interest equal to the amount of the mortgage; the mortgagor has an ownership interest equal to the value of the property. The vendor, who retains title to the property merely as security, has an interest equal to the unpaid balance of the purchase price; like the mortgagor, the vendee has an ownership interest equal to the property value.

Vendors or Vendees. The losses faced by vendors and vendees under conditional sales contracts have been described above. In other sales situations the party who holds title at the time the property is damaged or lost is the one responsible for the loss. The potential gain in such situations, of course, is the profits on sales.

In transactions in which the terms of sale are not clear as to when title passes, the courts have relied upon the method of billing and shipment as an expression of intent. All states have enacted the Uniform Commercial Code, which clarifies some of these questions. In general, the rules are as follows: (a) Goods shipped f.o.b. point of shipment places title in the buyer when goods are delivered to the common carrier, since the buyer is paying the costs of freight and the common carrier therefore is the buyer's agent. (b) Goods shipped f.o.b. point of destination transfers title to the buyer when goods are received from the common carrier, since the common carrier is the agent for purposes of shipment of the seller. (c) Goods shipped f.a.s. (or free alongside) passes the title to the goods when they are delivered intact alongside the conveyancing equipment, and therefore loss or damage during the course of shipment must normally fall upon the buyer. (d) Goods shipped c.o.d. (or collect on delivery) normally does not affect the passing of title. Such a provision in the bill of lading merely indicates that the shipper is retaining the right of possession in the goods until payment is made. Title passes to the buyer if he or she is to pay transportation charges at the time the goods are received by the carrier, but the seller reserves a lien on the property until payment has been made. (e) Goods shipped c.i.f. (or cost, insurance, freight) normally passes title at the time the goods are delivered to the common carrier at the point of shipment, and the insurance documents and title papers are given to the common carrier at that time.

Tenants. Tenants generally do not have any property exposures in their status as tenants, but three exceptions deserve notice. First, under common law, a tenant is responsible for damage to the premises caused by the tenant's negligence. The law of negligence is discussed in Chapter 6. Second, some leases require that the tenant return the property to the landlord in as good a condition as it was received, wear and tear excepted. Such a provision makes the tenant responsible for accidental losses to the property as well as losses caused by the tenant's negligence. On the other hand, under some leases, the tenant escapes liability for either accidental losses or losses caused by his or her negligence. Third, the tenant may make some improvements to the real estate from which he or she expects to obtain some benefit. If these improvements are by law, contract, or custom removable by the tenant when the lease expires, the tenant has an ownership interest. If these improvements are not removable and, as explained above, the tenant is negligent or responsible under the lease for damage to the building, the improvements become part of the potential building loss. If the improvements are irremovable and the lease may be canceled if the building is severely damaged, the tenant suffers a time element loss.

Bailees. A bailee is a person who has possession of personal property belonging to others. The bailee can be a laundry, a warehouse, a garage, or some other business that cleans, repairs, processes, stores, or otherwise works on property belonging to others. As will be observed in Chapter 6, in the section "Bailee Liability Exposures," the obligation of the bailee for damage to the property is normally dependent upon the nature of the bailment. In general, however, a bailee is responsible for damage to the bailed property only if he or she is negligent.

Representative of Owner. Sometimes, because of an agreement made prior to the loss or because of a desire to maintain customer goodwill, bailees assume responsibility for accidental losses to customers' property even though they are not negligent. A bailee who follows this practice has an interest in the property as representative or agent of the owner.

Other Interests. Some other interests that may give rise to property loss exposures are described briefly to indicate the wide variety that exists.

Businesses granted easements may develop an interest in the property to which they are attached. An *easement* is a right granted by the owner to another to use his or her real property. Examples are the right to drive or walk through the grantor's building or to use the building for certain storage purposes. The right is acquired by either express or implied grants. An easement can also be obtained (by what the law calls *prescription*) by using the property over a long period of time. Depending upon the deed, the easement rights may be binding only upon the immediate parties or may pass to the successors of both parties.

Licenses may also create such interests. A *license* is a personal privilege given by the owner to another to use his or her real property for some specific purpose, such as placing on it an advertising sign. Normally, licenses are revocable at the will of the owner of the property, but in some cases the licensee spends considerable money improving his or her license and the privilege is not easily revoked. Although a licensee cannot be as certain that his or her right will continue as a business granted an easement, the licensee will nevertheless suffer a loss if the property is damaged.

A final interest that more commonly affects families than businesses is a life estate. A *life estate* gives a tenant full use of certain land and buildings during his or her lifetime. Upon the tenant's death, interest in the property passes to a re-mainderman, who becomes the owner of the property. Both the life tenant and the remainderman will suffer a loss if the property is damaged or destroyed. The life tenant will lose the use of the property for the rest of his or her life; the remainderman loses the ownership interest he or she will eventually acquire.

VALUATION OF POTENTIAL PROPERTY LOSSES

Once the risk manager has identified the organization's exposures to property losses, the task of valuing the amount at risk still remains. Several alternative methods are recognized by appraisers and others working professionally in the field of valuation. In general, these methods are not precisely suited to risk assessment because appraisals often are focused on objectives other than risk assessment. In fact, no single appraisal method fits every purpose to which appraisals are put. This statement may disappoint students who believe that the "right" or "true" method for valuing property and the associated ownership interests can be found in the proper reference manual, but unfortunately the issue is too complex to be captured with a single measurement method.

An example may clarify the point. An asset's *book value* is the value reported for the asset on the organization's financial statements. Book value is defined as the asset's original cost less accumulated depreciation. When the asset is acquired, the book value is the purchase price; the book value gradually declines to reflect depreciation charged against the organization's income. These depreciation charges are an accounting entry that allocates the cost of the asset over a time period. After the end of this period, book value for the asset is zero.

For certain types of real estate, 27.5 years is the period over which the cost is written off. Would anyone argue that the organization has suffered no loss if this type of real estate acquired 28 years ago is demolished in an earthquake? Surprisingly, the answer is yes, but only for determining the extent to which the earthquake damage affects U.S. taxable income. As far as the U.S. Treasury is concerned, no loss has occurred if the asset's book value is zero.

Methods for Valuing Owners' Property Exposures

Most readers will recognize that an economic assessment of damage usually would not be based on book value, despite the book value method being suitable for tax purposes. This observation merely illustrates the need to recognize the objectives toward which an appraisal is oriented. In risk assessment, *the objective is to estimate the economic burden of the damage on the organization's owners.* In the case of a publicly held firm, for example, an ideal assessment of possible damage would reflect the difference between the firm's market value prior to the damage and the market value afterward. The firm's market value is the value of its outstanding securities, so this valuation method would estimate the effect of, say, a factory explosion on the market value of the firm's securities.

Most readers also will recognize the almost insurmountable practical difficulties involved in estimating the effect of property damage on the market value of a firm's securities. Despite these difficulties, the basic objective of the valuation method should be recognized when judging the suitability of any particular method: to estimate the economic burden of the damage on the organization's owners.

Most valuation methods used in risk assessment are based on estimated repair or replacement costs. Three commonly used methods are discussed below: (1) market value, (2) replacement cost, and (3) replacement cost less physical depreciation ("actual cash value"). These methods are based on the assumption that the owners wish to repair or replace the property following damage. When this assumption does not hold, valuation is based on the present value of cash flows from the asset prior to damage. Repair or replacement may not occur if the possibility of abandonment is present or if the asset cannot be replaced for other reasons. Valuation when repair or replacement may not occur is discussed as a fourth possibility below.

Market Value. The market value of real or personal property is what a willing seller will accept and a willing buyer will pay for the property in an "arm's length" transaction on the date the property is valued. In valuing *real property*, market value can be estimated using prices at which comparable properties have traded recently, assuming trades involving comparable property can be found. Market value depends upon the supply and demand for a particular type of property at a point in time, so estimates based on market values should be interpreted with possible fluctuations in mind.

The market value of real property reflects the opportunity to use the property immediately. The change in a property's market value after a loss (if it could be measured) reflects the loss of this opportunity (e.g., lost income). Especially for new property, the reduction in market value may be greater than the cost of restoration. In other words, a damage estimate based on market value includes a net income loss as well as a direct loss. Moreover, the market value of a structure usually includes the value of the lot whose location may greatly affect the market value and which is not subject to damage by physical perils such as fire.

Market value poses fewer difficulties for valuing *personal property* and is commonly used. Personal property that is readily obtainable in established markets may be valued according to current purchase or invoice prices. For example, a typewriter can be valued quite easily by obtaining the purchase price of similar typewriters either in the new or used market. Published sources of market value estimates can be helpful in making these valuations, but they have the shortcoming of being based on averages. Personal property whose condition differs significantly from the average should be valued on its own characteristics rather than the average for property of its type and age.

Replacement Cost New. Replacement cost new is the cost of brand-new property that is not identical to the damaged property but meets current specifications. For example, a risk manager may determine what it would cost to replace a building by another that is equivalent in terms of space or volume and of reasonable, current design. In estimating building replacement cost, risk managers can use appraisal information services that periodically publish construction price indexes for various types of buildings in localities throughout the country.

Replacement cost is less affected by subjective considerations than are some other valuation methods, which is an advantage. A disadvantage arises when replacement cost exceeds market value. For example, an insurance benefit based on replacement cost may create an incentive to cause loss because the insured is paid more from the insurance than from selling the property. Insurance contracts often control this problem by requiring replacement as a condition of the replacement cost benefit.

Perhaps the most important argument in favor of replacement cost is that most losses are partial and restoring damaged property to its condition prior to the loss usually requires new materials. The fact that a roof is 10 years old does not in any way diminish the cost of replacing it with a new roof—and the new roof serves the same function as the old one. Also, the true cost to an organization of restoring damaged property generally exceeds the direct expenditure because of other unplanned costs (e.g., production delays). If existing property is performing its function adequately and the organization plans to replace it with new property in the event of damage, replacement cost does not overstate the true cost of damage unless the benefit from replacing old property with new more than compensates the organization for these unplanned costs.

Replacement Cost New Less Physical Depreciation and Obsolescence. In many property-loss valuations, risk managers begin with replacement cost but subtract an allowance for physical depreciation, economic obsolescence, or both. Their reasoning is that new property has greater value to a business than old property. The older the property, the more likely a risk manager is to argue that this is true. An organization should recognize, however, that an unexpected loss will force it into a replacement decision that it otherwise would not face and that replacement will require additional financing. The risk manager should determine what position the organization wishes to take on this matter. In recent years, replacement cost has gained favor as a method for property-loss valuations.

Insurance contracts often use replacement cost less physical depreciation as a measure of damage to property. As will be explained in Chapter 17, insurance contracts refer to the concept as "actual cash value," although courts have interpreted this phrase in other ways as well. Replacement cost insurance often is available as an alternative to actual cash value coverage.

An estimate of physical depreciation and economic obsolescence is somewhat subjective, a shortcoming of this valuation method. Physical depreciation is an estimate of effects from age and wear and tear. Economic obsolescence is illustrated by a change in fashion or design. Property differs in the extent to which its value is affected by these factors, and individuals can differ in their estimate of the effects.

In valuing personal property on either this basis or the basis of replacement cost new, one must be careful to include all the costs (e.g., transportation and installation costs) that would be incurred in obtaining the replacement. The risk manager should also recognize that the same property has different replacement costs as it moves through the channels of distribution—from the manufacturer to the wholesaler to the retailer to the ultimate consumer. Finally, in assessing possible damage to real or personal property, one should include the expense of cleaning up debris.

Valuation When Repair or Replacement Does Not Occur. Circumstances in which repair or replacement do not occur are quite plausible. For example, replacement of a unique object, such as work of a deceased artist held for display, may not be possible. When the asset is not repaired or replaced, the economic burden of the damage on the organization's owners is their loss of the present value of the asset's future earnings. The effect of possible loss to a unique asset is assessed by estimating the present value of the asset's contribution to the organization's future earnings.

Another example is when the possibility of abandonment is present, that is, when an organization might maintain an existing operation but elects to abandon it following serious damage. The possibility of abandonment complicates loss assessment, as shown in Neil Doherty's text *Corporate Risk Management* (Doherty, 1985). However, the principle identified above still prevails when the asset is abandoned: the economic burden of the damage on the organization's owners is their loss of the present value of the asset's future earnings.

For the abandonment issue to arise, values associated with the undamaged asset (i.e., prior to loss) must be sequenced in the following order: (1) the asset's replacement cost, (2) the present value of its future cash flows, and (3) the market value of the undamaged asset, with replacement cost being the largest and market value the lowest. For example, an asset whose replacement cost is $700,000 is a candidate for possible abandonment when its market value is only $200,000 if the asset currently is contributing cash flows whose present value is $400,000. Such a condition might arise, for example, in an old retail store located in a deteriorating area of a city. The asset's cash flows are sufficient to continue operating the store (present value of $400,000) because selling the asset would yield only $200,000. However, the owners will not elect to replace the asset if completely destroyed because the replacement cost ($700,000) exceeds the present value of the asset's cash flows by $300,000.

The preceding condition is necessary for the abandonment issue to arise; abandonment never becomes a consideration unless the condition is present. The narrow circumstances under which the abandonment issue arises become evident by considering other circumstances. If the present value of the asset's cash flows exceeds the asset's replacement cost, the damaged asset always will be repaired or replaced because this action always is to the benefit of the organization's owners. If the present value of the asset's cash flow is less than the asset's market value, presumably the organization never will own it prior to damage because selling it provides a gain relative to the value of retaining ownership.

Although the condition is required for the abandonment issue to arise, abandonment is not an automatic result. For abandonment to actually occur, the *damage* (i.e., the economic burden on the owners of restoring the asset's function) must exceed the present value of the asset's cash flows (in the above example, $400,000). For damage less than $400,000, restoring the asset's function benefits the organization's owners. In other words, abandonment will not occur unless damage exceeding the present value of the asset's cash flows occurs.

Even if damaged property is replaced, the effect of the loss on the firm will include the temporary interruption of earnings while the property is being restored. In deciding whether to abandon damaged property, therefore, the test should consider the temporary reduction in the earnings stream. The result is that reinvestment may not be justified when the effect of the temporary interruption is considered. Regardless of whether the firm decides to reinvest, the present value of the earnings lost because of the interruption should be recognized as an additional loss. If the property is replaced, the total property loss should be the direct loss plus the earnings interruption loss. The valuation also should consider extra expenses, such as the cost of negotiating new financing to restore a damaged asset.

Methods of Valuing Other Interests

As noted above, an owner may also suffer indirect property losses. A loss to property damaged because its environment is altered is valued the same way as direct losses. Similarly, if a building is severely damaged, making it necessary to tear down what remains, the value of the remaining section is determined the same way as a direct loss. If one pair of a matched set or an essential part of a machine is destroyed and cannot be replaced, the decline in value of the remaining parts may vary from almost zero to their complete value depending upon their relationship to the destroyed part.

Representatives of owners, tenants, bailees, and vendors or vendees, depending upon who holds the title, can estimate their potential losses in the same way as owners. In some instances, the cost of replacement without any deduction for depreciation is the proper measure. For example, under a lease, the tenant may be required to replace the damaged or destroyed property with new parts or a new building. Secured creditors face the loss of the unpaid balance of the secured debt.

TIME ELEMENT LOSSES: A FURTHER LOOK

The direct and indirect property losses are often not the only losses that occur when property is damaged, destroyed, or taken. Until that property is replaced or restored to its former condition, the organization may suffer a reduction in its net income (revenues less expenses) because it loses the use of that property—in whole or in part. As a result, either (1) revenues are decreased or (2) expenses are increased.

Although in many instances the time element loss will far exceed the direct and indirect property losses, organizations tend to be less aware of net income exposures than direct and indirect property exposures. Risk managers also find it more difficult to measure the loss potential of net income exposures because of the many variables involved. This section describes the leading net income exposures and their loss potential.

Decreases in Revenues

The major ways in which revenues may be decreased as a result of an accidental loss to property include (1) a loss of rent, (2) an interruption in the firm's operations, (3) an interruption in the operations of important supplies or customers, and (4) smaller net collections on accounts receivable.

Loss of Rent. If a building is accidentally damaged or destroyed, and the tenant is not responsible for the payment of rent during the period the property is untenantable, the landlord loses the rent, less any noncontinuing expenses, for the time necessary to restore the structure to a tenantable condition.

The responsibility of the tenant in case the property becomes untenantable is usually specified in the lease. Typically the landlord is responsible for the loss of rent, but this is not always true. If the lease is silent, common law holds the tenant responsible, but most states have statutes that excuse the tenant from the rental payments. (If the tenant *is* responsible, the landlord's risk manager may still prefer to include this exposure in the risk analysis but recognize that it has been handled through a noninsurance transfer.

Interruption in Operations. Because assets are damaged or taken, a business or other organization may have to suspend or reduce its operations. For example, a department store may have to close its doors or part of the store until the assets are repaired or replaced. Assets that, if damaged or taken, might cause such a shutdown include the store premises, furniture and fixtures, or merchandise for sale. A manufacturer may have to cease or reduce production until it replaces assets such as the plant, machinery, patterns and dies, raw material inventories, or goods in process. As these examples imply, it is customary to measure the loss to a mercantile or service business in terms of the reduction in sales. The loss to a manufacturing firm depends upon the reduction in production—not sales. The loss a manufacturer might suffer because of a loss to its finished goods is considered below. A third example is the reduction of tuition income suffered by an educational institution or a day-care center when its facilities are damaged.

The loss caused by such a business interruption would be (1) the net profit the business would have earned if there had been no interruption plus (2) the expenses that continue despite the interruption. Illustrative of such continuing expenses are the payroll of certain key employees, services performed by others under contract, interest expense, depreciation and taxes on undamaged property, and some portion of advertising and insurance expenses.

The period of the shutdown or reduction in operations will vary according to what assets are damaged or taken and the nature of the direct or indirect loss. Sometimes partial damage to a vital asset can cause the organization to shut down for an extended period. To this period must be added the time required after operations are resumed to achieve normal sales or production volume. Some organizations never return to normal.

The net profit loss will depend upon the state of the economy as well as circumstances peculiar to the industry and the individual organization. Trend, cyclical, and seasonal factors should be considered in estimating the loss. The estimate of continuing expenses will be influenced by similar considerations.

Pro forma income statements for various shutdown periods provide a useful framework for estimating these losses.

Contingent Business Interruption. Some businesses depend so much upon receiving raw materials, power, or merchandise from a single supplier that interruption of that supplier's operations will, in turn, interrupt the organization's production or sales. Similarly, a business may be so dependent upon sales to a single customer that if the customer's operations, and consequently its purchases from the business, are slowed by damage to or taking of its assets, the business will also suffer a business interruption loss. This loss, called a *contingent business interruption loss,* depends upon how much the organization depends upon a single supplier or customer, the susceptibility of those suppliers and customers to interruption losses, and the likely restoration period.

Increases in Expenses

Expenses may be increased because of an accidental loss in a variety of ways including (1) extra expenses incurred to keep the business operating, (2) cancellation of a valuable lease, and (3) the loss of use by a tenant of irremovable improvements and betterments.

Extra Expenses. Newspaper publishers, dairies, dry cleaners, banks, and other businesses that believe they must continue operating to preserve their relationships with customers could suffer irreparable damage if damage to or taking of their assets interrupted these operations. If their customers are forced to turn to their competitors for temporary service, they may lose a large portion of these customers forever. Consequently, these organizations would probably incur extra expenses to continue as near normal operations as possible.

To estimate the extra expenses that might be incurred in such a situation, the risk manager, in conjunction with others in the organization, should develop a plan that will be followed after an accident to continue operations. The plan serves two purposes. First, the plan itself will permit the organization to proceed more expeditiously following the accident than if there were no pre-loss planning. Second, the plan provides a reasoned estimate of the extra expenses that will be incurred to continue operations.

The extra expenses might include such items as the cost of moving to and from temporary quarters; the extra rent for those quarters; the rental of temporary equipment; higher prices for rush orders of raw materials, supplies, or merchandise; additional transportation charges; and higher labor costs. Generally, these extra expenses are higher the first 30 or 60 days following a loss than subsequently.

In addition to those organizations that believe they must maintain their operations to keep their customers, certain organizations such as a public utility are required to maintain continuous service. Sometimes an organization has both an extra expense and a business interruption exposure. For example, a diversified organization may render services or manufacture products, some of which cannot and others of which can be discontinued. Another organization may be willing to interrupt its operations in the short run but prefer to operate with alternate facilities at extra expense in case of an extended shutdown.

In addition to incurring extra expenses to continue operations, the organization may incur some extra costs to expedite repairs, thus shortening the period operations are either shut down or continued elsewhere.

Cancellation of Lease. Many leases provide that if the building is damaged by at least, say, 50 percent, the lease is canceled either automatically or at the option of either party. The tenant suffers if the property is worth more than the rent it pays or if it has paid a bonus or advance rental payment that is not refundable.

Rental Value Higher than Rent. Sometimes a long-term lease on a building calls for a contract rent that is less than the rental value of equivalent premises elsewhere. Such a lease is valuable to the tenant. If the lease provides for cancellation automatically or at the option of the landlord and such a loss does occur, the landlord would probably ask for a higher contract rent equal to the building's rental value. The tenant, therefore, faces a potential loss equal to the present value for the remainder of the lease of the difference between the rental value and the contract rent. The shorter the time remaining under the lease, the smaller this present value. If, in addition to having the lease canceled, the business must move to new quarters, the rent difference is only part of the loss. The organization will also incur the cost of moving to a new location and the additional costs, if any, of operating at the new location.

The calculation of the present value of the difference between the rental value and the rent is illustrated in the following example. A business has a lease under which it pays $5000 a month to rent space whose current rental value is $7000. The unexpired term of the lease is four years or 48 months. The organization estimates that the rental value will remain $7000 for the remainder of the lease period. If the lease is canceled, the organization will lose the difference between $7000 and $5000, or $2000, paid at the *beginning* of each month for 48 months. The present value or lump-sum equivalent value of this loss is the amount that, invested at a certain rate of interest, would permit monthly withdrawals of $2000 for 48 months. The appropriate interest is the after-tax return the business could earn on a safe, liquid investment during those 48 months. A 6 percent rate of return (0.06/12 per month) will be assumed in this example. The present value of this stream of monthly differences is $85,586.

This $85,586 *leasehold interest* will decline as the unexpired term of the lease shortens. For unexpired terms of 36, 24, and 12 months, for example, the leasehold interest will be respectively $66,070, $45,352, and $23,354.

Because leases tend to be written for shorter periods now than in the past and rents are often related to some index that reflects increases in the owner's costs, this type of loss receives less attention today than it did formerly.

Bonuses or Advance Rental Payments. If the organization has paid a bonus to secure a lease or has paid the last month's rent in advance and neither payment is refunded in case the lease is canceled, the organization faces an additional leasehold interest loss. Each of these two types of loss will be illustrated below. To simplify the presentation, annual rental payments will be assumed instead of monthly payments.

To illustrate the bonus loss, assume that an organization paid a bonus of $30,000 to secure a 10-year lease. If the lease is canceled with four years remaining, what is the organization's loss because of the bonus payment? Two calculations are necessary. First, an immediate payment of $30,000, assuming, say, a

6 percent interest rate, has the same present value as $3845 paid at the beginning of each year for 10 years. Second, the present value of $3845 paid at the *beginning* of each year for the four remaining years, assuming a 6 percent interest rate, is $14,123, which is the leasehold interest loss because of the bonus.

The advance rental payment loss is much easier to calculate. The loss is the advance rental payment itself, say, $60,000. That amount, if invested now, would yield $3600 interest at the end of the next three years plus the $60,000 required to pay the rent at the beginning of the fourth year.

Irremovable Improvements and Betterments. Sometimes a tenant makes improvements to a rented building that cannot be removed when the tenant leaves the building. An organization makes this investment because it believes the improvements will have use value while it occupies the premises. What loss does the tenant sustain if these irremovable improvements are damaged or destroyed?

If the lease requires the landlord to repair the improvements, the tenant loses only the use of the improvements while the repairs are being made. This loss becomes part of the broader business interruption loss.

If the tenant is responsible under the lease for accidental damage to any part of the building, including the improvements, the cost of repairing damage to the improvements becomes part of a large responsibility described earlier. The loss of use of the improvements while repairs are being made would be part of the business interruption loss.

What will the organization lose if the lease does not specifically cover the restoration of improvements? If the tenant intends to replace the improvements, it should recognize a potential property loss equal to the cost of replacing the improvements with no deduction for depreciation. The loss of use of the improvements during the repair period would be part of the business interruption loss. If the tenant would not restore the improvements, the loss could be calculated as if the original cost of the improvements was a bonus paid at the time of the improvements. In practice, it is customary to use a more simple pro rata approach. To illustrate, if improvements costing $30,000 were made at the beginning of a 10-year lease and destroyed at the end of six years, it is assumed that 40 percent of $30,000 or $12,000 has been lost. This pro rata approach ignores the fact that the improvements may not decline uniformly in value over the lease period, the time value of money, and the effects of inflation.

If the tenant's lease is canceled because of the accidental loss, as explained in the discussion of leasehold interest, the pro rata method described in the preceding paragraph can be used to calculate the loss. It makes no difference in this case whether the improvements were actually damaged by the accident.

PROPERTY-LOSS FREQUENCY AND SEVERITY DATA

As noted in Chapter 3, most firms will not generate enough experience of their own from which the risk manager can estimate the probable loss frequency and

TABLE 5.1. Estimated Structural Fires and Damage by Class of Property, 1989

Class of Property or Use	Fires		Damage	
	Number	Percent	$ Millions	Percent
Residential	513,500	74.6	3,998	61.3
One- and two-family dwellings	402,500	58.5	3,335	51.2
Apartments	96,000	14.0	541	8.3
Hotels and motels	6,500	0.9	87	1.3
Other residential	8,500	1.2	35	0.5
Storage in Structures	44,500	6.5	673	10.3
Stores and Offices	34,500	5.0	703	10.7
Special Structures	32,000	4.7	293	4.5
Industry, Utility, or Defense	24,500	3.6	406	6.2
Public Assembly	17,500	2.5	286	4.4
Institutional	12,500	1.8	43	0.7
Educational	9,000	1.3	116	1.8
TOTAL FIRES	688,000	100.0	6,518	100.0

(Details may not add to totals because of rounding.)

Source: Accident Facts, 1991 edition.

severity. Some external sources of accident data that may prove useful to the risk manager are *Insurance Facts*, an annual publication of the Insurance Information Institute, and *Uniform Crime Reports*, an annual publication of the Federal Bureau of Investigation. For example, *Insurance Facts* contains information on fires, tornadoes, earthquakes, and automobile collisions.

Table 5.1 illustrates the type of data available from published sources. Shown in Table 5.1 are the estimated number of structural fires and the resulting damage in the U.S. during 1989. These data are only averages that do not reflect characteristics that distinguish one property exposure from another, such as the nearness of fire-fighting facilities or the use of sprinkler systems to contain fire damage. Also, the data would be more useful if the losses were related to units of exposure, such as the number of structures exposed to possible fire damage during the year. Without further detail concerning these issues, data such as shown in Table 5.1 offer only a rough estimate of possible damage amount or its likelihood. The lack of detailed estimates is typical for many risks under the jurisdiction of the risk manager; information available to estimate fire damage usually results in this risk falling at level 2 uncertainty (see Chapter 1 for a discussion of levels of uncertainty).

Statistical exhibits filed by insurers with state insurance departments sometimes contain loss-frequency and severity data. The risk manager can obtain these data when they are available. Some insurers develop such data for internal use but the public seldom has access to such information. Public agencies, such as the state department of motor vehicles, may also gather data of interest to risk managers.

Key Concepts

property exposure: Exposure to risk from the damage, destruction, or taking of property.

peril: The cause of a loss. Examples are fire, windstorms, water leakage, and vandalism.

direct property loss (gain): A loss (gain) that occurs because property that is damaged, destroyed, or taken by a specified peril (enhanced) must be repaired or replaced.

indirect property loss (gain): A loss (gain) that occurs because some property is adversely (favorably) affected by the fact that some other property is damaged, destroyed, or taken by a specified peril (enjoys a favorable outcome). For example, food in a refrigerator spoils when fire destroys a transformer.

market value: The amount a willing seller will accept and a willing buyer will pay for property on the date the property is valued. For risk management purposes, this method is more commonly used for valuing personal property than real property.

property interest: The rights that a business possesses in a piece of property; for example, as an owner, representative of the owner, or a secured creditor.

replacement cost new: The cost of replacing or repairing the property damaged, destroyed, or taken without any deduction for physical depreciation or economic obsolescence.

replacement cost new less depreciation and economic obsolescence: The cost of replacing or repairing the property damaged, destroyed, or taken less a deduction for physical (not accounting)

depreciation and economic obsolescence.

time element loss (gain): A decrease (increase) in revenues or an increase (decrease) in expenses that occurs because one loses the use of property that is damaged, destroyed, or taken a (greater than expected return or the asset).

rent loss: The loss of contract rent that occurs when a tenant is excused from paying rent when a building that is damaged or destroyed is rendered untenantable; also, the loss of the contract rent the tenant may be required to pay even though he or she cannot occupy the building.

business interruption loss: The profits that are lost and the expenses that continue when a business has to suspend or reduce its operations because assets are damaged, destroyed, or taken.

rental value loss: The loss of the cost of equivalent premises if an owner-occupant or a tenant cannot occupy a building that was damaged, destroyed, or taken, less any contract rent that may be discontinued.

extra expense loss: The extra amount a business spends to continue at least part of its operations if damage to or taking of its assets would otherwise interrupt its operations.

leasehold interest loss: The loss to a tenant, in case a building is damaged, of a valuable lease under which the rental value exceeds the rent.

improvements and betterments: Improvements made by a tenant to a building that cannot be removed if the tenant leaves the building.

Review Questions

1. The text classifies property exposures to risk in four ways. Name and explain briefly these four ways.
2. How does a direct property loss differ from an indirect loss?
3. Cite three illustrations of indirect property losses, gains.
4. Cite four illustrations of interests in property other than sole ownership.
5. Two or more organizations may have a property interest in the same real estate. Use three examples to illustrate the truth of this statement.

6. A firm purchases goods f.o.b. point of destination. At what point does the title pass to the organization? What other terms of shipment are possible and what is their effect upon the passing of title?

7. Twenty years ago an organization purchased a building, which was then five years old, for $200,000. The price was generally considered a bargain. The organization's current balance sheet states that the building is worth $200,000 less depreciation of $120,000. From these data can you tell what the direct loss would be if the building were totally destroyed by fire? If not, why not?

8. According to one construction index, the cost of building the structure described in question 7 has increased 50 percent over the past two years. The risk manager decides, therefore, to value the building at $300,000. Comment on this valuation.

9. How would you value the direct property loss sustained by each of the following if a building were destroyed by fire?
   a. The owner
   b. A bank that holds a mortgage on the property
   c. A tenant

10. Which property valuation method would you prefer—market value, cost of replacement new, or cost of replacement new loss physical depreciation and obsolescence? Why?

11. A firm intends to abandon a building if a fire destroys it completely.
    a. Why might a firm make such a decision?
    b. How would you value the direct property loss to the firm if such a loss were to occur?

12. Cite some sources of information concerning the frequency of property losses of various types.

13. How do time element losses differ from indirect property losses?

14. A building whose rental value is $24,000 a year is rented for $18,000 a year under a lease that has five years to run. The lease excuses the tenant from paying the rent if an accident renders the property untenantable. If the physical damage to the building exceeds 50%, the lease is automatically canceled.
    If a fire causes enough damage to the building to render it untenantable for six months but not enough to cancel the lease:
    a. What time element loss will the landlord suffer?
    b. What time element loss will the tenant suffer?

15. Assume the same facts as in question 14 except the fire is serious enough to cause the property to be untenantable for nine months and to cause automatic cancellation of the lease. At 6 percent interest the present value of $1 paid at the beginning of each year for five years is $4.4651.
    a. What time element loss will the landlord suffer?
    b. What time element loss will the tenant suffer?

16. A windstorm damages a manufacturing plant and a warehouse in which finished goods are stored until sold.
    a. What time element loss does the business suffer because of the damage to the manufacturing plant?
    b. What time element loss does the business suffer because of the damage to the warehouse?

17. A department store has been operating at a slight loss during the past year. Does it have any business interruption exposure?

18. Under what conditions would a contingent business interruption exposure exist?

19. Explain why an organization with a few large customers is less likely than one with many small customers to have difficulty collecting on its accounts receivable if its records are destroyed by vandals.

20. **a.** Why might a business consider itself to have an extra expense exposure instead of a business interruption exposure?

    b. Might both exposures exist?

21. Five years ago a business paid a bonus of $20,000 to secure a 10-year lease. If the lease is canceled, what will be the leasehold interest loss because of the bonus? Assuming 6 percent interest, the present value of $1 paid at the beginning of each year for five years is $4.4651; for 10 years $7.8017.

22. Five years ago a tenant spent $20,000 on irremovable improvements that it expected to use under a 10-year lease. If these improvements are destroyed and not replaced, what loss does the tenant suffer?

References and Suggestions for Additional Reading

BECKMAN, G. M., W. F. BERDAL, and D. G. BRAINARD: *Law for Business and Management* (New York: McGraw-Hill Book Company, 1975), part IV.

DOHERTY, N. A.: *Corporate Risk Management* (New York: McGraw-Hill Book Company, 1985), chaps. 7 and 8.

HARDY, CHARLES O.: *Risk and Risk Bearing* (Chicago: The University of Chicago Press, 1923).

HEAD, G. L., and STEPHEN HORN, II: *Essentials of Risk Management* (Malvern, Pa.: Insurance Institute of America, 1991).

Insurance Facts (New York: Insurance Information Institute, annual).

KEETON, R. E.: *Basic Text on Insurance Law* (St. Paul, Minn.: West Publishing Company, 1971), chaps. 3 and 4.

MEHR, R. I., and B. A. HEDGES: *Risk Management: Concepts and Applications* (Homewood, Ill.: Richard D. Irwin, Inc., 1974), chap. 7.

—— and ——: *Risk Management in the Business Enterprise* (Homewood, Ill.: Richard D. Irwin, Inc., 1963), chaps. 6, 8, and 9.

RODDA, W. H.: *Commercial Property Risk Management and Insurance, vols. I and II* (3rd ed., Malvern, Pa.: American Institute for Property and Liability Underwriters, 1988).

SMITH, MICHAEL L.: *Selection of Deductibles in Property and Liability Insurance,* unpublished doctoral dissertation, The University of Minnesota, 1974, chap. 5.

THOMAS, P. I.: *How to Estimate Building Losses and Construction Costs* (4th ed., Englewood Cliffs, N.J.: Prentice-Hall, Inc., 1983).

——, and P. B. REED: *Adjustment of Property Losses* (4th ed., New York: McGraw-Hill Book Company, 1977), chaps. 14, 16, and 17.

Liability Exposures to Risk

Learning Objectives

After you have completed this chapter, you should be able to:

1. Define *stare decisis* and briefly explain its effect on the American legal system.
2. Identify the four sources of law.
3. Explain the difference between civil and criminal law.
4. Explain the four points a plaintiff must make to prevail in an action based upon negligence.
5. List and distinguish among the defenses available to a defendant in a civil action.
6. Summarize and discuss major liability problem areas encountered by most organizations.
7. Define intentional torts and provide illustrations of an intentional tort.
8. Briefly identify the relationship between ethics and the law.

INTRODUCTION

Possibly the most significant source of risk and uncertainty for many organizations is the legal environment. The law establishes a web of rights and duties that influences virtually every decision an organization makes and every activity it undertakes. Under the law, rights define the range of activities or options available to individuals and organizations. These rights may be lost or infringed upon if care is not taken to protect them. As an illustration, Chapter 5 shows how the law regards property as a set of rights with respect to a physical asset. Hence, a zoning decision by a local government may impact upon an organization's easement interest in some property. Failure to assert that right may result in an economic loss to that organization.

Protection of rights is clearly important, but it is nevertheless true that the risk and uncertainty arising from "duties" imposed by the law is probably of greater concern to the typical risk manager. Chapter 6 is devoted to an exposition of those duties, or to put it in the vernacular of this textbook, an exposition of the "hazards from which liability losses arise." The chapter begins with an overview of the legal environment. Although reference will be made to differing systems around the world, the main emphasis is upon the United States system of law, which grows from English Common Law. English Common Law and legal tradition, in turn, have had an important influence on legal systems throughout the world, so much of the chapter's discussion can be generalized to other countries. Included in the introduction is a discussion of the different categorizations of the law and a description of the legal process. The chapter then turns to several significant problem areas for most organizations. Among the several topics is an overview of such issues as product and service liability, environmental impairment liability, and (briefly) workers' compensation. The chapter concludes with a short discussion of the relationship between the law and ethics.

A BRIEF INTRODUCTION TO LAW

The law concerns itself with relationships: relationships among individuals, organizations, and governments in all possible configurations. The purpose of law is to provide stability to the political, social, and economic systems in which people and organizations exist. At the same time that the law seeks to assure stability, however, it should also adapt to new developments, such as changing technology or new levels of scientific knowledge. For example, medical technology—such as DNA testing—is now forcing some serious rethinking about standards of evidence. Some legal systems place more emphasis on stability than on flexibility, yet however the emphasis is placed, in all systems the process of balancing stability with flexibility creates an underlying tension that affects virtually every aspect of the legal environment.

The American system of law is, perhaps, more flexible and evolutionary than other systems. Though this characteristic is due in great measure to the political and social environment, from this chapter's perspective it is also because the American civil justice system is based upon a *common law system*, as opposed to a *code law system* (although there are significant code law elements in the American system). Under a code law system, the law principally is established through legislation, or "codes," and its adjudication is effected through an inquisitorial method in which the judiciary essentially initiates and conducts a case to resolution. Common law was developed in England and is based largely upon judicial decisions. Through an adversarial presentation of a case, the judiciary hears the competing arguments between a "plaintiff" (the party alleging a wrong) and a "defendant" (the party accused of the wrong) and renders a decision. Since individual judicial decisions form the basis of common law, there is a clear possibility that such a system might become "capricious and revolutionary" rather than "evolutionary." This possibility is largely controlled through the important legal doctrine of *stare decisis* (roughly, "to stand by the decision"). Under *stare decisis*, the judiciary defers to relevant past decisions, and is guided by those decisions in resolving current cases. *Stare decisis* does not eliminate the possibility of the revolutionary decision or the novel application of past decision, but it does serve as an anchor to the common law system.

Risk managers in multinational organizations must be aware of the different systems of law around the world. Although much of Europe, North America, Australia, and some parts of Asia and Africa operate in a relatively similar common law environment, most of Central and South America, the Middle East, Asia and many parts of Africa function under a code law system (in the United States, Louisiana essentially has a code law system). These differences exist within a growing body of international law. Though nations and organizations may often elect to ignore international law, it is likely that international bodies, such as the United Nations and the European Community, will have increasing authority and influence as economic, political, and social matters become transnational in nature.

A somewhat related issue is the interaction of law and culture. Although law and culture is a subject beyond the scope of this textbook, it is useful to remember that even similar legal systems can look quite different when placed in different cultures. For instance, the widely noted litigiousness of American society is not seen to the same degree in Great Britain, though the legal systems are quite closely related. An explanation for the differences in litigation frequency would be complex, perhaps attributing the lower frequency in Great Britain to social and cultural homogeneity (and contrasting heterogeneity in the United States). Excessive litigation does not appear to be an inherent characteristic of the common law system.

Sources of Law

In America, the law arises from four principal sources: judicial decision (common law), constitutional law, legislative enactment, and administrative ruling. Common law will be covered in detail later in the chapter, so comments here are confined to constitutional, legislative, and administrative sources of law.

The basis for constitutional law is, of course, the United States Constitution. This document enunciates the rights and liberties of individuals, delineates the powers held by the national government vis à vis state governments, and details the nature of the powers held by the national government. Correspondingly, each state has its own constitution that is paramount within that state, but which defers to the U.S. Constitution when matters of common interest arise. The principal of "judicial review," established very early in American history, holds that the Supreme Court is the final arbiter regarding the constitutionality of all law.

At both the federal and state levels, legislatures have the power to establish laws (assuming executive approval, or an executive inability to sustain a veto) that have a significant effect on the legal environment. Thus, legislative enactment is a fundamental source of law. Whereas the common law tends to be evolutionary in nature, legislative lawmaking is—almost by definition—revolutionary. Legislatures do not necessarily rely upon precedent (*stare decisis*) to guide decisions and enactments, and are often proactive in extending or creating new law. Workers' compensation, securities regulation, bankruptcy law, and unemployment insurance are examples of legislative law.

The flexibility of legislative law, relative to common law, does cause problems. Notably, Congress and various state legislatures can (and do) enact laws that may be inconsistent or conflicting in application. For instance, a given state might have a workers' compensation statute that is quite different from those in neighboring states. This difference can have an effect on the competitiveness of that state in attracting employers. A more common problem arising from such differences is the administrative difficulty the risk manager of a nationwide company may have in complying with different workers' compensation systems. Some efforts have been made to harmonize certain legislative enactments between states. Perhaps the most well-known example is the Uniform Commercial Code (UCC), a legal code that now governs almost all aspects of commercial transactions.

Administrative law is a separate source of law. Administrative law arises from government agencies, bureaus, and regulatory bodies at the federal and state levels, promulgating rules specific to their areas of jurisdiction. Often, these administrative rules interpret broadly worded provisions of legislation applying to specific organizations or activities. In many respects, administrative law is confusing and complex because of the vast number of governmental bodies that develop and release hundreds of rules and directives each year. Notable sources of administrative law relevant to risk managers are the Occupational Safety and Health Administration, the Department of Labor, and the Environmental Protection Agency.

Types of Law

Another way to look at and understand the American legal system is to categorize the sources of law and the types of laws that arise from these sources. One commonly used approach classifies the law as either "public law" or "private law." Public law pertains to the powers and rights of governments and the relationships of governments to individuals and organizations. The three areas of public law are constitutional law, criminal law, and administrative law. Private law pertains to the governing of individuals and organizations and their relationships to one another. Private law includes tort law, contract law, property law, agency law, sales law, partnership/incorporation law, and commercial paper law.

A second classification scheme is to categorize law as federal law or state law. In America, there are essentially two parallel legal systems, one arising from federal law and the federal court system, and one arising from individual state law and court systems. While these systems largely are independent of one another, there are considerable points of overlap and mutual interest. Indeed, a plaintiff may sometimes be in the position to choose between pursuing a case in a state or a federal court. For introductory purposes, the state/federal classification scheme is limited in usefulness. However, from a typical risk manager's perspective, the distinction may be quite important.

A third useful classification scheme is to identify law as either "criminal" or "civil." Civil liability is distinguished from criminal liability by the nature and form of the action as well as by the penalties imposed. In a criminal action, the actual legal procedure is begun by the law enforcement officer on behalf of society or the state. For example, the district attorney or attorney general of either the federal or state government normally initiates the criminal action against the individual or organization. The penalty typically is a fine or a jail sentence.

A civil liability is brought by one party against another party for alleged wrongs. Penalties consist of indemnity for the loss, punitive damages imposed by the courts, restitution of the property or loss, injunctive relief precluding future conduct or action, and other remedies—including possession of the property or an accounting of the property entrusted. Civil actions are brought by the litigants at their own expense although court costs may be imposed on the losing party. In a criminal case, the standard of proof that must be met by the plaintiff is "beyond a reasonable doubt," that is, the judge or jury must be convinced of the defendant's guilt beyond doubts a reasonable person might have. In criminal liability cases, when it is clearly shown that the defendant is unable to hire legal counsel, the state will provide such counsel at its own expense.

Little more will be said regarding criminal liability and risk management, but further omission does not imply that criminal law cannot be an important issue for organizations and their officers. Criminal liability may be imposed in a number of situations in which the public at large is endangered because of activities undertaken by an organization (malicious and willful dumping of hazardous waste, for instance). Further, some state's attorneys general have demonstrated an increasing interest in pursuing criminal actions against directors and officers of organizations that have shown a reckless disregard for the safety of employees, customers, and others—the case of the deadly fire at the Imperial Foods chicken processing plant in North Carolina being a good recent example. Finally, some controversy exists as to whether a corporation can be held criminally liable (as opposed to the officers being held criminally liable), but convictions have occurred. Some scholars question the efficacy of trying such actions using criminal law rather than civil law, but the possibility of criminal conviction does extend to the organization itself.

Civil liability may be classified into the various sources of legal actions that may be brought to establish civil liability. Sources of civil liability can be classified into (1) those arising from contracts or similar agreements, (2) those arising from acts of omissions, which are called "torts," (3) those arising from fraud, error, or mistake, and so forth, referred to as "equitable actions," and (4) some actions and remedies that do not fall into the first three categories. As a point of reference, if constitutional law and administrative law are added to this list of sources, the classification encompasses the area of "private law" identified above. In a civil action, the standard of proof is the "preponderance of evidence," that is, the judge or jury weighs evidence presented by both the plaintiff and defendant. Hence, the burden on a plaintiff in a civil action is not as heavy as in a criminal action, when a higher "beyond a reasonable doubt" standard applies. The balance of this chapter will adopt the "civil law" focus.

Issues in the Legal Process of Civil Actions

In order to bring a civil action, it is not necessary that the type of action (tort, contract, equitable action, etc.) be named as such but merely that the theory of recovery be established for deciding the rights of the parties. For example, breach of contract may be considered a wrongful act and thus fit within the definition of a tort. The plaintiff's attorney may decide to bring the action in contract law to recover damages suffered as a result of the breach rather than to bring the action in tort law because of problems in establishing proof. It may be more difficult to show the legal duty of the defendant and actual negligent conduct than to show nonperformance of the contract obligation.

Establishing Civil Liability. It is said that the law protects only those persons who can afford it. Though this statement is an oversimplification, it makes an important point. The adversarial nature of the American legal system is based upon the presumption that the litigants will positively assert their rights in a particular matter. In other words, under civil law, if an individual chooses to sit upon his or her rights, they may not be preserved. Timeliness also matters; most states impose statutes of limitation that can bar forever an individual's ability to pursue redress.

This aspect of civil law, that individuals are responsible for protecting their interests, does appear generally to lead to a system in which justice and fair play prevail. However, the law does not profess to assure justice specifically, in each and every case, but to give each party the opportunity to have his or her "day in court." Having that day in court may be dependent upon the financial ability of the individual to obtain proper legal counsel.

The parties of a civil action must comply with all the statutes relating to legal process as well as statutes governing rules of evidence and methods of obtaining evidence. Generally speaking, the plaintiff in a civil action must carry the burden of proof by "the preponderance of the evidence" (as was mentioned above). Some jurisdictions in negligence actions shift this burden of proof during the course of the trial; such action depends upon the facts of the case and the legal principles involved. For example, under the doctrine of *res ipsa loquitur* ("the thing speaks for itself") the burden of proof may shift to the defendant. The doctrine may be applied in situations in which the plaintiff was injured under circumstances clearly establishing the possible negligence of the defendant. For instance, an engineering company was held responsible when a ceiling it had installed fell, causing bodily injury to a person below. The court reasoned that ceilings do not ordinarily fall unless someone was negligent, and that the defendant was solely responsible for the installation. Hence, the jury could conclude that the contractor was negligent unless he could prove otherwise.

The Legal Process. The entire process of litigation is very technical and almost always requires the skill and service of an attorney (small claims court being a notable exception). Despite this complexity, the legal process can be summarized. There are, potentially, five stages of a civil procedure. They are:

1. Pleadings
2. Pretrial
3. Trial
4. Appeal
5. Enforcement.

Pleadings. The purpose of this first stage is to serve notice that a complaint has been filed with the court and to determine issues of fact and issues of law. Issues of fact pertain to the event that gives rise to the complaint (lawsuit), while issues of law relate to the relevance of particular legal rules or doctrines to the specific event in question. During pleadings, the defendant is given an opportunity to respond to the complaint. A judgment may be rendered or a settlement proposed at any time during this step, but a number of cases are not resolved here and, therefore, move into "pretrial."

Pretrial. Although there may be considerable overlap with the first stage, pretrial proceedings consist mainly of evidence gathering. Under rules set forward by the law, each party is directed to develop its case through an independent investigation of the "facts." This process, sometimes known as "discovery," may involve the taking of depositions from affected parties, from witnesses, and from certain experts, and the use of interrogatories—which are usually a written set of questions to which the opposing party must provide sworn responses. Once again, the judge may rule on the case at the pretrial stage. A judicial ruling at this stage is usually referred to as a "summary judgment." As with the pleadings stage, both parties may resolve the case through settlement.

Trial. Rarely do cases actually reach the trial stage, but when that occurs the evidence is presented before a judge and jury (the parties usually may choose whether or not to have a jury). Each party has the opportunity to cross-examine the opponent's witnesses, experts, and usually the disputants. After cross-examination, the defendant may move for a "directed verdict" if he or she believes the plaintiff clearly has failed to establish a case. If this does not happen, closing arguments are made and the judge or jury deliberates and renders a verdict.

Historically, the role of the judge in litigation is not only to supervise the conduct of the trial by ruling upon proper procedures and admissibility of evidence, but also to hold the opposing attorneys directly accountable for their conduct. In the absence of a jury, the judge performs the function of "trier of fact" as well as determiner and interpreter of the law. The jury, when present, is traditionally limited to finding the facts of a case upon instructions from the judge as to the law.

Appeal. Either party may have cause to appeal a decision to a higher court (an "appeals court"). Usually, a case cannot be appealed on the facts of the case. Appeals must almost always be based upon matters of law, that is, erroneous instructions to the jury by the judge, or misapplication of some law. The appeals court will either affirm or reverse the lower court decision, and in some cases the verdict may be reversed and "remanded" for a new trial. Occasionally, appeal court decisions may be appealed to a higher level (often, the state or federal Supreme Courts).

Enforcement. At the point at which appeals are exhausted, the final verdict is enforced. Either the defendant is "released" from the allegation, or the defendant is ordered to comply with the verdict. As the above discussion makes evident, litigation is a time-consuming and costly process. Further, with court dockets overwhelmed at local, state, and federal levels, many legal experts have proposed that alternatives to the adjudication process be developed. One approach that has gained fairly wide acceptance is Alternative Dispute Resolution (ADR) (Carver and Vondra, 1994). ADR typically involves a formal arbitration or mediation process. Through the use of attorneys and other experts specializing in ADR, parties seek to resolve disputes outside the intensely adversarial environment of the courtroom. Although ADR is a relatively new phenomenon, it has been shown to be a useful method for reducing the costs of resolving disputes in many situations. A number of organizations now write ADR stipulations into contracts with customers, vendors, and co-venturers, which require a complainant to first utilize ADR in any contractual dispute with the organization.

The Determination of Awards. The nature and extent of the damages sustained by the plaintiff may be an issue of fact determined by the jury or judge, or it may be an issue of law determined by the judge. Evidence as to the exact amount and nature of damage suffered by the plaintiff is introduced and the kind of evidence admitted and the use of evidence is ruled upon by the judge as a matter of law.

Damages may be "special," "general," or "punitive." *Special damages* are compensation for tangible losses incurred by the plaintiff, such as the loss of earnings, medical bills, property repair costs, and legal fees. *General damages* are compensation for losses that are not directly measurable, such as pain and suffering. Both special and general damages are considered *compensatory damages,* in that they compensate the plaintiff for loss or injury. The losses for which special and general damages are awarded may have been incurred before the trial or be expected to occur in the future. For example, Chapter 7 will explain how future wage losses can be calculated. The allowance for physical and mental suffering, of course, is highly subjective. *Punitive damages* may be allowed when the conduct of the defendant is grossly negligent, reckless, and without regard to life or property. Jury awards, once determined, may be reduced by the court when they are held to be "unreasonable" for the injury sustained.

SPECIFIC LIABILITY PROBLEM AREAS FOR ORGANIZATIONS

We now turn our attention to several specific problem areas that are commonly encountered in the public and private sectors. Though not intended to be a comprehensive listing of all important liability issues, the following discussion does attempt to provide a general overview of the significant problems faced by most risk managers. Discussion begins with an overview of tort law, which underlies many of the specific problem areas highlighted in this chapter. This introductory information provides a transition between the general introduction above and the subsequent presentation of specific liability problem areas.

Tort Law

In general use, the word "tort" means "a wrong." Legally speaking, however, a tort is a civil wrong other than a breach of contract for which the court will provide a remedy in the form of money damages. Scholars often note that there is no satisfactory definition for the word tort and that it might be better to define a tort action by enumerating the things that it is not (Prosser, 1971). In that vein, it is noted that a tort is not a crime; it is not a breach of contract; it is not necessarily concerned with property rights or problems of government. Tort law occupies a large residual field of other types of legal actions. In this sense, tort is a miscellaneous classification that holds what cannot be put elsewhere in the law.

There are three basic types of torts: (1) intentional torts, involving conduct that may be by intention or design but not necessarily with the intention that the resulting consequences should occur, (2) unintentional torts, involving the failure to act or not act as a reasonably prudent person would have acted under similar circumstances, and (3) torts in which "strict" or "absolute" liability applies. In cases of strict liability, intent or fault of the defendant is not an issue.

Intentional Torts

The intentional tort field includes the type of conduct that can be identified as premeditated or planned but the consequences of which are not necessarily anticipated. Various specific kinds of intentional torts have been recognized by the courts. They include trespass, conversion, assault, battery, false imprisonment, and defamation of character, among others.

Trespass. Trespass consists of the entry of a person or a thing upon land in the possession of another without permission. This action is designed to protect the exclusive possession of land and its physical status or condition. The trespasser is responsible for damages caused by trespass, possibly including punitive damages and, in many states, a special statutory penalty.

Conversion. Conversion is the wrongful disposition and retention of personal property belonging to another. Conversion usually results from the failure of a person who had legal possession of personal property to return it as agreed. The penalties essentially are the same as for trespassing.

Assault. A person is assaulted when that person becomes apprehensive that he or she will be touched without consenting to such contact. Generally speaking, mere words, however violent, are not sufficient to amount to an assault. In order to have the essentials of an assault, there must be a clear and present danger evident to the plaintiff, and the apparent ability by the defendant to execute the threatened act. Damages may be awarded for physical illness resulting from the apprehension and, when present, for humiliation.

Battery. Battery is an unpermitted and unprivileged contract with another. An assault becomes a battery when contact is made. The gist of the action for battery is not the hostile intent to execute the touching but rather the absence of consent of the innocent party. Recovery is allowed for physical and mental harm.

False Imprisonment. False imprisonment or arrest is the illegal and unlawful confinement of another within the boundaries fixed by the defendant without legal justification and with the intention that the act or breach of duty shall result in such confinement. The restraint may be by means of physical barriers or by threat of force, either or both of which intimidate the plaintiff into compliance with the orders. The restraint upon the plaintiff's freedom also may be imposed by the assertion of legal authority that the defendant contends he or she possesses. Damages may be awarded for mere interference with the plaintiff's freedom of motion plus, if present, physical harm, loss of time, damage to reputation, and humiliation.

Defamation of Character. Defamation is a tort action that involves the invasion of the interest, reputation, and good name of a person by communicating to others information that diminishes the esteem in which the plaintiff was held, or excites adverse feelings or opinions against the plaintiff. Defamation can take place through either the twin torts of libel or slander, the first being written, the other, oral. In cases of libel or slander, truth is a defense, so failure to prove the falsity of the charge defeats the action.

Normally, proof of special damages is required; mere hurt feelings are not sufficient. In a few instances, the courts have established certain specific exceptions to the plaintiff's showing of special damages; these include the allegation that the plaintiff has committed specific crimes or possesses a loathsome disease, holding the plaintiff up to ridicule in his or her business, trade, profession, or office, and possibly the allegation that the plaintiff is given to unchastity.

In suits involving defamation of character, the courts have held that certain forms of privileged communications will not invoke liability under the tort of defamation. Absolute immunity from defamation suits has been granted, for example, to judges and members of grand or petit juries, members of legislatures, and certain executive officers of government in the discharge of their duties. Qualified or conditional privilege is extended to other interests in society, such as publishers of newspapers and magazines and commercial credit agencies. Newspaper accounts must be limited to the facts, and suits of defamation may not be brought if the facts are fairly and honestly presented, without any intent to do injury to the person's character. Commercial credit agencies investigating a person's character or financial reputation must have some specific objective in regard to a business or commercial interest and must make their inquiries honestly and carefully.

Other Intentional Torts. In addition to the above intentional torts, others have been recognized by the courts under varying circumstances. For example, invasion of privacy, malicious and unlawful prosecution, interference with family relations, and interference with contractual relations are intentional torts.

Unintentional Torts: Negligence

Most civil cases brought for personal injury or property damage involve the unintentional tort of negligence. The dividing line between an intentional tort and an unintentional tort is made in terms of the conduct of the defendant. The attorney bringing the case for the plaintiff must choose the theory of recovery that he or she is best able to prove. For example, one case involved a salesperson who attempted to demonstrate a fly spray by spraying the product profusely around a grocery store. The wife of the grocer, who was allergic to this particular product, developed a very serious injury as a result of inhalation of the fumes. The plaintiff's attorney in this case could have brought the action on a theory of negligence, namely, that the salesman did not act as a reasonably prudent person would have acted in failing to discover whether or not any possible injuries might result to the people who inhale such fumes. In the particular case, however, the action was brought on a battery charge, namely, that the spraying of the fly spray was intentional, and the touching of the plaintiff by this product was a battery committed on the grocer's wife, causing her great bodily harm.

Ingredients for a Cause of Action. A case alleging negligence requires the following ingredients for a cause of action.

1. Legal Duty to Act or Not Act. Legal duty implies that the plaintiff can show that the defendant should have used a legal duty of care in acting or failing to act in the manner involved. A legal duty of care is the normal basis of proving or showing the existence of negligence. The duty varies depending upon the situation and the parties involved, but in general, the law expects that individuals and organizations will act "reasonably" (sometimes referred to as the reasonable person standard).

2. The Breach of Legal Duty. The plaintiff must prove that the defendant clearly breached the legal duty to act or not act as a reasonable person would have under similar circumstances. The boundaries of reasonable behavior are set in the context of the facts and circumstances leading to injury.

3. Breach of Duty Was the Proximate Cause of Injury. The plaintiff must show that the breach of legal duty by the defendant was the proximate or closest cause in producing the injury to the plaintiff. The doctrine of proximate cause draws a circle around the scope of responsibility of the negligent offender and attempts to cut off those liabilities for which he or she should not be held responsible. For example, the courts inquire as to whether or not the defendant could have foreseen the consequences of that act when he or she engaged in it, whether the defendant created an unreasonable chance of harm to others, and whether the injuries were within the foreseeable consequences of the negligent acts. In addition, the plaintiff's exposure must be in the "zone of risk," namely, sufficiently close to the actual commission of the negligence in the first place, in order to make it foreseeable, there must be no separate intervening cause, and the physical forces unleashed by the defendant must bear some relationship to the ultimate injury that the plaintiff suffers.

4. Damages Sustained. In the showing of damages in a negligence action, the plaintiff may allege actual bodily injury or damage to property. The damages must be stated in terms that allow money awards to be calculated (see earlier discussion of special and general damages). Courts may allow recovery for mental suffering and pain or emotional distress caused by the alleged shock imposed as a result of the defendant's conduct. In one case, the court allowed recovery to a woman who was almost hit by an oncoming vehicle, finding that the mental anxiety resulting from such a near-miss produced shock and mental injury to the plaintiff.

Defenses Against Charges of Negligence. The defendant may be able to convince the court that he or she was not negligent and thus not responsible for the damages sustained by the plaintiff. However, even if the defendant is negligent, he or she may be able to assert additional defenses, such as those described below.

1. Assumption of Risk. Under the assumption of risk defense, the defendant argues that the plaintiff consented to the clear and present danger of the possible negligent conduct of the defendant and failed clearly to establish his or her objections to such conduct. The assumption of risk defense is often used in host-guest cases in the operation of vehicles when the driver's conduct is sufficiently bad and is known to the plaintiff guest. The driver in defense may allege that the guest in the vehicle did not leave the vehicle or clearly establish his or her objections to the negligent driving.

2. Contributory or Comparative Negligence. Another defense, contributory negligence of the plaintiff, may remove any claims against the defendant for alleged negligent conduct. The contributory negligence defense usually is asserted in states allowing the theory that parties who were both at fault should not be able to recover from one another. Automobile accidents at uncontrolled intersections commonly illustrate a situation in which both parties are at fault. Under a strict interpretation of the contributory negligence doctrine, neither party should collect because of the liability of the other. Statutes have been enacted in the United States to overcome shortcomings of the contributory negligence doctrine. For example, the Federal Employers' Liability Act, the Merchant Marine Act, and the State Railway Labor Act all provide that the contributory negligence of an injured worker shall not bar recovery, but that the worker's damages shall be reduced in proportion to his or her negligence. About 40 states, plus several Canadian provinces, have adopted similar "comparative negligence" rules by statute or court decision. For example, in Minnesota and Wisconsin, which have "partial comparative negligence" statutes, if the plaintiff's negligence is less than the defendant's negligence, money is granted for 100 percent of the plaintiff's injuries, less his or her own percentage of negligence. In Mississippi, which has a "complete comparative negligence" statute, each party receives 100 percent of his or her damages diminished by his or her own percentage of negligence. Table 6.1 illustrates the difference between these two statutes.

An offsetting doctrine to the contributory negligence defense is that of "last clear chance." In a state without a comparative negligence statute, the last clear chance doctrine offers a way to mitigate the effects of the contributory negligence defense. Under this doctrine, if the plaintiff can clearly show that his or her negligence had been spent and that the defendant had a last clear chance to avoid the injury, then recovery will be granted.

Even in contributory negligence states, claims are usually settled out of court on a more liberal basis than the legal doctrine would suggest. For example, assume that the plaintiff prevails only about half the time in cases with certain characteristics. An insurance adjustor representing the defendant may, in such cases, settle the claim for about half of what it would be worth. In the language of Chapter 1, the insurance adjustor would settle the claim for its "expected value." Courts in contributory negligence states also sometimes appear to ignore a small degree of negligence on the part of the plaintiff.

TABLE 6.1. **Comparison of "Partial Comparative Negligence" Statutes in Wisconsin and Minnesota with "Complete Comparative Negligence" Statute in Mississippi**

Damages	% of Negligence	*Recovery* Wisconsin and Minnesota	Mississippi
A $100,000	25	$75,000	$75,000
B $ 50,000	75	$ 0	− $12,500
			net of $62,500 to A

3. Charitable and Governmental Immunity Defenses. In the development of the common law concept of liability, the courts at various times have granted immunity to certain activities and institutions. Immunity has been granted to charitable institutions and the government itself, among others. These concepts of immunity, however, have been undergoing rapid change, and many states have virtually lifted the immunity.

In the case of charitable institutions, the theory of immunity from liability is based upon the concept that a charitable institution is a trust and that the property of a charity cannot be used to pay judgments. This concept would permit hospitals, nursing homes, and charities to conduct their activities without fear of legal liability for their negligence. The common law rule of nonliability has given way, however, to a more modern concept that the charitable institution is liable (1) to persons receiving benefit from its activities for injury caused by the negligence in the selection of employees, and (2) to anyone else for injury caused by negligent acts or omissions of its employees.

Governmental immunity is based in part on the archaic concept, "the king can do no wrong," but more commonly, this immunity is interpreted as a measure to preserve and protect the common good. That is, if governments were susceptible to legal actions alleging negligence and wrongdoing, the economic burden might prevent governments from providing services that would benefit the public at large.

Since the early 1960s, the rather broad protection enjoyed by governments has been eroded steadily. Unfortunately (for students of the subject), this erosion has not occurred uniformly throughout the nation, so summarization is difficult. Some state and local governments still retain significant legal immunity, while others virtually have no immunity. Some states permit lawsuits against local governments for almost any valid reason, but limit the maximum amount that may be paid on any claim. Other states do not "cap" liability but provide some degree of legal protection through other measures—for instance, limitations on joint liability with co-venturers. The federal government has waived its immunity under the Federal Tort Claims Act.

Though summarization of the present status of governmental immunity is difficult, one fairly common thread among the states is the effort to legally distinguish between "governmental" and "proprietary" functions. Governmental activities pertain to the "functions of governing," a somewhat vague concept that refers to those activities that are generally legislative in nature or that are purely governmental administrative activities (provision of police services, for instance). Governmental activities are considered appropriate, by many, for immunity to apply.

Proprietary activities are those activities that might reasonably be provided by the private sector—municipal power and light plants, garbage collection, street maintenance and repair, or operation of a public marina. Proprietary functions should not enjoy legal immunity, according to scholars who subscribe to this view.

The distinction between proprietary and governmental activities is useful only when an activity fits neatly into one category or the other, and unfortunately, this does not occur frequently.

Strict or Absolute Liability

In addition to unintentional and intentional torts, a third kind of tort involves "strict" or "absolute" liability. This is an important type of liability loss exposure area, for an organization held "strictly liable" is responsible for damages regardless of fault.

As was explained earlier, liability arising from an unintentional tort is based upon breach of duty. That is, the plaintiff will argue—indeed, must argue—that the defendant had a legal obligation to act in a certain way but failed to do so. That duty, or "standard of care," may sometimes be precisely described by laws, statutes, or rules, but in general terms the duty is to act reasonably. Earlier reference was made to the reasonable person standard. This standard requires that individuals act in a given situation with the due care and consideration a reasonable person would exhibit in the same situation. Needless to say, reasonableness is not a fixed standard.

However, there are a growing number of situations in which "acting reasonably" is not a sufficient defense. These are situations in which the concept of strict or absolute liability applies. The doctrine of strict liability is based not upon fault, but upon the nature of the activity that causes the damages. Over time, the law has established that some activities pose risks that are so far above the norm that the ordinary standard of care is not adequate. Indeed, the law has reasoned that an elevated standard of care is inadequate as well. Therefore, an organization engaged in such an activity is expected to bear the full cost of that activity, including the costs of damages inflicted on others. We might, in fact, argue that strict liability makes an organization the virtual insurer of those exposed to the actions and activities of the organization. Workers' compensation is perhaps the best known example of strict liability, though its particular characteristics make it a distinct and separate example (see limited discussion in this chapter and extensive discussion in Chapter 23). Other areas where strict liability does apply are situations in which an organization undertakes abnormally dangerous activities (working with explosives) and—most importantly—in a significant proportion of all product liability situations. Product liability will be discussed in some detail shortly.

We now turn our attention to several specific liability problem areas. While not all organizations encounter all these issues, they do represent a fairly broad illustration of the types of problems and issues most organizational risk managers will confront. The problem areas to be discussed are:

1. Liability arising from ownership, use, and possession of land
2. Liability arising from maintaining a public or private nuisance
3. Liability arising from the sale, manufacture, or distribution of products or services
4. Liability arising from fiduciary relationships
5. Professional liability
6. Agency and vicarious liability
7. Bailee liability.

Discussion will conclude with a presentation of some non-tort issues that also deserve special attention. They are:

8. Contract Liability
9. Employment Liability
10. Liability for Work-Related Injury
11. Motor Vehicle Liability.

To reinforce the real-world importance of these issues, readers are directed to Table 6.2, which shows the type of civil cases filed in federal courts during a recent survey period. As can be seen, the cases fairly closely replicate the general structure of the following discussion.

Liability Problem Area 1: Liability Arising from Ownership, Use, and Possession of Land.

Some serious liability exposures may be associated with the ownership, use, and possession of land. The life tenant, for example, has a certain duty to preserve and protect the property from future loss. In the excavation of land, the adjoining property owners are entitled to lateral support and are privileged to use drainage established by the natural terrain. The following discussion, however, will deal more exclusively with the liability exposures of a property owner or possessor to visitors on his or her property.

The legal liability of a landowner to individual visitors upon his or her property depends on the status that they occupy at the time of the visitation. The law has placed visitors into three classifications: trespassers, licensees, and invitees.

Liability to Trespassers. The owner of land is normally not bound to anticipate the presence of a trespasser, for the law assumes that the owner has the right to enjoy the safe and peaceful possession of his or her land without interference. A trespasser thus enters land without specific permission, expressed or implied, and must assume the unsafe conditions of the premises as they exist. However, most courts look with disfavor on the use of traps or similar devices designed to harm trespassers. Otherwise, the owner has no liability to an undiscovered trespasser who is injured because of the unsafe premises.

TABLE 6.2.   Selected Categories of Civil Cases Commenced in U. S. District
Courts, 12-Month Periods Ending June 30, 1986 Through June 30, 1990

133

CHAPTER 6
*Liability Exposures
to Risk*

Nature of Suit	1986	1987	1988	1989	1990
Contract Actions	88,352	69,606	62,811	61,975	46,039
Tort Actions	42,326	42,977	44,961	42,090	43,759
Product Liability:	12,459	14,153	16,166	13,408	18,679
Airplane	216	151	185	185	196
Marine	93	99	101	88	330
Motor Vehicle	656	649	623	662	575
Asbestos	5,463	7,776	10,715	8,230	13,687
Other	6,031	5,478	4,542	4,243	3,891
Other Personal Injury:	25,789	25,020	24,982	24,953	21,914
Airplane	738	719	762	711	834
Marine	4,095	3,641	3,061	3,023	2,961
Motor Vehicle	6,958	7,137	7,264	7,653	6,157
Assault, Libel and Slander	800	815	814	704	644
Federal Employers' Liability Act	2,635	2,437	2,540	2,639	2,741
Medical Malpract.	1,911	1,785	1,567	1,573	1,375
Other	8,652	8,486	8,974	8,650	7,202
Personal Property Damage	4,078	3,804	3,813	3,729	3,166
Actions under Statutes	113,392	114,942	119,514	118,131	118,465
Real Property Actions	10,674	11,586	12,209	11,217	9,505
Other Actions	84	74	139	116	111
TOTAL CASES	254,828	239,185	239,634	233,529	217,879

Source: *Annual Report of the Director of the Administrative Office of the United States Courts, 1990.*

A notable exception in the law relating to trespassers is found in the *attractive nuisance doctrine,* which imposes a special duty of care upon a person maintaining an artificial condition on land that attracts children. Generally speaking, trespassing children occupy the same position before the law as trespassing adults, but, because children lack as much judgment, many jurisdictions have placed special legal responsibility for injuries to such trespassing children when the injuries result from conditions of land that are highly dangerous to them. Under the attractive nuisance doctrine, children enjoy the status and protection of invitees, and, in some cases, the landowner has been held absolutely liable even though they were trespassers.

Liability to Licensees.   A licensee is defined as one who stands in no contractual relationship to the owner or occupier of the premises, but is permitted or tolerated thereon, expressly or impliedly, or inferentially, merely for his or her own interest, convenience or pleasure, or for that of a third person.

The common law holds that the possessor of land does not owe a licensee any duty to make the premises safe for his or her reception. However, the licensee is entitled to the same obligations as are owned to a discovered trespasser in a few states, that is, the landowner must use reasonable care for the licensee's protection to avoid injuring him or her by any active negligence and must provide warning of known concealed dangerous conditions. While the licensee is required to accept the premises as the possessor uses them, he or she is entitled to know the dangers that the possessor knows. Typical licensees include police and firefighters who enter upon the premises under license given by law. The personal benefit they receive is the ability to do their job, which often, of course, benefits the owner as well. Other licensees include door-to-door salespersons, solicitors for charities, and persons entering the premises without objection from the owner to avoid a rainstorm.

Liability to Invitees. The invitee—also called a business visitor—is a person invited expressly or impliedly, to come onto the land of the possessor for the business advantage of the possessor.

An invitee is a visitor to the premises for the benefit of the owner or occupier of the premises as well as of himself or herself. Examples are actual and potential customers, suppliers, mail carriers, garbage collectors, and persons making repairs. Social guests are usually considered licensees, but the exceptions are numerous enough to justify a high degree of care for their safety. The common law generally imposes a duty of reasonable care to make the premises safe for anyone accepting an invitation to do business thereon—a duty to inspect and to warn of dangers. The typical cases in this area of law have involved business visitors who engaged in specific transactions with the owner or occupier of the premises. The court held in a food-market case that a business invitation includes also the use of the parking lot, since parking is part of the business transaction. Therefore, the premises include not only the building but also any other property used in the business venture.

In some states, safe place statutes have reinforced the duties of care required of landowners or possessors of land open to the public. A safe place statute makes the owner of the property absolutely liable for injuries caused by frequenters or business visitors to his or her property when the injury is due to some unsafe condition. In bringing an action under the statute, the plaintiff does not have to show specific negligence with reference to the care or maintenance of the premises, but merely to show that the injury was caused by a defect.

Liability Problem Area 2: Liability Arising from Maintaining a Public or Private Nuisance

A business may be sued for maintaining a public or private nuisance in relation to the use and enjoyment of its premises. These nuisance actions require that the claimant show substantial harm as the result of some activity and indicate that the value gained by the user of the land is much less in proportion to the harm or risk that it creates. Public nuisance actions normally involve possible criminal liability for interference with the rights of the community at large. They may involve, for example, the construction of an unsafe roadway or the performance of business transactions corrupting the morals of the community.

Private nuisances, on the other hand, may be the cause of a civil action. They include such highly dangerous activities as blasting, storing explosives, drilling oil wells, or laying pipelines. They may also involve such things as keeping vicious animals, shooting fireworks in the street, ringing bells or blowing whistles, or making disturbances that may invade the quiet and solitude of others. An unpleasant odor, a whiff of smoke, or an increased fire hazard due to the presences of certain types of buildings may also be the basis of suit. Private nuisances that threaten the safety of others may expose the organization to absolute or strict liability.

Legislation such as the Clean Air Act, the Water Pollution Control Act, the Noise Control Act, the Water Quality Improvement Act, and the Comprehensive Environmental Response, Compensation, and Liability Act (CERCLA—but commonly called the Superfund law), regulates the manner in which businesses dispose of their wastes and regulate noise emission levels; violations of these regulations may expose the organization to civil suits as well as the penalties prescribed in the law. For example, CERCLA is designed to achieve the prompt cleanup of hazardous dump sites by creating a Superfund, which can be used to finance both public and private responses to an actual or imminent threat from the sites. The persons who are potentially liable to finance these efforts are the owner or operator of the facility that released or disposed of the toxic substance and any person or organization that arranged for the disposal of such a substance or accepted it for transport. The only defenses available to a defendant are an act of God, war, or an act or failure to act by a third party who does not have a contractual relationship with the defendant. The defendant may be held responsible up to $50 million for public and private response costs and damage to natural resources. Only the federal government can bring claims under this act, but other parties can bring actions under common law for losses they suffer because of pollution.

Superfund is widely criticized for a failure to fulfill its mission. The original 1980 budget for superfund anticipated $1.6 billion to be spent over five years to clean up hazardous waste sites. In 1994, there are some estimates suggesting that around 3000 cleanup sites will make the Environmental Protection Agency's cleanup list. So far, only 161 sites have been cleaned at a cost of $13.4 billion, and it is estimated that the average cost per site of cleaning up the remaining sites is $30 million. EPA Administrator Carol Browner estimates that the total cost of all environmental protection costs may exceed 3 percent of America's Gross National Product (RIMS, 1994).

In 1994, Congress is evaluating numerous modifications to Superfund, as part of the reauthorization process. Although it is always difficult to predict the outcomes of the legislative process, there is a strong likelihood that the program will push more responsibility onto the states, that there will be an effort to improve the efficiency of the cleanup process, and that there will be a financing role for the insurance industry.

Liability Problem Area 3: Liability Arising from the Sale, Manufacture, and Distribution of Products or Services

Special liability problems exist for businesses in relation to the manufacture, sale, or distribution of goods and services. Legal problems arise out of the sales contract itself, involving promises and obligations concerning the performance of the products or services sold. In addition, the product or service itself may be defective or manufactured and designed in a negligent manner so as to produce serious harm to those using it. Tied to the product itself may be the necessary services of delivery, installation, training, and maintenance, which may be negligently performed.

1. Breach of Warranty Actions Arising from Sales Contract. Breach of warranty actions arising from the sales of goods or services may be based upon either express or implied warranties. An *express* warranty has been defined as "an affirmation of fact or a promise by the seller relating to the goods which may serve as an inducement for the buyer to purchase the goods." If the purchaser relies upon the statement of the seller and the product does not meet these expressed guarantees or promises, then liability for the purchase price and the property damages resulting from the breach may be established by a suit based on breach of express warranty. It is important, therefore, in the sale of products that the retailer or seller does not make statements that go beyond the normal performance to induce the purchase.

In addition to the express warranty actions, the common law has established certain *implied* warranties attached to most sales contracts, the breach of which may give rise to liability. They are: (a) implied warranty of title, (b) implied warranty of fitness for a particular purpose, and (c) implied warranty that the goods are of merchantable quality.

In the sale of goods, the seller makes the implied warranty that he or she has title to the goods and may convey them free and clear of other claims in the absence of any expressed reservations. If it subsequently develops that the seller does not have this title, then he or she is liable to subsequent buyers for the purchase price and any other damage suffered as a result of breach of this warranty.

When goods are purchased by description or catalog number, the buyer may specify that the article ordered must be used to fit or fulfill a particular purpose. When the buyer specifically indicates to the seller that the article must be suitable for a particular purpose as a condition of purchase, and when the buyer relies on the skill and judgment of the seller concerning the capacity of the goods to fulfill this purpose, then failure of the product to perform accordingly may also result in legal liability. For example, if a particular type of furnace is installed to heat your home properly and you rely on the installer's skill and judgment concerning the size and type of furnace required, then failure of the product to heat your home may involve the seller in a liability resulting from breach of the implied warranty of fitness.

The third warranty of merchantability governs situations involving food or other products that must maintain a certain minimum quality. Goods are said to be merchantable when they are free from hidden defects and are fit for the use for which they are ordinarily intended. For example, during the 1950s Cutter Laboratories manufactured a polio vaccine that subsequently caused patients who had been vaccinated to contract the disease. Suits followed, and even though the manufacturer offered evidence to show it used great care and skill in manufacturing the vaccine, the court allowed recovery for breach of warranty of fitness.

2. Liability Arising out of Negligence. In addition to breach of warranty actions, many product or service liability suits are based on the tort of negligence. If liability is to be successfully proved, it must rest upon the fact that the defendant either created the condition or refrained from removing it, and that creation or nonremoval was the result of the defendant's carelessness. For example, actions have been successfully brought under this theory against manufacturers of canned tuna and soft drinks that contained deleterious substances.

3. *Strict Liability.* In a large number of circumstances, courts have held manufacturers responsible for injuries arising out of defective products without regard to negligence. Only the defect need be proved by the plaintiff. This finding of strict liability, as it is called, raises serious problems for the defendant manufacturer since it cannot defend itself by showing that it used proper and reasonable care. Such findings have become particularly common in recent years and have been applied to a wide variety of products.

In October, 1972, Congress passed the Consumer Product Safety Act, which (a) increased the responsibility of sellers to buyers *before* they are injured and (b) made it much more likely in many cases that injured consumers will be able to collect damages from sellers. The act requires the Consumer Product Safety Commission to develop product safety standards for consumer products that in its judgment have unreasonably large injury potential. These standards may deal with the performance, composition, content, design, construction, finishing, or packaging of the product. If the commission determines that no feasible product safety standard can be developed for a certain product, it can ban further distribution of the product.

Every manufacturer of a product that is made subject to safety standards must certify that the product complies with the relevant standard. Any manufacturer, distributor, or retailer who determines that a product is not up to standard or that it contains a potentially dangerous defect must report this fact to the commission. After a hearing, the commission may require the business (a) to give public notice of the defect and (b) to repair, replace, or refund the purchase price, the choice being left to the business.

The effect of this statute on civil suits varies greatly among jurisdictions. In some jurisdictions, violation of the Consumer Product Safety Act is held to be negligence per se. Unless the violator can show some justifiable excuse, the violation will be held to be a breach of duty. In other jurisdictions the violation is considered to be prima facie evidence of negligence. Consequently, the violator is presumed to be guilty of negligence, but the presumption is rebuttable. In the remaining states, the violation is merely one of the pieces of evidence of negligence to be considered.

Similar statutes dealing with the manufacture and sale of consumer goods are the Pure Food, Drug, and Cosmetic Act; the Federal Hazardous Substances Act; the Federal Insecticide, Fungicide, and Rodenticide Act; the Federal Flammable Fabrics Act; and the National Traffic and Motor Vehicle Safety Act.

Liability Problem Area 4: Liability Arising from Fiduciary Relationships

Fiduciary relationships have become a more important source of liability in recent years. Two important examples are (1) the responsibility of members of a board of directors to manage the assets of a corporation in the best interests of the stockholders and (2) the responsibility of employee benefit plan managers or administrators to the plan participants.

The fiduciary duties of corporation directors fall into two broad categories: (1) the duty of care and (2) the duty of loyalty. The duty of care means the directors must exercise their duties with the care a prudent person would exercise under similar circumstances. The duty of loyalty means the directors must discharge their duty in good faith and in a manner believed to be in the best interests of the corporation and the shareholders. Directors who do not comply with these duties may be subject to personal liability for their actions.

In addition to their potential liability as a member of the board as a whole, directors may expose themselves to personal liability as members of the audit committee, the executive committee, or other board committees. Tort actions may be (1) derivative or (2) nonderivative suits. *Derivative suits*, which are brought by stockholders, seek damages for the corporation. *Nonderivative suits,* brought by competitors, governmental units, individual stockholders or others, seek damages for losses they sustained themselves or for law violations.

The Employee Retirement Income Security Act (ERISA) of 1974 greatly increased the responsibility of persons who manage pension plan assets and of other employee benefit plan fiduciaries. The major features of ERISA will be described in Chapters 24 and 25. Under ERISA any person (including company officers or directors) who exercises any discretionary authority or control over the management or administration of the plan is considered to be a fiduciary. In general, a fiduciary must be an honest, prudent person who always acts in the best interests of the plan participants and their beneficiaries. Failure to meet this standard may expose the fiduciary to civil actions, fines, and other penalties.

Liability Problem Area 5: Professional Liability

Special liability problems confront persons who engage in professional pursuits or perform services requiring special care and skill. Courts have defined the term *profession* as follows: "The word implies professed attainment in special knowledge as distinguished from mere skill. A practical dealing with affairs as distinguished from mere study or investigation, and an application of such knowledge to uses for others as a vocation, as distinguished from its pursuit for its own purposes." In surveying the common law, however, one finds that although lawyers, doctors, dentists, accountants, architects, and other occupations involving advanced training and licensing are clearly professionals, some courts have added such unexpected groups as operators of pool halls and operators of school buses. On the other hand, one court excluded management consultants. One trend is clear, however; more occupations are qualifying for professional status, at least insofar as professional liability is concerned.

The rise of professionalism in the United States has produced interesting developments in civil law. The individual practitioner has discovered, sometimes after painful and expensive litigation, that his or her conduct is not measured by the common law tests of quality used in the ordinary relationships among individuals. On the contrary, the law has recognized that the professional calling imposes responsibilities far above those of persons engaged in less skilled or less intellectual pursuits.

The Malpractice Problem Facing the Professions. The necessity and desirability of imposing fairly rigid controls over professional conduct is certainly not denied by the patients or clients, and least of all by the professions themselves. Professional status, as we have indicated, is dependent upon the quality and sophistication of the services rendered by all practicing members. It is for that very reason that the individual professions have not looked only to legal censure to preserve the quality and stature of their services, but have imposed strict and rigid rules of self-control and self-policing as a matter of self-preservation. Actions to bring about disbarment, loss of certification or license, and finally expulsion from the organized profession are usually brought in the name of the professional organizations against the violating individual. Codes of professional ethics, which carefully summarize the moral responsibilities of the individual members, are promulgated and enforced by most professional groups. State practice and licensing laws are usually sponsored by the individual profession.

A problem arises for the professional practitioner, however, when the control and regulation takes the form of litigation by the client or patient concerning the particular standards and qualities of the individual's conduct. It is in these situations and with this type of legal control that the professional faces the severe test that may bring about complete failure and economic ruin.

The malpractice or liability action strikes at the very heart of the practitioner's greatest and most cherished asset, his or her professional reputation. The bad publicity arising from such a suit, even in situations in which the defendant is entirely innocent and the eventual outcome is entirely favorable, may spell complete ruin of a professional career that took a lifetime to build.

Loss of reputation and professional standing are not the only consequences of malpractice litigation. Final judgment may be rendered against the practitioner for tremendous sums for the injury caused by careless, unexpected, unpredictable, or unintentional blunders. The loss in terms of trial time in testifying in the defense of one's actions, the legal and court costs that are usually assessed to the loser, to say nothing of the emotional and physical strain of enduring the whole ordeal, are some of the other losses suffered as a consequence of litigation.

Liability Problem Area 6: Agency and Vicarious Liability

Agency relationships permeate organizational life in the public and private sectors. The law has addressed the issue of agency in its various aspects: the nature of agency, the responsibilities or scope of agency authority, the duty owed by an agent to the "principal," the duty owed by the principal to the agent, and so on. The purpose of this discussion is not to survey agency law, but rather to focus upon the narrow subject of liability arising from the actions and activities of agents. In discussing this issue, the somewhat broader issue of vicarious liability will be addressed.

In its most fundamental form, the agency relationship creates a somewhat unusual liability exposure for an organization, in that the organization might be held liable for the tortious acts of others. Those "others" are its agents: individuals who the law determines to be legally constituted representatives of the organization (called the "principal" in agency law). Providing the agent is acting within the scope of the agency duties, the principal will be held responsible for any negligent act: a responsibility that arises from the legal doctrine of *respondeat superior.*

Although *respondeat superior* may be a reasonable application of the general idea of "vicarious liability" (liability for the actions of others), it is a potential problem area for risk managers. This is because the principal cannot maintain rigid control over all its agents, and it may become liable for some action or activity it would ordinarily never condone or sanction. Further, since from the plaintiff's perspective suing General Motors is more attractive than suing an employee of General Motors (a characteristic of agency law often ascribed to the "deep pocket theory," which motivates the plaintiff to seek the defendant with the greatest ability to pay), the principal is likely to be a major target for suits alleging wrongdoing by employees or other agents. Agency law does permit the principal—once it has paid a claim—to seek to recover from the agent, but this is often as unattractive or unproductive to the principal as it is to the plaintiff.

Apart from *respondeat superior*, one of the more troublesome areas of vicarious liability relates to the contingent liability of an organization for the negligence of others hired as independent contractors. Initially, the law adopted the general rule that the employer was not liable for the tortious conduct of an independent contractor. The basic reason for this nonliability rule was that an employer was deemed to have no right of control over the manner in which the work is to be done, it being regarded as the contractor's own responsibility.

Opposed to this reasoning is the argument that the employer is the person primarily benefiting from the work; and, indeed, the general rule of nonliability has been largely whittled away. In the first place, some courts have held the employer liable for failure to select a competent contractor. Second, so far as the employer participates in the work of the contractor, negligence is borne by the employer. Third, some duties—general safety measures among them—are construed to be nondelegable by the employer. Finally, the law has basically determined that liability for inherently dangerous activities, whether performed by the contractor or the employer, may rest with the employer.

In many commercial activities, several organizations may engage in a joint undertaking. The law recognizes the right of a third party to bring a civil action against *any* or *all* of the joint venturers. The doctrine of "joint and several liability" holds that each or all of the co-venturers may be sued for the total damages, so in that sense the negligence of one is vicariously shared by all others. Joint and several liability does not apply in all co-venturing or agency situations, but it is somewhat controversial since the "ability to pay" for damages caused may sometimes supercede "fault" as a criterion for apportioning the burden of liability.

Liability Problem Area 7: Bailee Liability Exposures

In many commercial and noncommercial activities, personal property is surrendered to another for a temporary period. The person taking possession may perform some service pertaining to the property, borrow it for his or her own use, or keep it for the owner's benefit, after which time the property must be returned to the owner or lawful possessor. These transactions in which possession of personal property is vested in one person and eventual lawful right of possession vests in another are called *bailments.* The owner or original possessor of the goods is called the *bailor;* the person receiving possession for the temporary period is called the *bailee.*

Important liability questions arise concerning the rights and duties of the bailee for any possible claims that the bailor may make for damages while the property was in the custody and care of the bailee. In establishing the legal duty of care to be exercised by the bailee, the law has classified bailments into three general categories: (1) bailments for the benefit of the bailor (in which property is left with the bailee without any compensation for care and safekeeping), (2) bailments for the benefit of the bailee (in which case the bailee often borrows or uses the property involved for a period of time, usually without compensation to the rightful owner), and (3) bailments for the mutual benefit of the bailor and bailee (in which both parties benefit from the bailment, which may involve the repair, carriage, storage, or safekeeping of the property). Each party to the last-mentioned transaction receives some benefit; the bailor receives the service rendered by the bailee, for which he or she usually pays a fee to the bailee.

In establishing these three classes of bailment relationships, the courts clearly recognize different degrees of care required of the bailee. In a transaction for the exclusive benefit of the bailor, the bailee is required to exercise only slight care. In transactions for the exclusive benefit of the bailee, extraordinary care is essential. In other words, the law looks behind the purpose of the transaction and demands that the degree of care vary according to the respective benefits conferred on the parties involved. In a bailment for the mutual benefit of the parties, the law normally demands ordinary care on the part of the bailee, in other words, the degree of care that average individuals or organizations would usually exercise over their own property.

One of the more common commercial relationships involving bailment is the transport of goods by common carrier. The common carrier in receiving the goods performs the acts of a bailee and assumes certain duties of care with reference to the handling of such goods. The written contract for carriage, called a *bill of lading*, sets forth the terms and conditions of the bailment. The amount of care required of the common carrier, however, greatly exceeds that of ordinary care. Under the various bills of lading acts, for motortruck carriers as well as railroads and aircraft, the common carrier is liable for all loss of goods with the following exceptions: (1) an act of God, (2) action of an enemy alien, (3) exercise of public authority, (4) any inherent defects in the nature of the goods themselves, or (5) any negligence or fault of the shipper, including misaddressing the package or mislabeling the merchandise. Thus, the common carrier becomes virtually an insurer of goods, unless the loss or damage falls within the exceptions thus stated.

By statute, carriers by sea are responsible for losses to cargo being carried either to or from the United States only if they fail to exercise due diligence. Their responsibility for losses to domestic shipments can be similarly limited in the bill of lading. Under the Warsaw Convention, international air shipments are also subject to a negligence standard and a dollar limitation unless the bill of lading states otherwise.

Liability Problem Area 8: Contract Liability

Liability arising from contracts may be a significant issue for some organizations, particularly those that subcontract for many services. The formation of business contracts often creates risks, as parties are contracted to perform certain services, or provide goods at some specified level of quality. Further, there may be certain mechanical aspects of contracts that create additional obligations—a financial security deposit, collateral requirements, or certain audit commitments.

Organizations also commonly assume under contract, certain liability for losses to others for which they would not otherwise be liable. For example, under a lease, a commercial tenant may assume what otherwise would be the landlord's financial responsibility for injuries to third parties arising out of defects in the premises. Under a sales order, a manufacturer may assume what would otherwise be the responsibility of the wholesaler or the retailer for injuries to persons using the product.

Liability Problem Area 9: Employment Liability

Several important demographic and social trends are elevating the importance of employment liability as a risk management issue. The aging workforce has raised an awareness of age discrimination issues, while the entry of more women into the workplace has brought with it a greater sensitivity to matters related to sexual discrimination and harassment. The opening up of opportunities for minority groups, heretofore shut out of the primary job market, has raised matters of racial discrimination, representativeness, cultural sensitivity, and even preferential treatment. Finally, the pressures of international competition have resulted in a massive restructuring of the nature of work. "Downsizing" and "outsourcing" are but two of the most obvious trends with employment liability implications. The net result of these changes is heightened uncertainty for employers and employees. What is the nature of the employment relationship between a business owner and a leased worker? What about consultants who work on a full-time basis for a single client? What are the obligations of an employer to provide reasonable accommodations for workers with physical or mental challenges? It is difficult to imagine that a single manager can keep abreast of every aspect of employer-employee law, which is why it behooves a risk manager to develop an effective working relationship with human resource managers and legal counsel.

In general terms, the employer-employee relationship is governed by the rules of common law, which have been previously discussed. However, in a large (and growing) number of instances common law has been supplemented or superseded by statutory law. Workers' compensation, which is discussed elsewhere, is a well-known example of a statutory law applying to the employment relationship, but there are significant other examples. A few of the more important laws that shape employment liability are discussed briefly below.

National Labor Relations Act. Enacted in 1935, the NLRA provides that "the right to self-organization, to form, join or assist labor organizations, to bargain collectively through representatives of their own choosing, and to engage in concerted activities for the purpose of collective bargaining or other mutual aid or protection" is a federally protected right. In 1947, in response to the rapid growth of unions, Congress passed the Labor-Management Relations Act, which addressed some of the potential issues and abuses caused by the unions themselves.

Title VII of the Civil Rights Act of 1964. This title prohibits employment discrimination on the basis of race, color, sex, religion, or national origin in hiring, compensating, promoting, training, firing, and so forth. The title is enforced by the Equal Employment Opportunity Commission (EEOC). The EEOC may:

1. File a legal action against an employer in its own name or on behalf of a third party
2. Seek to resolve alleged violations through informal means
3. Investigate allegations of discrimination
4. Issue guidelines and regulations

Age Discrimination in Employment Act of 1967. The ADEA prohibits discriminating in hiring, firing, retention, and promotion on the basis of age alone. Unlike Title VII, the ADEA does allow a claimant to request a jury trial.

The Americans with Disabilities Act of 1990. The ADA forbids organizations above some minimum size from taking into consideration an applicant's handicap in the hiring decision. Also, organizations must make reasonable accommodations available to disabled workers and customers/visitors.

There are a number of other important statutes. The Family and Medical Leave Act, the Rehabilitation Act of 1973, the Vietnam Veterans Readjustment Act of 1974, the Equal Pay Act, the Occupational Safety and Health Act (discussed in Chapter 8), unemployment insurance (discussed in Chapter 22), and the Fair Labor Standards Act are but a few of the numerous examples that could be cited.

As mentioned above, the influence of statutory law on the employment relationship is only one characteristic of the employment liability problem area. The changing nature of work further complicates the question of employer liability. For instance, the increased use of temporary workers, leased workers, independent contractors, consultants, as well as schedule modifications such as job-sharing, flex time, and part-time employment raise many questions about the applicability of the common law and statutory law features of employment law. Perhaps the central risk management issue of the day is whether an employer is held to the same legal expectations and duties with these less traditional employment relationships. (Indeed, some of these employment relationships are driven by an employer's hope that these duties and obligations do not apply.)

Because of the newness of many of these work arrangements, the law is not unequivocal in application. However, it may be said generally that the courts do not look favorably on employment arrangements that exist mainly to avoid legal duties or obligations. The use of leased workers as a means of avoiding workers' compensation obligations is a commonly seen illustration of this practice. Also, the courts have tended to base their interpretation of the employer's obligation to a worker on the right of control over the work to be done. Thus, if an employer uses an independent contractor to perform some job, but the employer directly supervises the work, sets the day-to-day schedule and work load, and expects that consultant to participate in company meetings and other collective activities, then the courts are likely to rule that the employer owes that worker the same duty (in common and in statutory law) it owes a more conventional employee.

Liability Problem Area 10: Work-Related Injury

An employment relationship creates several responsibilities for the employer (and the employee). Perhaps the most important statutory responsibility for the typical risk manager is workers' compensation. Indeed, workers' compensation is such a significant topic that it is discussed in depth in a separate chapter, Chapter 23. However, a few brief comments are necessary here.

Each state in the United States (as well as the District of Columbia and a few other jurisdictions), and virtually every developed nation in the world has instituted a statutory system for addressing the problem of work-related injury. These systems impose a "no fault" concept on applicable injuries, diseases, and deaths. That is, if a worker is injured on the job or as a result of the job, certain benefits are paid to that worker regardless of fault. In exchange for that promise, workers waive their right to sue employers for those work-related injuries. Employers are mandated to make arrangements to finance the cost of the benefits paid to injured workers—most typically through the purchase of workers' compensation insurance.

As Chapter 23 explains, workers compensation is not a comprehensive system, at least not in America. There are several types of employment that are not covered, there are certain types of injuries and diseases that are not covered, and—arguably—the full extent of the injury is not always compensated. Nevertheless, a worker can expect generally to have benefits paid for medical expenses arising from the injury or illness, plus a replacement of some percentage of lost wages if the injury keeps the worker from working for some period. Rehabilitation, death, and funeral benefits may also be paid in relevant cases.

As a final note, employers retain potential liability for worker injuries and illnesses not covered under workers' compensation. This exposure is commonly referred to as "employers' liability," a term that sounds broad, but which usually refers narrowly to liability for physical injury not covered under workers' compensation.

Liability Problem Area 11: Motor Vehicle Liability

One of the most complicated and most widespread areas of potential liability in organization activity surrounds the use of automobiles and other motor vehicles. Organizations are usually aware that the ownership, maintenance, or use of a motor vehicle creates a serious liability exposure, but they often do not appreciate the complexity of magnitude of this exposure. The discussion here will deal briefly with the special factors affecting the finding of negligence and lia-

The Finding of Negligence and Liability. Despite the large number of states with no-fault laws, the law of negligence continues to play the most important role in automobile liability. Not all states have no fault laws, and none of the present no fault laws have completely abolished the application of tort liability. The finding of negligence relating to the use of vehicles normally depends upon a jury's decision as to certain questions of fact: (1) Did the defendant fail to have the vehicle under proper control? (2) Did the defendant fail to exercise proper lookout? (3) Did the defendant operate the vehicle at an excessive speed? An affirmative answer to any one of the three above questions will result in finding the defendant negligent. The owner of a vehicle, however, cannot be concerned only about his or her own driving habits and ability to meet the above negligence tests. Liability may also exist under certain conditions in the use of the owned automobile when it is operated by someone other than the owner.

The *law of agency* may impute the negligent conduct of the operator to the owner when the operator is acting as an agent of the owner. For example, if A asked B to go to the grocery store and purchase some articles, A could be sued if A's agent, B, operates A's vehicle negligently.

Financial Responsibility Requirements. In too many cases, automobile accident victims have not been compensated for their losses, despite the fact that under the law of negligence they have a legal right to recover their losses. The reason is that the negligent drivers have been financially irresponsible. State legislatures have responded to this problem through (1) financial responsibility laws, (2) compulsory automobile liability insurance, and (3) automobile compensation or no-fault laws.

Financial Responsibility Laws. Financial responsibility laws, the original and still a common approach, encourage, but do not require, all drivers to be financially responsible. These laws vary somewhat in details, but the following description of a typical law indicates the basic approach. First, if a person is convicted of certain offenses such as drunken driving, reckless driving, or speeding, that person must prove that he or she would be financially responsible for motor vehicle losses he or she may cause in the next three years. Second, on occurrence of an accident involving bodily injury or a stated minimum of property damage, the license of the operator and the registration of any car are suspended unless, or until, evidence of financial responsibility is filed with state authorities covering, up to the limits stated earlier, any damage for which a judgment might later be incurred. In some states motorists involved in accidents must also furnish proof of future financial responsibility, for, say, three years.

Compulsory Automobile Liability Insurance. Twenty-one automobile compensation or no-fault laws go beyond financial responsibility laws in that they require owners and drivers to purchase insurance that will pay the no-fault benefits and large portion of the residual liability claims. Compulsory automobile liability insurance, however, predates no-fault insurance and affects some owners and drivers in 15 states that do not have no-fault laws.

For many years most owners of public vehicles such as taxicabs and buses have been required to provide evidence of minimum financial responsibility. Similarly, interstate motor common carriers have been required to have insurance or some other evidence that they will be able to pay claims occasioned by bodily injuries to passengers or others or damage to cargo or other property. In a few states, young drivers or registrants have been required to post proof of financial responsibility.

Automobile Compensation or No-Fault Laws. Over half the population live in the 24 states plus the District of Columbia and Puerto Rico that have replaced the tort liability system in part with automobile compensation or no-fault benefits. Under these no-fault laws, automobile accident victims receive certain benefits regardless of who was at fault. The replacement of the tort system, however, has been far less complete than in workers' compensation and few states have joined the no-fault movement in recent years.

With a few minor exceptions, current compensation laws provide no-fault benefits only for bodily injuries, not for property damage. Otherwise the laws vary greatly among the states, the three most important areas of variation being the following:

1. The types of benefits provided on a no-fault basis and the dollar limits on those benefits.
2. Under what conditions tort actions are permitted (is the threshold a monetary or a verbal threshold and how high is the threshold?)
3. Whether first-party (no-fault benefit) insurance and residual liability insurance are compulsory.

If tort actions are not restricted in any way, many would question whether the law is truly a no-fault law. Because 10 states plus the District of Columbia place no restrictions on lawsuits, only 14 states have laws that are consistent with this more narrow definition.

In all but one of these 14 "true" no-fault jurisdictions, prescribed first party no-fault insurance is compulsory. Residual liability insurance covering the lawsuits that are still permitted in the home state and elsewhere is also compulsory up to some specified limits. Florida requires first-party no-fault insurance, but not residual liability insurance. The Michigan law, however, is of special interest because it provides more liberal no-fault benefits and imposes much more severe restrictions on lawsuits than the other state laws. This law covers on a no-fault basis unlimited reasonable medical and rehabilitation expenses, up to $1,000 funeral and burial expenses, and 85 percent of work loss up to $1,000 a month (adjusted for cost of living changes) for up to three years. These benefits are reduced only by benefits provided under any state or federal law, not other voluntary private insurance. Lawsuits are barred except in cases of death or serious injury, when economic losses exceed the no-fault benefits, or when the harm was intentionally caused.

The other 10 no-fault states plus the District of Columbia place no restrictions on lawsuits under the tort system. In 4 of these 10 states, no-fault insurance and liability insurance are compulsory, but the insured is always permitted to sue under the tort system.

In the three remaining states, no insurance is compulsory and no restriction is placed on lawsuits. These states require insurers to offer first-party no-fault benefits, but permit the insured to reject the coverage. Insurers often voluntarily offer such coverage in other states that have not passed no-fault statutes.

One common explanation for the previously noted plateauing of the no-fault movement is that premiums have risen more than was expected in no-fault states. During the no-fault debates, whether premiums would rise or fall was one of the key issues. Factors favoring a premium increase under a no-fault plan are the increase in the number of persons receiving benefits and the higher benefits paid to persons with large economic losses. Factors favoring a decrease are the reduction or elimination of pain and suffering allowances and possible reductions in claim adjustment costs. Because increases in wages and the cost of medical care were expected to increase premiums in both no-fault and fault states, the real test is whether, other things being equal, no-fault statutes increased or decreased costs. Several careful comparisons of premium increases in no-fault states with those in fault states suggest that in some states no-fault laws have increased costs; in other no-fault states, generally those with high tort thresholds, premium costs are less than they otherwise would be.

ETHICS, LAW, AND THEIR RELATIONSHIP TO RISK MANAGEMENT

"We didn't break any laws." Often today this phrase is used to justify some action that, while legal, carries with it an odor of impropriety. The fact that this defense rings hollow for so many underscores the point that law and morality are not synonymous. Ethical behavior is clearly something larger than legal behavior. The law obviously has an ethical basis. In the Western world, the law derives from Judeo-Christian thought as well as from ancient Greek and Roman moral philosophy. More modern influences on present day law can be found in the arguments of the moralists of the seventeenth and eighteenth centuries. In this sense, we could conclude that risk managers address moral and ethical issues when they manage the liability loss exposure. However, we would probably be uncomfortable with the conclusion of this reasoning for it would suggest that risk managers act morally only when morality aligns with the law.

This discussion does not intend to argue for any particular moral compass. It is not possible to provide the necessary depth of discussion to adequately expose readers to the competing theories of ethical behavior. Further, reasonable people may disagree on the value of these alternative views. However, it is useful for a management textbook such as this to assert the importance of morality in organizational life and affirm its value as an appropriate subject of discussion.

In risk management, the importance of the moral dimension of management decision making is perhaps more evident than in other areas. This is, in large part, due to the fact that risk management is principally concerned with the "consequences" of situations, actions, and activities. It is almost impossible to consider the management of any risk without directly confronting the moral or ethical aspects of the decision. Further, risk management is a function that may place the risk managers at odds with other managers—at least when policy is being formulated. In many instances, that is because the risk manager's orientation is toward the long-term; but importantly, it is also because the risk manager's role often becomes that of the chorus in a Greek tragedy—reminding the actors of their mortality, of the fickleness of Fortune, and of the consequences of their actions.

Key Concepts

tort A civil wrong other than a breach of contract.

negligence The most important nonintentional tort affecting risk management. Failure to do or not to do what a prudent person would have done in the same situation.

comparative negligence A defense for the defendant which reduces the award to the plaintiff by the percent of his or her contributory negligence.

damages The compensation that the plaintiff may recover in the courts for losses sustained. Consists of damages for personal injuries and property damage as well as punitive damages.

vicarious liability Liability for the negligent acts of others.

contractual liability Liability assumed under some contract, such as a lease, that would not be present except for the contract.

licensee A person on the premises with the consent of the owner. A licensee is owed more care than a trespasser, but less than an invitee.

breach of implied warranty A common cause of action in a product liability suit. The implied warranty may be that the seller had the necessary title, the product was suitable for the purpose it was sold, or that the product was of merchantable quality.

strict liability A legal doctrine under which a manufacturer is held responsible for injuries arising out of defective products, regardless of whether or not the manufacturer was negligent.

bailee liability The liability of a bailee for damage to property of others in his or her care, custody, or control.

malpractice liability The liability of a professional for errors or omissions in the pursuit of his or her profession.

workers' compensation The program created by statute that makes the employer, regardless of fault, responsible for most job-related injuries and diseases.

employers' liability The common law or special statutory responsibility of employers for job-related injuries and diseases caused by their negligence but not covered under workers' compensation.

financial responsibility law A law that causes automobile operators (owners) to lose their license (registration) if they are convicted of certain offenses, such as drunken driving, and cannot post proof of financed responsibility (usually insurance), or if they are involved in an accident involving bodily injury or a stated minimum amount of property damage and cannot post proof of financial responsibility for that accident and perhaps future accidents.

automobile compensation or no-fault law A law that permits occupants of cars and pedestrians injured in an automobile accident to collect certain medical and income replacement benefits regardless of who was at fault. Under some laws, the occupant victims collect from the insurer of the car they were occupying; under other laws they collect first under their own automobile insurance policies if they are so insured.

1. Distinguish between criminal liability and civil liability.
2. **a.** What are the various sources of legal actions that may be brought to establish civil liability?
   b. Is it possible for more than one source of legal action to exist in the same situation?
3. "Law does not protect those who sleep on their rights." What does this statement mean?
4. **a.** What is an intentional tort?
   b. Cite some examples of intentional torts.
5. Comment on the legal liability status of the following:
   a. A person whose dog bites a neighbor
   b. A newspaper columnist who accuses a government official of being a liar
   c. A member of Congress who, on the floor of the House of Representatives, calls a newspaper columnist a liar
   d. A department store that by mistake causes someone to be arrested.
6. In order to make out a cause of action for negligence, what must the plaintiff demonstrate?
7. **a.** In what way can the burden of proof be shifted from the plaintiff to the defendant?
   b. Why would this be an important shift?
8. The plaintiff in a particular case was totally and permanently disabled in a boating accident. At the time of the accident he was 30 years of age and was earning $30,000 a year. His boat was completely destroyed in the accident. What factors will be considered in determining how much the defendant will have to pay this plaintiff?
9. What defenses might be asserted by the defendant in a case involving negligence?
10. What types of legal actions might be brought to establish legal liability in each of the following cases?
    a. The casing on a power mower broke and injured the person mowing the lawn.
    b. A man became ill as a result of some impurities contained in a seasoning purchased by his wife.
    c. Some soft-drink bottles that a retailer had placed near a radiator exploded, causing serious injuries to some customers.
    d. A customer requested a refrigerator with a true freezer compartment. The store sold her instead a refrigerator with a section which, though colder than the rest of the refrigerator, was not a true freezer. The customer became ill as a result of eating some food that would have been kept fresh in a true freezer but was not preserved in her refrigerator.
    e. The steering wheel of car suddenly failed to work, and an accident resulted.
11. The strict liability doctrine has become more common in product liability cases. What does this mean?
12. What defects in employers' liability led to the passage of workers' compensation statutes?
13. In what sense is workers' compensation a no-fault program?
14. In your state must a person have insurance to operate a vehicle? If not, what action has your state legislature taken to protect the public against uninsured motorists? Is your state typical?
15. Would you favor the extension of no-fault beyond automobile and workers' compensation? Is so, why and to what areas?
16. Do you believe governmental entities and charities should be immune from tort liability? Why or why not?

References and Suggestions for Additional Reading

Automobile Insurance . . . For Whose Benefit? (New York: State of New York Insurance Department, 1970).

CARVER, T. B., and L. A. VONDRA, "Alternating Dispute Resolution: Why It Doesn't Work and Why It Does," *Harvard Business Review* (May–June 1994).

Corpus Juris Secundum (New York: The American Law Book Company, and St. Paul, Minn.: West Publishing Company, 1948).

Department of Transportation Automobile Insurance and Compensation Study (Washington, D.C.: U.S. Government Printing Office, 1970).

DEPARTMENT OF TRANSPORTATION: *State No-Fault Automobile Insurance Experience, 1971–1977* (Washington, D.C.: U.S. Government Printing Office, 1978).

DONALDSON, JAMES H. and DONALD HIRSCH: *Casualty Claims Practice* (5th ed., Homewood, Ill.: Richard D. Irwin, Inc., 1991).

HOLMES, OLIVER WENDELL, JR.: *The Common Law* (Boston: Little, Brown and Company, 1923).

KEETON, R. E., and J. O'CONNELL: *Basic Protection for the Traffic Victim* (Boston: Little, Brown and Company, 1965).

KULP, C. A., and J. W. HALL: *Casualty Insurance* (4th ed., New York: The Ronald Press Company, 1968), chap. 5.

MALECKI, D. S. (ed.): *Professional Liability: Impact in the Eighties* (Malvern, Pa.: Society of Chartered Property and Casualty Underwriters, 1983).

MALECKI, D. S., R. C. Horn, E. A. WIENING, and J. H. DONALDSON: *Commercial Liability Risk Management and Insurance*, vols. I and II (2nd ed., Malvern, Pa.: American Institute for Property and Liability Underwriters, 1986).

MANN, R. A., and B. S. ROBERTS: *Smith and Roberson's Business Law* (8th ed., St. Paul: West Publishing Company, 1991).

MEHR, R. I., and B. A. HEDGES: *Risk Management: Concepts and Applications* (Homewood, Ill.: Richard D. Irwin, Inc., 1974), chaps. 9–10.

National Commission on State Workmen's Compensation Laws, Report of the (Washington, D.C.: U.S. Government Printing Office, 1973).

———: *Compendium on Workmen's Compensation* (Washington, D.C.: U.S. Government Printing Office, 1973).

———: *Supplemental Studies for the National Commission on State Workmen's Compensation Laws*, vols. I–III. (Washington, D.C.: U.S. Government Printing Office, 1973).

PROSSER, W. L.: *Handbook of the Law of Torts* (4th ed., St. Paul, Minn.: West Publishing Company, 1971).

RISK AND INSURANCE MANAGEMENT SOCIETY, INC: *Position Statement of RIMS Regarding CERCLA (Superfund) Reauthorization* (New York: May 1994).

CHAPTER 7

Human Resource Exposures to Risk

Learning Objectives

After you have completed this chapter, you should be able to:

1. Explain why risk managers are interested in human resource loss exposures of employees.
2. Estimate the frequency of disability or death and identify sources of information for these estimates.
3. Describe the losses to employees and to families as a result of the employee's death, poor health, old age, or unemployment.
4. Calculate the loss of income to an employee's dependents as a result of the employee's death or poor health.
5. Identify losses beyond loss of income that may result from an employee's death or poor health and provide a rough estimate of their magnitude.
6. Explain the nature of business discontinuation losses.

INTRODUCTION

The productive resources of an organization include property (physical capital) and human resources (human capital). Preceding chapters have focused on exposures due to ownership of property and exposure to liability. The discussion now turns to assessing exposures related to the organization's human resources—losses that occur when individuals die, become injured or ill, reach an advanced age, or become unemployed for other reasons. Individual employees and their families bear the direct consequences of these losses. In the absence of measures to mitigate the effects of these losses, individual employees' concerns about these exposures and their efforts to manage them can affect their productivity and contribution to the organization's mission. Further, loss of human assets can have direct economic effects on an organization. Hence, risk managers have valid reasons for being interested in human resource exposures. This chapter describes the nature of human resource exposures and presents data on losses of individuals and organizations.

REASONS FOR CONCERN OF RISK MANAGERS

Many of the issues discussed in this chapter are related to the assessment of risks faced by an organization's employees, including but not limited to poor health, death, or providing for income after retirement. At first glance, these risks may seem remote to an organization's managers because they are borne by the employees and their dependents. The planning for and management of these risks would appear to be a matter of individual choice, so why should an organization's risk manager interfere in choices that could be left to individuals and households?

Valid reasons exist for risk managers' concern with human resource exposures of individual employees. Employer-sponsored programs providing benefits for death, poor health, and retirement are quite common; for many employers, the cost of these programs exceeds 20 percent of direct payroll. The prevalence of these programs suggests that these risks, whose direct effects are felt by individual employees, nonetheless are important concerns of employers. The rationale for these benefit programs is discussed more fully in Chapters 24 and 25; several basic considerations are summarized below.

The Issue of Cost-Efficiency

The employer's concern with human resource loss exposures often springs from self-interest. Employees' concerns about adverse effects possibly resulting from death or disability may affect levels of their productivity. Removal or lessening of these concerns frees energy of employees that can be harnessed to the benefit of the organization. However, the transfer of responsibility from individual employees to the organization is not necessarily an improvement unless the organization is more cost-efficient in the management of these exposures than the individual employees acting on their own. Programs providing benefits for death, poor health, or retirement are just one form of compensation to employees. The argument for the organization's involvement in these areas rests on this form of compensation being more cost-efficient than wages or salaries.

In some circumstances, the relative advantage of the employer is obvious. In the area of health care services, the bargaining power of most individual employees vis-à-vis health insurers and providers of health care services is weak, and most employees are poorly-equipped to monitor the delivery of health care services to themselves or to their dependents (employees of health care providers may be an exception). A large employer is better able to negotiate with health care providers, and the organization's risk manager may be able to effectively monitor the delivery of these services. A large employer may have the same type of advantage in negotiating favorable prices for life insurance coverage; as long as the amount of coverage provided is no greater than the amount each employee would purchase at the employer's favorable price, less-expensive life insurance purchased by the employer is in the mutual interest of both the employer and employees.

Sense of Employer Responsibility

Employers may be interested in the welfare of their employees because they feel responsible for their well-being. The employer may take pride in an insurance and retirement program that is the best in the industry or may simply believe that it is his or her duty to provide a good program.

Public Relations

Some employers may have little sense of responsibility for the welfare of their employees, but they know that the general public may attribute some responsibility to employers, and they recognize the value of good public relations.

Compliance with Government Regulations

The federal government and state governments have enacted several important laws, such as the Employee Retirement Income and Security Act of 1974, which impose certain requirements on employers with employee benefit plans. Failure to comply with these requirements may cause the employer to lose some tax advantages or to incur certain fines and other penalties.

Employer-Sponsored Programs Can Substitute for Welfare or Social Insurance

In most industrialized countries today, much of the burden of risk related to loss of human resources has been reallocated from individuals and families, who otherwise would bear these risks, to employers and governments. Programs sponsored by employers can serve as substitutes for government programs. Political pressure for enactment of government-sponsored welfare and social insurance may grow in the absence of employer-sponsored programs, and a government-sponsored program may be more expensive than a similar program managed by employers. Often employers bear a major share of the cost of government-sponsored benefit programs anyway, so an employer-sponsored program is likely to have greater appeal to employers if it is less expensive than a government-sponsored program. Appendix 7.1 at the end of this chapter provides a brief historical perspective on government and private approaches to managing human resource loss exposures.

A Word About Human Resource Exposure to Speculative Risks

Chapters 5 and 6 noted the presence of possibilities for "gain" occurring from an exposure to risk, and this is equally true for human resources. The exposure of a worker to a new piece of machinery can present the opportunity for improved productivity and job satisfaction. Likewise, organizations that finance the cost of their managers returning to school for MBAs might expect a positive return in the form of increased managerial and decision-making competency.

This chapter is based upon the premise that the negative consequences of risk are a principal concern of the risk manager. While this is true in practice, readers should not ignore the important possibility of gain that may arise from risk as well. In other words, risk management of human resource exposures is not limited to reducing the likelihood and severity of loss. It must also be understood to include activities that enhance the probability and magnitude of potential gains.

A theme that reemerges at several points in this textbook is the role of information in risk management. When risk managers contemplate human resource exposures, they recognize that training and education of the workforce (the "dissemination of information") can affect pure and speculative risks. A well-trained workforce will likely experience fewer injuries, will cause fewer accidents, and will be able to respond more quickly when accidents do occur. However, a well-trained workforce will also be more productive and typically will enjoy higher job satisfaction. Other factors contribute to productivity and job satisfaction, of course (compensation, relationships with management), but the point is illustrative. Risk management of human resource exposures should include a recognition of the opportunities for expanding the positive possibilities arising from speculative risks.

ASSESSING EXPOSURES OF EMPLOYEE: LOSS FREQUENCY

Households face human resource risk exposures due to four causes: (1) death, (2) poor health, (3) old age, and (4) other types of unemployment. The resulting losses to employees and their dependents fall into two categories: (1) loss of earnings and (2) additional expenses. The frequency and magnitude of each type of loss are discussed below.

Mortality Rates

Table 7.1 provides data on the probability of death. The data show, for ages in 5-year brackets, the proportion of the U.S. population dying within the next

TABLE 7.1. Proportion Dying within a Year and Prior to Age 65, by Attained Age, All Population Groups, United States, 1988

	Proportion Dying			*Proportion Dying*	
Age	Within A Year	Prior to Age 65	Age	Within A Year	Prior to Age 65
0	0.00999	0.20877	35	0.00172	0.17786
5	0.00029	0.19918	40	0.00222	0.16989
10	0.0017	0.19821	45	0.00317	0.15927
15	0.00063	0.19712	50	0.00498	0.14309
20	0.00109	0.19359	55	0.00796	0.11663
25	0.00119	0.18892	60	0.01261	0.07275
30	0.00135	0.18394			

Source: Derived from National Center for Health Statistics, *Vital Statistics of the United States, 1988*, vol. II, mortality, part A, section 6, Life Tables, page 10. Washington: Public Health Service. 1991.

year, and the proportion dying prior to age 65. For example, the proportion of 25-year-olds dying in the next year is 0.00119, slightly greater than one-tenth of one percent. The proportion of 25-year-olds dying prior to age 65 is 0.18892, or almost one in five. As the individual's age increases, the proportion dying within the next year increases while the proportion dying prior to age 65 declines.

Poor Health

Unlike the risk of death, the risk of poor health cannot be assessed meaningfully using only a single measure; the risk is too complex. One issue complicating the analysis is the possibility of multiple losses; it is possible and even likely that a given individual will be in poor health more than once during his or her life. Another complicating issue is related to the definition of the state giving rise to loss; the estimated frequency of poor health is related to how the condition is defined. Nearly every working person will experience at least one work-loss day from a health-related condition some time during his or her working life, but only a few will be unable to work for a continuous period lasting more than one year. In 1956, Congress authorized a continuing National Health Survey to secure information on health conditions in the United States. Tables 7.2 through 7.6 provide excerpts from portions of the 1990 Survey, classified by age and sex when such distinctions are made in the Survey data.

Disability Rates. Disability rates for the population offer one gauge of frequency of poor health. Tables 7.2 and 7.3 provide data on disability rates in the United States. Data in Table 7.2 reflect all causes of disability while data in Table 7.3 reflect injuries only. In Tables 7.2 and 7.3, disability rates are given per 100 person-years, so the rates are the number of disabilities that would be expected in a group of 100 individuals in a given age bracket living for one year. For example, Table 7.2 shows that 568.8 days of restricted activity would be expected in a group of males ages 18 to 44, or 5.688 per person. Only 302.5, or 3.025 per person, of those days would be expected to result in work loss.

Because the data in Table 7.3 reflect injuries only, the rates per 100 person-

TABLE 7.2. Disability Days per 100 Person-Years, by Sex and Age, United States, 1990

Age Group	Restricted Activity Days		Bed-Disability Days		Work- or School-Loss Days	
	Male	Female	Male	Female	Male	Female
All ages	600.8	803.0	260.3	349.9	292.9*	382.4*
Under 5 years	918.2	990.4	423.4	478.7	—	—
5–17 years	612.4	701.5	265.5	342.1	345.5	413.9
18–44 years	568.8	807.7	236.2	353.5	302.5	411.1
45 and over	551.1	809.1	246.6	320.6	209.5	270.4

* All ages 5 years and over.

Source: National Center for Health Statistics, *Current Estimates From the National Health Interview Survey, 1990*, series 10, no. 181. (Washington: U.S. Department of Health and Human Services, Public Health Service, December, 1991, Tables 37, 42, 46 and 48).

TABLE 7.3. Number of Episodes of Persons Injured per 100 Person-Years and Number of Associated Bed-Days, by Sex and Age, United States, 1990 (bed-days appear in parentheses)

Age Group	All Episodes		Motor Vehicle		At Work	
	Male	Female	Male	Female	Male	Female
All ages	27.5	20.3	2.3	2.2	6.7	1.5
	(81.4)	(86.8)	(22.8)	(17.4)	(35.6)	(18.6)
Under 18 years	34.3	22.6	1.1	2.4	—	—
	(18.6)	(27.8)	(1.8)	(9.7)	—	—
18–44 years	30.6	20.4	3.4	2.8	9.5	1.6
	(120.9)	(69.5)	(41.9)	(17.9)	(43.5)	(17.2)
45 and over	16.5	18.4	1.7	1.2	2.7	1.4
	(82.8)	(153.8)	(14.5)	(22.7)	(23.8)	(20.3)

Source: National Center for Health Statistics, Current Estimates From the National Health Interview Survey, 1990, Series 10, No. 181. (Washington: U.S. Department of Health and Human Services, Public Health Service, December, 1991, Tables 51 and 55).

years are smaller than in Table 7.2. For example, Table 7.3 shows that 30.6 injuries from all causes would be expected in a group of males ages 18 to 44. Of these injuries, 3.4 would be from motor vehicles and 9.5 would be at work. The associated number of bed-days appearing in parentheses reflect the severity of the injury. Data in Table 7.3 suggest that males ages 18 to 44 and females age 45 and over are susceptible to serious injuries.

Contact with Providers of Medical Care. The health of a population also is reflected in the frequency of contact with providers of health care services. Tables 7.4 and 7.5 provide data on frequency of contact with physicians and on hospital stays. Data in Table 7.4 show the number of contacts with physicians generally increases with age, with contacts that take place in hospitals (which presumably reflect more serious conditions) growing faster for males than for females. Table 7.5 focuses on hospital stays, by showing the percentage distribution of hospital stays for the U.S. population. For example, Table 7.5 shows that 91.2 percent of males ages 45 to 64 experienced no hospital stay during the year, while 0.8 percent had three or more hospital stays. Data in Table 7.5 show

TABLE 7.4. Number of Physician Contacts per Person-Year, by Sex and Age and Place of Contact, United States, 1990

Age Group	All Places		Office		Hospital	
	Male	Female	Male	Female	Male	Female
All ages	4.7	6.4	2.7	3.9	0.7	0.7
Under 18 years	4.4	4.3	2.6	2.7	0.6	0.5
18–44 years	3.5	6.2	2.0	3.8	0.6	0.8
45–64 years	5.6	7.1	3.1	4.4	0.9	0.8
65 and over	8.7	9.5	5.0	5.6	1.7	0.9

Source: National Center for Health Statistics, Current Estimates From the National Health Interview Survey, 1990, Series 10, No. 181. (Washington: U.S. Department of Health and Human Services, Public Health Service, December, 1991, Table 71).

TABLE 7.5. Percent Distribution of the Number of Short-Stay Hospital Episodes of Living Persons, by Sex and Age, United States, 1990

Age Group	None Male	None Female	1 Male	1 Female	2 Male	2 Female	3 or More Male	3 or More Female
All ages	93.7	90.6	5.0	7.7	0.9	1.2	0.4	0.5
Under 18 years	96.2	96.9	3.2	2.7	0.4	0.3	0.2	0.2
18–44 years	96.0	88.6	3.4	10.0	0.5	1.0	0.2	0.4
45–64 years	91.2	91.6	6.6	6.4	1.4	1.4	0.8	0.6
65 and over	82.2	84.4	13.4	11.5	2.8	3.1	1.6	1.1

Source: National Center for Health Statistics, *Current Estimates From the National Health Interview Survey, 1990,* Series 10, No. 181. (Washington: U.S. Department of Health and Human Services, Public Health Service, December, 1991, Table 73).

that the proportion of individuals being hospitalized at least once generally rises with age. The high proportion of females ages 18 to 44 receiving hospital treatment is largely due to the delivery of infants.

Old Age and Retirement

Even though many persons may not appreciate fully the seriousness of the potential financial losses associated with premature deaths, serious accidental in-

TABLE 7.6. Average Remaining Lifetime, Average Lifetime Beyond Age 65, and Proportion Surviving to Age 65, by Attained Age, All Population Groups, United States, 1988

Attained Age	Average Remaining Lifetime, Years	Average Lifetime Beyond Age 65	Proportion Surviving to Age 65
0	74.9	13.4	0.79123
5	70.8	13.5	0.80082
10	65.9	13.6	0.80179
15	61.0	13.6	0.80288
20	56.3	13.6	0.80641
25	51.6	13.7	0.81108
30	46.9	13.8	0.81606
35	42.2	13.9	0.82214
40	37.6	14.0	0.83011
45	33.0	14.2	0.84073
50	28.6	14.5	0.85691
55	24.4	14.9	0.88337
60	20.5	15.7	0.92725
65	16.9	16.9*	1.00000
70	13.6	13.6*	—
75	10.7	10.7*	—
80	8.1	8.1*	—
85	6.0	6.0*	—

*Average remaining lifetime.
Source: Derived from National Center for Health Statistics, *Vital Statistics of the United States,* 1988, Vol. II, mortality, part A, section 6, Life Tables, pages 6 and 10. Washington: Public Health Service. 1991.

juries or sicknesses, and extended periods of unemployment, the vast majority do fear these contingencies and recognize that some financial losses accompany them. Old age accompanied by loss or reduction in earnings is less often recognized as a source of financial problems until later in life.

At advanced ages, while a person's earning power usually stops or is considerably reduced, expenses continue. The person may prepare for this retirement period by saving and investing during his or her earning career, but (1) saving is neither painless nor automatic, and the amounts needed may be very great, and (2) the necessary amount is indefinite because it depends upon the length of the retirement period.

Table 7.6 provides data on survival past age 65 for the U.S. population. The data show, for 5-year age brackets, the average remaining lifetime, the average lifetime beyond age 65, and the proportion of individuals who survive to at least age 65. For example, Table 7.6 shows the proportion of 20-year-olds surviving to age 65 is .80641, or 80.641 percent. Table 7.6 also shows that the average 20-year-old lives another 56.3 years and can expect to live 13.6 years beyond age 65. The average lifetime and average lifetime beyond age 65 do not coincide for ages under 65 because of truncation. For a given age, the average lifetime considers the lifetimes of *all* individuals, including those who die prior to age 65. The average lifetime beyond age 65 considers lifetimes of *only* those individuals who survive *beyond* age 65.

Unemployment

Involuntary unemployment caused by economic factors—not mortality, poor health, or old age—is another threat to an individual's earning power. Most organizations provide coverage against unemployment through government-mandated unemployment insurance; many more provide indirect coverage through programs providing paid leave-of-absence or salary continuation benefits.

Published unemployment rates tend to understate the probability of an individual becoming unemployed. One reason for the understatement is related to the changing composition of the group of unemployed individuals; different individuals may become unemployed during a year in which the unemployment rate remains constant. As a consequence, the fraction of the population experiencing unemployment at some time during the year is greater than the stated rate. Also, only those individuals who are actively seeking work are considered unemployed; an individual who becomes discouraged because of market conditions and stops seeking work is not considered unemployed even though he or she may rather be working.

Table 7.7 provides selected statistics on U.S. unemployment rates as reported in the *Monthly Labor Review*. Other than a slight upward trend in unemployment rates after reaching a low point in 1989–1990, the data in Table 7.7 show a significant increase in duration in 1989, with continued increases afterward. Data reported in the *Review* can be used to provide more detailed estimates by category of employment, type of worker and duration of employment.

One characteristic of unemployment not captured in Table 7.7 nor in the previous paragraphs is the nature of the specific unemployment experienced by

Year	Unemployment Rates by Worker Category (pct.)			Mean Duration of Unemployment (wk.)
	Nonagricultural Private Workers	Government Workers	Agricultural Workers	
1987	6.2	3.5	10.5	6.5
1988	5.5	2.8	10.6	5.9
1989	5.3	2.7	9.6	11.9
1990	5.7	2.6	9.7	12.1
1991	7.0	3.2	11.6	13.8

Source: *Monthly Labor Review* (Washington: U.S. Department of Labor, Bureau of Labor Statistics).

an individual. Economists have long recognized that unemployment occurs for many reasons. Some unemployment is relatively benign or even positive in its effect, as when a worker is in the process of changing jobs (sometimes called "frictional unemployment"). Some unemployments are due to swings in the business or economic cycle, or arise because of seasonal variations in the demand for labor. This "cyclical" unemployment is, by definition, episodic and cyclically unemployed individuals commonly expect to return to work within some limited period.

There are other types of unemployment as well. "Structural" or "technological" unemployment arises when workers' skills do not match the needs of the labor market. For example, the skill level of a workforce may not be high enough to obtain the jobs that a particular industry may have available. As the structure of an economy shifts from, say, a manufacturing-based economy to a service-based economy, such unemployment is likely to be high.

Risk managers must be clear about the specific type of unemployment faced by their organization's employees, for each type raises very different issues. For instance, unemployment arising from structural or technological sources is likely to require an examination of retraining and educational strategies, whereas cyclical unemployment will be less effectively attacked through such efforts.

ASSESSING LOSS EXPOSURES: LOSS SEVERITY

Potential Loss of Earnings: Human Life Value

The magnitude of loss related to interruption of earnings is positively related to its duration. Especially in cases involving death or permanent disability of an employed individual, loss of earnings constitutes a major portion of the loss because the loss is permanent. The amount of loss to an employee's dependents can be assessed by estimating the income the dependents would have received from the employee if the employee had continued to work. A rough estimate can be obtained by (1) forecasting the annual after-tax income the employee would have earned each year until retirement, (2) for death as the cause of loss, subtracting the portion of the income that would have been used to finance the employee's own personal consumption, and (3) discounting the annual amounts to their present value. The resulting amount, the present value of the employee's annual after-tax earnings reduced to reflect personal consumption, is called the employee's *human life value*. For permanent disability, the employee's personal consumption would not be subtracted (step 2).

The estimation procedure is illustrated in Table 7.8 for an employee who dies at age 40 and expected to retire at age 65. The employee's annual salary is $50,000, on which income taxes of $8000 are paid. The remaining $42,000 is the annual amount available to finance the personal consumption of the employee and the dependents. If $14,000 is spent on the employee's personal consumption, the remaining $28,000 is available each year to finance the consumption of the dependents. If the dependents would have received the $28,000 each year until retirement, their income loss as a result of the death is the present value of $28,000 a year for 25 years. At a 5 percent rate of interest, the present value is $394,630, the amount shown at the bottom of the right-hand column of Table 7.8. This amount, the employee's human life value, represents the lump sum equivalent of the dependents' earnings loss. If the $394,630 were invested at 5 percent interest compounded annually, $28,000 could be withdrawn at the end of each year for 25 years, finally exhausting the fund at the twenty-fifth withdrawal.

Human Life Value Is Approximate. Although the procedure illustrated in Table 7.8 conveys the impression of an exact estimate, the required assumptions cause the estimate to be only a rough approximation. One obvious assumption is the forecast of the annual earnings themselves. Table 7.8 uses constant annual earnings to simplify the illustration. More realistically, earnings are likely to change as a result of the employee's career development and from changes affecting earnings generally (e.g., wage inflation). A second assumption concerns the portion of the employee's earnings available to finance the dependents' consumption. Table 7.8 assumes that the employee consumes $14,000 annually, leaving $28,000 as the claim of the dependents on the employee's earnings.

TABLE 7.8. Human Life Value of Employee Age 40, 5 Percent Interest Rate

Age	Annual Earnings	Income Taxes	Personal Consumption	Net to Dependents	Present Value of One Dollar	Present Value of Earnings
40	$50,000	$8,000	$14,000	$28,000	0.95238	$26,667
41	$50,000	$8,000	$14,000	$28,000	0.90703	$25,397
42	$50,000	$8,000	$14,000	$28,000	0.86384	$24,188
43	$50,000	$8,000	$14,000	$28,000	0.82270	$23,036
..	..	..	..	..	..	..
..	..	..	..	..	..	..
..	..	..	..	..	..	..
62	$50,000	$8,000	$14,000	$28,000	0.32557	$ 9,116
63	$50,000	$8,000	$14,000	$28,000	0.31007	$ 8,682
64	$50,000	$8,000	$14,000	$28,000	0.29530	$ 8,268
	$1,250,000	$200,000	$350,000	$700,000	14.09394	$394,630

More realistically, this claim is likely to vary over life cycles. The third assumption involves the interest rate. The illustration in Table 7.8 uses a 5 percent interest rate.

A fourth assumption concerns the timing of the earnings and consumption streams. The illustration in Table 7.8 considers only earnings and consumption that develop prior to the employee's retirement. Earnings terminate at retirement, but the employee's consumption usually continues beyond (the only case in which it would not is if the employee dies upon retirement). This issue would be incorporated in the estimate by considering the employee's earnings and consumption streams separately, taking the difference in the two respective present values. Under this approach, an employee's human life value could become *negative* prior to retirement, that is, when the present value of the employee's consumption exceeds the present value of remaining earnings.

A final set of issues involves consideration of benefits that may affect the dependents' earnings loss. Benefits provided to surviving dependents under Social Security programs or through employer-sponsored benefit programs offer an illustration. Often these benefits offset the loss, as when an employer-sponsored survivor benefit program provides an income benefit to the surviving spouse of a deceased worker. However, the possibility exists that considering the value of these benefits could increase the loss, as when a worker's death results in the termination of a pension benefit and resulting loss to a surviving spouse. Possible remarriage of a surviving spouse offers a final illustration. If these issues are not considered, the resulting human life value estimate tends to misstate the economic loss to the dependents.

Human Life Value in Wrongful Death Actions. Nothing about the procedure illustrated in Table 7.8 precludes consideration of issues such as life cycle consumption patterns and benefits that offset the earnings loss. These issues, however, tend to complicate the estimation procedure and make the estimate tentative in nature. From a legal point of view, the method illustrated in Table 7.8 closely resembles the procedure used in tort cases involving wrongful death. Although courts generally follow the procedure illustrated in Table 7.8, regional variations exist as to evidence that may be presented on estimates of the annual earnings amounts and on other assumptions affecting the final result. In general, a court's evaluation of a wrongful death claim considers evidence falling short of a full economic valuation. For example, some courts may not consider evidence on estimated income tax payments, instead basing compensation on pre-tax earnings. Few if any courts would consider evidence related to post-retirement consumption of the employee or the possibility of remarriage of a surviving spouse.

Effects of Changing Assumptions. A brief discussion of the consequences of changing the assumptions is helpful in understanding their effects. In general, human life value is proportional to the estimated annual earnings loss. Holding other factors constant, doubling the estimated annual loss in Table 7.8 to $56,000 doubles the employee's human life value to $789,260. The proportional relationship simplifies the estimation of the family's earnings loss if the employee is disabled. If the employee is permanently and totally disabled, the employee's $14,000 annual consumption would not be subtracted in estimating the loss of earnings to the family, leaving the annual earnings loss at $28,000 + $14,000, or $42,000. The estimated present value is a simple proportionate adjustment of the estimate in Table 7.8: ($42,000/$28,000)($394,630), or $591,945, the present value of earnings loss from total and permanent disability.

The effect of changes in the interest rate is more complex. In general, the estimated human life value is inversely related to the rate of interest; a higher rate of interest results in a lower human life value. Table 7.9 shows the effect of changing varying the rate of interest between zero and 10 percent, keeping the earnings loss at $28,000 per year for 25 years. At a zero rate of interest, the present value is merely the undiscounted earnings, or ($28,000)(25) = $700,000. At 10 percent interest, the present value is reduced to $254,157. Human life value decreases with higher assumed interest because higher investment earnings imply a smaller initial amount to fund the $28,000 payments each year.

When annual earnings are expected to increase by a constant percentage, the earnings loss can be approximated using constant earnings but discounting them at a rate equal to the *difference* between the rate of interest and the rate at which earnings increase. If the rate of interest is 7 percent and earnings are expected to increase at a 5 percent annual rate, the earnings loss can be approximated by discounting a constant earnings stream at $7 - 5 = 2$ percent interest; a closer approximation is $100[(1.07)/(1.05) - 1]$, or 1.9 percent. For example, if earnings currently are $28,000 but are expected to increase at a 5 percent annual rate, the present value at 7 percent interest is, approximately, $546,657, the present value of a constant $28,000 annual amount at 2 percent interest. Readers seeking a more detailed presentation of present value estimation techniques are referred to finance textbooks (e.g., Brealey and Myers [1991] chapter 2), where the subject is discussed extensively.

The Needs Approach

An alternative method for estimating potential earnings loss is called the *needs approach*. The needs approach estimates the present value of the income level re-

TABLE 7.9. **Human Life Value of Employee Age 40 at Selected Interest Rates, $28,000 Net Annual Earnings Loss to Dependents**

Interest Rate (Percent)	Present Value of Earnings
0	$700,000
1	$616,648
2	$546,657
3	$487,568
4	$437,418
5	$394,630
6	$357,934
7	$326,300
8	$298,894
9	$275,032
10	$254,157

quired by the dependents to maintain their life styles. Instead of considering the portion of earnings available to dependents (i.e., their resources), the needs approach identifies normal expenditures of the dependents and how these expenditures are affected by the employee's death. Typical income replacement needs include:

1. A readjustment income close to the actual loss of income for a short period during which the family is expected to readjust their needs and desires to their new circumstances
2. A reduced but still substantial income following the readjustment period and continuing until children, if any, are self-sufficient (normally to age 18)
3. A further reduced, but adequate, lifetime income for the spouse beginning after the end of the dependency period.

For example, the family whose income loss was estimated in Table 7.8 might have the following pattern of income replacement needs:

1. $2,600 a month during a two-year readjustment period following his or her death
2. $2,000 a month during the next 13 years until the one child, now age 3, attains age 18
3. $1,600 a month for the rest of the spouse's life beginning after the child reaches age 18.

As in the human life value method, the needs approach can consider potential resources that offset the family's income replacement needs, such as benefits provided to surviving dependents under Social Security programs. One would expect a careful evaluation using either approach to arrive at the same answer; if the employee's earnings are the resources that will be used to finance the dependents' consumption, estimates using either method should be identical. The human life value approach, however, is the conceptually correct way of addressing the issue from a risk management perspective because it focuses on the potential loss rather than the family's preferences concerning levels of consumption.

The point can be illustrated using an analogy. If an owner of a dwelling is asked to estimate the amount of fire insurance to purchase on the structure, the response usually reflects the possible amount of damage that could be caused by fire. Normally this estimate will be based on the replacement cost or market value of the dwelling structure, because this amount is what disappears if the fire occurs. By analogy, the employee's earnings disappear if the employee dies. More precisely, the dependents lose their claim to the employee's earnings as a result of the death. One would expect their living expenses to be related to the amount of this claim, but the relationship is not necessarily direct. Again by way of analogy, the owner of a dwelling may require shelter, but this requirement is indirectly related to the loss that occurs if the dwelling is lost to fire.

Despite the conceptual purity of the human life value method, practical considerations may weigh in favor of the needs approach. Financial planners often prefer the needs approach over the human life value method because of its simplicity and direct portrayal of family economic welfare. Also, the human life value method requires a projection of future earnings, while the needs approach only considers future living expenses.

Additional Expenses

The term "additional expense" implies an expenditure that would not have been made in the absence of the event giving rise to loss. The nature of additional expenses depends on the cause of loss being considered. An individual's death, for example, gives rise to funeral expenses, which in many cases can exceed $5000. The death also may give rise to other costs such as probate costs, inheritance taxes, fees of administrators and executors, and estate taxes.

Under this definition, ordinary living expenses of a permanently disabled person would not be considered an additional expense even though they constitute part of the family's loss. The observation that death terminates the employee's ordinary living expenses does not imply that they are an additional expense unless the employee's death is considered "ordinary." This use of the term would blur the distinction between ordinary expenses and additional expenses resulting from the loss. The cost of medical care to alleviate the disablement is an additional expense.

Financial consequences of additional expenses are evaluated in the context of costs that ordinarily would prevail in the absence of the loss-causing event. A $5000 funeral expense may seem large to a family with limited means. This expense, however, is evaluated relative to the level of expenses that would prevail if the individual had survived. For most individuals, $5000 is less than their ordinary living expenses over a reasonable planning horizon such as a year. Seen in this light, the $5000 funeral expense is not a major consideration.

Costs of Medical Care. In contrast, medical expenses are a major consideration for most families and individuals. Unfortunately, the complexity of medical care does not allow an economic assessment of magnitude using approaches as simplistic as the methods for measuring lost earnings. The level of medical expense resulting from an illness or injury depends on the medical procedures administered to alleviate the problem. Certainly the upper limit of medical expenses rivals or exceeds estimated earnings losses typical for most employed individuals, that is, medical expenses of $400,000 to $1 million for an individual have occurred but are unusual. The 1991 edition of the *Source Book of Health Insurance Data* reports (p. 68) that the average length of a hospital stay in the U.S. during 1989 was 7.2 days, with an associated cost of $4587.87. Interested readers are encouraged to consult the *Source Book* and other references listed at the end of this chapter for additional information.

The cost of a typical employer-sponsored medical expense insurance policy for a head of family ($4000 to $6000 per year in many communities, at the time of writing) far exceeds the cost of an insurance policy to fully reimburse the family's loss of earnings as a result of the employee's death; IRS tables on imputed cost of employer-sponsored life insurance suggest that a $1 million policy on an employee aged 30 costs $1080, approximately one-forth the cost of the medical expense insurance policy. The relative costs of the insurance policies suggest that, for most families, medical expenses are a more significant financial concern than possible loss of earnings.

In the U.S., the growth in health care costs over the last three decades has placed this risk at the forefront of issues affecting employees and their families. U.S. national health expenditures grew from 5.9 percent of gross national product (GNP) in 1965 ($204 per capita, in 1965 dollars) to 11.6 percent of GNP in 1989 ($2354 per capita, in 1989 dollars). Affected groups have pressured businesses and government to shoulder an increasing share of the resulting burden. Private business' share of U.S. expenditures for health services rose from 17.0 percent in 1965 to 29.7 percent in 1989. The share of federal and state governments also grew from 20.6 percent in 1965 (the year Medicare and Medicaid were established) to 30.6 percent in 1989 (figures derived from Lazenby and Letsch [1990] and Levit and Cowan [1990]). The topics of health care and health care benefits provided by employers and government programs are discussed further in Chapters 19, 22, and 24.

ASSESSING DIRECT EXPOSURES OF ORGANIZATIONS

Most of the human resource exposures of concern to the risk manager are indirect, such as exposures of individual employees for which the risk manager has a comparative advantage in negotiating terms of coverage. In some circumstances, the organization itself may be exposed to risks related to its human resources, such as the death or disability of an employee, a customer, or an owner. These exposures often arise when the ownership or control of an organization is vested in only a few individuals, which results in the fortunes of the organization being vulnerable to events affecting individuals. For large and especially for publicly-held organizations, these exposures are likely to be minimal or nonexistent. Potential losses to organizations related to these exposures are classified as (1) key-person losses, (2) credit losses, and (3) business-discontinuation losses.

Key-Person Losses

Certain employees stand out because of their skill, knowledge, or business contacts that are an important resource for the organization. The death or disability of these key persons may result in loss as a result of reduced sales, increased costs, or restriction of credit. The loss to the organization would appear to be the present value of the key person's contribution. For example, $250,000 of an organization's annual earnings may be attributable to the efforts of a key executive who withdraws only $100,000 in direct compensation. In this example, the loss to the organization's owners if the executive dies or is disabled would appear to be the present value of $150,000 a year for the remainder of the executive's working lifetime.

The assessment of this exposure is with respect to the interests of the organization's owners. The loss to the organization arises because the organization receives $250,000 a year from the executive's efforts, for which it pays only $100,000. One must question the reasons for this $150,000 shortfall in the executive's compensation. When the executive is the sole owner, for example, the $150,000 difference may be an accumulation for the executive-owner's retirement. The contribution ends with the executive's death, but so does the need for the accumulation. If the ownership of the organization is vested in individuals who are distinct from the executive, a distinction needs to be drawn between the exposure to loss arising from, say, the owners' dependence as members of the family headed by the executive and their exposure resulting from a business relationship. When their loss exposure arises from a familial relationship, the potential loss is evaluated as a dependents' earnings loss using methods explained earlier.

Creditors of an organization (including banks, trade creditors, and holders of an organization's bonds) may be concerned about the possibility of an organization's ability to repay debt becoming impaired following the death or disability of a key employee. Terms on which these creditors are willing to lend to the organization may be favorably affected if steps are taken to reduce the likelihood of the impairment. A similar argument can be made about the interests of employees, whose productivity may decline because of concern about possible loss of job security in the event of a key employee's death or disablement. The assessment of these exposures of lenders and employees is largely qualitative, focusing on issues such as business continuation and transfer of leadership.

Credit Losses

Many organizations extend credit to their customers. For example, financial institutions make loans to customers, and vendors of various types assume a creditor position as a result of the sale of securities, real estate, merchandise, and other types of property. Death, extended disability, or unemployment of a customer may either reduce the chance that the loan will be repaid or create a public relations problem if it is necessary to force repayment.

Business-Discontinuation Losses

Business-discontinuation losses can occur when an owner of a sole proprietorship, a partnership, or a closely-held corporation dies or is disabled. Especially when the owner is active in the management of the business, the death or disability can have severe consequences for the survival of the enterprise and for remaining owners. Business-discontinuation losses may arise independent from and in addition to any loss arising from dependence on earnings that would have been provided by the decedent.

Special Problems for Sole Proprietorships and Partnerships. Discontinuation of a sole proprietorship or a partnership is especially likely in case of death. In most states, the executor or administrator of the owner's estate must take immediate steps to liquidate the business assets unless the owner has expressly authorized the continuation of the business or unless all heirs are adults and they consent to the continuation of the business. Even if the executor or administrator is authorized to continue the business (1) until conditions for disposing of the business are more favorable, (2) as a long-term source of income for the family, or (3) until some heirs take over,[1] the return to the heirs is likely to be relatively low, and a shortage of working capital or other business problems may force the executor into a liquidation of the firm. A quick sale may also

[1] The executor or administrator remains personally liable to the heirs and the creditors unless they all consent to the continuance.

be necessary if a large portion of the personal estate plus the business estate[2] must be converted into cash in order to pay outstanding expenses, such as the costs of the owner's last illness, funeral expenses, taxes, and probate costs.[3] Even if some heirs take over, they may not succeed, and in the early years, at least, they will probably not be so successful as the decreased proprietor. Moreover, it might be necessary to liquidate some of the business assets in order to distribute equitable shares of the total estate to the other heirs.

Special Problems for Partnerships. In addition to these difficulties, the death of a partner poses a problem that is not present in the case of a sole proprietorship. Under the Uniform Partnership Act, which is in effect in about three-quarters of the states, if a partner dies, the partnership is dissolved, and the surviving partners must liquidate the business as soon as possible. The reason for this legislation is that each partner has the power to bind the partnership if he or she acts ostensibly in the interest of the partnership. Moreover, each partner has unlimited liability for the debts of the partnership. Consequently, the choice of one's partners is extremely important and is reserved for the partners themselves.

After a partner dies, the heirs may not want to continue as partners, or the surviving partners may not be willing to accept the heirs as partners. If the heirs and the surviving partners do continue the business, it may not be successful, and liquidation may be necessary at a later date. If the heirs intend to sell their interest to someone else, this person will have to be acceptable to the surviving partners before the business will be continued.

Special Problems for Close Corporations. The discontinuation problem in a close corporation is somewhat different and less obvious. Under this form of business organization, the owners hold stock in the corporation, and this stock is transferable to other persons. However, because the stock is closely held, it is not so marketable as the stock of public corporations. Under forced sale conditions, the heirs or surviving stockholders will probably suffer a sizable loss on the sale of the stock; a minority stockholder will suffer disproportionately.

Regardless of whether the deceased was a majority or minority stockholder, the best (although unsatisfactory) solution for the heirs and for the other stockholders may be to dispose of their stock in the business or to liquidate the business itself. The surviving stockholders, for example, will have to accept a successor to the deceased, who, if a majority stockholder, may run the business to their disadvantage or, if a minority stockholder, may constantly challenge the majority. The heirs of a majority stockholder may not be capable of exercising their power to run the business, and in spite of their majority stockholdings, the effective management may fall into the hands of the minority. This contingency could be to their detriment. The heirs of a minority stockholder (especially when they are not willing or able to be active in the firm) are at the mercy of the majority. If the deceased stockholder shared the ownership with the survivor, the

---

[2] The personal and business estates of a sole proprietor are not separated as are the estates of partners or stockholders in a close corporation. If the liquidation value of the business assets is less than business debts, the family estate will also shrink.

[3] It is estimated that on the average about one-third of the gross estate value is needed to meet these costs.

close working relationship that is necessary for a firm of this type may disappear. Even if no financial losses result in any of the above circumstances, life for the heirs and the survivors could be far from pleasant.

APPENDIX 7.1. HISTORICAL PERSPECTIVE: ALLOCATING THE BURDEN OF MISFORTUNE AND POVERTY[4]

The reallocation of risk[5] away from individuals and families to employers and governments can be understood as a natural reaction of humans facing an uncertain environment. Most societies have developed customs or formal programs for allocating loss to human resources away from the individuals who are directly affected and towards larger risk-bearing entities, such as (1) the family unit, (2) an organization such as an employer, village, or tribe, or (3) society through government programs. This section offers a historical and cross-cultural perspective on this issue by providing a brief description of selected programs and customers appearing at points in time in different cultures.

Analysis of human resource risk exposures focuses on four causes of loss: (1) premature death, (2) poor health, (3) excessive longevity (old age), and (4) unemployment. The first three causes give rise to *universal* risks that exist in every society. The risk of unemployment is not universal because it requires an employer-employee relationship. A self-employed shopkeeper or shepherd may be poor, but does not face the risk of unemployment.

Much of the allocation of risk from affected individuals and families to employers and governments has taken place during the twentieth century. Prior to the twentieth century, many families lived in rural areas and were largely self-sufficient. However, growing industrialization of Western countries during the last half of the nineteenth century and the increasing reliance of families on wage income created a climate favorable to the reallocation of families' risk exposures across large units. In the United States, the development of social insurance and employer-sponsored programs providing for welfare of employees occurred largely during the twentieth century, beginning somewhat earlier in Europe.

However, earlier systems existed thousands of years ago, although perhaps not as formal programs. Brinker, Klos and Kesselring (1982, ch. 1) trace the development of programs to alleviate poverty and misfortune through history to modern times. They identify documents describing social welfare programs existing as early as Ancient Elba and Ancient Egypt; they also recognize Old Testament admonitions as the foundation for Western beliefs concerning the obligations of society to the disadvantaged.

---

[4] Professor H. Wayne Snider of Temple University proposed this section offering a historical perspective. Professor Snider also contributed the material used to prepare the section.

[5] In this section, risk and loss can be used interchangeably because they are used in the context of government programs and customs. In this context, reallocation of risk and reallocation of loss usually are synonymous. For example, government programs allocating the cost of disability losses across the entire population also reallocate individuals' exposure to the risk of becoming disabled.

Premature Death

Although the risk of premature death is universal in that it exists in every society, it does not exist for an isolated individual. The risk does not exist for a Robinson Crusoe; it requires a dependency relationship. A death is premature if it occurs while an individual is a net producer, producing more than he or she consumes. The primary loss to the survivors is their claim to the deceased person's production. This claim may be financial, such as a claim to earnings, or in-kind, as a claim to services that the deceased person would have provided. For example, the death of a retired worker is not premature unless the individual is a net producer of services to others.

In estimating the loss from premature death, the value of foregone services is as much a part of the calculation as the lost income. Particularly in the case of a spouse who does not work outside the household, the value of these services can be substantial. Presumably, a spouse not employed outside the household is engaged in the activities providing the highest level of benefit to the household; if the spouse could provide a larger benefit to the household through gainful employment, presumably the spouse would have chosen this employment rather than directly providing household services. As a consequence, the household's loss from the spouse's premature death is greater than if this spouse had been earning income from employment outside the household.

In primitive societies, the family or tribe often provided resources to offset a loss due to premature death. In western Europe until the Middle Ages, the church was a primary source of social welfare. An early form of employment-related program occurred when merchant and craft guilds came into prominence during 1000 to 1400 A.D.; they provided care for members who became ill and for widows of guild members who died. Increasingly as societies developed, governments and employers have assumed these obligations, possibly with support from religious and charitable organizations. In the United States and other countries relying on private markets, privately purchased life insurance can provide additional protection to households against the financial consequences of premature death.

Poor Health

Two types of financial loss arise from poor health: reduced production (income and in-kind services, as in the case of premature death) and additional expenses of caring for the ill or injured person. Additional expenses, particularly expenses for medical care, loom as the largest component of this financial loss in the United States today.

Any definition of poor health has subjective elements. An individual's state of health tends to deteriorate with advancing age, confusing attempts to distinguish between poor health and age-related deterioration in health. Poor health could be defined as a state of health significantly below the state typical for an individual's age category, but this definition fails to account for burdens of poor health associated with increasing age. Also, an individual's motivation and desire can have important effects on the exposure to risk; a given handicap may disable some individuals but not others. As an example, Franklin Delano Roosevelt became President of the United States years after polio left him confined to a wheelchair. Further, programs to alleviate the risk of poor health can affect its incidence; the availability of benefits to replace lost income and to provide for medical care reduces the individual's financial incentives to return to productive activity. In the United States, an offsetting effect may occur as more facilities are required to become accessible by persons with physical handicaps.

Advances in medical technology have caused dramatic changes in the risk of poor health, particularly during the twentieth century. In primitive societies, medical care consisted of administration of folk remedies or medicines or was directed towards religious objectives. In the West prior to the twentieth century, medical care often was oriented toward providing comfort to the ill and an environment to foster natural healing, or preparing the affected individual for death. The development of antibiotics, vaccines, and other pharmaceutical products, together with other advances in medical knowledge have allowed lives to be preserved that previously would have been lost. However, the cost of some of these advances has been high. In a manner of speaking, the risk feeds upon itself. Modern medicine often preserves lives of individuals whose survival depends critically on the continued administration of high-cost medical procedures.

Excessive Longevity

Upon reaching old age, a net producer may be transformed into a net consumer. The risk of excessive longevity complements the risk of premature death, as one arises from living too long rather than dying too soon. The risk of excessive longevity is a universal risk, so most societies have developed methods for its treatment. Folklore of some societies, such as Eskimos and Native American Indians, holds that elderly tribe members who ceased being productive would leave the tribe for a place of solitude where they would die from starvation or exposure. In rural societies, family units often provide for aged family members by assigning tasks that are appropriate for the age category, such as household work for elderly who are frail.

Some elderly persons are fortunate enough to retain the capacity for productive activity far beyond the age at which most retire. Rules of organizations mandating retirement at a given age, such as 65, often disadvantaged these persons as well as depriving the organization of their accumulated wisdom and experience. Federal laws now prohibit mandatory retirement based on age only, altering individuals' exposure to the risk of excessive longevity. These laws provide another example of changes in the social or legal environment altering individuals' exposure to risk.

Even in developed, urban societies, many families continue to care for elderly and frail family members within the family unit. Often, declining health forces elderly persons to enter institutions, in many cases at considerable cost. In the United States, state and federal government programs provide a supplement when the resources of an elderly person are exhausted by lengthy confinement to a nursing home. Especially in the United States, increasing reliance on organized, formal methods of caring for the elderly, together with advances in medical technology, have dramatically altered the character and magnitude of risks related to excessive longevity.

Unemployment

Brinker, Klos and Kesselring (1982, p. 12) trace the origins of welfare programs including unemployment to practices followed during the middle ages in England and on the European continent. At that time, able-bodied idlers were provided strong incentives to work, and during some episodes begging was considered a crime. At times, treatment of able-bodied unemployed persons was harsh, including whipping or enslavement. The Elizabethan Poor Laws enacted and amended in England during 1597 to 1601 provided that vagrants were to be forced to work or be punished. However, the Poor Laws recognized the existence of involuntary unemployment, and persons who became involuntarily unemployed were spared physical punishment but sent to almshouses or workhouses.

Unemployment can be defined as being unable to find employment despite being willing and able to work. Unlike the risks discussed previously in this section, the risk of unemployment is not universal because it requires an employer-employee relationship to exist. As an example, much of the population of the United States during the nineteenth century lived in rural areas. For a family member who left the farm and became employed in industry, the option of returning to the farm could provide a cushion against possible unemployment.

The Industrial Revolution and the attendant growth in households' dependence on wage income resulted in the risk of unemployment becoming more prominent than when households were largely self-sufficient. Although the nineteenth century was marked by sharp economic depressions, federal legislation providing unemployment benefits was not passed until 1935, during the Great Depression.

Summary: Government- and Employer-Sponsored Programs in Society

Systems for allocating burdens of poverty and misfortune across groups are a natural reaction of humans to an uncertain environment. These systems can improve the collective well-being of a society's members. The improvement in welfare is an indirect consequence of individuals' economic activities becoming more efficient when they specialize. The absence of protective mechanisms leaves individuals vulnerable to events causing an inability to employ specialized skills. As a consequence of this exposure to risk, they may demand extra compensation to develop and employ specialized skills. Protective systems allow specialization without being fully exposed to these risks. If specialized economic activity is more efficient than every individual maintaining the same set of survival skills, protective mechanisms fostering specialization can improve the collective welfare of groups.

A system for allocating the burden of these risks is likely to be efficient if the burden resides in an entity that is able to monitor and control the risk and manage the consequences of loss. If effective risk management occurs at the level of the employer, low-cost programs can exist with control at the employer level. For example, the frequency of work-related injuries is likely to be affected by an employer's injury prevention efforts, which suggests allocating the cost of work-related injury to employers using a method that is sensitive to the frequency of the employer's work-related injuries. However, if the risk is due to factors that are systematic or widespread, or control at the local level is not effective, government intervention may be required. Programs of government intervention would be expected to develop (1) when individuals and employers are not effective at assessing an exposure to risk or (2) when control of problems, such as moral hazards, is not effective at the individual or employer level.

A given set of programs is a society's response to the environment at a point in time. Societies would be expected to develop programs that are efficient. Inefficient programs would not be expected to survive when societies compete for resources and markets. An inefficient system would place the society's members at an economic disadvantage relative to a society adopting a more efficient program, forcing changes in the inefficient system. However, superficial observations on the efficiency of a particular system may be misleading, particularly when the observation is made within another culture. For example, a public program to provide for the care of retired elderly persons may appear to provide no direct tangible rewards to productive persons, but it does relieve family members of the burdens of providing for the care of these persons, freeing their time for more productive activities.

Over time, programs to alleviate risk tend to evolve, accommodating changes in the nature of households' exposure to risk. Further, some of the changes in households' exposure may be traceable to the program itself. An example is the Medicare program in the United States, which improved access of the elderly to medical care. Access to medical care along with improvements in medical technology have lengthened the lives of elderly persons, particularly at the highest age brackets. In turn, the improved state of health of the elderly has increased the likelihood of elderly persons outliving their resources, particularly when high consumption of health care services is required to maintain life.

Key Concepts

human resource exposures Possible financial losses resulting from the death, poor health, retirement, or unemployment of an organization's employees. Although the direct effects of these losses fall on employees and their families, organizations have an indirect interest in assessing and managing these exposures.

earning power loss The present value of an individual's after tax earnings, reduced to reflect expenses that cease due to the cause of loss being considered. For death as the cause of loss, earnings would be reduced by the decedent's personal consumption expenditures. A more complete valuation would consider the effect of the loss on other benefits and the cost of replacing services that would have been provided in the absence of the event causing loss.

additional expense An expenditure that would not have been made in the absence of the event giving rise to loss, such as funeral expenses for a decedent and medical expenses related to a disability.

needs approach An approach to estimating the value of lost earnings based on reasonable consumption expenditures of survivors.

key-person loss The loss experienced by an organization as a result of the death or disability of an employee with critical skills, knowledge, or business contacts.

business-discontinuation loss The loss experienced by a sole proprietorship, a partnership, or a closely-held corporation when the death or disability of an owner causes the organization to go out of business.

Review Questions

1. Assessment of human resources exposures for a business includes assessment of exposures for individuals and their families.
   a. Explain this statement.
   b. Explain why a risk manager for a business may be concerned about possible losses to employees and their families that they could manage on their own.

2. One employee, age 30, earns $35,000 a year after taxes. Another employee, age 62, earns $55,000 a year after taxes.
   a. How would you compute the possible loss of earning power as a result of death for each employee?
   b. For which employee would the loss of earning power be greater? Why?
   c. How would you compute the possible loss of earning power from total and permanent disability? Why would this loss not be identical to the loss of earning power as a result of death?

3. Explain how you would estimate the possible loss of earning power for an employee age 35 who earns $55,000 a year after taxes if earnings are expected to increase at 3 percent a year. The interest rate is 6 percent.

4. Distinguish between the human life value and needs approaches to estimating possible loss of earning power as a result of death. Under what circumstances would the approaches yield different estimates? Why?

5. Identify three different types of additional expenses associated with death. For what types of persons would these additional expenses be major in comparison to estimates of lost earnings?

6. Rank and compare the following three probabilities:
   a. The probability of a person age 25 dying prior to age 65.
   b. The probability of a person age 25 surviving past age 65.
   c. The expected number of lost work-days due to disability during a one-year time period for a male age 50.

7. Compare the magnitude of additional expenses associated with poor health to those associated with death.

8. Give two reasons why published unemployment rates tend to understate the probability of an individual becoming unemployed during the year.

9. Identify characteristics of business firms that would make them vulnerable to key-employee or business-discontinuation losses.

10. Al and Bob are equal active partners in a thriving business. For the following individuals, identify potential losses if Bob should die in the next year:
    a. Bob's heirs
    b. Al.

11. The majority stockholder in a manufacturing firm held by only three stockholders believes that business-discontinuation losses are of no concern to his heirs because they will hold a majority position. Critically evaluate his belief.

References and Suggestions for Additional Reading

BLACK, K., and H. SKIPPER, JR,: *Life Insurance* (12 ed., Englewood Cliffs, N.J.: Prentice-Hall, Inc., 1994).

BRINKER, PAUL A., JOSEPH J. KLOS, and RANDALL KESSELRING: *Poverty, Manpower, and Social Security* (2nd ed., Austin, Texas: Lone Star Publishers, Inc., 1982).

GREGG, D. W., and V. B. LUCAS: *Life and Health Insurance Handbook* (3rd ed., Homewood, Ill.: Richard D. Irwin, Inc., 1973), chaps. 1, 2, 42, 43, 45–47.

LAZENBY, HELEN C., and SUZANNE W. LETSCH: "National Health Expenditures, 1989." *Health Care Financing Review* (vol. 12, no. 2, Winter 1990), pp. 1–26.

LEVIT, KATHARINE R., and CATHY A. COWAN: "The Burden of Health Care Costs: Business, Households, and Governments." *Health Care Financing Review* (vol. 12, no. 2, Winter 1990), pp. 127–137.

McGILL, DAN: *Life Insurance* (rev. ed., Homewood, Ill.: Richard D. Irwin, Inc., 1967), chap. 1.

MEHR, R. I., and S. G. GUSTAVSON: *Life Insurance: Theory and Practice* (4th ed., Austin: Business Publications, Inc., 1987), chaps. 19 and 21.

Monthly Labor Review (Washington: U.S. Department of Labor, Bureau of Labor Statistics).

NATIONAL CENTER FOR HEALTH STATISTICS: *Current Estimates From the National Health Interview Survey*, 1990 (series 10, no. 181, Washington: U.S. Department of Health and Human Services, Public Health Service).

NATIONAL CENTER FOR HEALTH STATISTICS: *Vital Statistics of the United States*, 1988 (Washington: Public Health Service, 1991).

REJDA, GEORGE E.: *Social Insurance and Economic Security* (4th ed., Englewood Cliffs, N.J.: Prentice-Hall, Inc., 1991).

Source Book of Health Insurance Data (Washington: Health Insurance Association of America, annual).

WILLIAMS, Jr., C. A., J. G. TURNBULL, and E. F. CHEIT: *Economic and Social Security* (5th ed., New York: John Wiley & Sons, Inc., 1982), chaps. 2, 6, and 12.

WHITE, E. H., and H. CHASMAN: *Business Insurance* (5th ed., Englewood Cliffs, N.J.: Prentice-Hall, Inc., 1986).

PART THREE

Risk Management Methods and Techniques

Part 3 redirects the reader's attention away from the "risks themselves" toward the methods, resources, techniques, and strategies for managing risks and the principles governing their management. Coverage of this broad subject area is organized into two sections: (1) an overview of risk management methods and (2) a discussion of the principles for selecting among these methods.

Section 1 offers an overview of risk control and risk financing techniques. Risk control methods are described in Chapter 8, which also discusses the relationships between risk control and other risk management tasks. Methods for financing losses and other costs of risk are described in Chapters 9 and 10. Because insurance offers an important alternative for risk financing, an overview of insurance concepts constitutes a major portion of these chapters. The discussion of insurance in Chapters 9 and 10 is not exhaustive, but is intended to identify the position of insurance in the full array of risk financing tools. A more detailed examination of insurance institutions, law and contracts appears later in Part 4.

Principles governing the selection of risk management methods are discussed in Section 2 (Chapters 11 and 12). Chapter 11 presents readers with a rationale for risk management in organizations. This presentation offers a conceptual framework for considering risk management decision problems. Chapter 12 applies this framework to specific analytical approaches that enable a risk manager (1) to evaluate possible methods and techniques and (2) to align risk management programs with overall objectives of the organization.

175

SECTION ONE:
AN OVERVIEW OF RISK MANAGEMENT RESOURCES AND METHODS

Section 1 describes major elements representing the array of tools, techniques, strategies, and options available for managing the risks whose assessment has been discussed in earlier chapters. Chapter 8 opens this discussion with an exposition of risk control techniques. Risk control techniques seek to avoid or prevent losses, or to reduce undesirable effects of losses and other costs of risk on an organization.

Chapters 9 and 10 address the subject of risk financing, which includes methods for an organization to assure that resources are available to reimburse losses. Chapter 9 first offers an overview of risk financing methods, then develops a framework for understanding the distinction between risk retention and risk transfer. Chapter 10 extends the discussion of risk financing to consider methods representing the broad array of risk financing tools often available to risk managers. As presented in Chapters 9 and 10, insurance is only one of the possible risk financing options, although an important one.

CHAPTER 8

Risk Control

Learning Objectives

After you have completed this chapter, you should be able to:

1. Distinguish between risk control and risk financing methods.
2. Explain the relationship between risk control and risk assessment.
3. Identify the positive and negative attributes of risk avoidance.
4. Distinguish between loss prevention and loss reduction activities.
5. Understand the benefits and costs of loss prevention and loss reduction.
6. Explain the purpose of the Occupational Safety and Health Administration (OSHA).
7. Identify examples of governmental involvement in risk control.

INTRODUCTION

Risk control methods seek to alter an organization's exposure to risk. More specifically, risk control efforts help an organization *avoid* a risk, *prevent* loss, *lessen* the amount of damage if a loss occurs, or *reduce* undesirable effects of risk on an organization. The application of techniques to achieve these ends may range from simple and low-cost to complex and costly. Risk control methods are exemplified by security systems to prevent unauthorized entry or access to data; by sprinklers and other fire control systems; by training programs to educate employees on techniques to reduce the likelihood of injury; by the development and enforcement of codes regulating construction, with the purpose of decreasing the vulnerability of structures to forces of nature; and so on.

In concept, risk control is an intermediate point between risk assessment and risk financing. Risk control efforts are prompted by an awareness and recognition of an exposure to risk. In turn, risk control efforts determine the extent to which undesirable effects of the risk are manifested within the organization. Ultimately, these undesirable effects translate into financial results. This sequential description implies that risk control is linked to risk assessment and to risk financing in important ways. These linkages become key points in understanding the thought process of a risk manager.

WHAT IS RISK CONTROL AND WHEN IS IT USED?

Effective risk control reduces an organization's exposure to risk. More formally, risk control includes *techniques, tools, strategies and processes that seek to avoid, prevent, reduce, or otherwise control the frequency and/or magnitude of loss and other undesirable effects of risk; risk control also includes methods that seek to improve understanding or awareness within an organization of activities affecting exposure to risk.*

The use of risk control methods in an organization can be based on criteria applying generally to nearly all areas of activity including risk management: a balancing of benefits against costs. In some instances, external influences such as state and federal governments mandate the use of risk control methods or provide other incentives affecting the use of risk control. Where such direct incentives are absent, an even-handed balancing of benefits and costs of risk control often tends to understate its true benefits. This statement is based upon three considerations: (1) the cost of risk financing is commonly greater than the cost of losses, (2) losses typically generate indirect or hidden costs that may not be revealed until the distant future, and (3) losses can have effects outside an organization.

Point 1 can be illustrated by considering insurance. The dollars spent for insurance include the insurer's charges for overhead, profits, taxes, commissions, and so on. To the extent that risk control can prevent a loss, the costs of the loss are saved but so are at least some of the administrative and transactional costs. Even in situations in which an organization self-finances losses, the savings derived would have to include administrative costs necessary to self-administer the claims.

Points 2 and 3 are important. Almost invariably, a direct loss will generate indirect, consequential, and time element losses. Some of the loss costs may fall on society or on others, as when an organization pollutes the environment. To the extent that losses are prevented or controlled, these costs are eliminated and the case for risk control is further strengthened.

THE RELATIONSHIP OF RISK CONTROL TO RISK ASSESSMENT

In Chapter 3 the subject of risk assessment was introduced and discussed. That discussion explained that risk assessment involves a thorough and critical analysis of the process through which gains or losses are produced. The study and analysis of the sequence of events leading to such outcomes is influential in the development of risk control solutions, since an understanding of how outcomes occur very often leads to insights into possible risk control methods.

The linkage between risk assessment and risk control becomes more explicit by considering the "risk chain," a concept that describes the process leading to loss as a linked chain of events. The "links" in this chain are:

1. The hazard
2. The environment
3. The interaction
4. The outcome
5. The consequences.

The hazard is the condition that might lead to a loss, for instance, an improperly maintained piece of heavy machinery. The environment is the context in which the hazard exists, for instance, the shop floor where the improperly maintained piece of machinery is located. The interaction is the process whereby the hazard interacts with the environment, sometimes having no effect and sometimes resulting in loss. For instance, a worker operating this improperly maintained equipment might suffer injury because a protective screen is not in place when a drill bit breaks. The outcome link is the immediate result of the interaction, in this case a serious eye injury. Finally, the consequences link refers not to the immediate outcome (the injury) but rather the longer-term consequences of the event; a workers' compensation claim, repair of the equipment, an OSHA penalty, and so on.

The risk chain is discussed here to show the relationship between risk assessment and risk control. As part of risk assessment, a risk manager is likely to analyze the nature of hazards within the organization, the environment in which these hazards exist, the potential outcomes when hazards interact with environment, the immediate outcomes of accidents and the longer-term consequences. While this analysis is occurring, however, the risk manager is quite likely to be considering possible strategies for managing a particular risk. For instance, an analysis of the previously described risk might suggest to the risk manager that machinery maintenance is a major part of managing the risk, so adopting maintenance protocols for this equipment may become the centerpiece of the risk management plan for this particular area. Readers interested in the risk chain concept are directed to Merkhofer's *Decision Science and Social Risk Management* (Merkhofer, 1987), which develops a similar idea.

THE RELATIONSHIP OF RISK CONTROL TO RISK FINANCING

Risk financing methods are used by organizations to provide resources for reimbursing the cost of loss (insurance, for example). Most organizations utilize some financing mechanism that transfers the risk to another party or they retain the risk and absorb the cost of losses internally. Risk control has a powerful relationship with risk financing because the control of risks can have a significant effect on the frequency and severity of losses that must be "financed."

The positive effects of effective risk control on an organization's risk financing costs are likely to occur irrespective of the particular risk financing methods used. If losses are retained, the benefit is obvious—losses do not occur and loss financing is not needed. Also, for most medium and large organizations, the pricing of insurance or other financing mechanisms is based upon the principle that, over time, the organization will pay almost the (if not *the*) full cost of its losses. That is, except for the rare catastrophic loss, most organizations above a certain size ultimately pay for all the losses they suffer. Therefore, any effort to control a risk will usually have a positive effect on the cost of financing. While this may seem obvious, the relationship sometimes escapes the attention of managers. As an illustration, many managers hold the view that an injured worker collecting workers' compensation benefits is "no longer the organization's problem" because "workers' compensation will take care of the worker." This comment could be made only if the manager fails to see that her organization's loss experience and risk control efforts directly influence the cost of its workers' compensation insurance.

As with risk control and risk assessment, the actual implementation of risk control and risk financing activities rarely occurs in a sequential manner. For example, an insurer may stipulate that certain risk control activities occur as a condition of the insurance (risk financing) contract. These activities might include the installation of a sprinkler system in a warehouse or the adoption of standardized safety procedures.

RISK CONTROL AND SPECULATIVE RISKS

The term "risk control" traditionally has been applied to methods addressing possible losses rather than gains. However, nothing about the concept of risk control requires it to be limited to "pure" risks. It is true that risk control methods are limited by an organization's ability to exert an influence on the frequency and severity dimensions of the risk; for instance, an organization may have almost no control over the risk of changes in the price of a widely held common stock. However, this does not preclude the application of risk control to "speculative" risks. This is especially the case because the organization frequently has control over its exposure to "uncontrollable" risks. The organization can avoid the uncontrollable investment risk mentioned above by not investing in that particular company.

The concept of risk control applies to all risks, whether or not gains are possible. For a business, profit is the difference between revenues and costs, both of which are uncertain. Most actions of managers affect both revenues and costs. The pure/speculative risk dichotomy fails to unambiguously classify the type of risks addressed by efforts such as quality control, which can have effects on both future revenues (through enhancement of perceived value) and future costs (through reduced warranty claims and reduced injury costs).

Risk control applied to speculative risk is exemplified by a business entering a joint venture with a foreign-based marketing organization as a means of gaining entry to a foreign market. On the one hand, the entry into a foreign market is a deliberate acceptance of a new exposure to risk. On the other hand, the joint venture agreement provides access to the skills, knowledge, and contacts of the foreign-based organization; it also creates an incentive for the foreign organization to work towards the success of the project. As a consequence, the use of the joint venture tends to mitigate the exposure. The form of risk control illustrated by this example can be described as *risk selection* or *selective exposure:* the deliberate choice by an organization of risks for which its knowledge and skills provide a relative advantage in risk-bearing. A well-designed mission statement for an organization can offer guidelines for selecting risks that are aligned with the organization's mission.

Most organizations today would be unfamiliar with this interpretation of risk control. For one thing, this definition seems to suggest the existence of an organization "master plan" for risk control. That is unlikely to be the case, because most organizations continue to rely on specialists to control risk: marketing managers control marketing risk, finance managers control financial risks, risk managers control pure risks, and so on. However, the fact that organizations do not, generally, coordinate their risk control activities does not mean there is no value in doing so.

RISK CONTROL TOOLS AND TECHNIQUES

Risk management has been described as an "art," because creativity seems to play an important role. The illustrations that follow emphasize that view. The activities that constitute one organization's risk control efforts may be quite different from the efforts of a similar organization in another part of the world. Organizations vary as to their desire for risk control, and any particular risk may be managed through a variety of techniques. Indeed, a comprehensive list of risk control applications would be virtually endless, limited only by the collective imagination of the risk management community.

Although risk control programs can vary from organization to organization as a consequence of creativity and innovation, a typology of risk control tools and methods still exists. Risk control tools and techniques can be categorized as *risk avoidance, loss prevention, loss reduction, information management,* and some types of *risk transfers.*

Risk Avoidance

One way to control a particular risk is to avoid the property, person, or activity giving rise to possible loss by either refusing to assume it even momentarily or by abandoning an exposure to loss assumed earlier. The first of these avoidance activities is *proactive avoidance,* while the second is *abandonment.*

Government and business risk management practices reveal several examples of *proactive avoidance.* A leading chemical firm once planned to conduct a series of experiments in a rural area containing a single small town. While preparing for the experiments, the researchers discovered that the venture might possibly cause extensive property damage to the community. The risk manager was asked to purchase insurance against this possibility, but only a few insurers were willing to provide the protection, and the premiums for insurance were much greater than the firm was willing to pay. Consequently, the firm decided against conducting the experiments.

A governmental entity recently was bequeathed a small amusement park.

The park, which contained a number of antiquated rides for children, was inspected by the risk manager who determined that the rides were extremely hazardous. After some negotiation between the government and the estate executor, the estate sold the rides for scrap and donated the vacant lot to the government. That government converted the lot to an "open space" park, which contains several gardens, fountains, and walking paths. In this case, one might argue that the government did not proactively avoid the source of the risk (the park), but it did avoid the hazards (the rides). Through such an example, readers can see that avoidance is not always a clear-cut matter. Indeed, in many circumstances, successful avoidance may be as much a matter of how the risk is defined as it is a matter of applying a technique.

Avoidance through *abandonment* is, perhaps, not quite as common as proactive avoidance, but it does occur. A risk manager of a university may recommend against serving alcoholic beverages at university-sponsored functions because of dram shop liability. A pharmaceutical firm may choose to discontinue the production of some particular product when reports of serious, and heretofore unknown, side-effects begin to surface. An apartment management firm may decide to remove a swimming pool from its premises upon learning that a majority of the renters have small children.

Avoidance is an effective approach to the handling of risk. By avoiding a risk, the organization knows that it will not experience the potential losses or the uncertainty that the risk may generate. However, it also loses the benefits that may have been derived from that risk. Indeed, this very fact often makes avoidance an unacceptable option. A particular activity—the production of some product, the provision of some service—may provide economic rewards whose expected value far exceeds potential loss costs at the margin.

There are other circumstances when avoidance simply is not possible. The more broadly the risk is defined (say, "property damage"), the more likely this is to be the case. For instance, the only way for an organization to avoid property damage is to sell all its physical assets. Or, for most college students, the most significant risk they face is likely to be their future earning potential, a risk that cannot be avoided. More narrowly, governments (and particularly the courts) may impose legal expectations that cannot be avoided. An employer cannot avoid the costs of financing the risk of unemployment because participation in the unemployment insurance program is mandatory. The Occupational Health and Safety Administration (OSHA) imposes the risk of fines for employers who fail to meet safety standards. Finally, such legal concepts as strict liability may impose a potential obligation or duty upon an organization that cannot be avoided.

The context of the decision to avoid also may make avoidance impossible. A risk does not exist in a vacuum, and a decision to avoid a risk might actually create a new risk elsewhere or enhance some existing risk. For instance, a city council was told that one of two bridges crossing a river in the city center was in a state of serious disrepair. In response, the council decided to close the bridge and divert all traffic to the second bridge. The increased traffic load made failure of the second bridge more likely to occur, and within a year that second bridge collapsed. Risks that most organizations encounter often are interrelated in some way, and the removal of one can adversely affect the risks remaining in the "risk portfolio."

Finally, a risk may be so fundamental to the organization's reason for being that avoidance cannot be contemplated. A mining concern may wish to avoid the risk of tunnel collapse, but true avoidance would mean leaving the mining business.

Loss Prevention and Loss Reduction

Loss prevention and reduction measures attack risk by reducing the number of losses that occur (i.e., loss frequency is reduced) or by mitigating the amount of damage when a loss does occur (i.e., loss severity is reduced). From a public policy perspective, loss prevention and reduction have the distinct advantage of preventing or reducing losses for both the individual organization and society while permitting the organization to commence or continue the activity creating the risk.

Loss Prevention. Loss prevention programs seek to reduce the number of losses or to eliminate them entirely. The earlier discussion of the risk chain is important to recall here, because loss prevention activities seek to intervene in the first three links in the chain: the hazard, the environment, and the interaction of hazard and environment. That is, loss prevention activities are focused on:

1. Altering or modifying the hazard
2. Altering or modifying the environment in which the hazard exists
3. Intervening in the processes whereby hazard and environment interact.

The examples of loss prevention activities below illustrate how these tactics focus upon each of the first three links in the risk chain.

Loss Prevention Activities That Focus on the Hazard

1. Hazard: Careless housekeeping
   Loss Prevention Activity: Training and monitoring programs
2. Hazard: Flooding
   Loss Prevention Activity: Dams, water resource management
3. Hazard: Smoking
   Loss Prevention Activity: Ban on smoking, confiscation of smoking materials
4. Hazard: Pollution
   Loss Prevention Activity: Handling protocols for use and disposal of polluting substances
5. Hazard: Icy sidewalks
   Loss Prevention Activity: Shoveling, salting, heated walkways
6. Hazard: Radioactive materials
   Loss Prevention Activity: Construction of appropriate barriers and containers
7. Hazard: Drunk driving
   Loss Prevention Activity: Prohibition, enforcement of ban, prison sentence

8. Hazard: Lack of information regarding some activity
   Loss Prevention Activity: Research

Loss Prevention Activities That Focus on the Environment

1. The Environment: A shop floor that could become slippery from oil spillage
   Loss Prevention Activity: Installation of absorbent, non-skid mats
2. The Environment: Interstate highways
   Loss Prevention Activity: Barrier construction, lighting, signs, and road markings
3. The Environment: Improperly trained workforce
   Loss Prevention Activity: Training
4. The Environment: Consuming public
   Loss Prevention Activity: Adequate product instructions and warnings
5. The Environment: The drug-addicted population
   Loss Prevention Activity: Counseling, treatment, detection
6. The Environment: Structures susceptible to fire
   Loss Prevention Activity: Fire resistive construction
7. The Environment: Unlighted central city parking facility
   Loss Prevention Activity: Lighting, escort, and security service
8. The Environment: Employees driving a fleet of delivery vehicles
   Loss Prevention Activity: Driver's education training

Loss Prevention Activities That Focus on Interactions of Hazard and Environment

1. The Interaction: A heating process that may overheat surrounding equipment
   Loss Prevention Activity: A water-cooling system
2. The Interaction: Improper lifting of heavy crates by employees
   Loss Prevention Activity: Lumbar support belts
3. The Interaction: Vehicle skidding on a slippery road
   Loss Prevention Activity: Antilock brakes
4. The Interaction: Telephone line repairworkers working in Minnesota in January
   Loss Prevention Activity: Proper clothing, cold-weather work protocols
5. The Interaction: Consumer use of a hazardous product
   Loss Prevention Activity: Safety features, customer assistance
6. The Interaction: A city council deciding on proprietary matters
   Loss Prevention Activity: Documentation of decision making, legal counsel review
7. The Interaction: An underground storage tank leaking fuel
   Loss Prevention Activity: Double-seal tanks
8. The Interaction: Moving a production facility to an underdeveloped country
   Loss Prevention Activity: Host-government relations activities, research

The purpose of these illustrations is not so much to identify the full scope of activities that constitute loss prevention as it is to give the reader a general sense of the variety of loss prevention activities; these illustrations also reinforce the point made earlier that loss prevention activities will likely be quite specific to the problem or risk confronting the organization.

Loss Reduction

Loss reduction programs are designed to reduce the potential severity of a loss. A sprinkler system is a classic example of loss reduction; because fire is required to activate the sprinklers, such a system does not reduce the probability of loss. Instead, a sprinkler system reduces the amount of damage if a fire occurs.

Loss reduction activities are post-loss measures. Although such measures may be planned prior to any loss, their function or purpose is to minimize the impact of losses that occur. Loss reduction programs are a tacit admission on the part of the risk manager that some losses will occur, despite an organization's best efforts. Therefore, steps should be taken to control the loss and reduce its potential severity.

Earlier, the concept of a risk chain was invoked to illustrate how loss prevention addressed the first three links in the chain. Loss reduction focuses upon the third link (occasionally) and the fourth and fifth links (more commonly): the interaction link, the outcome link, and the consequences link. A loss reduction effort may address the interaction link only insofar as the measure intervenes to stop a loss in progress. A clean-agent (gaseous) fire suppression system offers a good illustration: the interaction of hazard and environment results in the igniting of combustible materials. While this interaction is occurring, the gaseous suppression system responds and reduces the ultimate impact of the fire.

The fourth and fifth links are addressed after a loss has occurred and the risk manager must minimize the outcome and the consequences of the loss. For example, a worker suffers serious burns to his arms and legs. Assuring that this worker is sent promptly to a burn treatment center with the appropriate expertise is a loss reduction measure.

One widely used loss reduction measure is *salvage*. Rarely will a loss be total, and a risk manager may minimize the loss through salvaging the property. A car can be sold for scrap, while a damaged but repairable piece of equipment may be sold to a secondary market. Insurance companies employ salvage extensively to minimize the impact of losses they pay and risk managers have emulated this loss reduction technique.

A somewhat related loss reduction technique is commonly identified by the term *subrogation*. When an insurance company pays a claim to a policyholder, there may be an opportunity for the insurer to seek reimbursement from a negligent third party in the claim. After the insurer has paid the claim, the insured's common law right to collect from the negligent third party becomes "subrogated" (that is, it is transferred) to the insurer. If the insurer can successfully collect, its recovery has reduced the impact of the claim on the insurer. In a risk management setting, an employer who has a self-insured workers' compensation program may seek reimbursement for benefits paid to an injured worker by filing a lawsuit against a negligent third party who was responsible for injuring the worker (e.g., the manufacturer of an industrial machine that injures the worker).

As a practical matter, subrogation might also be reviewed as a loss reduction measure that addresses longer-term consequences of a loss. Subrogation is one type of *litigation management* tool, litigation management being a set of strategies or tactics that seek to control or reduce the impact of a legal action arising out of a loss that has occurred. Among the specific methods employed are arbitration, mediation, and other alternative dispute resolution tools; litigation strategy and philosophy; settlement strategies; and public relations efforts to manage the "court of public opinion."

Loss reduction seeks to reduce the impact of loss either through controlling the event as it occurs, controlling the immediate outcome of the event, or controlling the longer-term consequences of the event. *Catastrophe* or *contingency plans* are an integrated approach to loss reduction. A catastrophe plan is an organization-wide effort to identify possible crises or catastrophes and develop plans for responding to such events. Catastrophe planning usually involves a fairly lengthy process of research and evaluation that ultimately yields a contingency plan for possible use in the event of a catastrophe. Among the activities that might become part of a catastrophe plan are:

1. Cross-training employees
2. Back-up, off-site storage of computerized records
3. Updating of fire suppressant system
4. Securing of credit from lending institutions
5. Training of employees on emergency safety procedures
6. Disaster training/planning with fire department or similar governmental organizations (Federal Emergency Management Agency—FEMA—for example)
7. Cold- or hot-site backup computer facility
8. Construction modification, such as installation of firewalls
9. Development of community relations strategy
10. Creation of an Emergency Response Team or Committee.

As can be seen, catastrophe planning is similar to loss prevention activities in that specific activities are dictated by details peculiar to the organization's situation and preferences. Catastrophe plans vary considerably between organizations.

Catastrophe or crisis management is a topic that has become a separate topic of study in recent years. For example, Laurence Barton's *Crisis in Organizations: Managing and Communicating in the Heat of Chaos* (Barton, 1993) presents a thorough introduction to catastrophe management. Barton details the development of a crisis management plan, the designation of a crisis team, and the imposition of a level of crisis-preparedness on an organization. A technical understanding of catastrophe management is essential for the risk manager, but there is some danger in decoupling catastrophe management from the broader subject of risk management. Catastrophe plans are much less likely to succeed if imposed upon an organization that has no existing risk management culture in place at the time of a disaster.

A special case of loss reduction, suggested by Dr. George Head (Head, 1986), is duplication of an existing asset that is not used unless something happens to the original asset. Spare parts or duplicate machinery illustrate the concept. Duplication often is used in cases in which an indirect loss, such as loss, of use arises from direct damage to the asset. In such cases, duplication reduces the amount of damage if a loss occurs by reducing or eliminating the indirect loss. Duplication often serves in the dual roles of loss prevention and loss reduction. Duplication reduces the probability of an indirect loss because the duplicate may be available for use if the original asset cannot be used. Backing up computer files and storing the backup records off-site is perhaps the most vivid illustration of the value of duplication, since the loss of employee records, accounts receivable, transaction documentation, or other financial information could be a serious problem for an organization.

Separation offers a final illustration of a loss reduction technique. Separation is a technique by which an organization attempts to isolate its exposures to loss from each other instead of allowing them to be vulnerable to a single event. Fire walls within a structure are an example of separation; dividing the interior of the structure into a number of compartments separated by fire-resistant materials tends to confine the damage to a single compartment if a fire occurs. Another example of separation is a rule requiring employees in a retail establishment to move cash accumulations over a stated amount from cash registers to a more secure location, such as a bank vault. A third example of separation is a rule requiring the storage of vehicles in a fleet in diverse locations rather than a single place. The motive behind separation is to reduce any dependency between an organization's exposures to loss by reducing the likelihood that a single event could affect them all.

The act of separation does not necessarily reduce the chance of loss to a single exposure unit, although it tends to reduce the chance of a catastrophic loss. The effectiveness of separation may depend on the type of asset and the cause of possible loss. For example, storage of inventory in several warehouses dispersed throughout a one-square-mile area may reduce the likelihood of a catastrophic fire loss. If the warehouses are located in a coastal area, however, they still may be vulnerable to catastrophic damage from hurricanes.

Information Management

Chapter 1 explained how the reduction or resolution of uncertainty has economic value, and how information can reduce or resolve uncertainty. Information emanating from an organization's risk management department can have important effects in reducing uncertainty in an organization's stakeholders. To realize the maximum benefit from a loss control program, for example, the program's objectives and its favorable effects can be communicated to stakeholders having an interest in the outcome: employees, regulators, insurers, and for a government entity, taxpayers. Having an effective loss control program in place goes only part of the way toward meeting the organization's objectives if the information describing its effectiveness never reaches the organization's stakeholders whose interests are affected.

Communication from an organization's risk management department conveys information describing the effectiveness of loss control measures and the intent of the department's future actions. Loss occurs as a result of natural forces and the actions of humans, and uncertainty can arise from imperfect knowledge along either dimension. Lack of information can cause stakeholders to become uncertain about the nature of the organization's actions with respect to matters affecting their interests. Their uncertainty leads them to charge a higher price for their goods and services or to demand safeguards or restrictions having an unfavorable effect on the organization. Credible information from the risk management department can provide these stakeholders with the assurance that the organization has not and will not take actions that are detrimental to their interests.

Another area in which communication can reduce uncertainty involves individuals' awareness of the loss-causing process; the risk chain, for example. Knowledge of the process by which hazards evolve into injuries can reduce uncertainty in affected parties, as the awareness allows better forecasts of the consequences of actions. For example, employees' awareness of the circumstances leading to possible injury can alert them to situations requiring preventive action. One possibility for enhancing this awareness is a reporting method and system of rewards for employees who make suggestions leading to safer practices.

Risk Transfer

Risk transfer is a risk control tool that causes some entity other than the one experiencing the loss to bear the burden of the loss. Transfer may be accomplished in two ways. First, the property or activity responsible for the risk may be transferred to some other person or group of persons. For example, an organization that sells one of its buildings transfers the risks associated with ownership of the building to the new owner. A general contractor who is concerned about possible increases in the cost of labor and materials needed for the electrical work on a job to which he or she is already committed can transfer the risk by hiring a subcontractor (with a fixed price contract) for this portion of the project. This type of transfer, which is closely related to avoidance through abandonment, is a risk control measure because it attempts to eliminate exposure to potential loss that otherwise could strike the organization. Risk transfer differs from avoidance through abandonment because a transferred risk results in an exposure for some other entity. An abandoned risk is passed to no one.

Second, the risk, but not the property or activity, may be transferred—usually by contractual agreement. For example, a lease may shift to the landlord the tenant's responsibility for negligent damage to the landlord's premises. A retailer may assume responsibility for any damage to products that occurs after the products leave the manufacturer's premises even if the manufacturer otherwise would be responsible. A customer may give up the right to sue a business for bodily injuries and property damage sustained because of defects in a product or a service. The contracts that implement such transfers are called "exculpatory contracts." In a risk control transfer, the transferee (the party accepting the risk) excuses the transferor (the party transferring the risk) from liability. The transferor's exposure is eliminated. The above examples of exculpatory contracts, if upheld by courts, are risk control transfers. However, a promise by the transferee to reimburse the transferor for damage is *not* a risk control transfer, as the transferor still faces the risk. Such a promise is an example of a risk financing transfer, which is covered in the next chapter.

Although the distinction between risk control and risk financing transfer may appear to be semantic, it can have economic consequences when the transferee becomes insolvent or otherwise unable to pay for the damage. Also, a risk financing transfer may limit the transferee's liability, after which point the burden of loss again falls on the transferor. For example, leases of business property often require the tenant to reimburse the landlord for fire damage to the rented premises even if the tenant is not negligent. Under a purchasing agreement, a retailer may secure a promise from a manufacturer to reimburse the retailer for any payments to third parties arising from defects in the manufacturer's products. As part of a bailment agreement, a laundry may accept responsibility for damage to customers' property even if the laundry, except for the agreement, would not be liable. In each of these instances, the transferor bears the economic burden of damage if the transferee is unable to pay.

Risk control transfers involve only the transferor and the transferee; risk financing transfer, however, may involve others. A transferee cannot excuse a transferor from any liability the transferor may have to third parties because the third parties are not part of the agreement; the law does not allow the rights of third parties to be reduced by this transfer. The transferee can, however, agree to finance any losses that otherwise may have been financed by the transferor.

Unless a risk control transfer is declared illegal, it offers complete protection for the transferor. The burden of the risk falls completely on the transferee. Under a risk financing transfer, in contrast, if the transferee fails for any reason to provide the promised funds following a loss, the transferor bears the loss. A single agreement may result in a risk control transfer with respect to some potential losses and a risk financing transfer with respect to others. For example, a lease may excuse the tenant from responsibility for any damage to the premises (risk control) and obligate the landlord to finance any liability of the tenant to others arising out of activities on the premises (risk financing).

Nothing in the above discussion implies that a risk control transfer is costless for the transferor. Where a fixed price contract is used to transfer the risk of possible increases in the cost of labor and materials to a subcontractor, for example, the fixed price of the contract reflects the value of the risks being transferred. Recognizing this point, rational parties would be expected to transfer a risk only when the transferee possesses a relative advantage in controlling or otherwise managing and bearing the risk. Where the transferee is at a relative disadvantage, the price of the transaction from the transferor's point of view is affected adversely; the transferee charges too much to accept the responsibility for managing the risk.

RISK CONTROL, GOVERNMENT AND SOCIETY

Reasons other than self-interest motivate organizations to practice risk control. A number of private and nonprofit organizations promote and encourage risk control activities. Federal and state governments also promote and encourage risk control, and in some cases mandate that risk control activities be undertaken.

Private and Non-Profit Efforts

A partial listing of private and nonprofit groups active in the area of risk control suggests the range of activities and services. The National Safety Council is perhaps the most well-known of these groups. The Council includes among its members individuals, business firms, schools, government departments, labor organizations, insurers, and others. It assembles and disseminates information concerning many types of accidents, cooperates with public officials in safety campaigns, encourages the establishment of local safety councils, and helps members solve their own safety problems. Other examples are the American Insurance Association, an organization of insurers that publicizes the extent and causes of fire losses, investigates suspected cases of arson, grades municipalities according to the quality of their exposures to fire and their protection against fire loss, and suggests codes; the Underwriters Laboratories, another insurance-sponsored organization that tests equipment (television sets, electric wiring, safes, etc.) to determine whether it meets safety standards; the National Fire Protection Association, which establishes standards and codes, stimulates local loss control activities, and promotes fire safety, educates the public, and encourages its members, including public officials, to adopt its suggestions; the Insurance Institute for Highway Safety, which provides financial assistance for other organizations engaged in traffic safety work and also provides direct assistance in selected states; and the National Automobile Theft Bureau, whose name indicates its concern. Individual insurers also maintain engineering or loss control departments to study risks faced by their insureds, and suggest ways in which these risks might be reduced. Insurers also provide posters, films, pamphlets, and conduct safety classes.

Because unions are concerned with all matters affecting working conditions, they also are active in loss control. Unions tend to strongly support government regulations to improve workplace safety; they belong to the National Safety Council and similar organizations, and they often demand new or more intensive loss control from employers.

Governmental Efforts

Government is involved in loss control because (1) the public interest often requires the government to enact legislation requiring all industries to provide information, meet certain standards, and stop undesirable practices, and (2) the government can provide certain services, such as those of fire departments, more economically and efficiently than can scattered private firms. The government exercises this responsibility through a variety of educational efforts (pamphlets, posters, and conferences) and through statutes and codes regulating building construction, working conditions, safety equipment and safety clothing, maximum occupancy in rooms and elevators, sewage disposal facilities, and the operation of motor vehicles. This duty is met through inspections designed to enforce the statutes and codes, by police and fire departments, rehabilitation programs, the assembling and dissemination of statistical data related to loss prevention and reduction, and by the conduct and encouragement of research activities.

Economists note that certain aspects of some risks lead to a demand for government involvement. Two characteristics that should be mentioned are *externalities* and *public goods.* Externalities are costs or benefits that are not captured in the ordinary functioning of a market. Pollution is a commonly cited example of an externality. A manufacturing firm may pollute the environment, harming a neighboring community. The cost to the community will largely, if not completely, escape the pricing of the good produced by the polluter.

A public good is a good or service that cannot be limited to purchasers of the good. National defense is often cited as an illustration of a public good. By its nature, a national defense is available to everyone, whether they pay for that service or not. This inability to discriminate between buyers and nonbuyers leads to a phenomenon known as the "free rider." Free riders are those individuals or organizations that enjoy the benefits of a good or service while avoiding the cost or price of that service.

In both cases, externalities and public goods, the government may be expected to intervene to direct the costs of goods and services (or risks) to the appropriate parties.

Perhaps the best-known government intervention in the realm of risk management is the Occupational Safety and Health Administration. In late 1970, Congress passed the Occupational Safety and Health Act (OSHA), an extremely important piece of safety legislation. OSHA applies to private employers of one or more persons (the self-employed are exempted) engaged in a business affecting interstate commerce, except for some employers subject to special federal legislation such as the Federal Coal Mine and Safety Act. About three-fourths of the civilian labor force is affected. Federal government employees are covered under a separate federal program. State and local governments historically have been exempt. States may assume responsibility for developing and enforcing occupational safety and health standards under plans approved by the Secretary of Labor. The state standards must be at least as stringent as the counterpart federal standards. Many states have developed plans that have been accepted by the federal government. Indeed, many state plans impose standards that are stricter than the federal law. For instance, federal law requires states that assume responsibility for occupational safety and health to include governmental entities as covered organizations under OSHA.

Under the Occupational Safety and Health Act, the Secretary of Labor establishes safety and health standards and enforces compliance with these standards. Voluminous standards have been developed. Many are "consensus" safety standards previously developed as voluntary guidelines for business by private associations, such as the American National Standards Institute and the National Fire Protection Association. Other standards are based on federal regulations developed earlier for contractors and maritime industries. Still others are new standards proposed by the Secretary after consultation with an OSHA Standards Advisory Committee. Proposed new or revised standards must be published in the *Federal Register.* Interested parties have 30 days in which they can comment informally on the proposal. Affected parties also have 60 days after a standard is promulgated to challenge the standard before the U.S. Court of Appeals. An individual employer may apply for a temporary variance from a standard in order to have more time to comply. The employees of such an employer must be aware that the employer has applied for this variance and be allowed to appear at the hearing on the application.

Illustrative standards include:

1. All places of employment, passageways, storerooms, and service rooms shall be kept clean and orderly and in a sanitary condition.
2. Portable wood ladders longer than 20 feet shall not be supplied to workers (the standard on portable wood ladders alone fills more than 15 pages).
3. In the absence of an infirmary, clinic, or hospital in near proximity to the workplace which is used for the treatment of all injured employees, a person or persons shall be adequately trained to render first aid.

To check compliance with these standards, federal inspectors have the right to enter without notice, but at reasonable times, any covered establishment. An employee can also request such an inspection by describing in writing what he or she considers to be a serious violation of some standard. The name of the complaining employee may not be revealed to the employer. During an inspection the employer and an employee representative may, upon request, accompany the inspector. As a result of a court decision in the late 1970s, an employer can require the inspector to obtain a warrant for the search.

If an inspector discovers a violation that is more than *de minimus*, the inspector is directed to issue a written citation decribing the violation (*de minimus* means no direct or immediate relationship to job safety and health, e.g., no toilet partitions). This citation must be posted near the location of the violation. Within a reasonable time the employer must remove the hazard.

If death or serious physical harm could have resulted from the violation, the citation means a mandatory penalty up to $1,000. Less serious violations may entail smaller penalties, but the penalties still can range up to $1,000. If the employer fails to correct the violation within the time stated in the citation, he or she *may* be penalized up to $1,000 each day the violation continues. Penalties of $10,000 per violation may be levied for willful or repeated violations. If a willful violation results in the death of an employee, the employer is either fined $10,000 or imprisoned up to six months. These penalties are doubled if such a fatal willful violation is repeated. An employer can appeal citations before a judge acting on behalf of the three-member Occupational Safety and Health Commission, which administers the safety standards portion of the act. Any one of the three commission members can demand a review of the judge's decision by the entire commission. Commission orders may in turn be appealed to the U.S. Court of Appeals.

In addition to meeting certain health and safety standards, employers of eight or more employees must maintain and make available to government representatives accurate records of work-related deaths, illnesses, and injuries that cause the employee to miss work. These employers also must maintain records of injuries without lost workdays that result in medical treatment beyond first aid, diagnoses of occupational illness, and injuries involving loss of consciousness, restriction of work or motion, or transfer to another job.

Under a High-Risk Occupational Disease Notification and Prevention bill, also known as the "Right to Know" bill, the Department of Health and Human Services identifies hazardous substances and notifies current and past employees who have been exposed to these hazardous substances. Private employers are required to pay for medical screening of these employees and either provide other employment for a worker with an occupational disease or permit the worker to resign and receive one year's salary. Many employers object to the high costs, including workers' compensation costs, that this program imposes.

OSHA requires that employees be notified of their rights under the law. They must also not be discharged or harassed because they exercise these rights.

In the 1993–1994 session, both houses of Congress began considering several major reforms of OSHA. Although it is impossible to describe the outcome of these deliberations, certain features appear likely to emerge. First, employers may be required to take further steps to promote workplace safety, including the development of safety plans and the creation of safety committees to oversee the execution of safety plans. Reporting procedures are likely to change as well. The biggest change is likely to occur in the area of inspection and enforcement. Under various proposals, responsibilities for compliance may shift to the employers. For instance, it is possible that employers will be required to contract with a private inspection service and submit to an inspection—the report of which would be submitted to OSHA. Such a reform measure would allow OSHA to reduce its own inspection activities, while actually increasing the amount of safety inspecting that would be done.

As a final note, readers should be made aware of the great difficulty risk managers can face in keeping abreast of government mandates. At any given moment an organization may be required to understand and comply with dozens of regulatory mandates pertaining to risk control. Further, new directives and laws are emerging all the time, so risk managers need to spend a certain amount of time studying legislative activity. For example, between 1994 and 1998, most governmental risk managers will face over 20 new regulatory requirements (PRIMA, 1993). A partial listing of those requirements includes:

1. Five compliance provisions arising from the Americans with Disabilities Act.
2. Four new compliance directives from the EPA covering underground storage tanks.
3. Three new requirements promulgated by the EPA for municipal solid waste landfills.
4. Two new EPA requirements for the control and disposal of sewage sludge.
5. A special OSHA directive for working in confined spaces.
6. A second OSHA requirement covering the reporting of workplace injuries and illnesses.
7. Two new Department of Labor requirements arising from the Family and Medical Leave Act.
8. Two IRS directives which apply to pension nondiscrimination rules.

Key Concepts

risk control Those techniques, tools, strategies and processes that seek to alter the organization's exposure to risk by avoiding, preventing, reducing, or otherwise controlling the frequency and/or magnitude of risks and losses or gains.

risk selection   The control technique best described as the conscious acceptance of risk in accordance with an organization's overall goals, objectives, and risk-taking philosophy.

risk financing   Those tools and techniques used to finance the cost of risks and losses.

risk avoidance   A risk control technique whereby a risk is proactively avoided or abandoned after rational consideration.

loss prevention   Those strategies and activities intended to reduce or eliminate the chance of loss.

loss reduction   Those activities that minimize the impact of losses that do occur.

the risk chain   A simple model of accidents that interprets those accidents as consisting of five elements or "links": the hazard, the environment, the interaction, the outcome, and the consequences.

subrogation   The legal transfer of a right, discussed in this chapter as a loss reduction tool.

catastrophe management plan   An organization-wide loss reduction plan for controlling the indirect, consequential, and time element losses associated with a catastrophic event.

information management (as a risk reduction tool)   The use of information for the express purpose of reducing uncertainty, or for enhancing stakeholder awareness or knowledge of organizational risks.

the Occupational Safety and Health Administration (OSHA)   A significant government program that promulgates and enforces workplace safety standards.

Review Questions

1. Distinguish between risk control and risk assessment. How are they related?
2. What is the relationship between risk control and risk financing?
3. Give three examples of how risk avoidance might actually harm an organization.
4. How is proactive avoidance different from abandonment?
5. Consider some current event in which a loss has occurred, for example, Hurricane Andrew, the Los Angeles riots, the earthquake in Cairo, Egypt. Using the risk chain concept, break the event down into:
   a. The hazard
   b. The environment
   c. The interaction
   d. The outcome
   e. The consequences.
6. With respect to the event you identified in question 5, does this analysis suggest any possible risk control activities?
7. Classify each of the following as to whether they are loss prevention or loss reduction activities:
   a. Oily rags and paper are cleaned up or disposed of each day.
   b. Nonslip treads are placed on each stairway.
   c. Brakes on delivery vehicles are inspected each week.
   d. Safety meetings are held each month.
   e. A take-over target is evaluated for its past risk management activities.
   f. Machines are equipped with safety guards.
   g. All key employees are required to take an annual physical evaluation.
   h. A new product is manufactured during a slack period.
   i. Board of director decisions are recorded and documented.
8. Describe briefly the responsibilities imposed on employers by OSHA.
9. Why is separation considered a loss reduction activity?

10. Give two examples of non-insurance risk transfers.
11. Explain how risk control might apply to speculative risks.

References and Suggestions For Additional Reading

Accident Prevention Manual for Industrial Operations (8th ed., Chicago: National Safety Council, 1982).

BARTON, LAURENCE: *Crisis in Organizations: Managing and Communicating in the Heat of Chaos* (Cincinnati: South-Western Publishing Co., 1993).

DOHERTY, NEIL A.: *Corporate Risk Management* (New York: McGraw-Hill Book Company, 1985).

FACTORY MUTUAL ENGINEERING DIVISION: *Handbook of Industrial Loss Prevention* (New York: McGraw-Hill Book Company, 1959).

GREEN, M. R., and O. N. SERBEIN: *Risk Management: Text and Cases* (2nd ed., Reston, Va.: Reston Publishing Company, 1983).

HEAD, GEORGE L. (ed.): *Essentials of Risk Control* (Malvern, Pa.: Insurance Institute of America, 1986).

HEINRICH, H. W.: *Industrial Accident Prevention* (4th ed., New York: McGraw-Hill Book Company, 1959).

MACDONALD, DONALD L.: *Corporate Risk Control* (New York: The Ronald Press Company, 1966).

MALECKI, D. S., R. C. HORN, E. A. WIENING, and J. DONALDSON: *Commercial Liability Risk Management and Insurance* (2nd ed., Malvern, Pa.: American Institute for Property and Liability Underwriters, 1986).

MEHR, R. I., and B. A. HEDGES: *Risk Management: Concepts and Applications* (Homewood, Ill.: Richard D. Irwin, Inc., 1974).

MERKHOFER, MILEY W.: *Decision Science and Social Risk Management* (Dordrecht, Holland: D. Reidel Publishing Company, 1987).

PRIMA: "Selected Regulatory Compliance Dates," *Risk Watch* (vol. IX, no. 6, Arlington, Va., June 1993).

RODDA, W. H., J. S. TRIESCHMANN, E. A. WIENING, and B. A. HEDGES: *Commercial Property Risk Management and Insurance* (2nd ed., Malvern, Pa.: American Institute for Property and Liability Underwriters, 1983).

SIMONDS, R. H., and J. W. GRIMALDI: *Safety Management* (3rd ed., Homewood, Ill.: Richard D. Irwin, Inc., 1975).

SNIDER, H. W. (ed.): *Risk Management* (Homewood, Ill.: Richard D. Irwin, Inc., 1964).

WILLIAMS, C. A., Jr., G. L. HEAD, R. C. HORN, and G. W. GLENDENNING: *Principles of Risk Management and Insurance* (2nd ed., Malvern, Pa.: American Institute for Property and Liability Underwriters, 1981).

CHAPTER 9

Risk Financing Techniques I

Learning Objectives

After you have completed this chapter, you should be able to:

1. Explain the distinction between risk control and risk financing and give an example of an area in which the two activities overlap.
2. Explain how an organization's degree of control over a risk affects its willingness to retain the risk.
3. Give examples of contemporaneous, retrospective, and prospective risk financing methods.
4. List four elements required for a transaction to be insurance.
5. Explain the advantages and disadvantages of non-insurance transfer methods.
6. Explain why risk-bearing capacity is essential for retention.
7. Give two examples of services provided by insurers as part of their insurance coverage.
8. Outline the issues to be considered in choosing between retention and transfer.

INTRODUCTION

In most risk management programs, some losses occur in spite of the best risk control efforts. The failure to control all risks means that some measures must be taken to finance losses that occur. This chapter explains the concept of risk financing and discusses major characteristics of techniques that may be employed.

Losses can occur in carefully designed risk management programs, even when the risk manager's objective is to prevent *all* losses. Zero losses as an organizational objective is advocated in a philosophy growing out of the Quality Management movement. The "continuous improvement" approach asserts that continued movement toward zero losses is desirable because intangible benefits of loss prevention (improved public relations, worker satisfaction, and productivity) provide positive incentives that are difficult to incorporate into standard economic analysis. Despite the most vigorous loss prevention efforts, however, some losses still may occur.

For less aggressive loss control programs using standard cost/benefit methods of economic analysis, one would expect losses to occur. Driving losses to zero through vigorous loss control efforts, even if possible, may not be justified using standard cost/benefit analysis. At some point, the marginal cost of increasing loss prevention activities may exceed the marginal benefits of risk reduction. Beyond this point, loss prevention simply costs too much.

The philosophical perspective presented under the continuous improvement approach is distinct from the perspective of standard cost/benefit analysis. However, proponents of either approach concede that losses can occur despite vigorous prevention efforts. As a consequence, either point of view is harmonious with the discussion of risk financing in this chapter. Standard economic analysis allows some losses to occur because they are too expensive to prevent; when they occur, they must be financed. The quality improvement view also recognizes that some losses may be impossible to prevent using available technology, and these intractable losses must be financed.

Risk financing is a passive activity when compared with risk control. Whereas risk control is proactive, seeking to reduce the loss-producing aspects of an activity or property, risk financing techniques are reactive in the sense that they are activated only after a loss occurs. This is not to say that risk financing strategies and activities are unplanned. The risk assessment process plays an important role in helping the risk manager plan and implement a rational risk financing program. However, losses must occur before the financing mechanism comes into play.

From a slightly different perspective, risk financing can be summarized in the answer to the question "Who pays?" Whether by conscious design or by default, risk financing always occurs; someone always bears the financial consequences of losses. When the damage is great enough to cause the organization to default on its debt payments, for example, holders of the organization's debt bear the consequences. Few readers would consider default as a mark of a carefully planned risk management strategy, so little will be said concerning the possibility of default except to note its existence. However, the example serves as a reminder that the corporate form of organization is a risk-shifting mechanism; in most cases, the liability of stockholders is limited to the amount of their investment. Beyond the point at which the corporation's stock becomes worthless, the burden of additional losses is transferred to other stakeholders of the corporation.

A point should be made concerning the terminology in this chapter. Risk financing can be defined to encompass financing *risk* as well as financing *losses*. The discussion of risk financing in this chapter does not develop this concept, which raises a difficult analytical issue. Risk imposes significant costs on an organization, only some of which are recognized in the organization's financial reports. Part of the cost of risk is recognized through losses that occur, but other indirect costs occur as a result of uncertainty or less-than-efficient deployment of an organization's resources. In concept, these costs should be recognized and methods for financing these costs should be considered risk financing, yet standard reports rarely consider them. Certainly risk financing includes methods for paying the risk manager's salary or financing loss control measures, yet many reports do not incorporate these costs. However, methods for financing the latter activities are generally unremarkable, and are more appropriate to consider in a course in compensation theory, finance, or other areas of management. Nevertheless, it is important for readers to keep in mind that the impact of risk on an organization often goes well beyond the cost of losses that occur.

This chapter and Chapter 10 discuss organized, planned approaches to providing financial reimbursement for losses. This chapter provides a framework for analyzing the issue of risk financing and discusses general characteristics of risk financing methods. Chapter 10 applies these principles to specific risk financing methods, discusses several recently introduced approaches to risk financing, and outlines advantages and disadvantages of each method.

TYPES OF RISK FINANCING METHODS

Compared with risk control, the classification of risk financing methods is quite simple. Risk financing methods fall into two classes: *Retention* and *transfer.* Retention is an arrangement under which the entity experiencing the loss bears the direct financial consequences. In other words, the entity itself pays for the loss. Transfer is an arrangement under which some entity other than the one experiencing the loss bears the direct financial consequences. In other words, transfer implies that some other entity (such as an insurer) pays for the loss.

The use of the term "transfer" to describe a risk financing arrangement actually is misleading if the risk itself is not shifted. Often, risk financing transfer provides a means of reimbursing the cost of a loss that occurs. For transfer to take place in a literal sense, the risk itself should be shifted to another entity. Such a shift occurs with risk control transfers, which were discussed in the preceding chapter. Because "transfer" is commonly accepted as describing a class of risk financing methods, however, this text will continue to use the term in this sense.

Also, transfers normally imply compensation to the transferee, such as payment of a premium to an insurer. The transferor does not escape the ultimate economic burden of risk through transfer, only the direct and immediate financial consequences of a loss. Even under the risk control transfers discussed in the preceding chapter, one would expect the price of the transaction (e.g., contractual rent in a lease agreement) to reflect risks being transferred through the agreement.

Risk financing methods can be classified according to the time periods from which resources to pay for loss are drawn. If an organization has sufficient operating revenues, the financial burden of loss may be absorbed as a current expense, without any special advance planning. This method often is used by organizations (and individuals) without any awareness that risk management methods are being used. This approach is called *contemporaneous* risk financing.

When the potential loss is large relative to the organization's capacity, formal methods for spreading the cost of losses over more than one budgeting period are likely to appear. When funds are accumulated in advance of loss, the risk financing is *prospective* in that the accumulation anticipates a future loss. A separate trust fund established by a municipality with funds earmarked for payment of future work-related injuries is an example of prospective risk financing. When loss payments are spread across time periods following the occurrence of the claim, risk financing is *retrospective* in that payments reflect past losses. The planned use of borrowing to finance potential losses, with repayments coming from future revenues, is an example of retrospective risk financing. A line of credit used to finance losses is ambiguous with respect to this timing issue if some costs (e.g., commitment fees) are paid in advance of loss.

Clearly, retention may use retrospective, contemporaneous, or prospective risk financing. Perhaps less obviously, transfer can fit into any of these classes as well. The purchase of insurance coverage usually is prospective risk financing in that premium payments are made in advance of loss. However, insurers have adapted to increasing sophistication among buyers of commercial insurance by developing novel risk financing methods that are better described as contemporaneous or, less commonly, retrospective. For example, an insurer may reimburse claims under a program providing health care benefits to a group of employees using an account specifically dedicated by the employer to that purpose. These arrangements, called Administrative Service Only (ASO) programs, are common in health benefit programs provided by large employers. ASO programs, which may be administered by an insurer, are an example of contemporaneous risk financing. Other institutional arrangements for risk financing are described in Chapter 10.

RETENTION

The most common method of handling risk is retention by the organization. The source of the funds is the organization itself, including borrowed funds that the organization must repay. A modified form of retention is retention by a group to which the organization belongs, in which case the source of the funds is the group. This modified approach is examined in this chapter. Retention may be passive or active, unconscious or conscious, unplanned or planned.

Retention is *passive* or *unplanned* when the risk manager is not aware that the exposure exists and consequently does not attempt to handle it. By default, therefore, the organization has elected to retain the risk associated with that exposure. Few, if any, organizations have identified *all* their exposures to property, liability, and human resource losses. Consequently, some unplanned retention is commonplace and perhaps inevitable. For some organizations, the task of risk identification has been so poorly performed that far too much risk is being passively retained. A related form of unplanned retention occurs when the risk manager has properly recognized the exposures but has underestimated the magnitude of the potential losses. Liability exposures exemplify the type of potential loss that is often underestimated.

Retention is *active* or *planned* when the risk manager considers other methods of handling the risk and consciously decides not to transfer the potential losses.

Unplanned retention may, by chance, be the best approach to a particular exposure, but it is never a rational way of handling the matter. Whether active or planned retention is rational or irrational depends upon the circumstances surrounding the decision to retain the risk. Sometimes risks are retained that most persons would agree should not be retained, whereas other risks are not retained when they should be. For example, some businesses retain the risk of being sued on account of a product liability exposure when a transfer of this risk is possible and highly desirable. Other firms transfer the risk associated with small losses when these losses could rather easily be retained.

Self-insurance is a special case of active or planned retention. It is distinguished from the other type of retention usually referred to as *noninsurance* in that the organization has a large number of exposure units. Self-insurance is *not* insurance, because there is no transfer of the risk to an outsider. Self-insurers and insurers, however, share the ability, though in different degrees, to predict their future loss experience. Some writers would not consider a retention program to be self-insurance unless earmarked funds are accumulated in advance of any losses. Others discourage the use of the term because the organization does not transfer the risk.

Funding Arrangements

Formal funding arrangements for retention plans range from simply making no provision for advance funding to more sophisticated techniques, such as captive insurers and risk retention groups. Basic approaches are discussed in this section, with discussion of more sophisticated methods in Chapter 10.

No Advance Funding. Many decisions to retain property and liability losses do not involve any formal advance funding. The organization simply bears the losses when they occur. This approach cuts administrative detail to a minimum; but if the losses fluctuate widely from year to year, the organization may have to sell property on unfavorable terms in order to develop the cash required to meet the losses. Major losses are seldom financed through borrowing, partly because creditors consider retention of such large losses to be financial mismanagement. As a result, they either refuse to grant such credit or demand high interest rates. (Minor losses may be covered by borrowing, usually arranged in advance. The extra cost includes the charge for holding open the credit and the interest on any funds borrowed.) Another disadvantage of no advance funding is that the organization's operating statements can be unduly influenced by chance results.

Liability or Earmarked Accounts. A risk manager for a self-funding entity who is concerned about possible impacts of uninsured losses on the entity's financial reports might be tempted to create a liability account to absorb fluctuations in uncovered losses. Each year a provision for loss would be added to the account, with profits or other financial gains reduced by the same amount. When an uninsured loss occurs, its amount is deducted from the account rather than being deducted from the entity's profit. This procedure would smooth the reported effects of uninsured losses over time by deducting an estimate of the expected value of losses from profit each year rather than deducting the full value of a loss when it occurs. Technically, this earmarked account is not a funding method because it does not provide resources to finance losses. It is a bookkeeping method to account for the cost of losses.

Accountants are reluctant to allow earmarked liability accounts because they imply a level of financial certitude that is unrealistic for most self-funding organizations. In most real-world settings, insufficient statistical information is available to justify an automatic allocation to reflect anticipated losses. Instead, financial accounting standards require that losses be recorded when they are "probable and reasonably estimable." This requirement appears in the Financial Accounting Standards Board Statement No. 5 (FASB-5) and the Government Accounting Standards Board Statement No. 10 (GASB-10).

Both FASB-5 and GASB-10 promulgate a reporting standard that requires an entity to reflect and annotate "incurred losses" when they are deemed to be probable and can be reasonably estimated. "Requires" is a slight overstatement, for neither FASB nor GASB has enforcement authority to mandate the practice, but their statements do have teeth because certified public accountants cannot issue a clean audit if recommended practices are not followed.

"Incurred losses" are losses arising as a result of activity that has occurred during the reporting period and for which enough information is available to make a reasonable estimate of their amounts. The losses may not have been reported, however, and may not be paid for some time. Earlier, Chapter 4 discussed methods for projecting claim estimates using historical data on loss development. When sufficient information is present to determine that a loss has occurred and to make a reasonable estimate of its amount, public financial statements should reflect the full extent of the loss.

The expectation created by FASB-5 and GASB-10 differs from the creation of liability accounts as these reporting standards require the recognition of an uninsured loss when sufficient information is present to determine that a loss has occurred and to reasonably estimate its amount. In contrast, the amount credited to a liability account anticipates the eventual occurrence of a loss in the absence of sufficient information to ascertain its timing and amount. Such liability accounts are not a permitted accounting practice.

Earmarked Asset Accounts. An organization may hold cash or investments that can easily be turned into cash for the purpose of paying uninsured losses. This approach could be used when uninsured losses could possibly exceed the cash available for emergencies and the amount the organization could borrow. For example, a risk manager for a municipality could hold a trust fund account to pay for losses and avoid the necessity of seeking a temporary tax increase or additional borrowing authority when losses occur. A disadvantage of the earmarked asset account is the possibly low return on assets held as cash or near-cash when investing them elsewhere, especially within the organization, provides a higher return.

Captive Insurers. A captive insurer is an insurer that is owned by the insured. The parent organization establishes a captive insurance subsidiary that writes insurance against the parent's insured risks. Many of these captive insurance subsidiaries are domiciled in offshore islands such as Bermuda or the Cayman Islands. These captive insurers may write insurance for other parties that are not affiliated with the parent and also may be active in reinsurance markets (reinsurance is coverage written between insurers rather than with ultimate consumers of insurance).

The existence of captive insurers may seem puzzling to many readers. Because the insurer and insured are part of the same organization, the transfer of risk would not appear to be a motive when the captive writes coverage for the parent company's risk. However, benefits other than risk transfer may arise from insurance transactions, or insurance may be required as a result of regulation. Diallo and Kim (1989) argue that a captive insurer provides the parent company with access to these advantages or a means of satisfying the regulation, but without other disadvantages arising from insurance transactions with unaffiliated parties. In particular, costs related to possible moral hazards and adverse selection are not a problem in a transaction between the parent and the captive, for they both are part of the same organization.

The use of captive insurers is widespread, with thousands of them being organized since 1970. Considerations prompting the formation of captives and other issues related to their development are discussed in Chapter 10.

INSURANCE TRANSFERS

Insurance is an important part of risk management programs for organizations as well as individuals. Insurance is a risk financing transfer under which an insurer agrees to accept financial burdens arising from loss. More formally, insurance can be defined as a contractual agreement between two parties: the insurer and the insured. Under the agreement, the insurer agrees to reimburse "loss" (as defined in the insurance contract) in return for the insured's premium payment.

Elements of an Insurance Transaction

This definition of insurance focuses on the economic substance of the transaction, not necessarily legal implications. Four elements are required for an insurance transaction under this definition: (1) a contractual agreement, (2) a premium payment (or a promise to pay) by the insured, (3) a benefit payment conditioned on circumstances (usually of misfortune) defined in the insurance contract, and (4) the presence of a pool of resources held by the insurer to reimburse claims. Normally, premium payments accumulated from insureds constitute the pool of resources, although premium payments are not required for a transaction to be considered insurance. For example, a pure assessment mutual is a not-for-profit insurer that provides insurance to subscribers in return for their agreeing to be subject to assessments when losses occur. In the pure assessment mutual, the pool of resources is the collective promises of subscribers to provide funds in the event of assessment.

The *pool of resources* is a key element in this definition. Without the pool of resources, the transaction has no effect on economic performance, which is the substance of an insurance transaction. An obvious example would be an agreement to reimburse loss written by an entity that is known to be bankrupt. The agreement has no economic substance because the financial burden falling on the holder of the agreement in the event of loss is the same as it would be in the absence of the agreement. Also, an entity cannot insure itself; coverage provided by captive insurers do not fit this definition of insurance unless entities other than the insured provide resources that are subject to claims of the owner-insured.

Pooling of Resources Contrasted with Pooling of Risk

Some authors hold the pooling of risks to be a requirement for an insurance transaction. This "pooling of risk" requirement is based on a misinterpretation of the *law of large numbers*. As it would apply to a pool of insured risks, the law of large numbers asserts that the average loss *per insured unit* tends to fall close to the true expected loss—as the number of identical, independent insured risks becomes large. For example, if each insured pays a premium that exceeds the expected value of the loss, an increase in the number of insureds participating in the pool increases the probability that the pool will be able to pay all claims. Eventually, as the pool's size increases to very large numbers, the full reimbursement of all claims becomes a virtual certainty. The examples and problems presented earlier in Chapter 4 illustrate the central limit theorem, which is one version of a law of large numbers.

However, the "pooling of risk" concept fails to explain why the pool is able to provide a stronger guaranty as it becomes larger. The stronger guaranty is due to the pooling of resources, not the pooling of risks. In other words, the strengthening of the guaranty is not due to any tendency of independent risks to cancel each other. The "pooling of risk" explanation misinterprets the law of large numbers because it fails to distinguish between pooling of risks and pooling of resources. Smith and Kane (1993) show that the strengthening is driven by the pooling of contributions, not the pooling of risks. When each insured contributes a premium payment that exceeds the expected value of its insured loss, the pooling of resources eventually overwhelms the tendency of independently, identically distributed losses to deviate from their expected value.

Figure 9.1 demonstrates the effect of pooling in a way that allows the effects of "risk pooling" and "resource pooling" to be distinguished. Figure 9.1 shows the effect of pool size on the probability of failure (i.e., the probability that the pool's resources are not sufficient to pay all claims). The assumptions used to develop Figure 9.1 are: (1) each unit independently faces a possible loss of $100,000 whose probability of occurrence is 0.02; (2) each unit in the pool contributes a premium of $5000, which is 2.5 times the expected loss of $(0.02)($100,000) = 2000; and (3) the pool's initial capital is $100,000.

As shown in Figure 9.1, the probability of failure is zero with only one unit exposed to loss. Because the pool's initial capital is $100,000, the pool cannot fail with only one participant because the pool's resources are sufficient to guaranty performance. In fact, adding a second unit to the pool *increases* the probability of failure, which occurs if both units suffer a loss. As shown in Figure 9.1, adding additional units continues to increase the probability of failure until the

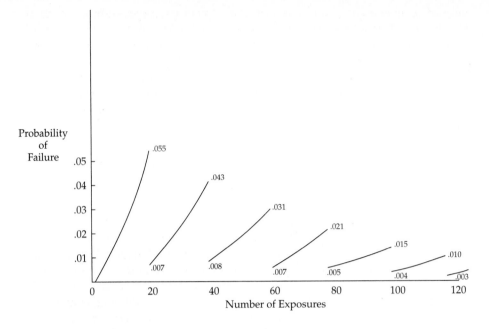

Assumptions:
$100,000 loss
.02 Probability of loss
$5000 Premium per exposure
$100,000 Initial capital

FIGURE 9.1. Pooling of exposures and probability of failure.

resources accumulated from the additional units are sufficient to absorb an additional loss. The accumulation of additional resources explains the discontinuities in Figure 9.1 at multiples of 20 units. Each time an additional 20 units are added, the resources accumulated from these units [(20)($5000) = $100,000] allow the pool to absorb an additional loss, and the probability of failure drops. Between these points of discontinuity, the entry of an additional unit *increases* the probability of failure. Eventually, the effect of adding additional resources tends to overwhelm the effect of adding a new risk to the pool, and the probability of failure drops to an arbitrarily low value as the number of pool participants becomes very large.

The effect of contributing new resources eventually overwhelms the tendency of adding a new risk to increase the probability of failure. By increasing the number of units in the pool, the probability of failure can be brought arbitrarily close to zero. However, Figure 9.1 shows the probability of failure *is* zero with only a single unit. The $100,000 initial capital provides the guaranty of performance with only a single unit. No matter how many units are added to the pool beyond the first unit, the probability of failure never *reaches* zero, instead only coming arbitrarily close.

The distinction between pooling of resources and pooling of risk clarifies our reason for requiring a pool of resources for an insurance transaction. To be insurance, a transaction must subject resources to possible claims. Clearly, a very wealthy individual could insure a single risk faced by another individual, an agreement that does not require any pooling of risk. As long as the resources of the wealthy individual are sufficient to ensure financial performance in the event of loss, the transaction meets the test implied in the above definition without involving any pooling of risk. In a pooling agreement in which each insured contributes a premium payment in excess of the expected value of the loss, the pooled resources are subject to claims of each insured.

Pooling Agreements and Combination

A pooling agreement can take the form of an agreement to share losses that occur among pool participants. For example, a group of municipalities may agree to share liability exposures arising from police and fire protection activities through a pooling agreement. Under the pooling agreement, the financial impact of the liability exposure tends to become more predictable *per municipality* as compared with its impact in the absence of the pooling agreement. Pooling of risk exposures also is called *combination,* which refers to the combining or pooling of losses arising from a large number of exposures. As a result of combination, the loss *per unit* tends to become more predictable. In a vehicle fleet in which damage to individual vehicles is pooled across the entire fleet, combination occurs when the fleet increases in size; accidental damage *per vehicle* in the fleet tends to become more predictable as the number of vehicles becomes large.

Most risk management texts, including previous editions of this text, consider pooling and combination as risk *control* methods because losses become more predictable. However, the preceding discussion of insurance transactions implies that most cases of pooling and combination are risk *financing,* not risk control. As the number of units in a pool increases, losses tend to become more predictable *relative to the number of units in the pool,* but not in absolute terms. The number of units in the pool serves as a proxy for the pool's risk-bearing capacity, and the pooling of this capacity eventually dominates the tendency of losses to deviate from their expected value. In most cases, a pool's risk-bearing capacity consists of financial resources, and the pooling of these resources is risk financing. Even when the pooling arrangement takes the form of a right to assess participants, the method should be classified as risk financing.

A possible ambiguity arises when a pooling agreement involves nonfinancial resources. For example, a group of electrical utilities could develop a crisis management team comprised of a variety of specialists identified within each participating utility. The objective of the team is crisis containment and damage mitigation, which clearly are loss control. Yet the team represents pooled resources; the act of pooling tends to result in the level of the team members' activity being more predictable than if each utility has its own team. Ultimately, the increased predictability translates into financial consequences. The observation that each utility's share of the cost is more predictable than the cost of each utility maintaining its own team suggests that the pooling of experts is risk financing.

This example only illustrates a weakness of the risk financing/risk control dichotomy; some practices may not fit clearly into either class. And as a practical issue, the failure of the classification system to unambiguously label the pooling of expertise should have no effect on a risk manager's willingness to evaluate the merits of the pooling arrangement and to adopt the practice.

NONINSURANCE RISK FINANCING TRANSFERS

Chapter 8 indicated that transfers could be risk control measures or risk financing measures. Risk control transfers (1) shift the property or activity itself to someone else, (2) eliminate or reduce the transferor's responsibility for losses to the transferee, or (3) cancel obligations that the transferor has assumed for losses to others. Risk financing transfers, in contrast, provide external funds that will pay for the losses that do occur. This section deals with noninsurance risk financing transfers. These noninsurance transfers differ from insurance in that the transferees are not legally insurers.

Most noninsurance risk financing transfers are accomplished through provisions in contracts dealing primarily with other matters, but some are achieved through contracts designed specifically for this purpose. Many of these contractual arrangements transfer financial responsibility for direct property losses or loss of income; some deal with human resource losses; most transfer financial responsibility for liabilities to third parties. The transfers differ as to the extent of responsibility shifted. At one extreme, the transferor shifts only his or her financial responsibility (vicarious liability) for the negligent acts of the transferee. At the other extreme, the transferor is to be indemnified for the types of losses covered under the contract no matter who (the transferee, some third party, or an act of God) caused the loss.

Some Examples

A few examples will suffice to illustrate the nature of these contracts. Under one lease, a landlord may be able to transfer to a tenant financial responsibility for damage to the rented property and bodily injuries to third parties that would in the absence of the lease be borne by the landlord. Under a second lease the tenant may be able to shift to the landlord financial responsibility for damage to the tenant's furniture caused by fire, no matter who was at fault. Under a construction contract the owner may be able to shift to the contractor some or all of his or her responsibility for injuries to the public occurring on the premises. A business shipping parcels by air, storing equipment in a warehouse, or sending its material to some other firm for further processing may through a special contract obligate the bailee to pay for losses in excess of its statutory or common law liability. A retailer may insist on a hold-harmless provision in its purchase contracts under which the manufacturer agrees to indemnify the retailer for any liability sustained because of defective products unless that defect was caused solely by the retailer's negligence.

HEDGING OR NEUTRALIZATION

As generic terms, hedging and neutralization describe actions whereby a possible gain is balanced against a possible loss. Hedging or neutralization of an existing risk uses a bet whose outcomes are opposite in sign to the outcomes of the existing risk. In this generic sense, an insurance policy could be considered a hedge against loss, but this use of the term would be overly broad and misleading. A more specific example of neutralization is an individual who has bet one way on the outcome of a sporting event neutralizing the risk by betting the other way as well.

In business, formal hedging often is used to offset the risk of fluctuation in raw materials prices or in foreign currency exchange rates. When a manufacturer enters a contractual agreement to sell a finished product at a fixed price in a foreign currency, it faces the risk of variation in the rate of exchange between currencies in the country where the product is sold and the country where the manufacturer is domiciled. Futures contracts offer one way to hedge this risk. A futures contract is a contract to deliver a fixed amount of the foreign currency at some point in the future, say six months. The contract is traded in a futures market at a price that depends on traders' assessments of future exchange rates between the foreign currency and other currencies.

A U.S. manufacturer of agricultural machinery, for example, may agree to deliver 1,000 tractors to a French distributor in six months at an agreed price of 165,000 French francs per tractor. If the current exchange rate between U.S. and French currencies is 5.5 French francs per U.S. dollar, the French selling price of each tractor translates into US$30,000 in current terms. The total amount of the transaction in current U.S. dollars is $30 million, or 165 million francs. If manufacturing and shipping costs are $28,000 per tractor, the manufacturer hopes to clear a profit of $2000 on each tractor. However, the actual profit of the manufacturer on the transaction depends on the exchange rate between French and U.S. currencies at the time the transaction is consummated, which is six months from now. If the value of the French franc rises relative to the U.S. dollar, the manufacturer's profit in U.S. dollars increases. If the value of the French franc declines relative to the U.S. dollar, the manufacturer's profit decreases.

One way that the manufacturer could hedge the risk of foreign currency fluctuation is to sell 165 million French francs at the current (or *spot*) rate of 5.5 francs per dollar. Such hedging action action could be called a *short hedge* or *short sale* because the manufacturer does not actually own the francs that are being sold. Instead, the manufacturer could borrow the francs from the inventory of a dealer in foreign currencies, promising to replace the borrowed francs using the proceeds from the sale of the tractors. The borrowed francs are currently sold in the foreign exchange market for US$30 million, locking in the manufacturer's eventual profit on the transaction.

Although hedging through the short sale described above could offer a method of neutralizing the foreign exchange risk, in practice the neutralization is more likely to take place with the use of *futures* contracts. As applied to currency markets, a futures contract is a promise to deliver a specified quantity of a stated currency at the end of a given time interval. The futures contracts are traded on organized exchanges, so the futures contract can be sold any time prior to expiration. The opportunity to sell on the exchange means that the owner of the contract is not required to make actual delivery of the currency. Instead, the contract is sold at the time the hedged transaction occurs.

The manufacturer already owns the tractor buyer's promise to deliver 165 million French francs in six months. If the manufacturer does not want to bear the foreign currency exchange risk from owning this promise, it can offset the foreign currency risk by directing a dealer in foreign currencies to sell a futures contract obligating the manufacturer to deliver 165 million French francs in six months. At the time payment is received for the tractors, the manufacturer buys back the futures contract. Any gain or loss on the tractor sale arising from changes in the foreign currency exchange rate is offset by a corresponding loss or gain on the futures contract.

The use of the futures contracts does not involve the inconvenience of dealing in large amounts of the foreign currencies themselves. It is easy to see how the futures transaction has hedged the manufacturer's exposure to the foreign currency exchange risk. If the value of the French franc drops to 6.0 francs per U.S. dollar (a drop in the franc's value means that each dollar buys more francs), the manufacturer's profit on the tractor sale declines. Due to the drop, the 165,000 French francs per tractor now convert to US$27,500, which is $500 less than the US$28,000 manufacturing cost. However, the loss on the sale of the tractors is offset by the gain on the futures transaction. When the value of the French franc declines to 6.0 francs per U.S. dollar, the dollar value of the futures contract also declines. The manufacturer holds a short position (i.e., has sold a futures contract), so a decline in the value of the futures contract means that the contract can be repurchased for less than it was sold. As a result, the gain on the futures transaction offsets the loss on the tractor sale. Similarly, a gain in the value of the French franc to 5.0 per U.S. dollar translates into an increased profit on the tractor sale, but offset by a loss on the futures transaction.

Hedging is risk management in a generic sense of the term. The earlier discussion in Chapter 2 of "financial risk management" implies that hedging is the generic mechanism that underlies virtually all of the instruments identified in that chapter, such as swaps, options, futures, and forward contracts. In concept, all of these risk financing mechanisms involve the acquisition of an asset whose return is negatively correlated with a currently held (or "underlying") asset. One who uses the term in this sense might describe the purchase of insurance as hedging, although this usage of the term is misleading. In general, hedging and neutralization are not available as risk financing options for most of the risks discussed in this text. Further information on hedging through futures, options, and forward contracts is available in modern finance texts such as Brealey and Myers (1991) or Chance (1989).

As a risk financing option, hedging more closely resembles insurance than retention. However, retention can be applied to any risk, at least in concept. Hedging and insurance tend to be used for different types of risk. Hedging generally is used to offset the risk of price movements, which is speculative in nature. Insurance generally is used to offset pure risk. Hedging is not insurance in the generally-accepted sense of the term. A hedging contract would not reimburse the owner of 1000 tractors for their loss at sea from the sinking of the vessel being used to deliver them to France, for example, while an insurance contract could. Hedging tends to be used for risk exposures arising from fluctuation in market prices rather than from physical damage. Presumably, market prices are beyond the control of the holder of the futures contract. Insurance tends to be used on risks involving physical damage or legal liability for damage, which often are partly under the insured's control.

The foreign currency exchange risk used as an example above illustrates this distinction because the tractor manufacturer's actions would not be expected to affect the U.S. dollar–French franc exchange rate; the risk is beyond the control of the manufacturer. However, a risk manager's loss prevention programs can have a dramatic effect on an organization's losses. In other respects, hedging and insurance have more in common than hedging and retention, although hedging and insurance have noticeable differences. Normally, the identity of the holder of a futures contract is immaterial to traders in the futures market, while the identity of the insured nearly always is a material consideration to the provider of insurance, often being the most important consideration.

CONSIDERATIONS AFFECTING CHOICE BETWEEN RETENTION AND TRANSFER

One would expect long-run advantages for organizations that replace insurance purchases with carefully planned retention programs. The nature of these advantages and the conditions required for them to develop are presented below. The discussion of advantages and disadvantages presumes sufficient *capacity for bearing loss,* which is an essential requirement for retention. This capacity must be sufficient to bear the maximum probable cost (MPC) associated with the risk, or retention becomes unwise (see Chapters 3 and 4 for a discussion of MPC). Without the required capacity, a risk manager is forced to seek alternatives other than retention. Although the point seems obvious, it can easily be forgotten if a risk manager focuses too closely on benefits expected in the long run.

The term "capacity" is used in a generic sense to denote physical, human and financial resources to offset or mitigate damage. At this point, risk control and risk financing overlap. As an example, the risk manager of an electrical utility may recognize that the corporate headquarters has individuals with the required skills to manage physical crises arising within the utility's distribution network. In the absence of an internally organized team, financial resources would be required to secure the needed repair services from suppliers outside the utility. In general, one would expect an internally organized team's familiarity with the utility's system, combined with their own specialized areas of training, to result in the team approach being superior to using resources outside the organization.

Although the risk management department usually operates within a budget, there is no particular reason that the evaluation of loss-bearing capacity needs to be in the context of a single budget period. A risk manager for a municipality may be able to create a separate trust fund to pay work-related injury claims, building the fund through regular contributions over several years. As this fund accumulates, retention levels in the workers' compensation coverage can be increased to levels that are commensurate with the capacity of the fund. The buffer created by this fund reduces the likelihood that an unexpected disaster would necessitate an extra allocation or an increase in municipal taxes. This example illustrates the importance of support and cooperation from higher levels of management, without which the fund is unlikely to exist or may fall prey to other needs within the municipality.

Legal, Economic, and Public Policy Limitations

Important limitations apply to transfers of risk, especially non-insurance transfers. First, the contract may transfer only part of the risk that the organization thought it had shifted to someone else. The risk manager should study the contract language carefully to determine its impact. Second, the language is often so complicated that legal action may be required for its meaning to become apparent. Third, because the courts are reluctant to change statutory and common law, they tend to interpret transfer provisions narrowly if given an opportunity. Broad shifts of responsibility are sometimes declared invalid because they violate public policy or are grossly unfair to the transferee. Fourth, because the contract provisions vary so widely, there are few precedents one can consult to determine how the courts will interpret a particular provision. Fifth, if the transferee is unable to pay the losses transferred, the transferor must pay the loss it thought it had shifted to someone else. Finally, the transferee, who now has the major incentive for loss control, may lack the expertise or authority for effective control.

Degree of Control

The organization's control over the risk has a strong effect on the attractiveness of retention programs. The larger the degree of control, the more attractive retention becomes relative to insurance. The reason for this conclusion becomes apparent by considering the moral hazard, which was discussed in Chapter 1. Insurance weakens incentives to prevent or reduce loss, because losses are compensated. The weakened incentives tend to increase losses beyond the levels that would prevail if the incentives were maintained. As a consequence, the premium for the insurance coverage is higher than would be the case if some mechanism for maintaining the loss-prevention incentives were present. The greater the degree of the insured's control over losses, the stronger this effect. The result of this effect is to increase the cost of insurance relative to retaining the loss.

Insurers are aware of this problem, of course, and continually search for ways to maintain loss-prevention and loss-mitigation incentives in their insurance coverages. Deductibles are one way of maintaining these incentives, as are other methods for returning part of the financial burden of loss to insureds. To the extent that these methods fail to restore the level of loss-prevention that would prevail in the absence of insurance, the cost of insurance is increased relative to retention. In general, retention increases the incentives of the organization to establish and maintain loss-prevention and loss-mitigation activities, for it is through retention that the organization reaps the fruits of these activities.

From a public policy view, society benefits when the burden of loss falls on the party best equipped to control loss-producing events. This principle would be reflected in transactions between informed parties in free markets. One would expect the price at which a transaction occurs to reflect any risks being transferred, which implies that the transaction most favorable to the parties involved is one in which the burden of loss falls on the party in the best position to manage the risk. Heimer (1985) attributes many insurance policy provisions to this principle: a rational allocation of the burden of loss. For example, insurance on cargoes being transported by sea have used a provision holding the insured party responsible for minor amounts of damage while providing full reimbursement for substantial damage. Heimer reasons that this provision was designed to maintain the insured's incentives for care in packing and stowage of the cargo, activities under the insured's control. Lack of care in these activities would be expected to lead to only minor damage, while major damage would more likely be the result of events beyond the control of the insured.

Insurance Loading Fees

The term "insurance loading fees" means the amount by which the premium for insurance coverage exceeds the expected value of loss reimbursements. These fees are an extra payment for insurance relative to the cost of retention; a payment over and above the amount the insured expects to receive in loss reimbursements. Holding other factors constant, higher loading fees increase the attractiveness of retention.

The loading charged by the insurer varies among lines, among insurers, and among insureds. For instance, in many property and liability insurance lines, the average ratio is 30 to 40 percent of the premiums charged. Life and health insurance written in connection with employee benefit plans usually has loading fees under 10 percent. Different insurers charge different loadings because they do not all render the same services or operate with the same efficiency. Large insureds are commonly charged a lower-percentage loading than small insureds because in their pricing insurers usually recognize that their expenses do not increase proportionately with the size of the insured.

Value of Services Provided by Insurers

The entire amount of insurance loading fees is not necessarily wasted money. In many instances, loading fees are used to provide services to insureds that they must provide themselves in the absence of insurance.

Loss adjustment and loss-control services provide the clearest illustration of this consumer benefit in property and liability insurance, but risk analysis services provided by the agent and the insurer must also be considered. If an employer self-insures a pension plan, it will probably have to engage a bank or trust company to invest the monies in the pension fund, and a consulting actuary to determine how much money should be placed in the fund each year. In most instances, the employer will save some, but not all, of the money that would be paid to an insurer to cover its loading; but in some instances the expenses would be higher. Insurers have the advantage that they can spread overhead costs over many insureds. They also may be able to service widespread operations more efficiently. Offsetting to some extent the loss of services provided by the insurer are the time and effort the risk manager would otherwise spend selecting the insurer, negotiating with the insurer the terms of the insurance contract and the price to be charged, and filing a proof of loss with the insurer.

Quality of Services. Some organizations believe that many of the services provided by insurers can be better performed internally or by some servicing agency. For example, some risk managers argue that if the organization pays its own claims, it will pay them more promptly and more equitably. They believe that the organization's own staff will resist unjustifiable claims that many insurers would pay. In addition, some managers are of the opinion that the organization gets more public relations value out of paying its own claims.

In response, insurers argue that organizations who settle their own claims tend to be less efficient and less effective because they lack experience. They also tend to be too lenient, especially with claims involving employees. This is particularly true if the organization has many small, widely dispersed locations and as a result must assign this responsibility on a part-time basis to someone at each location. The public relations value an organization obtains from settling its own claims may also be overestimated. In fact, dissatisfied claimants who may have been content to blame an insurer must now blame the organization itself.

Supporters of retention reply that if these counterarguments are correct, an experienced independent servicing firm can be hired to adjust the losses under a retention program.

The relative quality of the loss-control and general-administration services under a retention program and an insured program is another bone of contention. Supporters of both retention and insurance claim superiority on this score. Insurers claim the advantage of experience gained by working with many organizations over a long period of time; some can also claim the benefit of research staffs that are capable of studying specific problems. Yet the organization's own staff know the organization better, can concentrate on the organization's problems, and may receive more cooperation from other employees than would an outsider. In certain lines, such as boiler and machinery insurance, the insurer does provide important, highly specialized inspection services; in other lines, the organization's employees may be the experts. With respect to some losses, such as dishonest acts by employees, the mere involvement of an insurer who is not so likely to be sympathetic with a dishonest employee may reduce the chance of loss.

One of the main advantages claimed for retention is that the organization itself is more highly motivated to control losses when it will bear these losses itself.

In pension plans, a key consideration is the investment performance of the pension fund. Consequently the plan provider will want to compare carefully the investment advice and services available from insurers and from banks and trust companies that might service a self-insured plan.

In recent years, many insurers have "unbundled" their services. For example, if an organization decides to retain some property or liability exposure, it may be able to purchase from the insurer, say, its loss-control and claims-adjustment services. An organization with a self-insured pension plan may purchase administrative and investment services from an insurer.

Opportunity Costs

When the purchase of insurance involves a premium payment at the time the policy is issued, an evaluation of insuring the risk vis-à-vis retention should consider the investment income that could be earned during the time between payment of the insurance premium and ultimate payment of the claim. If a $100,000 premium is required to insure a given risk whose ultimate cost is estimated to be $100,000, the issue of investment income breaks the apparent tie in favor of retention. Investment income reduces the cost of a given claim; usually this issue is evaluated by comparing the present value of retention costs to the present value of insuring the risk.

In the absence of market restrictions or institutional constraints, one would not expect the opportunity set of investments to differ between insurers and organizations that might retain risk. Also, one would expect insurance premiums to reflect anticipated investment income. When insurers and insureds face identical opportunity sets and insurance premiums fully reflect anticipated investment income, the opportunity cost of using insurance is zero. Evaluation of possible opportunity costs would be based on a belief that the opportunity set of investments for insureds is not identical to the set for insurers, or the belief that the premium for insurance does not fully reflect expected investment income.

Tax Considerations

In general, insurance companies tend to receive favorable tax treatment relative to consumers of insurance. As a consequence, an insurer's cost of financing a given risk often is lower than the cost of the insured organization financing the risk itself. For liability insurance when a long time lag is expected between payment of the premium and payment of the insured claim, the favorable tax treatment arises primarily from rules allowing insurers to deduct from current taxable income their provision for future claim payment. An organization that pays these claims using its own funds, in contrast, cannot deduct payments from taxable income until "economic performance" occurs, which in most cases means actual payment of the claim. In other words, insurance companies are allowed to deduct a provision for loss at an earlier date than organizations that retain the risk and pay losses from their own funds.

Holding other factors constant, this tax-induced effect places insurers at the greatest advantage relative to heavily-taxed organizations, but the relative advantage declines when insurers are compared with organizations that are taxed lightly or not at all. The tax-induced effect is lowest when an insurer is compared with an untaxed entity, such as a nonprofit hospital or a municipality.

A full discussion of tax effects related to insurance is beyond the intended scope of this chapter and even of this text. Conclusions related to tax-induced effects are specific to the type of claim reimbursed by the financing method and the type of organization against whom the claim might be filed. For a tax-exempt organization, the issue of deductibility is irrelevant as long as the tax-exempt character of the organization's activities is maintained.

For example, a business corporation is allowed to deduct uninsured losses to property from its taxable income, but the deduction is limited to the book value of asset. If an asset has been fully depreciated on the corporation's books, no deduction is allowed if the asset is completely destroyed. However, the cost of fire insurance to finance the replacement of this asset if lost by fire normally would be deductible as a business expense.

As another example, employers who turn over funds to a bank or a trust company in connection with a properly structured self-insured employee benefit plan can deduct these contributions at the time they are made. Further, investment returns to the fund are not taxable income to the employer as long as the fund is used in connection with this employee benefit plan.

Whether these tax-related effects would reverse a choice of risk financing methods based on considerations such as legal limitations and the degree of control over loss is doubtful. When tax-related effects are believed to be important, experts in tax accounting and tax law may be consulted to evaluate appropriate methods for risk financing.

Retention May Be the Only Possible Method

In some cases, retention is the only possible (or at least the only feasible) tool. The organization cannot prevent the loss, avoidance is impossible (or clearly undesirable), and no transfer possibilities (including insurance) exist. Consequently, the organization has no choice. It *must* retain the risk. For example, an organization with a plant located in a river valley may find that no other method of handling the flood risk is feasible. Abandonment and loss control would be too costly, and in this particular area flood insurance is not available.

In many more instances, part, but not all, of the potential loss can be controlled or financed externally. For example, an organization may be able to purchase some flood insurance on a plant located in a river valley, but the insurance contract may exclude certain events and the insurer may limit its responsibility to some fraction of the possible losses. Sometimes insurance is not available unless the insured agrees to absorb the first part, say $50,000, of any loss. If these uninsured losses cannot be completely controlled or transferred elsewhere, the organization will be forced to retain them.

Summary

In summary, the choice between retention and transfer is based on considerations such as:

1. The maximum probable cost relative to the organization's capacity for bearing risk
2. Restrictions or legal limitations applying to risk transfers
3. The organization's degree of control over the risk

4. Loading fees associated with insurance coverages
5. The value of services provided by insurers as part of their insurance coverages
6. Opportunity costs related to investment of funds used to reimburse claims
7. The tax treatment of uninsured and insured losses
8. The availability of alternatives to retention.

Key Concepts

retention A risk financing method in which the entity experiencing a loss bears the financial consequences.

transfer A risk financing method in which some entity other than the one experiencing a loss bears the financial consequences.

planned retention Retention that results from active consideration of possible outcomes and a conscious decision to retain the risk.

retrospective financing A type of risk financing method in which loss payments are spread across time periods following the occurrence of the claim.

concurrent financing A type of risk financing method in which loss payments are absorbed as a current expense.

prospective financing A type of risk financing method in which resources are accumulated in advance of loss to absorb claims when they occur.

noninsurance transfer A risk financing method in which a contract other than insurance is used to transfer responsibility for loss to an entity other than the one experiencing the loss.

captive insurer An insurer that is owned by the insured or the group of insureds. Usually this ownership takes the form of owning the captive insurer's common stock.

hedging A financial transaction in which gains on one contract are used to offset losses on another transaction. Usually hedging involves two bets whose outcomes are opposite in sign.

Review Questions

1. Explain why a $1 million earmarked liability account on an organization's balance sheet has no effect on the organization's risk-bearing capacity.
2. List the four elements of an insurance transaction, explaining why the pool of resource is necessary for the transaction to be insurance. Give an example of a type of insurance in which the pool of resources is not cash or near-cash such as liquid investments.
3. Give two examples of noninsurance transfers.
4. Compare hedging and insurance transactions, listing two ways in which the transactions are similar and two ways in which they differ.
5. Explain how each of the following considerations affects the willingness of an organization to use retention:
   a. The organization's risk-bearing capacity
   b. The probable maximum cost associated with the risk
   c. The risk-bearing capacity of an entity to whom the risk could be transferred
   d. The organization's degree of control over the risk
   e. Loading fees of available insurance
   f. The skill of a liability insurer's legal staff in defending against claims
   g. The tax bracket of the insured organization.

References and Suggestions for Additional Reading

BREALY, RICHARD A., and STEWART C. MYERS: *Principles of Corporate Finance* (New York: McGraw-Hill Book Company, 1991).

CHANCE, DON M.: *An Introduction to Options and Futures* (Chicago: The Dryden Press, 1989).

DIALLO, ALAHASSNE, and SANGPHILL KIM: "Asymmetric Information, Captive Insurer's Formation, and Manager's Welfare Gain," *The Journal of Risk and Insurance* (vol. 56, no. 2, June 1989), pp. 233–251.

Financial Applications for Risk Management Decisions (San Rafael, Ca.: Firemen's Fund Insurance Companies and Risk Sciences Group, Inc., 1983).

GAUNT, L. D., and M. E. MCDONALD: *Examining Employers' Financial Capacity to Self-Insure Under Workmen's Compensation* (Atlanta, Ga.: Georgia State University College of Business Administration, 1977).

HAMMOND, J. D. (ed.): *Essays in the Theory of Risk and Insurance* (Glenview, Ill.: Scott, Foresman and Company, 1968).

HEIMER, CAROL A.: *Reactive Risk and Rational Action* (Berkeley: University of California Press, 1985).

LONG, J. D.: *Ethics, Morality and Insurance* (Bloomington, Ind.: Bureau of Business Research, Indiana University Graduate School of Business, 1971).

MOWBRAY, A. H., R. H. BLANCHARD, and C. A. WILLIAMS, JR.: *Insurance* (6th ed., New York: McGraw-Hill Book Company, 1969), chap. 5.

PFEFFER, IRVING, and D. R. KLOCK: *Perspectives on Insurance* (Englewood Cliffs, N.J.: Prentice-Hall, Inc., 1974), parts I and IV.

SMITH, MICHAEL L., and STEPHEN A. KANE: "The Law of Large Numbers and the Strength of Insurance." In: *Insurance, Risk Management and Public Policy: Essays in Honor of Robert I. Mehr* (Norwell, Massachusetts: Kluwer Academic Publishers, 1993).

WILLETT, A. H.: *The Economic Theory of Risk and Insurance* (Philadelphia: The University of Pennsylvania Press, 1951).

CHAPTER 10

Risk Financing Techniques II

Learning Objectives

After you have completed this chapter, you should be able to:

1. Identify the advantages and disadvantages of a captive insurer as a risk financing method.
2. Distinguish between a single-parent and group or association captives.
3. Explain the difference between insurance pools, risk retention groups, and purchasing groups.
4. Define and explain "risk" or "finite" insurance and distinguish it from conventional insurance products.
5. Characterize the degree of risk transfer in fully insured, minimum premium, and administrative services only insurance contracts.
6. Explain the form and purpose of a consumer cooperative and consumer proprietary insurer.

INTRODUCTION

Chapter 9 classified risk financing methods into two categories: retention and transfer. This two-way classification is based on the party bearing the financial consequences of loss. Under retention, the financial consequences of the loss are borne by the party to whom the loss occurs; under transfer, they are borne by some other party. Most risk financing programs use both types of risk financing, even on a particular risk. Full retention or complete transfer are rare. When insurance is purchased, for example, the insured usually bears some of the financial consequences of loss. Loss-sharing may take place through explicit policy provisions, such as deductibles and internal policy limits, or it may take place through provisions limiting coverage to certain aspects of loss but not to others. It may also occur unintentionally, as when a policyholder fails to pur-

chase adequate amounts of insurance to cover the value of property. Full retention is equally unusual in that a loss frequently becomes transferred at *some*
point. Such transfer can occur as a result of legal limits on liability, through limited liability inherent in the corporate form of organization, or perhaps through
bankruptcy law. Most risk financing programs, then, are a blend of transfer and
retention.

This chapter offers a description of a representative set of risk financing
methods. By focusing on a representative set rather than providing an inventory
of the full array, this chapter provides the background to appreciate the ways
that transfer and retention can be arranged. Risk financing methods are prolif-
erating at a rapid pace, and a complete inventory of available techniques could
be confusing, tedious, and rapidly out-of-date.

THE RISK FINANCING CONTINUUM

Pure retention and complete transfer might be imagined as two ends of a continuum, between which lie a variety of retention/transfer combinations. Some
financing techniques might be essentially retention with just an element of
transfer, while others are just the opposite. Some techniques are "half" retention
and "half" transfer. In many cases, the differences between these combinations
are subtle and may, in fact, be indistinguishable to the untrained eye. These distinctions, however, can be important. Whether a technique is considered "transfer" or "retention" can have important effects, because tax laws, generally accepted accounting principles, and civil law may treat retained losses and
transferred losses very differently.

The following discussion introduces several selected risk financing techniques that fall between full retention and complete transfer. Techniques at or
near the "transfer" end of the continuum include *guaranteed cost insurance, experience-rated plans,* and *retrospectively rated plans.* Techniques that may be found
near the center of the continuum include *consumer proprietaries/cooperatives, "self-
insurance pools," risk retention groups,* and *ASO/stop loss plans,* as well as a special
kind of transfer/retention approach that is manifested through *taxing authority.*
Techniques found at or near the retention end of the continuum are *captive insurance companies,* and *finite* or *risk insurance plans.*

Table 10.1 lists the risk financing methods listed above, in order of increasing levels of retention (methods at the bottom of a list have the highest degree
of retention); and classified by whether an insurer is involved in the technique.
The order of placement in the listing is approximate and should not be considered a strict ranking. The actual degree of transfer or retention in a particular
method depends on its specific provisions. For example, one hospital may use
a $1 million retention on its medical malpractice liability coverage while another
hospital purchases full coverage on the same risk. Both policies may be guaranteed cost insurance, yet the degree of retention differs dramatically between the
two coverages. For many hospitals, the $1 million retention may be tantamount
to full retention.

TABLE 10.1. Risk Financing Methods Classified by Presence of Insurer Involvement and Degree of Retention

FULL TRANSFER

Insurance Coverages	*Noninsurance Pooling and Retention Efforts*
Guaranteed Cost Insurance	Consumer Proprietaries/Cooperatives
Experience Rating	"Self-Insurance" Pools
Retrospective Rating	Group "Self-Insurers"
Paid Loss Retros	Pooling Through Taxing Authority
Minimum Premium (Stop Loss) Plans	Risk Retention Groups
Administrative Service Only Plans	Captive Insurers
Finite Risk Plans	

FULL RETENTION

TRANSFER OR MOSTLY TRANSFER TECHNIQUES

Insurance contracts and insurance pricing are subjects covered in detail in later chapters. For purposes of discussion here, however, a presentation of three generalized methods for pricing insurance illustrates subtle differences in the degree of risk transfer that can occur in insurance contracts.

Guaranteed Cost Insurance

Most organizations transferring risk through an insurance contract are likely to be offered "guaranteed cost insurance." Under guaranteed cost insurance, the insurer agrees to reimburse losses of the policyholder in exchange for a premium that is fixed at the time the contract is signed. The premium may be paid in a lump sum or in increments over the life of the policy.

Guaranteed cost insurance premiums are based upon the insurer's estimate of expected losses for organizations similar to the insured. For instance, the property insurance premium for a small sole proprietorship would be based upon expected losses of a class of similar sole proprietorships. This arrangement is risk transfer in a nearly pure form, since all of these sole proprietorships are paying a similar contribution to an insurer, *based upon the expected loss experience of the group as a whole.* Importantly, such a system does not formally recognize any individual insured's own loss experience in the computation of that insured's individual premium (though the premium may be later debited or credited to recognize the insured's past loss experience).

While the fact that an insured's premium is not directly influenced by that insured's own loss experience may appear to be a peripheral matter, in the context of a discussion of transfer and retention it is not. Risk and uncertainty are most fully transferred under a guaranteed cost arrangement. The individual insured has virtually no knowledge to make a quantitative assessment of the risk, which generally translates into a high level of uncertainty. In a similar sense, the insurer is assuming a higher level of uncertainty than under coverages in which the cost is not guaranteed because the insured is an unknown quantity with respect to loss experience and potential. This uncertainty is partly resolved through underwriting and risk-classification procedures that allow the insurer to use statistical information on a broad class of similar insureds to arrive at a premium for the coverage.

The guaranteed cost approach may be the only risk transfer approach available to small and medium sized public, private, and nonprofit organizations. Approaches that are "loss sensitive," that is, in which the premium is based at least in part on the insured's own loss experience, typically are not used for smaller insureds. One reason for this restriction is the lack of statistical credibility a small organization's past loss experience would have in reflecting its expected future losses. In general, loss frequency is low when the insured's scale of operation is small, resulting in low credibility. When the insured's scale of operation is large and the expected number of losses is high, the insured's own loss experience becomes a more credible (i.e., reliable) predictor of future losses inasmuch as the effect of loss prevention efforts (or lack thereof) becomes apparent in a short period of time. For an insured whose scale of operations is small, a longer time period is required to develop reliable estimates. Hence, premiums for small insureds are likely to be based on data grouping these insureds into a class.

Experience-Rated Insurance

Experience-rating (often called "prospective experience-rating") plans are risk transfer arrangements in which the insured's own past loss experience directly affects the premium. Such an approach differs from guaranteed cost plans because the insured retains some control over the cost in the sense that loss prevention efforts can reduce the number of losses and consequently reduce or control the premium.

Experience rating often is found on coverages in which a large number of units are exposed to loss (e.g., a large number of workers exposed to possible injury). The experience-rated premium is based on a weighted average of the insured organization's own loss experience and the loss experience typical for the class to which the organization belongs. The evaluation of loss experience is based primarily on the *number* of losses rather than the dollar amount. Consequently, 20 losses averaging $5000 each will have a greater effect on the experience-rated premium than a single loss of $100,000. The emphasis on the number of losses arises from a belief by insurers that loss control activities are likely to affect loss frequency, while loss severity often is a matter of chance.

The credibility or weight assigned to the insured's loss experience is a function of the number of units exposed to possible loss. For example, the loss experience on a group of 2000 employees may be assigned a credibility of 40 percent (0.4). A weighted average formula is used to weight the group's loss experience vis-à-vis the loss experience of a typical insured group:

$$CA + (1 - C)E$$

where C is the credibility or weight, A is the insured's actual loss per unit of exposure during the time period, and E is the expected loss per unit of exposure in a typical insured group. The weighting process applies to downward as well as upward adjustments. As an illustration of how the weighting procedure may be applied to workers' compensation insurance, the expected number of injuries for a typical insured group in a class (E) may be 2.00 per 100 worker-years. If the group's actual losses (A) are 1.50 per 100 worker-years and credibility (C) is 0.4, the weighting process yields:

$$(0.4)(1.50) + (1 - 0.4)(2.00) = 1.80$$

which is 90 percent of the expected number for a typical insured group (1.80/2.00). Using this adjustment, the experience-rated premium for this group would be 90 percent of the premium for a typical group. If the insured group's own loss experience were fully weighted in this adjustment (i.e., 100 percent credibility), a 25 percent reduction would apply, as actual losses are 75 percent of expected (1.50/2.00). However, the number of workers in the above example is not large enough to assign full credibility, so the 40 percent credibility cuts the adjustment to only 40 percent of the full-credibility value [i.e., (0.4)(25%) = 10%].

Experience-rated plans are available to medium-sized and large organizations whose own loss experience has some degree of statistical credibility. Other things being equal, the loss experience of a larger organization has greater credibility, and its own loss experience is very influential in the determination of its premium. Conversely a "smaller" medium-sized organization has less credible loss experience, so its premium is less influenced by its own past experience.

Experience rating is widely used in workers' compensation and general liability insurance, and has applications in almost every type of commercial insurance. Experience rating begins to move insurance contracts along the transfer/retention continuum away from full transfer. Although the insurer continues to bear the risk, in the sense that losses are paid by the insurer, the insured is now provided an incentive to control losses and hence the cost of the insurance through risk management efforts. Though this incentive to exercise control may appear to be an incidental consequence of experience rating, it actually represents a fundamental departure from full transfer. Direct control over the risk that determines the premium provides the insured with a degree of control over the cost of risk financing, which makes experience rating qualitatively different from a guaranteed cost approach.

Retrospective Rating

Insurance plans using retrospective rating (sometimes called *retrospective experience rating*) base the premium for coverage on the losses of the insured *during the policy period.* In other words, the premium for coverage is not known in advance but is determined after the end of the policy period. In concept, additional losses during the policy period translate directly into an increased premium, although the range over which premiums can fluctuate is subject to a minimum and a maximum. Over the range in which the premium directly responds to increased losses, retrospective rating resembles retention or self-insurance. When compared with experience rating, the cost of financing losses under retrospective rating is more responsive to losses. On the transfer/retention continuum, the increased responsiveness to losses moves retrospective rating toward retention and away from transfer.

Figure 10.1 illustrates the effect of losses in a coverage using retrospective rating. The minimum premium is paid regardless of losses experienced during the policy period. Over a range, increased losses translate into increased premiums, but the premiums are subject to an upper limit. Insured groups qualifying for retrospective rating may be allowed to choose from several different retrospective rating plans, with plans varying as to upper and lower premium bounds or the responsiveness of premiums to actual losses. Because retrospective rating may be used on coverages in which time may be required for the full amount of a loss to become evident, plans provide for provisional premiums with the possibility of subsequent adjustments. If the adjustment is upward, the business can be viewed as having, in effect, an open line of credit with the insurer until the adjustment is made. Because it may take several years after the policy period before the insured and the insurer can agree on what the still unpaid losses will cost, several adjustments may be necessary before the final retrospective premium is determined.

Retrospective rating is very responsive to fluctuations in the insured's experience. Insurers limit its use to very large organizations whose financial resources are adequate to absorb fluctuations due to loss experience. For large organizations with superior loss records, retrospective rating can be very attractive. It also can be attractive for an organization that expects significant improvement in loss experience relative to the record that prevailed in the past. Insurers sometimes require the use of retrospective rating when they expect a poor loss record.

FIGURE 10.1. RETROSPECTIVELY RATED PREMIUM RANGE.

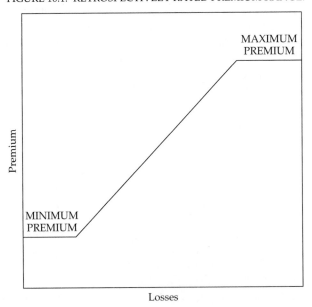

A modified form of retrospective rating, called a *paid loss retro*, has been in use for more than a decade. When compared with standard retrospective rating, a paid loss retro is closer to full retention but still has a few elements of transfer. As with standard retrospective rating, the range over which the premium varies may be subject to an upper limit. Under a paid loss retro, however, the insured organization agrees to reimburse the insurer for losses when they are paid, not when the accident or injury giving rise to the claim occurs. Beyond the initial premium paid at the beginning of the policy period, the insured pays the retrospective premium in periodic installments, with each installment being the claim payments and associated expenses actually paid by the insurer in that year. Future payments from accidents or injuries that already have occurred are not included in these periodic installments, but the insured agrees to reimburse the insurer for these payments when they actually occur.

This practice contrasts with standard retrospective rating, in which the retrospective premium includes a charge for the expected present value of future payments from injuries or accidents that already have occurred. When compared with standard retrospective rating, a paid loss retro more closely resembles a pay-as-you-go approach. An insured may prefer this approach because (1) the insured retains use of the premium dollars until payments actually are made, not when the liability is recognized and estimated, and (2) the premium does not depend on the insurer's *estimate* of future payments. In many respects, the paid loss retro is almost indistinguishable from ASO/stop loss plans discussed later.

TRANSFER/RETENTION TECHNIQUES

Consumer Proprietaries/Cooperatives

One of the hybrid risk financing mechanisms to emerge in recent years is a type of privately incorporated insurance pool; a phenomenon that can be described as a consumer proprietary or consumer cooperative insurance company. The terms "proprietary" and "cooperative" refer to the legal form of the pooling organization. Consumer proprietaries are private insurance pools that are "stock insurers" whose stocks are owned by their policyholders. For example, one pool received its initial capital from 68 sponsor corporations that purchased insurance from the pool. Other policyholders purchasing coverage subsequent to the formation of the pool also were required to purchase stock in the insurer. Two well-known examples of a consumer proprietary are X.L. Insurance Co. Ltd. and A.C.E. Insurance Co. Ltd., which have become major providers of large liability insurance policies that cover only losses in excess of a given amount.

The consumer cooperative form of insurer is older, at least in concept. Not-for-profit cooperatives that operate to benefit policyholders have existed for a long time. Protection and Indemnity (P & I) clubs, which are shipowner-owned mutual insurers providing liability insurance to members, offer an example of this type of pooling arrangement. The cooperative form of insurance operation is discussed extensively in Chapter 13. The topic of consumer cooperatives is brought up now because a permutation of this legal form has begun to appear in the movement toward group risk financing (self-insurance pools, risk retention groups, and insurance purchasing groups). For instance, a group of local governments may choose to incorporate a "self-insurance pool" as a mutual insurance company. The advantages of this form of organization lie in known regulatory treatment, some access to capital markets, higher levels of consumer confidence, and some administrative benefits. In many respects, such a mutual is indistinguishable from a larger mutual insurance company, but a close inspection reveals that the smaller number of policyholders limits the degree of risk transfer that may occur. As a simple illustration, such arrangements may adopt very aggressive "assessment" policies whereby the insurer can charge excess losses (that is, losses greater than those expected) directly to policyholders.

Depending on the reader's perspective, the consumer proprietary and co-operative insurers might be considered as being close to full risk transfer arrangements. While nearly full risk transfer may be the outward appearance, most such arrangements are not conventional risk transfer. For instance, the consumer proprietary usually requires the explicit assumption of a financial risk (investment in the pool) in exchange for the transfer of the insured risk. The limited size of the pool and the possibility of assessment actually may place additional risk on policyholders in that they may be forced to pay an extra assessment to cover unanticipated losses of other policyholders.

Self-Insurance Pools

The insurance industry has perceived governmental entities to be risky institutions: a perception that has existed for a long time. The reasons for this perception are varied, but are rooted in the fundamental nature of government where complexity, ambiguity, and even inefficiency complicate the underwriting of such organizations. Government and politics are difficult to understand, let alone insure.

Since 1970, governmental entities experienced two periods of crisis in terms of insurance availability and affordability: one period occurring in the mid-1970s and the other in the mid-1980s. During those two times, insurance for governmental risks (particularly liability insurance) was virtually unaffordable, if available at all. In response to these insurance crises, governments began to explore alternatives to the commercial insurance marketplace. A significant alternative to emerge from this period of time was the "self-insurance pool."

The phrase "self-insurance pool" is an oxymoron. Pools by definition involve more than one risk, so self-insurance is technically inconsistent with such an arrangement. A more descriptive title might be "risk financing pool," but the phrase "self-insurance pool" has become common enough to allow it to be used without misunderstanding.

Self-insurance pools are arrangements whereby participating entities mutually agree to "insure" one another. For instance, a dozen city governments may agree to finance the cost of workers' compensation by pooling member contributions to pay claims and administrative expenses. Usually, the entities involved must seek authorization from the state to begin such an organization, but the actual nature of that authorization varies widely from state to state. Operationally, these governments usually will contract with a third party administrator (sometimes an insurance brokerage firm) to provide for day-to-day administrative and managerial services. Premiums or contributions are paid to the pool, and these funds serve as the basis for financing the losses of the participating members and paying for administrative services.

On rare occasions, pools are incorporated as insurance companies. More commonly, a pool is incorporated under an intergovernmental cooperative agreement. State constitutions typically permit governments to join together to provide services that are of mutual benefit. This basis for incorporation is important, for it is the principal distinction between pools and insurance companies. Pools are not insurance companies (with a few exceptions), though they often appear indistinguishable from small mutual insurance companies. Legally, however, these pools are not insurers, so they are not subject to insurance regulation, certain insurance taxes and assessments, and they tend to restrict the actual risk transfer that occurs through the pooling contracts.

The first pools, which were formed in the mid-1970s during the first insurance "crisis," largely were limited to providing workers' compensation and general liability coverages. After an initial growth surge in the mid- to late-1970s, the growth rate in the pooling movement reached a plateau until the mid-1980s, when the second insurance "crisis" brought renewed interest in the pooling option. Since that time, the growth of the pooling movement has been dramatic. In 1994, there are over 400 pools in operation in the United States. Estimates of participation indicate that at least one third of the 84,000 governmental entities in the United States participate in pools, making pools the most significant single market for public sector risk financing in North America. Pools come in various types and sizes: some have as few as three participating members, while others have 1200 or more. Some pools are created solely by the participating members while others are created by sponsoring organizations. For instance, almost all state municipal leagues now sponsor a self-insurance pool for members. Although most pools are limited to one or two types of coverages (workers' compensation is a common coverage), a number of pools provide coverages ranging from general liability to employee benefits. The pooling phenomenon has not been adopted extensively by governmental entities lying outside the U.S. borders. There are a few pools in Europe and Australia (one in the United Kingdom was founded early in the twentieth century), but their formation and growth is not the result of the same factors that influenced pool growth in the U.S.

Although pools continue to proliferate (and show little sign of abating) they have come under growing scrutiny. Critics have questioned whether pools should be treated differently from commercial insurers, as many pools are virtually indistinguishable from the insurance companies they replaced. Further, as commercial insurers have reentered the government insurance market, questions have arisen over whether governments should be sponsoring risk financing arrangements that could be managed by the private sector, or whether governments should be competing with the private sector. Critics also have questioned whether pools have a long-term purpose, or whether they merely are a short-term response to a temporary emergency. The growth and size of the pooling community suggest that pooling will continue to be an important risk financing vehicle for governmental entities, but some of the present advantages of pools—favorable tax status, lack of regulatory oversight, avoidance of regulatory compliance costs, and product innovation—probably will diminish as legislatures and regulators focus their attention on these financial institutions.

Risk Retention Groups

The Liability Risk Retention Act of 1986 created new opportunities for creation of pools. Under this 1986 legislation, organizations are permitted to band together to set up (1) risk retention groups (RRGs) for retaining their liability exposures (other than workers' compensation) and (2) purchasing groups that can purchase liability insurance on a group basis for their members.

Retention Groups. An RRG is a corporation (or other limited liability association) whose primary purpose is assuming and pooling liability exposures of its members. The RRG members must have similar liability exposures by virtue of common or related premises or operations. RRGs closely resemble mutual insurers, and an RRG must be chartered and licensed as a liability insurance company under the laws, including the captive insurance law, of one state. From a functional point of view, an RRG is a special-purpose association owned by its members. It can provide both insurance and reinsurance coverages. Several states have enacted special licensing legislation for RRGs that excuses them from some of the obligations normally imposed on insurers.

The regulatory authority of other states in which the RRG operates is limited to specific areas, primarily insolvency and trading practices. For example, an RRG must comply with the state's unfair claim settlement practices law, pay certain taxes, designate the state insurance commissioner as its agent solely for receiving service of legal documents or service, and submit to an examination by the state insurance commission to determine the RRG's financial condition if the chartering state has refused to initiate such an examination.

In each state in which it intends to do business, the RRG must first submit a plan of operations or a feasibility study, which includes coverages, deductible, coverage limits, rates, and rating classification systems for each line of insurance to be offered. If the plan of operations changes, the RRG must submit a new plan. Each state also must receive a copy of the group's annual financial statement submitted to the chartering state. This statement must include an independent opinion on the adequacy of the RRG's reserves for insured but not yet paid losses and loss-adjustment expenses. Federal courts, at the request of a state insurance commissioner or some other party, may issue an injunction to stop the operations of an RRG if they find that the RRG's financial condition is "hazardous." The RRG is required to notify its members that the group may not be subject to all of the insurance laws and regulations of their state and that it does not participate in state insurance guaranty funds. Hence RRG members lack protection against insolvency they may be provided by state guaranty funds. For many organizations, limits on guaranty fund coverage make the absence of the coverage unimportant.

Despite these regulatory restrictions, the RRG offers important benefits over the retention alternatives available before the 1986 act. The RRG can be domiciled in the United States, it needs to be licensed in only one state, and no other state can require that its rates and policy forms be approved prior to their use. Some states have challenged this interpretation. The U.S. domicile is important because the Tax Reform Act of 1986 wiped out a tax advantage for member-owned offshore insurance companies. Previously, shareholders owning less than 10 percent of the offshore insurer's stock could defer paying taxes on their share of the insurer's earnings until they actually received it. Some observers believe that removal of this tax incentive and the opportunity to eliminate some of the expenses and inconveniences associated with using subsidiaries will cause many of these insurers to relocate. Others argue that offshore insurers continue to have the advantage of support services developed in Bermuda and other offshore domiciles. Offshore insurers also need not concern themselves about whether state insurance commissioners might use unclear provisions of the act to exercise more control than the owners find desirable.

The fact that the RRG need be licensed in only one state and only that one state can regulate its policy forms and rates enables the RRG to use the same policy form in all states and avoid many expenses and delays the group otherwise would encounter. For example, the RRG circumvents state laws requiring insurance to be purchased only from insurers licensed in that state.

The Liability Risk Retention Act of 1986 greatly expanded retention opportunities first created in a more limited way under 1981 legislation. As a consequence, the number of RRGs has grown. Under the Product Liability Risk Retention Act of 1981, only one major RRG covering about 11,000 home builders was ever formed because of the narrow scope of the act and the intense price competition among insurers that existed until late 1984. In January, 1987, the first RRG to take advantage of the 1986 act started to write professional liability policies for a potential market of 25,000 small and medium-sized accounting firms. Many other RRGs have been established since that time, including, for example, groups offering environmental pollution liability coverage to firms in the electronics industry, educators legal liability insurance to colleges and universities, and general and product liability for livestock and pet food producers. A trade association, the National Association of Risk Retention Groups, has been organized to lobby on behalf of its members and to provide support services.

Purchasing Groups. Purchasing groups authorized by the Liability Risk Retention Act are not ways of funding retention arrangements. Instead, they enable individual firms to purchase insurance from insurers, including RRGs, on a group basis, which is expected to produce more favorable policy terms and rates (due to, it is alleged, economies of scale). These groups, which lie closer to full transfer methods than do RRGs, are discussed in this section because they were made possible by the same act as RRGs. Like RRGs, purchasing groups must be composed of persons or entities with similar liability exposures by virtue of common or related premises or operations. Unlike RRGs, however, a purchasing group's primary interest need not be the insurance part of its activities. Also, the group need not be a corporation. For example, a trade association can create a purchasing group by passing a simple resolution. A major provision in the act exempts these groups from state laws that otherwise would forbid insurers from granting the group any advantages, even if experience-justified, concerning rates and policy forms.

A purchasing group intending to do business in any state must notify the state of its intention. The notice must specify the state of domicile, the lines and classifications of liability insurance they intend to purchase, the insurance company from whom they intend to purchase the insurance, and their principal place of business. The group must register itself with the state insurance commissioner of each state in which it does business and designate the state commission as its agent for the purpose of receiving service of legal documents or process. A state may require a person acting as an agent or broker for a purchasing group to obtain a license from that state, but the state cannot impose a residency requirement. A purchasing group may not purchase insurance from a risk retention group that is not chartered in the state or from a traditional insurer that is not licensed in the state unless the purchase is made through a licensed agent or broker in compliance with the state's laws and regulations regulating such purchases.

Group Workers' Compensation Self-Insurers. In many states, group workers' compensation self-insurance statutes typically permit two or more firms with combined net worth exceeding a specified amount (the amount varies from state to state) to form a joint arrangement. Under an indemnity agreement each member agrees to be jointly and severally responsible for all the claims and expenses incurred in any year in which the member belongs to the group. The members thus share the combined experience of the pool. Legally, these pooling arrangements are treated as self-insurers subject to special regulations. Group self-insurers commonly purchase excess insurance to cover large losses and use providers of claim-settlement services to administer claims. Group self-insurance programs also have been developed in connection with employee benefit plans.

The Identity of Pool Participants

One important issue in evaluating the effect of a risk financing method on an organization is identifying and measuring *what* risks are being transferred and retained. For example, a pooling arrangement may have the outward appearance of being transfer, but the pool's assessment provisions may leave pool participants exposed to the risk of adverse developments affecting pool members generally.

Equally important, many of the methods lying between full retention and complete transfer introduce another issue: *who* are the other participants. Particularly when a pool has only a few members, the identity of the participants can be a major consideration affecting the success of the pooling arrangement. Without sophisticated pricing techniques and monitoring arrangements, the character of pool participants' exposures and risk control techniques should be approximately equal. When they are not equal or at least perceived as being equal and monitoring is costly, the introduction of surveillance measures and differential pricing drives up costs and introduces the possibility of disputes, all of which lead to decreased efficiency. Hence the observability of participant's risk control activities can be a key issue affecting the viability of a pooling arrangement. Another key issue is the provision allowing withdrawal from the pool, including any withdrawal penalty.

Administrative Services Only (ASO)/Minimum Premium (MPP) or Stop Loss Plans

ASO plans are programs designed to provide administrative services on claims, possibly in conjunction with other financing services. Under such a program, a service provider supplies only the claims-settlement (or perhaps some other) services, while the plan sponsor finances the payment of the claims themselves. The service provider, who may be an insurance company, also may offer programs of full insurance or coverage only for claims exceeding a stated amount— often referred to as "stop loss" coverage. Other service providers specialize in providing only administrative services, a practice widely seen in the area of workers' compensation. In the area of health care benefits, the provider of administrative services often is an insurer that also can provide the stop loss cover. Under ASO and MPP or stop loss plans, the service provider uses the sponsor's funds to reimburse claims. Typically, the sponsor establishes an account at a bank, against which the service provider writes checks in favor of health care providers such as hospitals and doctors. Periodically the service provider provides information on funding levels to the sponsor, who then adjusts the deposit accordingly.

Presumably, the skill of the service provider is the rationale for a claims service only arrangement; the ASO arrangement provides the plan sponsor access to the claims settlement skills without entailing other costs of using insurance. In the absence of a provider of these services, the plan sponsor wishing to use retention is forced to provide the services itself. The ASO arrangement avoids fixed costs of establishing an internal claims settlement facility and also may reduce the likelihood of employee relations problems that could appear if the sponsor settled claims directly. In addition, a large service provider's bargaining power vis-à-vis providers of health care services may be an attraction; the ASO arrangement provides access to favorable rates negotiated with health care providers without other costs of using insurance.

Stop Loss or Minimum Premium Plan. A stop loss or minimum premium plan is a hybrid of retention and insurance for health benefits, so it is written by an insurer. As in the ASO plan, the insurer writing the plan provides claims settlement services with the plan sponsor paying the claims themselves. However, the insurer also guarantees a maximum cost (a stop loss) for a time period. Usually this maximum cost is stated in terms of a monthly health claims cost per employee. For example, the insurer may estimate an average monthly claim cost of $300 per employee, with a stop-loss at 125% of the estimated average, or $375. If the monthly claim cost exceeds $375, payment of the excess becomes the insurer's responsibility. Hence, the plan provides insurance not unlike that provided by an insurance policy with a deductible. This maximum cost guarantee resembles the maximum premium in standard retrospective rating plans. The high frequency of claims in health benefit programs and the close involvement of the insurer in claims settlement creates an obvious incentive for the insurer to control claims costs, especially when claims approach the stop loss level. Such a direct incentive is not present in an ASO plan, nor is it likely to be a consideration on insurance covering claims that occur infrequently.

Pooling Through Taxing Authority

This text addresses public- as well as private-sector risk management issues. Thus, a discussion of risk financing methods would be incomplete without mention of a special type of risk financing method available to many public entities. In the public sector, an entity that is authorized to set and collect taxes enjoys access to a risk financing method that generally is not available in the private or nonprofit sectors. Through its claim to taxes on assets held by taxpayers, the public entity has access to risk-bearing capacity that would not be expected to appear in private or nonprofit entities of comparable size. The cost of risk is spread over the tax base, which reduces the effect on any one taxpayer. A $100,000 unreimbursed loss becomes forty cents when spread across 250,000 households, a negligible effect on each individual household.

When the public entity pools through its taxing authority, it is pooling the risk-bearing capacity of the constituent households and organizations. The technique offers an excellent illustration of risk-bearing capacity and the effect of pooling. Here, the constituent households and organizations become their own insurer; not through pooling of losses, but through the pooling of their collective risk-bearing capacity. It is not difficult to imagine substantial capacity built from this source. A fifty-cent contribution from each of 250,000 households creates a fund that can absorb a $125,000 uninsured loss. If the fifty-cent contribution is an annual assessment, unused capacity at the end of the first year can be used to augment capacity from the following year's assessment.

In many respects, the payment of taxes (or at least a part of those taxes) may be construed as a premium payment. That premium payment, however, is not financing losses *directly* suffered by the taxpayer, but rather by the entity. In other words, the taxpayers are the insurers, and the entity is the insured: quite the opposite of what one might initially imagine. Yet, it is not possible to argue that taxing the citizenry is like buying insurance, or even like establishing a line of credit for financing losses. This is because in a democracy the entity is a legally constituted representative of the people, so it might be argued that the entity is the institutional embodiment of the taxpayers—and indeed, philosophically they are one in the same. Therefore the "people" must also be viewed as insureds, not just as insurers of the governmental entity.

The discussion of risk-bearing capacity as a requirement for retention appearing in Chapter 9 provides appropriate background for evaluating pooling through taxing authority against other risk financing methods. Practical considerations limit the extent to which risk-bearing capacity can be built using this method. Statutory restrictions on tax rates and other budgeting and political restraints affect the availability of funds. Even in large communities, households' resistance to tax increases imposes another limit. Also, a large retention fund not being used to reimburse current losses may prove tempting to officials as a source of funds for other activities.

Without raising the normative question of whether a government should rely upon its taxing authority to directly finance risk, there is a somewhat broader conceptual issue that merits a mention. Some observers argue that conventional insurance is unnecessary in a public entity with taxing authority since the tax base *is* insurance (at least in a generalized sense of the term). Discussion in Chapter 12 considers this argument and establishes some principles for thinking about such a issue. Nevertheless, establishing an awareness of the controversy is appropriate at this point because it alerts the reader to the fact that insurance-like risk financing can occur in different forms. In one sense, risk financing through pooling the risk-bearing capacity of the tax base might be seen as retention in that the citizens are jointly retaining the risks of their public institutions. In another sense, the public entity transfers risk to constituent households and other taxpayers. Such interpretations highlight the murky boundary between transfer and retention. The risk financing methods described in this chapter reveal that it is sometimes very difficult to identify precisely when some practice is no longer risk transfer, and precisely when that practice becomes risk retention. Transfer through taxation merely introduces the reader to a set of risk financing techniques that are fundamentally different from traditional commercial insurance risk transfer.

RETENTION OR MOSTLY RETENTION TECHNIQUES

Captive Insurers

As explained in Chapter 9, a captive insurer is an insurance operation that is owned by the insured. The parent company establishes a captive insurance subsidiary that writes coverage against the parent company's risks. A *group* or *association* captive is owned by the members of a sponsoring group or association for the purpose of insuring their risks. Captive insurers also may write insurance for other parties that are not affiliated with the parent company or sponsoring group. Captive insurers offer the parent company access to advantages of insurance transactions or a means of satisfying a regulation requiring insurance while avoiding some of the costs of securing insurance from unrelated entities. Most notably, costs associated with moral hazards and adverse selection would not be present in the parent company's purchase of coverage from a captive. These costs include underwriting expenses, agents' compensation, and costs of monitoring the insured's loss-prevention activities after coverage is written.

Fronting is a technique for using a captive insurer to provide coverage when there is a requirement that insurance be provided by an insurer licensed in the state. The licensed insurer, the "front," writes coverage for the parent company, but then reinsures the coverage with the captive. As a consequence of the reinsurance, the licensed insurer is reimbursed on a dollar-for-dollar basis for all losses paid to the parent company as long as the captive and its parent company remain solvent.

A paid loss retro accomplishes much the same result. Risk retention groups offer an alternative to fronting, as an RRG licensed in one state can offer the same coverage in other states without additional licensing.

The costs of forming a captive insurer are related primarily to regulation. Establishing a captive insurance subsidiary requires the parent organization to go through legal procedures necessary to form an insurer, but the cost of this process is likely to be minimal for an organization planning to use the captive extensively. The parent also must meet requirements of the jurisdiction in which the captive is formed, such as minimum levels of capital and minimum numbers of policyholders. Premiums paid to a captive insurer are subject to the state tax on premium income, levied by the state in which the purchase of coverage takes place. This premium tax, which typically is about 2 percent of the premium (but can be higher), also would apply to insurance purchased from an unrelated entity but usually would not apply to risks retained other than through captives. Some states, however, have proposed a premium tax levy on retained risks. Hence the premium tax normally is a cost of using a captive insurer as compared to retaining the risk. Also, a captive may be required to participate in state-managed pools designed to guarantee coverage to individuals who are denied coverage through voluntary channels ("assigned risk pools").

Until recently, the relatively few regulatory restrictions in offshore locations, such as Bermuda, allowed them to dominate locations in the United States. The remoteness of these offshore locations is not necessarily an obstacle. Many captives do not have a physical presence (such as a home office) in the jurisdiction in which they are incorporated, their presence being essentially a set of documents filed with regulators. More recently, a number of states including Colorado, Delaware, Georgia, Hawaii, Tennessee, Vermont, and Virginia, have changed their laws to encourage the formation of "domestic" captives.

Tax advantages of using captive insurers arise from the favorable tax treatment of insurers compared with organizations that retain risk. The favorable tax treatment is under pressure from the U.S. Internal Revenue Service, which has challenged the tax treatment of transactions between captive insurers and their parent companies in a number of cases. Hence, the favorable tax treatment is subject to the risk of being disallowed. In general, cases involving captive insurers whose coverages are written solely or primarily with the parent company have not been allowed the tax treatment accorded insurance transactions. The result has been to deny favorable tax treatment to insurance transactions between a parent and a captive unless the captive writes a significant amount of coverage with unaffiliated parties. This principle was notable in a set of three decisions of the U.S. Tax Court in 1991: the *Amerco,* the *Harper,* and especially, the *Sears* case. In the Sears case, Sears owned an insurance company (Allstate) whose coverages were written primarily with unaffiliated insureds. The Tax Court ruled that Allstate's writing of coverage for Sears was an insurance transaction for tax purposes.

Even when a captive insurer's coverages are written solely against the parent company's risks, a captive insurer still provides the parent company with access to reinsurance markets. Reinsurance is coverage exchanged between insurers rather than sold in primary or direct insurance markets. Fewer regulatory restrictions apply to reinsurance transactions than to primary insurance, which leaves the parties free to design coverages tailored to individual needs and circumstances. The benefit of access to reinsurance markets is not affected by the tax treatment of transactions between the captive and the parent.

Finite or Risk Insurance Plans

Perhaps the most current area of risk financing innovation is a set of approaches that might be considered "banking arrangements." Such plans are self-financing programs (perhaps with an element of risk transfer) that involve the formal participation of a "bank." The bank need not be a bank in the popular sense of the term; rather, it is a separate entity that arranges and manages the plan for a self-insured entity.

In its simplest form, a banking arrangement might be nothing more elaborate than a line of credit that an organization may draw on in the event of unexpected losses. A somewhat more elaborate banking arrangement is the formal issuance of debt to finance losses. Some governmental entities in the 1980s, while facing an absence of commercial insurance, issued bonds to finance losses or to capitalize a risk fund. Some self-insurance pools experimented with this approach as a means to generate surplus or a financing base. Although never very popular (the practice requires assuming a financial risk in order to finance losses), structured debt-financed programs have some merits, possible cash flow stabilization being the most significant. (Readers should note that many organizations finance losses through borrowing, so the preceding statement narrowly applies to more formalized debt-based financing arrangements.)

The previous illustrations underscore a fundamental difference between banking arrangements and pooling. In banking arrangements risk is spread across *time* rather than across *exposures*. That is, whereas a pool (or a government with taxing authority) accepts the risks of many members (or accepts risks on behalf of the citizens), and spreads the costs of losses across these members (taxpayers), a banking arrangement involves the retention of risk with the objective of spreading costs of losses across time. Arguably for the largest organizations, a banking arrangement and, say, a retrospectively rated insurance plan would be indistinguishable. The two plans would be indistinguishable for the largest insureds because they pay the full cost of their losses in both the long and the short run. For smaller organizations, purchasing conventional insurance coverage offers one way to stabilize the costs of losses by exchanging an irregular pattern of losses for a regular pattern of premium payments. Likewise for the organization using a banking arrangement; it is substituting a regular pattern of bond or letter/line of credit payments for the irregular pattern of losses and loss payments.

"Finite insurance" or "risk insurance" (also, "risk reinsurance") represents a second generation of banking arrangements. In principle, it is based upon a structured self-financing plan that seeks to stabilize risk costs over time. Although there is a wide variation among specific plans, finite insurance plans commonly involve the creation of a managed account of money. The "policyholder" capitalizes the account through premium payments, and this account is the principal source of cash for financing losses. The contract is set for a limited period of time, usually three to five years and the premiums are expected to be paid over that time. The finite insurance provider may offer administrative services, may structure some type of excess insurance to cap losses, and may provide additional guarantees, such as interest rate guarantees for the managed account. Other banking services, such as cash management or letters/lines of credit, may be included as part of the contract. Finally, if—after the contract period—there is a positive fund balance, that balance is returned to the policyholder.

"Excess insurance" may be part of a finite insurance arrangement, but the amount of risk transfer is minimal. One common arrangement is for the policyholder and the insurer to share in losses when the account is exhausted, with the policyholder bearing the greater percentage of excess losses. For instance, the contract might stipulate that if losses exhaust the account, the policyholder pays for 80 percent of the excess while the insurer covers the remaining 20 percent. The premium for this excess insurance may not be fully payable unless losses actually exhaust the account.

There are three purported advantages of finite insurance. The first is cash accumulation. Finite insurance serves as a vehicle for establishing a fund that can be drawn upon in the event of a significant loss, that is, funds are sequestered so "raiding" cannot occur without difficulty. This approach allows the risk manager to avoid drawing down the organization's line of credit to cover the loss. This advantage could be important to organizations that rely on borrowing or are heavily leveraged. Second, finite insurance may provide a tax advantage. If structured properly and viewed as insurance by the IRS, the arrangement resembles an "organizational IRA," in which the premiums are tax deductible, and the capital accumulation is not reported unless the fund is recouped. Third, finite insurance may provide cash flow stabilization. Like traditional insurance, the stable or budgetable "premium" replaces the uncertain and possibly large loss that could dramatically impact net income.

Finite insurance is controversial, with some critics suggesting that the benefits described above are illusory. Whether or not these benefits occur, finite insurance still represents a point in the retention/transfer continuum. Though certain transfer elements appear in the method, they tend to be peripheral to the central purpose, which is to provide a structured mechanism for retaining and financing the costs of loss.

The Increasing Importance of Risk Retention

Retention of property and liability exposures, broadly defined, has become increasingly important over the past 30 years, particularly with respect to liability exposures. Even if group captives, self-insurance pools, and risk retention groups, which have some transfer characteristics, are omitted, the growth has been dramatic.

Richard Sherman, a Coopers and Lybrand actuary, estimated in the late 1980s that the portion of the potential commercial insurance market served by retention plans had risen to about 10 percent by the late 1960s. The potential insurance market is assumed to be the premiums written by commercial insurers plus contributions to retention plans. In the mid-1970s, Sherman noted, retention's market share increased to about 25 percent and in the late 1980s had reached about 45 percent. He explained that when certain types of insurance became unavailable or available only at high prices, many commercial insureds shifted from commercial insurance to retention. When insurance became more available and prices dropped, these insureds tended not to return to commercial insurance.

Tillinghast, a major risk management and insurance consulting firm, has tracked retention practices since 1973 and reports similar findings. The consulting firm's data show retention's market share increasing from 1973 until about 1980 after which the share remained fairly constant until around 1985, when it trended upward again. Tillinghast estimates that today retention plans constitute roughly one-third of the commercial risk financing market. Based upon this longitudinal study of retention, Tillinghast concludes that retention programs, once established, tend to remain at least partly in place because of the time and effort required to set up a plan, the desire to be prepared for the next turn in the insurance market, and the withdrawal restrictions group captives and other group financing approaches place on members.

A 1993 analysis of the insurance market, conducted by Sedgwick (an international brokerage), concluded that retention and other nontraditional risk financing arrangements (captives, pools, finite risk insurance) now account for 43 percent of the total commercial risk financing market (Sedgwick, 1993). Sedgwick noted that it expected the nontraditional arrangements to continue to expand through the turn of the century.

Employee benefit plans have experienced a similar movement toward greater reliance on retention. For many decades more workers have participated in "self-insured" pension plans than in insured pension plans. Most large employers have shifted their medical expense plan for employees from an insured plan to a self-insurance program managed by insurers on an administrative services only basis or by independent servicing firms.

Key Concepts

guaranteed cost insurance An insurance arrangement whereby the insurer agrees to reimburse the losses of the policyholder in exchange for a premium that is fixed at the time the contract is signed.

experienced rated insurance An insurance arrangement whereby the insured's own past loss experience directly affects the premium charged. The degree of influence this loss experience has is tied to the statistical credibility of the insured's loss experience.

retrospectively rated insurance An insurance arrangement whereby the premium is based on the losses of the insured during the policy period. Subject to minimums and maximums, the premium is entirely based on the insured's own experience.

consumer proprietaries/cooperatives Two types of risk financing mechanisms whereby the members form a for-profit or not-for-profit arrangement to jointly finance the costs of a particular risk exposure. A significant characteristic of these arrangements is that they are usually incorporated as an insurance operation.

self-insurance pools A type of risk financing arrangement found in the public sector, pools are arrangements whereby public entities enter into an arrangement for jointly financing the cost of losses and the administrative costs of pool operation.

risk retention groups (RRGs) Risk financing arrangements authorized by federal law, RRGs are financing mechanisms whereby organizations in a common industry jointly finance the costs of liability and/or workers' compensation risks, either through an organized retention program or through a group purchase of commercial insurance.

administrative services only (ASO) An arrangement whereby a third party provides risk financing *administrative services*, but not the risk financing. Commonly used as part of a self-insurance plan, ASOs are often part of an arrangement that includes the purchase of some type of insurance.

captive insurers An arrangement operation that is owned by the insured and operates for the exclusive benefit of the owner/insured. Some types of captives do permit non-owners to insure in such a plan.

finite insurance A risk financing arrangement whereby the policyholder spreads the cost of risk over time, but does not transfer the risk to any other party.

Review Questions

1. How do guaranteed cost insurance, experience-rated plans, and retrospectively rated plans differ with respect to "degree of transfer"?
2. Why might it be advantageous for a large organization to try to move from an experience-rated plan to a retrospectively rated plan?
3. Explain how an experience-rated plan incorporates the insured's own loss experience into the premium.
4. How does a paid loss retro differ from the basic incurred loss retro?
5. What are consumer proprietaries and cooperatives, and how do they differ from one another?
6. Self-insurance pools are a major phenomenon in the public sector. Why were they created, and what do they do?
7. Explain how a group of organizations might form a risk retention group.
8. How might you support the statement: "governmental entities are 'insurance' "?
9. What are the advantages (to an organization) of forming a captive insurance company?
10. What are the principal characteristics of a typical finite insurance plan?

References and Suggestions for Additional Reading

BERLINER, BARUCH: *Limits of Insurability of Risks* (Englewood Cliffs, N.J.: Prentice-Hall, Inc., 1982).

DOHERTY, NEIL A.: *Corporate Risk Management* (New York: McGraw-Hill Book Company, 1985).

GOSHAY, ROBERT: *Corporate Self-Insurance and Risk Retention Plans* (Homewood, Ill.: Richard D. Irwin, Inc., 1964).

GREENE, MARK, and OSCAR SERBEIN: *Risk Management: Text and Cases* (2nd ed., Reston, Va.: Reston Publishing Company, 1983).

LALLEY, E. P.: *Corporate Uncertainty and Risk Management* (New York: Risk Management Society Publishing, Inc., 1982).

MACDONALD, DONALD L.: *Corporate Risk Control* (New York: The Ronald Press Company, 1966).

MEHR, R. I., and B. A. HEDGES: *Risk Management: Concepts and Applications* (Homewood, Ill.: Richard D. Irwin, Inc., 1974).

SEDGWICK: *Insurance Market Trends and Developments: 1993* (New York: Sedgwick James, Inc., 1993).

STEPHENS, V. M., W. S. MCINTYRE, and J. P. GIBSON: *Risk Financing: A Guide to Insurance Cash Flow Plans* (Dallas, Tex.: International Risk Management Institute, Inc., 1983 and updated periodically).

WILLIAMS, N. A. (ed.): *Risk Retention: Alternate Funding Methods* (Malvern, Pa.: Society of Chartered Property and Casualty Underwriters, 1983).

YOUNG, PETER C.: *Local Government Pure Risk Management Pools: Theory and Practice* (unpublished doctoral dissertation, University of Minnesota, 1988).

SECTION TWO
DECISION METHODS: OBJECTIVES AND ANALYSIS

Section 2 (Chapters 11 and 12) presents a framework for risk management decision methods. Earlier chapters have introduced readers to methods of risk assessment, to the nature of exposures to risk, and to techniques available for risk management. Section 2 offers a framework to unify these topics. Chapter 11 presents a rationale for risk management in organizations using finance theory applying to the private and public sectors. The emphasis in Chapter 11 is conceptual and theoretical. Chapter 12 presents methods for organizing, presenting, and analyzing data in risk management. The emphasis in Chapter 12 is on application, although the methods rely to a large extent on the theory developed in Chapter 11.

A Rationale for Risk Management in Organizations

Learning Objectives

After you have completed this chapter, you should be able to:

1. Explain why the rationale for an organization's purchase of insurance provides insight into the rationale for the practice of organizational risk management.
2. Explain how expected utility maximization by a risk-averse individual can be used to explain the individual's decision to purchase insurance.
3. Describe limitations of the expected utility rationale in explaining observed behavior.
4. Explain why changing from a context involving only a single asset to a context involving a portfolio of assets affects the method for determining an individual's demand for insurance.
5. Describe how securities prices would respond to risk management activities in a frictionless securities market.
6. Describe the rationale for risk management in the public sector.
7. Identify reasons other than risk aversion that can be used to explain the purchase of insurance by publicly held corporations.
8. Summarize the rationale for risk management in corporations and in the public sector.

INTRODUCTION

Traditionally, one important role of a risk manager has been to serve as liaison between an organization and its insurers. In fulfilling this role, the risk manager undertakes activities such as providing underwriting information, supervising the initiation and continuation of loss control programs vital to the organization's insurers, negotiating terms of coverage, and providing information required to favorably affect settlement of the organization's claims against insurers.

Even when the organization does not use insurance, these or similar activities survive in the risk management function. For example, a risk manager may collect and store the data required to defend the organization against legal liability or to satisfy regulators as to the organization's compliance with risk financing requirements imposed by statute.

The issues prompting the organization to manage risk are not necessarily identical to the issues leading it to purchase insurance. For example, cost reduction might be the reason for establishing a loss prevention program, a motive less likely to be served by purchasing insurance. In many large organizations, however, a rationale for risk management may be almost indistinguishable from a rationale for why the organization might purchase insurance. For example, a large self-insurance program for a state government may require the risk manager to perform almost the same functions that would be provided as part of conventional insurance: underwriting the state's agencies and departments, pricing the "coverage," providing loss-control services, and managing work-injury claims. An answer to the question "why do organizations buy insurance?" offers considerable insight into the reasons for the organization to adopt formal risk management programs.

Readers might presume that the motives leading an organization to purchase insurance are the same as the motives of individuals—insurance is purchased (or risk management is practiced) to provide protection against the consequences of unforeseen loss. Unfortunately, this answer fails to explain the demands for insurance of large, publicly held organizations whose resources rival those of insurers who might write coverage for the organization. This chapter shows why the protection-against-loss motive fails to explain organizations' demands for coverage. An understanding of why risk aversion fails to explain these transactions leads to a fuller understanding of the role of insurance, and hence risk management, for organizations as well as individuals. An alternative rationale is described that offers a way to identify the potential value contributed by an insurance institution and, by inference, the practice of risk management.

Appreciation of the motives for the purchase of insurance by organizations first requires that basis for individuals' demands for coverage be examined. The next section of this chapter describes how risk aversion and expected utility maximization can explain an individual's demand for insurance. Following sections extend the analysis, first to a portfolio setting in which diversification offers a low-cost method for reducing risk, then to a setting of frictionless markets, culminating in a rationale that can accommodate risk management in both the private and public sectors. Two appendixes to the chapter illustrate the rationale using two specific problems that have been discussed in the risk management and insurance literature: the value of a commitment to restore damaged assets and the effect of taxation on corporate insurance purchases.

EXPECTED UTILITY AND A RISK-AVERSE INDIVIDUAL'S DEMAND FOR INSURANCE

The acts of writing and acquiring insurance consume resources. The resources consumed represent a deadweight loss for the parties to the transaction. The

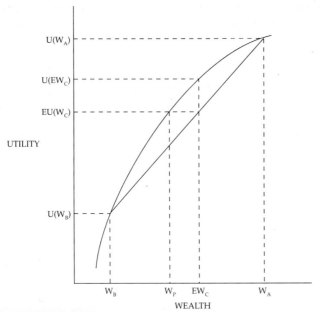

FIGURE 11.1. Utility as a function of wealth.

presence of these transaction costs implies that no specific demand for insurance would arise in an economy in which parties are equally informed and expected wealth is the only criterion used to evaluate choices. In such a setting, risk aversion can be used to explain an individual's demand for insurance. The explanation rests on a foundation laid by Von Neumann and Morganstern (1944), who explore the consequences of *expected utility* being used to explain an individual's preferences among risky alternatives. A risk-averse utility function can be combined with the assumption that the individual acts to maximize the expected value of his or her utility.

A *risk-averse* individual prefers less risk to more risk. Risk aversion implies that the individual is willing to devote a portion of wealth to an activity whose only effect is to reduce risk (in the sense of reducing possible variation in outcomes without affecting their expected value). A risk-averse utility function is illustrated in Figure 11.1, which depicts a situation in which an individual whose initial wealth is W_A faces the risk of a loss that reduces wealth to W_B. The utility function assigns a numerical value to the utility associated with holding a given level of wealth. For example, the function in Figure 11.1 assigns utility $U(W_A)$ to wealth amount W_A and utility $U(W_B)$ to wealth W_B. A utility function that is convex upward, such as the function shown in Figure 11.1, can be used to illustrate the effects of risk aversion. The convex upward function implies that the *marginal utility* of wealth declines as the level of wealth increases, that is, an additional dollar of wealth is less important when the individual is wealthy than when the individual is poor. Decreasing marginal utility of wealth is evidenced by the slope of a line tangent to the utility function, which decreases as the level of wealth increases. Conversely, the slope of a line tangent to the utility function increases at lower levels of wealth; the marginal utility of wealth increases as the level of wealth declines. As a consequence, a large loss has a disproportionate impact on utility as compared with the effect of a small loss.

The convex upward utility function illustrated in Figure 11.1 allows a geometric interpretation of risk aversion. The points lying on the straight line connecting the points $[W_A, U(W_A)]$ and $[W_A, U(W_B)]$ represent the expected value of wealth under gambles whose outcomes are wealth amounts W_A and W_B. The probabilities of the outcomes are directly proportional to the distances between the expected value of the gamble and the other possible outcome. For example, the point EW_C represents the expected wealth of one such gamble. The probability of loss, which results in wealth W_B, is $(W_A - EW_C)/(W_A - W_B)$, while the probability of no loss, which results in wealth W_A, is the complement: $(EW_C - W_B)/(W_A - W_B)$. The expected loss is $W_A - EW_C$.

With respect to the points lying on the aforementioned straight line, the geometry of Figure 11.1 implies that the proportions apply to the distances on the vertical axis that measures utility. For example, the ratio $[U(W_A) - EU(W_C)]/[U(W_A) - U(W_B)]$ is the same as the ratio $(W_A - EW_C)/(W_A - W_B)$. The convexity of the utility function implies that the utility of the expected wealth level, $U(EW_C)$, is greater than expected utility of holding the gamble, $EU(W_C)$, that is, $U(EW_C) > EU(W_C)$. In other words, a risk-averse individual prefers to pay the expected value of the loss $(W_A - EW_C)$, lowering wealth to EW_C, as opposed to facing the risk of loss. Regardless of the degree of risk aversion, the risk-averse individual fully insures if insurance is "actuarially fair" (i.e., the premium equals the expected value of insured claims). Somewhat more generally, a risk-averse individual prefers a stated level of wealth to a gamble with an identical expected value.

These conclusions are a consequence of the convex upward shape of the utility function. For a function that is convex upward, all points on a straight line drawn between any two points on the function lie beneath the function. This property is illustrated by the line drawn between the points $[W_A, U(W_A)]$ and $[W_B, U(W_B)]$. Except at the endpoints of the line, the straight line lies beneath the utility function.

The expected utility of the individual who faces the risk of loss is $EU(W_C)$, so the individual would be willing to pay for an insurance policy providing full reimbursement of the loss as long as the cost of the policy results in utility of at least $EU(W_C)$. In Figure 11.1, this premium would be $W_A - W_P$, where the ending wealth W_P gives rise to utility $EU(W_C)$. The *risk premium* is the difference between this largest premium and the expected value of the loss: $(W_A - W_P) - (W_A - EW_C)$, or $EW_C - W_P$. This risk premium represents an upper limit to the difference between the amount the individual is willing to pay for an insurance policy covering the loss and the expected value of the loss itself.

Limitations of an Expected Utility Rationale

Schoemaker (1982) provides a summary and review of literature on the expected utility approach. The principle of expected utility maximization is used widely to explain the behavior of individuals facing choices under risk, in part because expected utility offers an elegant approach. Also, the behavior of individuals does exhibit some characteristics of risk aversion. Unfortunately, empirical support for the expected utility rationale has not been strong. A growing body of empirical evidence appears to contradict expected utility approaches (see Tversky, Slovic, and Kahneman [1990]), although a theory to replace expected utility has not been widely adopted.

Even more severe limitations apply to using expected utility approaches to explain the behavior of organizations. Not only is the issue of whose utility governs the organization's choices unclear (e.g., the manager's or owners' utility), but the mechanism through which utility is aggregated into a collective function for the organization could be open to wide and inconclusive speculation. This limitation has long been recognized in the public finance literature. The application of utility theory to a public-sector environment requires the concept of a "social welfare (or utility) function" to be meaningful. In the early 1960s, Kenneth Arrow (1963) concluded that such a function could not be developed—a conclusion that subsequently became known as the impossibility theorem.

Further, expected utility and risk aversion fail to explain many phenomena related to insurance purchases, even by individuals. Many, if not most, demands for insurance by individuals arise in the context of some other transaction, so the question of whose utility governs the transaction can become a concern. In the case of life insurance, the buyer and the party reimbursed in the event of death frequently are not the same individual. Life insurance may be purchased to provide additional assurance of meeting financial commitments implied in, say, the formation of a family unit. Automobile insurance may be purchased to satisfy state-level statutes requiring financial responsibility. Dwelling insurance is purchased when lenders require insurance as a condition for mortgage closing.

The example of dwelling insurance being required by lenders is especially intriguing. Fire insurance is a typical requirement for a lender to resell a a mortgage in secondary markets after underwriting and closing. Although the borrower might seek coverage on the dwelling in the absence of a requirement by the lender, the existence of the requirement suggests otherwise for at least some borrowers. The reason for the insurance requirement is not evident. If insurance is viewed as merely a passive risk financing activity, the lender could allow some borrowers to leave property uninsured and charge them an extra amount to fund mortgages on which default occurs after fire. The absence of selling and underwriting costs would allow the lender to charge approximately one-half the cost of an equivalent fire insurance policy (the ratio of claim payments to premiums in fire insurance averages about 50 percent). Further, borrowers' incentives to prevent fires would be strengthened by the absence of insurance, especially if the amount of the mortgage were limited to leave the borrower with a substantial stake. These observations suggest that the insurance requirement could be detrimental to the interests of the partner to the mortgage transaction, which leads to a question about why the requirement exists.

THE DEMAND FOR INSURANCE IN THE CONTEXT OF A PORTFOLIO OF ASSETS

The preceding section shows that a risk-averse individual prefers paying the expected value of a loss to facing the possible loss itself. This conclusion does not necessarily extend into a portfolio setting, where an individual or organization holds a variety of assets. In a portfolio setting, the demand for any financial asset—including insurance—depends on correlations between all assets in the portfolio. Mayers and Smith (1983) and Doherty and Schlesinger (1983) are early papers addressing this issue. Later, Doherty and Schlesinger (1985) review the then already extensive literature on the issue.

For example, if a portfolio of risky assets includes two assets whose returns are negatively correlated, the holder of the portfolio would not be expected to fully insure either asset. When returns on two assets are negatively correlated, losses on one asset are hedged by gains on the other. Fully insuring either asset eliminates its natural hedging properties against the risk of the other asset. Even if insurance with no transaction costs were available (i.e., "actuarially fair" insurance priced at the expected value of claims), the holder of the portfolio would not be expected to fully insure either asset because insurance would eliminate the asset's natural hedging properties. This result overturns the conclusion derived earlier by examining a single asset in isolation: a risk-averse individual fully insures if actuarially fair insurance is available.

The concept of evaluating returns in a portfolio context is the basis for asset-pricing models that have become a cornerstone of finance literature. Chapter 8 of Brealey and Myers (1991) provides a summary of these models and their implications for asset pricing. Because this text is concerned with a specific application of asset pricing models—a rationale for risk management in organizations—only a few aspects of these models are considered.

The capital asset pricing model (CAPM) is perhaps the most widely known of the asset pricing models. The CAPM models the consequences of efforts by risk-averse individuals to diversify risk in their holdings of risky securities. When returns on risky securities have less than perfect positive correlation, risk-averse individuals hold diversified portfolios of securities. For individuals, diversification is a low-cost method of risk reduction. Diversification reduces risk because returns on a well-diversified portfolio exhibit less fluctuation than the returns on individual securities comprising the portfolio.

The collective efforts of individual investors to build their own portfolios determine equilibrium prices and returns on securities. Because risk on individual securities can be reduced at low cost by combining different securities into portfolios, security-specific risk does not affect the market price (and hence the return) of an individual security. Instead, its expected return reflects only the *systematic* component of risk, which the CAPM assesses as beta. Conceptually, beta is a measure of the vulnerability of a security's return to factors affecting security returns generally.[1]

The total risk of a security can be separated into two components: system-

---

[1] The beta of security i is $\beta_i = \sigma_{im}/\sigma_m^2$, where β_i is the beta of security i, σ_{im} is the covariance between the return on security i and the return on the CAPM "market portfolio" (a portfolio of risky securities whose composition is identical to the market) and σ_m^2 is the variance of the return on this market portfolio. The covariance σ_{im} can be rewritten as $\sigma_{im} = \rho_{im}\sigma_i\sigma_m$, where ρ_{im} is the correlation coefficient between the return on security i and the market portfolio, and σ_i and σ_m respectively are the standard deviation of the return on security i and on the market portfolio. This formula allows the expression for beta to be rewritten to highlight beta's role as a gauge of vulnerability: $\beta_i = \rho_{im}\sigma_i/\sigma_m$.

atic risk, which reflects vulnerability of the security's return to factors affecting security returns generally; and nonsystematic risk, which is particular to the specific security (recall Chapter 1's discussion of diversifiable and nondiversifiable risk).[2] Because nonsystematic risk can be reduced at zero cost though portfolio diverfication, it does not affect the equilibrium return of a security. In equilibrium, the only type of risk for which investors are compensated is systematic risk.

The type of distinction reflected in systematic and nonsystematic risk was noted early in the insurance literature. In distinguishing between fundamental and particular risk, Chapter 1 of Kulp's text on casualty insurance (1928) anticipated the distinction between systematic and nonsystematic risk that appears later in finance literature. The distinction in the finance literature can be traced to early work by Markowitz (1952) on portfolio diversification.

The CAPM envisions a securities market in which transactions are costless and individuals hold identical beliefs concerning the probability distributions of securities' returns. As a consequence of their identical beliefs, all investors hold risky securities portfolios whose composition is the same: a proportionate share of the market. Because the only risk that is compensated is systematic risk, security returns are positively related to beta.

Carried to an ultimate conclusion, the CAPM envisions a securities market in which the composition of every investor's portfolio is identical and security returns are linear in beta. In a frictionless market in which securities are the only risky assets, when individuals' probability beliefs are homogeneous and their utilities depend only on expected return and variance, individuals hold a replica of the market. Each security's share of an individual's holdings is identical to its share of the aggregate market. As a consequence, returns on individuals' risky securities portfolios under these conditions would be perfectly correlated.

Such a result makes no provision for insurance contracts, although the CAPM does offer a conceptual framework for considering how individuals would react to negative correlation between asset returns (an insurance contract's return is negatively correlated with the insured asset). Attempts to rationalize insurance contracts in such a framework typically postulate individuals being endowed with nonmarketable risks, such as claims to human capital or exposure to liability (see Doherty and Schlesinger [1985]). Insurance contracts exist to hedge these otherwise nonmarketable risks.

The attempts to extend the CAPM to accommodate possible demands for insurance lead to results that are analogous to the CAPM. An individual holds insurance to hedge otherwise nonmarketable risk. Beyond the risk-specific hedge, the composition of every individual's portfolio is a replica of the market, where the market is extended to include aggregate insurance holdings. In other words, beyond the risk-specific insurance contracts to hedge otherwise non-

---

[2] The variance of the return on security i is the sum of systematic and nonsystematic variance: $\sigma_i^2 = \beta_i^2 \sigma_m^2 + s_i^2$, where β_i is the beta of security i, σ_m^2 is the variance of the return on the market portfolio and s_i^2 is the nonsystematic variance of the security's return: $s_i^2 = \sigma_i^2 - \beta_i^2 \sigma_m^2$. The beta of a market-proportioned portfolio is 1.0 and its nonsystematic variance is zero.

marketable risks, every individual holds a market-proportioned portfolio of securities and a proportionate share of the supply of insurance. Returns on securities and insurance are linear in an extended beta, where the extension reflects vulnerability to factors affecting returns on insurance as well as on marketable securities. The concept of extending the methodology underlying the CAPM to consider assets with marketability restrictions appears in finance literature in work by Mayers (1972), Brito (1978), and Breeden (1979).

Limitations and Qualifications of Portfolio Approaches

The CAPM and related approaches as well as the expected utility approach summarized in an earlier section are models of an individual's decision problem. In general, such an approach would be expected to say little about the demand for insurance by organizations. In particular, the CAPM cannot provide a rationale for a resource-consuming insurance transaction between a publicly held insurer and another publicly held organization. The logic behind this assertion is simple. Diversification provides individuals with the opportunity to reduce security-specific risk at low cost. Managers acting in the interest of the organization's owners would not be expected to buy insurance and incur transaction costs because owners can accomplish the same result at lower cost by diversifying their holdings.

The argument becomes especially compelling when one recognizes that the owners of an insured organization also have an opportunity to be owners of a publicly held insurer that writes the coverage. The organization's managers would not serve the interests of owners by incurring transaction costs of insurance that represent a deadweight loss to the insurer and the insured organization. Owners of the insurer and the insured organization could accomplish the same allocation of risk at lower cost by adjusting their ownership shares of each entity.

THE EFFECTS OF RISK MANAGEMENT IN A FRICTIONLESS MARKET

Although the assumptions used to derive the CAPM do not suggest obvious motives leading organizations to purchase insurance, they offer a framework for considering the effects of risk management. The discussion appearing below merely summarizes investment criteria in a frictionless market. A more substantive discussion appears in Brealey and Myers (1991).

In a frictionless market in which securities are the only risky assets, when individuals' probability beliefs are homogeneous and their utilities depend only on expected return and variance in a single time period, an organization's actions, including its risk management activities, would be evaluated by considering expected return and beta. Under assumptions leading to efficient markets, all individuals have the same information and the same assessments of risks and returns. No action escapes the attention of investors or other holders of claims against an organization. Also, holders of claims make rational forecasts of the organization's future actions. In such a setting, prices react immediately to available information. Investors would adjust their holdings of an organization in response to actions of managers. In aggregate, investors' attempts to adjust their individual portfolios would determine the market value of the organization. If the organization adopts an activity whose risk and return reflect a better opportunity than implied in securities returns generally, the market value of the organization rises.

For example, an organization could improve reported profits in the current year by reducing its liability insurance coverage and adopting less expensive quality-control measures. But if markets are efficient, the short-run improvement in the reported profits would not necessarily increase the market value of the organization. Instead, the value of the organization would respond to investors' evaluation of the long-run effects of the actions. Their evaluation would include an assessment of the downward adjustment in customers' demands for the organization's products, the response to lower levels of product quality, and the lack of recourse against a third party (an insurer) for injuries caused by defects in the organization's products.

The assessments would cause shareholders to revise their forecasts of future earnings to reflect reduced consumer demand and higher levels of uninsured product liability claims. Also, the product liability insurer would adjust the price of coverage to reflect the organization's reduced efforts at quality control. The aggregate effect of these adjustments would be a change in the value of owners' holdings in the organization. The net effect would balance investors' assessments of reduced customer demand and increased future product-liability claims against the reduced insurance expenditures and reduced quality control expenditures.

This conceptual framework is not a literal description of market reaction to risk management efforts. Because risk management is a specialized area, few holders of claims against an organization are likely to become fully informed on details in an organization's risk management program. Fewer still will be able to make accurate long-run forecasts of their effects. However, the consequences of risk management policies become evident over time, and they affect investors' forecasts of earnings available for distribution. The only remaining issue then becomes the length of time required for holders of claims to develop accurate forecasts of effects that ultimately become evident.

The Function of Managers

The structure of an organization usually provides incentives for managers to act in the interests of the organization's owners. In publicly held corporations, for example, managers act as agents of the corporation's stockholders. In this role, managers act to increase the value of owners' holdings in the corporation. This value-increasing principle of management applies to managers in marketing, production, finance, human resources, and information systems as well as to risk managers. One also could argue that this same principle applies to nonprofit and public-sector organizations, although few readers would equate a citizen's interests in city government to a stockholder's interest in a corporation. In public and nonprofit organizations, the interests of stakeholders can encompass a wider and more diffuse set of issues than in private organizations.

The risk manager seeks to increase the value of the owners' holdings in the organization. In evaluating the issue of whether to undertake a risk management activity including the purchase of insurance, the risk manager adopts the view of an investor who might hold shares of the organization. The question to be considered is whether the investor would be willing to allocate the required resources to the activity. In making this judgment, the risk manager's specialized knowledge allows better long-run forecasts of the risk management decision's likely effects than investors may be prepared to make.

The value-increasing principle is an important organizing idea. However, the value-increasing *objective* offers little insight into the value-increasing *process*, which is the purpose of this book. The preceding 10 chapters of this text would be unnecessary if all the risk manager needs to know is that risk management seeks to increase the value of the organization. To state the point more plainly, it is less important to know *that* a manager seeks to increase the value of the organization than to know *how* to accomplish the goal.

Questions Left Unanswered

The question of "how" involves more than meets the eye. At first glance, readers might observe that cost-effective loss control measures are likely to increase the value of an organization—an observation that essentially is correct. Also, the elimination of deadweight costs, such as expenditures for vendor-provided services that duplicate activities already taking place within the organization, would be expected to increase value. However, some important risk management activities are not easily explained, as exemplified by the purchase of insurance.

In the long run, the purchase of coverage whose costs exceed direct benefits would appear to be against the interests of the organization's owners. Earlier, this chapter identified links between possible use of insurance by organizations and the activities of risk managers. A rationale for the purchase of insurance by organizations offers insight into risk management because the reasons for employing risk management programs are likely to rest on the same foundation as the rationale for insurance.

Business organizations expend substantial resources on the purchase of insurance coverage. The *1988–89 Property/Casualty Fact Book* (p. 27) reports that commercial purchasers accounted for more than half of net premiums written by property and casualty insurers in the United States during 1987. It is difficult to argue that expenditures of this magnitude could persist if they are against the interests of organizations' owners. It also is difficult to dismiss them as an aberration. Still, the purchase of coverage by organizations seemingly runs against the value-increasing principle.

A frictionless-markets framework also leaves unexplained the earlier-noted practice of requiring fire insurance as a condition for mortgage lending. Investors who hold mortgages in secondary markets would be expected to diversify their holdings to limit their exposure to adverse developments in a limited geographic area or type of property. This diversification could be achieved by holding a variety of securities backed by mortgages. Diversification would be expected to entail low transaction costs, allowing it to dominate insurance as a passive method for risk financing. Opportunities for diversification would be expected to improve as markets for trading these securities organize and become developed. The prediction would be that highly developed markets for securities backed by mortgages are accompanied by lower demand for insurance.

In fact, just the opposite pattern prevails. Investors require not only fire insurance but also insurance against failure to make timely payments of interest and principal. This type of coverage is provided by organizations such as the Federal Housing Administration (FHA), Government National Mortgage Association (GNMA), and the Mortgage Guaranty Insurance Corporation (MGIC) (See Lacy and LaMalfa [1985] and Bartlett [1989]). This demand for specific insurance coverage on each mortgage is especially puzzling in light of investors' general lack of protection against other conditions, such as declining interest rates. If interest rates decline, mortgagors are likely to refinance and prepay their mortgages, which lowers the value of a security backed by the mortgage.

A final question concerns the time period over which analysis is valid. The CAPM assumes a single time period such as a year. Many risk management activities (and other investments by organizations) require a time horizon longer than a single period for evaluation. Capital budgeting approaches appearing in finance texts adopt an approach extending the CAPM into a multiperiod setting. If the CAPM is applied to a problem whose time horizon extends beyond a single period, the results of a single-period model are being extended to a multiperiod setting. This extension of the CAPM for evaluating long-term projects is described later in Chapter 12.

Analysis of long-term investments is a topic that has been discussed extensively in the finance literature. Brealey and Myers (1991) offer an insightful and thorough discussion of methods for evaluating long term-investments and the determinants of their yields. The discussion of the topic appearing later in Chapter 12 is limited to providing a conceptual framework for considering long-term investment issues that arise as part of an organization's risk management process. Interested readers are urged to consult Brealey and Myers or other modern finance texts for further insight into the evaluation of long-term investments.

FRICTIONLESS MARKETS AND PUBLIC-SECTOR RISK MANAGEMENT

A rationale for risk management should apply to public as well as private organizations, although the objectives of government institutions may not be identical to those of private organizations. A brief consideration of whether the value-increasing principle could be adapted to public-sector risk management issues when markets are efficient is helpful in understanding differences between the public and private sectors.

Public Finance

The area of public finance offers a conceptual framework for understanding public organizations. Public finance is an area of economics concerned with understanding government's role in allocating limited resources and distributing the cost of government functions. Because public finance is a field within economics, the concept of a "market" serves as a paradigm for understanding the role of government in society. This common reliance on the concept of a market results in public finance and business finance using similar economic premises to address issues that arise in the two areas.

Two assumptions apply to analysis of issues in public finance: (1) societal welfare depends only on individuals' levels of satisfaction and (2) satisfaction is best realized through allowing individual preferences to determine the allocation of society's resources. Therefore, one important function of government is to promote market efficiency by assuring that markets function freely and competitively. If markets are inefficient or nonexistent, government may intervene. The intervention may range from the mere providing of advice to more stringent measures, such as regulation of business conduct, laws restricting business behavior, or, in extreme cases, the government provision of goods and services.

Economic efficiency is summarized through the "unanimity principle," or Pareto optimality: an allocation of resources is efficient when it is impossible to make one member of society better off without making someone else worse off. Two limitations are present in this method of policy analysis. First, the principle only identifies a set of allocations, not all of which may be equally desirable. One could, for instance, envision economic growth in which all additional benefits of new production accrue to a single individual, while no other person is made "worse off." The new allocations may be Pareto optimal but fail a test based on social equity.

Second, a literal application of the unanimity principle may require gainers from some policy to actually compensate losers. True enforcement of this requirement may be politically impossible. One widely recognized alternative to this restrictive view is the "compensation principle" embodied in the Kaldor-Hicks criterion. This principle loosens the strict application of Pareto optimality by asserting that a policy is acceptable if gainers *could* compensate losers and still benefit. The compensation principle resolves the operational restriction but does not address equity issues.

The idea that government should promote economic efficiency is controversial. Economic efficiency imposes a discipline on public decision making by forcing government officials to consider whether a particular government activity has positive economic effects. In an extensive analysis of the objective of promoting economic efficiency, Rhoads (1985) suggests that the application of concepts such as markets and utility to a public environment raises important issues. For instance, while it may be interesting to consider electoral politics as another example of a market—with candidates buying votes offered for sale by citizens—such analysis may fail to recognize motives behind political behavior. In a representative democracy in which the process of governance is an important issue, the motives behind political behavior can be as important as the behavior itself.

Proprietary and Governance Functions

For the typical public risk manager, Rhoads' concerns about public finance theory typically are not major issues. This statement can be explained by drawing a distinction between proprietary and governance functions in government. Proprietary functions are activities that could be performed or are performed by private business. Governance functions determine the structure of the legal, economic, and social environment in which activity takes place.

City, county, state, and national governments produce goods and services that are, or could be, provided by the private sector. Often, the outward appearance of the government enterprise renders it virtually indistinguishable from the private sector counterpart. The evolution of the political and social climate in developed nations continues to blur the distinction between the public, private, and nonprofit sectors. As governments expand the use of private vendors to provide public services and private organizations seek alliances with public entities to achieve mutual objectives, the distinction between the public and private sectors becomes less clear. A nonprofit day care center that contracts to provide day care services to welfare recipients with a portion of the resulting revenues dedicated to support a child welfare agency offers an illustration. Is the arrangement a government activity, a nonprofit activity, or possibly a for-profit operation?

Notwithstanding the blurred distinction between private and public enterprise, governments do serve unique governance purposes, such as guarantors of law, protectors of rights, enforcers of duties and obligations, and vehicles for expression of the will of the people. Cynics may observe that governments sometimes fail to live up to these responsibilities, but the performance of these functions still is reserved to the public sector.

The dual spheres of activity—"proprietary" and "governance"—give rise to some ambiguity in understanding the structure and function of government. Some observers look at proprietary activities of governments and conclude that their problem is they are "not run like a business." Others, in response, cite governance activities as clear proof that government cannot function as a business. Both points of view contain some truth. For instance, a government-run garbage collection service can operate under the same discipline as a private business. However, some controversy would be likely in a policy initiative that incorporates the buying and selling of rights (to release pollutants, for example). Even more controversial would be the possibility of democratic governments allowing markets for basic human rights—a move that would restore the institution of slavery. The "bottom line" found in a business statement of profit and loss has little meaning with respect to such issues. In truth, proprietary and governance spheres are not mutually exclusive, with some proprietary functions having political ramifications. Readers need only consider the possible effects of a county hospital considering changes in policies for emergency room admissions to appreciate the difficulty of separating purely proprietary functions from governance issues.

Governance Functions in Risk Management

Public-sector risk managers face two important problems. First, public finance—an area of economics that is amenable to explaining risk management—does not provide much insight into the "process" of government. Because process is important to a representative democracy, public finance overlooks an important element in public decision making. Although many proprietary issues arising for public-sector risk managers can be resolved using purely economic analysis, those incorporating governance functions or issues are likely to constitute a greater fraction of the total for a public-sector risk manager as compared with a risk manager in the private sector.

Fortunately for the writers and readers of this text, many risk management decisions in public entities involve issues that are largely proprietary in nature. For example, decisions related to participation in a risk-financing pool or setting safety standards for street repair crews are unlikely to require analysis of governance issues. On other risk management issues, however, political implications can become prominent. The location of a hazardous waste disposal site or the setting of hiring, firing, and promotion standards are examples, although these issues can have strong political overtones in the private sector too.

A rationale for risk management in organizations should be able to accommodate the dual spheres of risk management activity that are especially prominent in the public sector. In the public sector especially, political and governance issues may dominate purely economic considerations. In both public and private sectors, however, a large number of risk management issues can be resolved using economic analysis alone. The next section of this chapter presents a conceptual framework that can accommodate both points of view.

INSURANCE, RISK MANAGEMENT, AND STAKEHOLDER INTERESTS

The earlier frame of reference using efficient markets suggests an extension that may be used to rationalize insurance and risk management in organizations. The extended view considers an organization to be a collection of agreements between resource suppliers and managers. Organizations are formed to accomplish tasks whose completion is impractical or impossible using resources of individuals acting alone. Individuals provide resources to organizations, whose managers assemble the resources and employ them to accomplish the organization's mission. Often, the resources supplied by individuals are financial, as when individuals purchase common stock or lend funds to corporations. They also may take the form of in-kind contributions, such as labor or intellectual efforts.

In return for these resources, the organization's managers make commitments to compensate the individuals who provide them. When the commitment is to provide future compensation, the claim may appear as a liability on the organization's balance sheet. However, even legally binding commitments are not necessarily recorded as liabilities. For example, prior to 1993 corporations were not required to formally recognize a promise to pay retired employees' medical expenses as a liability.

Seen in this light, an organization is a collection of agreements directed towards a mission. The organization holds title to assets, but the organization itself is subject to claims of other organizations and individuals. Ultimately, all claims against organizations can be traced to individuals. Even government entities are owned by individuals, although the attribution of ownership interests is collective rather than to individuals by legal contract.

Individuals who supply resources to organizations often demand safe-guards to protect their claims. Suppliers of equity capital to corporations can protect their interests through voting rights to elect members of the organization's board, which is responsible for monitoring actions of managers. Other suppliers, such as lenders, may demand contractual safeguards against managers taking actions to the detriment of their interests, especially if the suppliers anticipate managers having incentives to take such actions. However, a set of contracts that anticipates all of the contingencies that can arise is likely to be cumbersome and may impose restrictions on managerial discretion that are inefficient.

Managerial Incentives

Typically, the structure of rewards to managers induces them to act as agents of owners, who hold a claim to the residual after other contractual commitments have been met. This reward structure may create an incentive for managers to take actions that benefit owners at the expense of parties holding other types of commitments. In corporations, managers' compensation may be tied directly to the value of the firm through stock options, providing a direct financial incentive to increase the value of the firm's common stock.

The court system imposes a countervailing force to managers' incentives to benefit owners at the expense of other parties. In extreme cases, court action can be used to enforce ethical responsibilities of managers and elected officials. Other types of internal and external monitoring, such as actions of regulatory authorities, can discipline managers' behavior.

Under the concept of an organization as a collection of agreements, individuals who hold indirect claims against an organization can affect the value of direct ownership claims. For example, potential lenders may change the terms on which they are willing to provide funds to a firm in response to the degree of security offered in the lending agreement. Ultimately, lending costs can affect earnings available for distribution to stockholders who have direct ownership claims.

The earlier example of an organization considering the termination of product liability coverage and reduced efforts at quality control offers another illustration. A customer has an indirect claim against the organization through the right to take legal action if injured by a defective product. Because judgments against the organization for defective products reduce earnings otherwise available to stockholders, the value of the organization's stock incorporates stockholders' assessments of future product liability actions. Also, customers' demands for an organization's products are likely to decline in response to perceived low quality, affecting expected future profit levels.

The organization's set of actions in response to these indirect effects or their possibility is called "stakeholder management" in literature on legal environment (see Chapter 5 of Dunfee et al. [1989]). Stakeholder management offers a framework for analyzing the demand for insurance by organizations and, by implication, demands for risk management. Some readers may question why, since stockholder risk aversion does not provide an adequate explanation of corporate insurance purchases, any stakeholder's risk aversion can explain these purchases. If stockholders can reduce risk in their holdings at low cost through diversification, other stakeholders should be able to use diversification too.

However, diversification may prove inadequate for reducing risks that comprise a substantial fraction of an individual's holdings. The career of an executive whose talents make a significant contribution to the organization exemplifies this problem. In fact, the owners of an organization would be expected to create incentives that tie a manager's welfare closely to an organization's performance in ways that make diversification ineffective. Part of the manager's compensation may be in the form of stock that must be held for the period of the manager's employment, subject to further restrictions on transactions the manager could use to offset the risk from holding a large stake in a single firm. The existence of the manager's claim creates a demand for insurance against events that are beyond the manager's control.

Also, being a stakeholder does not necessarily require that an organization's or individual's wealth appear on the balance sheet of the organization in which it holds a stake. Public sector activities exemplify this type of stakeholder interest. The residents in a community hold a collective interest in the community's water supply. Elected officials and representatives they appoint act as agents of the community's citizens in enforcing their collective interest against an organization that contaminates the water supply. Enforcement is accomplished through fines or by forcing the offender to shoulder the costs of removing the contaminants. However remote the effect might be, the fines and penalties or even their possibility affect the value of the organization.

Insurance can provide a signal concerning a firm's efforts at safety-related activities. The willingness of an insurer to write coverage against environmental contamination provides a signal to investors about the organization's efforts at controlling the release of contaminants. The willingness of an insurer to write product liability coverage reflects favorably on an organization's efforts at quality control, a signal that may increase consumers' demand for the organization's products.

Corporate Insurance Purchases

The above examples provides background for considering seven reasons other than stockholder risk aversion identified by Mayers and Smith (1982) to explain corporate insurance purchases: (1) insurance can be used to allocate risk away from stakeholders who have a comparative disadvantage in risk bearing, (2) insurance transaction costs may be lower than the expected value of bankruptcy costs, (3) an insurer may have a comparative advantage in claims administration, (4) an insurer may be used to monitor risk-creating activities, (5) insurance may strengthen incentives to follow patterns of investment implied when resources are contributed by investors, (6) insurance can reduce an organization's expected tax liability, and (7) insurance may reduce regulatory costs. With the possible exception of reason 6, which applies to taxable entities, these reasons also can be adapted to explain insurance in government and nonprofit sectors. Each of these reasons is explained briefly below.

Insurance can be used to allocate risk away from stakeholders who have a comparative disadvantage in risk bearing. If the equity of a corporation were large enough and its ownership were widely dispersed in an efficient market, all risk could be efficiently allocated to stockholders. The existence of other claims, such as those of employees and suppliers, creates incentive for insurance if these claims cannot be diversified effectively.

Insurance transaction costs may be lower than the expected value of bankruptcy costs. Bankruptcy is not a costless event. Bankruptcy costs include expenses such as costs of litigation to resolve disputes over competing claims. The expected value of these costs can be weighed against loading fees associated with insurance.

This type of reasoning can be extended to reflect other costs associated with financial distress. Borrowing funds to replace damaged assets or to reimburse liability claims offers an alternative to insurance, but the cost of borrowing may be affected by the incident creating the demand for borrowed funds. Payment of at least a portion of insurance loading fees may be justified by considering the extra cost of obtaining funds under conditions of distress. Remarkably, consideration of possible bankruptcy costs or extra costs associated with financial distress leads to effects that are nearly identical to the effect of risk aversion in individuals. These costs, which could be described as "worry costs," provide the motivation for a method to select retention levels described in Chapter 12.

An insurer may have a comparative advantage in claims administration. Benefits provided by insurance include not only claim reimbursement but also services related to the administration of claims. In the absence of insurance, these services are supplied from some other source. In liability insurance, for example, the insurer is obligated to provide legal defense services if a covered claim is filed against the insured. In effect, the insurer bonds its promise to provide legal defense services by agreeing to pay a judgment up to the policy limit if the defense fails. Purchasing coverage provides access to the insurer's skill and experience in defending the type of claim covered by the liability policy. The search costs required to identify equivalent legal defense skills in the event of a claim are avoided by purchasing coverage.

Health insurance for employees offers another example of a type of coverage in which claims administration is an important element of insurance coverage. If coverage is not purchased, the services required to administer claims must be supplied from some other source. Further, an insurer may have a relative advantage in negotiating with providers of health care services, further reducing the cost of coverage relative to the employer's direct reimbursement of claims. Administrative service only (ASO) plans, in which a health insurer provides only the claims administrative services, offer evidence of the value of these services.

Inspection and rating services provided as part of boiler and machinery coverage offer a third example. These services are provided at the time of underwriting, and they exemplify a service other than claims administration for which an insurer may hold a comparative advantage. Inspection and rating services provided by boiler and machinery insurers are valued highly enough by some purchasers that their value alone would warrant payment of the premium.

An insurer may be used to monitor risk-creating activities. After insurance is written, the insurer has a strong interest in monitoring activities that increase exposure to risk. In the absence of insurance, a manager's incentives might encourage the creation of risk. For example, a manager may have an incentive to shirk on safety-related activities if the manager's compensation is based on current reported profits and the effects of safety-related activities become apparent only after some delay. The incentive becomes stronger if the manager is near the end of his or her career. Insurance mitigates this effect by creating an incentive for the insurer to monitor this aspect of managers' activities.

Insurance may strengthen incentives to follow patterns of investment implied when resources are contributed by individuals. After a corporation issues debt, managers acting in the interest of stockholders may have incentive to undertake negative present-value risky projects. The truncated nature of the debt contract causes the investment in risky projects to result in a transfer of wealth from debtholders to stockholders. When the risky projects perform well, debtholders receive only the promised payment, while residual gains accrue to stockholders. When the risky projects' yields are too low to cover debt service charges, debtholders bear the burden of loss. Insurance can be used to mitigate this problem by affecting subsequent patterns of investment. Appendix 11.1 at the end of this chapter illustrates how insurance reduces an underinvestment problem.

The argument can be extended to consider insurance as a method for alleviating moral hazards in organizations. The incentive to undertake negative present-value risky projects after the issuance of debt merely illustrates how moral hazards can arise in this setting. When moral hazards are present, insurance can be used to strengthen guarantees provided by the organization. The exposure to liability of a corporate director offers an illustration. The corporation could write an agreement to indemnify the director if lawsuit arises out of the director's duties. Because the lawsuit could possibly arise from one of the corporation's own shareholders, the director faces the risk of default if the shareholder mounts a successful legal challenge to the indemnity agreement. In recognition of this possible conflict, the director may require insurance written by an insurer that is unrelated to the corporation employing the director.

A similar argument applies to liability insurance for a government official. With respect to risks affecting taxpayers generally, risk-neutrality is likely to hold in a government entity that can pool the resources of many taxpayers. However, the government official faces the possibility that taxpayer resources may not be available to cover some lawsuits or that legal action may be required to secure them. In this instance, the risk aversion of the government official gives rise to the demand for insurance coverage.

Insurance can reduce an organization's expected tax liability. A large uninsured loss may drive an organization's taxable income below zero. Negative taxable income results in the organization losing the current value of tax savings that result when business expenses are written off against taxable income. Instead, writeoffs such as depreciation may be deferred to future accounting periods, in which case their value is less than if written off currently. The use of insurance tends to smooth out possible fluctuations in an organization's taxable income, hence preserving the value of current writeoffs.

Liability insurance offers a second example. Current tax rules allow a liability insurer to establish a provision for loss (a *reserve*) in advance of actual claim payment. These rules do not extend to self-insurers, who generally can deduct these costs only when *economic performance* occurs, which in most cases means actual payment is made to the injured party. The right to write off future costs against current income reduces the cost of claims to the insurer, who in a competitive market would be expected to share these savings with insured customers. A third example involves tax rules related to property losses, which may encourage the use of insurance on depreciated property. These rules are described in Appendix 11.2 at the end of this chapter.

Insurance may reduce regulatory costs. A regulated industry may use insurance to build loss costs into the current rate structure. For example, an electrical utility may have difficulty convincing the regulatory board of the levels of future costs of current work-related injuries. The purchase of insurance against these injuries provides the kind of hard evidence required to incorporate these costs into current electrical rates. The use of insurance matches the current cost against the activity giving rise to the cost.

Summary: The Rationale for Insurance Purchases by Organizations

Many of the seven reasons in the Mayers-Smith (1982) rationale for corporate insurance purchases can apply to the public as well as to the private sector. The risk management and insurance literature, including previous editions of this text, has long recognized the value of insurer-provided services as well as possible benefits of insurance in offsetting expected costs of bankruptcy and financial dislocation. However, these features of insurance were viewed as secondary or incidental to protection against risk. As the size of an organization increases, features of insurance that may be secondary or incidental for individuals become increasingly prominent.

RISK MANAGEMENT IN ORGANIZATIONS

By inference, the rationale for organizations using insurance can be adapted to offer a rationale for risk management. The observation that organizations use insurance identifies one reason why organizations employ risk managers. The risk manager is the liaison between the organization and its insurers. A risk manager can provide evidence to insurers that favorably affects the terms on which they offer coverage. In the absence of an active risk management program, insurers' forecasts of an organization's losses are likely to be pessimistic. These pessimistic forecasts translate into higher insurance premiums.

However, the rationale for risk management in organizations extends beyond the scope of liaison with the organization's insurers. Some reasons for corporate insurance purchases envision the insurance providing a performance guaranty in some other transaction (e.g., replacement of an asset whose present value is positive). To the extent that a risk manager can design a program that provides the same type of guaranty, the program substitutes for insurance coverage while avoiding the transaction costs typically associated with insurance. For example, a trust fund dedicated to the payment of hospital medical liability claims may serve the same function as insurance covering the same claims as long as reasonable safeguards are incorporated into the trust fund agreement and the appropriate funding levels are used. A captive insurer may serve the same role.

The effectiveness of risk management in substituting for insurance is likely to be specific to the parties concerned and the nature of their incentives following a covered event. Ultimately, the demand for insurance may be driven by individuals' risk aversion, although the effects of risk aversion are manifested differently in organizations than in individuals. For example, a trust fund probably would not fully substitute for insurance to indemnify a corporate director or elected official against legal liability related to discharging his or her duties. The level of funding required for such a trust fund probably is too high to make it a practical substitute for insurance. Also, the director or elected official might reason that a trust fund arrangement is nearly as vulnerable to legal challenge as is a pure indemnity agreement.

Effective communication of risk management efforts is an important element in any organization's efforts at reducing uncertainty. Chapter 2 of this text asserts that the purpose of risk management is to enable the organization to move toward its goals and objectives on a direct, efficient, and effective path. Risk management is seen as a central management function, devoted to the management of uncertainty and its effect on the organization's progress toward its mission. Credible information can have a strong effect on stakeholders' levels of uncertainty, so communication of an organization's risk management efforts is an important link in the risk management process.

How These Principles Can Explain Mortgage Insurance

A question posed earlier in this chapter focuses on the practice of lenders requiring fire insurance coverage at the time a mortgage is written. The seven reasons for corporate insurance purchases can be reexamined to see which offer insight into the practice. The allocation of risk away from stakeholders who have a comparative disadvantage in risk bearing offers a possible explanation for a lender who continues to hold a large mortgage after underwriting, although this explanation is not very convincing. Mortgages typically are sold by lenders after underwriting and ultimately repackaged into mortgage-backed securities. If the use of insurance entails higher costs than diversification by holders of mortgage-backed securities, one would expect at least one lender who sells its mortgages to have discovered a lower-cost no-insurance alternative through experimentation.

Possible bankruptcy costs and a comparative advantage in claims administration offer more plausible explanations. An uninsured mortgagor might be expected to default on mortgage payments after a fire. Although such default is not synonymous with bankruptcy, the legal process of foreclosure consumes resources. Avoidance of these legal costs is balanced against insurance loading fees. A comparative advantage in claims administration also can explain insurance guaranteeing timely payment of principal and interest in the event of default under conditions other than fire. An insurer's comparative advantage in pricing and evaluating fire risks offers another explanation. A lender's skills are closely related to underwriting of mortgages, an activity that is only distantly related to evaluating, pricing, and monitoring of risks related to fire damage.

APPENDIX 11.1. THE VALUE OF A COMMITMENT TO RESTORE DAMAGED ASSETS

Mayers and Smith (1987) offer an illustration of conflicting incentives as they affect a firm's stockholders and bondholders. Their paper shows how insurance can overcome an underinvestment problem when a firm has risky debt in its capital structure. More generally, their approach shows how a commitment to restore damaged assets can increase the value of an organization.

The value of the commitment can be illustrated with an example. To simplify calculations, the example ignores the time value of money and assumes that cash flows are zero-beta. Relaxing either of these assumptions would not affect the nature of the conclusions. The example is an all-equity firm whose market value is $1 million in the setting of a single time period. The firm faces possible damage from explosion, in which case the salvage value of its assets becomes $200,000. The damage can be repaired at a cost of $600,000, and the firm's market value again becomes $1 million. The probability of explosion is 1/10. If the firm is not damaged by explosion, it will earn $66,667 during the period. These earnings are lost if explosion occurs.

Repairing the damage after an explosion would appear to be the rational course of action; the $600,000 expenditure increases the market value of the firm by $800,000. Thus, restoring the firm following explosion is a value-increasing activity. Presumably, owners of the all-equity firm would be willing to finance the restoration if an explosion occurs. Repairing the damage requires a $600,000 outlay to restore the firm's market value to $1 million, a net payoff of $400,000. If no explosion occurs, the payoff to owners of the all-equity firm is the firm's market value plus earnings, or $1,066,667. The value of the firm at the beginning of the period is the expected value of the cash payoffs: (1/10)($400,000) + (9/10)($1,066,667), or $1,000,000.

Suppose the firm issues debt with a face value of $500,000 and uses the proceeds to retire outstanding shares of equity. Holders of the debt receive $500,000, or, if less, the value of the firm's assets. How does this debt affect the incentive to restore the firm after an explosion? Equity holders would not be expected to provide $600,000 to repair the damage when the value of their claim to a restored firm will be less than $600,000. If control of the firm resides with equity holders and they cannot extract a payment from bondholders, they would be expected to default.

Furthermore, the market value of the firm declines when claimholders anticipate default. The value of bondholders' claims declines because payment becomes uncertain. Bondholders receive $200,000 if explosion occurs and $500,000 if the firm survives with no damage. The expected value of bondholders' claims is (1/10)($200,000) + (9/10)($500,000), or $470,000. Equity holders receive nothing if explosion occurs and $566,667 if the firm survives the period with no damage. The expected value of their claims is (1/10)($0) + (9/10)($566,667), or $510,000.[3]

The market value of the firm with debt in its capital structure is $470,000 + $510,000, or $980,000. Relative to the all-equity firm, the market value has declined by $20,000. Stockholder default following explosion implies that the $200,000 gain from restoration will be lost, and holders of claims against the firm price their claims accordingly. The forgone gain from restoration represents a deadweight loss to all claimholders. The expected value of this opportunity loss is (1/10)(200,000), or $20,000.[4]

A guarantee that restoration will take place in the event of explosion increases the value of the firm by $20,000. In the case of the all-equity firm, equity holders' pursuit of their own self-interest provides this guarantee. With debt in the firm's capital structure, the guarantee may take some other form. Thus, an insurance policy used for restoration can increase the value of the firm, even with an expense loading. However, it is not the insurance per se that increases the value of the firm; it is the guarantee that restoration will be undertaken if an explosion occurs. The insurance is incidental to this issue. Its role is to provide assurance that the positive present-value restoration will be undertaken if explosion occurs. Any other form of commitment sufficient to convince claimholders that restoration will follow an explosion can fulfill the same role.

Both the restoration and the commitment to restoration contribute to the value of the firm. Owners of the all-equity firm would be expected to favor the commitment when the debt is issued. Paradoxically, equity holders would be expected to oppose the commitment once the debt is outstanding.[5] Their opposition would be based on the decline in the value of their holdings; the commitment increases the market value of the debt by $30,000 while decreasing the market value of equity by $10,000.

This opposition would be detrimental to long-run performance when firms compete for assets as well as funds from investors. With a commitment to restore the asset, a firm's claimholders would be willing to contribute up to $1 million to fund the asset's acquisition. Without the commitment, claimholders are

---

[3] One might observe that bondholders could take control of the firm and restore damaged assets after stockholder default. In a practical setting, bondholder control of the firm would require a bankruptcy proceeding with attendant litigation expenses and delays.

[4] The $20,000 decline in the value of the firm is caused by the forgone restoration opportunity. This result can be confirmed by considering the market value of the all-equity firm under the assumption that restoration does not occur. In this case, the payoffs to equity holders would be the $200,000 salvage value of the assets if explosion occurs and $1,066,667 if the firm survives with no explosion. The expected value of these payoffs is (1/10)($200,000) + (9/10)($1,066,667), or $980,000, the same as the firm's market value with debt.

[5] On balance, stockholders bear the $20,000 decline in market value when the firm issues debt without a restoration commitment. If the all-equity firm issues debt without a commitment, the proceeds will be $470,000 and the market value of the firm's equity becomes $510,000. If the debt proceeds are paid directly to holders of equity, their wealth has declined from $1 million as owners of the all-equity firm to $980,000, the sum of the debt proceeds and remaining equity value. Having suffered this loss, stockholders have no incentive to provide the restoration commitment. Stockholders would benefit, however, by providing a restoration guarantee prior to issuing the debt.

willing to contribute only $980,000. A restoration commitment gives the firm a competitive advantage in bidding for assets and funds from investors.

261

CHAPTER 11
A Rationale for Risk
Management in
Organizations

When restoration is value-increasing, a commitment to restoration increases the firm's market value. In evaluating this issue, the market value of the firm considers the value of *all* claims against the firm, not just those of stockholders. The commitment to restoration also illustrates the importance of timing; stockholders would favor the commitment prior to issuing the debt but would oppose it once the debt is outstanding.

APPENDIX 11.2. TAXATION AND CORPORATE INSURANCE PURCHASES

As Chapter 9 explained, a corporation is allowed to deduct uninsured losses as well as premiums for insurance when computing income subject to taxation. Deducting these costs reduces the corporation's tax payment, so the after-tax cost of these expenses is lower than their pretax value. For example, a $1000 insurance expenditure becomes $1000(1 − $0.34) = $660 after taxes for a corporation taxed at a 34 percent rate. Similarly, a $10,000 uninsured loss becomes $10,000(1 − $0.34) = $6600 for this corporation.

The tax rules appear to be evenhanded in that they allow the corporation to deduct either an uninsured loss or the premium for the insurance to cover the loss. However, this presumed evenhandedness does not consider possible effects of widely fluctuating losses on a corporation's taxable income. A corporation that retains losses faces the possibility of their becoming unpredictably concentrated in a single year and driving taxable income below zero. A corporation whose taxable income becomes negative can carry the loss back to prior years' income and obtain a refund of taxes paid in those years. When carrybacks are exhausted, the loss is carried forward to reduce taxes that will be paid in the future. A corporation in this situation loses the favorable effect of a current tax reduction when costs are written off against taxable income.

By reducing possible fluctuations in taxable income, insurance protects against the loss of these tax shields. This observation can be used to explain the purchase of business interruption and liability coverages by corporations.

Tax rules favor the purchase of liability insurance in yet another way. A corporation is allowed to deduct an uninsured liability loss involving payments to an individual only when "economic performance" occurs. Economic performance occurs when payments are made to the injured individual. However, insurers are allowed to deduct the present value of the payments when they have enough information to make a reasonable estimate of the amount of liability. This differential tax treatment favors the use of insurance against losses requiring payments distributed over future time periods.

For example, an insurer that becomes liable to pay $50,000 a year for 20 years to an injured person can deduct the present value of the $50,000 payments from its current taxable income. Using an 8 percent interest rate, the present value of these payments is $490,905. If the current interest rate is 8 percent, an insurer could fund the $50,000 payments with a portfolio of bonds whose current value is $490,905 and pay no tax on the transaction. Ignoring the effects of expense loadings, an insurer would be willing to accept this liability for a premium of \$490,905. Using a 34 percent tax rate, the after-tax cost of this premium to an insured corporation is $490,905(1 - \$0.34) = \$323,997.30$.

The insured corporation can deduct each \$50,000 payment when it is made. Using a 34 percent tax rate, the after-tax payment becomes $50,000(1 - \$0.34) = \$33,000$. If the corporation were to set up a retention fund to cover these payments, it would need a fund large enough to provide \$33,000 a year for 20 years. However, the corporation is taxed on interest earnings from this fund; using the 34 percent tax rate, the 8 percent pretax interest rate becomes $8(1 - \$0.34) = 5.28$ percent after taxes. The present value of \$33,000 a year for 20 years at 5.28 percent is \$401,661.90, which is \$77,664.60 greater than the after-tax premium for the insurer to accept the liability with no transaction costs. This difference creates an incentive for the corporation to pass the liability to an insurer as opposed to setting up a retention fund and making the payments when they come due. This incentive is present even with transaction costs. If no uncertainty is involved in the estimated liability, the \$77,664.60 represents an upper limit on allowable transaction costs.

Prior to 1987, tax rules were even more favorable to liability insurance in that they allowed insurers to deduct the full estimated claim payment without discounting for the time value of money. Smith and Witt (1985) show how these tax rules provided an incentive for retroactive insurance covering MGM Grand Hotels for its liability in the November, 1980, hotel fire in Las Vegas.

A third way in which tax rules can favor the purchase of insurance over retention involves tax accounting methods for depreciable property. Accounting depreciation allocates the cost of an asset over time. In concept, accounting depreciation reflects wear and tear and aging on the value of an asset. In practice, accounting depreciation (at least for tax purposes) is determined by a rule that may bear little relationship to an asset's physical depreciation.

An asset's book value is original cost less accounting depreciation. For example, a warehouse costing \$2 million has a book value of \$2 million on the day of purchase. If the warehouse is depreciated over a 20-year period using a straight-line method, the book value is \$1 million after 10 years and zero after 20 years.

For a corporation that retains property losses, the deduction for an uninsured property loss is the asset's book value. For example, if the warehouse is destroyed on the day of purchase, the corporation can deduct \$2 million from its taxable income. If the warehouse is destroyed 20 years after purchase, no deduction is allowed because the asset is fully depreciated for tax purposes.

If insurance covers the destroyed warehouse, the insurance proceeds offset any loss deductible for tax purposes. For example, a corporation collecting a \$2 million insurance benefit for the warehouse whose book value is \$2 million reports no gain or loss. The corporation collecting a \$2 million insurance benefit for the warehouse whose book value is zero may be required to report a gain of \$2 million. However, if the insurance proceeds are used to replace the destroyed warehouse with another one costing \$2 million, the corporation is not required to report the \$2 million as taxable income. The book value of the replacement warehouse then becomes zero. In accounting language, the corporation has "deferred the gain" from the insurance proceeds by setting the book value of the new warehouse to be the same as the destroyed one.

The way that this rule can favor property insurance becomes apparent by considering the fully depreciated warehouse whose book value is zero. The discussion assumes that the destroyed warehouse is replaced with another one costing $2 million. If the corporation retains the loss, the new warehouse is treated like any other new investment: The book value of the new warehouse is $2 million, to be depreciated over 20 years. Thus, the economic loss to the retaining corporation is the $2 million outlay less the present value of reduced taxes from writing off the $2 million outlay over 20 years. If insurance is used, the economic loss is zero; the corporation's outlay is offset by insurance, but the new asset is fully depreciated on the day of purchase.

In effect, the purchase of insurance whose premiums are deductible allows the corporation to write off the expected difference between the insurance benefit and the asset's book value as an immediate charge. If the damage is retained, this difference is written off gradually through depreciation deductions. To make this point clear, suppose insurance costing $2 million is available on the day the warehouse is destroyed. On the surface, it would appear that the corporation would be indifferent to the insurance; the contract provides a $2 million benefit for a premium of $2 million.

However, this indifference does not necessarily survive when tax effects are considered. The after-tax cost of the $2 million insurance premium to the corporation taxed at a 34 percent rate is $2,000,000(1 − $0.34), or $1.32 million. In effect, the purchase of the tax-deductible insurance allows the corporation to write off the full cost of the destroyed warehouse as an immediate charge against income. In contrast, when the corporation retains the loss the same amount is written off gradually through depreciation deductions.

By purchasing insurance, the corporation does not gain in an absolute sense; instead, the gain is *relative to retaining* the loss. This gain would not occur with insurance on a new warehouse. The corporation would be indifferent between retaining the loss or paying the $2 million premium on the day the warehouse is destroyed. If the loss is retained, the $2 million uninsured loss is a charge against income. If the insurance is purchased, the same $2 million charge is taken, but as an insurance expense. Thus, tax-reduction motives tend to be stronger on assets that have been depreciated for tax purposes.

Key Concepts

claim against firm   A right to payment that can be asserted against the firm. The right may be exercised currently or at some future point in time. The right to exercise the claim may be contingent in that it can be exercised only under certain conditions.

claimholder   The organization or individual having the right to exercise a claim.

value of the firm   The total market value of all the outstanding claims against the firm.

stakeholder   An organization or individual having a right that can be exercised against another organization. The right does not necessarily take the form of a legal contract, but may exist through common law or the authority to regulate.

utility function   A function that ranks an individual's preferences among possible outcomes. The function may rank outcomes by assigning a numerical value to the well-being the individual experiences as a result of the outcome.

risk aversion A characteristic of an individual who prefers receiving the expected value of a bet over being exposed to the risky outcomes inherent in the bet itself.

systematic risk Risk arising from factors that affect a population generally. Because systematic risk affects all the members of a group in the same way, it cannot be reduced by pooling or diversification.

nonsystematic risk Risk that affects members of a population independently. Nonsystematic risk can be eliminated through pooling or diversification.

actuarially fair insurance Insurance coverage whose price equals the expected value of insurance claim payments.

capital asset pricing model (CAPM) A model of securities pricing in a market in which securities are the only risky assets, transactions are costless, and individuals hold identical beliefs concerning the probability distributions of securities returns.

public finance An area of economics concerned with understanding government's role in allocating limited resources and distributing the cost of government functions.

unanimity principle (Pareto optimality) A condition applying to an allocation of resources in society whereby it is impossible to make one member of society better off without making someone else worse off.

compensation principle (Kaldor-Hicks criterion) A principle that relaxes side payments between individuals that may be required to achieve a Pareto-optimal state by asserting that a policy is acceptable if gainers from the policy could compensate losers and still benefit.

proprietary functions Activities in the public sector that could be performed or are performed by private business.

governance functions Activities in the public sector that determine the structure of the legal, economic, and social environment in which activity takes place. These functions generally cannot be assigned to the private sector.

Review Questions

1. Distinguish between systematic and nonsystematic risk. Why do managers of large, publicly owned business firms have little incentive to reduce nonsystematic risk?
2. Explain why a risk-averse individual holding a portfolio of assets may fail to fully insure against loss to either one of the assets, even if the price of coverage is actuarially fair.
3. Explain how the objectives of a risk manager and a financial manager are similar and how they may differ.
4. Explain how the role of the risk manager with respect to a firm's insurers may depend on the issue being considered (e.g., loss prevention or negotiation with respect to an insurance recovery after loss).
5. A corporation's market value is $5 million when organized as an all-equity firm. If a fire occurs, the salvage value of the firm's assets is reduced to $1 million. Repairing the fire damage costs $2.5 million, in which case the firm's market value is restored to $5 million. The probability of fire is $0.05. The corporation's earnings if no fire occurs are $131,579.
   a. Would repairing the fire damage be rational for the owners of the all-equity firm?
   b. Calculate the expected fire damage.
   c. Calculate the payoff to owners of the all-equity firm if no fire occurs.
   d. The firm issues debt with a face value of $3 million. Would repairing the fire damage be rational for stockholders if they control the decision?
   e. Calculate the market value of the debtholders' claim against the firm. Calculate the expected value of the stockholders' claim against the firm.

f. Calculate the market value of the firm with $3 million face value of debt in its capital structure. Explain any change from the answer to question **a.**

6. Explain how tax considerations can increase the value to a corporation of insurance against:
   a. Business interruption losses
   b. Workers' compensation liability losses
   c. Losses to depreciable property.

7. Should a corporation's pension be considered in determining the value of the firm to its owners? Explain.

8. Define public finance and explain its relationship to business finance.

9. Can the theory of public finance fully explain the behavior of governments and politicians? If not, what aspects of the behavior does it fail to explain?

10. Explain the difference between the unanimity principle and the compensation principle.

11. Explain why the risk manager for a large municipality may purchase liability insurance coverage for an elected official despite the availability of lower-cost methods such as retention. If the cost of legal defense and claim payment for the official were retained, the cost would be allocated across the 1.5 million households comprising the municipality, with negligible effect on each tax bill.

12. Public finance economists often argue that politicians are utility-maximizing individuals in their public and professional roles. In this context, they may conclude that utility maximization usually means "getting (re)elected." Do you believe that getting elected is a politician's sole objective? Why or why not?

13. Distinguish between proprietary and governance functions in the public sector.

References and Suggestions for Additional Reading

ARROW, K. J.: *Essays in the Theory of Risk Bearing.* (Amsterdam: North-Holland, 1971).

————: *Social Choice and Individual Value.* (New York: John Wiley & Sons, Inc., 1963).

BARTLETT, WILLIAM W.: *Mortgage-Backed Securities.* (New York: New York Institute of Finance, 1989).

BREALEY, RICHARD A., and STEWART C. MYERS: *Principles of Corporate Finance.* (New York: McGraw-Hill Book Company, 1991).

BREEDEN, DOUGLAS T.: "An Intertemporal Asset Pricing Model with Stochastic Consumption and Investment Opportunities," *Journal of Financial Economics* (vol. 7, no. 3, 1979), pp. 265–296.

BRITO, O. NEY: "Portfolio Selection in an Economy with Marketability and Short Sale Restrictions," *Journal of Finance* (vol. 33, no. 2, 1978), pp. 589–601.

BROWNING, EDWARD K., and JACQUELINE M. BROWNING: *Public Finance and the Price System* (2nd ed., New York: Macmillan Publishing Company, 1983).

DOHERTY, NEIL A., and HARRIS SCHLESINGER: "Incomplete Markets for Insurance: An Overview," *The Journal of Risk and Insurance* (vol. 52, no. 3, 1985), pp. 402–423.

———— and ————: "Optimal Insurance in Incomplete Markets," *Journal of Political Economy* (vol. 91, no. 6, 1983), pp. 1045–1054.

DUNFEE, THOMAS W., FRANK F. GIBSON, JOHN D. BLACKBURN, DOUGLAS WHITMAN, F. WILLIAM McCARTY, and BARTLEY A. BRENNAN: *Modern Business Law* (2nd ed., New York: Random House, 1989).

KULP, C. A.: *Casualty Insurance.* (New York: The Ronald Press Company, 1928).

GOODSELL, CHARLES: *The Case for Bureaucracy.* (Chatham, NJ, Chatham House, 1983).

LACY, WILLIAM H., and THOMAS S. LAMALFA: "The Role of the Private Mortgage Insurance Industry," chapter 8 in James M. Kinney and Richard T. Garrigan (eds.), *The Handbook of Mortgage Banking* (Homewood, Ill.: Richard D. Irwin, 1985).

MARKOWITZ, HARRY: "Portfolio Selection," *Journal of Finance* (vol. 7, 1952), pp. 77–91.

MAYERS, D.: "Nonmarketable Assets and Capital Market Equilibrium under Uncertainty." In M. C. Jensen (ed.), *Studies in the Theory of Capital Markets* (New York: Praeger, 1972).

MAYERS, D., and C. W. SMITH, JR.: "On the Corporate Demand for Insurance," *Journal of Business* (vol. 22, no. 2, 1982), pp. 281–296.

———— and ————: "The Interdependence of Individual Portfolio Decisions and the Demand for Insurance," *Journal of Political Economy* (vol. 91, no. 2, 1983), pp. 304–311.

———— and ————: "Corporate Insurance and the Underinvestment Problem," *Journal of Risk and Insurance* (vol. 54, no. 1, 1987), pp. 45–54.

MIKESELL, JOHN L.: *Fiscal Administration: Analysis and Applications for the Public Sector* (Homewood, Ill.: Dorsey Press, 1982).

RHOADS, STEVEN E.: *The Economist's View of the World: Governments, Markets and Public Policy* (Cambridge, Mass.: Cambridge University Press, 1985).

SCHOEMAKER, PAUL J. H.: "The Expected Utility Model: Its Variants, Purposes, Evidence and Limitations," *Journal of Economic Literature* (vol. 20, no. 2, 1982), pp. 529–563.

SMITH, MICHAEL L., and ROBERT C. WITT: "An Economic Analysis of Retroactive Liability Insurance," *The Journal of Risk and Insurance* (vol. 52, no. 3, 1985), pp. 379–401.

STOKEY, EDITH, and RICHARD ZECKHAUSER: *A Primer for Policy Analysis* (New York: W. W. Norton & Co., 1978).

TVERSKY, AMOS, PAUL SLOVIC, and DANIEL KAHNEMAN: "The Causes of Preference Reversal," *The American Economic Review* (vol. 80, no. 1, 1990), pp. 204–217.

VON NEUMANN, JOHN, and OSKAR MORGANSTERN: *Theory of Games and Economic Behavior* (New York: John Wiley & Son, Inc., 1944).

1988–89 Property/Casualty Fact Book (New York: Insurance Information Institute).

Risk Management Decision Methods: Data Organization and Analysis

Learning Objectives

After you have completed this chapter, you should be able to:

1. Identify features that distinguish risk management problems from problems faced by managers in other areas.
2. Describe a process that a risk manager for a small organization can use to set priorities among insurance coverages.
3. Identify break-even points in a table of insurance premiums for different deductible levels.
4. Use insurance industry data to estimate thresholds for an organization's willingness to pay for claims management and other protection services.
5. Explain how the nature of an organization's exposure to possible loss affects its willingness to pay for claims management and other services related to insurance coverage.
6. Explain why the discount rate used to evaluate the present value of cash flows in a long-term risk management project can differ from the discount rate used to evaluate an organization's other long-term projects.
7. Use a risk-adjusted discount rate to evaluate the cash flows from a proposed long-term risk management project.
8. Explain how financing side-effects such as incremental addition to the organization's debt capacity can affect the evaluation of a long-term risk management project.
9. Explain how the method used to estimate risk-adjusted net present value for a publicly held business can be modified for use by a government entity.
10. Explain how commonly used financial ratios apply to risk management.

INTRODUCTION

With the conceptual framework offered in Chapter 11 as a background, readers are prepared to consider methods that can be used in making risk management decisions. The purpose of Chapter 12 is to describe techniques for organizing and presenting data in problems likely to confront a professional risk manager. The rationale for risk management in organizations appearing in Chapter 11 provides a framework for thinking about the risk management function, while Chapter 12 describes applications.

After reviewing several notable features that tend to distinguish risk management problems from problems faced by other managers, this chapter presents six decision-aiding tools that can be useful in organizing data for the evaluation of these problems. The tools are (1) a structured review of insurance coverage likely to be useful in smaller organizations, (2) a type of break-even analysis that can be useful in selecting retention levels, (3) a method to assist the risk manager in estimating the organization's willingness to pay for services related to insurance coverage, (4) an adaptation of capital budgeting techniques from finance literature to reflect characteristics of long-term risk management projects in the private sector, (5) a further adaptation of these capital budgeting techniques to reflect issues likely to appear in the public sector, and (6) a discussion of how financial ratios can apply to risk management.

The methods described in this chapter are intended to aid in two tasks: (1) analysis of problems requiring a decision, and (2) the presentation of recommended actions to other areas of management. In most cases, the methods do not determine which action is optimal. Rather, they aid in the identification and clarification of the issues and consequences of actions. The purpose of formally studying decision-making methods is to better understand the decision process: the assumptions that underlie the process and their validity, the relationship of the decision to broader organizational purposes, the consistency between the decision and other decisions made within the organization, the fairness of the outcome to affected parties, and the justifications for the eventual outcome. Ideally, an approach for analyzing issues and making decisions is anchored in the overall mission of the organization.

However, rigid application of decision-making methods can inhibit creative solutions to difficult problems. Managers often encounter issues in which innovative thinking and nontraditional methods of analysis can be valuable. Good managers typically have an ability to use intuitive approaches to problem solving as well as more formal and structured methods. Franklin Roosevelt, for example, was known to mystify aides with his ability to pull together seemingly unrelated pieces of information to offer a new—and frequently useful—way of looking at or solving a political or policy dilemma.

Decision-making methods must be adaptable to informal input and new methods of analysis. A successful manager develops an overall approach to decision making that finds some balance between three conflicting criteria: (1) the decision-making process should be "rigorous" (i.e., subject to a system that organizes ideas, objectives, or principles, such as a theory), (2) the method should be "flexible" (i.e., allow for insight, intuition, and adaptation), and (3) the process should be "practical" (i.e., understandable to the manager).

ELEMENTS COMMON TO RISK MANAGEMENT PROBLEMS

269

CHAPTER 12
*Risk Management
Decision Methods:
Data Organization
and Analysis*

Many of the challenges faced by risk managers are similar to challenges faced by managers in other areas. Issues related to setting budgets, deployment of human resources, and communication of outcomes to other managers exemplify such tasks. However, a number of features tend to distinguish risk management problems from problems faced by other managers, the most notable of which are: (1) time horizons, (2) measurement of costs and benefits, (3) possible uncertainty, (4) data credibility, (5) possible externalities, and (6) interdependent exposures. Often these features dictate the type of data required and the way the data are organized and presented for a risk manager to justify a program. Although these features can be present in areas other than risk management, collectively they tend to distinguish risk management problems.

Time Horizons

The evaluation of risk control efforts commonly requires a "long-run" view, perhaps as long as 20 years for evaluating a project requiring capital investment. Although a 20-year time horizon may be at the extreme, horizons of five years are common for the evaluation of loss-control efforts. Even risk financing issues may require a long-time horizon. For example, choosing between a claims-made or an occurrence form of coverage for medical liability involves issues that are likely to span periods longer than five years. Financing of risks related to loss of property often can be resolved using a time horizon of one or two years, but the significant challenges to a risk manager usually require a longer time horizon for evaluation.

Measuring Benefits and Costs

Often, the hallmark of successful risk management is the absence of unpleasant surprises. When a risk manager prevents or reduces losses, benefits come in the form of "things that don't happen." Benefits that take this form may be difficult to measure. For example, what type of data can a risk manager use to justify lumbar support belts as a measure to reduce lower-back injuries when the composition of workers' activities changes over time? How does the risk manager justify implementing a driver education program for drivers of delivery vehicles? The previously identified issue of the time horizon also becomes a concern in measuring benefits and associating them with the cost of activities that produced the benefits. For example, a smoking-cessation program may create a host of benefits over a 20-year period, during which many of the favorably affected workers become employed elsewhere. One of the beneficiaries may be a competitor who enjoys reduced costs of health care and employee absenteeism. A serious measurement problem arises in the design of programs to address risks that have not yet produced losses. Catastrophe or contingency planning is a good example of this issue, because—by definition—the event is not likely to occur. How are the benefits of such a program identified and associated with expenditures of time, effort, and money? Establishing a linkage between costs and benefits can become a major challenge for this type of effort.

Recognition of Uncertainty

Predicting future outcomes of current choices is an uncertain task. In many cases, a risk manager can only estimate probabilities, even when possible outcomes can be identified. In other cases, the outcomes themselves may not be fully identified and recognized. This issue, which was discussed in Chapter 1, is present in most business decisions and especially prominent in risk management. The risk measurement techniques presented in Chapter 4 require a level of information that ordinarily exists only when losses occur frequently. For losses that occur infrequently, cognition can affect both the identification and assessment of risk. A risk manager can try to estimate the effect of personal influences, biases, and preconceptions on the task of risk assessment, but such an effort requires unusual objectivity and impartiality. This issue was identified at a primitive level in the discussion in Chapter 2 of environmental sources of risk and uncertainty and again in the discussion in Chapter 3 of the Prouty method for risk assessment.

Data Credibility

Justification of risk management efforts often relies on data developed from past experience. Changes in the environment and in the nature of the organization's activities may make the data obsolete. Data trending and other adjustment techniques may cause the data to more accurately reflect current and future experience, but managers often are skeptical of modified data. Evolution of the conditions underlying the risk may be dramatic enough to render an estimate little more than a guess.

Recognition of Externalities

Externalities are economic costs that are not captured in the price of a good or service. Externalities represent a type of market failure in that the market pricing system does not account for all the costs of production. Pollution is frequently cited as an illustration. Pollutants emitted by a manufacturer in the course of production impose harm on neighboring communities whose residents may have no ability to directly charge the manufacturer. Neither the buyer nor the seller bears the cost of the pollution, except by coincidence. Costs of trash disposal provide another example. Only rarely does the cost of a product reflect eventual disposal of packaging or disposal of the product itself after reaching the end of its useful life.

Externalities need not always take the form of costs. Health care can provide examples of services having positive externalities. Having a patient who has contracted a highly contagious and possibly fatal disease hospitalized, quarantined, and cured benefits others in addition to the unfortunate patient.

While the possibility of externalities is not confined to risk management, externalities are commonplace in risk management activities. Pollution and product liability, workplace safety, and management of human resource loss exposures serve as examples of topics covered in this textbook having potential externalities. Common-law liability related to products, for example, can be explained as a social and legal mechanism compelling manufacturers to incorporate injury potential into the price of their products.

271

CHAPTER 12
Risk Management
Decision Methods:
Data Organization
and Analysis

Identification of Interdependency

Interdependent exposures are present when a single event can cause more than one loss. Possible interdependency can be an issue of critical importance to a risk manager. For example, fire damage to a manufacturing plant used in one stage of an integrated production process can affect other plants handling other stages of the process. Another type of interdependency occurs if an organization owns a number of properties along the same earthquake fault, even though the properties may be dispersed geographically. Four aircraft stored in the same hangar serves as a third example. Possible interdependency may be uncovered by risk assessment methods such as the flow-chart technique discussed in Chapter 3, but careful thought by the risk manager may be required to reveal an interdependency that is not obvious.

REVIEWING INSURANCE PRIORITIES

For a small organization, such as a retail outlet, that is not affiliated with a larger chain, a risk management program may be focused primarily on acquiring necessary insurance. Even large, financially sophisticated organizations typically purchase some insurance coverage. A method for reviewing priorities within available coverage can be helpful in either case.

As summarized at the end of Chapter 9, factors that are considered in deciding whether to retain a risk or transfer the risk by purchasing insurance include:

- The maximum probable cost relative to the organization's capacity for bearing risk
- Restrictions or legal limitations applying to risk transfers
- The organization's degree of control over the risk
- Loading fees associated with insurance coverage
- The value of services provided by insurers as part of their insurance coverage
- Opportunity costs related to investment of funds used to reimburse claims
- The tax treatment of uninsured and insured losses
- The availability of alternatives to retention.

The number of factors and the absence of any clear-cut method for assigning weights suggests that inconsistencies may arise if insurance purchase decisions are made piecemeal. Some types of coverage may be purchased when a careful evaluation would reveal that other risk management methods are better. Still other risks may be retained when insuring them would be a more efficient allocation of risk management resources. The existence of insurance price cycles (periodic swings in insurance prices and availability of coverage) implies that a periodic review of all available coverage may reveal priorities that have changed due to changing market conditions.

The setting of insurance priorities can be explained as a three-step process. The risk manager's knowledge of the risks faced by the organization and their importance relative to each other provides background information for these steps. The risk manager first assumes that insurance will be used if coverage is available. When more than one combination of coverage can be used, the risk manager selects the best combination for the risks facing the organization. For example, coverage against fire losses may be provided through a policy that is narrowly focused on fire and related perils, or provided as part of a policy covering a broad range of perils including theft. Whether the broad or narrow policy is better suited to the organization's exposures depends on the composition of its exposures outside those covered by the narrowly-focused policy.

This first step has two purposes: (1) it identifies uninsurable risks and (2) it converts a list of the organization's risks into a list of insurance policies available against these risks. The cost of each coverage offers a benchmark against which the risk manager can evaluate alternative risk management methods.

As a second step, the list of coverage is divided into three categories based on an evaluation of the factors identified in Chapter 9 and summarized above. In the third step, the risk manager reviews the coverage in each category to determine if other, more satisfactory methods are available. Each of these steps is explained in more detail below.

Initial Listing

In the first step, the risk manager must determine what combination of insurance coverages would provide the best protection against the losses to which the organization is exposed, on the assumption that the organization would prefer to buy insurance whenever it is available. To make this determination, the risk manager must understand insurance contracts and insurance pricing. The objective is to provide the most complete protection at the minimum cost. Because some of the risks faced by the organization may not be insurable, the risk manager is alerted through this analysis to the fact that these risks will have to be handled by some method other than insurance.

In addition to selecting the proper combination of coverages, the risk manager must select policy limits that provide as complete protection as possible. Generally, the policy limits in this initial listing should equal the maximum loss, but sometimes this loss may exceed the largest limit available. Losses in excess of the maximum available limit will have to be dealt with in some other way.

After the risk manager has determined the best combination of coverages and policy limits, he or she divides the resulting set of insurance contracts into three groups: (1) essential coverages, (2) desirable coverages, and (3) available coverages.

The *essential* contracts include those that are compulsory because they are required by law (e.g., automobile liability insurance, workers' compensation insurance) or by contract (e.g., group health insurance required under a union contract or property insurance required under a mortgage). Another type of insurance protection in this category is coverage against "high severity" losses that could result in a financial catastrophe for the organization. Liability losses might be an example of this type.

The *desirable* contracts provide protection against losses that could seriously impair the operations of the organization but probably would not put it out of business. Business interruption insurance might be an example of this type.

The *available* contracts include all the types of protection that have not been included in the first two classes. These contracts protect against types of losses that would inconvenience the organization but would not seriously impair its operations unless several of them occurred within a short period. Insurance against breakage of glass might be considered an available coverage.

273

CHAPTER 12
Risk Management
Decision Methods:
Data Organization
and Analysis

Revised Listing

After the initial listing has been completed, the risk manager then reviews the contracts in each group to determine which of these losses might be more satisfactorily handled in other ways. For example, contracts that might be dropped from the essential category would include contracts covering:

1. Losses that can be transferred to someone other than an insurer at a smaller cost than the insurance premium.
2. Losses that can be prevented or reduced to such an extent that they are no longer severe.
3. Losses that happen so frequently that they are fairly predictable, thus making self-insurance an attractive alternative because of expense savings.

In making these decisions, the risk manager can weigh the advantages and disadvantages of other methods presented in earlier chapters or can apply the more structured approaches explained later in this chapter. Few, if any, contracts will be dropped from the essential category. Compulsory insurance must be purchased, while contracts covering potential catastrophic losses usually will be purchased unless they satisfy conditions (1) or (2) above or the risk itself can be avoided.

The discussion up to this point has been in terms of types of losses, but it also may be possible to divide any particular type of loss into two (or more) subtypes, depending upon the amount of the potential loss. For example, although the maximum possible loss of a given type is $1 million and the coverage against this loss is therefore an essential coverage, losses of $500 or less may be either so predictable or so unimportant that the risk manager would regard this type of insurance on the first $500 of loss as at best "available insurance" with only the excess being essential. The types of deductibles and excess insurance available from insurers would limit what could be done along these lines.

The risk manager then subjects the desirable coverages to the same type of analysis. The case for noninsurance methods is stronger with respect to these coverages because the consequences of not insuring are less severe. Still, this insurance is desirable, and unless some other method of handling the loss is at least as attractive, insurance should be purchased. As in dealing with essential coverages, the risk manager may decide to buy the insurance with a provision for partial retention.

The available contracts rate the lowest priority. Some available contracts will be attractive to a particular risk manager because the insurer will perform certain services that are more expensive purchased elsewhere. For example, although potential glass damage may be limited in its severity, the risk manager may believe that the rapid replacement service provided by the insurer justifies payment of the premium. Insurance against some relatively unimportant property losses may become attractive if the premium is, in the eyes of the risk manager, a bargain price. With respect to many of the available coverages, however, other risk management tools will appear more convenient, will cost less to apply, or will have other advantages.

The threefold classification does not set the total budget for insurance. If the budget is large enough to buy all essential coverage but only some of the desirable coverage as well, the method does not tell the risk manager where to draw the line. The method does, however, suggest rough priorities for allocating an insurance budget. It also focuses attention on the consequences of not insuring and identifying other more efficient methods for managing the exposure.

For many small organizations, risk management may end once insurance priorities are established and the insurance budget is allocated. Establishing insurance priorities at least imposes some discipline and consistency on the decision process. Clearly, the method fails the "rigor" test identified earlier in this chapter. It also receives a low grade on the "flexibility" dimension, although the method's "practical" attributes allow it to be used by managers without training in risk management. For a small organization whose risk management options are limited to the purchase of insurance, the method's reliance on insurance is of little concern.

IDENTIFICATION OF BREAK-EVEN POINTS

A break-even point can be a useful point of reference in making retention decisions, particularly on retentions at low levels. The break-even point may refer to either a chance of loss, an expected number of losses in a time period, or a time period required to recover an invested amount.

The calculation of a break-even point is illustrated in the example below, which states the premium for a property insurance policy on which two deductible levels are available:

Deductible Amount	Annual Premium
$1000	$3500
$5000	$3000

The question to be answered is which deductible amount to select. The effect on the insured of choosing a deductible of $5000 instead of $1000 depends on the distribution of covered losses, of course. One approach to estimating a break-even point is to assume that all losses that occur will exceed the larger of the two deductibles, in this case $5000. Under this assumption, the deductible affects only the amount recovered when a loss occurs, not the number of covered losses. The calculation of a break-even chance of loss also assumes that, at most, one loss can occur during the period of coverage.

From the perspective of an insured who has chosen a $5000 deductible, reducing the deductible to $1000 is like buying a policy providing $4000 of a coverage over the $1000 deductible; that is, the additional coverage applies only to losses in excess of $1000, and pays at most $4000. The $4000 of coverage costs $3500 − $3000, or $500. If all losses that occur exceed $5000, the break-even probability of loss is 500/4000, or 1/8.[1] In terms of loss frequency, a loss once every eight years results in the insured breaking even. A risk-neutral insured would be indifferent between the two deductibles at a loss frequency of one loss every eight years.

The break-even point is only a point of reference. The risk manager compares the break-even point with his or her estimate of actual loss frequency. How often does a loss of $5000 or more occur? The risk manager's knowledge of the risk being insured is critical in answering this question. If the risk manager believes that on average such a loss occurs every four years, the $1000 deductible looks like a bargain in that the expected recovery is twice the additional premium. (The risk manager also might question how long the insurer will continue to offer this price as the frequency of covered losses becomes evident.) Also, the method provides a screening device to alert a risk manager to retention decisions for which savings are small relative to the amount retained. A break-even loss frequency of 1/100, for example, implies that up to $100 may be required to fund a loss left uncovered by a decision that generated one dollar in premium savings.

Limitations

The break-even point is a simple calculation, and the result is not sophisticated. The break-even point can be considered a first cousin to the "payback" method that has been used in financial analysis of investment projects. The payback method considers the time period required for the investment in the project to be recovered; that is, the time period required for the cash generated from the project to equal the initial investment. For example, a project requiring an initial investment of $500,000 that generates cash inflows of $150,000 a year has a payback period of 500,000/150,000 = 3.33 years.

The use of payback is widely criticized in the finance literature (see Brealey and Myers [1991, p. 76]). The payback measure fails to consider benefits accruing after the initial investment has been recovered, which is a major flaw. For example, two projects requiring identical $500,000 outlays and generating identical $150,000 yearly inflows have the same payback period even though their lifetimes beyond the payback period are not the same. Also, payback fails to consider the time value money (i.e., its use value over time) in a meaningful way.

Setting retention limits using break-even points is subject to the same type of criticism applied to payback: break-even points fail to consider a lot of infor-

---

[1] The insured breaks even (in the sense of expected value) if the premium equals the expected recovery from the insurance. If p is the probability of loss, the expected value of the additional recovery from choosing a deductible of $1000 instead of $5000 is the additional recovery times the probability of loss, or ($4000)(p). When the expected value of the additional recovery equals the additional premium, ($4000)(p) = $500, or p = 1/8.

275

CHAPTER 12
Risk Management
Decision Methods:
Data Organization
and Analysis

mation. However, few risk managers would use a break-even point as the sole criterion for evaluating a proposed retention level. All that the break-even point provides is an element of data that is evaluated alongside other information bearing on the possible outcomes of the decision. The break-even point is an element of data that is simple to calculate and interpret.

As a method of financial evaluation, net present value (NPV) analysis improves on payback by (1) recognizing the time value of money and (2) reflecting all the inflows and outflows associated with a project. In risk management, NPV analysis is especially useful for decisions involving whether to invest in long-term loss control projects. NPV analysis of a long-term loss control project is illustrated in later sections of this chapter. NPV analysis also is useful for risk financing decisions requiring long-term commitments (e.g., whether to establish a captive insurer). For risk financing decisions involving only short-term commitments and planning horizons, however, a straightforward comparison of benefits and costs without regard to timing often provides sufficient information.

One might argue that successful risk management programs often are distinguished by aggressive retention of risks, associated with active loss prevention and risk control programs. The transition to this type of risk management effort usually requires a deliberate long-term commitment, with the raising of retention levels constituting an early step. This sequence of steps creates an impression that risk financing decisions can be long-term commitments, but in fact most risk financing is short-term. The long-term commitment in successful risk management programs is to active loss prevention and risk control, while many if not most risk financing decisions can be reversed quickly. One might attempt to analyze the purchase of insurance using a 10-year horizon, for example, but the required data could be open to wide speculation (e.g., at what price will the insurer renew in year 8?)

When an insurer enjoys a comparative advantage at loss control and claims administration activities that overcomes insurance loading fees, sophisticated techniques are not required to decide whether to purchase insurance. In this case, the insurer's advantage can be identified using a straightforward comparison of loading fees against the cost of the insured providing its own loss control and claims administration services. Even when the insurer does not have this comparative advantage, a broader scope of analysis still may reveal advantages to using insurance. Included among the issues considered in this broader analysis are the reasons identified in Chapter 11 that may justify an organization's use of insurance coverage. The following section suggests one method of estimating benchmark values for an organization's willingness to pay for services provided as part of insurance coverage.

WILLINGNESS TO PAY FOR CLAIMS MANAGEMENT AND OTHER SERVICES RELATED TO INSURANCE COVERAGE ("WORRY COSTS")

The purchase of insurance may be prompted by worry or concern about the effects of a loss that might occur. For individuals, this concern is manifested in risk aversion: a willingness to pay more than the expected value of a loss for an insurance policy to cover the loss. Some insurance purchases by organizations may be prompted by individuals' risk aversion, although the effects of risk aversion appear differently in organizations than in individuals. Insurance can serve as a guaranty of performance for some other commitment. Liability insurance for the member of a corporation's board of directors or an elected official illustrates the purchase of coverage that can be traced to an individual's risk aversion.

277

CHAPTER 12
Risk Management
Decision Methods:
Data Organization
and Analysis

The career of an organization's risk manager is tied to the performance of the risk management function, for example, so the risk manager's personal risk aversion may affect the use of insurance. If the risk manager underestimates the probable maximum cost of a business interruption by $500,000 and as a consequence purchases a policy whose limit turns out to be $500,000 less than the actual loss sustained after a fire, the risk manager's career path may be adversely affected by the error. Although the foregoing example implies that the risk manager's aversion toward the risk of adverse career changes may affect the estimation of probable maximum cost, the authors are not going to suggest that the risk manager's utility function be incorporated directly into the choice of coverage limits. In choosing the limit on the business interruption policy, the risk manager acts as an agent of the organization's owners.

Consider an example in which a risk manager uses a combination of insurance and self-funding to cover an organization's losses. In the long run, an organization that sets aside a yearly amount equal to the expected value of losses not covered by insurance will be able to fund these losses. However, the possibility exists that losses in any year may exceed the amount set aside, leading to possible disruption of the organization's progress towards its mission. The disruption itself, which may take the form of additional financing costs or in extreme cases bankruptcy costs, can cause the effect of a loss to be greater than its nominal amount would indicate. When the expected value of these additional costs exceeds the loading fees associated with insurance, the purchase of insurance is a lower expected-cost alternative than self-funding.

Categories of Risk Management Costs

More generally, the cost of an organization's risk management program can be classified into four categories:

1. Cost of insurance premiums
2. Payments for losses not covered by insurance
3. Cost of loss-related services, risk control efforts, and other program costs
4. Cost of financial disruption, distress, or worry concerning possible nonperformance.

The sum of items 1 and 2 is the direct cost of financing losses. In general, costs falling into categories 1 and 2 are directly observable. Category 3 includes some indirect costs, such as legal defense costs or amounts paid to a third party administrator who reimburses employees' claims for health care services. Category 3 also includes costs of loss prevention and damage containment programs. Following a suggestion by Douglas Barlow, a former RIMS President and risk manager for Canada's Massey-Ferguson, Ltd., RIMS defines the sum of 1, 2, and 3 to be the "cost of risk" (RIMS [1990]).

Costs falling into category 4 are indirect and often not observable. For a member of a corporation's board of directors or an elected official, these costs are exemplified by the increase in compensation required to induce the director or officer to serve in the absence of insurance, less the expected value of covered claims and defense costs. In the example presented in appendix 11.1 on the use of insurance to mitigate an underinvestment problem, the expected value of the foregone investment opportunity in the absence of insurance falls into category 4. A third example is the extra costs of securing financing for retained losses under conditions of financial distress and legal fees associated with foreclosure or bankruptcy proceedings. Brealey and Myers (1991, ch. 18) discuss costs of financial distress as they affect use of debt financing.

Whenever item 1, the cost of insurance, is less than the combined increase in items 2, 3 and 4 that results when losses are retained, the purchase of coverage reduces risk management costs. In organizations, costs falling into category 4 are analogous to an individual's *risk premium* identified in Chapter 11: the difference between the largest premium the individual is willing to pay and the expected value of the loss. Previous editions of this text identified category 4 as a "worry value" to link these costs with the concept of risk aversion for individuals.

Use of Insurance Data to Estimate Costs

Insurance industry data on insurance costs classified into categories similar to 2, 3 and 4 can be helpful in assessing cost levels likely to be borne by an organization that retains a risk that otherwise could be insured. Two illustrations of the procedure appear below. The examples are based on data in Table 12.1, which uses data presented later in Chapter 14 (Table 14.1) for fire insurance and for Workers' Compensation insurance.

The insurance cost data in Table 12.1 are expressed as a ratio to premiums *written* or premiums *earned*, depending on whether the cost arises from the *writing* of insurance (e.g., underwriting costs) or the *providing* of insurance coverage (e.g., loss adjustment costs). A premium is written when coverage is put in force, while a premium does not become fully earned until the end of the period of coverage (e.g., 12 months after the premium is written on a one-year policy). Accounting issues related to insurance coverage are discussed in more detail in Chapter 15, especially in the two appendices.

To keep the presentations straightforward, both examples presented below assume that the expected value of losses is unaffected by the decision to retain or insure. In other words, the examples ignore the increased incentives to prevent loss that a decision to retain creates. If an insurance policy covers a loss whose expected value is $10,000, the illustration assumes that the expected value remains at $10,000 if the insurance is discontinued.

For fire insurance, Table 12.1 shows losses incurred of 56.8 percent of premiums. Does this figure imply that the remaining 43.2 percent of premium represents a long-run average reduction in risk management costs if the organiza-

TABLE 12.1. Ten-Year Average Ratios for Workers' Compensation and Fire Insurance, United States Property-Casualty Insurers, 1983–1992 (figures in percentages)

Type of Insurance	Ratio to Premiums Earned		Ratio to Premiums Written		Ratio to Premiums Earned	Ratio to Premiums Earned		
	Losses Incurred	Loss Adjustment Expenses Incurred	Commissions and Brokerage Incurred	Other Underwriting Expenses Incurred	Dividends to Policyholders	Combined Ratio After Dividends	Investment Gain & Other Income	Overall Operating Ratio
Fire	56.8	4.9	18.0	19.5	0.5	99.7	5.2	94.6
Workers' Compensation	83.1	11.0	5.1	13.6	6.6	119.3	14.4	104.8

Source: Best's Aggregates and Averages: Property-Casualty (1993 edition).

tion retains the risk of fire damage instead of purchasing coverage? This question can be answered by examining other categories of insurance costs shown in Table 12.1 and reflecting on the nature of the activities that might generate this type of cost.

Table 12.1 also illustrates the effect of investment income on the cost of insurance. Investment effects are evenhanded if the same set of investment opportunities is available to insurers and organizations choosing to retain risk, so the illustrations based on Table 12.1 do not consider possible investment effects. For fire insurance, Table 12.1 shows investment gain and other income of 5.2 percent of premiums, which implies that fire insurers had $105.20 of resources for every $100 of premium income. Of this amount, $0.50 was returned to policyholders as dividends, leaving $104.70 to reimburse losses and to fund other activities. The small investment gain relative to premiums reflects the short delay between payment of premiums and payment of insurance claims and other expenses that would be typical for fire insurance.

Table 12.1 classifies insurance-related expenses into three categories: loss adjustment expenses, commissions and brokerage, and other underwriting expenses. Depending on the type of insurance, some but not all of these expenses represent avoidable costs. For example, the underwriting process in fire insurance may generate recommendations for improved fire prevention and control activities. In the absence of insurance, a risk manager may seek comparable services from service organizations. The insurer's experience in providing these services creates the possibility that the services may be less cost-effective when purchased from other sources. The writing of insurance creates an incentive for the insurer to identify potential hazards, an incentive that is not as strong when these services are provided separately.

A risk manager's knowledge of the risk that could be insured and his or her experience with service organizations are helpful in arriving at these estimates. As an illustration, a risk manager may estimate that one-half of loss adjustment expenses, commissions and brokerage, and other underwriting expenses in fire insurance represent costs that can be avoided by retaining fire damage. Hence $(1/2)(4.9 + 18.0 + 19.5)$, or 21.2 percent, of premium is the long-run expected value of expense savings from retaining fire losses.[2] Using these assumptions, the estimated expected value of net savings is 21.2 percent of premium. A decision to retain fire losses that could be covered by a policy whose annual premium is $50,000 would be expected to generate annual savings of (0.212)($50,000), or $10,600.

However, this estimate has not considered costs falling into category 4: cost of financial disruption, distress or worry concerning possible non-performance (*"worry costs"*). These hidden or indirect costs are weighed against estimated savings to arrive at a decision. In other words, the question to be answered by the risk manager is whether the reduction in these worry costs that can accompany the purchase of insurance justifies payment of insurance loading fees.

Worry Costs and the Nature of the Exposure to Loss

The risk manager's knowledge about the nature of the exposure to risk and the resources for reimbursing loss are critical in judging whether the reduction in worry costs justifies payment of insurance loading fees. For example, if the policy being considered is a blanket fire insurance contract covering 70 retail outlets, each valued at approximately $80,000, the risk manager might choose to retain if the outlets are dispersed widely enough that a single fire would not be expected to damage more than one outlet. The reasoning in this choice might be that the expected annual savings ($10,600) or the premium savings ($50,000) compare favorably to the maximum exposure to damage from a single event ($80,000).

Note that the estimated savings level already takes into account the expected value of fire damage. By retaining the risk of fire, the organization avoids paying the $50,000 fire insurance premium. Of this $50,000, 56.8 percent, or $28,400, is the estimated expected value of retained fire damage. This estimated expected value of retained fire damage amounts to about 35 percent of the value of a single outlet.

The expected level of expenses for inspections and loss-related services is $10,600, or 21.2 percent of premium. These inspections and loss-related services are possibly purchased from service organizations. The remaining one-half of loss adjustment expenses, commissions and brokerage, and other underwriting expenses, or $10,600, is net savings not considering worry costs. The total of these amounts ($28,400 + $10,600 + $10,600 = $49,600), is the difference between the $50,000 premium and the sum of: (1) the 0.5 percent dividend and (2) the 0.3 percent difference between 100 percent and the combined ratio.

The nature of the exposure to possible damage can dramatically affect the

---

[2] Possible insurer profit is not considered in the illustrations presented in this chapter. In theory, one could argue that retention generates additional savings of the difference between 100 percent and the combined ratio, or 0.3 percent of premium. For coverage such as fire insurance, under which the time lag between premium payment and claim payment is short, the difference between 100 percent and the combined ratio approximates the share of premiums that funds the insurer's profit. This approximation becomes more biased on coverage such as liability insurance where typical time lags are longer and investment income constitutes a significant share of claim payments. As a consequence, estimating the share of premium constituting insurer profit is impractical using data such as shown in Table 12.1.

281

CHAPTER 12
*Risk Management
Decision Methods:
Data Organization
and Analysis*

worry costs that are weighed against estimated net savings. For example, the total amount at risk on the 70 retail outlets is $5,600,000, that is, (70)($80,000). The same total amount could be at risk in a single $5,600,000 office building at one location. Even though the total amount at risk is the same in both cases, the maximum exposure to damage from a single loss is much larger for the office building. A $5,600,000 loss might be expected to result in considerable disruption in all but the largest organizations, leading to higher worry costs. Even though the total premium savings and composition of expected retained costs might be identical in both situations, a typical organization would be more likely to retain the risk of fire damage for the 70 retail outlets than for the single office building.

The above presentation of the method assumes that the expected value of the fire damage ($28,400, or 56.8 percent of the premium) is not affected by the decision to retain. More realistically, the estimate would incorporate the effect of loss-control methods induced by a decision to a retain fire damage. The difference between the expected reduction in fire damage and the cost of additional loss-control methods represents additional savings that worry costs must overcome. Also, the presentation does not take into account timing issues, which involve calculating present values. In particular, loss adjustment expenses reflect activities that would take place at the time of loss, while commissions, brokerage fees, and other underwriting expenses reflect activities associated with the writing of coverage. The implied adjustment is to estimate the present value of savings in loss adjustment costs rather than their nominal value. The same type of adjustment could apply to the expected value of the fire damage itself. These additional steps are not included in the above presentation to simplify the description of the method.

The same type of procedure can be applied to a decision to retain a workers' compensation exposure, although the numerical values will change. The figures in Table 12.1 show a different composition of expenses for workers' compensation than for fire insurance. Investment gains are more than twice as large relative to premiums (14.4 percent versus 5.2 percent for fire insurance), reflecting the longer delays to claim settlement typical for workers' compensation. Loss adjustment expenses are higher in workers' compensation, but a risk manager would seriously question whether much of these expenses would be saved by retaining the workers' compensation exposure. Most of the loss adjustment expenses in workers' compensation are generated in managing and reimbursing claims from injured employees, activities that will continue if the exposure is retained.

Whether much of the category identified as "other underwriting expenses" would be avoided by retaining the exposure is doubtful also. Workers' compensation insurers often provide consultation on matters related to safety as part of the underwriting process, and the value of this advice should be considered in estimating the savings that may result from a decision to retain.

In fact, one would expect loss-prevention and claims-reduction activities to increase if the workers' compensation risk is retained, causing expenses in this category to rise. Familiarity with the situations giving rise to possible work-related injury places the employer in the best position to identify sources of injury and allocate resources to injury-prevention and claim-reduction efforts. Retention creates a direct financial incentive for the employer to manage these efforts actively. This incentive is not as strong for an insurer who writes coverage against the workers' compensation risk because most insurance plans provide a mechanism for passing part of increased costs back to policyholders through higher premium charges. As noted earlier, possible loss-reducing effects of a decision to retain an exposure are not considered in the presentations based on Table 12.1.

A risk manager's knowledge of the type of events leading to injury and the availability of injury-prevention and claim-reduction services from service organizations influences estimates of potential savings. For example, a risk manager may estimate that the entire amount of commissions and brokerage fees plus one-half of the underwriting expenses represent costs that can be avoided by retaining the workers' compensation exposure. Using the figures in Table 12.1, savings of $5.1 + (1/2)(13.6)$, or 11.9 percent of premium, would be expected long-run savings from a decision to retain workers' compensation claims. These estimated long-run savings are weighed against the worry costs resulting from the choice to retain these claims. For example, $595,000 would be the estimated annual savings on a policy whose annual premium is $5 million. Weighed against these savings is the potential exposure to liability and possible disruption if a large claim or series of claims were to materialize. Because workers' compensation is a statutory liability, statutory limits on an employer's liability play a role in this phase of the evaluation.

Limitations

Tailoring data on insurance industry average expenses to fit a particular organization's exposure to loss may require skill and imagination. In particular, costs falling into category 3, the cost of loss-related services, risk control efforts, and other program costs are not as readily observable as premium costs and claim costs, categories 1 and 2. Attributing costs of loss prevention programs to identifiable areas of activity may prove difficult. For example, how is the cost of a fire prevention program allocated between manufacturing and the related administrative office?

Also, as noted earlier, an insured who retains a loss exposure may have an incentive to allocate more resources to loss-control activities than an insurer writing coverage against the same exposure. Possible effects of this incentive lend additional subjectivity to the evaluation of retention decisions. Additionally, many loss-control efforts take on the character of long-term programs and capital projects, making a direct comparison with claim costs and premium savings more complicated. The next section of this chapter discusses the evaluation of long-term efforts such as loss control.

EVALUATING LONG-TERM PROJECTS IN PUBLICLY HELD CORPORATIONS

A risk management program may include long-term projects requiring a portion of an organization's capital outlays. These projects may take the form of proposed facilities or modification of existing facilities to incorporate risk control features. As examples: an educational institution located in an urban area may consider the installation of new lighting to improve campus safety during hours of darkness; a common carrier may consider the development of an information system to improve cargo tracking and reduce theft.

283

CHAPTER 12
*Risk Management
Decision Methods:
Data Organization
and Analysis*

A methodology for evaluating proposed capital outlays can be an important part of a risk manager's knowledge. When a risk management department has a separate budget, the ability to evaluate competing proposals is important in allocating the capital budget. If capital outlays are allocated at some other level, an understanding of the methodology for evaluating proposed outlays can be important in drafting and arguing for the proposal.

The topic of capital budgeting is an important part of the finance literature, and capital budgeting is a major part of a financial manager's responsibilities. A substantial portion of modern finance texts such as Brealey and Myers (1991) or Ross, Westerfield, and Jaffe (1993) is devoted to developing a conceptual framework for evaluating and financing proposed capital outlays. Exploring the full scope of the methodology in a few pages of a risk management text would not be a realistic goal. The following material summarizes the approach as it relates to the risk management principles developed so far. Readers who wish to acquire enough knowledge to apply the methodology to proposed capital projects are advised to consult a modern finance text such as Brealey and Myers or Ross, Westerfield, and Jaffe.

Valuation of a Project in an Efficient Market

The principle that was summarized at the end of Chapter 11 is: risk management policies in publicly held business organizations serve the interests of investors who own the organization. In serving the interests of the organization's owners, a risk manager may recognize how interests of other stakeholders can conflict with interests of stockholders. In choosing a policy to resolve the conflict, the risk manager balances the interests of both parties. A successful policy is in the interests of both parties. One example appearing in Chapter 11 is the corporation purchasing liability insurance for a member of its board of directors. The risk manager purchases liability insurance for a member of a corporation's board when it is in the mutual interest of both the corporation and its board member to provide coverage that way.

The same rule applies to evaluation of long-term projects. The efficient markets framework discussed in Chapter 11 sets a benchmark for initial evaluation of the project. Initially, the risk manager adopts the perspective of an investor who might hold shares in the organization. The question to be answered is whether this investor would be willing to allocate the required resources to the project. If returns forecast from the project compare favorably to returns available on investments generally, the required funds will be provided by the hypothetical investor. The risk manager's specialized knowledge becomes helpful in forecasting the returns offered by the project.

Project evaluation begins with forecasting *cash flows* associated with the proposed project. A cash flow is the *after-tax* marginal effect of the project on the organization's cash position. Cash flows should not be confused with earnings.

In particular, noncash charges, such as depreciation, generate cash inflows when they reduce taxable income and taxes. For most loss prevention and reduction projects, cash inflows often take the form of reduced expenses or reduced claims. A reduction in expenses is a cash inflow because the organization's cash position is improved relative to its level had the project not been adopted. The after-tax effect is considered because revenues and expenses directly affect tax payments. For example, reduced expenses increase tax payments. Similarly, the initial outlay to acquire an investment project is a cash outflow. An example presented in Table 12.2 illustrates the estimation of cash flows from an investment project.

Under the efficient markets framework discussed in Chapter 11, securities are the only risky assets, individuals' probability beliefs are homogeneous, individuals' utilities depend only on expected return and variance, and returns on securities are linear in beta. The rate of return offered by a security having a known beta in a single time period is $r = r_f + ß(E_m - r_f)$, where r is the rate of return of the security, r_f is the rate of return on a riskless investment,[3] ß is the beta of the security and E_m is the expected rate of return on a market-proportioned portfolio of risky securities. The difference $E_m - r_f$ is the *market risk premium*, the expected reward for risk bearing implied in security returns generally. Intuitively, beta measures systematic (or nondiversifiable) risk relative to the market.

The return offered by any proposed investment should compare favorably with returns on securities generally. Hence an investment yielding a cash flow having a known beta in a single time period is required to offer a return at least as large as the return on a security having the same beta. For example, the riskless rate of interest may be 5 percent. If the expected return on a market-proportioned portfolio of risky securities is 13 percent, the market risk premium is $13 - 5 = 8$ percent. The required return for an investment having a beta of 0.75 is $5 + (0.75)(13 - 5) = 11$ percent. The required return for a riskless (zero-beta) cash flow is 5 percent.

The Brealey-Myers Adjusted Present Value Method

Brealey and Myers (1991) offer several methods for evaluating proposed investment projects, including an adjusted present value method. The methods they propose all use the same conceptual framework but differ in the way they are applied to specific projects. Their adjusted present value method, which is based on an asset-specific beta, can be summarized in five steps:

1. Forecast the after-tax cash flows from the project.
2. Estimate the beta of the cash flows from the project.
3. Use the estimated beta to calculate the rate of return offered to investors by securities carrying the same level of risk as the proposed project.
4. Use the required return estimated in step 3 to calculate the net present value (NPV) of the project's cash flows.
5. Adjust NPV for possible side-effects of the project, such as additions to a firm's debt capacity.

[3] In empirical work, the riskless rate of interest usually is taken to be the rate of return on short-term U.S. Treasury securities.

TABLE 12.2. Evaluation of Cash Flows from Installation of Proposed Lighting System in Employee Parking Ramp

Income Tax Rate: 34 Percent
Risk-Free Rate of Interest: 5 Percent
Expected Return on Market Portfolio: 13 Percent

Case I: Beta of 0.75

Required Rate of Return: 5 + 0.25(13 − 5) = 11 Percent

End of Year	Amount Invested	Cost Savings	Savings in Claim Costs	Operating Expense	Depreciation	After-Tax Cash Flow	Discount Factor	Present Value
0	($100,000)	—	—	—	—	($100,000)	1.0000	($100,000)
1	—	$22,000	$10,000	($12,000)	$10,000	$ 16,600	0.9009	$ 14,955
2	—	$22,000	$10,000	($12,000)	$10,000	$ 16,600	0.8116	$ 13,473
3	—	$22,000	$10,000	($12,000)	$10,000	$ 16,600	0.7312	$ 12,138
4	—	$22,000	$10,000	($12,000)	$10,000	$ 16,600	0.6587	$ 10,935
5	—	$22,000	$10,000	($12,000)	$10,000	$ 16,600	0.5935	$ 9,851
6	—	$22,000	$10,000	($12,000)	$10,000	$ 16,600	0.5346	$ 8,875
7	—	$22,000	$10,000	($12,000)	$10,000	$ 16,600	0.4817	$ 7,996
8	—	$22,000	$10,000	($12,000)	$10,000	$ 16,600	0.4339	$ 7,203
9	—	$22,000	$10,000	($12,000)	$10,000	$ 16,600	0.3909	$ 6,489
10	—	$22,000	$10,000	($12,000)	$10,000	$ 16,600	0.3522	$ 5,846
								($ 2,239)

Case II: Beta of 0.25

Required Rate of Return: 5 + 0.25(13 − 5) = 7 Percent

End of Year	Amount Invested	Cost Savings	Savings in Claim Costs	Operating Expense	Depreciation	After-Tax Cash Flow	Discount Factor	Present Value
0	($100,000)	—	—	—	—	($100,000)	1.0000	($100,000)
1	—	$22,000	$10,000	($12,000)	$10,000	$ 16,600	0.9346	$ 15,514
2	—	$22,000	$10,000	($12,000)	$10,000	$ 16,600	0.8734	$ 14,498
3	—	$22,000	$10,000	($12,000)	$10,000	$ 16,600	0.8163	$ 13,551
4	—	$22,000	$10,000	($12,000)	$10,000	$ 16,600	0.7629	$ 12,664
5	—	$22,000	$10,000	($12,000)	$10,000	$ 16,600	0.7130	$ 11,836
6	—	$22,000	$10,000	($12,000)	$10,000	$ 16,600	0.6663	$ 11,061
7	—	$22,000	$10,000	($12,000)	$10,000	$ 16,600	0.6227	$ 10,337
8	—	$22,000	$10,000	($12,000)	$10,000	$ 16,600	0.5820	$ 9,661
9	—	$22,000	$10,000	($12,000)	$10,000	$ 16,600	0.5439	$ 9,029
10	—	$22,000	$10,000	($12,000)	$10,000	$ 16,600	0.5083	$ 8,438
								$ 16,589

Steps 1 through 4 of the evaluation procedure assess the project as a stand-alone investment financed entirely by equity. The resulting NPV is an estimate of the project's value under the assumptions leading to the efficient market, assumptions that were discussed in Chapter 11 of this text. Step 5 adjusts this efficient-market value to reflect aspects of financing the project not contemplated in efficient-market assumptions.

Steps 1 through 4 can be understood in the context of the assumptions leading to an efficient market. Under these assumptions, cash flows from the project would be evaluated using their expected return and beta. The question addressed in steps 1 through 4 is whether cash flows generated by the project are sufficiently large to compensate holders of equity for the risk associated with the project, where risk is measured by beta. Formally, the procedure is to use the project's beta to estimate a risk-adjusted return required on the project and use the adjusted return to discount the project's cash flows. Our initial description of the process bypasses the issue of how asset betas are estimated.

A Benchmark Valuation

Steps 1 through 4 of the procedure are illustrated in Table 12.2, which analyzes a proposal to install new lighting equipment in an organization's employee parking ramp. The ramp is located in an area of a city where crime is a concern. The installation of the new lighting fixtures is expected to reduce the need for other security measures, such as guards, and also reduce the number of crime-related losses and injuries related to employees going from and coming to the premises at night.

The proposed lighting system has an expected lifetime of 10 years and costs $100,000 to install. Annual operating costs are $12,000. Each year of its life, the lighting system is expected to save the organization $22,000 in security costs, such as providing additional guards during night hours. In addition, the lighting system is expected to save another $10,000 in reduced claims for employee injuries. The lighting system is assumed to have zero salvage value after the 10-year period. The organization faces a 34 percent tax rate on income, and straight-line depreciation is used on the lighting system. At the end of each year, the after-tax cash flow generated by the project is the increment in after-tax income plus the value of the tax shield (i.e., reduction in tax) resulting from deducting depreciation: $(1 - 0.34)(\$22,000 + \$10,000 - \$12,000) + (0.34)(\$100,000/10) = \$16,600$. If the present value of the $16,600 after-tax cash flow as valued by investors is greater than the $100,000 required to fund the lighting system, the value of the organization increases when the lighting system is installed.

In Table 12.2, the riskless rate of interest is 5 percent, the expected rate of return on a market-proportioned portfolio of risky securities is 13 percent, leading to a market risk premium of $13 - 5 = 8$ percent. Table 12.2 shows the evaluation of the cash flows for two cases: a beta of 0.75 and a beta of 0.25. From the perspective of hypothetical investors, the present value of the $16,600 annual cash flows depends on the beta of these flows. In case I, in which the beta is 0.75, investors require a return of $5 + 0.75(13 - 5) = 11$ percent. In case II, in which beta is 0.25, investors require a return of only $5 + 0.25(13 - 5) = 7$ percent.

The net present values appearing at the bottom of the right-hand columns for each case show how estimated betas affect the value of the project. In general, increasing the beta increases the required return and decreases the present value of distant cash flows. When the required return is 11 percent, investing in the project generates a net *loss* of $2239. Under the efficient market assumptions, investing in this project if its beta is 0.75 causes the value of the organization to decline by $2239. However, if the required return is only 7 percent, investing in the project leads to a net *gain* of $16,589. Where the project's beta is only 0.25, investing in the project causes the market value of the organization to increase by $16,589.

287

CHAPTER 12
*Risk Management
Decision Methods:
Data Organization
and Analysis*

How Is the Value of Beta Determined?

The preceding example shows that the value of beta and the implied rate of return required on the project can have important effects on the estimated value of a project. This observation leads to an obvious question: how can betas be estimated? In concept, beta measures the vulnerability of the project's cash flows to factors affecting security returns generally (e.g., the state of the economy). For types of investments that are typical for an organization's line of business, an analyst may assume a beta that is typical for the organization's own experience or for investment projects in a particular industry or line of business related to the project.

However, the value of the investment project in a setting of an efficient market depends on the beta of the *project*, not the organization. The character of projects under consideration by a risk manager is likely to differ from the character of the organization's other projects, with the possible exception of an organization engaged in the business of selling loss-prevention and loss-reduction services. If the project differs from the type typically undertaken in the course of the organization's business, the analyst should consider how this difference affects the level of beta estimated for the project and hence the level of required return. It seems plausible to consider the possibility of *negative* betas when loss-control projects are being evaluated. A negative beta could occur, for example, if claim costs are inversely related to the state of the economy (i.e., claims increase when the economy is performing poorly).

With respect to the lighting project illustrated in Table 12.2, the cash flows from the project fall into four categories: (1) cost savings, such as reduced expenditures for security guards, (2) savings in claim costs, (3) operating expenses, such as electrical power and maintenance, and (4) depreciation. An analyst could question whether these categories are related to the organization's primary line of business. Typically, an organization's investment projects are related to the primary line of business because their cash flows are directly related to sales. A direct relationship between sales and the cash flows of a loss-control effort such as the proposed lighting project is unlikely. To the extent that sales affect the level of the organization's activity generally they could have an indirect effect on operating expenses, but no other relationship is apparent between the lighting project's cash flows and the organization's sales.

An analyst then could consider how cash flows falling into the four categories listed above might be related to security returns generally. Expenditures for security and the cost of crime-related claims are likely to have a negative relationship with the state of the economy. That is, if the state of the economy declines, crime-related losses and expenditures for security against these losses are likely to increase. Hence savings in these areas would tend to increase as the state of the economy declines, leading to a negative beta. However, the beta of the project's operating expenses could be positive to the extent that the level of these expenses tends to follow economic trends generally. The beta of the depreciation tax flows is likely to be near zero.[4]

As the above issues affect the evaluation of the proposed lighting project, they point toward a beta near zero. A careful consideration of the four categories into which the project's cash flows fall does not suggest a strong relationship with factors related to the state of the economy generally. At worst, a weak positive relationship might be expected between the cash flows on the lighting project and returns on risky securities generally (e.g., a beta perhaps as high as 0.25, which still leads to acceptance of the project). However, this opinion holds only with respect to the lighting project under consideration. In general, one would not expect a strong positive relationship between factors affecting securities returns generally and cash flows on loss-control projects, but a careful analyst should consider the possibility for each project under consideration.[5]

Adjusting Estimated NPV for Possible Side-Effects

A final step in the analysis of long-term projects is to adjust NPV for side-effects of financing the project. These side-effects are exemplified by (1) considering the cost of issuing new securities to finance a project or (2) adjusting for the tax deductibility of interest payments on debt used to finance the project. For example, if the project requires the organization to issue new common stock with issuance costs of 7 percent of the proceeds, the firm must issue $107,527 of common stock to finance the project. The $7527 issuance cost would be added to the cost of the project.

With respect to the tax deductibility of interest payments on debt used to finance the project, the analyst considers how much the acceptance of the project adds to the organization's debt capacity (i.e., what proportion of the project lenders would be willing to finance with debt at the organization's usual cost of borrowing). The present value of the tax shields from the use of this debt is *added* to the estimated value of the project, as the tax shield reduces the cost of the project. The tax shield is the organization's expected tax rate times the interest payment on the outstanding debt balance, the amount by which the interest payments reduce the organization's tax liability.

For example, the Chief Financial Officer of the organization considering the lighting project may believe that lenders are willing to provide 40 percent of the funds required for the lighting project (i.e., $40,000) at 9 percent interest, the rate at which the firm customarily has borrowed. The addition to the organization's debt capacity declines over the 10-year lifetime of the project, which suggests a

---

[4] A nonzero beta for depreciation tax flows could occur because the firm's tax bracket is related to its earnings, which in turn may be affected by general economic trends. For example, adverse economic trends could cause the firm's earnings to decline to the point where taxes becomes zero and the value of the firm's tax shields evaporates. This logic would assign a positive beta to the cash flows arising from tax shields.

[5] Some loss-control efforts can have a positive relation to sales. If product-safety measures reduce the proportion of products having defects that could cause injury, the cash flows from these efforts increase with higher sales levels.

level-payment mortgage loan to finance 40 percent of the outlay required for the project. The rate of discount applying to the tax shields is the same as the 9 percent interest charged on the loan, assuming that the tax shields are as risky as the interest payments that generate the shields. At 9 percent interest, the present value of the interest payments on a 9 percent 10-year $40,000 mortgage with annual payments is $15,845.84. If the organization's tax bracket is expected to remain at 34 percent during the 10-year period, the present value of the tax shields is $5387.59.

289

CHAPTER 12
Risk Management
Decision Methods:
Data Organization
and Analysis

A more detailed discussion of methods for adjusting NPV for side-effects of financing the project would go beyond the intended scope of this section. The above discussion merely summarizes the adjusted present value method. Readers who wish to directly apply this technique to project evaluation are urged to review Brealey and Myers (1991), especially Chapter 19. After explaining the adjusted present value method, Brealey and Myers suggest the use of adjusted discount rates as an alternative, in which the adjusted discount rate reflects the business risk of the project and financing side effects. Our discussion of project evaluation retains the adjusted present value method to keep focused on likely differences between loss control projects and the type of project typically considered by an organization.

EVALUATING LONG-TERM PROJECTS IN THE PUBLIC SECTOR

The evaluation of long-term projects can be organized into three tasks: (1) identifying benefits and costs of a project, (2) estimating the nominal value of these benefits and costs, and (3) setting a discount rate that translates future benefits and costs into their effects on current resources. The successful evaluation of any long-term project involves these three tasks, whether the project is owned privately or is owned by a public entity. In the private sector, benefits and costs usually appear as direct cash flows. Managers of public entities may consider benefits and costs that are not in the form of cash, although the framework for their evaluation can be the same as for the private sector. In other words, the basic features of the adjusted present value framework offered by Brealey and Myers need not change because the project's owner is public rather than private. The actual benefits and costs of a project and the discount rate may not be identical to those for a private organization owning the same project, but the framework should perform as well in a public as in a private setting.

The differences between project analysis in public and private entities can be determined by focusing on the three tasks identified above. For a public entity, the cash flows arising from a project are not taxable (unless they arise from an activity the IRS deems as for-profit). If the cash flows are not taxable, the analyst considers the present value of the nominal flows, with no adjustment for depreciation. The absence of taxation also implies that no tax advantage is present for debt financing, although financing side-effects could arise if tax-exempt securities such as special revenue bonds are used to finance a project.

A second difference may arise in considering effects that would be external if the project were held privately. In a public entity, few if any effects are external because the project is owned collectively. For example, a lighting system for a parking lot in a community hospital may reduce crime in the surrounding areas as well as on the hospital premises. If the project is financed by the community as a whole, the evaluation may extend to consider such external effects that are not likely to be considered by a private employer. Although a private employer whose objectives include community service may consider benefits that are external to the firm, private analysts are likely to overlook them in project evaluation.

However, the efficient markets framework discussed in Chapter 11 still sets a benchmark for initial evaluation of the project. The analyst adopts the perspective of a member of the community who might hold a share of the proposed project. The question to be answered is whether this community member would be willing to allocate the required resources to the project. If returns forecast from the project compare favorably to returns available on investments generally, the required funds will be provided by the hypothetical community member. The analogy with the investor in the private organization should be clear: the member of the community has the same access as private investors to projects offering market risk and return. The method for evaluating a project does not change because its ownership is transferred from private to public.

The example of the proposed lighting project can be used as an illustration. The illustration, which is presented in Table 12.3, focuses narrowly on the direct savings attributable to adopting the project. Annual cash flows are the savings in expenditures for security, reduced claims for employee injuries, less annual operating costs, or $22,000 + $10,000 − $12,000. No adjustment for tax applies because the flows are not taxable. Hence the evaluation of the project balances the net $20,000 annual inflow against the $100,000 cost of the project. At an 11 percent interest rate, the NPV of the project is $17,784. At a 7 percent rate, the NPV becomes $40,468. The absence of taxation increases the estimated value of the project for both levels of required return. When the flows were taxed, the project did not meet the test of an 11 percent required return, although it still met the 7 percent threshold.

Allocating Cost Burdens

On long-term projects in the public sector, the issue of fairness in allocating cost burdens arises in ways less likely to occur in the private sector. Ideally, parties who benefit from the project should bear its cost burden, with the allocation of cost being contemporaneous with the provision of the benefits. The issuance of bonds whose proceeds are used to finance current costs of work-related injuries is inappropriate, for example, because the bonds shift to future generations part of the costs of currently provided services. The discussion of public finance in Chapter 11 alludes to this issue, which is not resolved by the "unanimity" or "compensation" principle. Pareto optimality only requires a project's benefits to outweigh its costs, for example, but is silent on whether the parties bearing the costs are identical to the parties to whom the benefits accrue.

In the example of the lighting system for the parking ramp, a public sector risk manager considers whether the individuals who benefit from the installation of the system are the same as the individuals bearing the cost burdens. If

TABLE 12.3. Evaluation of Cash Flows from Installation of Proposed Lighting System in Employee Parking Ramp

Untaxed Public Entity
Risk-Free Rate of Interest: 5 Percent
Expected Return on Market Portfolio: 13 Percent

Case I: Beta of 0.75

Required Rate of Return: 5 + 0.25(13 − 5) = 11 Percent

End of Year	Amount Invested	Cost Savings	Savings in Claim Costs	Operating Expense	Cash Flow	Discount Factor	Present Value
0	($100,000)	—	—	—	($100,000)	1.0000	($100,000)
1	—	$22,000	$10,000	($12,000)	$ 20,000	0.9009	$ 18,018
2	—	$22,000	$10,000	($12,000)	$ 20,000	0.8116	$ 16,232
3	—	$22,000	$10,000	($12,000)	$ 20,000	0.7312	$ 14,624
4	—	$22,000	$10,000	($12,000)	$ 20,000	0.6587	$ 13,174
5	—	$22,000	$10,000	($12,000)	$ 20,000	0.5935	$ 11,870
6	—	$22,000	$10,000	($12,000)	$ 20,000	0.5346	$ 10,692
7	—	$22,000	$10,000	($12,000)	$ 20,000	0.4817	$ 9,634
8	—	$22,000	$10,000	($12,000)	$ 20,000	0.4339	$ 8,678
9	—	$22,000	$10,000	($12,000)	$ 20,000	0.3909	$ 7,818
10	—	$22,000	$10,000	($12,000)	$ 20,000	0.3522	$ 7,044
							($ 17,784)

Case II: Beta of 0.25

Required Rate of Return: 5 + 0.75(13 − 5) = 7 Percent

End of Year	Amount Invested	Cost Savings	Savings in Claim Costs	Operating Expense	Cash Flow	Discount Factor	Present Value
0	($100,000)	—	—	—	($100,000)	1.0000	($100,000)
1	—	$22,000	$10,000	($12,000)	$ 20,000	0.9346	$ 18,692
2	—	$22,000	$10,000	($12,000)	$ 20,000	0.8734	$ 17,468
3	—	$22,000	$10,000	($12,000)	$ 20,000	0.8163	$ 16,326
4	—	$22,000	$10,000	($12,000)	$ 20,000	0.7629	$ 15,258
5	—	$22,000	$10,000	($12,000)	$ 20,000	0.7130	$ 14,260
6	—	$22,000	$10,000	($12,000)	$ 20,000	0.6663	$ 13,326
7	—	$22,000	$10,000	($12,000)	$ 20,000	0.6227	$ 12,454
8	—	$22,000	$10,000	($12,000)	$ 20,000	0.5820	$ 11,640
9	—	$22,000	$10,000	($12,000)	$ 20,000	0.5439	$ 10,878
10	—	$22,000	$10,000	($12,000)	$ 20,000	0.5083	$ 10,166
							($ 40,468)

the benefits from the system are widespread—extending to the community at large—the fairness issue is a minor concern. However, if the benefits accrue to a select few—say, employees of a business located next to the ramp—then the fairness issue becomes a legitimate concern. Ordinarily, the fairness issue would not reverse a decision to install, but may influence methods used to finance the project. For example, a government may choose to produce the bulk of financing through dedicated user fees (i.e., parking fees) and recognize that benefits accrue to the surrounding neighborhood by providing a subsidy from general revenues.

The question of fairness, while not absent from capital budgeting in the private sector, may be an explicit factor in public sector capital budgeting. The issue arises in the private sector if one category of a claimholder (e.g., stockholders) can take self-interested actions that reduce the value of claims held by another category of claimholder. Ordinarily, claimholders in the private sector place safeguards against possible expropriation through measures such as bond covenants. Although covenants are possible in the public sector too, the nature of activities in the public sector makes them less useful as a safeguard. Especially when public projects touch on matters involving civil rights, property rights, taxation, the conflict between state and federal jurisdiction, international relations, and the tension between majority rule and minority rights, questions of fairness become important. In such cases, political considerations can be as important as purely economic issues in the evaluation of a proposed project.

USE OF FINANCIAL RATIOS IN RISK MANAGEMENT

Financial ratios offer a convenient way to summarize an organization's financial condition and to compare performance among organizations. Some ratios can offer helpful guidelines to a risk manager in setting retention limits because they reflect the level of resources available to reimburse loss. Other ratios can offer a guide to replacement of damaged assets when the ratios reflect opportunities for employing resources elsewhere. When ratios are based on accounting data, as is typically the case, they should be interpreted with caution. In particular, asset values may be distorted by accounting entries based on historical cost.

An organization's ability to retain risk is influenced by financial characteristics, such as degree of leverage (debt) and liquidity. Leverett (1992, p. 27-2) observes that "materiality" is another concern. He defines materiality in its legal sense as anything an outsider making a financial decision would regard as improper. He notes that the possibility of a financial event, such as a retained loss that could be deemed as material, is likely to require an explanatory note in an organization's financial statements. Financial officers, Leverett observes, do not like notes.

The discussion below is limited to a few selected financial ratios that can be directly related to constraints on a risk manager's actions. Chapter 27 of Brealey and Myers' (1991) finance text discusses the use of ratios in financial analysis generally. Three categories of financial ratios are likely to be of interest to a risk manager: (1) leverage ratios, (2) liquidity ratios, and (3) market-valuation ratios.

Leverage Ratios

Leverage ratios measure the extent to which an organization is in debt. Financial analysts use the term leverage because the use of debt magnifies the effect of earnings changes on stockholders. Debt is a fixed obligation. Stockholders receive residual earnings after all other fixed obligations are met, so a high level of fixed obligations causes the effect of a given change in earnings to be magnified in earnings available to shareholders. For example, the earnings of an all-equity organization might be $1 million. If earnings increase by 10 percent to $1.1 million, earnings available to shareholders of the all-equity organization also increase by 10 percent. If the same organization were to have $500,000 in fixed interest payments, however, the effect of the change in earnings is magnified. When earnings are $1 million, $500,000 is available to shareholders. When earnings increase to $1.1 million, earnings available to shareholders increase to $600,000, a 20 percent increase. The presence of the debt magnifies the 10 percent increase in earnings into a 20 percent increase in earnings available to shareholders.

293

CHAPTER 12
Risk Management
Decision Methods:
Data Organization
and Analysis

Because leverage operates on the downside as well as the upside, high leverage increases the vulnerability of the firm to changes in the business environment. Leverage magnifies the effect of losses as well as gains. High leverage is likely to limit risk management flexibility in other ways. Holders of debt usually impose direct restrictions on an organization's actions through side agreements called *bond covenants*. For example, a bond covenant may require the purchase of fire insurance on an asset pledged as collateral.

One commonly used leverage ratio is the ratio of long-term debt to net worth:

$$\text{Long-term debt to net worth ratio} = \frac{\text{Long-term debt}}{\text{Net worth}}$$

For example, a 1:1 ratio implies equal amounts of debt and equity financing. In calculating this ratio, long-term debt often includes the present value of payments under long-term leases. The logic behind including lease payments is they represent a fixed long-term commitment with many of the characteristics of debt.

Another measure of leverage is the times interest earned ratio:

$$\text{Times interest earned} = \frac{\text{Earnings before interest and taxes} + \text{Depreciation}}{\text{Interest}}$$

The times interest earned ratio measures the extent to which interest payments are met from cash generated in an organization's operations. A high ratio reflects a substantial cushion, that is, earnings can decline substantially without necessarily impairing the organization's ability to meet fixed interest payments. For example, a ratio of 12.0 implies that interest payments could still be met (although barely) if cash generated from operations declines to only one-twelfth its current level.

Liquidity Ratios

Liquidity ratios measure the extent to which an organization can raise cash, particularly in the short run. In a broader sense, the term liquidity refers to the ease with which an asset can be converted to cash. Bank deposits and marketable securities frequently traded on large securities exchanges are examples of liquid assets. Real estate and specialized machinery used in production are examples of illiquid assets.

Liquidity ratios reflect how much cash a firm can raise in a short time period. Although an illiquid asset might be valuable, converting it to cash may require time and effort. Consequently, liquidity ratios consider cash and assets that can easily be converted to cash in a short time. An organization's *current assets* are assets that are likely to turn into cash shortly. *Current liabilities* are obligations that should be met in the near future. The difference between current assets and current liabilities is *net working capital,* the net amount of cash the organization expects to generate in the near future (e.g., in the next 60 days). The measure of net working capital can be important to a risk manager because it reflects internally generally cash during the near future. Net working capital represents an upper limit to internally generated cash available to finance unexpected short-term developments, including the reimbursement of uninsured claims and payment of expenses related to managing a crisis. One commonly used measure of liquidity is the ratio of net working capital to total assets:

$$\text{Net working capital to total assets} = \frac{\text{Current assets} - \text{Current liabilities}}{\text{Total assets}}$$

If the value of this ratio is 0.05, for example, an organization expects to generate enough cash in the near future to finance its normal operations and provide a margin for contingencies of 5 percent of total assets (in terms of book value). This contingency margin could be used to finance unexpected losses.

A second measure of liquidity is the current ratio, which measures the extent to which current assets cover current liabilities:

$$\text{Current ratio} = \frac{\text{Current assets}}{\text{Current liabilities}}$$

A current ratio of 1.0 indicates that assets that the organization expects to be converted into cash in the near future are just sufficient to meet short-term liabilities accruing during the same period. A ratio below 1.0 indicates that outside financing (e.g., borrowing) may be needed, while a ratio above 1.0 indicates that the organization's operations will generate a cash surplus in the near-term.

An organization's inventory is included in current assets. An organization's inventory may be less marketable than widely traded securities and amounts owed to the organization by its customers. The acid-test ratio is a more stringent test of liquidity based on these more marketable assets:

$$\text{Acid test ratio} = \frac{\text{Cash} + \text{Marketable securities} + \text{Accounts receivable}}{\text{Current liabilities}}$$

An even more stringent test of liquidity is to leave accounts receivable out of the calculation. The ratio of cash plus marketable securities to current liabilities measures the proportion of short-term liabilities that could be met by the organization even if all its own accounts become uncollectible.

Unfortunately, none of these liquidity ratios capture an organization's borrowing capacity. In evaluating an organization's capacity to absorb retained losses, a risk manager also considers the willingness of lenders to provide needed funds. This type of information is reflected in the leverage ratios described earlier. Other things being equal, lenders are less willing to lend to heavily indebted organizations than to organizations carrying little debt.

Market-Valuation Ratios

295

CHAPTER 12
Risk Management
Decision Methods:
Data Organization
and Analysis

Market-valuation ratios capture the reaction of stockholders to actions of the organization's managers. The price-to-earnings (P-E) ratio is a commonly used measure of the stockholders' valuation of an organization's earnings:

$$\text{Price-to-earnings ratio} = \frac{\text{Market price of common stock}}{\text{Earnings per share}}$$

It might appear that a high P-E ratio could magnify the effect of an uninsured loss. For example, would a P-E ratio of 15 imply that a $100,000 reduction in earnings due to an uninsured loss translates into a $1.5 million reduction in the value of the firm? Probably not. A high P-E ratio usually is regarded as a sign of stockholders' beliefs that the organization's earnings will grow at a high rate. Assuming this belief is correct, the effect of an uninsured loss on the value of the organization reflects stockholders' beliefs concerning the effect of the loss on their previous projections concerning future earnings.

A second market-valuation ratio discussed in economics and finance literature is Tobin's q, named after the work of economist James Tobin (1969):

$$\text{Tobin's q} = \frac{\text{Market value of firm}}{\text{Replacement value of assets}}$$

Tobin's q cannot be calculated directly from the book values typically reported on a firm's financial statements. In the estimation of Tobin's q, all amounts are marked to their market value.[6] The market value of the organization includes all of its debt and equity, priced at market value. The replacement value of assets is what it would cost the organization to replace all its assets, using current market prices. A value of Tobin's q above 1.0 could reflect stockholders' beliefs concerning the efficiency with which an organization has deployed assets or it could reflect an organization's franchise value arising from patent protection or brand image.

Tobin's q offers a measure of an organization's incentive to invest. A ratio above 1.0 implies that assets are worth more deployed in the firm than their market prices generally. This interpretation has been a subject of controversy, however, as researchers have found successful firms whose value of Tobin's q is less than 1.0. Possible estimation errors in evaluating market values of securities (e.g., closely held or thinly traded securities) and replacement values of assets (e.g., special-purpose machinery) could limit the reliability of Tobin's q as a measure of efficiency.

In the finance literature, Tobin's q has been used to predict gains and losses in takeover attempts (see Lang, Stulz and Walkling [1989]). As Tobin's q would apply to risk management, one would expect to see active loss-control and crisis-planning efforts at firms whose value of Tobin's q is above 1.0. An organization whose ratio is less than 1.0 may be content to abandon an asset following damage, as the implied market value of restoration appears to be less than its cost.

---

[6] The *replacement value* in the denominator of Tobin's q is not the same as *replacement cost* in insurance coverage. In Tobin's q, the replacement value of the firm's assets is their current value, marked to market. Replacement cost in insurance coverage is the cost of a brand-new asset.

Key Concepts

time horizon The number of years into the future that are allowable in evaluating cash flows arising under a long-term investment project.

matching The process of associating benefits with expenditures possibly giving rise to the benefits.

data credibility The degree of belief or certainty that can be associated with data.

interdependency A condition that exists when a loss to one segment of an operation increases the likelihood of loss to another segment.

externality An economic cost that is not captured in the price of a good or service.

essential coverage Insurance coverage that either is compulsory or covers losses whose occurrence could threaten the attainment of the organization's mission.

available coverage Insurance coverage that may be purchased primarily for convenience.

break-even point A condition in which the cost of insurance coverage equals the expected value of claim payments provided under the coverage.

risk premium As applied to an individual's behavior in purchasing insurance, the risk premium is the difference between the largest premium the individual is willing to pay and the expected value of the loss.

worry cost As applied to an organization's decision whether to purchase insurance, the worry cost is the difference between the largest premium the organization is willing to pay and the expected value of tangible benefits pro-

vided by the coverage in the form of claim reimbursements and other insurance-related services.

market risk premium As applied to securities prices and expected returns, the market risk premium is the difference between the expected return on a portfolio of securities whose proportions are those of the market and the return on a riskless asset.

cash flow The marginal effect of an investment project on the cash position of an organization during a given period of time.

discount rate A rate of interest used to discount future cash flows to reflect the timing of their occurrence.

risk-adjusted discount rate A rate of interest used to discount future cash flows. The rate of interest is adjusted to reflect vulnerability of the cash flows to systematic factors affecting security returns generally.

tax shield An accounting entry that reduces an organization's tax liability during a time period, possibly as a result of a cash outlay during some other period. Depreciation deductions are an example.

leverage ratio A financial ratio measuring the extent to which an organization is in debt.

liquidity ratio A financial ratio measuring the extent to which an organization can raise cash, particularly in the short run.

market-valuation ratio A financial ratio measuring the reaction of stockholders to actions of an organization's managers.

Review Questions

1. Explain how each of the following aspects of risk management problems tend to differ from the same aspects of problems faced by managers in areas other than risk management: (1) time horizons, (2) measurement of benefits and costs, (3) possible uncertainty, (4) data credibility, (5) possible externalities, and (6) interdependent exposures.

2. Under the method for reviewing insurance priorities, what criteria determine whether a type of insurance coverage is "essential," "desirable," or "available"?

297

CHAPTER 12
*Risk Management
Decision Methods:
Data Organization
and Analysis*

3. Should a risk manager automatically buy all essential coverages before considering any desirable or available coverage? Why or why not?

4. The data appearing below apply to an organization's worker's compensation coverage. Use the data in the table to estimate the largest value of expected claim frequency for which the organization will consider the $1000 deductible in lieu of full coverage (i.e., break-even loss frequency). What assumptions are required for the estimate to be valid?

Deductible Amount	Annual Premium
$0 (full coverage)	$3500
$1,000	$3000

5. The data appearing below are 10-year average ratios for commercial auto physical damage (i.e., collision) insurance. A risk manager believes that her firm can avoid paying the entire amount of loss adjustment expenses, commissions and brokerage, and other underwriting expenses by retaining the firm's exposure to auto physical damage claims. Using her assumption and the values in the table below, calculate the expected value of the firm's savings from retaining claims covered by a policy whose premium is $35,000 per year.

Ratio to Premiums Earned		Ratio to Premiums Written		Ratio to Premiums Earned	Ratio to Premiums Earned		
Losses Incurred	Loss Adjustment Expenses Incurred	Commissions and Brokerage Incurred	Other Underwriting Expenses Incurred	Dividends to Policyholders	Combined Ratio After Dividends	Investment Gain & Other Income	Overall Operating Ratio
52.4	6.6	15.3	14.7	0.4	89.4	2.7	86.6

Source: Best's Aggregates and Averages: Property-Casualty (1993 edition).

6. A risk manager is considering the installation of new ventilating equipment in an area in which employees use volatile solvents. The equipment has an expected lifetime of five years and costs $250,000 to install. Annual maintenance and other operating costs are $5000. Each year of its life, the ventilating equipment is expected to reduce the employer's retained work-injury costs and expenses related to having employees avoid excessive exposure to solvents by $35,000. In addition, the insurer that writes the employer's workers' compensation insurance is willing to reduce the premium for coverage by $45,000 a year if ventilating equipment is installed.
The employer faces a 34 percent tax rate on income, and straight-line depreciation is used on the ventilating equipment.

a. Calculate the annual cash flows from installing the ventilating equipment.

b. Assume that the riskless rate of interest is 6 percent, while the expected rate of return on a market-proportioned portfolio of risky securities is 12 percent. If the cash flows from the ventilating equipment are zero-beta, should the ventilating equipment be installed? Why or why not?

c. If the cash flows from the ventilating equipment have a beta of 1.0, should the ventilating equipment be installed? Why or why not?

d. What value of beta do you believe is likely to apply to the ventilating equipment? Do you believe that the value is more likely to lie near zero or 1.0? Why?

e. Evaluate the proposed installation of the ventilating equipment if the employer is an untaxed government employer. Explain any changes in your answers to parts **a** through **d**.

7. Use the data in the financial statements appearing below to calculate (1) the long-term debt to net worth ratio, (2) the times interest earned ratio, (3) the ratio of net working capital to total assets, and (4) the current ratio. Briefly explain the significance of each ratio to a risk manager.

Summary Balance Sheet ($Millions)

Assets		Liabilities	
Current assets	$ 681	Current liabilities	$ 457
Property, plant and equipment	486	Long-term debt	298
Other assets	116	Deferrals	71
Total assets	$1,283	Total liabilities	$ 826
		Stockholders' equity	$ 457

Summary Earnings Statement ($Millions)

Revenues	$1,724
Cost of raw stock	349
Payroll	748
Depreciation	49
Interest	43
Other expenses	393
Total expenses	1,582
Earnings before taxes on income	142
Income taxes	47
Earnings from continuing operations	95
Loss from discontinued operations	(8)
Net earnings	87

References and Suggestions for Additional Reading

BREALEY, RICHARD A., and STEWART C. MYERS: *Principles of Corporate Finance* (New York: McGraw-Hill Book Company, 1991).

BREEDEN, DOUGLAS T.: "An Intertemporal Asset Pricing Model with Stochastic Consumption and Investment Opportunities," *Journal of Financial Economics* (vol. 7, no. 3, 1979), pp. 265–296.

LANG, LARRY H. P., RENE M. STULZ, and RALPH A. WALKLING: "Managerial Performance, Tobin's Q, and the Gains from Successful Tender Offers," *Journal of Financial Economics* (vol. 24, 1989), pp. 137–154.

LEVERETT, E. J., JR.: *Risk Management and Insurance* (Athens, Georgia: University of Georgia, unpublished manuscript, 1992).

ROSS, STEPHEN A., RANDOLPH W. WESTERFIELD, and JEFFREY F. JAFFE: *Corporate Finance* (Homewood, Ill., Richard D. Irwin, Inc., 1993).

TOBIN, JAMES: "A General Equilibrium Approach to Monetary Theory," *Journal of Money, Credit and Banking* (vol. 1, 1969), pp. 15–29.

RIMS: *Cost of Risk Survey* (Chicago: Published by Tillinghast Inc. and the Risk and Insurance Management Society, annual, 1990).

Insurance Institutions and Coverages

Chapters 13 through 19 provide an introduction to the insurance industry and to insurance coverages. Although insurance is only one risk management tool, in most organizations the risk manager is responsible for issues related to insurance. Consequently, knowledge of insurance is important to most risk managers. Chapter 13 discusses the insurance industry and identifies the principal conceptual and institutional features of that industry. Chapter 14 focuses on insurance pricing and its relation to other insurance functions. Chapter 15 discusses financial aspects of the industry, with particular emphasis on evaluation of financial performance. Chapter 15 also provides an introduction to insurance regulation. Chapter 16 discusses legal characteristics of insurance, with emphasis on insurance as a "legal contract."

Chapters 17 through 19 represent something of a departure from more conventional discussions of insurance contract analysis. Typically, textbooks present a unified approach to analyzing contracts—whether they are prop-

erty, liability, or human resource related. The authors believe that the differences between property and liability insurance contracts, life insurance contracts, and health insurance contracts are significant; so much so that a discussion of contract analysis must be separated into three largely distinct presentations. Chapter 17 looks at property and liability insurance contracts, but with a very pragmatic orientation. What situations are covered by property and liability contracts, and how is the reimbursement for loss determined? An analytical approach to evaluating contracts is presented. The focus of Chapter 17 provides a glimpse into the types of contracts that constitute the typical risk manager's property and liability insurance portfolio. Chapters 18 and 19 provide a similar discussion, but focus on human resource risk exposures: life insurance (Chapter 18) and health insurance (Chapter 19). This introduction to life and health insurance provides the background for later discussions of employee benefits, business life insurance, and pensions.

CHAPTER 13

An Introduction to the Insurance Industry

Learning Objectives

After you have completed this chapter, you should be able to:

1. Explain the difference between insurance and bonding.
2. Identify and explain the costs and benefits of insurance.
3. Identify the characteristics of ideally insurable risks.
4. Discuss the roles of underwriting and claims management in insurance.
5. List six ways in which insurers can be classified.
6. Distinguish a stock insurer from a mutual insurer, a Lloyds Association, and a reciprocal exchange.
7. Describe how insurers can be classified according to their pricing policies.
8. Explain the major marketing systems used by insurers.
9. Describe the operations of groups of insurers, cooperative underwriters' associations, and reinsurance associations.

INTRODUCTION

In previous chapters, insurance is presented as but one of many risk management tools available to the risk manager. While this view is appropriate conceptually, insurance concepts are important background influencing the everyday world of risk management. Indeed, even when insurance is not used, insurance markets influence the practice of risk management. For example, price movements in insurance markets can influence an organization's willingness to substitute insurance for other risk financing methods. Also, the design of risk financing methods that substitute for commercial insurance may be patterned after commercial insurers. Readers need only recall self-insurance pools; public organizations modeled along the lines of insurance companies and created precisely because commercial insurance was either unavailable or unaffordable.

The principles and concepts that flow from the study of insurance have a general impact on risk management, because the concept and theory of risk is at the core of the study of insurance. Virtually every temporal aspect of insurance suggests a strong relationship with risk theory. For instance, the existence of reinsurance can be explained by considering the effect of the law of large numbers on insurance. Or, the industry's concern with "adverse selection" can offer important lessons to managers of benefit programs. To put it slightly differently, the study of insurance can provide readers with an institutional, practical, and managerially oriented window into the more esoteric realm of risk theory.

In fact, knowledge of risk gained through an understanding of insurance may be the one unique knowledge area of the risk management discipline. Risk management is acknowledged to be interdisciplinary, and its specialness is generally viewed as arising from a combining of knowledge from a number of areas—strategic management, finance, law, safety engineering, and so on. However, knowledge of risk via the study of insurance is unique to the discipline, so it is essential that insurance be included in a broader study of risk management.

After introducing several conceptual and functional issues, this chapter looks at insurance as an institutional phenomenon. Insurance is commonly made available by organizations that assume risk and indemnify losses. Since most readers are familiar with this face of insurance, it is an appropriate starting point. Discussion will focus on the descriptive characteristics of the industry: legal form of organization, marketing methods, types of products sold, types of customers. A central objective is to provide readers with basic vocabulary and a framework for understanding the complexities of the insurance industry today.

FOUR CONCEPTUAL ISSUES

Before discussing the institutional characteristics of the insurance industry, four issues are briefly addressed. They are (1) the benefits and costs of insurance, (2) the characteristics of insurable risks, (3) the distinctions between insurance and gambling, and (4) the distinctions between insurance and bonding. Each of these issues has institutional ramifications, but is essentially conceptual in nature.

Benefits and Costs of Insurance

Insurance, like most institutions, presents society with both benefits and costs. The benefits, which are numerous, are fairly obvious to most readers, though the implications of these benefits may not be as apparent.

Benefits

Indemnification. The direct advantage of insurance is indemnification for unexpected loss. Organizations suffering loss are restored or at least moved closer to their former economic position. The advantage to these organizations is obvious. Society also gains because resources are restored to production, tax revenues are increased, and other possible costs are reduced.

Reduction of Uncertainty. Prior to the purchase of insurance, the potential insured bears the risk associated with possible uninsured damage or exposure to liability. As a consequence, an insured who is aware of the exposure to risk is uncertain about the outcome. The insurance transfers financial consequences of loss to the insurer, who then becomes responsible for reimbursing loss and providing other loss-related services according to the provisions of the insurance agreement. If the insurer's resources are sufficient to honor its contractual commitments and the insured accurately interprets the terms of the insurance coverage, the purchase of insurance substitutes a known cost (the insurance premium) for a possibly larger, but unknown amount (the amount of damage). This substitution would be expected to reduce the insured's anxiety and uncertainty.

From this description, it would seem as though nothing has happened other than the substitution of one party's obligation (the insurer's) for that of another party (the insured). Any reduction in the insured's uncertainty would appear to give rise to a corresponding increase in uncertainty for the insurer. Although this point of view offers a factual description of the statistical or accounting effects of a single insurance transaction, at the same time it fails to recognize an important economy of scale arising when an insurance organization writes a large number of policies.

When an insurer charges a premium that exceeds the expected value of losses on each policy and writes a large number of policies on independent risks, the excess of premiums over the expected value of losses provides a cushion against possible variation of losses. As the number of policies becomes large, the cushion tends to grow at a faster rate than the tendency of claims to deviate from their expected value. This cushion reduces the insurer's uncertainty about claims possibly exceeding the pool of resources. As a consequence, uncertainty for an insurer writing a large number of policies is smaller than the insured's uncertainty prior to purchasing coverage.

However, nothing in the preceding discussion implies that the insurer's uncertainty and risk are zero. Although the insurer may be less concerned than the insured about claims under an individual policy, the insurer still faces risk from a portfolio of insurance policies. One type of risk arises when a common factor affects a large portion of the policies in the same way. Hurricane Andrew, an economy-wide change in auto repair costs, a change in rules regarding employment rights for disabled workers, or an increase in crime rates are examples of common factors affecting insurance costs. A second type of risk arises from the pricing function; the insurer may underestimate claim costs, particularly on a new type of coverage. Also, an insurer may underestimate the degree of adverse selection in a line of coverage or may fail to anticipate moral hazards induced by changing a policy provision to cover a new type of claim.

Insurers specialize in writing insurance and providing loss-related services, such as legal defense against liability. This specialization often creates a relative advantage for the insurer in activities such as claims management and forecasting claims costs. Together, the large pool of resources and expertise in claims forecasting and pricing tend to provide the insurer with an advantage in risk bearing relative to the insured.

The relative advantage of insurers in risk bearing gives rise to two benefits when insurance is used to cover risk. First, the reduction in uncertainty and anxiety allows the insured's energies to be focused on activities in which the insured has a relative advantage. For example, the purchase of property and liability insurance for a construction contractor allows the contractor's attention to be focused on matters such as scheduling of labor and materials acquisition, which may be critical to success in the construction business. Second, the insurer's expertise is applied to the situation giving rise to possible loss. Insurers often provide guidance and advice to customers on issues such as loss prevention and reduction, and insurers often have a relative advantage in claims management.

Funds for Investment. Insurance premiums normally are paid in advance of losses and held by insurers until the time of claim payment, which allows insurers to invest these funds until claims are paid. Earnings on invested funds partly offset the cost of insurance claims, the benefit of which can be passed through to policyholders in the form of reduced premiums. However, the net result of these investment-related effects would be neutral in a perfect investment market. In an economy in which insurers and policyholders are equally informed about investment opportunities and markets for investment are frictionless, insurers would make the same provision for future claim payment as their policyholders would make in the absence of insurance (see earlier discussion in Chapter 11 about frictionless investment markets). An argument that investment-related effects of insurance lead to a net benefit requires a presumed advantage for insurers in the process of investing funds held for payment of future claims.

Two reasons can be advanced for presuming that insurers have advantages relative to their policyholders in this type of investment. One reason is related to timing. An insured holding funds for future claim payments would be expected to invest these funds in liquid assets—ones that can be converted to cash quickly. Self-funding of claims would require liquid investments because the timing of payments is uncertain. To the extent that an insurer writing a portfolio of policies is better able than policyholders to predict the timing of claim payments, some of the funds held for this purpose are freed up for longer-term investments. The net effect of these funds being freed up for longer-term investments would be a lowering of long-term yields required to induce investors to forsake short-term for longer-term investments. Second, the consolidation of premiums from a large number of policyholders allows insurers to specialize in this type of investment, an advantage that policyholders acting on their own would not be expected to possess (except possibly policyholders specializing in the business of investment services).

The *1992 Life Insurance Fact Book* shows that life insurers provided about 18 percent of the total funds supplied to United States money and capital markets in 1991, an increase from 8.4 percent in 1970 (Best's, 1992, page 86). Mutual funds was the only category of financial institution whose share of the 1991 market exceeded the life insurance industry's share. Fire and casualty insurance companies' share of the 1991 market was about 5.2 percent. Fire and casualty companies' share was smaller than the share of the life insurance industry because their contracts typically cover a shorter period of time and consequently accumulate fewer premium dollars in advance of claim payments. Private non–life insurance company pension plans' share of the 1991 market was about 13.6 percent, while the share of state and local government retirement funds was about 11.8 percent. In aggregate, the share of money and capital markets attributable to insurance companies and pension plans was slightly under 48.8 percent.

Loss Control. The writing of insurance gives the insurance industry a direct interest in loss control. After the insurance contract is written, the prevention and reduction of losses results in smaller payments under the coverages. The interest in loss prevention manifests itself at the level of the individual policyholder and in aggregate. For example, an insurer that writes theft insurance may provide financial incentives to install theft-prevention devices through reduced premiums or more favorable settlement of losses occurring when such devices are installed. As another example, insurers writing contracts to pay benefits in the event of death may have a financial interest in improving longevity of covered lives. As a consequence, life insurers may support research into methods to prolong life.

Aid to Small Business. Insurance can allow a small business to engage in activities requiring resources that are beyond its capacity. A regulation requiring businesses to demonstrate financial responsibility for work-related injury offers an example. A large business may be able to demonstrate that its resources are adequate to fund work-injury claims without an insurance guaranty. The resources of a smaller employer are less likely to meet this test, in which case, the purchase of workers' compensation coverage offers an alternative for satisfying the requirement. Also, the purchase of insurance provides the small employer with access to the insurer's knowledge and skill in managing the exposure to risk, allowing the employer to focus its attention on the primary line of business activity.

Costs

Although the advantages arising out of the existence of an insurance industry are sizable, insurance is not without its costs.

Operating Expenses. Insurers incur expenses such as loss-control costs, loss-adjustment expenses, expenses involved in acquiring insureds, state premium taxes, and general administrative expenses. These expenses, plus a reasonable amount for profit and contingencies, must be covered by the premium charged. In real terms, workers and other resources that might have been committed to other uses are required by the insurance industry. The following data illustrate the magnitude of these expenses, excluding the amounts for profits and contingencies. Page 76 of the *1992 Life Insurance Factbook* reports that life insurers in 1991 used about 11.5 percent of their total income to pay expenses, excluding taxes. In terms of premium income, these expenses were about 16.9 percent; but the inclusion of investment income reduces the percentage relative to the insurers' total resources. Property and liability insurers typically use between 30 and 40 percent of their premium income to pay expenses, including loss-adjustment expenses, but excluding federal income taxes. For property and liability insurers, investment income is not considered in this calculation because it is only a minor part of their total resources. The *1990 Source Book of Health Insurance Data* (pp. 26, 28) shows expenses of health insurers to be about 11 percent of premiums.

Moral Hazard. A second cost of insurance is the moral hazard (which was introduced in Chapter 1). Insurance coverage reduces the insured's incentives to prevent loss or to contain the amount of damage when loss occurs. In extreme cases, losses may be deliberate, such as arson or staging of automobile accidents to collect insurance proceeds. Less extreme examples of moral hazards include exaggeration of damage to increase recovery for loss or increased consumption of medical services when the services are insured (sometimes referred to as "morale hazard"). Because the moral hazard increases losses relative to their amount in the absence of insurance, the extra burden constitutes a deadweight loss to both the insurer and the insured. The insurance industry has developed information-sharing methods and other investigative techniques to reduce extreme cases of moral hazards, which often constitute fraud. Less-than-extreme cases of moral hazards are more difficult to detect and overcome, and at some point the allocation of additional resources to overcoming moral hazards is not justified. As a result, some degree of moral hazard exists in virtually every type of insurance. Insurers and insureds have a mutual interest in overcoming the effects of moral hazards, and many policy provisions such as deductibles and other cost-sharing methods can be explained as attempts to control moral hazards.

The Benefit-Cost Tradeoff. The size of the insurance industry suggests that, in many instances, the benefits of insurance far outweigh the costs created by its existence. To the extent that insurers can reduce these costs, the scope of the insurance industry can expand. Insurers are constantly trying to reduce their costs through innovations in such matters as administrative procedures and marketing methods. Selling insurance to groups of persons instead of to individuals is a prime example. The creation of the moral hazard itself is offset, at least in part, by the loss-control activities of insurers. Moral hazard is specifically attacked through such measures as reporting services on suspicious fires, a systematic index of automobile personal-injury claims against all member insurers (which helps to reveal fraudulent claims), and close investigations of suicide claims. Morale hazard is most effectively handled by pointing out the direct relationship between premiums and losses and the sizable indirect losses and inconveniences that are not covered by insurance.

Characteristics of Insured Risks

Insurance can be a useful device for managing risk, but its use tends to be associated with risks having features in common. The following discussion applies primarily to privately purchased insurance, although some of the observations carry over to publicly provided coverages as well.

Insured Risks Tend to Be Pure Risks

Most insured risks are pure risks. Nothing in the nature of speculative risk precludes the writing of insurance, but the market for such coverages appears to be small. (This statement assumes that contracts such as options and futures are not defined as insurance). In fact, insurers and other financial institutions have experimented with insurance on speculative risk by, for example, guaranteeing a minimum return on an investment. Although these ventures are noteworthy exceptions to the rule, nearly all insurance is written against pure risk. The reason for this restriction can be related to the concept of insurance and consideration of possible moral hazards and adverse selection. Unless the insured has no control over the exposure to risk, insurers avoid writing coverage that makes the insured better off after an insured event as compared with the case in which no loss occurs. Were such a coverage to be written, moral hazards and adverse selection problems would be likely to develop. When moral hazards and adverse selection problems become prevalent, the market for insurance is likely to fail because policyholders become unwilling to pay the cost of coverage.

Webster's dictionary defines insurance as a system of protection against loss in which individuals agree to pay certain sums for a guarantee that they will be compensated for loss. Unless the insurance payoff is triggered by a loss that is at least as great as the insurance benefit, the insurance creates an incentive to cause the insured event to occur. As a consequence, moral hazard and adverse selection problems are strong unless the contract's payoffs occur only when accompanied by a loss at least as large as the insurance benefit. Because the payoffs occur only as a result of a loss at least as large as the insurance benefit, the "covered risk" is a pure risk. A possible exception would be the above-mentioned guarantee on investment return, although the covered event (failure to achieve a minimum return) resembles a pure risk; also, the coverage applies to outcomes over which the insured presumably has little control and the insurer's ability to forecast outcomes is at least as good as the insured's.

Conditions Affecting the Insurability of Risks

In addition to being pure risks, insured risks tend to possess certain features that enhance their insurability. A risk could be considered an ideally insurable risk if it satisfies the four conditions discussed below.

1. A large number of units are independently and identically exposed to the risk, whose importance is great enough to create an interest in insurance among persons responsible for the units. The large number of units is required for an accurate estimate of the expected value of the loss. The importance of the risk ensures that a large number of the persons in control of the units are likely to purchase coverage. The requirement that exposures to risk be independent is essential for the law of large numbers (or the central limit theorem) to hold.

Parenthetically, in addition to independence and identically distributed losses, a proof of the central limit theorem requires finite variance. A proof of the law of large numbers (more exactly, the weak law of large numbers) does not require that the variance exist. However, the central limit theorem offers a stronger result. The central limit theorem asserts that the distribution of the average loss per unit in a large pool converges to a normal distribution, after which the variance in the average loss per unit in the pool (making the standard deviation inversely proportional to the square root of the number of units). The weak law of large numbers uses a weaker set of assumptions (i.e., variance need not exist), leading to a weaker result. The weak law asserts only that losses per unit converge to the expected value, but the law is silent on how rapidly the convergence occurs.

When the exposures are independent and the insurance premium exceeds the expected value of the loss, the insurer's resources for reimbursing loss tend to grow at a faster rate than the deviation of pooled losses from the expected value (see the earlier discussion of insurance in Chapter 9, or Smith and Kane, [1993]). As a consequence, the probability that the insurer's resources are sufficient to pay all insured claims tends to approach 1.0 as the number of insured units becomes large. When the exposures are not independent, increasing the number of policyholders does not necessarily increase the probability that the insurer can honor all claims. If losses are identically distributed and perfectly correlated, for example, insurance is ineffective—the risk faced by each unit is identical to the risk they face collectively.

For a proof of the law of large numbers, the requirements that exposures be identical is not as critical as the requirement that they be independent. However, similarity among exposures can be important to an insurance or pooling agreement for other reasons. When the exposures are not identical, estimation of the expected value of the loss (for the purpose of setting premiums) becomes complicated because characteristics of each exposure must be considered. Also, the number of exposures required to achieve a given level of predictability tends to increase relative to when exposures are identical. The law of large numbers still is likely to hold if exposures are independent, but insurance is less effective when exposures are heterogeneous (see Billingsley, 1986).

2. The loss should be definite or determinate in time, place, cause, and amount. If the event triggering the insurance benefit is defined vaguely or the method for determining reimbursement is indefinite, the possibility of disputes with claimants or other loss adjustment problems is created. The cost of these disputes is a deadweight loss to both insureds and insurers. Under a typical contract, the loss must occur at a certain time and place, be caused by a covered peril, and be measurable or defined in the contract itself (e.g., through the policy limit).

3. The expected loss over some reasonable operating period should be calculable. This requirement is related to the preceding condition that the loss be definite or determinate because the accumulation of loss experience becomes difficult when losses are defined vaguely. The condition that the expected loss be calculable is necessary if the premiums are to be set at the level necessary to produce with some certainty a reasonable, but not excessive, profit or operating margin for the insurer. Conditions 1 and 2 must exist before condition 3 can be satisfied, but in addition, condition 3 requires the expected loss to either be fairly stable over time or otherwise predictable.

4. The loss should be fortuitous or accidental from the viewpoint of the insured. From a public policy viewpoint, it is clearly unwise to insure a person against an intentional loss. It is also unwise to insure against losses that are certain to occur, such as wear and tear, or that are easily preventable.

Practical Limits to These Conditions. Few if any insured risks meet all these requirements fully, although they all are present to some degree in risks that are insured. The second and third requirements are essential. If the event giving rise to an insurance benefit and the resulting loss amount are not defined clearly, disputes over the definition of the insured event and the determination of the benefit amount are likely to occur. If the expected loss cannot be estimated, determination of the cost of coverage is not possible.

The first and fourth conditions are least likely to hold in practice. Many insured risks are not independent of each other, and aggregate claim payments on portfolios of insured risks exhibit cyclical swings. Although the lack of independence increases the difficulty of writing insurance, the problem is reduced through reinsurance coverages purchased by insurers and other risk management methods. Also, some insurers are willing to write coverage on unusual or unique risks, where large numbers do not exist.

In a strict sense, the fourth condition requiring the loss to be accidental rarely holds. Many insured accidents are preventable, but costs associated with monitoring the insured's behavior limit the extent to which insurers can require loss prevention. Some provisions in insurance contracts can be explained as maintaining insureds' incentives to prevent and otherwise control losses. However, the principle still remains: the greater the insured's degree of control over losses, the less applicable the insurance mechanism. Insurance reduces the insured's incentives to prevent and otherwise control losses: the greater the degree of control by the insured, the more dramatic the effect.

Often, the issues detracting from the insurability of a risk are related to behavior of insured persons, particularly if the insured can conceal information related to the likelihood of this behavior. These problems, earlier defined as *adverse selection* and *moral hazards,* have strong effects on the development of insurance markets. In situations in which these problems are too great, the market for insurance against the risk does not develop because insureds are unwilling to pay the price of coverage priced to consider these problems. A similar problem is related to coverage disputes. If the covered event or the amount of payment is defined vaguely, coverage disputes are likely to arise. The cost of these disputes is a deadweight loss to both the insurer and the insured. These costs could be avoided by the insurer paying all claims, but the coverage would be expensive. If vaguely worded coverages in which the insurer pays all claims were more efficient than clearly worded but restricted coverages, presumably the marketplace would have discovered the more efficient alternative.

Another issue affecting the insurability of a risk is the presence of substitutes for the coverage, either through government programs or even the legal system itself. Private insurance cannot be expected to compete against a program receiving a government subsidy; why would individuals and organizations purchase coverage that offsets a benefit already provided by government or through the legal system? For example, dwelling owners are likely to be reluctant to purchase flood insurance if they believe that government disaster relief will be provided in the event of a serious flood.

Some risks whose insurability is questionable have nevertheless been insured because of the importance to the public of providing protection against a given peril, because of social pressures, because the risk is expected to become insurable in the future, or for some other reason. Insurers differ widely in their appraisal of many risks. Some insurers are anxious to insure risks that others flatly reject as uninsurable. Some insure risk to which only a few units are exposed because they seek predictability only for their total writings.

Regulatory Constraints

Most state laws prohibit the writing of life insurance by property and liability insurers and vice versa. This constraint, however, can be bypassed in various ways, for example, by writing the other type of insurance through a subsidiary. Many state laws also list the kinds of insurance that can be written by any insurer. If the type of insurance is not on the list, it cannot be written. Many lists include "any line approved by the state insurance commissioner," in which case lines not specifically mentioned may be approved—but only after a process that may not be worth the effort. This restriction was of greater importance in the past than currently. State laws prescribe the minimum capital and surplus a domestic insurer must have to transact business. These minimum requirements vary with the kinds of insurance the insurer intends to write.

Another factor that may defer entry into a new line is how state insurance departments regulate rates for the field the insurer is about to enter. Certain lines sometimes require substantial red tape, making entrance into those lines much less attractive. The effect of regulation on the profitability of insurers in that line must also be considered.

Common law developed through court interpretations of statutes and through resolving civil disputes has been another factor in determining whether a given type of risk is insurable. One example is the rule prohibiting payment of life insurance policy proceeds to a beneficiary who murders the insured. Another example, discussed later in Chapter 16, is the legal doctrine of insurable interest. This doctrine requires the insured to possess an insurable interest in the object or situation being insured in order to collect under insurance coverage. An insurable interest is demonstrated by the insured showing that he or she suffers an economic loss as a result of the insured event.

Other Constraints

An insurer may wish to enter a certain line but may conclude that its present staff, such as actuaries, underwriters, and claims adjusters, are not capable of writing and servicing this new line at a profit. Hiring new staff may not be easy, and the reactions of existing staff to new people, especially if they command higher salaries, may cause some serious problems.

"Reinsurance" facilities for the new line may also be needed. The interest of the insurer in writing the new exposure may be conditional on its ability to protect itself against catastrophe losses (which may occur even among exposures that for practical purposes are independent) and against substantial losses on single exposures.

"Financing" may also be a problem. To write more insurance at what the insurer considers an acceptable premium-to-net-worth ratio may require the insurer to seek more funds from its stockholders or to generate more surplus from internal operations.

"Custom and tradition" cannot be ignored. Most insurers hesitate to pioneer in areas that have not been successfully tested by other insurers. Despite the fact that the exposure under consideration appears to meet all the requirements established for a commercially insurable exposure, they may be reluctant to enter a new area.

In conclusion, it should be noted that a risk that is generally uninsurable today may be considered insurable at some future date because of some change in the risk itself, because of improvements in the technical knowledge or other abilities of insurers, or because some more compelling reasons are introduced for insuring the risk.

The insurance industry experiments with new coverages and new provisions in their existing coverages to determine whether they can be insured. One example of such an experiment is coverage sold to individual investors that guarantees these investors prompt and full payment of interest and principal on specified municipal bonds. (A related coverage, sold to the issuer of the municipal bond, guarantees the payment of interest and principal to the purchasers of bonds issued by the insured municipality. This coverage is more closely related to surety bonding.) Under a second coverage, a home warranty program sold to real estate agents for distribution free to buyers of used homes, the insurer promises to pay the buyer during the first six months or year of home ownership the cost of repairing major structural defects and mechanical failures of heating, plumbing, and electrical systems. The real estate agent is responsible for seeing that prospective used homes are inspected and that sellers have made necessary repairs before the houses are listed for sale.

Distinguishing Insurance from Gambling

Insurance transactions sometimes are confused with gambling. The transactions resemble each other in two respects: both the insured and the gambler may collect more than they pay out, and the benefit payment is determined by chance event. However, the insurance benefit offsets a loss, while gambling winnings normally do not depend on any misfortune affecting the holder of the contract. Thus, insurance addresses a risk that is independent of the contract, while the gambling "contract" creates the risk.

Distinguishing Insurance from Bonding

As used in risk management, the term "bond" has a special meaning. A bond is a guarantee of honesty or of the capacity to perform an act. When used to guarantee honesty, the bond is called a *fidelity bond.* Bonds guaranteeing the capacity to perform an act are called *surety bonds.* Fidelity and surety bonds are commonly used in business transactions when an organization wishes protection against adverse consequences of other individuals' or organizations' acts. For example, a lending institution may use a fidelity bond to provide protection against embezzlement by employees. In this case, the fidelity bond is a guarantee of employees' honesty. As another example, a school board may require construction contractors who wish to bid on the construction of a new school building to furnish surety bonds. In the case of the school building, the surety bond guarantees the contractor's capacity to complete the project. If the contractor becomes insolvent prior to completing the construction, for example, the provider of the coverage provides the resources to complete the project.

Bonding transactions resemble insurance in many respects. Often the providers of bonds also provide insurance. In particular, the typical fidelity bond closely resembles insurance. The typical surety bond, however, can be distinguished from insurance in three respects:

1. A typical surety bond has three parties to the contract: the *principal,* the *obligee,* and the *surety.* The principal is the party whose capacity is guaranteed. The obligee is the party who receives the benefit if the principal defaults. The surety is the provider of the coverage. In contrast, insurance contracts usually involve two parties: the insurer and the insured.
2. Surety bonds can and do cover intentional losses, while insurance contracts normally exclude losses caused intentionally by the insured. If a loss is covered by a surety bond, however, the surety has the legal right to turn to the principal for reimbursement.
3. Typically, a surety bond is issued following a careful investigation of the principal's capacity. As a consequence, few if any losses would be expected, and most of the premium for the coverage would be consumed in the investigation and underwriting effort. In contrast, most insurance contemplates a significant portion of the premium being used to reimburse insured losses.

INSURANCE FUNCTIONS AND SERVICES

A number of business functions are performed in writing and servicing insurance. Many of these functions have counterparts in other business organizations. For example, the functions performed by human resource departments and marketing departments are performed in insurers with much the same purposes as in other business organizations. However, several functions have special significance to the insurance business, and the performance of these functions can materially affect the character of the coverage provided by an insurer. Some of these functions entail the performance of insurance-related services that can be valuable to insured individuals and organizations. The performance of these functions also consumes resources, which means that these functions are related to the price of insurance. Chapter 14 focuses specifically on methods used to price insurance, so an understanding of these functions provides useful background information on their role in the pricing process. For this reason, and for the inherent importance in understanding these functions, this chapter turns to a brief discussion of (1) underwriting, (2) inspection, engineering, and loss prevention, (3) investment, and (4) loss adjustment (or claims management).

Underwriting

The underwriting process determines which applicants are eligible for insurance coverage. An insurer normally rejects some applicants and accepts others. The criteria used to screen applicants can range from rigid to lenient. At one extreme, an insurer using a strict underwriting policy applies stringent standards to determine eligibility, possibly rejecting many applicants. At the other extreme, a "guaranteed issue" policy is issued to virtually all applicants, with few if any criteria used to screen their eligibility.

The purpose of underwriting is to control adverse selection and assemble a group of insureds whose loss potential is homogeneous. When loss potential is homogeneous, the same insurance premium can be charged across insureds. When a strict underwriting policy creates an insured group whose loss potential is low, the group members benefit by having premiums reduced to reflect fewer-than-average losses. Conversely, the premium for a "guaranteed issue" coverage would be expected to reflect a lack of safeguards against adverse selection. Because the underwriting process itself consumes resources that are reflected in premiums for coverage, applicants whose loss potential is better-than-average benefit from strict underwriting only if the process is cost effective.

In some cases, an underwriting decision is not merely one of acceptance or rejection, but may involve the decision on the issuance of a particular type of policy or even provisions within the policy. For example, an applicant whose theft loss record is poor may be issued a policy that excludes theft losses but is standard in other respects. Another possibility is imposing a larger deductible on theft losses than on other losses. In some cases, the underwriting process is directly linked to pricing; the insurer may be unwilling to issue a policy at standard rates to an applicant, but may be willing to issue the same policy with a surcharge.

When preparing a proposal for securing insurance coverage and data backing the proposal (sometimes called an "underwriting submission"), an organization's risk manager should recognize that a high level of uncertainty for an insurer is likely to increase the price of coverage. The more high-quality information the insurer has to evaluate exposure to risk, the more likely the price of coverage reflects the true expected value of claims. Such information often includes data such as a listing of buildings and other property together with their locations and an up-to-date valuation; a listing of the organization's other exposures or activities creating loss potential together with a record of the organization's effort to control them; a history of uninsured and insured claims, together with a record of their settlement; and a record of outstanding and settled liability claims including the settlement history of each claim. The withholding of information that reflects adversely on claims potential is not likely to improve the position of the risk manager's organization vis-à-vis its insurers. Failure to reveal important information can result in disputes with the insurer or expensive litigation, and may be grounds for the insurer to deny claims.

Inspection, Engineering, and Loss Prevention

Services such as inspection, engineering, and loss prevention guidelines can be an important part of an organization's insurance coverage. For example, these loss-control services are an important element of fire insurance coverage provided by the Factory Mutual Insurance Companies and the Industrial Risk Insurers discussed later in this chapter. As another example, workers' compensation insurers frequently offer guidance on issues related to worker safety. Inspection and engineering services often comprise the largest benefit from coverage on heavy industrial machinery, refrigerating equipment, and boilers ("boiler and machinery" coverage).

From the viewpoint of an insurer, the cost effectiveness of loss control services can be evaluated by balancing the reduced insurance claims against the direct cost of the loss control activities required to prevent or mitigate the damage. Such an evaluation is unlikely to reflect indirect costs associated with injury or damage that are borne by the insured. These indirect costs, which can exceed the level of direct costs, were discussed earlier in Chapter 3. Particularly when an insurer possesses a relative advantage in providing loss control services, the evaluation of indirect costs may warrant loss control expenditures beyond the optimal point considering only the insurer's burden. If part of the burden of claims falls on the insured with the insurer bearing only the remainder, one would expect the insurer to invest a smaller amount in loss control than the insured and insurer would jointly invest if they were to reach mutual agreement on the issue.

Investment

The timing of insurance claims relative to payment of premiums may create the opportunity to earn investment income. When premiums are received by the insurer prior to payment of insurance claims, investment income earned on these funds augments the resources available to pay claims (a point discussed earlier in this chapter). As a consequence, the amount required to fund a given claim to be paid at some future time is less than the amount of the claim. For example, a $100,000 claim to be paid at the end of two years can be funded currently with $90,703 when the current interest rate is 5 percent [i.e., $(\$90,703)(1.05)^2 = \$100,000$].

Longer holding periods and higher investment rates of return increase this effect. The effect is minimal when funds are held by the insurer for only a short period (e.g., under most fire insurance policies, coverage applies for only a year and most claims are settled quickly) or when funds are not transferred to the insurer in advance of claim payment (e.g., under a paid loss retro plan). Life insurance prices are determined using methods that formally consider investment income; these procedures are illustrated in an appendix to Chapter 14. Prices for property and liability insurance are less likely to be developed using methods that formally consider investment income. When competition among insurers is present, however, insurers are forced to consider investment income in pricing their policies or lose business. Even when competition among insurers is not present, the failure to consider investment income in pricing insurance increases the attractiveness of alternative risk financing methods, such as retention. An insurer that holds a monopoly would expect to lose business to these alternative risk financing methods unless its price is competitive with these alternatives.

Loss Adjustment

The loss adjustment process determines the level of compensation for an insured claim. The insurance contract creates a legal obligation for the insurer to reimburse a covered claim, but the level of compensation and the effort required to establish the level of the insurer's responsibility can be strongly influenced by the insurer's administrative practices. One example of an administrative issue affecting loss adjustment is the type of evidence required by a property insurer to establish that (1) property was damaged by a peril for which the policy provides coverage and (2) the value of the property. An administrative procedure requiring formal legal evidence of ownership and an appraisal for every item of damaged property would be expected to lengthen the settlement process and reduce the level of compensation as compared with a procedure requiring less detailed information. In other words, the insurance contract creates minimum obligations that the insurer cannot escape without facing the possibility of legal action, but administrative procedures followed by the insurer in claims adjustment can significantly affect the level of compensation and the effort required to collect it.

In liability insurance, the loss adjustment services may be the most important benefit provided by the coverage. The typical liability insurance policy requires the insurer to defend claims against the insured alleging injury or damage arising from an act covered by the policy, even if the claim appears groundless. The value of these defense services can be significant, especially when the insured does not possess the skills, experience and network of contacts to mount a successful legal defense. With respect to liability claims, legal defense services are damage mitigation or loss reduction; in some cases, the value of the legal services by itself may justify the purchase of coverage. In a manner of speaking, a liability insurance policy is a contract to provide legal defense services, in which the insurer has bonded its promise to provide these services by holding itself responsible for paying judgments up to the policy limit if the defense is unsuccessful.

Holding other factors constant, generous claims settlement practices would be expected to increase insurance claims, while rigorous claims settlement practices would cause them to fall. The net effect on the price of insurance depends on the balance between the cost of claims administration and its indirect effect on the level of claims. Also, rigorous claims adjustment necessitates activities such as detailed record keeping for policyholders to support claims. The costs of administration on both sides of the agreement are a deadweight loss to both parties to the insurance transaction.

With respect to preparing the data to support an insurance claim, a risk manager should recognize that complete, well-organized data to support a claim are likely to lead to faster and more exact claim settlement. For a property insurance claim, such data include an inventory of properties, both damaged and undamaged, together with their associated values; an account of measures to protect property from further damage, together with their cost; measures to reduce the length of the business interruption period, along with their estimated effects; and estimated costs to repair or replace the damaged property.

Summary

With the exception of the investment function, the above-described activities affect the level of insurance claims from a group of policies, but the act of performing these functions consumes resources. Their indirect effects are the result of these activities on the level of insurance claims, while their direct effects are related to the cost of performing the functions. Some interdependence is present between the functions. For example, an insurer could maintain a constant price on its coverage while tightening underwriting standards and at the same time adopting more generous claims settlement procedures. Such changes might increase the appeal of the coverage to policyholders who were careful in preventing losses and not inclined to overstate claims, even in the absence of insurer scrutiny. Another possibility is insurance coverage on which very little investigation is performed to verify statements on the application, the investigation instead being performed when the first claim occurs. One can envision a number of different blends of these functions, each appealing to policyholders whose preferences and willingness to pay are consistent with the functional emphasis and final price associated with the particular blend.

THE INSURANCE INDUSTRY TODAY

Types of Insurers

Insurers can be classified into two broad categories: *Life* insurers, who in the United States can write life and health insurance, and *Nonlife* insurers, who can write insurance other than life insurance. Table 13.1 provides a summary of premium income of life and nonlife insurers across regions of the world. Data in Table 13.1 show the division of world premiums between nonlife and life in-

TABLE 13.1. Insurance Premium Volume by Continent

Continent	Nonlife Insurance			Life Insurance		
	1988 Premium Income (US $m)	Real Change from 1987 (pct.)	World Share (pct.)	1988 Premium Income (US $m)	Real Change from 1987 (pct.)	World Share (pct.)
North America	268,355	1.6	48.34	189,583	2.8	30.78
Central and South America	6,843	7.6	1.23	1,771	7.6	0.29
Europe	179,679	5.1	32.37	169,320	13.0	27.49
Asia	85,102	13.4	15.33	237,563	21.3	38.57
Africa	5,204	3.6	0.94	7,230	2.9	1.18
Australia and New Zealand	9,917	0.2	1.79	10,433	4.0	1.69
Total	555,110	4.6	100.00	615,900	12.6	100.00

Source: Sigma, Swiss Reinsurance Company, economic studies, 4, 1990.

surance to be roughly equal, with life insurance premiums being somewhat larger and showing a higher growth rate. Europe and North America account for over half of world premium volume, although Asia's growth rates are higher than other regions. By any measure, the insurance industry is large. *Sigma*, the source of data for Table 13.1, shows nonlife premiums in the United States to be 5.25 percent of gross domestic product (GDP), while life premiums are 3.65 percent of gdp.

Over 5,000 private insurers write insurance in the United States. They can be classified in various ways, of which the following are the more important: (1) by the type of insurance written, (2) by the legal form of business organization, (3) by domicile and admission status, (4) by pricing policy, and (5) by marketing method. Government insurers can also be classified under each of these categories, but these categories are much more meaningful in the private sector. Consequently, government insurers will be discussed only as a legal form of organization.

Type of Insurance Written

Table 13.2 provides a summary of payments made during 1989 in the United States toward the cost of insurance coverages and other programs providing retirement or health benefits. These data, which cover private purchases of insur-

TABLE 13.2. 1989 United States Premium Volume or Funding Allocation by Category of Insurer and Type of Coverage

Category of Insurer	Type of Coverage	$ millions
Property-Liability Insurance	Stock Insurers	143,191
	Mutual Insurers	52,236
	Reciprocal Exchanges	13,250
	Lloyds Associations	158
Life Insurance	Ordinary Life Insurance	57,558
	Group Life Insurance	13,120
	Credit Life Insurance	1,996
	Industrial Life Insurance	616
Health Insurance	Blue Cross / Blue Shield	56,000
	Self-Insured and HMO Plans	89,100
	Private Insurance	108,000
	Medicare*	94,300
	Medicaid*	64,900
Retirement Programs	Private Plans with Insurers	57,640
	Federal OASDI Program	251,591
	Federal Civilian Retirement System	30,072
	Railroad Retirement System	4,069
	State and Local Government Plans	44,057

*Benefit payments.
Sources: *Life Insurance Factbook*, *Best's Aggregates and Averages*, and *Source Book of Health Insurance Data*.

ance as well as benefit programs sponsored by governments and employers, provide a gauge for the size of the categories discussed in the following pages.

One of the most obvious distinctions that can be made in the insurance industry is based on the type of insurance written. Three methods of classifying insurers are of particular interest here. First, insurers can be classified according to whether they are primarily or solely (1) originating, primary, or direct insurers, or (2) reinsurers. Primary or direct insurers emphasize sales to the general public, while reinsurers insure those portions of the direct business that the direct insurers for one reason or another do not wish to retain. In other words, the reinsurer's customer is (almost always) a primary or direct insurer. Reinsurance will be discussed in Chapters 14 and 15.

By a second method of classification, insurers can be grouped according to whether they write life, health, property, or liability insurance, or some combination of these major divisions of insurance. Some insurers write only one of the many kinds of insurance under one of these major divisions; others write practically all kinds of insurance under all these divisions. Many insurers fall between these two extremes.

Within the field of life insurance, coverages and insurers can be classified into *branches,* which are categories based on characteristics of the coverages and the systems used to market them. These categories are not distinct, partly because the life insurance coverages on which these categories originally were based have evolved in ways that allow them to overlap. Life insurance falls into four branches: *ordinary, group, credit* or *industrial* insurance. Industrial insurance often is called *home-service* or, less commonly, *debit* insurance.

In terms of premium volume, *ordinary* life insurance is the largest branch. The *Life Insurance Fact Book* defines ordinary insurance as life insurance providing coverage of $1000 or more sold to individuals with premiums payable on an annual, quarterly, or monthly basis. Within the branch of ordinary insurance, a variety of coverages exist. The category is broad enough to encompass policies as heterogeneous as term, insurance, endowments, and credit life insurance covering loans whose term exceeds 10 years (these coverages are later examined in Chapter 19).

The *Fact Book* states that *group* life insurance usually is issued without a medical examination to a group of people under a master policy. Groups to which the coverage is provided include employee groups and members of an association. The individual group members do not actually receive a contract but are issued certificates as evidence of coverage.

Credit life is coverage issued in conjunction with a loan agreement to repay the outstanding loan balance if the debtor dies prior to making the final payment. The *Fact Book* does not define "credit life insurance," but data on life insurance holdings provided by the *Fact Book* limit credit life to coverage written on loans whose duration is 10 years or less. Using this classification, data on life insurance on loans whose duration exceeds 10 years are included with ordinary life insurance.

The *Fact Book* defines *industrial* life insurance as coverage issued in small amounts, usually less than $1,000, with premiums payable on a weekly or monthly basis. Premiums are generally collected at the insured's home by an agent of the company (sometimes called a "debit agent").

The third method of classification is closely related to the second. Insurers are often classified according to whether they market "commercial lines" or "personal lines" insurance. Commercial lines of insurance are all types of insurance that are marketed to organizations, while personal lines insurance are those types of insurance marketed to individuals and families. Many insurers market both types of insurance, but the issues and practices that surround each type of insurance can be quite different. The *Property-Casualty Fact Book* (Best's) shows that United States premiums for property and liability insurance are divided about equally between commercial and personal insurance.

Legal Form of Business Organization

Probably the best-known classification of insurers is according to the legal form of business organization. Three major classes exist—private proprietary insurers, private cooperative insurers, and governmental insurers—but each of these classes includes a variety of subclasses.

Proprietary Insurers. Proprietary insurers almost always are characterized by profit-seeking owners who are responsible for the management of the firm and who bear the risks of the insurer. There are two types of proprietary insurers: (1) stock insurers, and (2) Lloyds Associations.

The stock insurer is a corporation whose owners are stockholders. The stock may be held by the public and traded in an organized stock exchange, or the ownership may be concentrated in a few individuals. Many stock insurers are closely held. The operations of a stock insurer closely resemble the operations of profit-seeking corporations in any line of endeavor. The stockholders elect the board of directors, who delegate management responsibilities to the officers of the insurer. Stockholders receive dividends declared by the board of directors and may sell their shares of stock to others. The dividends and the market value will depend to a large extent upon the success of the operations of the insurer. The corporation possesses a cushion against unfavorable years consisting of the capital and paid-in surplus subscribed by the stockholders and the additional surplus retained from gains during years of favorable operation. This cushion permits stock insurers to follow their customary practice of charging policyholders a definite premium (subject, in some instances, to a retrospective rating plan, discussed in Chapter 14).

Lloyds Associations derive their name from the resemblance between their operations and those of Lloyd's of London. Lloyd's of London (known as the Corporation of Lloyd's since it was incorporated in 1871) is an association of individuals who underwrite insurance as individuals. The association provides certain services, such as underwriting information, policy writing, loss adjustments, and office space; screen prospective members; and prescribes certain regulations aimed at maintaining the financial solvency of members. The association was formed in 1769 by a group of underwriters who gathered at Edward Lloyd's coffeehouse to transact their business.

At its peak, Lloyd's listed about 32,000 members—or so-called "names"—whose personal wealth was pledged to insurance written through Lloyd's of London. After financial difficulties experienced by Lloyd's during the late 1980s, membership began to decline. Until 1969, an underwriter had to be a citizen of the British Commonwealth. The insurance decisions are made by lead underwriters who have the authority to commit names who belong to his or her "syndicate." Over 365 syndicates have been formed, ranging from a few members to thousands of members. Each name may belong to more than one syndicate. Although the insurance is provided through syndicates, a member is not legally responsible for the failure of other names or of other syndicates to fulfill their promises. Syndicates or names not participating in the particular contract are technically outsiders to the entire transaction.

The persons who wish to be names are carefully screened with respect to their financial status and moral integrity; their liability is unlimited; their accounts are supervised by the association; they must deposit with the corporation a substantial amount of cash or approved securities or a satisfactory letter of credit as security behind the member's commitments; and the association maintains a central guarantee fund to which all members contribute, which can be used to pay any unsatisfied obligation. In addition, the reputation of Lloyd's of London is jealously guarded by the membership.

Lloyd's of London names possess almost unlimited freedom with respect to the types of insurance they may write and the rates they may charge. Members, in fact, differ with respect to these matters, although there is a tendency to follow the established leaders in certain fields. This extreme flexibility has led to some of the unusual contracts attributed to Lloyd's of London, but most of the insurance written is less spectacular. Half the insurance written is reinsurance; marine insurance is the major direct line. Because individuals are the insurers, only short-term life insurance contracts are written, and the volume of business is small.

Since the late 1980s, Lloyd's of London has experienced financial troubles although the difficulties have not affected all syndicates equally. In addition to suffering large losses, questions of financial and underwriting mismanagement have arisen, and a series of investor-lead suits have been filed against some Lloyd's underwriters. Further, Lloyd's was named in a suit filed by several American State's Attorneys General alleging illegal pricing and underwriting practices. Lloyd's response to these troubles is not yet developed, but the future success of Lloyd's will be closely followed by the insurance industry; precisely because it is such an influential player in international insurance markets. Recently, Lloyd's of London adopted a new regulation allowing corporations to join as members, with limited liability applying to corporate members.

Lloyds Associations in the United States pattern their operation after those of Lloyd's of London, but the United States Lloyds differ from the original Lloyd's. The number of underwriters is very small; their financial resources are meager compared with those of Lloyd's of London underwriters; their liability may be limited; an attorney-in-fact speaks for all the underwriters in the association; and the insurance operations are almost always restricted to one state (usually Texas). Only about 60 associations are currently in operation. The insurance written by over half these associations is completely reinsured by some other insurer—usually a stock insurer. Also, several states have authorized the formation of insurance exchanges patterned after Lloyd's of London.

Cooperative Insurers. Cooperative insurers are organized for the benefit of their policyholders, who elect the management and provide the risk-bearing capital of the insurer. Three major classes of cooperative insurers are: (1) advance premium mutual corporations, (2) assessment mutual associations or corporations, and (3) reciprocal exchanges, sometimes referred to as "interinsurance exchanges." Three other types of cooperative insurers, which are usually regulated under a distinct section of the state insurance laws, are fraternals, mutual savings bank insurers, and medical and dental expense prepayment associations, such as Blue Cross and Blue Shield and Delta Dental.

The *advance premium mutual* is a corporation owned by its policyholders. The corporation sets premium rates at a level that is expected to be at least sufficient to pay the expected losses and expenses and to provide a margin for contingencies. Policyholders receive dividends, if any, declared by the board of directors, the dividends representing the amount by which the premium and other income exceeds the needs of the insurer. The surplus built up out of past operations serves as a cushion against years of poor experience.

The contracts issued by the advance premium mutual may be *accessable* or *nonassessable.* If assessable, the assessment may be unlimited or limited. In either case, however, the mutual usually does not expect to exercise this right, though it may be forced to do so. Nonassessable policies can be issued by mutuals whose surplus is strong enough to satisfy the state requirements on this score. Most advance premium insurance contracts are nonassessable.

Advance premium mutuals write almost 40 percent of the life insurance in force and almost 23 percent of the property and liability insurance premiums. Although some mutuals write all types of property and liability insurance, most mutuals engage in a much more limited operation. The first mutual insurer in the United States, the Philadelphia Contributorship for the Insurance of Houses from Loss by Fire, founded in 1752 by Benjamin Franklin and others, still operates. This insurer and a few others issue perpetual policies. The insured pays a very large initial premium the first year and nothing thereafter. The investment return on the premium is sufficient to pay the costs of the insurer and to return a dividend to the policyholder. The initial premium is returned when the insured drops the insurance.

Assessment mutuals differ from advance premium mutuals in that they always have the right to assess their policyholders and the chance of an assessment is high. A "pure" assessment mutual would charge an initial premium large enough to cover the expenses that will be incurred even if no losses are experienced and would assess the policyholders to pay any extra costs arising in connection with losses. At the other and much more common extreme, the assessment mutual would collect an initial premium sufficient to pay expenses and typical losses. Assessments are levied whenever unusual losses occur, the assessment in some instances being limited in advance to some specified amount. Some mutuals, legally termed "assessment mutuals," have never levied an assessment and could, in fact, be classified as advance premium mutuals.

Property assessment mutuals often write fire insurance or farm property insurance. They usually confine their operations to a county or counties and at most operate in a few states. Protection and indemnity (P & I) clubs are shipowner-owned mutual insurance associations providing property and liability insurance to owners of ocean-going cargo vessels. Some P & I clubs are quite large.

Reciprocal exchanges resemble advance premium mutuals although they are not corporations but unincorporated associations. Also, the association is not technically the insurer. Instead, the association makes it possible for the policyholders to insure one another individually and not jointly. Each member of the reciprocal insures and is insured by every other member of the reciprocal. This reciprocal exchange of contracts is the essence of the arrangement. In order to simplify the administration of the agreement, each subscriber receives only one contract, which states that he or she is in effect exchanging contracts with other members of the association. The administration of the agreement is in the charge of an *attorney-in-fact,* who performs such duties as soliciting new members, rejecting undesirable applicants, paying losses, investing funds, and establishing premiums. Additionally, individual accounts are maintained for each member, the accounts of the association being the sum of the accounts of the members. The accounts are credited with the premiums and a share of the investment income and debited with a share of the expenses and losses. Deficiencies in the account can be repaired by an assessment, which may be limited. A surplus in the account may result in a dividend.

In practice, it often is difficult to distinguish a reciprocal exchange from an advance premium mutual. First, undivided surplus funds are commonly kept in addition to the individual surplus accounts, and in many instances the undivided surplus funds replace completely the individual accounts. Second, because assessments are seldom necessary, the distinction between individual liability and joint liability almost never becomes effective. In fact, if sufficient undivided surplus funds exist, states permit the issuance of nonassessable contracts.

About 50 reciprocals exist today. They write no life insurance and only about 6 percent of the property and liability insurance. Many reciprocals are associated with a trade association or an automobile association, but a few are multiple-line insurers seeking with considerable success insureds of all types in most states. One of the largest automobile insurers in the United States is a reciprocal exchange.

A key factor in the success of a reciprocal exchange is the attorney-in-fact. The prospective subscriber should examine carefully the ability and reputation of the attorney-in-fact as well as the power of attorney that prescribes the authority and duties. In some cases, a policyholders' advisory committee may exist. This committee can be important because the attorney-in-fact, who has nothing to lose from the failure of the reciprocal other than a job, may be tempted to increase the volume of business, regardless of its quality, because reimbursement is on a commission basis. However, many excellent, progressive reciprocals can be found.

Before leaving the subject of cooperatives, readers should recall the Chapter 10 discussion of group retention arrangements, most notably risk retention groups, self-insurance pools, and multiple employer trusts. These organizations are very similar to cooperative insurers, and are often indistinguishable from one another. For instance, a significant percentage of government self-insurance pools probably could be classified as reciprocal exchanges or assessment mutuals without appreciably stretching the definition of those types of insurers. As a result, the different treatment afforded retention groups and cooperative insurers (especially by regulators) has become something of a conceptual problem as these organizations have come to more closely resemble one another.

Governmental Insurers. The last form of organization to be discussed is the government insurer. The principle government insurers are operated by the federal and state governments, but some are local government agencies. In most instances, the government plans are intended to be self-supporting, but in a few instances a direct subsidy exists. In all cases, the governmental unit probably would supply funds in time of financial distress.

The federal government insurers include the largest insurance operation in the United States, the Old-Age, Survivors, Disability, and Health Insurance program (OASDHI, discussed fully in Chapter 22) under the Social Security Act. Other important federal government insurers include the Railroad Retirement Board (benefits under the Railroad Retirement System), the Veterans Administration (serviceperson's life insurance and veteran's mortgage and property improvement loan insurance), the Postal Service (insurance on parcel post and registered mail shipments), the Federal Housing Administration (mortgage and property improvement loan insurance), the Federal Deposit Insurance Administration (insurance on bank deposits), the Federal Savings and Loan Insurance Corporation (insurance on savings and loan shares), the National Credit Union Association (insurance on credit union shares and deposits), the Federal Crop Insurance Corporation (insurance on farmer's crops against natural hazards), the Nuclear Regulatory Commission (nuclear energy liability protection in excess of that available from private sources), the Maritime Administration (war risk marine insurance binders, which become effective during time of war after private insurance is canceled), the Export-Import Bank of Washington (protection on exports against insolvency of the purchaser and such political losses as inconvertibility of foreign currencies), the Overseas Private Investment Corporation (insurance on business properties abroad against expropriation or other political losses), the National Insurance Development Fund (direct crime insurance), the National Flood Insurance Fund (flood insurance), and the Securities Investor Protection Corporation (protection for investors in case of brokerage house insolvencies).

The two most important types of state insurers are unemployment insurance funds, which exist in all states, and workers' compensation funds, which exist in 22 states. Of the 22 workers' compensation funds, 6 are monopolistic, meaning that they are the sole providers of workers' compensation insurance. The remaining 16 are competitive funds, that is, they compete with commercial insurers. The existence and performance of state workers' compensation funds is important to risk management, and these funds are discussed in Chapter 23.

Other state funds include temporary disability insurance funds in California, Hawaii, New Jersey, New York, and Rhode Island; a life insurance fund in Wisconsin; and funds operating within the Torrens title system in California, Massachusetts, North Carolina, and Ohio.

Domicile and Admission Status

State insurance regulators classify private insurers as domestic, foreign, or alien insurers, depending upon whether they are organized (1) under the laws of the particular state, (2) of some other state, or (3) outside the United States (and, of course, the same terminology applies in other nations). All domestic insurers must be authorized by state insurance officials to conduct an insurance business. Foreign and alien insurers are considered to be *admitted* insurers if they have been licensed by the state insurance officials (or national government, if other than the United States). An *unlicensed* or *nonadmitted* insurer cannot be represented by agents within the state unless a *surplus lines insurer* operating under the state's *surplus lines* law. Under these laws, surplus lines' agents or brokers (described in the section below under "Marketing Methods") are permitted to place insurance with nonadmitted insurers meeting certain requirements if such insurance is not available from admitted insurers. Some insurers are admitted in one or more states and nonadmitted in others.

Pricing Policy

Insurers can be classified according to whether they issue participating or nonparticipating contracts and according to whether they subscribe to the services of a rating organization.

Participating or Nonparticipating. The holder of a participating policy shares in the experience of the insurer through dividends, assessments, or both. Nonparticipating insurance does not provide for sharing of the insurer's experience. The same insurer may issue participating and nonparticipating insurance. Insurers issuing participating insurance include some capital stock insurers (mostly life insurers), most advance premium mutuals, all assessment associations, and most reciprocal exchanges. Nonparticipating insurers include most stock insurers (for at least part of their business), some advance premium mutuals, and some reciprocal exchanges.

Some participating insurers set their rates at a high level to permit the payment of large dividends, while others establish lower rates and expect to declare lower dividends. Some advance premium mutuals and reciprocal exchanges issue nonassessable contracts, fix rates at the lowest feasible predictable level, and pay no dividends.

Independent or Rating Organization Insurers. The classification of pricing policy arose when many property-liability insurers set rates in concert using service or rating bureaus. This classification does not apply to life and health insurance, in which each insurer sets its own rates independently. Today, a property-liability insurer may subscribe to the services of the Insurance Service Office (ISO), an organization that remains after the consolidation of what once was a system of regional rating bureaus that collected data from member insurers and used the data to prescribe premium levels for member insurers. ISO no longer sets rates for members, but still collects loss data from member insurers and publishes summaries of the data for members to consider in setting premium levels. ISO also develops standard contracts ("bureau forms") and has them approved for use by state regulators. Hence an ISO subscriber has these preapproved forms available when it wishes to write coverage in a particular state, instead of developing its own policies and awaiting approval from the state regulatory official having jurisdiction over insurance.

Marketing Methods

Private insurers may market their product in four different ways: (1) through independent agents, (2) through employees (often called sales representatives) on a direct-writing basis, (3) through exclusive agents, or (4) through brokers. A particular insurer may use more than one of these methods.

An *independent agent* is a representative who may act on behalf of two or more insurers. The agent is an independent businessperson who receives a commission as compensation for his or her services and who retains the right to renew the insurance contracts of his or her customers with a different insurer. The agency expiration list, which records the names and addresses of present policyholders and the dates their policies expire, belongs to the agent, and if the agent and the insurer agree to sever their relationship, the insurer cannot give any information in this list to a new agent. Independent agents may write their own policies and handle all financial transactions (billing, collecting, and extending credit) with their insureds. Increasingly, however, independent agency insurers have been able to reduce selling and servicing costs, including commissions, and to strengthen their relationships with their insureds.

Despite their independent status, independent agents have the authority to commit immediately the insurers they represent to insure most applicants. These representatives are considered legal agents of the insurers they represent. They can bind insurers legally, and any information provided to the agent is legally presumed to be provided by the insurer.

Direct writers sell insurance through commissioned or salaried (plus bonuses) employees, called sales representatives, who represent only the insurer employing them. Generally, the insurer does more of the policy writing, billing, and collection work under this system than under the agency system. Sales representatives usually have the power to bind the insurer they represent and are legally that insurer's agents. In some cases, insurance is marketed directly by advertisements inviting mail or phone applications.

Exclusive agency insurers occupy a position somewhere between independent agency insurers and direct writers. Like direct writers, these insurers require exclusive representation (at least for their regular business), regard the policyholders as their customers, and perform much of the administrative work in behalf of the agent. However, the agents are regarded as independent businesspersons and are always reimbursed on a commission basis. Typically, though, the renewal commission is less than the commission on newly generated business.

The leading examples of exclusive agency insurers are some leading mutual property and liability insurers and almost all life insurers, regardless of the form of business organization. In life insurance, however, the renewal commissions usually belong to an agent who has completed a certain period of service, even if he or she leaves the insurer.

The *brokerage system* is a fourth and final category of marketing method. Unlike the insurer's representatives discussed above, in principle brokers are independent businesspersons who do not represent any insurer. Brokers offer to analyze risks for their clients and to shop among insurers to place specialized coverages or to obtain the best price. For their services, brokers receive a commission from the insurer. Some insurers accept and even encourage the direct placement of insurance with brokers, while others require the placement through one of their agents.

Because brokers are not legal agents of the insurer, they cannot bind any insurer, and no insurer can be held responsible for brokers' mistakes. However, in several states, statutes make the broker the agent of the insurer with respect to the acceptance of premium payments from the insured. In other states, this practice is customary and in many instances has been supported by the courts.

Brokers often have considerable experience in the insurance business and an extensive network of contacts with insurance suppliers built through this experience—at least the best ones do. Brokers are especially important in placing insurance on unusual risks or when very large amounts of coverage are requested. Many brokers are members of business organizations ("brokerage houses") that specialize in providing risk management consulting as well as brokerage services for business clients. These risk management consulting services include engineering, appraisal, actuarial, and claims management for health benefit programs—services that otherwise might be performed by insurers as part of their insurance agreements but are offered separately ("unbundled") by brokerage organizations.

Some states do not license brokers, in which case, an insurance marketing representative must be a legal agent of the insurer. In a state allowing both brokers and agents, a given representative may function in the capacity of agent with respect to insurers he or she represents and in the capacity of broker in other instances.

In most states, *excess and surplus lines brokers* or *agents* may be licensed to obtain insurance from *nonadmitted* insurers, which are insurers not licensed to write a line of insurance in a state. Under these statutes, the excess line broker or agent must demonstrate that the insurance sought is not available in the admitted market, pay the state premium tax, and post a bond guaranteeing that he or she will comply with the statute. Surplus line agents or brokers are sometimes also agents or brokers engaging in regular business, but more often they are specialists serving ordinary agents and brokers and sharing their commissions with them.

In order to place insurance with underwriters at Lloyd's of London, a buyer of coverage must operate through a Lloyd's broker. This fact poses a problem for a buyer outside the United Kingdom because authorized Lloyd's brokers tend to be located in London. For instance, in the United States, Lloyd's underwriters can be represented with respect to all lines of insurance only in two states, Illinois and Kentucky. However, in a number of states, Lloyd's and other nonadmitted insurers can be represented by an excess and surplus lines broker. In the other states, technically, the buyer must contract a Lloyd's representative in Illinois, Kentucky, Canada, or London, but it is customary for a licensed agent to conduct the negotiations in the insured's name. Most American insurance with Lloyd's of London is insurance that is not readily available in the local market or reinsurance purchased by American insurers. Nevertheless, about 40 percent of the premium volume developed by Lloyd's underwriters is purchased by insureds or insurers in the United States.

Although Lloyd's is licensed only in two states, the underwriters agree in the insurance contract to submit to and abide by the decisions of United States courts. Moreover, they have established an American trust fund for the specific protection of United States policyholders.

Finally, a notable recent trend has been the growth of mergers, acquisitions, and cooperative ventures between non-Lloyd's brokers and their Lloyd's counterparts, and today most major worldwide brokerage houses have a "Lloyd's presence."

Groups and Cooperative Reinsurance and Underwriting Associations

In addition to individual insurers, the insurance market includes important (1) groups, (2) underwriters' associations, and (3) reinsurance associations.

A *group* (or fleet) of insurers includes two or more insurers operating under common ownership or management. In the United States, most large insurers are groups or members of groups. In some cases, 80 or more organizations will operate within a group, with many carrying similar names and methods of operation. The insurer's marketing representatives may be able to place coverage with a number of insurers within the group.

In some cases, insurers within a group can be formed to specialize in writing specific lines of insurance or within certain geographic areas. For example, a property and liability insurer must form a separate life insurance company to write life or health insurance, and vice versa. In many cases, insurance company groups have formed (or been acquired by) business organizations providing a wide array of financial and other services to clients, including stock brokerage, financial planning, investment counseling, estate planning, real estate brokerage, risk management consulting, and even brokerage services with other insurers. These combinations suggest a belief that organizations offering a wide array of services can compete more effectively than specialized organizations.

Underwriters' Associations may be formed when insurers cooperate to underwrite some or all of the policies they issue. These cooperative underwriting organizations are generally associated with one or more of the following conditions: (1) a unique or particularly hazardous exposure, (2) very high policy limits, or (3) a need for highly specialized talent. Some examples will illustrate the nature of these associations.

The Factory Mutual Insurance Companies includes three mutual insurers specializing in property insurance for sprinklered properties of superior construction. Typically, one of the three insurers writes a direct policy, and the other two members act as reinsurers, the percentage of risk reinsured by each insurer being indicated in a rider to the contract. The association provides appraisal, inspection engineering, loss-adjustment, and rate-making services for its members.

The stock insurers' equivalent (in many ways) of the Factory Mutuals is Industrial Risk Insurers (IRI), an organization of about 43 of the leading stock insurers and devoted to the underwriting of highly protected properties. IRI issues its policies directly, and its liability is uniformly apportioned among the member insurers. Unlike the Factory Mutuals, IRI operates through agents, and its member insurers write only a small portion of their business through IRI.

Property and liability insurance for the operators of atomic reactors is supplied by two associations, American Nuclear Insurers (a stock insurer pool) and the Mutual Atomic Energy Reinsurance Pool, which reinsures the exposure of six insurers operating as the Mutual Atomic Energy Liability Underwriters. Their coverages are discussed further in Chapter 21.

United States Aircraft Insurance Group handles the aviation insurance business of its stock members. IRM (formerly Improved Risk Mutuals) serves its mutual members in about the same way as the IRI serves its stock members. Assigned risk pools or joint underwriting associations in some property and liability lines, such as automobile and workers' compensation insurance, insure applicants unable to procure insurance directly (and tend to be organized by state regulators).

Insurers also organize associations to provide reinsurance facilities. Most *reinsurance associations,* such as the Workers' Compensation Reinsurance Bureau and the Mutual Reinsurance Bureau, reinsure members only. Reinsurance pools are much more common in property and liability insurance than in life and health insurance.

Key Concepts

insurable risk A loss exposure that is insurable by a private or public insurer. Few, if any, such risks meet the requirements of an ideally insurable risk.

underwriting The functional process of an insurer that involves the evaluation of risk and the acceptance of risk in accordance with the insurer's underwriting philosophy.

loss adjustment The functional process of an insurer that involves the investigation and resolution of claims in accordance with the insurer's claims resolution philosophy.

stock insurer A proprietary insurer owned by stockholders who elect a board of directors.

mutual insurer A cooperative insurer owned by its policyholders.

participating insurer An insurer whose policyholders participate in the experience of the insurers through dividends, assessments, or both.

independent agency insurer An insurer that markets its services through independent agents who may represent many insurers.

direct writer An insurer that markets its services through its own employees.

broker A person or organization that "shops the market" in behalf of the prospective insured; unlike an agent, not legally an agent of the insured. Some brokers are broker-agents.

independent insurer An insurer that sets its own prices and does not subscribe to a rating organization.

group of insurers Two or more insurers operating as a team under common ownership or management.

Review Questions

1. Describe the role of insurers as financial intermediaries.
2. The existence of insurers presents certain costs.
    a. What is the nature of these costs?
    b. How can these costs be reduced?
3. Insurance is almost exclusively concerned with pure risks. Why is this true? Will it always be true?

4. What are characteristics of an ideal insurable risk?

5. Do all risks covered by private insurers satisfy the characteristics cited in Question 4?

6. Why might private insurers insure a risk whose characteristics differ considerably from those of an ideal insurable risk?

7. Why might government insurers be able to write certain risks that all or more private insurers would decline to write?

8. "Underwriting is the process whereby risks are accepted or rejected." Does this statement accurately state the purpose of underwriting? Why or why not?

9. Insurers may adopt numerous different approaches to loss adjustment, from paying virtually all claims to rigorously fighting the payment of most claims—and, of course, gradations between those two extremes. Describe a kind of insurance in which a highly consumer-oriented pay-all-claims approach might be advisable, and explain why it is advisable. Describe a kind of insurance in which a rigorous approach would be important, and, again, explain why.

10. How can insurers be classified according to the types of insurance they write?

11. "Stock insurers, which are always nonparticipating, independent agency, proprietary insurers, write most of the premium volume in all branches of insurance."
    a. In what respects is this statement false?
    b. In what respects is this statement true?

12. Lloyd's of London is internationally renowned for its insurance activities, but technically Lloyd's is not an insurer. Explain this statement.

13. Some risk managers refuse to purchase insurance from mutual insurers because they believe that all mutual policies are assessable. Are they correct in their reasoning?

14. Compare the following types of insurers with respect to (1) the controlling group, (2) the liability of the "owners," that is, whether it is joint and several or individual, and (3) ownership of the surplus.
    a. Reciprocal exchange
    b. Advance premium mutual
    c. Lloyds Association
    d. Capital stock insurer.

15. The Buttonwood Mutual is legally a small township mutual operating in one state on the assessment basis.
    a. Should an insured be surprised if the management collects an assessment each year?
    b. Do all assessable mutuals levy assessments?

16. The Gray Company is considering the formation of a captive insurer. Which of the following legal forms would be easiest to establish? Why?
    a. Capital stock insurer
    b. Advance premium mutual insurer
    c. Reciprocal exchange.

17. a. Which government insurers compete with private insurers?
    b. Which government insurers provide insurance not available from private insurers?

18. An insurer domiciled in another state wishes to sell insurance in your state.
    a. If this insurer is not licensed by your state insurance department, what terms would you use to describe its status in your state?
    b. Why is this status important to insureds? to the insurer?

19. All participating insurance is sold by cooperative insurers, and all cooperative insurers sell only participating insurance. Comment on the truth or falsity of this statement.

20. a. What is the function of a rating organization?

b. Contrast the importance of rating organizations in property and liability insurance with that of rating organizations in life and health insurance.

21. Does the fact that an insurance representative calls himself or herself an agent or a broker mean that he or she is functionally what the term implies?

22. What is a group or fleet operation?

23. The Factory Mutuals and the Industrial Risk Insurers are two major underwriting associations.

a. In what ways do these two associations resemble one another?

b. In what ways do they differ?

24. Will all insurers soon become part of an integrated financial services institution? What characteristics would you expect to favor integration of insurance with other financial services?

References and Suggestions for Additional Reading

ATHEARN, J. L., S. T. PRITCHETT, and J. T. SCHMIT: *Risk and Insurance* (6th ed., St. Paul, Minn.: West Publishing Co., 1987).

BERLINER, BARUCH: *Limits of Insurability of Risks* (Englewood Cliffs, NJ: Prentice-Hall, Inc., 1982).

Best's Aggregates and Averages (Oldwick, NJ: Alfred M. Best Company, Inc., annual).

Best's Insurance Reports, Property-Casualty (Oldwick, NJ: Alfred M. Best Company, Inc., annual).

Best's Insurance Reports, Life-Health (Oldwick, NJ: Alfred M. Best Company, Inc., annual).

BILLINGSLEY, PATRICK: *Probability and Measure* (2nd ed., New York: John Wiley & Sons, 1986).

DORFMAN, M. S.: *Introduction to Insurance* (3rd ed., Englewood Cliffs, NJ: Prentice-Hall, Inc., 1987).

GREENE, M. R., and J. S. TRIESCHMANN: *Risk and Insurance* (6th ed., Cincinnati: Southwestern Publishing Company, Inc., 1984).

MEHR, ROBERT I., E. CAMMACK, and T. ROSE: *Principles of Insurance* (8th ed., Homewood, Ill.: Richard D. Irwin, Inc., 1985).

1990 Source Book of Health Insurance Data (Washington, D.C.: Health Insurance Association of America).

REJDA, GEORGE E.: *Principles of Insurance* (2nd ed., Glenview, Ill.: Scott, Foresman and Company, 1986).

SMITH, MICHAEL L., and STEPHEN A. KANE: "The Law of Large Numbers and the Strength of Insurance," *Insurance, Risk Management and Public Policy: Essays in Honor of Robert I. Mehr* (Norwell, Mass.: Kluwer Academic Publishers, 1993).

VAUGHAN, E. J.: *Fundamentals of Risk and Insurance* (4th ed., New York: John Wiley and Sons, Inc., 1985).

WEBB, B. L., J. J. LAUNIE, W. P. ROKES, and N. A. BAGLINI: *Insurance Company Operations*, vols. I and II (3rd ed., Malvern, Pa.: American Institute for Property and Liability Underwriters, 1984).

WILLETT, A. H.: *The Economic Theory of Risk and Insurance* (Philadelphia, Pa.: The University of Pennsylvania Press, 1951).

The Pricing of Insurance

Learning Objectives

After you have completed this chapter, you should be able to:

1. Explain the process by which target loss ratios are determined.
2. Describe how state law and business considerations affect insurance pricing and rating procedures.
3. Describe two loading methods used to get general rate levels: the pure premium method and the loss ratio method.
4. Describe the principal rating procedures used to determine insurance premiums: individual rating, class rating and modification rating.
5. Describe the factors affecting rates and how principal rating procedures are applied to lines of insurance, such as marine insurance, workers' compensation insurance, fire insurance and automobile insurance.
6. Describe the role of rating organizations across three lines of insurance: automobile insurance, workers' compensation insurance, and life insurance.
7. Explain how the price of life insurance coverage is determined.

INTRODUCTION

This chapter identifies factors affecting insurance prices and explains their relationship to the price of coverage. An understanding of these issues can be valuable in carrying out a risk manager's responsibilities. Risk managers often serve in the role of liaison between their organizations and the insurance industry, especially in matters such as providing data to support an application for insurance coverage, negotiating terms of coverage, or in negotiating settlement of insurance claims. These activities have direct counterparts within insurers, and risk managers who understand their effects from the viewpoints of insurers can use this knowledge to develop strategies for reducing the cost of coverage for their organizations. An understanding of these issues also helps risk managers identify characteristics of their organizations that affect the price of their insurance coverage.

Correct pricing of insurance is the foundation of an insurer's financial security and solvency. Important problems emerge if the premium does not accurately reflect the risk being insured. If the price is too low, the insurer will not accumulate sufficient resources to cover claims and provide claim-related services. If the price is too high, competitors will draw away customers. Either problem can reduce an insurer's financial security, the assessment of which is discussed in Chapter 15. The discussion of financial assessment of insurers is more meaningful if readers are first exposed to the subject of insurance pricing.

Unlike automobiles or computers, insurance is a product for which the costs of goods sold is not known until some future date. Insurance companies, therefore, must utilize special techniques and methods for product pricing. This chapter discusses those techniques and methods and provides several illustrations of pricing methods as they are applied to specific types of insurance.

In addition to the more pragmatic reasons listed above, knowledge of insurance pricing and its relationship to other insurance functions has a conceptual value. Organizations practicing retention are, in an informal sense of the term, "insurers" of their own risks. In such cases, the risk manager's thought processes and actions resemble an insurance company's planning and operations. That is, underwriting corresponds with risk assessment, pricing corresponds with risk measurement and risk financing, loss control corresponds with risk control, and claims management corresponds with risk reduction.

TERMINOLOGY AND BASIC CONCEPTS

Insurance Rate and Insurance Premium

The terms "insurance rate" and "insurance premium" often are used interchangeably in ordinary conversation, although they have distinct meanings in the insurance business. An *insurance rate* is the price per unit of coverage or unit of exposure. An *insurance premium* is the total price of coverage. For example, a $50,000 premium for $10 million of fire insurance coverage implies a rate of $0.50 per $100 of fire insurance. Fire insurance often is priced using a rate per $100 of coverage, with the insured choosing the total amount of coverage.

Pricing and Rating Procedure

In this chapter, the term *pricing* refers to methods used to determine general rate levels, while the phrase *rating procedure* refers to methods for determining the rate applying to a specific exposure. Often, the rating procedure recognizes special characteristics of an exposure for which coverage is sought. For example, the general level of automobile insurance rates is set by evaluating issues such as accident rates and the legal climate in an area, while the rate applying to a specific vehicle is determined by a rating procedure that evaluates the type of vehicle, its intended use, and characteristics of the principal driver.

Claims Data

The reader should recognize that most insurance prices rely on claims data. The connection may be direct, through formulas that formally recognize loss experience such as experience rating methods or ASO plans. The connection also may be indirect, as a consequence of an insurer's beliefs about the expected value of insured claims for a typical exposure and its beliefs about how basic data can be modified to reflect special characteristics of the exposure being insured. The sections of Chapter 4 related to claims development and probability estimates may be reviewed to provide background for understanding how data are incorporated into the pricing process.

Loading and Target Loss Ratios

In many lines of insurance, the term *loading* is used to describe the process used to develop insurance rates from data on insurance claims. The loading process adjusts estimated (or actual) claim costs to account for the cost of administering the insurance claims and providing other services associated with insurance. These services and their effect on insurance prices were discussed in Chapter 13: underwriting, inspection, engineering and loss prevention, investment, and loss adjustment. Loading also may include an allowance for uncertainty and profit.

The concept of loading can be illustrated with an example. If the estimated expected value of claim costs on a policy is $100,000 and expenses associated with providing insurance-related services are assumed to be 40 percent of the premium, the final premium for coverage is $100,000/(1 − 0.4), or about $166,667. Forty percent of the premium, or $66,667, is the loading fee, while the remaining sixty percent ($100,000) is the expected claim cost.

The above-described loading process is based on an assumption that the cost of providing insurance-related services is proportional to the insurance premium. For many insurance-related services, this assumption can be directly related to methods used in practice to determine the level of compensation. For example, agents' commissions often are based on premium volume, as is the state tax on premium income of insurers. For loss control services and claims-adjustment activities, however, the basis for assuming a proportional relationship seems less clear. On the one hand, an increase in the expected number and size of claims would be expected to increase an insurer's efforts at loss control and claims adjustment. As a result, one might reasonably expect to see a positive relationship between claims costs and the level of an insurer's expenditures on loss control and claims adjustment. On the other hand, one would not expect an insurer to increase loss control efforts and its scrutiny of claims unless such activities are expected to decrease claims. If an insurer allocates resources efficiently, one might just as reasonably expect to see a negative relationship between the level of claim costs and an insurer's expenditures on loss control and claims adjustment activities.

The apparent dilemma can be resolved by considering the pricing process that would be used by an insurer with perfect foresight. The illustration does not consider investment income, the inclusion of which would not change the qualitative description of the process. With perfect foresight, an insurer could accurately forecast the effect on claims costs of additional expenditures on activities such as loss control and claims adjustment. The insurer would allocate resources to these activities as long as an additional dollar of allocation reduced claim costs by more than one dollar. An optimal allocation of resources to these activities would result in the last dollar of expenditure reducing claim costs by one dollar.

Once an insurer achieved the size required to realize economies of scale in writing and servicing insurance, however, one would expect to observe an approximately proportionate relationship between claim costs and *optimal* expenditures on activities such as loss control and claims adjustment. After the insurer reaches a size required to be efficient, changes in the level of these expenditures would merely reflect an adjustment for the insurer's scale of operations. In other words, within a particular type of coverage, the ratio of claims adjustment costs to claim payments would be expected to be stable once the insurer reached an efficient scale of operations. By implication, the ratio of these two costs to premiums also would be stable.

This description suggests a process leading to a *target loss ratio*: the ratio of claim costs to premiums that occurs when an optimal amount has been allocated to activities related to the writing and servicing of insurance. The resulting level of claims expressed as a ratio to premiums is the (optimal) target loss ratio. Later in this chapter, the target loss ratio method is compared with other methods for pricing insurance.

One would expect the target loss ratio to vary across types of insurance coverage due to variation in methods of claim adjustment and in technology available for loss prevention, and for the transmission, evaluation, and storage of underwriting information. For example, the processing of claims for health care services under group health insurance coverage is highly automated, which suggests that claims administration under this type of coverage should consume only a small fraction of the premium dollar. In contrast, the administration and settlement of claims in coverage for medical liability exposures would be expected to consume substantial resources.

Table 14.1 provides data on average ratios for U.S. property-casualty insurers during a recent 10-year period as reported in *Best's Aggregates and Averages*. The data in Table 14.1 are expressed as a ratio to premiums written or premiums earned, depending on whether the activity arises from the writing of insurance (e.g., underwriting costs) or the providing of insurance coverage (e.g., loss adjustment costs). The ratios appearing in Table 14.1 are industry-wide averages over a 10-year period, classified by type of coverage. They are not necessarily optimal, even within a particular type of coverage. However, variation across types of coverage is likely to reflect characteristics peculiar to the type of coverage. For example, investment gains and loss adjustment expenses are large relative to premiums earned in medical malpractice insurance, in which significant time and effort often is required to negotiate claim settlement. Underwriting expenses are high in surety, burglary and theft, and boiler and machinery coverage, reflecting the substantial resources allocated to risk evaluation and underwriting in these types of coverage.

TABLE 14.1. Ten-Year Average Performance Ratios by Type of Insurance, United States Property-Casualty Insurers, 1983–1992 (figures in percentages)

Type of Insurance	*Ratio to Premiums Earned*		*Ratio to Premiums Written*		*Ratio to Premiums Earned*	*Ratio to Premiums Earned*		
	Losses Incurred	Loss Adjustment Expenses Incurred	Commissions and Brokerage Incurred	Other Underwriting Expenses Incurred	Dividends to Policyholders	Combined Ratio After Dividends	Investment Gain & Other Income	Overall Operating Ratio
Fire	56.8	4.9	18.0	19.5	0.5	99.7	5.2	94.6
Allied Lines	59.1	6.4	15.8	17.2	0.4	99.0	4.2	94.8
Farmowners Multi Peril	67.0	8.2	17.1	15.1	0.6	107.9	5.0	102.9
Homeowners Multi Peril	72.2	10.3	16.7	14.4	0.5	114.1	5.2	108.9
Commercial Multi Peril	57.4	15.1	17.6	18.2	0.3	108.6	9.3	99.3
Ocean Marine	69.0	7.9	18.9	14.2	0.2	110.2	9.6	100.6
Inland Marine	52.1	5.6	16.9	19.0	0.3	93.8	3.6	90.2
Group Accid. & Health	93.3	4.7	5.9	9.1	0.1	113.1	14.4	98.7
Other Accid. & Health	66.7	4.8	15.1	15.9	0.0	102.5	5.2	97.3
Workers' Compensation	83.1	11.0	5.1	13.6	6.6	119.3	14.4	104.8
Other Liab.	66.4	26.5	11.2	14.0	0.4	118.4	21.1	97.3
Medical Malpractice	73.7	32.1	4.2	10.1	2.4	122.5	36.8	85.8
Aircraft	71.1	7.1	13.8	13.5	0.0	105.6	10.6	95.0
Private Pass. Auto Liab.	78.7	13.0	9.2	13.9	0.8	115.6	9.9	105.7
Commercial Auto Liab.	73.3	12.9	13.2	14.9	0.7	115.0	11.3	103.7
Pvt. Pass. Auto Phys. Damage	61.7	8.1	9.5	13.6	0.8	93.8	2.4	91.5
Commercial Auto Phys. Damage	52.4	6.6	15.3	14.7	0.4	89.4	2.7	86.6
Fidelity	42.3	7.3	13.6	18.9	0.1	82.3	9.3	73.0
Surety	36.5	10.5	19.9	27.6	0.5	95.0	13.4	81.6
Burglary & Theft	24.2	5.9	16.0	24.0	0.6	70.7	4.4	66.3
Boiler & Machinery	46.9	4.7	11.7	37.4	0.6	101.3	5.1	96.2
Reinsurance	83.9	5.8	21.5	5.9	0.0	117.2	17.5	99.6
Other Lines	72.5	4.8	7.3	21.1	0.1	105.8	13.8	92.0
All Types Combined	70.5	12.2	11.7	14.5	1.4	110.3	10.3	100.0

Source: Best's Aggregates and Averages—Property-Casualty (1993 edition).

Other Factors Considered in Pricing Methods

Sophisticated pricing methods have been developed that consider the timing as well as the amount of insurance premium receipts, insurance claims costs, and costs of insurance-related services. The timing issue incorporates opportunities to earn investment income into the pricing methodology. Some of these methods also consider possible correlation between these insurance-related cash flows and returns on risky securities. The correlation issue arises when the capital asset pricing model (CAPM) is used to price insurance. The CAPM holds that prices of individual securities and their expected returns are based on their correlation with returns on a diversified portfolio of risky securities. When extended to insurance, the CAPM predicts the price of insurance coverage that would prevail in a perfect market, in which the only risky investments are marketable risky securities. The CAPM and other sophisticated pricing methods often are used to provide guidelines for insurance regulators in setting regulated prices and judging the fairness of a loading process. Cummins and Harrington (1986) present alternative methods for determining the rate of return on property and liability insurance in a regulatory context.

PRICING OBJECTIVES

An insurer's pricing policy is influenced by law and by business considerations. State law usually requires rates for property and liability insurance to be *reasonable, adequate* and *not unfairly discriminatory.* Insurance rates are reasonable if, on average, they are not too high. If insurance rates are too high, they provide a profit to the insurer that is excessive. Insurance rates are adequate if, on average, they are high enough to maintain the solvency of insurers. Adequate rates are sufficient to cover expected claim payments and the insurer's expenses of operation, possibly including a margin for adverse developments.

Insurance rates do not discriminate unfairly if each insured pays his or her "fair share" of the cost burden. The fairness requirement means that rate differentials among insureds should reflect differences in expected losses and expenses for these insureds, although the application of this requirement can be subjective. Strict *rate parity* between insureds would require that A should pay twice as much as B when the expected value of A's insurance claims and expenses are twice the level of B's. The objective of *rate equity* allows other considerations, such as social objectives, to influence rates, as equity only implies lack of bias. For example, the goal of having all persons insured for their medical expenses may allow subsidies to groups least able to afford health insurance, with the subsidy provided by groups better able to afford coverage.

State law usually requires life insurance rate to be adequate and not unfairly discriminatory. Competition in life insurance markets is presumed to keep life insurance rates from becoming unreasonable. Health insurance rates generally are subject to the same standards that apply to life insurance; however, some states have laws prohibiting the approval of a health insurance policy if the benefits provided by the policy are unreasonable in relation to the premium.

Although these objectives are legal requirements in many states, they also reflect expected outcomes when competition among insurers is present. When competition is present, an insurer whose rates are unreasonably high will be underbid by competing insurers, forcing the insurer to lower rates or lose business. At the other extreme, an insurer whose rates are inadequate ultimately becomes insolvent and is withdrawn from the market. Competition also prevents discrimination; an insurer who undercharges one class of insureds at the expense of another class will be underbid by competing insurers on the overcharged class, whose members will migrate to insurers offering lower rates. In turn, the undercharged class will migrate to the discriminatory insurer because of its low rates. Competition from other insurers ultimately forces the discriminatory insurer to increase rates for the undercharged class and lower rates for the overcharged class if it wishes to remain in business.

Business considerations also suggest other criteria. The rating procedure must be workable, understandable, impossible (or at least difficult) to manipulate to the insured's advantage, and relatively inexpensive to apply. If necessary, some accuracy may be sacrificed to attain these goals. The rates should be responsive to changes in the long run, but because of the adverse public relations, and administrative costs associated with frequent rate changes, the rates should be stable in the short run. Finally, the rating procedure should encourage loss-control activities. The rating procedure recognizes the effect of loss-control activities by providing a rate adjustment to reflect loss-control efforts. One would expect the rate adjustment to at least equal the change in expected claim payments and expenses. For example, when the installation of a security system reduces the expected value of insured theft claims and expenses by 40 percent, one would expect a 40 percent reduction in the premium for theft coverage. Some authorities have advocated stronger incentives, citing benefits accruing to society generally as a result of loss-control activities.

Public policy considerations may suggest the socialization of some risks on some basis other than private parity. For example, in order to keep the price of automobile insurance within reach of younger drivers, older drivers may be asked to pay more than their "fair share" of the total costs. This objective competes with the unfair discrimination standard noted earlier and requires special pricing arrangements. Also, some criteria that might be related to loss experience may not be socially acceptable. For example, a few states have prohibited the use of age, sex, and marital status in pricing automobile insurance.

BASIC PRICING METHODS

Loading Methods in Standard Insurance Products

For insurance coverage in which the insurer bears most or all of the risk associated with financing the cost of claims, two methods can be used to determine general rate levels: (1) the *pure premium approach* and (2) the *loss ratio approach.* The two methods are closely connected, and in practice may be combined. Both methods use pooled data based on a large number of insureds to estimate expected claims costs, which in the final result are loaded to compensate for costs of insurance-related services and to provide an allowance for uncertainty, profit, or other factors considered in the pricing process. The pure premium approach adjusts rates to produce a *target pure premium per unit of exposure,* such as vehicle-year or $100 of payroll. The pure premium is an allowance for expected claim payments per unit of exposure. The loss ratio approach adjusts rates to produce a *target loss ratio,* which is a desired ratio of claims (or losses) to premiums.

The pure premium approach can be used when a representative unit of exposure can be determined. This approach has been used in workers' compensation and automobile insurance, in which the units of exposure are respectively, $100 of payroll and one vehicle-year. A unit of exposure is standardized to reflect the level of claims expected from a typical or representative insured, often near the average for the insured population. For example, data on workers' compensation insurance may show that $50 million of claims arose under workers' compensation insurance on $6.25 billion of covered payroll. The $6.25 billion of covered payroll represents 62.5 million units of $100 payroll. Hence the pure premium indicated by these data is $50/62.5, or $0.80 per $100 of payroll. The pure premium is loaded for expenses and profit to arrive at a final rate.

The loss ratio approach can be used when a representative unit of exposure is not convenient. For example, in fire or marine insurance, the criteria used to arrive at final rates vary significantly among insured units. Basing rates on unique combinations of these criteria would result in a complex classification system with only a few exposures appearing in each combination. Instead, the loss ratio approach adjusts the base rate applying to a large group of exposures, leaving the determination of the final rate for a given exposure to the insurance provider who applies the rating criteria. In concept, the loss ratio represents the portion of the insurance premium returned to policyholders in the form of insurance claim payments. For example, a loss ratio of 60 percent implies that, on average, policyholders received insurance benefit payments equal to 60 percent of premiums.

The first step in the loss ratio approach is to estimate the lost ratio that would have occurred during some representative period of time if current rates were in effect. This estimate, called the *actual loss ratio (r),* is then compared with a *target loss ratio (R).* The difference as a proportion of the target ratio $(r - R)/R$, represents the proportionate change in current rates that would have produced the target loss ratio. For example, if the target loss ratio is 65 percent and the actual loss ratio is 70 percent, a proportionate rate increase of $(0.70 - 0.65)/0.65$, or about 7.7 percent, would have produced the target ratio.

The method used to determine the target loss ratio is described earlier in this chapter. The target loss ratio is the ratio of claim costs to premiums that occurs when an optimal amount has been allocated to activities related to the writing and servicing of insurance. In a market in which insurers compete through pricing and by offering services, premiums are at a level that compensates insurers for (1) the cost of expected claim payments, (2) the cost of services provided as part of the insurance process, and (3) payments to providers of capital placed at risk in the writing of insurance. Of these three categories of costs, categories 1 and 2 typically constitute over 95 percent of premiums, leaving a small amount to compensate providers of risk-bearing capital.

The large share of the premium allocated to payment of claims and reimbursing the cost of insurance-related services implies that most of the variation in observed loss ratios among different types of coverage is due to the cost of providing services related to the insurance process. For example, one would expect high underwriting costs to reduce the loss ratio, and vice versa. This reasoning suggests that a target loss ratio is based on an insurer's estimate of optimal allocation of premiums among categories of insurance costs: negotiation and payment of claims, underwriting and loss control efforts, agents' commissions, and brokerage fees. Earlier, Table 14.1 presented historical data on these allocations by type of insurance coverage.

Loading in Claims-servicing Agreements

The loading concept extends to claims-servicing agreements in which the insurer bears little if any risk associated with financing the cost of claims. These agreements, which were described earlier in Chapter 10, are exemplified by administrative service only (ASO) and retrospective rating plans. Group benefit plans, especially plans offering coverage for health care services, often use an approach in which the insurer provides only services related to the settlement of claims and is compensated for providing these services. These plans may use an agreed-upon claims-servicing fee or a formula-based method for determining the insurer's reimbursement. For example, the following formula or a slight variation has been used to determine charges for retrospectively-rated insurance coverage:

$$\begin{array}{c} \text{Retrospective} \\ \text{premium} \end{array} = \left[\begin{array}{c} \text{basic} \\ \text{premium} \end{array} + (\text{Claims}) \left(\begin{array}{c} \text{Claim-conversion} \\ \text{factor} \end{array} \right) \right] \left[\begin{array}{c} \text{Tax} \\ \text{multiplier} \end{array} \right]$$

The retrospective premium is subject to stated maximum and minimum premiums. The basic premium includes an allowance for the cost of insurance-related services that do not vary with losses and an insurance charge related to claims exceeding the level that results in the payment of the maximum premium. The claim-conversion factor compensates the insurer for claims-processing activities, while the tax multiplier provides an allowance for the state tax on premium income or other costs that vary with premiums.

To illustrate the operation of the formula, assume that the minimum premium is $51,000, the maximum premium is $131,500, the basic premium is $23,600, the claim-conversion factor is 1.125, and the tax multiplier is 1.078. If claims during the policy period are $40,000, the retrospective premium is [$23,600 + ($40,000)(1.125)][1.078], or $73,950.80. Claims of $21,075.41 or less result in payment of the minimum premium, while claims exceeding $87,453.47 trigger payment of the maximum premium. In this illustration, the loading for claim-processing activities is 12.5 percent of claims, while the loading for taxes is 7.8 percent of the premium.

Dividends

About one-fourth of the property and liability insurance in force and almost one-half of the life and health insurance in force is advanced premium participating insurance, which provides for the payment of dividends to policyholders. Because insurance costs depend upon these dividends as well as the initial premiums, dividend practices are a consideration in insurance pricing. Dividends paid by an insurer depend on its profitability, although insurers often use smoothing techniques to reduce fluctuations in dividends.

The risk manager is interested not only in the general level of dividends but also in their distribution among insureds. Most property and liability insurers return the same percentage dividend, say, 10 percent, to all insureds purchasing a particular policy. Sometimes the dividends vary by classes or broad groups of classes, and in some instances, particularly in workers' compensation insurance, the dividend varies with the loss experience of the particular insured and the size of the insured's premium. Under this last practice, the large insured with good experience obtains the most substantial return. Less common practices vary the dividend according to either the loss experience or the premium size but not both.

Life insurance dividends are apportioned according to a detailed formula. The three most important sources of dividends for a life insurer are (1) savings in mortality costs because actual death rates are less than estimated, (2) savings in the allowances for expenses, and (3) investment returns in excess of those assumed in computing the premiums. The most common plan for distributing available excess funds among the insureds is the "three factor method." The essence of this method is that each insured receives a dividend from each of the three sources listed above, adjusted to reflect the policy's type, issue age, and issue year. Dividends on policies where cash values are small are most affected by savings in mortality costs. Expense savings go mainly to those insureds paying large expense loadings and, if no size discount is applied to the initial premiums, may be greater for larger contracts. Policyholders whose contracts have large cash values receive the largest dollar return from the excess investment return. There is a tendency for dividends to increase with the age of the contract because the cash value and the share in the excess investment return increase over time.

PRINCIPAL RATING PROCEDURES

Insurance rating procedures can be divided into three major categories: (1) individual or judgment rating, (2) class or manual rating, and (3) modification rating, usually referred to as "merit rating."

Individual or Judgment Rating

Under individual or judgment rating, each insured is charged a unique premium based largely upon the judgment of the person setting the rate, supplemented perhaps by whatever statistical data are available and by a knowledge of the premiums charged similar insureds. Judgment rating takes into account all known factors affecting the exposure, including competition from other insurers. Under this method, the rating procedure is unique for each insured.

At some point in every rating process, human judgment becomes a consideration. However, the reliance on judgment as the sole consideration is not common in insurance today. Commercial insurance on ocean-going vessels and their cargoes and, to a lesser extent, other transportation insurance rates are set in this fashion. Individual rating is used in other lines of insurance only for unusual exposures that cannot be handled under the other two rating methods, and it is used in pricing reinsurance. Risk managers of large organizations are more likely to encounter this method than are other risk managers. Some risk managers of giant organizations that self-insure the more common exposures and seek outside protection only for the unusual may encounter individual rating on almost all of their organization's coverage.

Class Rating

Under class rating, insureds are classified according to a few observable characteristics, and the insureds in each class are charged the same rate. This method of rating is often referred to as "manual rating" because the class rates are printed in a manual used to determine the rate for the insured. Under this method, the person applying the rates to determine the premium does not set overall rate levels. Except for determining the correct class for the insured, the person applying the rates has no decisions to make and, at least in theory, the rate should be the same for an individual insured, no matter who applies the rate. Determining the correct class, however, may involve judgment, and the risk manager should check to see that his or her organization has been placed in a favorable class.

Besides simplifying and speeding up the application of the rates, class rating makes it possible to use statistical methods more extensively in making the rates. Class rating groups together similar insureds to improve the accuracy of forecasts. Class rating is used widely for individual life insurance and health insurance rates, automobile insurance rates, homeowner's insurance rates on dwellings, and general liability and workers' compensation rates for small organizations.

Fire Insurance Class Rates. In fire insurance, class rates generally are used to price such exposures as dwellings, private garages, small apartment houses, and small mercantile and manufacturing properties. The factors considered in classifying insureds are (1) the type of occupancy, (2) whether the property is a building or movable personal property, (3) the grade of the community fire protection, (4) the construction (generally brick, frame, or fire-resistant), and (5) the amount of insurance purchased. Charges may also be added for substandard conditions.

One important factor affecting fire insurance rates in a community is the ability of the community's fire alarm, fire department, and water system to minimize the property damage once a fire occurs. Class 1 communities have the greatest suppression ability, Class 10 the least.

Large buildings in a community may be assigned to their own class that cannot be higher than the class assigned to the community for smaller buildings. A risk manager may be able to reduce his or her fire rates and those of neighbors by convincing the community to take steps to improve its grade.

Automobile Liability Insurance Class Rates. Most private passenger automobile liability insurance is class-rated. The rating procedure typical for private passenger cars is illustrated by way of example, portions of which may not apply in a particular regulatory environment. For example, the use of age and sex of the driver or the territory in which the vehicle is garaged has come under criticism in some jurisdictions. The typical rating procedure adjusts a *base premium* for the vehicle upward or downward to reflect special characteristics of the vehicle and its intended use. The adjustment applies a *rating factor,* which is the sum of a *primary factor* and a *secondary factor,* to the base premium. For each car to be insured under the contract, a base premium is determined from the rating manual. The base premium depends only upon the policy limits desired and the territory in which the car will be principally garaged. Because smaller claims are much more likely than large claims, the base premium does not increase proportionally with the policy limit.

The primary rating factor varies among insureds depending upon the use of the automobile (pleasure, but not driving to work; driving to or from work with a one-way mileage less than 15 miles; driving to or from work that is 15 miles or more away; business use; or farm use), the age and sex of those who customarily use the car, whether youthful operators are married, whether youthful operators own the car or are principal operators, whether youthful operators have completed an approved driver-training course, and whether youthful operators are good students. For youthful drivers there are only two use categories: (1) pleasure, but not driving to work and not farm use; and (2) all other. The primary rating factor divides insureds into 161 classes. For example, if the car is used only for pleasure driving and the only operator in the household is a female driver, aged 30 to 64, the primary rating factor is 0.90. If the car is used by this female operator to drive to work for a one-way distance of less than 15 miles, the factor is 1.15. Business use would increase the factor to 1.35. If a car used only for pleasure driving is owned by an unmarried male 17 years of age without driver training and with low grades, the factor is 3.50. A driver-training course and good grades would reduce this factor to 2.50. Other things being equal, the rates for youthful male owners decrease each year until they are 21, remain stable until age 25, at which time they would again decrease but still retain an extra charge until age 30, at which time they are no longer considered to be youthful owners.

The secondary rating factor depends upon whether more than one car is being insured, the type of car (standard performance, intermediate performance, high performance, or sports car), and the number of driving record points assessed against the insured under a safe-driver insurance rating plan. Under this plan, the insured is assessed one point for each accident during the past three years causing bodily injuries or property damage exceeding $200 involving a car operated by the named insured or a resident relative. However, no point is assigned if the named insured can demonstrate that another person is responsible for the accident; for example, if the insured has secured a judgment against the other person or if the automobile was lawfully parked at the time of the accident. Up to three points may be assigned for various traffic convictions such as driving while intoxicated. The factor is zero for a person insuring only one standard-performance car with no points. If the person were insuring two or more cars, the factor would be -0.15. For a person with four points insuring a single standard-performance car, the rating factor is 2.20.

The final step is to multiply the base premium by the sum of the primary and secondary rating factors. For example, assume a base premium of $200 for a given territory and policy limits. A youthful male owner, aged 17, without driver training, with low grades, and with four points under the safe-driver plan would pay $200(3.50 + 2.20) = \$1040$ to insure one standard-performance car. A driver-training course, good grades, and no safe-driver plan points would reduce the premium to $200(2.50 + 0.00) = \$500$.

Workers' Compensation Insurance Class Rates. About 70 percent of the employers purchasing workers' compensation insurance are class-rated. Their payroll is divided into classes on the basis of the type of industry (banking, for instance), the occupation of the employee (clerical office employee) or the industrial operation performed (manufacturing concrete at the job location by a contractor constructing bridges). Generally, the entire payroll falls into one class determined by the industry except for clerical office employees, drivers, and certain other "standard exceptions." Because the payroll (to which the rate per $100 of payroll must be applied to determine the premium) can be estimated only at the beginning of the year, the insured pays a deposit premium, which is adjusted after an audit at the end of the policy period.

Modification Rating

Under modification or merit rating, the rate distinguishes among insureds in the same rating class on the basis of differences in expected losses or expenses per exposure unit. The rate distinctions may be based on differences in past experience, size of exposure, or a detailed analysis of the quality of the exposure. Four principal modification rating methods are discussed below: (1) schedule rating, (2) experience rating, (3) retrospective rating, and (4) premium-discount plans.

With some exceptions, these plans are reserved for larger organizations. A small relative difference between the modified rate and the class rate becomes important only when the premium is large; the loss experience of a particular insured becomes credible only when the number of exposure units is large; the expenses associated with modification rating become justified only when they result in substantial dollar premium changes; and expense savings may require a large scale of operation to become significant.

Schedule Rating. Under schedule rating, the modification is based upon a comparison between some specified characteristics of a standard insured and the corresponding characteristics of the insured being rated. The person applying the schedule adds a charge to the standard rate for each way in which the rated insured is worse than the standard and subtracts a credit for each way in which the rated insured is better. Often the characteristics considered in the schedules and the charges and the credits are precisely stated, and two persons applying the same schedule will arrive at approximately the same result. Other schedules are so highly flexible—the characteristics are so vaguely defined and the credits and charges can fall anywhere within a broad range (e.g., up to 55 percent)—that schedule rating approaches individual rating. Regardless of whether the schedule is flexible or inflexible, the persons constructing (not applying) the schedule are forced to rely almost entirely on their judgment in choosing the characteristics to be compared and in evaluating their importance.

One great advantage of schedule rating is that an analysis of the schedule will reveal those areas in which the quality of the insured's exposure could be improved. As such, schedule rating is a boon to loss-control efforts because it enables the insured to estimate the premium savings associated with a loss-control measure.

Detailed, inflexible schedule rating is declining in importance because a detailed schedule is expensive to apply and because the less flexible schedules have placed too much emphasis upon tangible or physical factors. The most important application of detailed schedule rating is the pricing of fire insurance and some transportation insurance for most commercial exposures. Highly flexible schedules are in common use in such lines as automobile liability, general liability insurance, and, more recently, workers' compensation.

Experience Rating and Retrospective Rating. Experience rating and retrospective rating are claim-sensitive rating methods. Both of these methods recognize the claims activity of the insured organization in setting the rate for insurance coverage. Of the two methods, retrospective tends to be the most claim-sensitive. As a general rule, these rating methods are available only to large organizations. A detailed description of these rating methods appeared in Chapter 10.

Premium Discount Plans. Premium-discount plans reduce rates for large-premium insureds on the ground that they are likely to experience more favorable expenses merely because they are large. The most important premium-discount plans are those recognizing that not all the expenses of servicing an insured increase proportionately with the size of the premium. Premium-discount plans usually apply a table of discounts to the premiums otherwise charged. For example, if the premium is $15,000, the amount in excess of $5000 may be discounted 10 percent to produce a premium of $14,000

Fire Insurance Schedule Rates. In fire insurance, schedule rates apply to most insureds who are not class-rated, which often are large organizations. A Commercial Fire Rating Schedule is used in many states to determine the schedule rate following the procedure described below. First, a detailed inspection is used to classify the exposure according to construction (e.g., thickness of walls, concealed spaces), occupancy (manufacturing, wholesale grocery), exposure (construction, occupancy, and distance from adjacent buildings), and protection (automatic sprinklers, guards). Using this information, the schedule rate is then determined by a rather complex procedure, which (1) adds charges to the rate for ways in which the particular exposure is considered to be more expensive to insure than a standard exposure located in the same community, and (2) subtracts credits for ways in which the particular exposure is considered less expensive to insure. The features to be included in the schedule and the charges and credits are based on an evaluation of overall past experience, some controlled experimentation, and the combined judgment of the persons who drafted the schedule. One attraction of this form of schedule rating is that it gives the risk manager an incentive for loss control by providing the business with detailed information on the factors affecting its rate, and on the financial impact of making changes in the exposure itself.

The schedules used to rate large insureds and superior properties with approved automatic sprinklers (called highly protected risks, or HPR) give the person applying the schedule much more leeway in determining the features to be considered and the charges or credits to be added to or subtracted from the rate.

Under an expense modification plan, large insureds may, if the insurer agrees, have their schedule rate reduced to reflect (1) savings in acquisition costs or other expenses, and (2) favorable features, such as training of employees, not recognized in the more common schedules. The discount is most likely to be granted when there is competition for the insured's account.

A large firm that operates at two or more locations may be eligible for a multiple-location rating plan, which enables the insured to reduce the rate otherwise payable by (1) a premium size or quantity discount credit, (2) a credit based on the extent to which the property values are dispersed, and (3) a modification for better than average experience.

Automobile Insurance Modified Rates. Modification rates can apply to automobile liability insurance on vehicle fleets. Important modification rating plans include a fleet-rating plan, an experience-rating plan with or without a schedule-rating supplement, and retrospective rating.

The automobile fleet plan provides discounts if five or more automobiles under one ownership are insured. An experience-rating plan also is available for fleets of automobiles. In most states, the experience rate may be further modified according to a flexible schedule. The schedule provides for a maximum credit of 25 percent and a maximum debit of 20 percent based on broad directives concerning management, employee characteristics, condition of equipment, and safety organization. The experience and schedule rate may in turn be reduced if the expenses—usually commissions—incurred in producing the business are smaller than normal. A retrospective rating plan is available for large fleets. The retrospective rating plan follows the rating procedure for plan V described below in connection with workers' compensation insurance rates.

Workers' Compensation Insurance Modified Rates. Modification rating plans are important in workers' compensation insurance. These include an experience-rating plan, a premium-discount plan, several retrospective-rating plans, and, in some states, a flexible schedule rating plan. Experience rating and retrospective rating were first developed as worker's compensation insurance rating tools.

An insured whose annual premium at manual rates would average about $2500 must be experience-rated. The detailed plan cannot be discussed here, but we should note that it is a carefully and objectively designed experience-rating plan.

If the insured's annual premium exceeds $5000, the premium is subject to a discount because of expense savings. The discounts are tabled and increase as the premium increases. Two sets of discounts are provided, stock discounts and nonstock discounts. Nonstock discounts are smaller because the insurers using these discounts prefer to pay dividends.

As an alternative to the premium-discount plan, an insured whose annual premium exceeds $5000 may elect to be retrospectively rated under plan I, II, III, or IV. In practice, however, insurers usually limit retrospective rating to insureds paying annual premiums of at least $25,000. Some require a $100,000 or higher premium. Each of these plans specifies the set of maximum and minimum premiums corresponding to the *standard premium*—the premium that would be paid without the benefit of retrospective rating or premium discounts. The formula for determining the retrospective premium is given earlier in this chapter.

Under plan I, the maximum premium is the standard premium, and the minimum premium exceeds the basic premium. At most, the insured loses the premium discount. Under plan II, the maximum premium is greater than the standard premium, but the minimum premium is less than the plan I minimum. In other words, the possible fluctuation in the premium is much greater than in plan I and the basic premium is considerably less. Plan III has the same maximum premium as plan II, but the minimum is less since it is the basic premium times the tax multiplier. Plan III produces a lower premium than plan II only when experience is favorable, as its basic premium is higher than under plan II. Plan IV is characterized by a lower maximum premium than either plan II or plan III, and the minimum premium is lower than under plan I. It is suitable for insureds who find plan I too conservative and plans II and III too risky.

To illustrate these differences, assume that an insured has a $50,000 standard premium. In one state, the ratios of the basic, minimum, and maximum premiums to this standard premium would be shown in Table 14.2. For example, under plan II the basic premium would be $12,350, the minimum premium $27,450, and the maximum premium $68,500.

Instead of electing plan I, II, III, or IV, an insured may elect plan V. Plan V has two distinctive characteristics. First, the insured may, subject to the consent of the insurer, select any reasonable set of minimum and maximum premiums. In other words, plans I, II, III, and IV are special cases of plan V. Second, plan V can be applied, separately or in some combination, to workers' compensation insurance, automobile liability insurance, general liability insurance, automobile physical damage insurance, burglary insurance, and glass insurance. Because plan V is so flexible, it has become more popular among eligible insureds than plans I, II, III, or IV.

RATING ORGANIZATIONS

As discussed in Chapter 13, a rating organization is an association that provides assistance to members in setting insurance rates. In the United States today, two major rating organizations are present: the Insurance Services Office (ISO) and the National Council on Compensation Insurance (NCCI). ISO is the major rat-

TABLE 14.2. Examples of the Ratios of the Basic, Minimum, and Maximum Premiums in Plans I to IV

Plan	Basic premium, percent	Minimum premium, percent	Maximum premium, percent
I	37.4	71.4	100.0
II	24.7	54.9	137.0
III	29.9	29.9 × tax multiplier	137.0
IV	29.8	60.2	118.5

ing organization for all major lines of property and liability insurance except workers' compensation.

ISO's influence on rate levels today is greatly diminished relative to the strong rate-setting authority vested in rating bureaus during the first half of the twentieth century. In the United States prior to 1950, rating bureaus were regional associations that had a strong influence on insurance rates and coverages. In some states and in some lines of insurance, rating bureaus had the authority to compel insurers to become members and use rates set by the bureau. Mehr and Cammack (1972) document that as late as 1966, courts upheld bureau pricing rules that strongly restricted price competition, despite the obvious conflict between the legal framework applying to insurance pricing and the pricing of other goods and services.

Gradually, the influence of rating bureaus in lines other than workers' compensation insurance has diminished. As late as the 1970s, rating organizations for these lines were a system of regional rating bureaus that collected insurance claim data from subscribing insurers and used these data to develop suggested insurance rates. By that time, however, rating bureaus in most situations could only suggest rate levels with no authority to compel membership and adherence to published rate levels.

The influence of rating bureaus has continued to diminish as a result of market pressures and changes in the regulatory climate for insurers. The system of regional rating bureaus eventually consolidated into ISO, a single organization for the entire United States. ISO no longer publishes suggested rate levels to members, but provides summaries of insurance claim data for members to consider in setting premium levels.

NCCI is the major United States rating organization for workers' compensation insurance. Many states also have state-domiciled private rating organizations or state-controlled rating organizations that influence rates. Rates for workers' compensation insurance are closely regulated in many states. A major role of NCCI and these other rating organizations is to provide testimony at regulatory hearings that consider changes in these rates.

APPENDIX 14.1. PRICING OF INDIVIDUAL LIFE INSURANCE

Life insurance rates are influenced by three major determinants: (1) expected mortality rates in the insured population, (2) investment income earned by the insurer on invested premium income, and (3) expenses incurred in operating an insurance enterprise and in providing insurance-related services. The procedure in this appendix illustrates how these determinants are incorporated into rates for standard or traditional life insurance coverages, in which the insurer promises a stated dollar benefit in return for a stated premium.

Class rates predominate in individual life insurance. For standard lives, the rates for a particular contract depend upon the age at issue, sex, and, in most cases, upon the face value of the contract. The class rates for substandard lives also depend upon the severity of their impairment or the dangers associated with their occupation.

Life insurance class rates can be and are established on a much more mathematically precise basis than is possible in the other lines of insurance. The primary reasons why life insurance rating can be more precise than rating in other lines are: (1) because all losses are total and a fixed amount is paid in case of death (or survival under an annuity contract), the only loss information required is the probability of death at each age, and (2) the mortality rates at each age, although subject to long-term trends, are fairly stable in the short run. Furthermore, because all insurers classify standard lives in the same simple way, the experience of several insurers can be combined to provide highly credible experience.

The combined experience on a large number of lives forms the foundation for a mortality table showing mortality rates for each age. On the assumption that some arbitrary number of persons, such as 1 million, is alive at the initial age in the table, the table shows the number of these persons who will survive to each subsequent age. These numbers allow the survival rates and death rates to be calculated.

The 1980 Commissioners Standard Ordinary Table, which is reproduced as Table 14.3, serves as an example of a mortality table. The title of the table reflects its source and use: (1) the National Association of Insurance Commissioners (NAIC) has approved its use for valuation of reserves and (2) the table applies to ordinary insurance on standard lives. Mortality rates estimated using this table are not necessarily unbiased estimates of mortality rates in the population. The mortality rates are (1) graded to reduce chance fluctuations and (2) loaded to provide a margin of safety in life insurance policy reserve valuations. With these qualifications in mind, Table 14.3 provides a basis for illustrating the method used to price life insurance.

Life insurance rates, unlike property and liability insurance rates, depend explicitly on an interest rate assumed in the rate calculation. The interest rate usually corresponds to a conservative assessment of the rate of return the insurer will earn on investment. Assume that a person, age 35, wants to pay one lump sum for a $1000 five-year term insurance contract. What is the appropriate lump sum on the assumption that the 1980 CSO mortality rates and a 4 percent interest return will be maintained and that expenses can be ignored? This lump sum is called the "net single premium." Assume that this person is one of the 949,171 persons who, according to Table 14.3, have survived to age 35.

According to Table 14.3, out of this group of 949,171 persons, 2003 will die in the first year, 2121 in the second, 2268 in the third, 2432 in the fourth, and 2623 in the fifth. To simplify the calculation, assume that these death claims, each for an amount of $1000, are paid at the end of the year in which the death occurs.

TABLE 14.3. 1980 CSO Mortality Table

Age	Male Number living	Male Number dying	Male Probability of dying	Female Number living	Female Number dying	Female Probability of dying
0	1,000,000	4,180	.00418	1,000,000	2,890	.00289
1	995,820	1,066	.00107	997,110	867	.00087
2	994,754	985	.00099	996,243	807	.00081
3	993,770	974	.00098	995,436	787	.00079
4	992,796	943	.00095	994,649	766	.00077
5	991,853	893	.00090	993,883	755	.00076
6	990,960	852	.00086	993,128	725	.00073
7	990,108	792	.00080	992,403	715	.00072
8	989,316	752	.00076	991,688	694	.00070
9	988,564	732	.00074	990,994	684	.00069
10	987,832	721	.00073	990,310	673	.00068
11	987,111	760	.00077	989,637	683	.00069
12	986,351	838	.00085	988,954	712	.00072
13	985,513	976	.00099	988,242	741	.00075
14	984,537	1,132	.00115	987,501	790	.00080
15	983,405	1,308	.00133	986,711	839	.00085
16	982,097	1,483	.00151	985,872	887	.00090
17	980,614	1,638	.00167	984,985	936	.00095
18	978,976	1,743	.00178	984,049	964	.00098
19	977,237	1,819	.00186	983,085	1,003	.00102
20	975,416	1,853	.00190	982,082	1,031	.00105
21	973,563	1,860	.00191	981,051	1,050	.00107
22	971,703	1,836	.00189	980,001	1,068	.00109
23	969,867	1,804	.00186	979,933	1,087	.00111
24	968,063	1,762	.00182	977,846	1,114	.00114
25	966,301	1,710	.00177	976,732	1,133	.00116
26	964,591	1,669	.00173	975,599	1,161	.00119
27	962,922	1,647	.00171	974,438	1,189	.00122
28	961,275	1,634	.00170	973,249	1,226	.00126
29	959,641	1,641	.00171	972,023	1,264	.00130
30	958,000	1,657	.00173	970,759	1,311	.00135
31	956,343	1,702	.00178	969,448	1,357	.00140
32	954,640	1,747	.00183	968,091	1,404	.00145
33	952,893	1,820	.00191	966,687	1,450	.00150
34	951,073	1,902	.00200	965,237	1,525	.00158
35	949,171	2,003	.00211	963,712	1,590	.00165
36	947,168	2,121	.00224	962,122	1,693	.00176
37	945,047	2,268	.00240	960,429	1,815	.00189
38	942,779	2,432	.00258	958,614	1,956	.00204
39	940,346	2,623	.00279	956,658	2,124	.00222
40	937,723	2,832	.00302	954,534	2,310	.00242
41	934,891	3,076	.00329	952,224	2,514	.00264
42	931,815	3,127	.00356	949,710	2,725	.00287
43	928,688	3,594	.00387	946,985	2,926	.00309
44	925,094	3,876	.00419	944,059	3,135	.00332
45	921,218	4,192	.00455	940,924	3,349	.00356

(Continued)

TABLE 14.3. (Continued)

	Male			Female		
Age	Number living	Number dying	Probability of dying	Number living	Number dying	Probability of dying
46	917,026	4,512	.00492	937,575	3,563	.00380
47	912,514	4,854	.00532	934,012	3,783	.00405
48	907,660	5,210	.00574	930,229	4,028	.00433
49	902,450	5,604	.00621	926,201	4,288	.00463
50	896,846	6,018	.00671	921,913	4,573	.00496
51	890,828	6,503	.00730	917,340	4,871	.00531
52	884,325	7,039	.00796	912,469	5,201	.00570
53	877,286	7,642	.00871	907,268	5,580	.00615
54	869,644	8,314	.00956	901,688	5,960	.00661
55	861,331	9,019	.01047	895,728	6,350	.00709
56	852,312	9,767	.01146	889,378	6,733	.00757
57	842,545	10,523	.01249	882,645	7,088	.00803
58	832,022	11,308	.01359	875,557	7,416	.00847
59	820,714	12,122	.01477	868,141	7,761	.00894
60	808,592	13,002	.01608	860,380	8,148	.00947
61	795,590	13,954	.01754	852,232	8,633	.01013
62	781,636	15,000	.01919	842,599	9,246	.01096
63	766,636	16,145	.02106	834,353	10,029	.01202
64	750,491	17,367	.02314	824,324	10,922	.01325
65	733,124	18,636	.02542	813,402	11,867	.01459
66	714,488	19,898	.02785	801,535	12,825	.01600
67	694,590	21,144	.03044	788,710	13,747	.01743
68	673,446	22,351	.03319	774,963	14,600	.01884
69	651,095	23,550	.03617	760,363	15,481	.02036
70	627,545	24,795	.03951	744,882	16,470	.02211
71	602,750	26,099	.04330	728,412	17,649	.02423
72	576,651	27,477	.04765	710,763	19,098	.02687
73	549,174	28,909	.05264	691,665	20,826	.03011
74	520,265	30,274	.05819	670,839	22,762	.03393
75	489,991	31,452	.06419	648,077	24,782	.03824
76	458,539	32,341	.07053	623,295	26,783	.04297
77	426,198	32,869	.07712	596,512	28,657	.04804
78	393,329	33,000	.08390	567,855	30,352	.05345
79	360,329	32,808	.09105	537,503	31,900	.05935
80	327,521	32,372	.09884	505,603	33,365	.06599
81	295,149	31,723	.10748	472,238	34,575	.07360
82	263,426	30,886	.11725	437,481	36,048	.08240
83	232,540	29,826	.12826	401,433	37,145	.09253
84	202,714	28,431	.14025	364,288	37,817	.10381
85	174,283	26,656	.15295	326,471	37,903	.11610
86	147,627	24,520	.16609	288,568	37,309	.12929
87	123,107	22,103	.17955	251,259	36,010	.14332
88	101,004	19,521	.19891	215,249	34,048	.15818
89	81,483	16,891	.20729	181,201	31,518	.17394
90	64,592	14,325	.22177	149,683	28,552	.19075
91	50,267	11,912	.23698	121,131	25,301	.20887

(Continued)

TABLE 14.3. (Continued)

351

CHAPTER 14
The Pricing of
Insurance

	Male			Female		
Age	Number living	Number dying	Probability of dying	Number living	Number dying	Probability of dying
92	38,355	9,721	.25345	95,830	21,927	.22881
93	28,634	7,792	.27211	73,903	18,587	.25151
94	20,842	6,167	.29590	55,316	15,450	.27931
95	14,675	4,842	.32996	39,866	12,651	.31732
96	9,833	3,781	.38455	27,215	10,226	.37574
97	6,052	2,906	.48020	16,989	8,069	.47497
98	3,145	2,069	.65798	8,920	5,850	.65585
99	1,076	1,076	1.00000	3,070	3,070	1.00000

Because of the one-year time lag and because of the assumed interest return, it is not necessary to collect $2,003,000 to pay the death claims occurring the first year. The necessary fund is only ($2,003,000)(0.9615) or $1,925,884 because this amount invested for one year at 4 percent will yield $2,003,000. The amount that must be collected to meet the claims payable at the end of the second year is ($2,121,000)(0.9246)^2, or $1,961,077, because this amount invested for two years at 4 percent will yield $2,121,000. A similar procedure is followed for the other three years. The complete computation is shown in Table 14.4. The increasing importance of the interest assumption in the later contract years is obvious.

The net single premium is equal to this fund divided by the number of individuals alive at age 35, the initial group. In this case, the net single premium is $10,137,931/949,171, or $10.68.

If the five-year insurance contract is purchased with five annual premiums instead of a single premium, the five-annual premiums will have to be greater than a single premium payment at the beginning of the five years, because (1) not all insureds will live to pay the five annual premiums and (2) the amount available for the insurer to invest will, on average, be smaller.

The annual premium is paid by only those group members who are alive on the premium due date. Using the assumption that premiums are paid at the be-

TABLE 14.4. Computation of Net Single Premium for $1000 Five-Year Term Insurance Issued to a Group of Individuals at Age 35 (see text for details)

(1) Contract year	(2) Death claims	(3) Present value of $1 payable at end of year, 4%	(4) Present value of death claims (2) × (3)
1	$2,003,000	$0.9615	$ 1,925,884
2	2,121,000	0.9246	1,961,077
3	2,268,000	0.8890	2,016,252
4	2,432,000	0.8548	2,078,874
5	2,623,000	0.8219	2,155,844
		Total	$10,137,931

ginning of the year, the mortality table can be used to calculate the lump-sum equivalent of a $1 annual premium. This lump-sum equivalent is the present value of premium receipts per dollar of annual premium payable by group members who survive to the beginning of each year.

Under the assumption that premiums are paid at the beginning of the year, all 949,171 insureds will pay $1 on the issue date, but only 947,168 insureds will pay $1 one year later, and because of the loss of interest on this money, its present value is only ($947,168)(0.9615), or about $910,702. Similar computations are made for the other years and are summarized in Table 14.5.

This present value of the $1 premium payment per policyholder is $4,375,602/949,171, or $4.61. The present value of $2 premium payments would be twice this value, $3 premium payments three times this value, and so forth. Consequently,

$$\text{Desired annual premium} \times \text{Present value of \$1 premium payments} = \text{Net single premium}$$

or

$$\text{Desired annual premium} = \frac{\text{Net single premium}}{\text{Present value of \$1 premium payments}} = \frac{\$10.68}{\$4.61} = \$2.32$$

Although these principles have been stated in terms of a specific example, they are general in their application. For example, in order to determine the net annual premium for a straight life policy, the only difference would be that the period of coverage would be extended to include 65 contract years, that is, to age 100, at which time it is assumed that all 949,171 group members will have died.

The above example illustrates the calculation of *net premiums,* which provide an allowance for expected death claims only. *Gross premiums,* which are premiums actually charged for coverage, are adjusted to provide an allowance for expenses and profit using procedures similar to loading methods in property and liability insurance.

TABLE 14.5. Computation of the Present Value of a One Dollar Annual Premium Received from the Survivors of a Group Initially Age 35 (see text for details)

(1) Contract year	(2) Premium payors	(3) Present value of $1 payable at beginning of year, 4%	(4) Present value of $1 premium payments, (2) × (3)
1	949,171	$1.0000	$ 949,171
2	947,168	0.9615	910,702
3	945,047	0.9246	873,790
4	942,779	0.8890	838,131
5	940,346	0.8548	803,808
			Total $4,375,602

Methods used to determine gross premiums for life insurance coverage may consider issues that would not be expected to affect property-liability insurance premiums, such as persistency. Especially on whole life coverage, a large portion of the administrative and marketing expense is incurred when the coverage is written. This first-year expense includes compensation paid to the agent who sells the policy and the expense of underwriting and issuing the coverage. Typically, the large first-year expense is amortized over premiums paid during the first five or ten years the policy is in force. If the coverage is discontinued prior to the end of the amortization period, and the insurer has no means of recouping the unamortized expense (e.g., a chargeback to the agent who sold the policy), a loss occurs. To the extent that these persistency-related losses can be anticipated at the time coverage is written, the method used to determine gross premiums can take them into account.

Although the issues considered and methods used to determine loading levels can be complex, in practice the procedure used to load net premiums may appear simple. For example, an insurer may add to the net premium a percentage of the premium plus (1) a constant per $1000 of insurance, or (2) a constant per $1000 of insurance and a constant per policy.

Key Concepts

loading   A process used to determine insurance premiums by adjusting the expected value of claim payments to provide an allowance for the cost of insurance-related services, uncertainty, and profit.

rating procedure   The method used to determine the rate for an individual exposure, as contrasted with the method used to determine overall rate levels.

rate parity   A condition whereby the rate applying to every insured group is the same multiple of the respective group's expected value of claim payments.

rate equity   A condition whereby rates are not biased against any group.

class rating   A rating method under which the rate depends upon a set of characteristics that define a class. For example, a fire-resistant building with an approved roof used as a small office building in a community with excellent fire, water, and police facilities.

schedule rating   A more refined version of class rating in which the rate depends upon a more detailed analysis of the exposure's characteristics. Schedules vary in the degree of flexibility they permit the person determining the rate.

experience rating   A rating method under which the insured's rate depends at least in part on the insured's own prior loss experience.

retrospective rating   A rating method under which the insured's premium depends upon the insured's own contemporaneous loss experience subject to minimum and maximum premium constraints.

Review Questions

1. What is the relationship between the insurance rate and the insurance premium?
2. What does "loading" mean? How does it relate to the premium that a policyholder will pay?
3. This chapter discusses "target loss ratios" in some detail. Define "target loss ratio"and explain its purpose.

4. Most state laws require that property and liability insurance rates be "reasonable," "adequate," and "not unfairly discriminatory." What do these terms mean?

5. What is the difference between "rate equity" and "rate parity?"

6. What role do dividends play in the determination of the ultimate premium paid by policyholders?

7. In the past, insurance losses totaled $132 million. Premiums at current rates were $200 million. If insurers need 40 percent of their premiums to pay their expenses and earn a reasonable profit, should premium rates be increased or decreased? How much?

8. How can a risk manager make use of the results of schedule rating?

9. Identify three risks in which individual or judgment rating might be used.

10. What types of business firms are class-rated by fire insurers?
   a. Are fire insurance class rates based on statistical analysis?
   b. How can a class-rated organization cut its rate?

11. Are the automobile liability insurance class rates paid by persons in a medium-sized city based solely upon the automobile liability experience in that city? Explain your answer.

12. Describe briefly the basic approach to schedule rating in fire insurance.

13. What is the difference between schedule rating and class rating?

14. On what basis should a firm decide among workers' compensation retrospective-rating plans I, II, III, IV, and V?

15. Review the discussion of experience-rated and retrospectively rated plans in Chapter 10.
   a. What distinguishes experience-rated plans from schedule-rated plans?
   b. If given a choice, why might a risk manager prefer retrospectively rated plans over experience-rated plans?
   c. How are experience-rated plans similar to classification-rated plans? How are they different?

16. Rating organizations are less important in property and liability insurance than they formerly were. What are rating organizations? Why are they less important today?

References and Suggestions for Additional Reading

BLACK, K., and H. SKIPPER, JR.: *Life Insurance* (10th ed., Englewood Cliffs, N.J.: Prentice-Hall, Inc., 1988), chaps. 19–23, 25, 27.

CUMMINS, J. DAVID, and HARRINGTON, SCOTT E. (EDS.): *Fair Rate of Return on Property-Liability Insurance* (Hingham, Mass.: Kluwer-Nijhoff, 1986).

BOWERS, N. L., JR., H. U. GERBER, J. C. HICKMAN, D. A. JONES, and C. J. NESBITT: *Actuarial Mathematics* (Itasca, Ill.: The Society of Actuaries, 1986).

FREIFELDER, L. R.: *A Decision Theoretic Approach to Insurance Ratemaking* (Homewood, Ill.: Richard D. Irwin, Inc., 1976).

HARTMAN, G. R.: *Ratemaking for Homeowners Insurance* (Homewood, Ill.: Richard D. Irwin, Inc., 1967).

JORDAN, C. W., JR.: *Life Contingencies* (2nd ed., Chicago: Society of Actuaries, 1967).

KALLOP, R. H.: "A Current Look at Workers' Compensation Ratemaking," *Proceedings of the Casualty Actuarial Society* (vol. LXII, nos. 117 and 118, May and November, 1975), pp. 62–133.

KULP, C. A., and J. W. HALL: *Casualty Insurance* (4th ed., New York: The Ronald Press Company, 1968), chaps. 11 and 19–22.

MCGILL, D. M.: *Life Insurance* (rev. ed., Homewood, Ill.: Richard D. Irwin, Inc., 1967), chaps. 8–12.

MEHR, ROBERT I., and EMERSON CAMMACK: *Principles of Insurance.* (Homewood, Ill.: Richard D. Irwin, Inc., 1972), pp. 790.

MEHR, R. I., and S. G. GUSTAVSON: *Life Insurance: Theory and Practice* (4th ed., Dallas: Business Publications, Inc., 1987), chaps. 23, 24.

PFEFFER, IRVING, and D. R. KLOCK: *Perspectives on Insurance* (Englewood Cliffs, N.J.: Prentice-Hall, Inc., 1974), chaps. 22, 25, and 26.

Proceedings of the Casualty Actuarial Society (annual).

SEAL, HILARY L.: *Stochastic Theory of A Risk Business* (New York: John Wiley & Sons, Inc., 1969).

STEPHENS, V. M., W. S. MCINTYRE, and J. P. GIBSON: *Rick Financing: A Guide to Insurance Cash Flow* (Dallas: International Risk Management Institute, Inc.).

Transactions of the Society of Actuaries (periodic).

WEBB, B. L., J. J. LAUNIE, W. P. ROKES, and N. A. BAGLINI: *Insurance Company Operations* (3rd ed., Malvern, Pa.: American Institute for Property and Liability Underwriters, 1984), vol. II, chaps. 9–10.

Insurance Regulation and Financial Assessment

Learning Objectives

After you have completed this chapter, you should be able to:

1. Describe and briefly explain the purposes of insurance regulation.
2. Explain why competition alone is not considered an adequate regulator of insurance.
3. List the general statutory powers and duties of state insurance commissioners.
4. Present arguments for and against state regulation of insurance.
5. Tell what steps states have taken to improve the availability of insurance.
6. List the major factors affecting an insurer's financial strength.
7. Describe how asset and reserve valuations and reinsurance affect an insurer's financial strength.
8. Calculate and evaluate the expense ratio of a property and liability insurer.
9. Identify where you can get information needed to evaluate an insurer's financial strength, service and cost.
10. Describe the system of state-level insurance guaranty associations and identify restrictions on guaranty association coverage that may be important to risk managers.

INTRODUCTION

An insurance contract is a promise to perform, with performance conditioned on future chance events. The insurer's ability to make good on this promise is not fully evident at the time the contract is signed. A rationale for regulation of the insurance industry rests on two premises: (1) the public's interest in assuring that insurers perform on their promises and (2) the amount and type of information required to evaluate an insurer's ability to perform.

Insurance regulation can have both indirect and direct effects on the practice of risk management. Regulation generally affects the availability of insurance coverage and the price at which coverage is offered. The state tax on insurers' premium income (the "premium tax") and some states' requirements that insurers subsidize pools to guarantee affordable coverage to all applicants (e.g., a joint underwriting facility or assigned risk pool) offer examples of regulations affecting availability and price of coverage. Because insurance offers one method for financing an organization's exposures to risk, changing conditions in the market for insurance indirectly affect an organization's risk management program.

Direct effects of regulation can occur as a consequence of rules related to conduct in the market. States have procedures that must be followed for coverage to be written by unlicensed insurers ("excess and surplus lines" insurers). A risk manager seeking coverage for an unusual or exotic exposure may be required to comply with these requirements if coverage is not available from a licensed insurer. The "fronting" technique described in Chapter 10 offers another example of a direct effect. Fronting is a way to use a captive insurer to provide coverage when a state has a requirement that insurance be provided by a licensed insurer. The licensed insurer, the "front," writes coverage for the parent company, but then reinsures the coverage with the captive. A third example is participation in risk financing arrangements, such as risk retention groups, which can be subject to state regulations applying to insurance.

One purpose of regulation is to protect the public interest. In some instances, insurance regulation may afford the same level of protection to the risk manager's organization as it does to the public generally. However, to an increasing degree, this level of protection may not be as available or as important to a large organization as it is to most individuals, partly because the level of sophistication among risk managers is growing. Insurance regulators are unlikely to be sympathetic to a claim that a sophisticated consumer of insurance was an innocent victim of financial manipulation. Consequently, the burden of independent evaluation of insurers is falling more heavily on organizational managers of risk than on members of the public generally. The necessity of independent analysis makes financial evaluation of insurers important to the risk management profession.

Two overlapping topics are studied in this chapter: (1) regulation of the insurance industry and (2) methods for assessing the financial condition and performance of insurers. The chapter first provides an overview of insurance regulation. The purpose of the overview is to develop an understanding of what aspects of insurance are regulated, why the regulation is necessary and how the regulation is accomplished. The issue of solvency, which is at the heart of insurance regulation, dominates the second half of this chapter. The discussion of solvency assessment is designed to help readers understand factors influencing an insurer's ability to meet its obligations, knowledge that provides the background for methods of analysis.

358

PART FOUR
Insurance
Institutions and
Coverages

OVERVIEW OF INSURANCE REGULATION

Reasons Why Insurance is Regulated

In the United States, few if any businesses escape regulation. Many business regulations apply in an even-handed manner across different types of businesses; regulations applying to weighing and measuring instruments, to advertising disclosures, and to fair employment practices are examples. In most instances, however, determination of the terms of business transactions is left to market forces. Banking and insurance are notable exceptions to the reliance on free markets and competition as the primary forces setting prices and terms of transactions. Four characteristics of insurance make it a special target for regulation:

1. Elimination of the marginal firm under a competitive environment is contrary to the basic purpose of the insurance institution, namely, to guarantee performance of future contingent financial obligations. Financial solvency is the foundation of public confidence in the private insurance mechanism and historically has been the primary objective of regulation.
2. The consumer is unable to evaluate the insurer's promises of future performance as well as he or she can evaluate tangible goods and services.
3. Complete freedom of entry of new insurance firms is not desirable because of the fiduciary nature of the policyholder-insurer relationship and the resulting opportunities for fraud and financial speculation by unregulated promoters.
4. Intensive unregulated competition in marketing insurance may produce unfair loss-adjusting practices, misleading policy language, and monopolization, all of which are recognized to be against the public interest.

Level of Government at Which the Regulatory Function Exists

The knowledge about why insurance is regulated still does not address the important political question: "who regulates?" Some nations regulate at the national level because local government has neither the structure nor wherewithal for the task—the United Kingdom is an example. Other nations, such as Japan, also choose to regulate at the national rather than the local level, although local regulation technically might be possible. Finally, some nations choose to regulate at the local (rather than national) level; the United States is an example. In the United States, most regulation of insurance emanates from state-level government.

The assertion that state regulation was "chosen" as the approach in the United States is not entirely accurate. Rather, state regulation is an outgrowth of political forces that have ebbed and flowed over the past 150 years. Indeed, though state regulation of insurance generally has been a settled matter for some time, considerable growth of the federal role has occurred since 1950. The political climate in the 1990s seems conducive to further expansion of the federal role.

Advocates of state regulation of insurance claim the following advantages:

1. State regulation has created a regulatory environment that has assured a financially strong, solvent, and vital insurance industry. In other words it works.
2. Insurance contracts are purchased to meet local exposures and risks. Local supervision is adaptable to local needs and concerns.
3. State supervision encourages innovations and experimentation. In several instances in which uniformity is desirable, the National Association of Insurance Commissioners (NAIC) has served as a forum for developing model legislation and procedures.
4. Federal supervision of insurance, if poorly administered, would affect adversely the entire private insurance business. Spotty or inept insurance supervision in a limited number of states does not seriously impair the activities of insurers and the needs of insurance consumers in the other states where supervision is proper and fair.
5. Most legal disputes involving insurance reflect issues of legal liability and of contract law, which are matters of state law and rulings by state courts. Financial and procedural regulation of insurance at the state level is a logical extension of this jurisdiction.

Advocates of federal insurance regulations assert the following advantages to their approach:

1. Insurers operating in more than one state have to deal with more than one regulator. Dealing with two or more regulators and differences in state statutes, administrative rules, and court decisions is inefficient and costly.
2. The quality of state regulation varies greatly among states. Federal regulation would give consumers in all states equal protection.
3. Federal regulators would be more talented and capable than those in most states. A federal insurance department would be better financed relatively than state departments, and a federal agency would have more authority, prestige, and status. Federal regulators also should be better able to resist pressures from the insurance industry, especially those reflecting local interests.
4. Businesses and other organizations often have operations in more than one state, and interstate commerce often transports articles across state boundaries. When insurance applies to these operations and articles, regulation at the state level creates possible anomalies and jurisdictional disputes. A system of uniform federal regulation would reduce or eliminate these problems.

HISTORICAL DEVELOPMENT OF STATE INSURANCE REGULATION

Mowbray and Blanchard (1955) trace the regulation of insurance to medieval Europe, but find little evidence that regulation of insurance existed in colonial America before the War for Independence. Aside from a few local mutual fire insurance companies and the Presbyterian Ministers' Fund that issued survivorship annuities, Mowbray and Blanchard claim there were no organized insurers in the colonies later forming the United States. However, a number of insurers were incorporated near the close of the eighteenth century, beginning with the Insurance Company of North America in 1794.

The earliest insurers established in the United States received their charters from state governments or were incorporated under state statutes, as were other business institutions. Early regulations pertaining specifically to insurance dealt with the licensing of agents and insurers, contract provisions, and investments. The two primary objectives of regulation during this early period were raising tax revenues and assuring financial solvency.

Development of Commission Regulation

In 1851, New Hampshire appointed a three-member commission to examine insurers annually. In 1852, Massachusetts established a Board of Insurance Commissioners, composed of a secretary, treasurer, and auditor, charged with general enforcement of the insurance laws. Several other states created similar boards around the same time. By these acts, the modern system of state supervision came into existence. It was not until 1859, however, that New York became the first state to appoint a single insurance commissioner.

The most famous of the early insurance commissioners was Elizur Wright, who served as a member of a two-member board in Massachusetts from 1858 to 1867. As a professor of mathematics, Wright had become interested in the mathematics of level-premium life insurance, the development of reserves, and nonforfeiture laws. In 1858, Wright secured passage by the Massachusetts legislature of a bill that required life insurers to maintain reserves that recognize the insurers' liability to pay future benefits. As commissioner of insurance, he also secured passage of a nonforfeiture law and developed methods of reporting and accounting that became the blueprint for the sound development of private life insurance.

The Legal Precedent for State Insurance Regulation. In 1866, a bill was introduced in the U.S. Congress that would have established federal regulation of insurance, but no action was taken. Three years later, the United States Supreme Court held, in *Paul v. Virginia* (1869), that the issuance of insurance is not a transaction of commerce within the meaning of laws giving the federal government the authority to regulate interstate commerce. Instead, the Court held, an insurance transaction is a local transaction governed by local laws. This finding, which was upheld for a 75-year period, removed the regulation of insurance from the jurisdiction of the federal government.

The dispute in *Paul v. Virginia* involved a Virginia law requiring nonresident insurance agents to deposit security and become licensed before soliciting business in the state. Samuel Paul, an agent for a group of New York insurers, refused to deposit the required security before selling fire insurance in Virginia. He was arrested, convicted, and fined. Paul appealed the conviction, arguing that Virginia's requirement for licensing was illegal interference by a state in interstate commerce. The Supreme Court's refusal to uphold his position set an important precedent for the development of state insurance regulation. This decision and subsequent decisions upholding the position stimulated state legislatures to establish administrative agencies to supervise insurance companies. By 1871, practically all states had established commissions to supervise and control insurers.

With the evolution of many separate state insurance commissions and their crazy quilt of insurance regulations, it became apparent that some form of national association was needed to eliminate many of the inconsistencies in state regulations. The New York superintendent of insurance requested a meeting of all state insurance regulators. At this first meeting in 1871 the National Association of Insurance Commissions was formed. Since that time the NAIC has continued to meet, at first annually and later semiannually, to discuss technical and legal problems relating to the development of uniform legislation and administrative solutions to the major problems confronting insurance regulators. All states now contribute to the work and the budget of the NAIC and have participated actively in its long list of legislative and administrative solutions. Several of the important accomplishments of this rather loosely knit organization are:

1. Creation of the valuation committee to establish uniformity in market values of stocks and bonds held by insurance companies
2. Development of the annual statement forms that serve as a basis for insurance company reports to state insurance departments
3. Development of administrative procedures for integrating supervisory activities
4. Drafting of uniform legislation.

The Armstrong Investigation. The period 1875 to 1900 was characterized by growing public resentment against the life insurance industry. Much of the resentment was the result of extravagance by life insurers and their disregard of policyholder rights. During the period, many life insurers failed to remain solvent. The growing public resentment culminated in demands for an investigation of the life insurance industry. In 1905, the New York legislature appointed an Armstrong Committee to examine life insurance companies doing business in New York, with the purpose of reporting to the next session of the legislature on revisions of laws applying to life insurance.

The committee's report was critical, finding a number of instances in which policyholders' interests were disregarded and company practices were extravagant. Policyholders of mutual companies were found to have no meaningful control over company affairs. Agents' commissions and salaries of company officers were believed by the committee to be too high. The committee report also was critical of deferred dividends, a practice followed on some types of coverage that held out the promise of large benefits to a few individuals who continued their policies in force for a given period of time (e.g., 15 years) and survived the period. Similar policies, which had been promoted in Europe during 1670 to 1745, were known as "tontines." By 1900, a growing list of abuses in the deferred dividend system led to the concept being regarded as against the public interest. Cooper (1972) and Jennings and Trout (1982) offer historical perspectives on the issues of tontines and their uses.

The work of the Armstrong Committee was reflected in changes in the New York Insurance Code adopted in 1906 and later years. Because of the importance of New York in financial affairs, the regulations adopted by New York set a pattern for regulations in other states.

The Southeastern Underwriters Association Decision

It would be incorrect to assume that state regulation of insurance was not challenged between 1850 and 1944. The inadequacy of state regulation served as the basis for legislation that was proposed in the U.S. Congress in 1866, 1905, 1906, 1914, 1915, and 1933. In each of these years, sponsors of legislation contended that state insurance regulation was inadequate and that the federal government should exercise control. However, not until the Temporary National Economic Committee (TNEC) conducted its investigations investigations in 1939 and 1940 was a detailed critique of state insurance regulation prepared.

The criticisms developed by the TNEC culminated in an important case involving an action against the Southeastern Underwriters Association alleging that 200 stock fire insurers had violated the Sherman Antitrust Act. Not only did the insurers involved sell over 90 percent of the fire insurance in the six states in which they operated, but by continued agreement and concerted action they were able to fix premium rates and agents' commissions and use boycotts and coercion to force the purchase of a particular insurer's insurance. The following coercive devices were scored in the indictment:

1. Failure to provide reinsurance for noncomplying insurers
2. Withdrawal of agents' licenses when they represented competing insurers
3. Threatening consumers doing business with non-SEUA insurers with boycotts when they attempted to satisfy their other insurance needs
4. Policing by rating bureaus and local boards of insurance agents directed toward the activities of their own members, with boycott and other forms of intimidation imposed to enforce the terms of their programs.

Litigation first developed on the issue of the jurisdiction of the federal government over insurance and was raised on demurrer by the insurers. The demurrer was sustained in the lower courts but reversed by the United States Supreme Court in a 4-to-3 decision. The opinion of the Court, written by Justice Black, distinguished this case from those starting with *Paul v. Virginia* on the basis that the earlier cases involved the validity of state statutes, and that this was the first case squarely presenting the question of whether the commerce clause grants Congress power to regulate insurance when conducted across state lines. The Court determined that the federal government could regulate insurance either as interstate commerce or as a matter that affects interstate commerce and pointed out that the practices attacked under the indictment violated the Sherman Antitrust Act. The trial on the facts never took place since the indictment was dismissed by agreement between the parties after the decision on jurisdiction.

The Consequences of the SEUA Decision

The SEUA decision established federal jurisdiction over the activities of insurance conducted across state lines. This did not mean, however, that state regulation was entirely precluded, since some insurers practices and activities were predominantly intrastate in character and thus subject to only state regulation. As a consequence of this important case, the courts established a dual system of regulation, with the state commissioners enforcing state law with respect to intrastate commerce and opening the possibility of federal regulations to the extent that the insurance business was considered interstate commerce.

The most important federal statutes that might be involved in any interstate regulation of insurance are:

1. *The Sherman Act.* The Sherman Act is designed essentially to prevent restraints to free competition in business transactions. In particular, this act would apply to all cooperative insurance activities. For example, the act would make illegal certain agreements or concerted actions with reference to the making of rates and the apportionment of risks under reinsurance pools. Agreements that relate to the appointment of agents and commission levels would also be subject to question.
2. *The Clayton Act.* Section 14 of the Clayton Act prohibits contracts "where the effects of such activities substantially lessen competition or tend to create a monopoly." The Clayton Act would prohibit in the insurance field certain stock acquisitions, interlocking directorates, unfair price discrimination, and brokerage agreements that may substantially lessen competition.
3. *Robinson-Patman Act.* Section (*a*) of the Robinson-Patman Act prohibits unlawful price discrimination between different purchasers of commodities of like kind and quality that tends to create a monopoly.
4. *Federal Trade Commission Act.* The Federal Trade Commission Act gives the FTC the power to investigate within reason and to restrain unfair trade practices.

In particular, activities of rating bureaus could be construed as price-fixing under the Sherman Act. This possibility created considerable uncertainty about the role of rating bureaus and application of antitrust statutes to pooling of loss data among insurers.

Enactment of the McCarran-Ferguson Act (Public Law 79:15, 15 U.S.C.A. 1012)

As a result of the Southeastern Underwriters case, Congress was petitioned by the insurance business and the state insurance departments to enact clarifying legislation that would continue the jurisdiction of the states over insurance. In attempting to draw the dividing line between the areas of jurisdiction of the federal and state governments, Congress sought to establish by the McCarran-Ferguson Act (Public Law 79:15, most commonly called Public Law 15) the preeminence of state insurance laws. In order to cover any gaps that may exist in inadequate state legislation, however, the act further suggested that "the Sherman Act, the Clayton Act, and the Federal Trade Commission Act would be applicable to the business of insurance to the extent that such business is not regulated by state law" and that agreements to boycott, coerce, or intimidate would be subject to the Sherman Act. The purpose of this provision essentially was to place responsibility on the states to set their regulatory houses in order and to dispel the threat of federal intervention unless state legislation proved inadequate.

Action by the States since 1944

From 1945 to 1960, state regulation of insurance emphasized three objectives: (1) preserving financial solvency of insurers, (2) regulating rates to avoid excessiveness, inadequacy, or unfair discrimination in pricing, and (3) controlling trade practices to encourage fair competition and marketing. During the decade of the 1960s, these objectives were expanded to encompass consumer needs and services that should be rendered by private insurers. Evidence of this expansion appears in a 1968 statement of Richard E. Stewart, then New York State Superintendent of Insurance, who argued that the purpose of insurance regulation is to help insurance consumers "get the most for their money." Within this broad purpose, Superintendent Stewart identified three specific objectives:

1. Insurance must be available to all who want and need it.
2. The insurance product should be of high quality and reliability. Contract provisions should be clear and fair; arbitrary cancellations should be prohibited; and consumers should be protected against insurer insolvencies.
3. Insurance prices should be as low as possible, not subject to large and sudden changes, and fair as among policyholders.

Many of the changes occurring in state-level regulation of insurance since 1960 can be related to these objectives. Some states have become notably aggressive in regulating insurance rates and availability of coverage. State-level initiatives mandating lower insurance prices or increased availability of coverage that have occurred in California and Florida provide evidence of this trend.

To provide insurance for those consumers who cannot purchase automobile and workers' compensation insurance through voluntary channels, many states have required insurers operating in the state to set up some facility for accepting most, if not all of these applicants. The four approaches used in automobile insurance will serve as an example of what can be done. Under an *automobile insurance plan,* each insurer doing business in the state is assigned its proportionate share of applicants who have been rejected by voluntary demands according to the ratio of its premium volume to the total state premium volume. Under a *joint underwriting association,* agents submit these applications to a few insurers who have agreed to service them. All insurers, however, share the expenses and profits or losses. Coverage under both these approaches may be limited to liability insurance in an amount that will satisfy financial responsibility requirements. The rates exceed those charged by insurers in the voluntary market except by those specializing in substandard applicants. In 1972 Maryland established a *state fund* to insure drivers unable to obtain insurance in the voluntary market. The fund is supported by premiums, a tax on insurers, and a charge added to drivers' license fees.

These three approaches have been criticized for (1) the higher-than-normal rates they charge and (2) the stigma attached to the special attention paid to insureds under the plan. Consequently, some states have established *reinsurance facilities* to which insurers can transfer the risk on insureds they prefer not to insure. The insured pays the same premium as other insureds in the same rating class and is unaware of the transfer to the facility. All insurers in the state share the experience of the underwriting pool. Under this approach some special arrangements must be made to prevent insurers from making excessive use of the reinsurance facility.

States also have taken steps to improve availability of coverage in other "troubled" lines. A medical malpractice insurance crisis during the 1970s caused many state legislatures to establish medical malpractice liability joint underwriting associations composed of all insurers writing liability insurance in the state. The U.S. Congress acted to address other problems that arose in providing insurance on properties in urban core areas, flood insurance on real property, and theft insurance. In all three instances, Congress has enacted legislation designed to improve the supply of insurance.

In accordance with and in some cases prior to the mandate given to the states under Public Law 15 to enact legislation that would adequately regulate insurance, most states passed what is referred to as the *Unfair Trade Practices Act for Insurance.* The purpose of this statute is "to prohibit and define unfair methods of competition and unfair and deceptive acts or practices in the business of insurance." Other states, while not enacting the model bill, have laws that have the same effect in regulating insurance advertising and trade practices.

Under these laws, unfair methods of competition are defined as follows:

1. Misrepresentation and false advertising in policy contracts
2. False information in advertising generally
3. Defamation of persons engaged in insurance
4. Boycott, coercion, and intimidation
5. Filing of false financial statements
6. Paying or receiving rebates
7. Unfair rate discrimination

Because of the difficulties in enforcing insurance regulations against out-of-state unlicensed insurers, the National Conference of Commissioners on Uniform State Laws developed a model *Unauthorized Insurers Process Act,* which attempts to give jurisdiction over foreign insurance companies operating within a given state. Section 5 provides that:

> . . . issuance or delivery of a policy of insurance by an unauthorized and unlicensed insurer to citizen or resident of the adopting state should be deemed to constitute designation of that state's insurance official as the attorney in fact upon whom legal process may be served.

The specific practice that this legislation attempted to control was a mail-order insurer operating in unlicensed areas.

Action by the Federal Government since 1944

The interest in federal regulation of insurance did not end with the enactment of Public Law 15. The current system of state regulation continues to be a source of tension between state and federal authorities. Also, the concept of federal regulation of insurance often has been supported by significant portions of the insurance industry. Several noteworthy actions of federal legislators, courts and administrative agencies are listed below:

1. Regulation of variable annuities and other equity-type contracts offered by life insurers, which were held by the Supreme Court as *not* constituting "the business of insurance" (as described by Public Law 15) and therefore not exempt from the Securities and Exchange Act of 1933 and the Investment Company Act of 1940. This decision established jurisdiction of the Securities and Exchange Commission over these types of investments.
2. Creation of the federal riot reinsurance, flood insurance, and crime insurance programs.
3. Three reports on the insurance industry by the Federal Trade Commission staff. The first, completed in 1979, recommended that physicians' organizations not be permitted to control Blue Shield plans. The second, also released in 1979, described rates of return on the savings element in life insurance contracts and urged more complete cost disclosure requirements. The third, which was financed by the FTC, was a study of the economics of insurance discrimination. It was published privately in 1980, not by the FTC, because Congress decided in 1980 to limit FTC insurance studies to those requested by Congressional committees. In 1983 the House Committee on Energy and Commerce directed the FTC to study the advantages of the different types of life insurance policies and the adequacy of consumer information provided by life insurers.
4. A Justice Department report, completed under the Ford Administration, advocating a dual system of regulation. Under this system insurers, at their option, could obtain either a federal or a state charter. Insurers who chose a federal charter would be exempt from state regulation on some but not all aspects of their operations. For example, rates, reserves, and investments would be subject to federal standards, but contract provisions would continue to be regulated by the state. A bill also would have established a Federal Insurance Guaranty Fund to supplement the state guaranty funds described later.
5. A 1979 report by President Carter's National Commission for Review of the Antitrust Laws which recommended repeal of P.L.15. This commission investigated several industries with antitrust immunities, not just insurance. Five options were considered for the insurance industry: (1) dual federal-state charters, (2) outright repeal of P.L.15, (3) a more narrow exemption for joint industry activities, (4) a policy statement favoring open competition over more restrictive rate regulation and a more limited and rigorous interpretation of the present exemption, or (5) the status quo. In its final report, adopted in January, 1979, the Commission recommended that:
   a. The current broad antitrust immunity granted by P.L.15 be repealed. In its place, Congress should enact legislation affirming the lawfulness of a limited number of essential collective activities.
   b. States should place maximum reliance on competition in pursuing their regulatory objectives.
   c. Relevant congressional committees or a special commission established by the President should study further the economic regulation of insur-

ance with special emphasis on equity and discrimination, availability and affordability, and the appropriate role of federal legislation.

6. A 1979 report by the General Accounting Office that questioned the effectiveness of state regulation of insurance, especially in regulating the financial and trade practices of insurers, automobile insurance policies, and insurance availability. The GAO has since then made several other important studies related to risk management and insurance.
7. Passage of the Product Liability Risk Retention Act of 1971 and, what is more important, the Liability Risk Retention Act of 1986 that created risk retention and insurance purchasing groups.
8. A proposed Financial Services Competitive Equity Act that would have permitted banks, through holding company structures, to engage in almost all financial service activities, including insurance marketing and ownership of an insurer.
9. A bill introduced in 1987 that would subject insurers to federal antitrust laws but preserve the power of the states to tax and regulate the industry.

In summary, regulation of the private insurance industry appears to be in a state of flux, with the areas of federal and state activity rapidly changing. The trend of expanding federal activities indicates a narrowing of state jurisdiction and a reformation of the present system of regulation. The lack of clarification of the boundary lines between federal and state jurisdiction, with the overlapping of jurisdiction and interest with regard to the activities of the insurance business point to increased conflict and litigation in the future.

The role of private insurance in the economy is an important one. The challenge that confronts government is the working out of a system of regulation—through effective legislation and effective enforcement—to adequately protect the public interest and to preserve the many benefits of private insurance.

THE STRUCTURE AND FUNCTIONS OF STATE INSURANCE REGULATION

Functional Organization of State Commissions

In every state and the District of Columbia, one or more officials are specifically charged with administering state insurance laws. By far the most common designation given to these officials is *insurance commissioner*. The prevailing administrative organization of the insurance department is that of a single head with one or more subordinates. The most common method of selecting the insurance commissioner is by executive appointment, but other personnel in the department are usually selected under civil service.

General Statutory Powers and Duties

The state insurance commissioner's duties typically consist of such activities as licensing insurers and agents, auditing detailed financial statements submitted annually by insurers, examining insurers periodically with respect to their financial strength and their market conduct, acting on consumer complaints, regulating rates, approving policy language and structure, and managing the conservation or liquidation of insurers with financial difficulties.

Preservation of Insurer Solvency

One major objective of state regulation historically has been the preservation of the financial integrity of insurers. In accomplishing this objective, insurance departments have directed much of their activity toward periodic examination of insurers' financial affairs. Most insurance departments examine insurers at least once every three years. In the interim between examination dates, insurers are required to file detailed annual reports concerning all their financial activities. In addition, the insurance commissioner may at any time choose to conduct special investigations or examinations or to request special information.

As a practical matter, most insurance departments are not adequately staffed to examine the affairs of all insurers, both domestic and foreign, that are doing business within their borders. Therefore, insurance departments feel the greatest responsibility toward careful examination of insurers domiciled within their own state. In addition, they participate with other insurance departments in what is referred to as a convention or zone examination, which enlists examiners from several states for checking the affairs of insurers doing business beyond the borders of the state in which the insurer's office is located. Most states, following an NAIC recommendation, conduct two different examinations: a financial condition examination and a market conduct examination.

Insurance departments also enforce state laws concerning investment activities of insurers. State statues, for example, describe certain types of securities that may be purchased and place restrictions on the distribution within the portfolio. Difficulties may arise in the regulation of investments when insurers do business in states with differing investment statues. Fortunately, the states have followed the principle of recognizing the power that another state has over a corporation to the extent that it does not offend public policy of the recognizing state. Following this rule, an insurer seeking to become licensed in a state other than its home state may be admitted, even though its investments only substantially comply with the general state statutes governing those investments. However, the applying insurer must comply absolutely with its own state's investment statutes.

With respect to other matters, such as the kind of business that can be written and commission or expense limitations, the statute may demand that the insurer conduct its operations within and outside the state in accordance with the standards established for domestic insurers. The reasoning here is that the ability of the insurer to fulfill its obligations to policyholders within the state depends upon its total operations.

Capital Requirements

States also prescribe minimum capital requirements for an insurer to be licensed to write coverage. The required capital provides buffer against adverse developments in the insurer's loss experience and also creates a financial incentive for the insurer's owners to have the insurer managed effectively.

Historically, required capital has been stated as a fixed dollar amount, such as $5 million. In 1992, the NAIC modified the standard for life and health insurers by basing the required amount of capital on the riskiness of the insurer. The NAIC plans to extend the approach, called *risk-based capital (RBC)*, to property-liability insurers effective with financial statements covering operations during calendar 1994. Under RBC, the level of required capital is based on the riskiness of the insurance being written and on the riskiness of the investments owned by the insurer to support the payment of insurance claims.

RBC applied to life and health insurers classifies risk into four categories: asset risk (C-1), insurance risk (C-2), interest rate risk (C-3), and business risk (C-4). Asset risk is exemplified by possible default on mortgages of bonds held by an insurer. Insurance risk is exemplified by possible adverse fluctuation in mortality rates under life insurance contracts issued by an insurer. The vulnerability of the insurer's asset values to changes in market rates of interest exemplifies interest rate risk (C-3). The C-4 risk is intended to reflect other business risks not captured in the other three categories, such as possible assessments from state-level guaranty funds.

Levels of the four categories of risk are determined using an insurer's financial statement entries weighted by a factor representing the riskiness of the item. For example, bonds backed by the U.S. Government may be assigned a factor of zero while residential mortgages 90 days overdue may be assigned a factor of 0.01 if not insured or otherwise guaranteed. The weights applied to the financial statement entries are aggregated to determine a threshold level that determines when the insurer requires further scrutiny. Once the insurer's capital falls below the threshold, decreasing amounts of capital invite increasing levels of regulatory action.[1]

RBC applied to property and liability insurers follows the same basic principles applied to life and health insurers, although the RBC formula is more complex. The RBC formula for property and liability insurers is based on risks classified into six categories: investments between affiliates (R0), fixed income investments, such as bonds (R1), equity investments in other than affiliates (R2), credit risk (R3), loss and loss adjustment reserve risk (R4), and written premium risk (R5). Category R0 reflects intercompany agreements and investments. Categories R1 and R2 reflect risk in assets held purely for investment reasons. Category R3 (credit risk) is exemplified by possible inability to collect on reinsurance coverage. (The issue of reinsurance is discussed later in this chapter.) Categories R4 and R5 reflect the risk in the insurer's underwriting policies.

An alternative to RBC used in the European Community is a cash-flow approach that focuses on the adequacy of the insurer's assets to meet insurance claims as they emerge. This approach bases the assessment on the expected inflows and outflows of the insurer's operations.

---

[1] The NAIC has been working to develop consistent rules for classification and valuation of assets and liabilities. In the June 8, 1994 issue of the *Wall Street Journal,* Scism (1994) describes regulators' concern with the issuance of "surplus notes" by mutual insurers. When issued by an insurer, a surplus note is a promise to make a series of interest and principal payments that is subordinated to all of the insurer's other obligations, including claims on insurance contracts. According to the article, regulators consider the surplus note to be a contribution to capital for the issuing insurer but may allow the acquiring insurer to count surplus notes as investment-grade debt, despite its equity-like features.

Rate Regulation

Insurance commissioners also have authority over the pricing of insurance. Almost half the states have adopted a model property and liability insurance rating law, developed by the NAIC in the late 1940s, which has five important features:

1. All rates must be reasonable, adequate, and not unfairly discriminatory, but these standards are not defined.
2. Rates and rating plans must be filed. The commissioner can request supporting information.
3. The filed rates cannot be used until a specified waiting period, which may be extended by the commissioner, has expired or until the rates have been specifically approved. In practice, the waiting period has sometimes been extended for many months. Because of this provision this rating law is known today as a *prior approval law.*
4. Rates that are permitted to go into effect may be subsequently disapproved.
5. Insurers may belong to or subscribe to the services of a rating organization.

The existence of the model law, however, does not imply uniform regulation. Methods used to regulate insurance rates (and availability) vary among types of coverage and geographic areas. Even within a given state, some types of coverage may be regulated heavily while others experience little regulatory intervention. Depending on the state or type of insurance, one or more of the five provisions of the model rating law (or its equivalent) may become prominent. Nearly every state has at least one type of insurance to which a prior approval law applies, although many states rely on competition among insurers to set rates. States tend to regulate personal coverage, such as health or automobile insurance, more heavily than commercial coverage, although some types of commercial insurance (e.g., medical malpractice insurance) have been subject to episodes of regulation too. Strict regulation of rates often is accompanied by other regulations designed to make coverage more available, such as a requirement that insurers participate in an assigned risk pool or contribute to a fund that subsidizes insurance issued to applicants whose loss potential is high.

State-level Guaranty Associations

Fifty-two jurisdictions (including Puerto Rico) have enacted a guaranty fund statute to protect policyholders from the consequences of an insurer lacking the financial capacity to pay claims. The system of guaranty funds, which began with a life and health guaranty association created in New York in 1941 and covering only domestic insurers, recently became complete. The District of Columbia enacted a statute covering life and health insurance effective July 22, 1992, the last of such statutes.

Although the New York guaranty association existed as early as 1941, the movement toward state-level guaranty associations did not gain momentum until 1970. Public interest in creating some system for protecting policyholders was prompted by a wave of insolvencies among substandard automobile insurers in the late 1960s. By 1980, all but a few states had property-liability guaranty associations. The interest in extending the concept of guaranty associations to life and health insurance came somewhat later; in 1980, for example, fewer than half the states had guaranty fund statutes applying to life and health insurance. The failure of several large life and health insurers during the 1980s and early 1990s prompted the remaining states to enact guaranty fund statutes applying to life and health insurance.

Insurance Regulation and Financial Assessment

Typical Provisions of Property-Liability Guaranty Funds. Most of the guaranty fund statutes are patterned after NAIC model laws, although the statutes differ on issues such as levels of coverage and the basis for assessing the cost of uncovered claims. The typical guaranty fund statute assesses insurers for the cost of claims left uncovered by an impaired or insolvent insurer (New York's property-liability guaranty fund collects funds in advance). Assessments are based on premium volume of the insurer for the covered type of insurance in the state in which the claims arise. Some states segment the assessment using as many as five or six types of insurance, while others make few if any distinctions. Assessments typically are limited to 1 or 2 percent of premiums.

Table 15.1 summarizes available data on provisions of property-liability

TABLE 15.1. Property-Liability Guaranty Association Provisions

	Dollar Limit	Number of Jurisdictions
Explicit Limits of Liability		
Limit on refund of	Unlimited	1
unearned premiums	$100,000	1
	$25,000 per policy	1
	$10,000 per policy	2
	$10,000	4
	less than $10,000	5
	No Coverage	4
Limit applying to	$500,000	1
claims other than	$300,000	36
workers' compensation	$150,000	3
	$100,000	8
	other	1
Other Limitations or Exclusions		
Punitive damage exclusion		8
Net worth limitations		9
Provisions for Segmentation of Assessment		
No segmentation		15
WC, auto, all other		19
Auto, all other		7
Other segmentation		10
Recoupment Provisions		
No recoupment		1
Premium tax offset		17
Recoupment allowed		29
Explicit policy surcharge		4

Source: National Conference of Insurance Guaranty Funds.

guaranty associations. The typical property-liability guaranty fund statute identifies three types of insurance for assessments: workers' compensation, automobile, and all other. When an automobile insurer becomes insolvent, for example, the guaranty association assesses member insurers based on their automobile insurance premium volume. However, the "all other" applies only to types of insurance covered by the statute, not necessarily any other type of insurance. For example, surety bonds and insurance against defects in real estate titles normally are not covered by the property-liability guaranty fund statute. Also, a separate statute applies to life and health insurance.

Other provisions, such as limits of liability and limits on refund of unearned premiums, are summarized in Table 15.1. These limitations are likely to be noteworthy for risk managers of large organizations, although possibly less important than casual analysis might suggest. In general, explicit limits of liability are less likely to apply to workers' compensation than to other types of insurance. Also, the importance of a per-claim limit depends on how the guaranty association interprets the term "claim." While the limit could be important for fire insurance covering $50 million of property, for example, it may be less significant for an organization facing 1000 liability claims of $50,000 each. For large organizations, however, the net worth limitations are likely to be binding. The typical net worth limitation denies coverage for claimants whose net worth exceeds $50 million.

The recoupment provisions allow insurers to recover the cost of their assessments. The most common provision, used in 29 states, allows insurers to consider the cost of assessments when insurance rates are set. Four states allow insurers to levy an explicit surcharge. Seventeen states allow insurers to offset guaranty fund assessments against their liability for the state tax on premium income, effectively transferring the cost of assessments to the state treasury.

Typical Provisions of Life-Health Guaranty Funds. Table 15.2 summarizes explicit limits of liability of life-health guaranty associations. The typical statute covers direct, non–group life, health and annuity contracts, but also applies to certificate holders of group contracts issued by member insurers (e.g., employees covered by an employer-provided group insurance policy). However, aspects of contracts not guaranteed by the insurer, under which the risk is borne by the policyholder are not subject to coverage. An example of an uncovered risk would be a contract to accumulate funds for retirement whose performance is based on a portfolio of common stock, except as to minimum performance guarantees provided by the insurer. Limitations also apply to unallocated annuities, which include guaranteed investment contracts (GICs) held by pension plans. Contracts issued by nonprofit hospital or medical service corporations or health maintenance organizations often are not covered. Pension plans also are not covered, except to the extent that guarantees provided by licensed insurers apply to the plan (e.g., when an employer purchases retirement annuities at the time of an employee's retirement).

Financial Experience. Tables 15.3 and 15.4 provide an overview of the financial experience of guaranty associations during recent periods. The data clearly show a growing number of insurer failures and growing level of assess-

TABLE 15.2. State Life and Health Guaranty Association Explicit Limits of Liability, per Covered Individual or Contract Holder

	Dollar Limit	Number of States
Death benefits	$500,000	2
	$300,000	28
	$250,000	1
	$100,000	1
Cash values	$100,000	12
Present value of annuities	$500,000	2
	$300,000	1
	$100,000	27
Health/disability benefits	$500,000	1
	$300,000	3
	$200,000	2
	$100,000	21
Aggregate benefits	$500,000	3
	$300,000	39
	$250,000	1
	$200,000	1
Unallocated annuities (per contract holder)	$5,000,000	10
	$2,000,000	1
	$1,000,000	5
	Not Covered	20

Source: National Organization of Life and Health Insurance Guaranty Associations.

ments during a period in which the number of guaranty associations was increasing. One might be tempted to infer a cause-effect relationship: attributing an increased number of failures to a lack of financial discipline induced by the increasing presence of guaranty association safety nets. However, one could just as easily, and perhaps more realistically, interpret the growing number of guaranty associations as a response to growing public concern about insurer insolvency. The data also reflect the pure effect of a growing number of guaranty associations; even if the frequency and level of insolvencies remained constant across the time period, the growth in the number of guaranty associations would lead to increasing total assessments and an increase in the number of covered insolvencies.

Although Tables 15.3 and 15.4 show assessments that are large in absolute terms, the assessments still are less than 1 percent of insurer resources. For example, the $574,814,170 life-health guaranty fund assessment shown in Table 15.4 for the year 1991 compares with $263,860,150,000 premium income or $398,699,792,000 total income (including investment) for the entire U.S. life and health insurance industry. As a percentage of these resources, the assessment is, respectively, about 0.218 or 0.144 percent. However, should the levels of insolvencies cause the growth rate of assessments to exceed the growth rate for insurer income, burdens associated with insurer insolvency will increase, leading to higher levels of public concern.

TABLE 15.3. Property-Liability Guaranty Fund Net Assessments and Net Expense, 1981–1991

Year	Number of Failures	Net Assessment	Net Expense
1981	2	49,772,896	41,228,932
1982	3	41,109,087	40,090,893
1983	7	30,565,410	24,733,701
1984	27	107,497,362	37,388,686
1985	26	297,339,284	132,632,384
1986	26	512,044,332	382,434,306
1987	15	902,848,663	497,947,230
1988	21	464,840,383	496,461,598
1989	23	708,045,183	534,279,612
1990	NA*	443,272,668	542,993,523
1991	NA*	429,891,033	427,802,799

*NA, data not available.

Source: National Conference of Insurance Guaranty Funds.

FINANCIAL ASSESSMENT OF PROPERTY-LIABILITY INSURERS

The possibility of insurer insolvency, together with limitations on guaranty fund coverage for large organizations, creates a need for independent financial evaluation of insurers by risk management professionals. Even in the absence of solvency concerns, methods for evaluating financial performance of insurers are useful in selecting providers of insurance coverage to organizations. Analysis of an insurer's financial reports usually focuses on these two issues: *solvency assessment* and *financial performance.*

Although the two areas of analysis overlap, distinct concerns are present in each one. Solvency assessment is concerned with the riskiness of an insurer as

TABLE 15.4. U.S. Life and Health Insurance Companies Declared Insolvent or Impaired and Preliminary Estimate of Insolvency Amount, 1982–1992

Year	Number of Insurers	Preliminary Estimate of Insolvency Amount	Guaranty Fund Assessments
1982	4	19,780,419	8,215,692
1983	8	46,457,066	57,347,772
1984	16	187,226,708	29,549,142
1985	9	36,618,828	24,894,551
1986	13	1,064,103,420	30,206,217
1987	18	107,022,733	85,254,374
1988	13	59,076,039	79,371,852
1989	44	719,116,281	160,652,158
1990	29	249,283,527	152,617,220
1991	35	3,418,134,576	574,814,170
1992	16	113,751,692	not available

Source: National Organization of Life and Health Insurance Guaranty Associations.

related to its financial strength: the likelihood that it will be able to honor future claims on contracts it has written, even under adverse circumstances; its vulnerability to unforeseen events. Issues such as the effects on the insurer of a major windstorm, a worsening of automobile accident rates, or a decline in returns on a category of investment are likely to be central in solvency assessment. Assessment of financial performance shifts the focus to profitability issues: the rate of return to investors, the insurer's returns on investment and returns to policyholders.

The measures used to evaluate these issues, such as loss ratios, combined ratios, reserve deficiencies, and so on can be discussed by persons without any familiarity with their meaning. For example, one only needs to know that the upper limit of the "usual range" for the premium-to-surplus ratio is 300 percent (i.e., 3:1) to be able to evaluate whether an insurer's ratio is within bounds considered normal. However, the meaning and significance of these measures becomes much clearer with some understanding of insurance accounting principles. Appendices 15.1 and 15.2 at the end of this chapter offer a brief introduction to principles of accounting for insurance organizations.

Measures of Performance and Solvency

A few commonly used performance and solvency measures are discussed below. Very few if any of the yardsticks discussed in this chapter are meaningful when examined as isolated measures. These yardsticks are most useful when taken as a group of measures, compared against industry averages or other benchmarks for the type of coverage under examination. Performance ratios vary across types of insurance, with much of the variation due to the composition of services provided by insurers as part of the insurance agreement. Levels of service also can vary among insurers within the same type of coverage, causing their performance ratios to differ for otherwise similar coverage. Earlier, in Chapter 14, Table 14.1 offered data on average performance ratios for U.S. property-casualty insurers during a recent 10-year period as reported in *Best's Aggregates and Averages*. The figures reported in Table 14.1 can serve as benchmark values if more specific information is not available.

The *loss ratio* is perhaps the most widely used measure. The loss ratio usually is calculated as the ratio of *losses incurred* (often, including expenses of settling these losses) to *premiums earned*. Usually the loss ratio (as well as the other ratios discussed below) is expressed as a percent. In concept, the loss ratio represents the portion of the premium returned to policyholders as insurance benefits. If an insurer were to write a group of 1-year fire insurance policies, collecting premiums at the beginning of the year and reimbursing all claims by the end of the year, the loss ratio would be the ratio of claim payments to premiums.

In actuality, the loss ratio usually is an estimate, primarily because the value of incurred losses usually is not known with certainty at the time coverage is provided. Many types of insurance provide coverage for claims that will be paid subject to substantial time lags (e.g., liability insurance), and an insurer writing a portfolio of policies can only estimate the claims that will arise under the coverage yet to be provided under the unexpired policies in the portfolio. Part of the skill in writing insurance is the ability to accurately forecast these claims.

Other things being equal, a high loss ratio implies that a high proportion of the premium is returned to the policyholder as insurance benefits and loss-related services. On the surface, a high loss ratio would appear to indicate favorable insurer performance. However, a persistent high loss ratio also may be associated with financial difficulty when an insurer's claim payments consistently exceed its resources. Also, when losses incurred include the cost of settling claims, a high loss ratio could result when an insurer expends a large amount of resources resisting policyholder claims. As a consequence, loss ratio data tend to be most useful when considered alongside other performance measures discussed below and compared with industry averages for the type of coverage under examination.

The *expense ratio* is another frequently used performance measure. For most insurers, detailed data is available that allows the calculation of many different types of expense ratios, including ratios for claims adjustment expenses. As the term is commonly used, however, the expense ratio usually refers to underwriting expenses. The (underwriting) expense ratio usually is calculated as the ratio of *underwriting expenses incurred* to *premiums written.* In concept, the expense ratio represents the portion of the premium consumed in the act of writing the coverage. Included in these expenses are costs associated with evaluating the insured's exposure to loss, compensation paid to the agent who served in the role of the insurer's intermediary, and the state tax on premium income. Because most of these costs are associated with the act of *writing* coverage (as compared with *providing* coverage), the expense ratio is calculated using premiums written rather than premiums earned.

Other factors held constant, a low expense ratio implies that a small proportion of the premium is consumed in the act of writing coverage, presumably leaving the rest to reimburse claims. Hence a low expense ratio would appear to indicate favorable insurer performance. However, a low expense ratio also may indicate that an insurer allocates few resources to underwriting, a practice that could lead to adverse selection and result in high premiums. Considered in isolation, a high expense ratio is not necessarily a sign of inefficiency. A high expense ratio would be expected to occur when an insurer carefully underwrites coverage. As a consequence of careful underwriting and selection procedures, the group of policyholders eligible for coverage may experience few losses and enjoy premiums that are low. As is true for other measures discussed in this section, expense ratio data tend to be most useful when considered alongside other performance measures and compared with industry averages for the type of coverage under examination.

In medical expense insurance, particularly group coverage in which the primary role of the insurer is to provide claim settlement services (e.g., administrative service only or minimum premium plans), expense ratios may reflect all costs other than claim reimbursement. For these plans, the administrative expense ratio is simple to interpret. Even though the interpretation is straightforward, however, a low expense ratio is not necessarily a sign of efficiency. Some administrative services, such as claim reviews and monitoring of utilization, may improve the efficiency of health care services, hence reducing the total premium.

The *combined ratio* is the sum of the *loss ratio* and the *expense ratio.* Insurer performance reports often include a combined ratio after dividends, which is the sum of the combined ratio and the ratio of policyholder dividends to net premiums earned. The combined ratio is a measure of insurer profitability that does not consider investment income. In concept, a combined ratio above 100 percent implies that estimated insurance claims and administrative expenses exceed premium income. A combined ratio below 100 percent implies that the writing of coverage produced an (estimated) underwriting profit, even without considering investment income.

Combined ratios exceeding 100 percent (i.e., an underwriting loss) are not unusual, particularly in liability insurance. The writing of coverage still may be profitable even with a combined ratio above 100 percent if claim payments are subject to delay. The delay allows the investment of funds allocated to payment of claims, and the resulting investment income offsets the underwriting loss. In types of coverage such as workers' compensation that involve substantial lags between providing coverage and payment of claims, combined ratios exceeding 110 percent may occur.

The *operating ratio* is *combined ratio* less the *net investment income ratio,* which is the ratio of *net investment income* to *net premiums earned.* In concept, the operating ratio measures an insurer's profitability per dollar of premium. If an insurer were to write only a group of 1-year fire insurance policies, collecting premiums at the beginning of the year and reimbursing all claims by the end of the year, the operating ratio would correspond exactly to profitability. For this insurer, an operating ratio in excess of 100 percent would imply a loss, even after investment income is considered. Because the operating ratio considers investment income, it is a more reliable measure of profitability than the combined ratio.

If possible lags in claim payment for the type of coverage are taken into account, a high combined ratio or high operating ratio is an unfavorable sign with respect to an insurer's solvency. A combined ratio below 100 percent implies that an insurer is profitable, although the converse is not necessarily true. An operating ratio above 100 percent is an unfavorable sign, although the type of coverage also should be considered. For types of coverage such as fire insurance, in which claim payment occurs quickly, an operating ratio above 100 percent is an unhealthy sign. For other types of coverage, such as Workers' Compensation, that involve substantial delays in claim payment, operating ratios above 100 percent may occur without necessarily impairing solvency.

The *premium-to-surplus ratio* is the ratio of net premiums written to policyholders' surplus. The premium-to-surplus ratio is a measure of an insurer's leverage, that is, the degree to which the insurer is vulnerable to adverse developments. *Policyholders' surplus* is the difference between an insurer's assets and liabilities, corresponding to *net worth* for other business organizations. Policyholder's surplus represents a cushion against adverse developments: an upper limit to the amount by which liabilities could increase or assets could decrease with the insurer still being able to honor all insurance claims. The premium-to-surplus ratio measures premium volume relative to this cushion.

Other things being equal, a high premium-to-surplus ratio implies that the insurer is vulnerable to adverse developments. For example, a premium-to-surplus ratio of 200 percent implies that policyholder's surplus is one-half of premiums written. At a premium-to-surplus ratio of 200 percent, an operating ratio of 150 percent for only a single year (admittedly, an adverse development) would completely exhaust surplus (i.e., the operating loss is one-half of premiums, the same as the level of surplus). However, if the premium-to-surplus ratio were only 100 percent, two years with an operating ratio of 150 percent would be required to exhaust surplus.

Some analysts consider the *policyholders' surplus ratio*, which is the ratio of surplus to liabilities. The policyholders' surplus ratio is a direct test of the adequacy of assets to meet liabilities estimated at a point in time. Expressed as a percent, the policyholders' surplus ratio is the largest percentage decrease in value of assets that could take place with the insurer still being able to meet estimated claims.

Table 15.5. lists audit ratios used by the NAIC to provide an initial assessment of a property-liability insurer's financial condition. When more than several of an insurer's ratios fall outside the usual range, the insurer is identified by the NAIC as requiring further examination. A number of other ratios and financial tests may be used to supplement the ratios appearing in Table 15.5. The measures discussed in this chapter and listed in Table 15.5 serve as an introduction to possible tests. A discussion of other tests to quantity solvency and performance appears in *Best's Key Rating Guide, Property-Casualty.*

The Issue of Reinsurance

Reinsurance is insurance coverage written between insurance organizations. Most insurance organizations participate in reinsurance markets as either buy-

TABLE 15.5. Insurance Regulatory Information System (IRIS) Audit Ratios

Audit Ratio	Usual Range (percent)
Leverage	
1. Premium-to-surplus	300% or less
2. Change in premiums written from prior year	−33% to 33%
3. Surplus released through reinsurance to adjusted surplus	25% or less
Profitability	
4. 2-Year operating ratio	100% or less
5. Net investment income to average invested assets	5% or more
6. Change in surplus to current-year surplus	−10% to 50%
Liquidity	
7. Liabilities to liquid assets (cash or near-cash)	105% or less
8. Agents' balances or uncollected premiums to surplus	40% or less
Reserve Adequacy	
9. 1-Year reserve development* to surplus	25% or less
10. 2-Year reserve development* to surplus	25% or less
11. Estimated current reserve deficiency† to surplus	25% or less

*Change in estimated liability for losses and expenses from value originally reported.
† Estimated amount by which the current liability for losses and expenses is understated.

ers or sellers, and sometimes as both. In many cases, reinsurance transactions occur between affiliated insurers, such as insurance companies within the same group. A few organizations specialize in writing reinsurance coverage. Broadly speaking, an insurer can be classified as (1) an *originating, direct,* or *primary* insurer if it emphasizes coverage written for the public and for noninsurance organizations, or (2) a *reinsurer* if it emphasizes coverage written for insurers. Many direct insurers also write coverage for other insurers as well as originating coverage.

Reinsurance can serve a number of purposes, but the most important for assessing an insurer's solvency are related to pooling and diversification. Other uses of reinsurance are to retire completely or in part (in an area or a line of business, for example) from the insurance business, to transfer insurance from one member of a group of insurers to another, and to obtain advice from an outsider (the reinsurer) with respect to a particular insured or a new line of business. The major contribution of reinsurance to insurer solvency, however, is the more widespread distribution of resources for reimbursing loss it makes possible. Reinsurance can reduce an insurer's vulnerability to a single event, thereby improving the range of coverage and other services that the insurer is able to provide policyholders. For example, the managers of an originating insurer may believe that writing policies providing coverage over $100,000 is not prudent considering the insurer's financial resources. Reinsurance for coverage in excess of $100,000 allows the insurer to write coverage with larger limits rather than forcing policyholders to seek coverage elsewhere.

Another possibility is related to geographic concentration: in the absence of reinsurance, an insurer may be reluctant to continue writing coverage in a limited geographic area because of vulnerability to a catastrophic event, such as a hurricane or large fire. Reinsurance providing coverage when losses in a single event exceed the primary insurer's financing capability allow the insurer to specialize in serving a limited geographic area. Such specialization allows the insurer to develop detailed knowledge and familiarity with the local market, the benefits of which would not be likely to develop in the absence of reinsurance.

A standard reinsurance contract does not exist, and reinsurance transactions are largely unregulated. As a consequence, parties to a reinsurance transaction are free to determine policy terms and conditions, and coverage can take many forms.

At one extreme is *facultative reinsurance,* which is arranged on a particular exposure. The advantages of this approach are the opportunities for tailor-made protection and for underwriting advice from the reinsurer. The disadvantages are the delay, the possible failure to obtain coverage, and the administrative expenses involved. At the other extreme is the *automatic treaty,* under which the ceding insurer (the insurer for whom coverage is provided) agrees to pass on to the reinsurer all business included within the scope of the treaty, the reinsurer agrees to accept this business, and the terms—for example, the premium rates and the method of sharing the insurance and the losses—of the agreement. The advantages and disadvantages are the counterparts of those cited for facultative reinsurance. An example of an arrangement between these two extremes is the *facultative treaty,* under which the terms are set but neither the ceding insurer nor the reinsurer is obligated to participate in the arrangement with respect to any particular business.

Reinsurance agreements may distribute the insurance and the losses in several different ways. Four of these distribution methods are described for illustrative purposes:

1. Under a *quota-share* split, the insurance and the loss are shared according to some preagreed percentage. For example, if a $100,000 policy is written and the agreed split is 50-50, the reinsurer assumes one-half of the liability; the insurer and the reinsurer each pay one-half of any loss.

2. Under a *surplus-share* agreement, the reinsurer accepts a portion (possibly 100 percent) of the insurance in excess of a stated amount, and the loss is prorated according to the amount of insurance assumed. For example, if the reinsurer accepts 100 percent of the coverage in excess of a $100,000 stated amount, the reinsurer's liability under a $200,000 policy would be ($200,000 − $100,000)/$200,000 or 1/2 of any loss. Under a $100,000 contract the reinsurer would accept no liability. Under a $160,000 contract the reinsurer would pay 3/8 of any loss.

3. Under an *excess-loss* arrangement, the reinsurer agrees to pay that portion of the loss incurred under an individual contract in excess of some specified amount, such as $100,000.

4. *Catastrophe* reinsurance, like excess-loss reinsurance, requires the reinsurer to pay excess losses, but in this instance the losses are those incurred by the insurer as a result of a single event under all contracts covered under the agreement. For example, the reinsurer might be obligated to pay the amount by which total losses incurred by an insurer in a single hurricane exceed $1 million, after adjusting for losses reinsured in other ways.

Variations are possible under all these methods. For example, the reinsurer may pay only 80 percent of the excess loss under the excess-loss method. In all lines and under all arrangements, the reinsurer may limit the maximum amount for which it is responsible. For example, catastrophe reinsurance may be purchased in layers. Under the first layer, the reinsurer might pay 80 percent of the first $10 million of losses in excess of $500,000. Under the second layer, the reinsurer might pay 90 percent of the losses in excess of $10,500,000.

FINANCIAL ASSESSMENT OF LIFE AND HEALTH INSURERS

The financial assessment of life and health insurers can be an important topic to risk managers for at least three reasons. First, life and health insurers commonly administer health benefit programs provided by organizations to their employees. Second, investment products offered by life and health insurers are often used to fund pension programs applying to employees. Third, deferred compensation and supplemental pensions applying to executives often are funded by life insurance. The financial performance of the insurer and the likelihood of the insurer being able to honor claims can be an important issue, as the funding burden often rests on the risk manager's organization.

As is true in property-liability insurance, financial assessment of life and health insurers focuses on two issues: *solvency assessment* and *financial performance*. Unfortunately, the prevalence of long-term coverage in life insurance and the variety of investment-related products and services offered by the life and health insurance industry make single-period performance measures, such as a loss ratio, impractical except for short-term coverage, such as medical expense insurance or short-term group life insurance.

An example can be used to illustrate the point. Effective in 1988, some (but not all) states discontinued the required reporting by health insurers of "premium equivalents" on ASO and minimum premium health insurance plans. These plans, described earlier in Chapter 10, are agreements to provide claims-adjustment services, with the health insurer drawing payments in favor of health care providers from an account maintained by the sponsor of the health insurance pan. The *premium equivalents* are the amounts that would have been paid as premiums to the insurer if the coverage had been standard insurance.

The reasoning behind the accounting change, which was adopted in some states, is that few if any of the insurer's assets are at risk in these financing agreements, especially under the ASO plan. However, the nonreporting of premium equivalents makes the determination of expense-to-premium or benefit-to-premium ratios impossible, except at the level of the individual plan. Presumably, the plan sponsor is provided reports that allow these performance measures to be calculated, but these performance measures are hidden from the public generally. The use of ASO and minimum premium plans grew rapidly during the 1980s and early 1990s, in part because expenses under these plans were lower than under standard insurance. The accounting change caused data that would have reflected favorably on the performance of the health insurance industry to become less accessible to the public.

If the data on premium equivalents were incorporated into the insurer's financial statements, they would be useful only in the context of the particular type of coverage. Also, if an insurer were writing minimum premium health plans along with standard life insurance coverage, the level of security implied by asset holdings of a given amount and composition would be unclear unless assets were segregated according to type of coverage. A similar observation would apply to a life insurer writing both guaranteed investment contracts (GICs) as well as standard life insurance; both types of contracts would need to be considered in evaluating the level of security implied by an investment portfolio of a given size and quality. The risk-based capital (RBC) rules that were discussed earlier in this chapter are an effort to base an evaluation of an insurer's riskiness on these types of distinctions.

Under long-term contracts written by life and health insurers, liabilities may develop unfavorably relative to levels estimated when the coverage was written. Such adverse developments are likely to occur gradually, possibly as a consequence of the coverage being underpriced. Gradual development implies the opportunity for corrective action, such as adjustment of dividends on participating contracts and pricing adjustments on contracts issued after the adverse developments become apparent. However, the same type of generalization does not apply to adverse developments for the insurer's investments. Investment returns on marketable securities can move quickly enough to make an insurer unable to provide guaranteed returns, particularly on long-term coverage. As a consequence, financial assessment of life and health insurers often focuses on the quality and composition of the insurer's investment portfolio, the evaluation of which easily constitutes an entire textbook. Finance texts such as

Brealey and Myers (1991) offer significant insights into methods for the type of evaluation.

Performance Assessment

Published data are available to evaluate returns from long-term life insurance coverage. These data may take the form of a direct comparison of guaranteed returns or other guarantees provided under life insurance policies. They also may take the form of cost comparisons across stated holding periods, preferably in comparison to a benchmark investment. The *interest-adjusted cost* method is perhaps the most widely-used, and has been endorsed by the NAIC and a life insurance industry committee. Two indexes are in common use: an interest-adjusted surrender cost index and an interest-adjusted payments index. Both are calculated as a rate per $1,000 of coverage to allow comparison across policies.

The *interest-adjusted surrender cost index* evaluates the coverage over a fixed holding period, such as 20 years. The following illustration assumes a fixed-premium contract providing a cash surrender value at the end of the 20-year holding period (cash surrender values are explained later in Chapter 18). For this contract, the interest-adjusted surrender cost index is the difference between the annual premium and the annual deposit that would yield the surrender value and the stream of dividends paid under the contract. The motivation for the index is to calculate the difference between the amount paid for the coverage and the value accumulated under the contract, converted to an equivalent annual amount.

Assume that the annual premium per $1000 of coverage for a life insurance policy is $13.00, the contract pays a dividend of $3.00 at the end of each year, and the cash surrender value is $270.00. Using an assumed interest rate of 5 percent, the annual deposit required to yield the $270.00 cash value at the end of 20 years is $270.00/34.719, the 34.719 being the amount accumulated at the end of 20 years from a $1.00 annual deposit at the beginning of each year. The $3.00 dividend received at the end of each year would accumulate to ($3.00)(33.066) at the end of 20 years, so the annual deposit required to produce this amount would be ($3.00)(33.066)/34.719. Hence the 20-year interest-adjusted surrender cost index for this policy is:

$$\$13.00 - \frac{(\$3.00)(33.066) + \$270.00}{34.719}, \text{ or } \$2.37.$$

The *interest-adjusted payments index* does not consider the surrender value but takes dividends into account, so it represents the difference between the annual premium and the deposit required to yield the stream of dividends. The motivation for the payments index is to calculate the difference an equivalent annual deposit that would have been required to maintain the coverage for the 20-year period. Continuing with the example developed above, the 20-year interest-adjusted payments index is:

$$\$13.00 - \frac{(\$3.00)(33.066)}{34.719}, \text{ or } \$10.14.$$

SOURCES OF INFORMATION

383

CHAPTER 15
Insurance Regulation
and Financial
Assessment

The last decade has seen an explosion in access to data and financial information. Risk managers have access to a wide array of data and analysis, some of which may be retrieved from continuously maintained and updated data sources over telephone lines or other means of electronic transmission (i.e., "on line" sources). For example, the A. M. Best Company maintains an on-line data service based on data provided to state insurance departments which it offers to subscribers for a fee. A. M. Best also provides these data in tape format. Because these data are reported to insurance regulators and are, in most cases, public documents, similar data are available in the state insurance departments in printed rather than on-line format. The printed format is not as convenient for analysis as data in machine-readable form, so insurance department data would most likely be restricted to a few specific questions or issues. Also, state insurance departments are not equipped to respond to requests for extensive data.

However, the continuing rapid expansion of data storage and processing capabilities implies that access to insurer financial data on a large-scale basis could occur within a few years. Such access would be likely to increase the value of analytical skills for risk managers and for consulting services that provide financial analysis.

Analysis of insurer financial strength and performance also is available in published form. A. M. Best Company has an extensive array of publications in this area, although their one-time dominance in this field has been challenged significantly by other rating services provided by financial rating organizations such as Moody's, Standard & Poor's and Weiss Research, Inc. Private rating services available through insurance brokerage houses or financial consultants are another source of information whose availability is likely to expand. Several widely distributed published sources of insurer rating information are listed below.

Best's Key Rating Guide, Life-Health provides a quantitative assessment of life insurers' profitability, leverage, and liquidity. *Best's Insurance Reports, Life-Health* presents each year the background history of most life and health insurers, the types of coverage they write, the states in which they operate, and detailed financial data. Each insurer is assigned a financial size category depending upon the net worth and one of six policyholder ratings based on Best's opinion of the relative financial strength of that insurer. The six policyholder ratings are A+ and A (Excellent), B+ (Very Good), B (Good), C+ (Fairly Good), and C (Fair). The rating is based on Best's assessment and weighting of five factors: (1) competent underwriting, (2) cost control and efficient management, (3) adequate reserves for undischarged liabilities of all types, (4) net resources adequate to absorb unusual shock, and (5) soundness of investments. Because of the large proportion of insurers receiving high grades, the major value of these ratings is that they tell the risk manager what insurers he or she should probably avoid. The ratings can also prove useful when a risk manager is approached by an insurer about which he or she knows little or nothing. If this insurer has a C grade, the risk manager would hesitate to consider it. On the other hand, the insurer may be graded A+, in which case the risk manager would be willing to investigate the insurer further. Comparative comments are also made on investment yields, expenses, mortality costs, lapses and surrenders, and net costs. *Best's Flitcraft Compend* indicates principal policy provisions, premium and dividend rates, and settlement option values used by most life insurers. Interest-adjusted cost data are also provided on both a payments and a surrender cost basis. *Best's Settlement Options* contains tables of settlement option values and, in addition, describes in detail the practices of most insurers with respect to settlement options. *Who Writes What in Life and Health Insurance* lists the contracts and underwriting practices of leading life and health insurers. *Time Saver for Health Insurance* analyzes policies and rates of health insurers.

Best's Aggregates and Averages, Life-Health reports composite data on the U.S. life insurance industry and on segments of the industry. The *Argus Chart of Health Insurance* provides data on individual and group health insurance written by commercial insurance companies. Some state insurance departments also prepare reports on health insurance written within the state. These reports may be the only convenient source of data on regional organizations, such as health maintenance organizations or other prepaid health care plans.

In property and liability insurance, *Best's Key Rating Guide, Property-Casualty* occupies a position analogous to *Best's Key Rating Guide, Life-Health* position in life and health insurance. The *Key Rating Guide* provides a quantitative assessment of property-liability insurers' profitability, leverage, and liquidity. Similarly, *Best's Insurance Reports, Property-Casualty* occupies a position analogous to *Best's Insurance Reports, Life-Health. Who Writes What* is analogous to *Who Writes What in Life and Health Insurance. Best's Aggregates and Averages* reports important financial data for leading insurers and the industry. The *Fire, Casualty, and Surety Bulletins* provide up-to-date information on leading property and liability insurance coverages and important legal interpretations.

In 1983 Standard & Poor's Corporation started an Insurance Rating Service that rates the claims-paying ability of over 225 insurers engaged in life insurance, property insurance, liability insurance, mortgage insurance, bond insurance, and reinsurance. Insurers are placed in one of eight categories, ranging from AAA to D, with a plus or minus sign sometimes being added. The rating depends upon seven factors: industry risk, insurer characteristics, underwriting performance, investment activities, earnings protection, leverage, and financial flexibility.

Other sources of information are contacts with individual insurers and agents who can supply specimen contracts and premium information; contacts with other insureds, especially those facing the same problems; meetings such as those sponsored by the Risk and Insurance Management Society; and the insured's personal experience.

Of the three factors to be considered in selecting an insurer, service is not only the most difficult factor to evaluate but also the one about which objective information is most scarce. Some state insurance departments report how promptly individual insurers pay workers' compensation claims; a few report the proportion of claims contested for each insurer. At least one department, New York, has ranked automobile insurers according to the number of complaints settled in favor of the insured relative to their automobile insurance premiums written. *The National Underwriter,* a leading insurance weekly, presents annually for a long list of automobile insurers the ratio of suits outstanding to premiums earned.

Although useful, this published information is limited to selected lines, types of service, or times. The risk manager can consult his or her counterparts in other organizations, but the value of their opinions depends upon their objectivity, their experience, and the similarity of their risk problems to those of the manager making the investigation.

APPENDIX 15.1. AN INTRODUCTION TO PROPERTY-LIABILITY INSURANCE ACCOUNTING

Financial statements filed with insurance regulators nearly always are based on *statutory accounting principles (SAP)*, as contrasted with *generally accepted accounting principles (GAAP)* used by most other businesses. Financial statements using GAAP are less biased toward conservatism than those using SAP, so financial statements using GAAP more closely reflect the "true" financial conditions (in the sense of a market value) of the business. Under SAP, in contrast, solvency concerns are paramount. The objective of SAP is to present a conservative assessment of an insurer's financial condition. Normally, financial statements prepared using SAP tend to overstate liabilities and to understate assets. Although these misstatements result in a conservative assessment of the insurer's financial condition, they may not improve the effectiveness of solvency assessment methods because they apply in the same way across all insurers of a given type. For example, if the rankings of 10 insurers using financial statements prepared under SAP are identical to the rankings under GAAP, either set of principles is equally effective for ranking the 10 insurers.

Tables 15.6 to 15.8 present financial statements of a representative property-liability insurance company. The figures in these tables, which are based on data in *Best's Aggregates and Averages, Property-Casualty*, 1992 edition, approximate what would be the entries for a property-liability insurer that was near-average in all respects for the insurers on which the Best's report is based. Entries that normally are a small fraction of the total (e.g., less than 1 percent) have been omitted. Any correspondence with the figures for any existing property-liability insurer is entirely coincidental, although the figures reflect entries that would be typical for the industry.

The Balance Sheet. Table 15.6 is a balance sheet for the representative property-liability insurer. Many of the assets appearing on the left-hand side of the balance sheet, particularly those appearing in the first group (bonds, preferred stock, common stock, mortgage loans short-term investments, and accrued interest), require little discussion except as to valuation techniques. These assets consist of marketable securities (or other investments that could be sold), issued by entities unaffiliated with the insurer. These assets are held primarily for investment purposes and are, for the most part, marketable. The valuation of these assets can be fairly straightforward. If stated in terms of market values, these amounts would represent the cash that could be obtained if the assets were sold to satisfy the claims arising from policies sold by the insurer.

However, SAP may prescribe valuation methods that do not accurately capture market values (e.g., amortized cost for bonds), so the reported values may misstate the cash-equivalent of the investment portfolio. The possibility of mis-

TABLE 15.6. Representative Property-Liability Insurance Company Balance Sheet

Assets (000)		Liabilities and Surplus (000)	
Bonds	154,299	Loss Reserves	106,361
Preferred Stock	4,111	Loss Adj. Exp. Res.	20,400
Common Stock	24,377	Commissions, Taxes, Expenses	3,196
Mortgage Loans	2,584	Unearned Premium Reserve	34,904
Short-term Investments	10,734	Reinsurance Funds	3,492
Accrued Interest	3,313	Other Liabilities	5,191
Total	199,418	Total Liabilities	173,544
Investment in Affiliates	12,064	Paid-up Capital	2,859
Premium Balances	20,587	Assigned Funds	29,072
Reinsurance Funds	4,284	Unassigned Funds	33,420
Other Assets	2,542	Policyholders' Surplus	65,351
Total	238,895	Total	238,895

Source: Computed from data in *Best's Aggregates and Averages: Property-Casualty,* 1992 edition.

statement has prompted insurance regulators to request supplemental schedules detailing market values of these assets. As a practical matter, the trade in some of these investments may be so thin (e.g., for some mortgages or tax-exempt bonds) that some accounting rule may provide a reasonable alternative to market valuation.

The second group of assets (investment in affiliates, premium balances, reinsurance recoverable, and other assets) also represents resources to satisfy claims against the insurer, but the valuation of these assets for the purpose of satisfying claims is less certain. Investment in affiliates is securities issued by an entity closely related to the insurer, such as insurers held by the same holding company. The valuation of securities issued by related insurers is less certain than other securities because problems in one member of a group of affiliated insurers may imply problems with other members of the group. Premium balances are amounts owed the insurer, but not yet received, for policies already issued. For example, premium balances would include premiums paid to insurance agents that have not yet been forwarded to the insurer (if uncollected for more than 90 days, insurance regulators will not allow agents balances to be considered). Reinsurance funds include recoveries under reinsurance contracts, for which claims have been filed but payment has not yet been received. Much of the amount reported as reinsurance funds is likely to be claims with affiliated companies, the valuation of which is less certain than claims filed with unaffiliated insurers.

The total of assets on statements filed with insurance regulators reflects only *admitted assets,* which are assets insurance regulators will consider in determining the insurer's level of security. Reinsurance contracts written by an unlicensed reinsurer, for example, would not be considered by an insurance regulator because recoveries from contracts issued by an unlicensed reinsurer are uncertain when compared with contracts issued by affiliated companies that are licensed. Other investments whose performance is uncertain also may not be considered.

Liabilities, which appear as entries on the right-hand side of the balance sheet, require some elaboration. The first group of entries (loss reserves; loss adjustment expense reserves; reserves for commissions, taxes, and expenses; unearned premium reserves; reinsurance funds; and other liabilities) primarily are *reserves*. A *reserve* is an estimated future liability; an accounting recognition of a payment that will occur some time in the future. Because insurance claims constitute most of an insurer's liabilities and most of these claims will arise in the future, reserves constitute nearly all of the liabilities of a property-liability insurer. As is evident from Table 15.6, loss reserves constitute almost two-thirds of liabilities.

Loss reserves represent the estimated value of future insurance claims under policies already written, including claims that have not yet been reported to the insurer (i.e., incurred-but-not-reported, or IBNR claims). Historically, property-liability insurers have reported reserves net of reinsurance. For example, if an insurer writes a group of property insurance policies on which it expects $5 million in claims but reinsures 80 percent of claims, $1 million is reported as the reserve. The reserve for loss adjustment expenses is the estimated level of expenses required to settle these claims. Entries for loss reserves and the reserve for loss adjustment expenses are advance recognition of future costs whose amounts only can be estimated.

The entry for commissions, taxes, and expenses is a recognition of sales commissions, taxes, and other expenses owed on policies already written. For example, this liability would include amounts owed to sales agents for coverage they have written but for which the commission has not yet been paid. The unearned premium reserve is a liability recognizing collection of insurance premiums in advance of the period of coverage. Formally, the unearned premium reserve is the required refund to policyholders if the insurer were to cancel every policy in force; the portion of the premium corresponding to the unexpired term of coverage. For example, the unearned premium reserve on an annual-premium policy that has been in force for three months is 3/4 of the premium, as 1/4 of the premium has been "earned."

Reinsurance funds (when appearing as a liability) includes the liability for claims under reinsurance contracts written by the insurer where a claim has been filed but not yet paid. Much of this amount is likely to be claims from affiliated companies, as was the case when reinsurance funds is shown as an asset. The discussion of Table 15.8 appearing below clarifies this issue of reinsurance with affiliated insurers.

The second group of entries on the right-hand side of the balance sheet (paid-up capital, assigned funds, and unassigned funds) contains the components of *policyholders' surplus,* one important measure of an insurer's level of security. Policyholders' surplus is the difference between assets and liabilities, analogous to *net worth* reported for other business organizations. In concept, policyholders' surplus is a cushion against adverse developments. Subject to the above-noted qualifications as to valuation and others as to reinsurance appearing below, policyholders' surplus represents an upper limit to the amount by which liabilities could increase or assets could decrease with the insurer still being able to honor all insurance claims.

Within policyholders' surplus, the distinction between assigned funds and unassigned funds is related to whether a purpose has been designated. For example, a portion of the surplus may be held as a cushion against the development of adverse trends in loss experience or as a buffer against a possibly catastrophic event.

The Summary of Operations. Tables 15.7 and 15.8 provide a summary of the insurer's financial activities during the year. Table 15.7 is a summary of operations, including an income statement, flow-of-funds statement and the associated change in policyholders' surplus and change in funds. Table 15.8 is a summary of underwriting expenses, reinsurance written (assumed), and reinsurance acquired (ceded). Reinsurance is coverage exchanged between insurers, as contrasted with direct or primary coverage written for noninsurance organizations and individuals. Reinsurance assumed consists of coverage written on behalf of other insurers, while reinsurance ceded consists of coverage written by other insurers on behalf of the ceding insurer.

In Table 15.7, the *income statement* and associated *change in policyholders' surplus* constitute the left-hand side of the exhibit. Income statement entries are based on *accrual* methods of accounting; the effect of an activity on the income statement is recognized when the right to receive a payment, or the liability to

TABLE 15.7 Representative Property-Liability Insurance Company Summary of Operations

Income Statement (000)		Flow of Funds Statement (000)	
Premiums Earned	91,684	Premiums Collected	91,796
Losses Incurred	62,787	Losses Paid	56,865
Loss Expense Incurred	11,587	Loss Expense Paid	10,232
Underwriting Expense Incurred	24,403	Underwriting Expense Paid	24,159
Dividends to Policyholders	1,148	Dividends to Policyholders	1,102
Net Underwriting Income	− 8,241	Funds from Underwriting	− 562
Investment Income	15,181	Investment Income	15,089
Investment Expense	1,088	Investment Expense	944
Income Taxes	1,823	Income Taxes	1,571
Net Operating Income	4,029	Funds from Operations	12,012
Change in Policyholders' Surplus		Change in Funds	
Net Operating Income	4,029	Funds from Operations	12,012
Realized Capital Gains	1,983	Realized Capital Gains	1,983
Unrealized Capital Gains	5,542	Capital and Surplus Paid In	871
Capital and Surplus Paid in	818	Capital and Surplus Paid Out	− 2,540
Capital and Surplus Paid Out	− 2,517	Other Changes in Funds	695
Increase in Policyholders' Surplus	9,855	Change in Funds	13,021

Source: Computed from data in *Best's Aggregates and Averages: Property-Casualty*, 1992 edition.

make a payment, becomes fixed and the amount can be determined. For example, premiums earned are premiums attributable to coverage already provided. On a 1-year advance-premium policy that has been in force for 5 months, 5/12 of the premium is earned.

Losses incurred is an estimate of insurance claims that are attributed to coverage provided during the year. Although these claims are recognized and the amount of liability has been determined, actual payment may be delayed, perhaps significantly (e.g., a lag of 5 to 10 years). The actual delay, which is not evident from data in the summary of operations, depends on the type of coverage under which the claim arises. Substantial delays can occur in some types of liability insurance (this delay often is called the "long tail"). However, payment of claims under property insurance usually occurs quickly. In some cases such as workers' compensation and in determining federal taxable income, estimated insurance claims are discounted to a present value. In most cases, estimated claims are recognized at the expected nominal value at time of payment ("ultimate" value).

Loss adjustment expenses incurred is an estimate of expenses involved in settling the above-recognized claims. This amount is an estimate of a future payment rather than an amount actually paid during the year. In contrast, *underwriting expenses incurred* is the expense associated with underwriting activities during the year, most of which are amounts that have been paid rather than estimated payments. Dividends to policyholders, which are accounted for as a return of premium, are the final entry used to determine *net underwriting income.*

In Table 15.7, net underwriting income is negative, which means that estimated outlays for the representative insurer exceeded premium income. The underwriting loss is offset by investment income, the two entries immediately following (investment income and investment expense). After subtracting an allowance for the estimated federal income tax liability, *net operating income* is the final entry. As shown in Table 15.7, investment income more than offsets the underwriting loss, leading to a positive net operating income.

The effect of income-statement figures on policyholders' surplus is detailed in the statement of change in policyholders' surplus that appears below the income statement. In essence, the statement of change in policyholders' surplus provides the connection between the income statement and the year-to-year changes in the balance sheet. Net operating income is adjusted to reflect investment activities not reported as part of investment income, primarily capital gains realized on securities sold, and unrealized capital gains on securities that the insurer continues to hold. A second adjustment reflects changes in capital, such as additional contributions from investors and surplus distributed to stockholders as dividends. The change in policyholders' surplus is the net value of these entries.

The right-hand side of Table 15.7 is the flow-of-funds statement and associated change in funds. While entries on the income statement were developed using accrual accounting methods, entries on the flow-of-funds statement are developed on a cash basis. Hence, entries on the flow-of-funds statement more closely reflect effects of the insurer's activities on its cash position. For example, the entry for losses paid represents actual claim payments during the year, regardless of when the event giving rise to the liability for payment occurred.

An example may help to make the distinction clear. On the insurer's balance sheet, the loss reserve represents the total liability for future claim payments. Payment of a claim reduces the liability, while writing new coverage causes a new liability for losses to accrue. Assuming that the insurer's estimated liabilities faithfully reflect ultimate claim payments, the difference between loss reserves at the end of two adjacent years is identical to losses incurred during the year, less the value of losses paid during the year.

Table 15.8 completes the summary of operations by providing a summary of underwriting expenses and reinsurance. Data in Table 15.8 offer a means of evaluating underwriting activities and assessing the magnitude of reinsurance activities relative to the insurer's other operations. The accounting for reinsurance transactions requires an explanation of terminology. The entries alongside the row designated *direct* require the least explanation. Direct premiums written represents premiums received by or on behalf of the insurer for coverage written for noninsurance organizations and individuals during the year. The commissions on direct business represents compensation paid to the insurer's representatives who placed this coverage in force (or, if not yet paid, the recognition of the liability for payment).

As explained earlier, reinsurance is coverage written between insurance organizations. When an insurer purchases reinsurance, it *cedes* the liability to the reinsurer, which *assumes* the liability of the ceding insurer's behalf. Hence, *reinsurance assumed* entails liabilities accepted from other insurers, while *reinsurance ceded* entails liabilities transferred to other insurers and reinsurers.

TABLE 15.8. Representative Property-Liability Insurance Company Summary of Underwriting Expenses and Reinsurance (000)

	Premiums Written	Commissions
Direct	97,247	10,351
Reinsurance Assumed	59,548	8,095
Reinsurance Ceded	(64,659)	(8,834)
Contingent		600
Net (Including Contingent)	92,136	10,212
		Other Underwriting Expenses
Salaries		4,606
Taxes, Licenses, Fees		3,168
Other Expenses		6,417
Total Underwriting Expense Incurred		24,403
Reinsurance Assumed		
From Affiliates	47,459	
From Non-Affiliates	12,089	
Reinsurance Ceded		
To Affiliates	48,430	
To Non-Affiliates	16,229	

Source: Computed from data in *Best's Aggregates and Averages: Property-Casualty,* 1992 edition.

Often, the nominal value of the liability is greater than the payment required for the reinsurance. For example, an insurer that cedes a newly written policy transfers the liability for this policy (the unearned premium reserve) to the reinsurer. If the reinsurer assuming the obligation had sold the policy directly to the ultimate customer, it would have incurred underwriting expenses when the coverage was put into force. If the policy is priced correctly, the fact that it already has been underwritten means that the nominal value of the liability overstates its true value. The insurer assuming the obligations recognizes this overstatement through a *ceding commission,* a payment to the ceding insurer.

Typically, the ceding insurer remits the net amount: the ceded amount less the ceding commission. Hence, the ceding commission is the amount by which the transaction increases the ceding insurer's surplus, that is, liabilities decrease by the amount of reinsurance ceded but assets decrease by only the ceded amount less the ceding commission. Although, in the above example, the ceding commission reflects underwriting activities of the originating insurer, other factors also can affect the ceding commission. For example, a substantial time lag until claim payments reduces the value of assets required to fund the payments, which would be expected to increase the ceding commission. Ceding commissions are negotiated between the reinsurer and the originating insurer, so parties to the transaction are free to set the commission at a level they believe appropriate.

For reinsurance assumed, the entry under premiums written reflects liabilities accepted by the insurer, while the entry under commissions reflects the ceding commissions payable to the insurers from whom the liability was accepted. The entries for reinsurance ceded are complementary. For example, the commissions on reinsurance ceded *reduce* the payment to the reinsurer. The entry under contingent commissions includes amounts payable to reinsurers contingent on their experience under coverage they have assumed.

The bottom half of Table 15.8 shows that most of the representative insurer's reinsurance activity is with affiliated insurers. This type of loss sharing is typical between members of the same group. For example, Table 15.8 shows that only about 20 percent of the reinsurance assumed is from unaffiliated insurers, leaving the remaining 80 percent as liabilities accepted from affiliates. A similar finding applies to reinsurance ceded; about 25 percent was ceded to unaffiliated insurers, with the remaining 75 percent ceded to affiliates.

In Table 15.8, reinsurance assumed is approximately 61 percent of direct premiums, while reinsurance ceded is about 66 percent of direct premiums. Even though the magnitude of reinsurance transactions is large relative to direct premiums, for an average insurer the ceding and assuming transactions will net approximately to zero. Certainly the transactions between affiliated insurers will net to zero if the affiliated group reports consolidated figures. The slight excess of reinsurance ceded over reinsurance assumed implies that the average insurer is a net consumer of reinsurance supplied from outside the U.S. insurance industry.

Proposed Changes in Accounting for Reinsurance. The accounting for reinsurance transactions has been subject to controversy, especially with respect to multi-period coverage. In late 1992, the Financial Accounting Standards

Board (FASB) enacted FAS 113 which applies to insurer financial statements using GAAP starting in 1993. FAS 113 imposes new standards for reporting reinsurance transactions. Initially the standards apply only to publicly held insurers that are required to report to investors using GAAP. However, many features of FAS 113 are likely to become incorporated into SAP if they reveal important data.

Following is a brief summary of a few significant features of FAS 113. Indefinite-duration contracts are likely to be accounted for as deposit arrangements rather than reinsurance. Accounting for this type of contract as a deposit would require the ceding insurer to recognize a loss at the time it becomes known rather than spreading the effect of the loss over several accounting periods covered by the reinsurance agreement.

For a contract to be considered reinsurance under FAS 113, a significant insurance element must be present: the coverage must involve uncertainty concerning significant variation in either the timing or amount of payments by the reinsurer. Also, ceded losses are no longer deducted from gross losses, as was allowed previously. Instead, the amounts are entered as reinsurance receivable, an asset.

These changes affect the reporting of a multi-period reinsurance agreement under which the insurer agrees to reimburse the reinsurer for loss payments by the end of the agreement period. These agreements, often called "finite risk" contracts, closely resemble banking or deposit arrangements in that they place few of the reinsurer's resources at risk. Under FAS 113, the full amount of a loss that occurs is reported at the time of occurrence, and reinsurance recoveries that are triggered by the loss are amortized over the settlement period. The changes imposed by FAS 113 are likely to improve the quality of information concerning reinsurance activities that is revealed to analysts.

Summary. Property-liability insurance accounting blends accrual accounting and cash accounting in an unusual way. In cash accounting, the effect of a transaction on financial statements is not recorded until payment is made or received. Most individual's accounting records, including tax statements, use cash accounting. Organizations are more likely to use accrual accounting methods. Under accrual accounting, the effect of a transaction is recognized when the events giving rise to the right to receive payment or the liability to make payment have occurred. For example, a business using accrual accounting may recognize revenue from a sale at the time goods are shipped in response to an order, even though payment is not received for some time. By the same token, the costs associated with filling the order are recognized as an offset to the yet-to-be-received revenues. The principle that motivates these accounting entries is the contemporaneous matching of revenues and costs: the costs of producing a unit of output are matched against the revenues from selling the unit.

When a property-liability insurer writes a policy, the expenses associated with issuing the policy are immediately recognized against income. However, the premium received from the contract is not immediately taken into income, because it is not yet "earned." Instead, the premium is earned over the period of coverage. At the time the policy is written, the insurer's unearned premium reserve increases by the full amount of the premium. As a consequence, underwriting expenses are recognized twice on a newly issued contract, at least as far as they affect reported income and surplus. First, they are recognized as an expense and as a cash outlay (or a liability for payment) at the time the policy is written. Second, they are recognized when the full amount of the premium is added to the unearned premium reserve, the increase in which offsets reported income and surplus. The portion of the unearned premium reserve that could be attributed to underwriting expenses already paid represents "hidden surplus" that will be released as the premium is earned. One motive for reinsurance is to release this surplus without waiting for the premium to become earned.

In another important respect, insurance accounting differs from accounting for other organizations. For most organizations, costs of operation are evident at the time financial reports are prepared. For a property-liability insurer, however, costs consist primarily of claims that will be paid under outstanding policies plus the cost of settling these claims. These costs are unknown but can be estimated, and may not materialize for a long time. Because the liability for these claims arises from providing the coverage under the newly written policies, the matching principle mentioned above offsets these estimated future costs against the revenue earned when the coverage is provided.

APPENDIX 15.2. AN INTRODUCTION TO LIFE INSURANCE ACCOUNTING

Because of the special rules applying to health insurance and the short-term nature of most health insurance coverage, the introduction provided below focuses on life insurance accounting. Medical expense insurance, which comprises most of the health insurance purchased today, more closely resembles property-liability insurance than life insurance. Conceptually, the accounting for medical expense insurance follows rules similar to those applying to property-liability insurance.

Compared with accounting for property-liability insurers, principles of insurance accounting applying to life insurance coverage are relatively straightforward. As is true for property-liability insurers, life insurance financial statements filed with insurance regulators follow statutory accounting principles (SAP). The distortion of asset values is a possibility under SAP, leaving the evaluation of asset quality and composition as a concern in financial assessment of life and health insurers. The evaluation of liabilities involving guarantees other than life insurance (e.g., guaranteed investment contracts) is an additional concern.

Tables 15.9 and 15.10 present financial statements of a representative life-health insurance company. The figures in these tables, which are based on data in *Best's Aggregates and Averages, Life-Health*, 1992 edition, approximate what would be the entries for a life-health insurer that was near-average in all respects for the insurers on which the Best's report is based. Entries that normally are a small fraction of the total (e.g., less than 1 percent) have been omitted. Any correspondence with the figures for any existing life-health insurer is entirely coincidental, although the figures reflect entries that would be typical for the industry.

The Balance Sheet. Table 15.9 is a balance sheet for the representative life-health insurer. As was true in the case of property-liability insurance, many of the assets shown on the balance sheet require little discussion except as to val-

TABLE 15.9. Representative Life and Health Insurance Company Balance Sheet

Assets (000)		Liabilities and Surplus (000)	
Bonds	361,118	Policy Reserves	413,217
Preferred Stock	4,734	Policy Claims	8,505
Common Stock	26,802	Policy Dividend Accumulations	8,731
Mortgage Loans	120,379	Dividend Reserve	5,790
Real Estate	16,430	Policyholder Premiums	2,237
Policy Loans	29,011	Guaranteed Investment	
Separate Account Assets	96,192	Contracts	57,493
Other Assets	60,062	Other Contract Deposit Funds	36,830
		Commissions, Taxes, Expenses	5,464
		Other Liabilities	22,796
		Securities Valuation Reserve	8,730
		Separate Account Business	95,148
		Total Liabilities	664,941
		Capital	1,407
		Contingency & Other Reserves	3,736
		Surplus	44,644
		Total Capital & Surplus	49,787
Total Admitted Assets	714,728	Total Liabilities & Surplus	714,728

Source: Computed from data in *Best's Aggregates and Averages: Life-Health,* 1992 edition.

uation techniques. These assets primarily consist of bonds (50.5 percent) and mortgage loans (16.8 percent) issued by entities unaffiliated with the insurer. These assets are held primarily for investment purposes and are, for the most part, marketable. Two asset categories, policy loans and separate account assets, require additional discussion.

The entry for *policy loans* is the outstanding balances on loans against policies having a loan option. This option, which is discussed further in Chapter 18, provides the policyholder with the right to borrow a stated percentage of the amount the policyholder could receive if the policy were surrendered for cash. When the option is exercised, the outstanding loan is an asset for the insurer. The loan option levies an explicit interest charge on the borrowed amount, which then becomes investment earnings to the insurer.

The entry for *separate account assets* is the value of assets held separate from the insurer's other holdings. Separate account assets are not subject to the regulatory restrictions usually applying to life insurer investments. Separate accounts may be invested in common stocks, which allows them to be used to fund agreements based on common stock investment portfolios such as group pension funds, some annuity contracts, and variable life insurance contracts. Separate accounts are not commingled with the insurer's other assets, instead being held and managed separately. The motive behind these accounts is to utilize the insurer's investment skills without being subject to the usual regulatory restrictions applying to life insurer investments.

The right-hand side of the balance sheet presents the liabilities and surplus of the life insurer. *Policy reserves* constitute the bulk (over 60 percent) of the liabilities. Policy reserves quantify the life insurer's liabilities to policyholders under all outstanding contracts. Formally, policy reserves are the present value of future life insurance benefits less the present value of future premium receipts under these contracts. The present value of future life insurance benefits is the current amount required to fund benefits promised under all contracts in force. The present value of future premiums is the current amount equivalent to expected future premium income receipts if these contracts remain in force. The difference between the present values of future benefits and future premiums represents the current amount that would fund the obligation incurred to date under these contracts.

Usually, the calculation of policy reserves follows methods prescribed by statute, using a specified mortality table and interest rate. An example of a mortality table (the 1980 Commissioners Standard Ordinary Table) was presented in an appendix to Chapter 14. As is standard under SAP, the valuation technique overstates the liability, for two reasons. First, mortality rates are "loaded" to accommodate possible adverse selection. Second, the interest rate used in the evaluation of reserves is lower than the interest rates that are expected to prevail over the periods of coverage.

The next three entries are relatively small and require little explanation. *Policy claims* include death claims under policies that have been filed but not yet paid. *Policy dividend accumulations* recognize the obligation of the insurer under participating policies in which dividends have been left on deposit with the insurer to accumulate at interest. *Policy premiums* include premiums paid on policies that have been applied for but not yet issued.

The entry for *guaranteed investment contracts (GICs)* represents the liability of the insurer under investment contracts providing guaranteed returns. These contracts, which have been popular for funding group pensions and some individual annuity contracts, are an investment product sold by the life insurance industry. The entry for *other contract deposit funds* represents the insurer's liability under other investment management agreements in which assets have been commingled with the insurer's other assets.

The next two entries requiring explanation are the *securities valuation reserve* and *separate account business.* The securities valuation reserve is established to absorb fluctuations in market values of bonds and other assets, to smooth the effect of variation in asset values on reported earnings and surplus. In the absence of a securities valuation reserve, changes in asset values would be posted to current earnings, where they would affect amounts available for immediate distribution as dividends. The long-term nature of life insurer liabilities is used to justify the gradual amortization of these changes over future time periods.

Recently, the NAIC replaced the securities valuation reserve with the interest maintenance reserve (IMR) and the asset valuation reserve (AVR), which will appear on financial statements filed after 1993. The IMR and AVR are similar in concept to the securities valuation reserve, although they more specifically focus on two risks affecting earnings and surplus: (1) the change in asset values due to interest rate movements and the resulting change in the ability of a portfolio of assets to support a stream of promised payments, and (2) possible defaults on fixed income investments, such as mortgages, and movements in prices of marketable investments, such as common stock and real estate.

The entry for *separate account business* recognizes the insurer's liability under separate account agreements. Although it is the second largest liability of the insurer, it very closely nets to zero against the assets held under these agreements.

The next three entries comprise the last category on the right-hand side of the balance sheet: *total capital and surplus.* Total capital and surplus is the difference between assets and liabilities. As is true for a property-liability insurers, these entries constitutes a cushion against adverse developments. Subject to qualifications concerning valuation methods, total capital and surplus represents an upper limit on the amount by which liabilities could increase or assets could decrease with the insurer still being able to honor its contractual commitments.

The Summary of Operations. Table 15.10 provides a summary of the insurer's financial activities during the year. Most of the summary requires little explanation or comment. The magnitude of investment income is noteworthy; for life insurers, investment income constitutes a more significant portion of total income than for property-liability insurers. In Table 15.10, investment income constitutes 26.7 percent of total income. For the typical property-liability insurer's summary of operations presented earlier in Table 15.7, investment income constitutes 15.3 percent of total resources (net investment income plus premiums earned).

The insurer's outlays include *benefits* such as death benefits, *expenses* such as underwriting expenses and salaries of employees, *commissions* paid to agents as compensation for successful sales efforts, and *dividends to policyholders.* The *change in reserves,* while not being an actual cash outlay, represents the change in the insurer's liability to policyholders. The change in reserves arises from three sources: (1) new reserves on contracts issued during the year, (2) the increase in reserves on policies that were outstanding during the entire year, less

TABLE 15.10. Representative Life and Health Insurance Company Summary of Operations (000)

Premium Income	124,053
Net Investment Income	50,132
Other Income	13,262
Total Income	187,447
Benefits	96,894
Expenses	15,482
Commissions	10,708
Change in Reserves	34,886
Dividends to Policyholders	7,204
Other Disbursements	13,677
Gain before Federal Income Tax	8,596
Federal Income Tax	2,411
Net Gain after Federal Income Tax	6,185

Source: Computed from data in *Best's Aggregates and Averages: Life-Health,* 1992 edition.

(3) the reserves that were extinguished on policies that terminated during the year as a result of death, maturation of the policy, or voluntary termination by the policyholder (lapsation).

Key Concepts

loss ratio   The ratio of losses and loss-adjustment expenses incurred to premiums earned, usually expressed as a percent. The loss ratio is an estimate of the value of insurance benefits and loss-related services relative to premium payments.

expense ratio   The (underwriting) expense ratio is ratio of underwriting expenses incurred to premiums written. In concept, the expense ratio represents the portion of the premium consumed in the act of writing the coverage.

combined ratio   The sum of the loss ratio and expense ratio.

policyholders' surplus   The difference between the value of an insurer's assets and the insurer's liabilities. Policyholders' surplus represents a cushion against adverse developments: an upper limit to the amount by which liabilities could increase or assets could decrease with the insurer still being able to honor all insurance claims.

premium-to-surplus ratio   The ratio of net premiums written to policyholders' surplus. The premium-to-surplus ratio is a measure of an insurer's leverage, that is, the degree to which the insurer is vulnerable to adverse developments.

policyholders' surplus ratio   The difference between an insurer's assets and its liabilities divided by its liabilities. One measure of an insurer's financial strength.

audit ratios   Ratios derived from an insurer's financial statement that are useful in assessing its financial strength. Audit ratios are part of the Insurance Regulatory Information System.

reserve   A balance sheet entry recognizing an estimated liability for future payment of insurance claims, expenses, or other outlays.

joint underwriting association   A servic-ing arrangement to provide insurance to consumers who are unable to secure coverage through usual channels. A few insurers agree to service the coverages issued by the association, but profits and losses of the association are spread generally throughout insurers writing the type of coverage provided through the association.

guaranty association   A state-level arrangement to reimburse claims against insurers that become insolvent. Usually the required funds are obtained through assessments against insurers writing coverage in the state.

risk-based capital (RBC)   A regulatory method for determining the capital required to write a given type of insurance coverage. Under RBC, the required capital is based on the riskiness of the type of coverage and the riskiness of the insurer's asset holdings.

statutory accounting principles (SAP)   A set of accounting rules for reporting transactions and values of assets and liabilities. The primary concern under SAP is the insurer's ability to meet its obligations. SAP present a conservative assessment of the insurer's financial position.

generally accepted accounting principles (GAAP)   A set of accounting rules for reporting transactions and values of assets and liabilities that portrays an unbiased assessment of the insurer's financial position.

admitted assets   Assets whose value is considered by an insurance regulator in determining an insurer's capital requirements. If an asset is not admitted, its value does not count in determining whether the insurer meets the state's solvency requirements.

reinsurance   Coverage purchased by an insurer to transfer part or all of the financial burden associated with a group of insurance contract it has written.

originating insurer In a reinsurance transaction, the insurer that writes coverage with an individual or a noninsurance organization in which part or all of the coverage is reinsured is called the originating, primary, or direct insurer.

reinsurance ceded In a reinsurance transaction, the value of a liability transferred by an insurer to a reinsurer.

reinsurance assumed In a reinsurance transaction, the value of a liability acquired by a reinsurer from an insurer.

ceding commission In a reinsurance transaction, the difference between the value of a liability transferred to a reinsurer and the payment required to compensate the reinsurer for accepting the liability.

separate accounts Assets managed by an insurer under an agreement to provide investment-related services. Separate account assets are not commingled with the insurer's other assets and not used to meet contractual insurance liabilities. As a consequence, these assets are not subject to the regulatory restrictions usually applying to life insurer investments.

state insurance commissioner The state official charged with administering the state insurance laws.

Paul v. Virginia The 1869 case in which the United States Supreme Court held that Congress had no authority to regulate insurance as interstate commerce.

Southeastern Underwriters Association decision The 1944 decision in which the United States Supreme Court held that Congress could regulate insurance either as interstate commerce or as a matter that affects interstate commerce.

prior approval law A rate regulatory law that requires that the state insurance commissioner approve the rates filed by an insurer before they can be used.

interest-adjusted cost indexes A surrender cost index and a payments index that are commonly used to compare the cost of life insurance among insurers.

Review Questions

1. "Permitting insurance practices to be determined under conditions approximating perfect competition is neither desirable nor possible." Comment on the truth or falsity of this statement.

2. What are the objectives of current insurance regulation? How have these objectives been influenced by the "age of consumerism"?

3. **a.** What was the nature of insurance regulation prior to the appointment of state insurance commissioners?
   b. Explain the role of the National Association of Insurance Commissioners.

4. The state insurance department has extensive regulatory authority over the solvency of insurers. Indicate the scope of this authority with specific examples.

5. Another important objective of insurance regulation is the prevention of unfair trade practices. Indicate the scope of this authority with specific examples.

6. **a.** An insurer wishes to raise its automobile liability insurance rates 10 percent. What procedure must it follow?
   b. Can this insurer join with other insurers to establish a common price? Explain your answer.

7. Prior to 1944 the states had the exclusive right to regulate insurance. What was the legal basis for this authority?

8. **a.** What was the nature of the federal complaint against the Southeastern Underwriters Association that gave rise to a history-making decision by the United States Supreme Court?
   b. What ruling did the Court make, and how did it reach this decision?

9. Security is generally considered to be the most important consideration in selecting an insurer.
   a. What is meant by security?
   b. What variables determine the security of an insurer?
10. The balance sheet for insurer A indicates unearned premium reserves equal to 10 percent of liabilities and loss reserves equal to 80 percent of liabilities.
   a. What is the unearned premium reserve?
   b. What is the loss reserve?
   c. What types of insurance does this insurer probably write?
11. Financial analysts often subtract a fraction of the unearned premium reserve from the total liabilities and add it to the surplus to determine the policyholders' surplus ratio.
   a. What is the policyholders' surplus ratio?
   b. Why do financial analysts correct the unearned premium reserve?
   c. Describe briefly the 11 NAIC property and liability audit ratios.
12. Reinsurance affects an insurer's solvency and its ability to service its policyholders. How?
13. Distinguish between facultative reinsurance, facultative treaty reinsurance, and automatic treaty insurance.
14. An insurer wishes to enter into one of the following reinsurance arrangements:
   a. A quota-share arrangement with the ceding insurer retaining 60 percent of any loss
   b. A surplus-share arrangement, under which the ceding insurer will retain policy amounts up to $100,000
   c. An excess-loss arrangement, under which the ceding insurer will retain all losses under $100,000
   How much will the reinsurer pay under each of these arrangements if the loss is
   (1) $40,000 under an $80,000 policy?
   (2) $40,000 under a $200,000 policy?
   (3) $200,000 under a $200,000 policy?
15. a. How does catastrophe reinsurance differ from the arrangements cited in question 14?
16. Insurer A reports an expense ratio of 0.30 while insurer B reports an expense ratio of 0.45. Does this mean that insurer A is the more efficient insurer?
17. What sources can the risk manager consult to obtain information concerning an insurer's financial strength, service, and cost?
18. A nonparticipating $10,000 straight life insurance policy would cost $150 a year and at the end of 20 years its cash value would be $2700. Calculate, assuming a 5 percent interest rate,
   a. The interest-adjusted surrender cost index
   b. The interest-adjusted payments index
19. Life insurers control more than twice as many assets as property and liability insurers. Why?
20. How do life insurers determine reserves?
21. To what extent is there a redundancy in the policy reserves of life insurers?
22. State three arguments for and three arguments against federal regulation of insurance.
23. Distinguish between each item in the following pairs: earned premiums and written premiums, incurred losses and paid losses.
24. Explain how you would calculate an expense ratio for an administrative service only (ASO) group medical expense coverage plan.
25. Outline the basic provisions of the typical guaranty fund statute and explain some of its shortcomings for the risk manager of an organization.

References and Suggestions for Additional Reading

Argus Chart of Health Insurance (Cincinnati: National Underwriter Company, annual).

Best's Aggregates and Averages: Property-Casualty (Oldwick, N.J.: A. M. Best Company, annual).

Best's Aggregates and Averages: Life-Health (Oldwick, N.J.: A. M. Best Company, annual).

Best's Flitcraft Compend (Oldwick, N.J.: A. M. Best Company, annual).

Best's Key Rating Guide: Life-Health (Oldwick, N.J.: A. M. Best Company, annual).

Best's Key Rating Guide: Property-Casualty (Oldwick, N.J.: A. M. Best Company, annual).

Best's Settlement Options (Oldwick, N.J.: A. M. Best Company, annual).

BREALEY, RICHARD A., and STEWART C. MYERS: *Principles of Corporate Finance* (New York: McGraw-Hill Book Company, 1991).

COOPER, ROBERT W.: *An Historical Analysis of the Tontine Principle.* (Philadelphia: The S. S. Huebner Foundation for Insurance Education, The University of Pennsylvania, 1972. Distributed by Richard D. Irwin, Inc. for the Foundation).

Credit Review: S&P's Insurance Rating Service (New York: Standard & Poor's Corporation, revised periodically).

CUMMINS, J. DAVID, and SCOTT E. HARRINGTON (EDS.): *Fair Rate of Return on Property-Liability Insurance* (Hingham, Mass.: Kluwer-Nijhoff, 1986).

———, and S. N. Weisbart: *The Impact of Consumer Services on Independent Insurance Agency Performance* (Glenmont, N.Y.: IMA Education Research Foundation, 1977).

Federal Register, issues containing directives of the Federal Insurance Administration.

Fire, Casualty, and Surety Bulletins (Cincinnati: The National Underwriters Company, monthly), sections on Federal Insurance Administration programs.

GERATHEWOLD, KLAUS: *Reinsurance Principles and Practice,* vols. I and II, Verlag Versicherungswirtschafte e. V. (Available in the UNited States from Englewood Cliffs, N.J.: Underwriting Printing and Publishing Company, 1980 and 1983.)

HANSON, J. S., R. E. DINEEN, and M. B. JOHNSON: *Monitoring Competition: A Means of Regulating the Property and Liability Business,* vols. 1 and 2 (Milwaukee: National Association of Insurance Commissioners, May, 1974).

Insurance Facts (New York: Insurance Information Institute, annual).

Insurer Profitability: A Long-Term Perspective: U.S. Property/Casualty Insurance Compared with Other Industries, 1970–1986 (New York: Insurance Services Office, Inc., April, 1987).

JENNINGS, ROBERT M., and ANDREW P. TROUT: *The Tontine: From the Reign of Louis XIV to the French Revolutionary Era.* (Philadelphia: The S. S. Huebner Foundation for Insurance Education, The University of Pennsylvania, 1982. Distributed by Richard D. Irwin, Inc. for the Foundation).

KIMBALL, S. L.: *Insurance and Public Policy* (Madison: University of Wisconsin Press, 1960).

———, and H. S. Denenberg: *Insurance, Government, and Social Policy* (Homewood, Ill.: Richard D. Irwin, Inc., 1969).

Life Insurance Fact Book (Washington, D.C.: American Council of Life Insurance, annual).

Meeting the Insurance Crisis of Our Cities: A Report by the President's National Advisory Panel on Insurance in Riot-Affected Areas (Washington, D.C.: U.S. Government Printing Office, 1968).

MEHR, ROBERT I., and EMERSON CAMMACK: *Principles of Insurance.* (Homewood, Ill.: Richard D. Irwin, Inc., 1972.

MEIER, KENNETH J.: *The Political Economy of Regulation: The Case of Insurance* (Ithaca, N.Y.: State University of New York Press, 1988).

MOWBRAY, ALBERT H., and RALPH H. BLANCHARD: *Insurance* (4th ed., New York: McGraw-Hill Book Company, Inc., 1955).

PATTERSON, E. W.: *The Insurance Commissioner in the United States* (Cambridge, Mass.: Harvard University Press, 1927).

NATIONAL Association OF INSURANCE COMMISSIONERS: *NAIC Life Risk-Based Capital Report Including Overview and Instructions for Companies.* (Kansas City, Mo.: National Association of Insurance Commissioners, 1993 (annual).

Paul v. Virginia, 8 Wall 183 (1869).

Proceedings of the National Association of Insurance Commissioners (semiannual).

Property-Liability Insurance Accounting (5th ed., Durham: N.C., Insurance Accounting & Systems Association, Inc., July 1991).

Reports of the Subcommittee on Antitrust and Monopoly, U.S. Senate, on various aspects of the insurance industry (Washington, D.C.: U.S. Government Printing Office, periodically since the late 1950s).

SCISM, LESLIE: "Surplus Notes of Insurers May Attract Institutions Now That New Rules Loom," (*The Wall Street Journal,* June 8, 1994), p. C1.

Time Saver for Health Insurance (Cincinnati: The National Underwriter Company, annual).

TROXEL, T. E., and C. L. BRESLIN: *Property-Liability Insurance Accounting and Finance* (2nd ed., Malvern, Pa.: American Institute for Property and Liability Underwriters, 1983).

Using the NAIC Insurance Regulatory Information System: Life and Health and Fraternal Insurance (Milwaukee: National Association of Insurance Commissioners, revised periodically).

Using the NAIC Insurance Regulatory Information System: Property and Liability Insurance (Milwaukee: National Association of Insurance Commissioners, revised periodically).

Who Writes What (Cincinnati: The National Underwriter Company, annual).

Who Writes What in Life and Health Insurance (Cincinnati: The National Underwriter Company, annual).

CHAPTER 16

Legal Aspects of
Insurance Contracts

Learning Objectives

After you have completed this chapter, you should be able to:

1. Explain why the legal definition of insurance is so important and how it varies among jurisdictions.
2. Describe the characteristics of an insurance contract that subject it to a special body of law.
3. List the four conditions that must be satisfied to make an insurance contract a valid contract.
4. Explain how an insured might lose his or her coverage because of concealment, a misrepresentation, or a breach of warranty.
5. Describe the importance to insureds of waiver and estoppel.
6. Tell the extent to which insurance contracts are standardized and the ways in which this standardization is accomplished.
7. Describe the authority of insurance agents and brokers with respect to committing insurers to coverage, changing provisions of insurance contracts, and in accepting information disclosed by insureds.

INTRODUCTION

An understanding of the structure and legal interpretation of insurance contracts can be important to a risk manager, for several reasons. One reason is fundamental in deciding whether to use insurance or some other method: the risk manager should know what the insurer promises to do under the contract. If the risk manager decides to purchase one of the insurer's conventional products, an ability to analyze these coverages is valuable in choosing from among these products. If conventional products are not suitable, the risk manager should understand the consequences of drafting a tailor-made insurance contract instead of accepting a standard form. In either case, the risk manager should understand the rights and responsibilities of the insurer and insured under the contract.

This chapter first discusses what types of agreements the law considers to be insurance and why the distinction between insurance contracts and other agreements can be important. Other topics include: the requirements for any contract including insurance to be valid, special features that tend to distinguish insurance from other contracts, some rules on disclosure of information by the insured, legal doctrines affecting the rights of an insured who violates a contract condition, and the extent and nature of insurance contract standardization.

A LEGAL DEFINITION OF INSURANCE

The issue of whether a particular contract is *legally* considered insurance is not purely semantic (see Denenberg [1963]). The law applying to insurance can differ from the law applying to other transactions in important ways. First of all, the issuance of insurance coverage by an organization raises the issue of whether the organization is in compliance with the laws and regulations governing insurance.

Second, the question may be raised in a civil action whereby one party alleges certain rights that flow from insurance contracts. These actions may include suit to recover a promised benefit under the alleged policy, a return of premiums paid, or a money judgment for damages suffered by the claimant because of insurance coverages promised. The courts in these cases have tended to favor the theory that the claimant should recover from organizations holding themselves out as providing such benefits. What may be determined to be insurance in such civil actions, however, may not be held to be "doing a business of insurance" as related to state regulation.

Third, the issue may be raised in bankruptcy proceedings since the Bankruptcy Act excludes insurance corporations from the operation of the act. This exclusion has had the effect of shifting defunct insurers to an elaborate procedure and process of liquidation under state insurance laws and administration. The system of state-level guaranty associations discussed in Chapter 15 is part of this administrative procedure.

Finally, courts have been asked to rule on what is insurance in administering our tax laws. Insurance companies are entitled to special treatment regarding deductions for reserves, investment income, and accounting treatment of expenses. The United States Supreme Court has held that a state's classification of an organization as an insurer is an important test in determining whether the tax administration and treatment accorded insurers applies, unless the classification has been grossly misused to hide the true purposes of the organization.

Case law shows clearly that there is no single legal definition of insurance. Certain tests that are often applied to the business or transaction in question are:

1. Is there a risk of economic loss to the beneficiary or insured
   a. Independent of the contract itself?
   b. Outside the control of either party?
   c. That may be distributed among those who are subject to loss?

2. Is this risk assumed by the insurer or promisor?
3. Does the contract incorporate a plan to distribute the cost of the loss among a group exposed to risk?

Case law and commentary on the subject contain the following, sometimes contradictory, examples of what the courts have held to be or not to be insurance (*American Jurisprudence,* 1982). Transfers that are considered insurance in one state may not be considered insurance in another. Warranties are particularly troublesome. In general, when a manufacturer, contractor, or distributor promises to replace a product or redo work if the product or work proves defective, the warranty is not considered insurance. If the warranty covers only (or in addition) accidental losses, the warranty probably will be considered insurance. Warranties also have been considered insurance when the promise to protect the buyer against defects in the product is made by an outsider, not the manufacturer, contractor, or distributor. For example, some insurers now sell warranty insurance on new cars. Table 16.1 offers a few examples of agreements that courts have held to be insurance and a few other examples of similar agreements where courts have held otherwise.

REQUIREMENTS FOR A VALID CONTRACT

To be legally enforceable by the courts, a contract must meet four requirements. The set of four requirements applies generally to all contracts, insurance being no exception. Their application to insurance is specialized because of the nature of the insurance agreement and the large body of case law that has developed on insurance issues. The four requirements are: (1) *offer and acceptance,* (2) *con-*

TABLE 16.1. Examples of Agreements

Insurance	Not Insurance
Indemnity for loss by theft	Lightning-rod salesman's guarantee
Indemnity for loss by death of cattle	Bicycle repair contract issued by a bicycle association
Contracts guaranteeing the performance of, or indemnifying against the non-performance of, certain contracts	Agreement to protect employer from striking employees
Comprehensive guarantee of auto tires	Tire warranty promising a price adjustment if tire fails because of faulty construction or materials
Contracts for replacement of plate glass, if broken	Provision in lease making the lessor responsible for replacement of a chattel injured by fire
Newspaper promises to pay a stated amount to a person killed in an accident if at the time he had a copy of the newspaper on his person	Contract entitling members of groups to medical services free or at reduced rates
Contracts guaranteeing the value of corporate stock on a certain date	Agreements for service and repair of defective parts of fluorescent fixtures
Comprehensive care guaranteed for an abortion for a flat fee	Long-term disability plan offered through trust agreement to employees

sideration, (3) *legal capacity of parties*, and (4) *purpose not contrary to public interest*. These four requirements are explained below.

1. Offer and Acceptance. For a contract to be enforceable, evidence of agreement must exist. Without a "meeting of the minds" between the parties, no contract is present. The evidence does not need to be in writing, as verbal agreements can be contracts. Of course, a written contract usually is stronger evidence of agreement than the parties' recollection of verbal exchanges.

A contract exists after one party makes a definite, valid offer that is accepted by the other party. What the law deems an offer or an acceptance of the offer depends a great deal on the circumstances and parties to the transaction. In the typical insurance transaction, the offer is made by the applicant when he or she applies for insurance. If the insurer rejects the offer but agrees to provide coverage subject to a surcharged rate or other modifications, the insurer often is deemed to make a counteroffer. The counteroffer must be accepted by the applicant prior to its withdrawal for the agreement to become effective.

2. Consideration. The consideration requirement means that something of value must be exchanged by each party to the agreement. For example, an agreement to give a gift is not an enforceable promise because the recipient gives nothing in exchange. The contract is not enforceable unless each party gives up a right, power, or privilege that he or she already has in exchange for an equivalent renouncement by the other. The contract is enforceable, however, even if one person promises to do much more than the other.

Under an insurance contract, the consideration made by the insurer is the promise to pay. A promise to pay can be deemed consideration even if actual payment does not occur. The consideration made by the insured is the payment of the premium or the promise to pay. For example, an insured may agree to be subject to possible assessments at the end of the coverage period.

3. Legal Capacity. The parties to a contract must be legally capable of entering a contractual agreement. Insane or intoxicated persons are not considered competent to make contracts. Minors (persons under age 18 in some states and under 21 in others) may void a contract to which they are a party as long as they do so prior to attaining the age of majority. However, minors cannot void contracts for "necessities" (food, clothing and shelter, for example). Only the minor has the option to void the contract, and if the minor does not exercise the option prior to attaining the age of majority, the contract is valid.

Insurers are presumed competent if they meet statutory requirements to be licensed. Insurance is not considered a necessity, but the rule with respect to minors has been modified in some states to permit minors to enter into legally enforceable life insurance contracts as early as age 14. The courts of a few states deny the rights of minors to void an insurance contract, on the ground that since the insurer has fulfilled its promise, the contract has been executed.

4. Purpose Not Contrary to Public Interest. A contract whose purpose is against the public interest will not be enforced. For example, a contract to commit a crime is unenforceable. Although an agreement to commit a criminal act offers a clear application of the principle, the requirement extends further. The *insurable interest* requirement illustrates how the requirement can extend into contracts which will not be enforced even though their purpose may not be criminal. The absence of an insurable interest for the insured (or, in life insurance, the beneficiary) usually makes the insurance contract unenforceable.

An insurable interest is present when the occurrence of the insured event results in a loss for the insured or the beneficiary. For example, a dependent spouse or child has an insurable interest in the life of an employed head of family. A creditor who has loaned funds for which property has been pledged as collateral has an insurable interest in the property. An owner of property has an insurable interest in the owned property, one that may exist at the same time as the creditor's.

In property insurance, the insurable interest must exist at the time of the insured event. For example, a property owner who transfers ownership to another party but continues insurance coverage on the property cannot collect under the coverage. A creditor cannot collect under a policy on property pledged as collateral if the loan has been repaid.

In life insurance, however, the insurable interest is required only when the contract is written. For example, a husband who takes out a life insurance policy on his wife can collect the policy proceeds even if the two are divorced at the time of her death. An exception applies if the husband murders his former wife—as a matter of public policy, a beneficiary who murders the insured cannot collect the policy proceeds.

In the absence of an insurable interest requirement, an insurance contract would amount to a wager against insured events, which is against the public interest. Strong moral hazards would be an obvious problem created by the availability of such a wager.

DISTINGUISHING FEATURES OF INSURANCE CONTRACTS

All contracts must meet the four requirements discussed above. Insurance contracts are subject to the same basic law that governs all types of contracts. However, one can be knowledgeable about the general law of contracts and know little about the law applying to insurance. A special body of law has developed around legal problems associated with insurance. A set of special features discussed below applies to insurance contracts. Some of the features may apply to other types of contracts, although often in special instances only and usually not as an entire set. Taken as a whole, the features discussed below tend to distinguish insurance contracts.

Personal Contract

Insurance contracts are personal contracts. Although the subject of a property insurance contract is an item of property, the contract insures the *legal interest* of a person or an entity, not the property itself. Suppose the insured is the owner. If the owner sells the property, the new owner is not insured under the contract unless the insurer agrees to an assignment of the insured's rights to the new owner. This aspect of the coverage reduces the likelihood of moral hazards that could arise if the identity of the insured were not known by the insurer. The identity of the insured person or entity is an important factor in the insurer's decision to insure the property. In many cases, the contract may insure the legal interest of more than one individual or entity, as when the contract insures a lender's interest in property pledged as collateral for a loan.

Unilateral Contract

Most insurance contracts are *unilateral* contracts. The term unilateral means that courts will enforce the contract in one direction only, against one of the parties: in this case, the insurer. After the insured has paid the premium for coverage, the insured's part of the agreement has been fulfilled. Under these circumstances, the only party whose promises are still outstanding is the insurer. If the insured has a valid claim to benefits under the contract, the courts may be used to force the insurer to perform its part of the agreement.

A contract is said to be *executed* with respect to a party when that party has no further outstanding promises. A contract is *executory* when outstanding promises still remain. After the premium is paid by the insured, the typical insurance contract is executed with respect to the insured and executory with respect to the insurer. The typical property insurance contract does not become executed with respect to the insurer until the promised benefits are paid or the end of the coverage period is reached with no claims occurring. In a sense, many liability insurance contracts may never become executed with respect to the insurer if they provide coverage for events occurring during the policy period. Even many years after the end of the coverage period, the possibility exists that a claim may appear for injury arising from an event that occurred during the policy period.

A typical contract other than insurance is *bilateral,* which means that courts may be used to force performance of either party. For example, a written sales agreement may be enforced against either the buyer or seller. In contrast, most insurance contracts are unilateral after the premium has been paid. An exception to the unilateral nature of insurance could occur if the insured were to promise to pay the premium at some future point in time, with the promise inducing the insurer to provide coverage prior to the payment of the premium. In this case, the insurer could use the courts to force the insured to make good on the promise.

In the typical insurance contract in which the premium is paid in advance of the coverage period, the insured cannot be forced to perform. The typical annual premium life insurance policy offers a good example. At any point in time, the insured may choose to cease making premium payments, and the insurer has no recourse against the insured. The life insurance coverage ceases or the nature of the promised benefit changes when premium payments terminate, of course, but the insurer cannot force the insured to continue paying the premium. The only direction in which the contract will be enforced is against the insurer. If premium payments are made in a timely fashion, the insurer can be forced to pay the promised benefit when the insured event occurs.

Conditional Contract

Insurance contracts are conditional contracts. Although only the insurer can be forced to perform after the contract is effective, the insurer can refuse to perform if the insured does not satisfy certain conditions contained in the contract. For example, the insurer need not pay a claim if the insured has increased the chance of loss in some manner prohibited under the contract or has failed to submit a proof of loss within a specified period.

Another condition that appears in most liability insurance contracts is a requirement that the insured assist the insurer in the investigation of circumstances surrounding the event giving rise to a claim, including testimony in court if needed. Failure of the insured to provide this assistance may allow the insurer to deny payment of the claim.

Aleatory Contract

Aleatory contracts have a *chance element* and an *uneven exchange.* Insurance contracts and gambling contracts are aleatory contracts. Under an aleatory contract, the performance of at least one of the parties is dependent upon chance. An aleatory contract also involves an uneven exchange: one of the parties promises to do much more than the other party. The chance element allows the exchange to be uneven without the contract being to the disadvantage of either party.

The aleatory and conditional nature of insurance contracts are two of their most important legal characteristics. These characteristics also cause some confusion in the general public. Most noninsurance contracts are *commutative,* which means that an exchange of equal values occurs. Unwittingly, many people also employ this concept when thinking about insurance. They fail to realize that only by coincidence (or over a very long period of time) will an insurance contract result in an exchange of equal values. However, the uneven exchange is not a flaw in the contract, but a fundamental feature of a contract that is both conditional and aleatory.

Contract of Adhesion

When legal disputes arise over the meaning of contract language, courts usually follow a principle holding the writer responsible for wording a provision clearly. If the wording of a contract provision is unclear or ambiguous, courts usually will construe the provision against the party responsible for drafting the provision. In most insurance transactions, insureds are not allowed to participate in the drafting of the insurance contract. Because insurance contracts typically are presented to insureds on a take-it-or-leave-it basis, insureds are not held responsible for unclear or ambiguous contract provisions. Rather, unclear or ambiguous provisions are construed in favor of insureds.

This principle often is stated as an *ambiguity rule:* if a provision in a standard insurance contract is ambiguous, courts will interpret the provision in a manner favorable to the policyholder. Courts frequently refer to this characteristic of insurance when they interpret ambiguous insurance contract provisions in favor of insureds.

The ambiguity rule is less likely to apply when the insured participates in drafting the insurance contract or when the insurer is not solely responsible for contract wording. For example, risk managers of large organizations often bargain with insurers over the wording of the contract, called a *manuscript policy*. Brokers or other service organizations also may negotiate on behalf of customers over the working of contracts. Another example is a state or other legal authority dictating the wording of a contract.

When a loss occurs, the extent of coverage applying to the loss is determined by applying the words used in the contract to the set of circumstances giving rise to loss. The chain of events resulting in loss may never have been contemplated by either the insurer or insured when the contract was drafted. Particularly in claims negotiation, the analyst should consider the meaning of a contract provision, phrase, or term in the context of the entire contract. Words such as "value" or "loss" are particularly sensitive to context, and an insured who was not allowed to participate in drafting the contract is likely to have these words interpreted in his or her favor.

For example, a contract insuring a building during its construction may reduce recovery if the insured carries an amount of insurance less than the building's reported "value" without defining precisely what the term means. In the case of an existing structure, the term "value" is likely to be interpreted as "actual cash value" if a policy reimburses the actual cash value of a loss. The meaning of "value" is less clear with respect to a building under construction. Cost of materials and labor? Market value of the structure? If value is interpreted to mean the cost of materials and labor, should current cost or historical cost be used? Particularly when the cost of building materials has changed since the project was begun, the loss settlements implied by these different interpretations could differ dramatically.

A word or phrase examined within an isolated sentence may acquire new meaning when the surrounding language or its use in other parts of the contract is considered. Unless the identical word or phrase is used in other parts of the contract, the insured may be able to convince an arbitrator, a judge, or a jury that a reasonable person could interpret a word used in one part of the contract differently when it is used in another part of the contract. Recognizing this possibility, many insurance contracts contain a section defining important terms and phrases. In other cases, insurers allow courts to define the meaning of contract terms. When this option is used, the insured has an important ally in the ambiguity rule: How would a reasonable person interpret the word or phrase in light of the other provisions in the contract?

Contract of the Utmost Good Faith

Insurance contracts are contracts *uberrimae fidei* or of the utmost good faith. Both parties to the contract are bound to disclose all the facts relevant to the transaction. Neither party is to take advantage of the other's lack of information. The legal questions involving this characteristic usually center on the disclosure of information by the insured. These legal questions are important enough to merit the separate treatment given in the section "Disclosure of Information by the Insured" later in this chapter.

The legal foundation for doctrines related to disclosure of information rests on principles established long ago for insurance on ocean vessels and their cargoes. Many of these coverages were written without an opportunity for the insurer to inspect or evaluate the vessel. Often the coverage was written after the voyage was under way. Consequently, a large degree of good faith was imposed on the insured regarding honest and full disclosure of circumstances bearing on the likelihood of loss.

Valued and Indemnity Contracts

When an insured event occurs, provisions in the contract determine the benefit amount. Insurance contracts commonly are classified according to the method for determining the benefit amount. A *valued contract* pays a stated amount if the insured event occurs. An ordinary life insurance contract is an example of a valued contract—the contract pays the stated benefit when the insured person dies. The only issue influencing the benefit amount is whether the insured event has occurred. The benefit amount may depend on the circumstances surrounding the insured event (for example, the benefit may be larger if death is due to an accident). In this instance, however, the benefit amount still depends only on the issue of whether the insured event (in this case, accidental death) has occurred.

In effect, a valued contract is an agreement between the insurer and insured as to the value of the damage if the insured event occurs. The parties to such an agreement avoid the cost of disputes over the value of the loss. Such disputes are likely to occur if the value of the loss is subjective or is subject to a large margin of error. The value of a loss occurring when a human dies is an obvious example. Valued contracts also are used to insure objects whose value is difficult to determine, such as antiques or objects of art.

A *contract of indemnity,* the other category, seeks to reimburse the insured for loss. Most property and liability insurance contracts are contracts of indemnity. Under a contract of indemnity, the amount of benefit depends on the size of the loss. A small loss results in a small payment (or perhaps no payment). A large loss triggers a larger payment. Because the benefit amount is conditioned on the size of the loss, contracts of indemnity nearly always contain language stating how the amount of loss is to be measured (e.g., replacement cost, actual cash value, or per diem amount).

Interpreted in a strict sense, the principle of indemnity would imply that the insured is fully restored to his or her condition prior to loss. In other words, the payment of the insurance benefit would leave the insured exactly as before the insured event, no better or no worse. In fact, very few insurance coverages achieve this result. An insurance policy providing such a benefit would make the insured indifferent to whether a loss occurs, very likely leading to decreased vigilance in loss prevention and control. A more accurate characterization of this principle is the statement that a contract of indemnity provides a benefit whose amount is conditioned on the size of the loss. The indemnity principle does require, however, that the insured does not benefit financially from the occurrence of the insured event. The insurance benefit should do *no more* than restore the insured to its condition prior to the loss, or else moral hazards are likely to occur.

Many insurance contracts fall somewhere between the extremes of a pure contract of indemnity or a pure valued contract. Most property and liability contracts, for example, impose upper limits on the amount of the benefit. The upper limit causes the coverage to resemble a valued contract when a loss is large enough to trigger the payment of the maximum benefit. However, a few policies do not contain an explicit dollar limit—automobile physical damage (collision) insurance often is written without an explicit upper limit. The term *valued policy* often is used to describe a contract that may be written without an upper limit, but in which an upper limit is imposed. Physical damage insurance on an antique or special interest vehicle may be written under a valued policy, for example. An *agreed amount endorsement* is used for the same purpose.

Many states have enacted a *valued contract law* applying to insurance on real estate. A valued contract law requires the insurer to pay the full limit of the policy in the event of a total loss. The payment of this amount does not consider the loss to the insured, instead being the limit of the policy. Such a statute has the effect of converting a contract of indemnity into a valued contract when total destruction of the insured premises occurs. The theory behind these statutes is they provide a disincentive for insurers or their agents to encourage insureds to overinsure property. In the absence of such a statute, an insurer's liability would be limited to the amount of loss, so overinsuring would increase premium income without increasing the insurer's liability. The valued contract law would create a moral hazard if property is overinsured, so the enactment of such a statute provides an incentive for insurers to avoid overinsurance.

A Contract Employing Subrogation

Subrogation is a common-law doctrine that applies when loss is caused by a party other than the insured. The subrogation doctrine transfers to the insurer the insured's common-law right of recovery against the third party, at least to the extent that the insurer has reimbursed the loss. The absence of subrogation would imply that the insured could collect twice for losses caused by other parties: once from the insurer, and once again from the party the law holds responsible. Allowing double recovery would be likely to increase moral hazards. The subrogation doctrine prevents such double recovery by assigning the insured's common-law right of recovery to the insurer. Even if the insurer chooses not to exercise this right, the doctrine prevents the insured from collecting twice.

For example, suppose vandals set fire to an insured structure, causing a $100,000 loss. If the vandals are apprehended, the owner of the property has a common-law right to recover the $100,000 from the vandals. If the loss has been reimbursed by insurance, however, the insured's right of recovery is transferred to the insurer. The insurer then has the right to recover from the vandals whatever amounts it paid to the insured for the loss. If the insurer paid $95,000 to the insured for the loss, the insurer can take legal action to recover $95,000 from the vandals. The insured still retains a right to recover the $5000 unreimbursed portion of the loss, but the insured cannot take action for the $95,000 belonging to the insurer.

If legal action results in recovery from the vandals, the allocation of the recovery between the insurer and the insured varies among jurisdictions. Keeton (1971, pp. 158–168) identifies three possible rules, the first of which is supported by court precedents: (1) the insurer receives no payment until the insured is fully indemnified, (2) the recovery is prorated between the insurer and insured according to their respective unreimbursed losses, and (3) the insurer is reimbursed first. If $20,000 is recovered from the vandals causing the $100,000 loss discussed above, of which the insurer has reimbursed $95,000, the insured would recover the following amounts under each rule: (1) $5000; (2) $1000; (3) $0.

The subrogation doctrine applies to most property and liability insurance contracts and to some types of health insurance. However, the subrogation doctrine does not apply to life insurance. If an individual dies as a result of an accident, for example, a surviving dependent has the right to take legal action against the person responsible for the accident. In determining the amount payable to the dependent in the wrongful death action, any life insurance benefits payable to the dependent are not considered by the court. Further, the life insurer that provided the death benefit has no cause of action against the person responsible for the accident.

DISCLOSURE OF INFORMATION BY THE INSURED

An insurance contract, as was noted earlier, is a contract *uberrimae fidei*. Consequently, an insurer is entitled to rely upon information provided by the insured and to seek some relief if this information is incorrect. When an insurer disputes payment of a claim because incorrect or incomplete information was provided by the insured, the insurer's argument to the court hearing the dispute will be based on one of three legal doctrines: *breach of warranty, misrepresentation,* or *concealment.* These doctrines are specific as to the types of insurance and the nature of the statements to which they apply. The discussion of these doctrines appearing below first considers them as common-law doctrines, not modified by any special statutes. The effect of statutes modifying these common-law doctrines then is considered.

The legal doctrines discussed below appear in order of the standard they impose on the insured. As a general rule, courts are likely to impose a higher standard of disclosure on professional risk managers of large organizations than on individuals and owners of small businesses. In particular, the rules of disclosure related to insurance on ocean vessels and their cargoes can be quite harsh—the doctrine of warranty often applies to these ventures. However, a professional risk manager or a shipowner is likely to be knowledgeable about the effects of contract conditions and rules of disclosure because the professional status provides economic incentives to learn about these issues.

Also, these legal doctrines are discussed as they apply to coverages other than life insurance. Although the qualitative nature of the doctrines applying to disclosure does not change dramatically between life insurance and other coverages, life insurance (and some health insurance) coverages issued in the United States become *incontestable* if the insured survives a period of time. In life insurance in the United States, this period of time cannot exceed two years. Once the policy becomes incontestable, the insurer cannot deny coverage because of inaccurate or incomplete disclosure of information on the policy application.

Breach of Warranty

A *warranty* is a condition in an insurance contract. A statement achieves the status of a warranty if it becomes a condition of the insurer's promise. Courts are not likely to give it this status unless the contract clearly indicates that the insured's answer is a contract condition. A question may also arise as to whether the warranty is affirmative or promissory. An *affirmative warranty* states a condition that is supposed to exist on the date the statement is made; a *promissory warranty* states a condition that is to exist throughout part or all of the policy period. For example, an automobile insurance policy contains an affirmative warranty stating that no insurer has canceled an automobile insurance policy covering the insured during the past three years. A burglary policy contains a promissory warranty stating that during the policy period the burglar-alarm system described in the policy will be maintained in proper working order.

If a court construes a statement as a warranty, it may allow the insurer to deny coverage if there has not been nearly literal compliance with the statement. The effect of this doctrine can be very harsh with respect to insureds. All the insurer needs to show to deny coverage is that the warranty was breached, even if the breach was unintentional and not related to the loss. For example, a ship owner may warrant that certain maintenance procedures will be followed on an insured vessel. If the maintenance procedures are not followed and the ship sinks in a storm, the insurer may be allowed to deny the claim even though the failure to comply with the warranted condition had nothing to do with the ship's sinking.

Warranties often are written statements incorporated into the insurance contract. In the absence of any statutory modification, the practice commonly followed by insurers of stapling a copy of the application to the contract would make every statement in the application a warranty. However, as described in a later section on statutory modifications, courts are unlikely to be this harsh except in insurance on ocean vessels and their cargoes.

In summary, a court may allow an insurer to deny coverage if there has not been literal compliance with a warranted condition. Because the effect of this doctrine on insureds is harsh, courts are reluctant to apply it except to knowledgeable professional buyers of coverage. Instead, courts are likely to apply the doctrine of *representation*, increasing the burden of proof required for the insurer to deny coverage. A representation is a statement made by the insured in applying for insurance. In order to deny coverage because the insured's representations were inaccurate or incomplete, the common law typically requires the insurer to show that the inaccurate statements influenced the insurance transaction or the information was deliberately incomplete. These requirements are discussed below under the headings *misrepresentation* and *concealment*.

Misrepresentation

A misrepresentation is an inaccurate or untrue statement, usually made in response to a question from the insurer. The statement may express a *fact* or an *opinion.* An opinion is a statement about an issue involving judgment or about which the insured lacks the expertise to make a factual statement. For example, an insured's response to a question "Are you in good health?" usually is construed as an opinion, as only a physician has the expertise to make a factual statement on this issue. A statement of fact, however, involves matters where the insured is presumed to have the required knowledge and expertise. For example, a response to the question "Have you been seen by a physician for a medical condition during the past six months?" presumably is a matter about which the insured would be expected to know the correct answer.

Under common law, an insurer can successfully plead misrepresentation of a *fact* if it can show that the factual information is (1) incorrect and (2) material. A fact is considered *material* if its disclosure would have altered the terms of coverage. The insurer does not need to show that the misstated fact was connected to the loss for which coverage is being denied. All the insurer needs to show is that the information would have caused the insurer to withdraw its offer or to change the terms of coverage. For example, an insurer can demonstrate materiality by showing that the premium for coverage would have been higher if the correct information had been disclosed.

If the misrepresentation involves an opinion rather than a fact, the insurer also must show that the misrepresentation was *intentional.* Intent could be shown by proving that the insured was aware of information that would not be evident to the insurer but deliberately misstated the information to induce the insurer to offer coverage. The following cases illustrate these concepts: Assume that a property insurer includes in its application a question concerning the existence of other insurance and that the applicant answers the question incorrectly. To deny a claim successfully later, the insurer must prove that the incorrect answer affected its underwriting decision. The insurer need not prove that the insured intended to deceive. If an applicant for a life insurance contract responds affirmatively to a question asking whether his or her health is good, the answer is considered an opinion. To contest a claim successfully on the ground that this opinion is a misrepresentation, the insurer must prove that the answer was incorrect, material, and fraudulent.

Concealment

Concealment is the failure to reveal information known to the insured that is not such common knowledge that the insurer would be expected to be aware of it. In other words, concealment is a failure to disclose information when the law imposes the duty to reveal. With respect to most types of insurance other than on ocean vessels and their cargoes, the common law requires the insurer to prove that the concealed information was *material* and the concealment was *intentional.* In showing whether concealed information was material, practices followed by other insurers may be introduced as evidence and in some states have become the standard to be applied (Patterson, 1957).

With respect to insurance on ocean vessels and their cargoes, the common law requires the insurer to prove only that the concealed information was *material.* The common law doctrine of concealment is much more harsh with respect to ocean marine insurance than with respect to other kinds of insurance, because at the time ocean marine insurance law was being developed, the courts believed that insurers needed protection. Communications were very poor, and insurers were often asked to insure vessels thousands of miles away. In fact, the vessels were insured "lost or not lost," and some had already been sunk or damaged. Consequently, an ocean marine insurer can successfully plead concealment if it can show that the fact concealed was material. Note that the concealed information need not have actually contributed to the loss that the insured refused to pay. An insurer could claim that some information the insured concealed with respect to some cargo was material even if a loss to the cargo had nothing to do with the fact concealed.

The ocean marine insurer need not prove that the concealment was intentional; in fact it is sufficient for the insurer to show that the applicant should have had the information. Other types of insurers, however, must prove that the applicant *intentionally* concealed some facts that he or she knew to be material and that would not be apparent from an inspection of the exposure. This additional requirement reduces substantially the insurer's reliance upon the doctrine of concealment, because fraud is difficult to prove and failure to prove intent may result in a countersuit. The following situation illustrates the application of this rule. Suppose that at the time a risk manager applied for fire insurance the building next door was on fire and that he or she did not report this fact to the insurer. This fire did not reach the insured building, but three weeks later a fire in the basement caused extensive damage. The insurer could probably successfully deny the insured's claim if it could prove that the risk manager knew about the fire next door and intentionally did not report the danger to the insurer. The materiality of the concealed fact would be evident. The fact that the claim that is being denied did not arise out of the unreported fire is inconsequential. On the other hand, if the risk manager did not know about the fire next door, the insurer would not be able to deny the claim successfully.

Statutory Modifications

The common law doctrines described above, particularly (but not limited to) the breach of warranty doctrine, were harshly applied during the eighteenth and early nineteenth centuries, and many insurers took advantage of insureds by denying claims on the basis of breaches that clearly were not material. As a result, many state legislatures have enacted statutes modifying the common law. These state statutes can be grouped into four classes:

1. Statutes declaring that all statements by the insured shall, in the absence of fraud, be deemed representations and not warranties. These statutes are limited for the most part to life and health insurance. All states in the case of life insurance, and most states in the case of health insurance, have statutes of this sort.
2. Statutes permitting the insured to recover unless the breach of warranty or, in some instances, the fact misrepresented either (a) increased the "risk" (meaning chance or severity of loss) or (b) materially affected the hazard assumed by the insurer. The type (a) statute seems to imply that the materiality will be determined by using the standard of a prudent insurer instead of

the standard of the individual insurer in question. These "increase-the-risk" statutes are the most common modification of the case law affecting property and liability insurance.

3. Statutes permitting the insured to recover unless the breach of warranty or the fact misrepresented actually "contributed to the loss." Common law requires only that the breach or the misrepresentation affect the insurer's decision to write the policy. Such a breach or misrepresentation may not have contributed in any way to a loss that occurs after the policy is in effect. Very few states have legislation that modifies the common law this radically.

4. One statute (New Hampshire) providing for a reduction in the amount paid under a fire insurance contract if the insured makes a nonfraudulent misrepresentation that does not contribute to the loss. The reduction depends upon the premium paid relative to the premium that would have been paid if the fact had not been misrepresented.

In practice, insurers should have little difficulty in proving the materiality of almost any statement by the insured that is made a condition of the insurer's promise. As a result, despite academic and legal interest in the distinction between the doctrines of misrepresentation and breach of warranty, relatively few court decisions depend on this difference (Keeton, 1971).

Another relevant provision found in most life and health insurance contracts is the entire contract provision, which states that the policy, including the endorsements and attached papers, constitutes the entire contract. Because of this provision, an insurer wishing to void a policy or contest a claim on the basis of misstatements by the insured must refer to statements contained in a written application attached to the policy.

RIGHTS OF INSURED AT VARIANCE WITH POLICY PROVISIONS

In denying the right of the insurer to void a contract on the grounds that the insured violated some condition in the contract, concealed information, or misrepresented some fact, the insured may cite the doctrines of (1) waiver and estoppel or (2) reasonable expectations.

Waiver and Estoppel

Legal scholars and some courts distinguish between waiver and estoppel. A *waiver* is the voluntary relinquishment of a *known* right, whereas *estoppel* prevents a person from asserting a right because he or she has acted previously in such a way as to deny any interest in preserving that right. A waiver usually involves a statement to the insured that he or she need not worry about compliance with some condition in the contract or in disclosing certain information. Most courts appear to use the doctrines interchangeably. For example, it is common to read that the insurer waived this right and is, therefore, estopped from asserting this right at a later date.

Whether the insured will be successful in claiming a waiver depends in part upon the time when the waiver was supposed to have occurred. The court decisions can be divided into three categories depending upon when the waiver supposedly took place:

1. *Before the contract becomes effective.* Waivers by the insurer during this period are likely to result in a valid contract because, the courts reason, the insured is in a vulnerable position since he or she has not received the contract. For example, if the insured has already breached a condition in the contract on the date it is issued and the insurer or its agent knows about this breach, the courts will usually hold that the insurer has waived the condition with respect to the breach.
2. *After the contract is issued but before any loss.* This period is the most difficult to discuss because of the tremendous variance in court decisions. It is possible to state, however, that the insured is less likely to be successful in claiming a waiver during this period than in either of the other two. It is also possible to state that courts in reaching their decisions consider (a) the degree of ambiguity in the breached condition, (b) the authority of the insurance representative who is supposed to have been aware of the breach, (c) the kind of action that is supposed to have constituted a waiver, and (d) the seriousness of the breach.
3. *After the loss.* This third period offers the best opportunity for the insured to claim a waiver. Insurance adjusters must be careful not to require too much of the insured before they admit their liability; if they do, they may be held to have waived any breached conditions. Insurance adjusters, by first denying liability, have also been held on occasion to have waived post-loss requirements, such as the submission of a proof of loss within a specified time.

An insurer may attempt to preserve an option to later deny an insurance claim through the issuance of a *reservation of rights letter.* This letter provides notice to the insured or claimant that the insurer reserves the right to later deny the claim if evidence is revealed that would allow the assertion of this right. The reservation of rights letter is issued in the belief that the letter allows the insurer to begin processing the claim as if it intends to make payment while still allowing the option of later denying the claim. If the insurer later denies the claim, the reservation of rights letter could be used by the insurer as evidence that its actions in processing the claim did not constitute a waiver of its right to deny the claim.

For example, evidence later may later be revealed that the claim is fraudulent or a contract condition was breached. When the insurer denies the claim using this evidence, the insurer may use the reservation of rights letter against the claimant who asserts that the doctrine of waiver or estoppel prevents the insurer from denying the claim. Without the reservation of rights letter, the claimant might argue that the later denial of the claim implies that the insurer's actions in processing the claim as if it intended to make payment were in *bad faith,* a charge that could entitle the insured to additional recovery.

Reasonable Expectations

As noted earlier, insurance contracts usually are contracts of adhesion. Courts, therefore, tend to interpret ambiguous provisions in favor of the insured. Two additional principles explain many court decisions that are not adequately handled under the contract of adhesion or the waiver and estoppel doctrines. Under the first principle, an insurer is not permitted an *unconscionable advantage* in an insurance transaction. Under the second, the objectively *reasonable expectations* of applicants and intended beneficiaries will be honored even if those expectations would have been negated by painstaking study of the policy provisions. Two important corollaries of this principle are that (1) policy language will be interpreted from the lay person's point of view, not that of a sophisticated underwriter, and (2) even if the language is clearly understandable, the insurer must show that the insured's failure to read such language was unreasonable. Deviations from the reasonable expectations doctrine can be found, but according to one authority "insurance law appears to be moving in the direction the principle indicates" (Keeton, 1971, p. 357).

The reasonable expectations principle is illustrated by the following case. A man planning a round trip on a scheduled airline purchased an airplane trip policy that did not cover travel on other than scheduled airlines. On his return trip, his flight was canceled but the airline arranged for him and two others to charter a special flight with a firm operating under an air-taxi certificate. The plane crashed and the insured was killed. The insurer denied coverage on the ground that the insured was not at the time a passenger on a scheduled airline. The court, in a split decision, held the insurer liable. It argued that the contract was ambiguous and that "in this type of coverage, sold by a vending machine, the insured may reasonably expect coverage for the whole trip which he inserted in the policy, including reasonable substituted transportation necessitated by emergency."

The reasonable expectation doctrine also explains the decisions in some cases in which the insurer delivered a policy that deviated significantly from the coverage for which the insured had applied or in which the insurer reduced the coverage in a renewal policy without informing the insured.

AUTHORITY OF AGENTS

Most insurance is written by organizations, such as insurance corporations. Even if a risk manager negotiates coverage directly with an officer of the insurer, the officer acts in the capacity of agent for the insurer. More commonly, a risk manager employs the services of a professional intermediary or such as an *agent* or *broker* who represents one of the parties to an insurance transaction. These representatives were discussed briefly in Chapter 13. An understanding of the legal authority of representatives can be important when disputes arise over the disclosure of information or modification of terms of coverage.

Agent's Authority to Commit Insurer to Coverages

Although the term "agent" is applied frequently to insurance representatives, the legal meaning of the term is not specialized to insurance, and not all insurance representatives are agents. Legally, the term recognizes a relationship between two parties, a *principal* and an *agent*. Under the agency agreement, the principal delegates authority to the agent to act on its behalf. After the delegation occurs, actions of the agent lying within the scope of the agency agreement are binding on the principal. For example, an insurer may delegate to its agent the authority to issue its standard automobile liability insurance contract providing coverage up to $100,000. This authority, commonly called *binding* authority, allows the agent to issue the insurer's standard automobile liability contract with limits of $100,000 or less, collecting the premiums for the coverage on the insurer's behalf. The provisions of policies issued within the scope of the agency agreement are legally binding on the insurer, as if the insurer had issued the contract directly.

The authority of the agent to act on behalf of the insurer rests primarily on the terms of the written agency agreement. The authority provided explicitly in the agency agreement is called *expressed authority*. However, the agent's authority is not necessarily limited to the explicit scope of the agency agreement. The public is not expected to know the terms of the agency agreement. If an agent's actions reflect the authority the public would reasonably expect the agent to possess, *implied authority* may exist for the agent to bind the insurer through these actions. Often implied authority is present when such authority is a reasonable extension of the written agency agreement. For example, it would be reasonable to assume that an agent has authority to accept premium payments on behalf of the insurer. This implied authority could be used to bind an insurer to continued coverage when an agent accepts a late premium payment, even though the agency agreement may be silent on the issue.

A third type of authority, called *apparent authority,* could exist when an agent acts beyond the scope of the agency agreement and the insurer does not protest. For example, an agent could issue a type of coverage lying outside the scope of the agreement. If the insurer does not object to the agent's act and honors the coverage, their acquiescence may be construed as granting apparent authority to issue the coverage.

In most cases, the agent's power is limited to the expressed authority granted in the agency agreement, extended to include implied and apparent authority allowed by law. In the case of a true *general agent,* the scope of authority is very broad. A true general agent is empowered to act on behalf of the principal in all matters. For example, a true general agent could sell the principal's assets or buy assets on behalf of the principal. Except for rare instances, an insurance agent's authority is not this broad. A few executive officers of some insurance corporations may be general agents of their corporations. Some insurers grant broad underwriting and claims management authority to a *managing general agent* who manages the insurer's affairs related to a type of coverage or in a geographic area.

A *broker* usually functions as an agent of the insured. Hence, a broker does not have the legal authority to bind coverages unless the broker also is an agent of an insurer. The broker's function is to analyze the customer's exposure to risk and make recommendations concerning coverages. If the customer accepts a recommendation, the broker then solicits coverage from possible insurance suppliers.

Agent's Authority in Accepting Information Disclosed by Insureds

Because an agent represents an insurer and acts in the insurer's capacity, information revealed to the agent is presumed to be revealed to the insurer. While restrictions imposed by the insurer on an agent's authority are binding on the agent and may be grounds for action by the insurer against the agent, these restrictions are not necessarily binding on the agent's clients unless the clients are made aware of them or reasonably would be expected to know them. For example, an insured who notifies an agent of a claim is presumed to have notified the insurer. If the agent fails to forward notice of the claim to the insurer, courts usually will not allow the insurer to deny the claim because notification was not timely.

As discussed earlier under the doctrines of warranty and representation, an insured's failure to provide accurate or complete underwriting information can be a legal basis for an insurer's denial of coverage. Because information revealed to an agent is presumed to be in the insurer's possession, an agent's failure to forward unfavorable underwriting information to the insurer is not likely to be a valid legal basis for denial of coverage. However, a practice commonly followed during application for coverage is for the agent to interview the applicant and fill out the application form using the client's responses to the interview questions. As a final step, the agent asks the applicant to sign the form. The applicant's signature on the form attests to the accuracy of the responses, so prudent risk management principles would suggest that the applicant review the form for completeness and accuracy.

A separate issue arises about verbal or written statements by an agent about the nature of coverage when these statements conflict with contract provisions. For example, an agent could state that a policy provides flood coverage when the contract contains an explicit flood exclusion. The *parol evidence rule* holds that the provisions of the written contract determine the rights and responsibilities of the parties. In other words, oral or written statements of the agent cannot modify the provisions of a subsequently issued written contract. The most recent evidence of agreement between parties determines their rights and responsibilities. When this evidence is in writing, evidence of other previous agreements cannot modify the terms of the written contract.

However, the possibility exists that a subsequent agreement, even if verbal, could be construed as a new contract. For example, an agent could provide instructions to an insured on the reporting of a claim that conflict with the reporting requirement in the written contract. Because the instructions are given subsequent to the issuance of the insurance contract, a court could construe them as a new agreement. Evidence on the insured's awareness of limitations on the agent's authority would be important in resolving such a dispute. Normally, agents do not have the legal authority to modify contract terms (unless they are general agents), but a question could arise about whether a client would be aware of this restriction. Certainly a professional risk manager would be expected to know of such a restriction, but an owner of a medium-sized business might reasonably argue ignorance on this issue.

A broker acts as an agent of the insured, so no presumption exists that information provided to a broker has been forwarded to the insurer. Also, statements by the broker have no effect on the insurer's rights and responsibilities unless the broker also serves in the capacity of the insurer's agent.

STANDARDIZATION

In many respects, insurance contracts tend to be standardized among insurers and even among types of coverage. Although a contract offered by one insurer may not appear to resemble the same type of contract offered by another, analysis of the two contracts often reveals that the two coverages have a great deal in common. Several forces tend to favor standardization of insurance contracts. (1) The meaning of standard contracts and standard contract provisions tends to become established over time as a consequence of court decisions. A new and untested provision opens the possibility of unintended new interpretations, making insurers reluctant to depart from established wording. (2) Provisions whose meaning has been established allow a more accurate estimate of the expected claim payment than untested provisions. (3) Standard provisions tend to simplify administration and training procedures for employees such as loss adjusters. (4) Conflicts are less likely to arise when two or more insurance contracts apply to a loss if provisions of the two contracts are similar.

Bureau forms developed by the Insurance Services Office (ISO) and other rating organizations that were discussed in Chapter 13 offer examples of standardized coverages. These forms are developed by the rating organization and approved by state insurance departments for use by insurers who subscribe to the services of the rating organization. The declining influence of rating organizations that was discussed in Chapter 13 is likely to have increased the variety among insurance coverages offered today, although the wording of contract provisions in bureau forms is an important force shaping the structure of insurance coverages offered by all insurers.

Standardization of insurance contracts often is promoted by state insurance departments through their authority to approve or disapprove contract forms. The interest of insurance departments promoting standardization arises from their duty to protect policyholders from meaningless or unfairly priced coverages. In a few cases, state statutes may prescribe the wording of insurance contracts. The Standard Fire Policy, which in the past was the foundation for all fire insurance, is prescribed word for word by statute. At one time, all insurers writing fire coverage on real property were required to use this prescribed policy, but the requirement largely has disappeared. Provisions that appeared in the prescribed policy have been incorporated into more readable (and in most cases, broader) contracts that have replaced the prescribed policy.

A less restrictive regulatory approach that fosters standardization is the enactment of statutes mandating minimum standards that must be met by all coverages of a given type. An insurer is free to substitute its own provision as long as it meets the minimum standard prescribed in the statute. This approach is illustrated by state laws applying to life insurance prescribing minimum values that must be provided to a policyholder who ceases premium payments. State laws also prohibit life insurance exclusions applying to suicide occurring after the policy has been in force more than two years. Standardization also occurs when insurance provides benefits required by statute such as workers' compensation.

Key Concepts

contract of adhesion   A contract drafted by one party to which the other party must adhere. Most insurance contracts are contracts of adhesion drafted by the insurer, which causes courts to interpret ambiguous provisions in favor of the insured.

contract *uberrimae fidei*   A contract of the utmost good faith. Both parties to the contract must disclose all the facts they have relevant to the transaction. Insurance contracts are contracts *uberrimae fidei*.

concealment   Failure by the insured to reveal certain facts he or she knows that are not such common information that the insurer should also know them. Except in ocean marine insurance, an insurer must prove intent and materiality to deny a claim based on concealment. A concealment is material if the fact concealed would have caused the insurer either not to write the insurance or to write it under substantially different terms.

misrepresentation   An incorrect answer by the insured in response to a specific question by the insurer. To deny a claim, the insurer must prove only the materiality of a misrepresentation of a fact.

breach of warranty   A failure to meet a contract condition which may include representations made by the insured that are incorporated into the contract. Under common law, an insurer need not prove either intent or materiality to deny a claim on the basis of a breach of warranty. Statutes have modified this doctrine considerably.

contribute-to-the-loss statute   A statute found in a few states that requires insurers claiming misrepresentation or breach of warranty to show that the fact misrepresented actually contributed to the claim the insurer refuses to pay.

waiver and estoppel   Doctrines under which the insured claims that the actions of the insurer or its agent are inconsistent with later denial of a claim on the basis of some violation by the insured.

standardized contracts   Contracts that are uniform, at least in part, as to content or both content and language. Insurance contracts are standardized to a large extent by law or voluntarily.

parol evidence rule   A legal doctrine stating that prior agreements cannot affect the terms of a written contract.

expressed authority   The authority granted by an insurer to its agent through explicit provisions in the written agency agreement.

implied authority   The authority possessed by an agent that is not granted explicitly in the agency agreement but the public would reasonably expect the agent to possess because of the agency agreement.

apparent authority   The authority possessed by an agent when the agent acts beyond the scope of the agency agreement and the insurer does not protest.

principal   The party to an agency agreement who delegates authority to an agent to act on its behalf.

general agent   An agent having authority to act on behalf of the principal in all matters.

Review Questions

1. A tire manufacturer offers to repair or replace any tire that for any reason fails to give trouble-free service for 18 months. Is this an insurance transaction?
2. Which characteristic of an insurance contract probably led to the following court decisions?

a. An ambiguous provision in the contract was interpreted in favor of the insured.

b. A contract covering the former owner of a building was held not to protect a new owner because the insurer had not consented to an assignment of the contract.

c. The insurer was held not responsible for a loss because the insured failed to submit a proof of loss within the proper time period.

3. A 16-year-old boy purchases an automobile insurance contract. At the end of the policy year, he demands the return of his insurance premium.

a. On what basis does he make this request?

b. Will he be successful?

c. What other insureds may be legally incompetent to purchase insurance?

4. An employee signed an application for individual life insurance on January 10. She did not pay any premium at that time. The underwriter at the home office of the insurer accepted the application on January 17 and mailed the contract to the agent that afternoon for delivery to the employee. When the agent called at the employee's home with the policy, he discovered that the employee had died. Is the insurer liable if the employee died on January 12? On January 18?

5. How would you answer question 4 if the employee paid the first premium with her application?

6. In its application for fire insurance, a firm failed to reveal that a disgruntled stockholder had threatened to set the building on fire if the president did not grant him an interview by the end of the week. The following week the building burned to the ground as the result of an accidental explosion.

a. Was the concealed fact material?

b. Can the insurer successfully deny liability in this instance?

7. An automobile insurer customarily asks an applicant whether any insurer has canceled his or her automobile insurance during the past three years. The new risk manager of a firm answers in the negative because he believes no cancellation has occurred; but actually a contract was canceled 18 months ago. The insurer issues the contract, and two months later there is a collision loss.

a. Was this misrepresentation material?

b. Can the insurer successfully deny liability?

8. a. What is the nature of the statutory modifications of the common law doctrine of warranties?

b. How important is the warranty doctrine today?

9. a. At the time an automobile insurance contract was being negotiated, the risk manager told the insurance agent that the firm's two automobiles were encumbered under a conditional sales agreement, but the agent did not note this fact in the application. Since this information is important to the insurer, it refused to pay a loss under the contract when it discovered the omission. Will the insurer be successful in its denial of the claim?

b. A risk manager informed her agent during the policy period that a building would be unoccupied beyond the period permitted under a fire insurance contract. The agent assured her that the period of nonoccupation would make no difference, but the insurer reacted differently following a loss. What is the probable outcome?

10. In his application for individual life insurance, an employee stated in reply to a direct question that he had not visited a doctor in the past three years. The employee's answer appears on a written application attached to the contract. Five years after purchasing the contract, the employee died, and the insurer discovered for the first time that the employee had visited a doctor several times in connection with a pain in his chest.

a. Will the statement made by the insured be considered a warranty?

b. Is the insurer liable for the face amount of the contract?

11. Since automobile liability insurance is required or highly encouraged in all states, it has been suggested that each state legislature enact a statutory automobile liability insurance policy. What would be the advantages and disadvantages of such action?

References and Suggestions for Additional Reading

American Jurisprudence, vol. XLIII (2nd ed., Rochester, NY: Lawyers' Cooperative Publishing Co. and San Francisco: Bancroft-Whitney Co., 1982), sections 4–16.

DENENBERG, H. S.: "The Legal Definition of Insurance," *Journal of Insurance,* vol. XXX, no. 3 (September, 1963), pp. 319–343.

GREIDER, J. E., M. L. CRAWFORD, and W. T. BEADLES: *Law and the Life Insurance Contract* (5th ed., Homewood, Ill.: Richard D. Irwin, Inc., 1984).

KEETON, R. E.: *Basic Text on Insurance Law* (St. Paul, Minn.: West Publishing Company, 1971).

LORIMER, J. J., H. F. PERLET, F. G. KEMPIN, and F. R. HODOSH: *The Legal Environment of Insurance,* vols. I and II (3rd ed., Malvern, Pa.: American Institute for Property and Liability Underwriters, 1987).

MEHR, ROBERT I., and EMERSON CAMMACK: *Principles of Insurance* (Homewood, Ill.: Richard D. Irwin, Inc., 1972).

PATTERSON, EDWIN W.: *Essentials of Insurance Law* (2nd ed., New York: McGraw-Hill Book Company, 1957).

———, and W. F. YOUNG, JR.: *Cases and Materials on the Law of Insurance* (4th ed., Brooklyn, N.Y.: The Foundation Press, Inc., 1961).

VANCE, W. R., and B. M. ANDERSON: *Handbook on the Law of Insurance* (5th ed., St. Paul, Minn.: West Publishing Company, 1951).

Insurance Contract Analysis: Property and Liability Coverage

Learning Objectives

After you have completed this chapter, you should be able to:

1. Describe how a typical property or liability insurance contract is structured.
2. Explain why insurers put exclusions in insurance contracts.
3. Analyze an insurance contract to determine what events are covered.
4. Distinguish between claims-made and occurrence forms of liability insurance and explain the importance of the distinction to risk managers.
5. Show by example the operation of a coinsurance clause typically found in property insurance contracts and explain the purpose of the clause.
6. List four ways that deductibles can be classified and give examples of each type.
7. Explain how layered coverage can be built using excess policies and why the layering approach is used.
8. Identify two specific risk management activities in which skill in analyzing insurance contracts is necessary.

INTRODUCTION

For risk managers of organizations, the skills required to analyze insurance contracts are almost a necessity because others in the organization often rely on the risk manager for guidance on issues related to insurance coverage. Unfortunately, the typical insurance contract is a long, complex document with wording that may be tedious and repetitive. The difficulty lies not with interpreting individual sentences. Most sentences found in modern insurance contracts can be understood with moderate effort (portions of some marine insurance contracts are an exception, as some wording developed hundreds of years ago has survived in these contracts). Rather, the problem often involves the reading of, say, 15 pages of small print, then integrating the sentences into a meaningful framework. What the insurance analyst needs is a set of roadmaps or guides, which this chapter provides for property and liability insurance contracts.

The blame for difficult-to-understand coverage does not lie entirely with the insurance industry. Economic and legal forces often force insurers into wording that lay persons would find difficult to comprehend. First, insurance tends to be practical for only a narrow set of risks, which the contract must set out clearly. Second, in most cases, the insurer is solely responsible for drafting the contract, in which case courts hold the insurer responsible for wording the contract clearly. Insurers attempt to word coverage to leave little room for interpretation beyond what was intended when the coverage was developed and for which the premium was determined.

Contract Analysis and Claims Negotiation

One context in which the analysis of insurance contracts arises is when a claim possibly covered by insurance occurs, particularly if coverage is denied by the insurer. In this situation, the purpose of the analysis is to negotiate claim settlement, perhaps for a claim that was not envisioned by either the insurer or insured when coverage was purchased. Environmental liability imposed on users of waste disposal sites offers an example. The parties to the coverage may not have envisioned the problem arising if the contract was written 30 years ago, so the contract language may not explicitly address the problem. However, a reasonable interpretation of the contract language still may allow coverage.

Subtle changes in the definition or interpretation of contract terms or provisions can dramatically affect recovery for loss. As an example, a manufacturer of fertilizer purchases a product liability insurance contract that provides $100 million coverage with a $50,000 deductible per occurrence. A batch of contaminated fertilizer is sold through dealers to 1000 farmers, whose crops are ruined. The meaning of the term "occurrence" is critical to the settlement of this claim. If the *sale* of fertilizer to the farmer is deemed the occurrence, the manufacturer may be required to retain up to (1000)($50,000) = $50 million of claims. If the *manufacture* of the entire batch of fertilizer is deemed to be the occurrence, a single $50,000 deductible applies but the $100 million coverage limit may be a concern. Under either point of view, attention is focused on the terms of coverage and their meaning.

Coverage Analysis, Risk Financing, and Risk Identification

A second context in which the analysis of insurance contracts arises is when a set of risks is identified for which insurance may be an appropriate risk financing technique. Analysis in this situation involves a broad set of issues, as it requires the analyst to consider (1) possible motives for holding coverage and (2) how well a set of coverages responds to these motives. However, consideration of possible motives for holding coverage intertwines coverage analysis with the process of risk identification and assessment. In practice, coverage analysis and risk identification may be inseparable.

A BASIC CONSIDERATION: UNDERSTANDING CONTRACT STRUCTURE

427

CHAPTER 17
Insurance Contract
Analysis: Property
and Liability
Coverage

Subject to the authority of the state insurance regulator to approve or disapprove policy forms, insurers are free to determine the structure and wording of their contracts. Despite this freedom to experiment with contract language, many insurers' coverages share a great deal in common. The similarity is due in part to the narrow set of circumstances in which insurance tends to be useful and the economic and legal forces that have shaped insurance coverage over time. However, the similarity does not imply that the wording of contracts is identical, only that the coverages are similar. Questions concerning the level of coverage for a particular claim or the suitability of the contract for a given purpose often require a detailed analysis of the contract.

The Initial Review

As a first step, an insurance analyst often quickly reviews the titles of major contract sections to determine the contract's structure and organization. Most insurance contracts are organized into major sections, each headed by a section title that indicates the nature of the material appearing in the section. This initial review alerts the analyst to the location of contract provisions likely to bear on a particular issue, particularly if the analyst is familiar with the wording of standard contract provisions.

Two formats are commonly used to organize insurance contracts: the *jacket* plus *form* arrangement and the *self-contained contract.* Under the first format, the complete contract consists of two parts: (1) a policy or jacket, containing a set of provisions applying to a number of types of coverage, and (2) a form, which is combined with the jacket to make a complete contract. The jacket may be a double-sized sheet of paper that is folded in the middle, with the form inserted into the jacket to make a complete contract. Under the second format, the self-contained contract does not consist of two distinct parts, being instead a single unified document.

Making the distinction between these two formats can simplify analysis. When a contract uses the jacket plus form arrangement, the analysis usually starts with the form, not the jacket. The form is the portion of the contract that makes the coverage specific to the risk being insured. The form contains provisions such as a listing of the perils and the covered property. The jacket usually contains provisions applying to a number of policies, so it usually is examined after analysis of the form suggests that coverage applies. For example, the jacket may contain a set of general exclusions applying to a series of coverages. Unless the analyst is concerned about the issue of whether a specific exclusion applies to the coverage, the analysis usually begins by determining what the policy covers, not what it excludes.

Unfortunately, the appearance of the word "form" does not necessarily imply that the contract is organized using the jacket plus form method. For example, many dwelling coverages use the term "form" (e.g., Homeowner's Form 3) while using a self-contained format. The issue of contract organization is best determined by a review of the major contract section headings rather than relying on the appearance of a particular heading or phrase.

Major Section Headings

A section heading usually appears at the head of each major section of an insurance contract. Clauses within each section also may be headed by boldface titles. The words in these headings usually reflect the nature of the provisions in the section or clause. Often commonly understood phrases such as "property insured," "perils insured," or "duties in the event of loss" appear as section headings. Some section headings have a meaning that is more specialized. A few typical headings are identified and explained below.

Declarations. The *declarations* identify the insured; describe the property, activity, or life being insured; state the types of coverage purchased, the applicable policy limits, and the term of the coverage; and indicate the premium paid for each separate coverage purchased. The purpose of the declarations made by the insured is to give the insurer sufficient information to enable it, with information from other sources, to issue the desired contract at a proper price. These declarations are subject to the legal doctrines of concealment, misrepresentation, and breach of warranty discussed in Chapter 16.

The declarations in an insurance contract typically constitute the first page or pages of the contract, often taking the form of a table in which information identifying the insured objects or situations is filled in. Because the declarations identify the objects or situations being insured, they are an important part of the contract. To avoid later disputes or unexpected denial of claims, an insurance analyst should verify that the information appearing on the policy declarations is complete and correct and that the desired coverage is provided.

Insuring Agreements. The *insuring agreements* state what the insurer promises to do. The insuring agreements describe the characteristics of the events covered under the contract. A section of the insuring agreements may also define certain terms used in the contract.

Many insurance contracts have more than one insuring agreement, particularly contracts providing both property and liability insurance in the same document (e.g., *multi-peril* or *package* contracts). In some insurance contracts, insuring agreements are diffused throughout the contract to such an extent that they are not easily isolated. This diffusion has been accompanied on some multi-peril coverage by the use of an insuring agreement that is vacuous: a statement that the insurer agrees to provide the insurance described in the contract in return for payment of the premium and compliance with policy provisions. Some contracts, particularly ones providing traditional or narrowly focused coverage, still adhere to traditional, explicit wording on insuring agreements, such as, ". . . this company . . . does insure . . . to the extent of the actual cash value of property at the time of loss . . . against all direct loss by fire, lightning and by removal . . . except as hereinafter provided. . . ." (excerpts taken from the insuring agreement on a Standard Fire Policy).

Exclusions. The *exclusions* limit the coverage provided under the insuring agreements. They may exclude certain perils, property, sources of liability, persons, losses, locations, or time periods. The exclusions usually serve one or more of the following purposes:

429

CHAPTER 17
*Insurance Contract
Analysis: Property
and Liability
Coverage*

1. To except losses that the insurer considers to be uninsurable. Intentionally caused losses are excluded, not only because they violate the accidental-loss standard, but also because public policy requires such an exclusion. Ordinary wear and tear losses are excluded because they are not accidental.
2. To reduce moral hazards. For example, freezing of an automobile radiator is not covered under an automobile insurance contract because an insured can easily prevent this loss with antifreeze. This purpose is closely related to the reason for excluding wear and tear losses as not accidental.
3. To exclude losses that are traditionally covered under other contracts or that require some special underwriting or rating. For example, an employer's liability for injuries to employees is generally excluded under liability insurance covering the premises because this liability is usually covered under workers' compensation or employers' liability insurance, and because the extent of exposure is measured by payroll units, which may not be an appropriate measure for other liability exposures. Another example is the exclusion in theft insurance policies of losses covered under employee dishonesty insurance.
4. To lower the premium for protection against exposures that would add to costs but which some persons do not have or do not consider important. For example, automobile liability exposures are usually excluded from general liability insurance. This exclusion permits insureds who have no automobile liability exposures to pay less for their general liability insurance.
5. To produce a limited coverage that can be sold at an attractive rate. An insurer is more likely to seek this objective through a narrow insuring agreement.
6. To exclude coverage the insurer is not prepared to service or licensed to write, such as boiler and machinery insurance, which emphasizes careful insurer inspections of the boiler and machinery. Another example is automobile insurance covering losses outside the United States and Canada.

Some exclusions merely clarify what should be apparent from the insuring agreement. For example, the fire insurance policy may exclude losses caused by riot unless fire ensues, in which case it covers the fire loss only. If this exclusion were omitted, the coverage would not be any greater, because a riot is not a fire, and fire and lighting are the only perils specified in the insuring agreement.

Conditions. The *conditions* define terms used in the other parts of the contract, prescribe conditions that must be satisfied before the insurer is liable, and may describe the basis for computing the premium. Most conditions describe the rights and obligations of the insured and the insurer following a loss.

Riders, Endorsements, and Extensions. *Riders* or *endorsements* may be included as part of the coverage. These terms describe provisions that are added to standard contracts. Although the terms sometimes are used interchangeably, the term "rider" usually refers to a separate agreement attached to a life insurance contract. For example, a rider may provide an additional benefit whose amount is expressed as a percent of the death benefit provided by the underlying life insurance contract. The rider does not modify the meaning of any provision in the contract to which it is attached, which distinguishes it from an endorsement. The rider, however, may not have meaning except as part of another contract.

The endorsement usually changes a provision in the contract to which it is attached. It may add or delete an exclusion, for example, or (re)define a term used in the contract. Policyholders often assume that endorsements improve the coverage provided by the contract (as in "my contract was endorsed to cover theft losses"). However, endorsements can remove coverage just as well as they provide it. Some endorsements, for example, may serve to define perils in ways that eliminate coverage courts have found the standard contract to provide.

An *extension* is a contract provision that may take the form of either a rider or an endorsement. For example, an extension may increase the limit of coverage applying to theft losses or include types of property not covered under a standard contract. Usually the term "extension" is used to describe a contract provision that broadens the coverage or relaxes the conditions for coverage to apply.

The purpose actually served by the extension, however, depends on the insurer's strategy in designing the contract. For example, an extension frequently found on dwelling policies includes lawns, trees, shrubs, and other plants within the scope of coverage if the loss is caused by a peril appearing on a list within the extension. An examination of many such lists reveals that windstorm does not appear as a covered peril, despite property such as the dwelling structure being covered for windstorm losses. The final outcome is to deny coverage for windstorm losses to lawns, trees, shrubs, and other plants. From the viewpoint of the insurer, one approach that would achieve this result might be to provide coverage under the standard contract for losses to lawns, trees, shrubs, and other plants, but list windstorm as an excluded peril for this type of property. The other approach is to provide limited coverage for this type of property through the extension. The approach using the extension may be easier to defend if a dispute on the issue goes to court.

Section Headings Do Not Provide Full Disclosure. Unfortunately, major section headings do not always alert the analyst to everything that appears in the section. Only a careful reading of the section will reveal all the information. For example, a section heading in a contract may say "perils insured," followed by a listing of the causes of loss covered by the contract. Under the peril "windstorm or hail" the contract may state that the peril is not defined to include damage to property inside the structure unless the direct action of wind or hail first damages the building and the damage is caused from rain, snow, or sleet entering through the resulting opening. This provision has the effect of excluding damage to property inside the building caused by rain entering through a roof that has become leaky as a result of age, or through a window left open. Presumably this type of loss is under the direct control of the insured. Providing coverage for this type of loss could seriously weaken the incentive for the insured to prevent its occurrence, ultimately increasing the cost of coverage.

431

CHAPTER 17
*Insurance Contract
Analysis: Property
and Liability
Coverage*

A FRAMEWORK FOR ANALYSIS

After the analyst has learned the organization and format of the contract, a detailed examination of policy provisions is the next step. The second reading, which proceeds slowly and carefully, seeks answers to three basic questions, which can be stated in sequence. (1) Is the loss covered? (2) If so, for how much? (3) What procedure must be followed to secure payment of benefits? These three questions form the core of analysis. Nearly any issue related to the scope of insurance coverage can be formulated in terms of these three questions, which are supported by further inquiries. When the first question's supporting inquiries are included, the framework appears as below:

1. Under what circumstances would the insurer be responsible for the loss? What events are covered?
   a. What perils are covered?
   b. What property or source of liability is covered?
   c. What persons are covered?
   d. What losses are reimbursed?
   e. What locations are covered?
   f. What time period is covered?
   g. Are there any special conditions that do not fall into any of the other six categories that may suspend or terminate the coverage?
2. If the insurer is responsible for the loss, how much will it pay?
3. What steps must the insured take following a loss?

The remainder of this chapter is organized to provide a detailed breakdown of these three questions as they pertain to property and liability insurance. Most of the chapter focuses on the first two questions: (1) events covered and (2) amount of recovery.

PROPERTY INSURANCE: EVENTS COVERED

Determining whether an event is covered by a property insurance contract is a bit like running the gauntlet. An accident or occurrence is insured only if it meets every one of the tests implied in the seven supporting inquiries, *a* through *g*, listed under question 1 above. That is, the peril must be covered, the property must be covered, the legal interest of the person or entity seeking recovery for damaged property must be insured, and so on. Failure to meet any one of the tests implies that the insurer is not liable. For example, if an accident meets every one of the tests except that it occurs at a location where coverage is not provided, the insurer can deny the claim.

Perils Covered

Relevant considerations in determining what perils are covered are (1) whether the contract is a named-perils or an all risks contract, (2) how the covered or excluded perils are defined, (3) the excluded perils, and (4) the chain-of-causation concept.

Named-Perils and All Risk Contracts. *Named-perils contracts* specify the perils covered. Loss by any peril not included in the list is not covered. In addition, exclusions may except losses caused by the named peril under certain circumstances (e.g., a fire caused by war).

All risk contracts cover all perils not otherwise excluded. In other words, a named-perils contract lists the included perils; an all risk contract names the excluded perils. All risk contracts sometimes cover losses beyond one's wildest imagination because the insurer has not excluded the particular cause of loss. For example, one insurer paid a claim because a police officer's horse licked paint off a car.

All risk contracts (1) generally provide broader coverage than named-perils contracts, and (2) permit the insured to consider explicitly all the perils to which he or she might still be exposed if the contract is purchased. In some instances the all risk contract replaces two or more named-perils contracts that would require more effort to administer and that might provide overlapping coverage. A disadvantage of all risk contracts is they generally are more expensive than named perils contracts that are equivalent in other respects. Furthermore, the insured may not want or need protection against some of the perils, known or unknown, included in the all risk contract.

A so-called "all risk" contract often used to insure owner-occupied dwellings illustrates the distinction. This contract provides all risk coverage on the dwelling structure but named-perils coverage on moveable personal property within the structure, such as furniture and appliances. Suppose an open, full can of paint is accidentally dropped down the stairs in the dwelling, with the spilled paint damaging the floor, walls, trim, and furniture. Is the peril covered? To determine the answer to this question, the analyst needs to distinguish between damage to property considered part of the structure (e.g., the floor, walls, and trim) and damage to other property. The coverage on the structure is all risk, so the analyst would examine the contract's exclusions to see whether any of them might be interpreted to deny coverage for loss to the structure. The coverage for other property (e.g., furniture) is on a named-perils basis, so the analyst would examine the list of covered perils to see whether a reasonable person could interpret any of them to afford coverage for the damage to furniture.

Perils Defined. A few contracts define covered perils. For example, burglary may be defined as "the felonious abstraction of insured property from within the premises by a person making felonious entry therein by actual force and violence, of which force and violence there are visible marks" on the exterior of the premises. Sometimes a peril is defined in a statute. For example, most states have statutes that define a riot as: (1) a violent or tumultuous act against the person or property of another by (2) three or more persons. The second part of this definition is important in distinguishing between a riot and and an act of vandalism.

433

CHAPTER 17
*Insurance Contract
Analysis: Property
and Liability
Coverage*

Often, perils are defined through court decisions. Courts, for example, have defined the following: windstorm, explosion, accident, collision and fires. Their interpretation of "fire" is particularly important. According to the courts a fire has not occurred unless there has been a visible flame or glow. Scorching and consequent blackening, for example, may not have involved any fire. The courts also have held that the fire must be a "hostile" fire, not a "friendly" fire. A hostile fire is one that has escaped from its proper confines. If an object is accidentally thrown into a fireplace, the loss is not a fire loss because there has been no hostile fire. Some courts, however, also consider a fire raging out of control to be a hostile fire even if the fire remains in the proper confines.

Excluded Perils. Whether the contract is written on a named-perils or an all risks basis, the exclusions affect what perils are covered under the contract. Sometimes courts add exclusions not mentioned in the contract. For example, fires are excluded under fire insurance contracts if they are caused by war or are intentionally set by public authorities (except to prevent the spread of fire). The contract may not exclude fires set intentionally by the insured, but the courts have held that to cover them would be contrary to public policy. Automobile comprehensive insurance covers all perils except collision, wear and tear, mechanical or electrical breakdowns, freezing, war, and confiscation by duly constituted public authorities.

Chain-of-Causation. When a sequence of events leads to loss that might be insured, courts may be asked to interpret whether the policy covers a peril set in motion by some other peril. For the purpose of illustration, suppose a windstorm blows down power lines that set fire to some leaves raked into a corner of a yard. The smoke from the burning leaves blows through an open window in the dwelling located in an adjacent yard, causing smoke damage to draperies and upholstered furniture. The sequence is illustrated in the chronologic chain shown below.

Windstorm → Fire → Smoke Damage

Suppose that the owner of the dwelling where the smoke damage occurs has an insurance policy covering only one peril: fire.[1] The question is whether the fire policy provides coverage for smoke damage.

As a general rule, a court presented with the above set of circumstances would tend very strongly toward finding in favor of coverage for the insured, particularly if the insured is legally unsophisticated. The legal doctrine that most likely would apply is the *chain-of-causation* doctrine, which would afford coverage for a peril set in motion by a peril named in the contract. In the above case, the smoke damage was caused by a fire, which is the peril named on the contract. This finding does not necessarily require that the fire occur on the insured premises, only that the damage be a consequence of the fire. Under the

---

[1] This assumption only serves to illustrate the chain-of-causation concept. A dwelling policy providing coverage for only the fire peril would be unusual in the United States today.

chain-of-causation doctrine, a policy providing coverage for a peril not only covers damage caused by the peril, but also damage caused by a peril set in motion by the named peril.

A somewhat harsher doctrine (from the viewpoint of the insured) is the *proximate cause* doctrine. A court applying this doctrine would consider the *foreseeability* of the loss: whether a reasonable person could foresee that the smoke damage would be a consequence of leaves catching fire. The court would make this judgment after considering remoteness of the peril from the damage: the physical distance between the site where the peril occurs and location of the damage; and how much time elapsed between the appearance of the peril and the damage. Whether any intervening causes appeared would be an additional consideration. In the above illustration, the connection between the fire and the resulting damage is fairly close, so a court would be likely to find in favor of coverage. The more remote the connection, the less likely the court is to find coverage.

The windstorm is the *actual cause* of the smoke damage, in that the loss would not have occurred in the absence of the windstorm. To require that the peril be the actual cause of loss would be very harsh with respect to the insured, as windstorm is not a covered peril. However, suppose the policy covers windstorm only, not fire. The sequence of events connecting the windstorm to the smoke damage may appear so improbable as to make it unlikely that a court would find windstorm to be the proximate cause of the smoke damage. The issue is whether a reasonable person could foresee that a windstorm could lead to smoke damage.

Fortunately for most unsophisticated insureds, courts are unlikely to apply a doctrine even as harsh as proximate cause. When the holder of coverage is a legally sophisticated professional, a court may be more willing to apply the proximate cause doctrine, reasoning that sophisticated professionals are likely to be aware of coverage limitations and set up appropriate safeguards.

Concurrent Causation. In 1983 the California courts advanced a new doctrine of *concurrent causation* which has caused insurers to make some important changes in property insurance contracts, especially those providing all risks insurance. In the first case citing this doctrine, heavy rainfall caused floods in the city of Palm Desert. Policyholders with all risk policies whose homes were damaged by the flood claimed that their losses were caused by the community's negligent management of flood-control facilities, which was not among the excluded perils. Insurers argued that the losses were caused by flood, which was an excluded peril. The court sided with the policyholders, reasoning that if two or more perils cause a loss, an all risk policy covers the loss if any one of these perils is not excluded. In another case a house slid off a ravine following a mudslide. Mudslide was an excluded peril. However, a contributing cause was a sewer drain that would have released subsurface waters if it had not been damaged by a sewer contractor. The insurer had to pay the claim because the damaged sewer drain was not an excluded peril.

Most, if not all, cases to date have involved flood and earth movement losses, but insurers feared that the concept might be extended to other excluded perils and to exclusions under named-perils contracts as well as all risk contracts. To counter this trend, insurers have replaced "all risk of direct physical loss" with "risk of direct physical loss." More importantly, the list of exclusions is preceded by a statement that the exclusions apply regardless of any other causes or event contributing concurrently or in any sequence to the loss. Named-perils contracts contain similar language relative to certain exclusions such as governmental action, nuclear hazard, and war.

435

CHAPTER 17
Insurance Contract
Analysis: Property
and Liability
Coverage

Property Covered

Property insurance contracts may be written to cover either real property or personal property, or both. Covered real property (i.e., real estate) usually is identified specifically in policy declarations. If coverage applies to personal property, the property may be specifically identified in a list or *schedule*. Coverage may apply more broadly to all personal property not specifically excluded (*unscheduled* personal property). An intermediate approach is to apply coverage to a category of property (e.g., machinery, vehicles, or jewelry).

The unscheduled approach is convenient for insureds because it (1) does not require the effort to identify and list all property prior to the occurrence of a loss, (2) alerts the insured to types of property that are not covered, and (3) allows coverage to apply to property acquired after the coverage is put into force. One disadvantage to the unscheduled approach is the cost, which usually is higher than coverage applying to specifically identified items. Possible disputes over the existence or valuation of property that is totally lost are another possible disadvantage. A lack of evidence on the existence of property or its value may lead to disputes over coverage, the cost of which are a deadweight loss to the insurer and insured. Scheduling covered property provides evidence as to the existence and valuation of property (the valuation often is based on a professional appraisal).

If the contract covers a business building, the building coverage typically applies to machinery used for the service of the building, such as plumbing, air-conditioning, heating apparatus, and elevators. It also includes ovens, kilns, furnaces, and the like, under most conditions. Awnings, screens, storm doors, window shades, and the like, if owned by the building owner, are considered part of the building. Finally, personal property, such as janitors' supplies, fuel, and the like, that is used solely in the service of the building is covered under the building coverage. Commonly excluded under the building coverage are excavations, underground flues and drains, and foundations below the surface of the ground.

Contracts covering personal property commonly exclude automobiles, airplanes, animals, money, and securities. Contracts covering specific types of property may exclude specific subtypes of items (for example, a policy may cover a contractor's construction equipment but not its trucks).

Persons Insured

Property insurance contracts identify the organizations or individuals whose legal interests are insured. In some contracts, only one individual is insured. Under other contracts, the coverage extends to include interests of a number of organizations or individuals. Covered individuals may include the named insured's family, guests, legal representatives, secured creditors, customers, or employees. These other persons may be protected against losses to their own property or their liability to the named insured for damage to his or her property. They may be covered automatically or only at the option of the named insured.

Clauses Protecting the Interest of Lenders. Secured creditors such as a mortgage company, lending institution, or automobile finance company are provided special treatment under property insurance contracts. The usual procedure is to include a *mortgage clause* (or, in automobile insurance, a *loss payable clause*) in the contract protecting the owner's interest. This clause obligates the insurer to pay the lender even if the property owner has violated a contract condition in a way that allows the insurer to deny the owner's claim. This special treatment applies only if the violation is not within the control or knowledge of the lender. The lender's recovery is limited to its insurable interest (e.g., the outstanding mortgage balance). If the clause results in the insurer paying the lender when it would have otherwise denied the claim, the insurer has a legal right to take action against the owner for the amount paid to lender.

For example, a business may own a $500,000 warehouse pledged as collateral for a $350,000 mortgage loan. If the owner purchases a fire insurance policy providing $500,000 of coverage on the warehouse and names the lender in the mortgage clause, the lender can collect in situations in which the owner's claim would be denied. If the owner deliberately sets fire to the warehouse and burns it to the ground, the lender still can collect up to $350,000 despite the insurer's denial of the owner's claim. The lender still is protected as long as the breach of contract was not within the control or knowledge of the lender. After the lender is paid, the insurer assumes the lender's rights against the owner for the $350,000 mortgage balance. The insurer has no obligation to the owner if the owner deliberately set the fire.

Under more typical circumstances, in which the owner has not violated a contract condition, the insurer usually makes payment jointly to the owner and the lender. Ideally, the lender releases funds to the insured for repairs. Another possibility is the lender claiming its share of the insurance payment and reducing the loan balance by the payment amount. This second possibility would result in the owner being forced to seek a new loan for funds to make repairs. The lender might take this second sequence of actions if terms on which new loans are issued are more favorable to lenders than terms on the loan in existence at the time of loss.

Clauses protecting the interest of lenders usually require that the lender be given separate notice of cancellation if the contract is cancelled. If the coverage is cancelled because the owner fails to pay the premium, the contract usually requires the insurer to offer the lender an opportunity to pay the premium.

Assignment. An organization's or individual's interest may become insured through *assignment.* For an assignment to be effective, the insurer's consent is required. Consent of the insurer is required because assignment may change the level of hazards. Following a loss, however, an insured can assign to another person any claim he or she may have against an insurer. The assignee does not become a party to the contract but can collect only what the insured could have collected without the assignment.

437

CHAPTER 17
Insurance Contract
Analysis: Property
and Liability
Coverage

Losses Reimbursed

Property insurance contracts typically reimburse some but not all aspects of a loss. Unless the contract is written specifically to cover indirect loss (e.g., business interruption coverage), property insurance usually reimburses direct loss caused by an insured peril. In addition, many property insurance contracts reimburse indirect losses, such as debris removal expense and, in the case of dwellings, additional living expense. Chapter 5 of this text explained the distinctions between direct, indirect, and time element losses.

Locations Covered

Property insurance contracts may be written (1) on a specified locations basis or (2) as a floater or floating insurance, in which case they cover losses anywhere within a specified area that is not excluded. To illustrate, some contracts provide protection only if the loss occurs at one specified location; others cover all locations anywhere in the world that are not specifically excluded. Between these two extremes lie other possibilities. For example, policies may cover losses at any one of a number of specified locations, at specified locations plus any new locations acquired by the insured, or anywhere within the United States and Canada that is not specifically excluded. Sometimes the coverage is more restricted as to perils, property, persons, or other features at certain locations.

Time Period Covered

The policy term for most property insurance contracts is usually one year, but it may be some fraction of a year (for example, six months) or some multiple of a year (for example, three years). Some surety bonds run until canceled.

Of particular interest are the hours at which the coverage begins and terminates—for example, noon or midnight—and the basis for identifying the time of the loss—for example, standard time or daylight saving time at (1) the address of the named insured or at (2) the place of loss. Sometimes the coverage does not begin until some event occurs, such as the departure of a ship or the award of a contract to a successful bidder.

The inception and termination dates of coverage usually are stated in the declarations of a property insurance contract. As long as the damage caused by the insured peril commences prior to the expiration (and not prior to inception), the entire loss caused by that peril is subject to coverage.

A fire starting at 10:00 A.M. but not extinguished until 5:00 P.M. on a day when coverage expires at noon offers an illustration. The fire is covered on the same terms that would apply if the contract had not expired that day. Another type of loss that is likely to extend beyond the time period of coverage occurs when business interruption insurance applies to operations using specialized equipment or facilities. For example, a fire may destroy a factory during the last week of coverage under a business interruption policy. If the factory is shut down for eight months, most of the resulting business interruption loss accrues outside the period of coverage. The coverage applies as if the entire period of interruption occurred prior to the termination date of the policy. This example demonstrates the importance of looking well ahead when negotiating provisions of business interruption coverage, particularly on manufacturing operations using specialized facilities or equipment.

Cancellation. Insurance contracts may be canceled only by mutual agreement of the parties to the contract unless the contract contains a provision to the contrary. Most property insurance contracts contain a cancellation provision that gives both the insured and the insurer the right to cancel the contract prior to the expiration date. Neither need give any reason for requesting the cancellation. If the insurer cancels the contract, the cancellation is effective a stated number of days after the insurer notifies the insured, and the insurer must return a *pro rata* portion of the premium to the insured. The required period of advance notice runs from midnight on the day on which notice is given. In many contracts "notice" means mailing of the notice, in which case the insured may receive less effective advance notice than the number of days stated in the contract.

If the insured cancels the contract, the cancellation is effective as soon as he or she notifies the insurer. The insurer must return a *short-rate* portion of the premium. The short-rate return is less than a pro rata return because the insurer is permitted to recognize that most of the expenses other than losses have already been incurred. For example, the short-rate refund after 180 days on a one-year contract is 40 percent. The short-rate cancellation also discourages the purchase of insurance to cover only the more hazardous parts of the policy period.

Other Conditions Restricting Covered Events

After analyzing the nature of covered events using the six criteria described above, a risk manager may identify other restrictions that do not fit easily into these six categories. Often these restrictions take the form of contract conditions that must be met for coverage to apply. For example, a fire insurance contract may suspend the coverage while there is any increase in the hazard within the knowledge or control of the insured, such as a change in occupancy from a retail store to paper manufacturing, without notification to the insurer.

PROPERTY INSURANCE: AMOUNT OF RECOVERY

As explained in Chapter 16, most property insurance contracts are contracts of indemnity. Typically, the contract reimburses loss as defined in the terms of coverage. Hence, the contract section explaining how the loss amount is determined (the *measure of loss*) is a starting point in determining the insured's recovery. The insurable interest requirement is a second basic consideration, as the payment is limited to the amount of the insured's legal interest. Other provisions placing explicit limits on recovery for loss are common in property insurance contracts. Some of these provisions are designed to prevent insureds from benefiting as a result of events against which they have insured themselves. Other provisions are designed to lower the cost of coverage or to make the contract more acceptable to either the insurer or insured.

439

CHAPTER 17
*Insurance Contract
Analysis: Property
and Liability
Coverage*

Measure of Loss

Two measures of loss are common in property insurance: replacement cost and actual cash value (ACV). These terms were introduced in Chapter 5. Replacement cost is the amount required to repair or replace the damaged property with brand-new property similar in kind and purpose, using current material costs and current labor rates. Actual cash value is a smaller amount, with the reduction reflecting an allowance for already-existing physical depreciation of the property immediately before the damage occurred (i.e., ACV = replacement cost less physical depreciation). Of the two measures, replacement cost is less likely to lead to disputes over the claim amount because the measure is easy to determine objectively. An allowance for physical depreciation is partly subjective, so the use of ACV may increase the likelihood of disputes. Balanced against the effect on possible disputes is the possible effect on the moral hazard. In concept, basing the reimbursement on replacement cost tends to overreimburse the loss, possibly leading to a moral hazard.

Despite possible effects on the moral hazard, a trend has developed toward replacement cost as a measure of loss, particularly on contracts with significant deductibles. Deductibles are effective at controlling moral hazards, and their amount is easy to assess objectively. Thus, a replacement cost policy with a large deductible may be more effective at controlling a possible moral hazard than an equally expensive ACV policy with a smaller deductible. Also, many replacement cost coverages require the insured to actually undertake replacement to become entitled to reimbursement based on replacement cost.

Time-element coverage that reimburses income losses (e.g., business interruption contracts) typically use the sum of net profit plus continuing expenses as the measure of loss. Continuing expenses include amounts that must be expended for the business to survive, such as contractual salaries or expenditures required by law. Some business interruption policies, particularly those written on retail outlets, provide a *per diem* benefit, which is a stated per-day reimbursement for each day that the retail outlet is closed due to the insured peril. In effect, the use of a per-diem benefit makes the policy a valued contract. Other coverages that may use a valued contract approach include contracts to reimburse lost rental income for a landlord or to reimburse the cost of a substitute rental vehicle while an insured vehicle is being repaired. For some coverage on property whose valuation is subjective, an *agreed amount endorsement* or similar provision is used to place a specific amount of coverage on an item of property.

Insurable Interest

Property insurance contracts also promise to pay the insured no more than his or her insurable interest at the time of the loss. An insured possesses an insurable interest if he or she would lose financially if the property is damaged. The extent of the possible financial loss measures the amount of the insurable interest. A sole owner's insurable interest is measured by the possible loss to the insured property, whereas a part owner's insurable interest is limited to his or her share of the loss. A secured creditor, such as a mortgagee, has an insurable interest equal to the outstanding balance on the debt, which includes amounts paid by the creditor to continue coverage that the owner has allowed to lapse. Other examples of insurable interests are the liability interest of a bailee in property in his or her care, custody, or control; the interest of a bailee or of some representative of the owner who acts as an agent for the owner; and the interest of persons holding judgments against the owner. Although the interest of a general creditor is considered to be too distant to justify an insurable interest, the creditor achieves an insurable interest when and if he or she obtains a judgment against the owner.

The insurable interest need not exist at the time the insurance is purchased. Bailees, for example, may purchase insurance on all the customers' property that they expect to come under their control within the next year. The interest must exist, however, at the time of the loss.

Duplicate Coverage

Limiting the insured's recovery under the contract to his or her interest in the loss may not be enough to make the insurance contract one of indemnity. The insured could still purchase several contracts and collect under each contract unless there were provisions preventing this duplicate coverage. Property insurance contracts contain three types of provisions dealing with this problem.

One possibility is for other insurance to be prohibited, in which case the existence of other coverage could constitute a breach of warranty. An approach this harsh is not typical. More commonly, the loss is allocated between policies, assuming that each policy would apply in the absence of other coverage. Three allocation methods are in common use: (1) the primary and excess approach, (2) contribution by equal shares, or (3) contribution by limits.

Under the primary and excess approach, one of the policies is designated as "primary" with the other policies "excess." The entire loss is allocated to the primary policy until the limit of the policy is exhausted, at which point the excess policy covers, but only to the extent that the loss exceeds the limit of the primary policy. Under contribution by equal shares, each insurer contributes equal amounts until the limit of its policy has been exhausted or none of the loss remains, whichever comes first. Under contribution by limits, each insurer's share of the loss is the ratio of its policy limit to the total of all limits applying to the loss.

For example, a $25,000 loss would be allocated between a primary policy whose limit is $20,000 and an excess policy whose limit is $30,000 as follows: $20,000 to the primary policy and $5000 to the excess policy. Under the contribution by equal shares approach, each of the two policies would bear $12,500 of the $25,000 loss. The contribution by limits approach would prorate the loss according to the respective policy's limit. A total of $30,000 + $20,000 = $50,000 of coverage applies, 3/5 of it provided by the policy with the $30,000 limit and 2/5 of it provided by the policy with the $20,000 limit. $15,000 of the $25,000 loss (3/5) would be allocated to the policy with the $30,000 limit, with the remaining $10,000 allocated to the other policy.

In any given insurance contract, the allocation method applied may vary according to circumstances. The type of loss that occurs and provisions in the other policies applying to the loss may affect the method that applies. In property insurance, the prorating approach often is used if two polices that are similar apply to the same loss (e.g., two fire insurance policies). If the two policies are dissimilar (e.g., a property floater specifically identifying a stolen item of jewelry and other policy providing coverage on unscheduled personal property, a category that includes the jewelry), the policy more specifically identifying the property and circumstances often is primary, with the broader policy providing excess coverage.

441

CHAPTER 17
*Insurance Contract
Analysis: Property
and Liability
Coverage*

Contract Limits

When a policy limit appears on a property insurance contract, the limit usually is interpreted as a maximum amount the insurer will pay to the insured for a loss. Especially for a very large loss, the policy limit may constrain the level of reimbursement for loss.

A single contract may have more than one policy limit. The size of the limit may depend on the peril causing the loss, the person to whom payment is made, the type of property, or the location where the loss occurs. Property insurance contract limits may be classified according to (1) whether there is an explicit dollar limit, (2) whether the limits apply to specific coverage or blanket coverage, (3) whether they are special internal limits, (4) whether the limits differ depending upon the perils, persons, types of loss, or locations covered, and (5) whether the limits are responsive to changes in the values of the property covered.

Most contracts cover losses up to a stated number of dollars, but some contracts, illustrated by most automobile physical damage insurance, do not include a dollar limit. In these contracts, the policy limit is in effect the maximum possible loss to the property less the deductible.

If a single contract limit applies to many types of property at one location or property at two or more locations, this insurance is called *blanket* coverage. If different limits apply to narrowly defined types of property or to the same type of property at different locations, the insurance is called *divided* or *specific* coverage. For example, one limit may apply to a building, another to machinery, and still another to contents, or one limit may apply to contents at one location with a different limit applying to contents at another location. The effect is the same as if a separate contract had been written on each division of property, each having its own policy limit.

The major attraction of blanket coverage over specific coverage is the flexibility it provides by making the face amount of insurance available to cover losses to any item covered under the contract. On the other hand, blanket insurance may cost more and be subject to more severe coinsurance (see below) and other restrictive provisions.

Blanket policies providing the same type of coverage at several locations but containing only a single limit are likely to *prorate limits* according to values exposed to damage at each location. For example, the owner of three retail stores may wish to insure all three stores using a blanket fire insurance policy for all three locations. Suppose the values of the stores at each location are: location A, $1 million; location B, $2 million; and location C, $5 million. The percentage of total value ($8 million) at each location can be used to prorate the limit: 12.5 percent at location A, 25 percent at location B, and 62.5 percent at location C. If the owner of the stores were to purchase only $5 million of coverage in the belief that $5 million is the maximum amount exposed to damage at any one location, a prorating provision would make the stores underinsured at all locations. In this illustration, only 5/8 of the policy limit, or $3,125,000 applies at location C if the limit is prorated.

An *internal limit* is a limit applying to a special category of property, usually property whose value is high relative to its weight. Property insurance providing coverage on broad categories of property often places internal limits on property such as jewelry, furs, and art objects. For example, personal property may be subject to a $50,000 limit, subject to a $2000 internal limit applying to loss by theft of jewelry. The internal limit does not create additional insurance, however, so the $50,000 overall contract limit still applies to personal property as a class.

Most property insurance limits are fixed at the beginning of the policy period, but some limits vary according to actual or expected changes in the value of the property covered. For example, automobile physical damage insurance is seldom written with stated dollar limits. Instead, the maximum payment under this insurance is the value of the car, which may vary during the policy period. Varying limits also are found in policies using a provision that may be called an *inflation guard,* in which the amount of coverage is adjusted using the construction price index in a community or some other index of prices. Some contracts adjust the coverage a fixed percentage each year or month, an adjustment that may correspond to the rate of increase in prices of covered objects, but only by coincidence.

Another type of policy whose limit varies over time is a *reporting form,* in which the insured provides periodic reports of the values exposed to possible damage. The insurer adjusts the amount of coverage in accord with the values reported by the insured. A reporting form might be used to insure inventory whose value fluctuates widely over time, as may occur for a retailer or a clothing manufacturer. Another use of a reporting form might be to insure a building under construction. One approach that could be used in a reporting form used to insure inventory is to set a provisional amount of coverage and provisional premium when the policy is issued. The amount of coverage during the policy period would be adjusted according to the values reported by the insured. At the end of the contract period, the insurer determines the final cost of coverage by applying its rates against the reported values.

The principal advantage of reporting forms is that the insured is never overinsured or underinsured. For a large insured with multiple locations, the price is also usually more attractive than for equivalent nonreporting insurance. The principal disadvantage is the effort involved in making the periodic reports.

Coinsurance and Other Insurance-to-Value Requirements

When a loss occurs to property, in most cases the damage is partial rather than total. The possibility of partial damage creates an incentive for policyholders to carry less than full coverage on the property, as will be explained later on. In response to this incentive, insurance contracts covering property where partial damage is possible often contain a clause that reduces recovery for loss when the amount of insurance is less than a minimum imposed by the contract.

443

CHAPTER 17
Insurance Contract
Analysis: Property
and Liability
Coverage

The coinsurance clause is one type of contractual *insurance to value* requirement (a phrase adopted by Head [1971]), and a commonly used one. The replacement cost clause is another form of this requirement found in contracts that use replacement cost as a measure of loss. Insurance-to-value requirements are common in time-element coverages, such as business interruption insurance. Various types of insurance-to-value requirements have been in use for over 100 years.

Unfortunately, the term "coinsurance" also is used to describe contractual loss-sharing agreements (especially in health insurance), so the term often is misunderstood. In property insurance, the coinsurance clause is *not* an agreement to apportion the loss between parties to the contract. Rather, the coinsurance clause creates a contractual incentive for the policyholder to carry an amount of coverage close to the value of the property being insured. The incentive is created by reducing the benefit if the amount of insurance fails to meet the specified minimum. In fire insurance, the typical coinsurance clause reduces the recovery for loss if the amount of coverage is less than 80 percent of the value of the property.

A fire insurance policy providing $800,000 of coverage on a warehouse can serve as an illustration. The amount of coverage required by the coinsurance clause is called the *coinsurance requirement*. If the value of the warehouse is $1 million or less, the $800,000 amount of coverage meets the 80 percent coinsurance requirement. If no other limitations on recovery are present, the policyholder recovers the full amount of loss up to the policy limit. If the value of the warehouse is $1.5 million, however, the amount of coverage required by the 80 percent coinsurance clause is (0.8)($1.5 million) = $1.2 million. The amount of coverage ($800,000) is only two-thirds of the required amount ($1.2 million). The coinsurance clause reduces recovery for loss to two-thirds of the loss amount, as shown in the formula below:

$$\frac{\text{Amount of insurance}}{\text{(Coinsurance percent)(Value of property)}} \times \text{Loss}$$

$$\frac{\$800,000}{(0.8)\ (\$1.5 \text{ million})} \times \text{Loss} = 2/3 \times \text{Loss}.$$

In the above illustration, the recovery for an $18,000 loss would be $12,000. The amount by which the recovery would increase if the required amount of insurance had been purchased is the *coinsurance penalty,* in this case $6000. The failure to meet the coinsurance requirement causes a proportionate reduction in recovery for small as well as large losses. In the above example, the recovery for a $60,000 loss would be $40,000, or a $20,000 coinsurance penalty.

The above illustration can be extended generally to other insurance-to-value requirements with only minor modification. For example, a typical *replacement cost clause* will base the reimbursement on the *replacement cost* of the loss if the amount of coverage is at least 80 percent of the *replacement value* of the property. *Business interruption* policies often base the required amount of coverage on *annual gross earnings* (sales less cost of goods sold).

The Rationale. The operation of the coinsurance clause may appear mysterious when encountered for the first time, especially if the encounter involves a claim. A policyholder may be especially resentful when an increase in the value of covered property causes an amount of insurance that was adequate at the time of purchase to later result in a coinsurance penalty. In the above illustration, the warehouse may have been worth only $1 million at the time coverage was placed, later increasing in value to $1.5 million.

The rationale for coinsurance becomes clear by considering the method typically used to price fire insurance and other property coverage. When partial losses are possible, this pricing method creates an incentive to underinsure that the coinsurance clause attempts to overcome. Typically, fire insurance is priced by establishing a rate per unit of coverage, so the final premium is proportionate to the amount of coverage. For example, a $0.75 rate per $100 of fire insurance coverage may apply to an office building. If $1 million of fire insurance is purchased, the premium is ($0.75)(1,000,000/100) or $7,500. If $10 million of coverage is purchased the premium becomes $75,000.

Suppose that the value of the office building is $10 million, and any fire loss that occurs will either be $1 million or $10 million. The building owner who purchases only $1 million of coverage pays one-tenth as much as if $10 million of coverage had been purchased. In the absence of a coinsurance clause, however, purchasing only $1 million of coverage does not reduce recovery for loss to one-tenth its value with $10 million of coverage, except for a total loss. The possibility of partial losses creates this disparity. Either amount of coverage would result in full recovery for a $1 million loss in the absence of coinsurance, for example.

The coinsurance clause reduces this disparity by stating a required amount of coverage relative to the value of the property. The required amount of coverage serves as a target. Purchasing only one-half of required amount of coverage reduces both the premium *and* the recovery for loss by 50 percent. By reducing the insured's recovery when less than the required amount of coverage is purchased, the coinsurance clause creates an incentive to insure to a high proportion of value.

Limitations. Coinsurance and other insurance-to-value clauses have been a source of disputes between insurers and policyholders who were not aware of the requirement. In response to the potential for misunderstanding, the insurance industry has experimented with alternatives. Usually these alternatives result in the insured relinquishing control over the amount of coverage. For example, one alternative used on dwelling insurance policies substitutes a requirement that the insured accept the insurer's recommended amount of coverage along with an inflation guard. The policy also requires the insured to report any significant additions to the dwelling. In return for the insured's acceptance of these conditions, the replacement cost clause is waived (policies on owner-occupied dwellings usually contain a replacement cost clause in lieu of a coinsurance clause). The cost of inspections are a disadvantage of this alternative, particularly if applicants decline to purchase the recommended coverage.

Coinsurance tends to become impractical when verification of the value of covered property is difficult. For example, the adequacy of the amount of coverage is unlikely to be an issue for a blanket policy covering a large corporation with international operations. For such an organization, prices and other terms of coverage are likely to be negotiated in a manuscript policy, and a technical issue such as the limit of coverage relative to the total value of covered property is unlikely to become important, even if the contract contains a coinsurance clause.

Deductible Clauses

A deductible is an amount subtracted from the loss to determine the insured's recovery. Under a typical flat dollar deductible, recovery is not triggered until a loss exceeds the deductible, in which case the recovery is the amount by which the loss exceeds the deductible. For example, a policy with an $1000 flat deductible provides no recovery for an $800 loss. For a loss of $1400, the policy provides a $400 recovery.

Deductibles are a partial retention device used to determine the point at which the financial consequences of loss become transferred to an insurer. The rationale for choosing retention levels appeared in Chapter 9. The discussion appearing below focuses on the different types of deductibles and methods used to determine deductible amounts.

Deductibles can be classified in a number of ways. A deductible may apply to each item damaged, to each person insured, to each occurrence, to each accident, or to total losses during the policy period. A deductible applying to total losses during the policy period is called an *aggregate deductible.* Deductibles applying on some other basis (e.g., each accident) usually are called *specific deductibles.* A specific deductible may be used in conjunction with an aggregate deductible. For example, a $1000 deductible may apply to each accident with a $5000 aggregate deductible applying to total losses during the policy period. If 10 accidents averaging $700 per accident occur during the period of coverage, the $5000 aggregate deductible limits the insured's financial responsibility to $5000.

Instead of being stated in terms of a dollar amount, a deductible may be a percentage of the loss, a percentage of the limit of the policy, or, in time element coverage, a waiting period. Workers' compensation statutes often impose a waiting period that is waived retroactively if the disability extends beyond a stated period of time, such as four weeks. Under a one-week waiting period retroactively waived after four weeks, two weeks' benefits would be paid for a disability lasting three weeks; if the disability lasts five weeks, benefits are paid for the entire five-week period.

Although deductibles are most commonly stated as a flat dollar amount, other forms combining the above approaches have been used. Earthquake coverage often imposes a deductible stated as a percentage of the value of the structure. A deductible could be a percentage of the loss, not to exceed a stated dollar amount. A *disappearing deductible* that was used on policies covering

445

CHAPTER 17
Insurance Contract
Analysis: Property
and Liability
Coverage

owner-occupied dwellings until the late 1970s imposed a deductible whose amount decreased as the size of the loss increased. For example, a $100 deductible that disappears at a loss of $500 can be fashioned by having a policy pay 125 percent of the amount by which a loss exceeds $100, subject to the further condition that losses of more than $500 are paid in full. Under this coverage, a $300 loss results in a benefit of (1.25)($300 − $100), or $250.

A more extreme form of this arrangement, called a *franchise*, was once common in ocean marine insurance on cargo. Franchises often were stated as a percentage of the value of the cargo. A benefit was not triggered until a loss exceeded the franchise amount, but any covered losses were paid in full. For example, insurance on $100,000 of cargo using a 5 percent franchise would provide no benefit for a $4000 loss, but a $10,000 loss would result in a $10,000 benefit. As a practical matter, franchises were used only when a loss near the franchise amount was very unlikely. Because covered losses were paid in full, an insured would have a strong incentive to exaggerate the amount of a loss that was slightly less than the franchise amount.

PROPERTY INSURANCE: PROCEDURE FOR SECURING PAYMENT OF BENEFITS

Normally, the burden of proof is on the insured to show that a loss covered by the contract has occurred and to provide evidence on the value of the loss. Many of the requirements for the insured to become entitled to payment of benefits are stated in a separate section specifically addressing the issue. The requirements usually are related to issues such as notification of the insurer during a specified time following the discovery of loss and the type of evidence required to support valuation of the claim. Insureds should be aware that these requirements are conditions of coverage. Failure to meet the conditions may prejudice or invalidate the insured's right to recovery. Other conditions in the contract not related to providing evidence of loss also may invalidate the right to recovery. For example, suspension of protective safeguards identified in an endorsement or interference with an insurer's subrogation rights may invalidate rights to recovery.

LIABILITY INSURANCE: EVENTS COVERED

Situations Triggering Coverage

Liability insurance reimburses amounts that insured persons become legally obligated to pay as a result of injury to others or damage to their property. Many insurance policies distinguish between liability arising from *bodily injury*, which involves physical injury or death of another person, and *property damage* involving damage to property belonging to others. Some liability contracts cover *personal injury*, a broad term that includes bodily injury as well as injury that is not physical. Defamation of character is an example of a personal injury that is not bodily injury.

Liability insurance may be written to cover liability arising from specifically identified *sources of liability* or, more broadly, to provide comprehensive coverage. The narrower coverage identifies specific sources of liability, such as the ownership, maintenance, or use of premises; the manufacture or distribution of products or services; the practice of accounting; or the ownership, maintenance, or use of a motor vehicle. These specifically identified sources of liability may be further limited through exclusions. For example, automobile liability insurance may exclude situations in which the vehicle is used as a taxi or a bus.

Comprehensive liability insurance covers all sources of liability except those specifically excluded. For example, a comprehensive liability insurance policy may cover all sources of liability except the ownership, maintenance, or use of a motor vehicle, a large watercraft, or an airplane. When compared with coverage for specifically identified sources of liability, the advantages and disadvantages of comprehensive liability insurance closely resemble those discussed earlier in two other comparisons: all risk coverage as compared with named-perils coverage, and coverage applying to personal property on an unscheduled basis as compared with a scheduled basis.

Accident, Occurrence, and Claims-made Liability Policies. Some liability insurance contracts provide coverage for injury or damage that results from an *accident.* Typically, an event that occurs at an identifiable point in time can be considered an accident. Accidents usually happen suddenly, although courts have held that unintended or unexpected consequences of an act can be considered accidents without a requirement that they also occur suddenly. A liability insurer would not consider the gradual pollution of a landfill with industrial waste to be an accident, because the pollution did not happen suddenly. However, some state courts have required insurers to honor claims related to pollution despite an exclusion in their policies for pollution that is not "sudden and accidental." The courts reasoned that the pollution was not intended or expected. At the time of writing, about all that can be said on this issue is a policy that covers liability arising from accidents is unlikely to cover an event occurring gradually without litigation between the insurer and insured.

Many liability insurance contracts provide coverage for injury or damage resulting from an *occurrence* during a period of time coverage is in force. Occurrence is a broad term that includes accidents as well as events that happen over an extended period of time, often due to exposure to harmful conditions. An occurrence need not be sudden. Liability insurance providing coverage for occurrences is considered broader than a policy providing coverage for accidents if the two policies are equivalent in all other respects. Gradual pollution would fit within the general definition of occurrence, although liability insurance contracts providing coverage for occurrences attempt to exclude gradual pollution on other grounds. Losses caused intentionally by an insured organization or person are specifically excluded on many policies, and courts are likely to exclude intentional acts as a matter of public policy.

An *occurrence policy* covers liability for bodily injuries or property damage that occurs during the policy period no matter when the claim is made. Often the claim is made shortly after the injury or damage occurs, but sometimes it is

447

CHAPTER *17*
Insurance Contract
Analysis: Property
and Liability
Coverage

made many years later. The principal reason for the late claim is that the injury or damage may not manifest itself until many years after the exposure. For example, a claim for bodily injuries caused by exposure to asbestos in 1960 may not be made until 1995.

The meaning of the term "occurrence" also has been a subject of litigation, especially when injury occurred due to exposure over a period of time to a harmful substance, such as asbestos. One legal doctrine, called the *exposure doctrine*, holds that the injury occurs as the person is exposed to the substance. Under the exposure doctrine as applied to insurance, the liability for injury rests on the insurer or insurers whose coverage was in force during the period of exposure. An alternative *manifestation doctrine* holds that the injury occurs when symptoms of injury become evident. Under the manifestation doctrine as applied to insurance, the liability for injury rests on the insurers whose coverage was in force when the symptoms of injury become evident. A third approach combines the two doctrines. Under the *triple-trigger doctrine* the liability rests on all policies providing coverage during the period of exposure *and* manifestation.

During the 1970s and early 1980s, the increasing proportion of late claims, the higher awards late claimants tended to receive because of inflation, and other factors increased insurer pricing uncertainties to the point where insurers sought for many insureds (for example, physicians with medical malpractice exposures) an alternative approach.

That alternative is a *claims-made policy*. Under a claims-made policy the insurer is responsible only for claims "made" (usually defined in terms of notification) during the policy period, subject to the further restriction that the occurrence giving rise to the claim (e.g., for a surgeon, the date surgery was performed) must have taken place after the *retroactive date*. Usually the retroactive date is the first date that coverage for the exposure is written by the insurer. For example, on June 1, 1994, a surgeon may purchase claims-made medical liability insurance with a retroactive date of June 1, 1994. If the policy covers a one-year period and a claim is filed on November 15, 1994, the date of the surgery giving rise to the claim must be after June 1, 1994 for coverage to apply. Also, if the coverage is allowed to expire on May 31, 1995, claims made subsequent to expiration are not covered, even for occurrences that took place during the policy period.

Normally, renewals of coverage with the same insurer will keep the original retroactive date: June 1, 1994. If the coverage is renewed with the original insurer on June 1, 1995 and a claim is made on September 10, 1995, the claim is covered as long as the occurrence took place after June 1, 1994. If the surgeon later decides to purchase a new claims-made policy from a different insurer, the new coverage will use a new retroactive date, usually the date coverage is first purchased from the new insurer.

Hence, the selection of a new insurer carries the risk that a claim may arise from an occurrence that took place prior to the new retroactive date. A similar problem may occur when the surgeon retires or when an insurer imposes a new, later retroactive date. Continued coverage using the same retroactive date requires continued renewals with the same insurer, although continuation of the

449

CHAPTER 17
*Insurance Contract
Analysis: Property
and Liability
Coverage*

policy does not prevent the insurer from imposing a new retroactive date. Often insurers are willing to continue providing coverage for claims made after the expiration of a policy ("tail" coverage). A policy may guarantee that tail coverage will be offered if the original coverage is not renewed or if a new retroactive date is imposed. The tail coverage applies to occurrences that took place between the original retroactive date and the new retroactive date or date of nonrenewal.

Claims-made forms are common in commercial liability insurance, especially on policies covering professional liability or product liability exposures. For some types of exposure to liability, coverage is available under both occurrence and claims-made forms. One would expect an occurrence form to be more expensive than a claims-made form that is equivalent in other respects, perhaps much more expensive.

Persons Insured

Liability insurance contracts, like property insurance contracts, may be limited to the named insured or extended to include other persons. Other possibilities are the insured's family, legal representatives, employees, friends permitted to drive his or her car, tenants who occupy a building he or she owns, and distributors who market a product he or she manufacturers. An automobile insurance contract normally covers anyone driving a covered car with the permission of the named insured; however, it does not cover any such person who uses the car while working in a business of selling, servicing, repairing, or parking automobiles.

Losses Reimbursed

In addition to paying settlements or court or statutory awards to the claimant, liability insurance contracts provide services such as investigation of the claim; negotiation and, it is hoped, settlement with the claimant; defense of the suit, if this proves necessary; payment of premiums on bonds and of court costs that may be incurred in connection with the claim; and payment of expenses incurred by the insured in cooperating with the insurer. Some contracts include a medical payments section under which medical expenses incurred by injured persons are paid without regard to the insured's liability.

Locations Covered

Liability insurance providing coverage only at designated locations is called *premises* liability insurance. For example, a landlord might purchase premises liability insurance applying at the location of rental property.

Coverage provided under vehicle liability insurance contracts typically is restricted as to territory, for example, North America. Coverage provided under business liability insurance may not be restricted as to where the injury occurs, but may require that the injury arise from the act of a person whose home is located in a stated territory or from a product made or sold in the stated territory.

Time Period Covered

As explained above, an occurrence policy provides coverage for amounts the insured becomes legally obligated to pay as a result of injuries that occur during the policy period, whenever the claim is filed. A claims-made policy provides coverage for claims that are filed during the policy period as long as the injury occurs after the retroactive date.

Cancellation. Most liability insurance contracts include a cancellation clause that allows the insurer or insured to cancel prior to the expiration date. If an occurrence policy is cancelled or otherwise not renewed, the insurer still is liable for injuries that occurred during the period of coverage, whenever the claim is filed. Claims-made policies usually provide the insured with the right to purchase coverage for claims that are made after the period of coverage arising from occurrences prior to the end of coverage ("tail" coverage), but at additional expense.

State law may restrict an insurer's right to cancel coverage. Automobile liability insurance contracts covering the owners of private passenger automobiles usually prohibit the insurer from canceling the contract except for a few specified reasons, such as nonpayment of premiums or revocation of the insured's driver's license or motor vehicle registration. Such a restricted cancellation provision is required by law in most states. Most states also restrict the right of insurers to cancel homeowners' and other residence contracts. Some of these statutes pertain to contracts written for businesses as well as for households.

LIABILITY INSURANCE: AMOUNT OF RECOVERY

Most liability insurance contracts obligate the insurer to pay amounts the insured becomes legally obligated to pay as a result of covered injury to others. In addition, the insurer is obligated to provide legal defense services for the insured against liability claims to which the coverage applies, even if the claims appear without merit. Most liability insurance contracts also state that the insurer's obligation to defend ceases when the limit of coverage has been exhausted by payment of judgments. Such a provision may allow an insurer to abandon the defense of a claim by tendering payment of the policy limit to the court.

Contract Limits

Until recently most liability insurance contracts usually contained separate limits applicable to awards or settlements (1) for bodily injuries and (2) for property damage. Some still do. Until 1973, most bodily injury limits stated first, the maximum amount payable on account of the injuries sustained by one person, and second, the maximum amount payable per occurrence. For example, under a $25,000/$50,000 contract the insurer would pay no more than $25,000 for claims arising out of injuries to one person. If two or more persons were injured in the occurrence, the insurer was not responsible for more than $50,000 of their combined claims, each individual claim being subject first to the per person limit. If two injured persons had claims of $40,000 and $20,000, respectively, the insurer would pay $25,000 plus $20,000, or $45,000. If three injured persons each had claims of $20,000, the insurer would pay $50,000. The property damage limit was usually a stated amount per occurrence. A major revision of an important group of liability insurance contracts in 1973 abolished the per person limit but maintained separate per occurrence limits for the bodily injury and property damage coverages.

451

CHAPTER 17
*Insurance Contract
Analysis: Property
and Liability
Coverage*

Single-limit liability insurance contracts are now common. A maximum amount is payable per occurrence, regardless of the number of persons involved and the mix of bodily injuries and property damage. Because of this flexibility, a $25,000 single-limit contract provides better coverage than either a policy with $10,000/$20,000 bodily injury limits and a $5000 property damage limit or another policy with a $20,000 bodily injury limit and a $5000 property damage limit.

Aggregate limits state the maximum amount the insurer will pay because of occurrences covered during the policy year, regardless of the number of occurrences, claimants, or insureds. Aggregate limits were relatively uncommon until the Insurance Services Office introduced its new commercial general liability insurance policy in 1987. As will be explained in Chapter 21, that policy contains two aggregate limits—one applicable to product liability claims, the second to other covered liability claims.

When an aggregate limit appears on a policy, it often is used in conjunction with a specific limit applying to each accident or occurrence. For example, a liability insurance contract with specific/aggregate limits of $1 million/$5 million provides coverage of $1 million per occurrence, subject to the further limitation of $5 million for all occurrences during the policy period. Without the aggregate limit, the insurer could be liable for up to $100 million if 100 occurrences arise during the policy period. For example, 100 persons could be injured when a prescription drug becomes contaminated before being dispensed to customers. A court may define the sale of a drug to be the occurrence to which the coverage applies, in which case the per-occurrence policy limit could apply 100 times. The aggregate limit further defines the insurer's maximum liability when multiple occurrences are possible.

However, the interpretation of insurance contract provisions as they apply to a particular set of circumstances is a matter of court rulings. For example, an insurer that wrote a series of five one-year policies during 1980 to 1984, each with a limit of $1 million, may be held liable for up to $5 million under the triple-trigger or exposure doctrines if the period of exposure encompasses the five years of coverage. The triple-trigger and exposure doctrines were discussed earlier in this chapter as they have been used to define the term "occurrence." It is possible that courts may find the amount of coverage to be the *sum* of the limits of policies written across several years, even if only one person is injured.

Medical payments coverage, often written in conjunction with liability insurance, is usually subject to a specified dollar limit per injured person. The medical expenses must also be incurred within a specified period of time following the accident. Sometimes a limit per accident also applies.

Workers' compensation policies do not place any dollar limit on compensation benefits other than those prescribed by statute.

Defense and Settlement Costs. Traditionally, defense costs and other costs of negotiating settlements in liability insurance have been covered without explicit limits. Further, many liability coverages require the insurer to defend against even frivolous lawsuits. This obligation, along with increasing costs of litigation, has created an incentive for insurers to experiment with contractual limits on defense costs. The imposition of such limits has been resisted by regulators and policyholders.

Under many liability coverages, the insurer can end its obligation to defend by tendering the policy limit to the court. The use of this option raises an ethical issue, particularly if the option were used by an insurer after it had managed a defense poorly. The same type of issue arises when limits on defense costs are considered. For example, one might envision a contract whose policy limit applies to the sum of defense costs and claim settlements. Such a limitation creates an incentive for the insurer to abandon the defense when the amount expended on defense costs approaches the policy limit. Abandonment could create hardship for the insured, particularly if the insurer had managed the defense poorly. By way of comparison, the traditional arrangement offers a stronger incentive for the insurer to continue the defense by requiring the insurer to tender the full policy limit as a cost of exercising the abandonment option.

Duplicate Coverage

As in property insurance contracts, duplicate coverage provisions in liability insurance prevent the insured from collecting twice for the same loss. The methods that can be used to allocate the loss between two or more policies were discussed earlier in the analysis of property insurance.

Excess-of-Loss Coverage

When risk managers for large organizations purchase insurance, the coverage typically involves substantial retention through means such as large deductibles. Coverage may apply only when the loss exceeds a stated threshold amount, or loss in excess of, say, $100,000. *Excess-of-loss* coverage (often shortened to *excess* coverage) provides reimbursement only when the covered loss exceeds the stated threshold. Although the excess coverage approach also can be used in property insurance, the phrase "excess coverage" most commonly appears in connection with liability insurance. Excess coverage was discussed earlier in connection with reinsurance transactions. In concept, excess of loss coverage resembles insurance with a deductible, although the legal structure of the two coverages may not be identical. Also, as is shown below, the concept of excess-of-loss is easily generalized to *layering* of coverages, a method used to construct coverages with the large limits often employed in risk management for organizations.

The threshold loss amount after which coverage applies may be called the *attachment point,* that is, the point at which coverage attaches to the loss. As an illustration, an excess policy may provide $1 million of coverage for losses in excess of $100,000 (sometimes a shorthand phrase "$1 million excess over $100,000" is used). This policy provides no reimbursement until a loss exceeds $100,000, the attachment point. For losses in excess of $100,000, the policy reimburses only to the extent the loss exceeds $100,000. The policy pays nothing for a loss of $80,000, for example, and pays $40,000 towards a $140,000 loss.

453

CHAPTER 17
*Insurance Contract
Analysis: Property
and Liability
Coverage*

The limit of coverage is $1 million. This limit would be reached at a loss of $1.1 million. Normally, the policy limit is the maximum benefit paid by the policy, not a maximum covered loss. The policy reimburses loss to the extent that the loss exceeds $100,000, so the $1 million policy limit is not exhausted until the loss exceeds $1.1 million.

To further illustrate the point, consider a policy providing $1 million of coverage excess over $1 million. Does this policy provide any coverage? The answer is yes. The policy provides a benefit when the loss exceeds $1 million, but only for the excess. The maximum benefit under the policy is $1 million, which is paid when a loss of $2 million or more occurs. The attachment point is the smallest loss at which coverage begins to apply, and the sum of the attachment point and the limit is the smallest loss triggering payment of the policy limit.

Large amounts of coverage (for example, $100 million of product liability insurance) typically are written in layers, with each layer being an excess policy. Normally, the attachment point on a layer is the loss amount that would result in payment of the policy limit on the underlying layer. The policy providing $1 million of coverage excess over $100,000 serves as an example. The attachment point on the next layer would be $1.1 million, the loss resulting in payment of the policy limit. If coverage for losses up to $15 million is desired, the limit on this next layer would be $13.9 million. An attachment point of $15 million would apply for coverage beyond this second layer. Table 17.1 illustrates a layering approach combining a third layer with these first two to provide coverage for losses up to $100 million. The table also shows how three loss amounts would be apportioned between these layers.

The layering shown in Table 17.1 could result from placement activities of a broker, who may be unable to place the entire amount of coverage with a single insurer. This layering takes place on the coverage itself, as contrasted with a situation in which an insurer writes the entire amount and reinsures much of the coverage with other insurers. An insurer writing one of the layers may specialize in writing coverage at this level, especially if the skills required to underwrite vary across different layers. In liability insurance, for example, claim frequency would be expected to be greater in the lower as contrasted to the upper layers. An insurer whose skills lie in negotiating settlement of smaller

TABLE 17.1. Layering of Policies to Provide Coverage for Losses up to $100 Million

Insurance Layer	*Amount of Recovery*		
	$75,000 Loss	$1 Million Loss	$50 Million Loss
$1,000,000 XS* $ 100,000	$0	$900,000	$1 million
$13,900,000 XS* $ 1,100,000	$0	$0	$13.9 million
$85,000,000 XS* $15,000,000	$0	$0	$35 million
$99,900,000 XS* $ 100,000	$0	$900,000	$49.9 million

*XS = excess over.

claims might specialize in writing lower layers, leaving upper layers to be written by insurers specializing in providing financial capacity for events occurring infrequently.

Umbrella Liability Insurance

Umbrella liability insurance is a type of excess liability insurance written in conjunction with a set of two or more underlying liability insurance policies. Instead of applying on the same basis as a single type of underlying policy, umbrella liability insurance is excess insurance over two or more policies. Usually, one of the conditions of the umbrella policy is that the underlying policies be kept in force. However, umbrella liability insurance coverage may apply to losses not covered by underlying policies. For example, an umbrella liability insurance contract may apply to personal injury, while the underlying policies apply more narrowly to bodily injury. Some umbrella policies impose a deductible when its coverage applies to a loss not covered by one of the underlying policies.

For example, an umbrella policy may be used when a business firm wishes to extend the limits on its commercial auto policy and commercial general liability policy to $20 million. The umbrella policy may be written in conjunction with a commercial auto policy with a limit of $500,000 per occurrence and a commercial general liability policy with a limit of $1 million per occurrence. When a loss occurs that exceeds the limit of either underlying policy, the umbrella policy covers the loss to the extent that the loss exceeds the limit of the underlying policy. Umbrella liability insurance is discussed further in Chapter 21.

Deductibles and Other Provisions for Loss-Sharing

Contract provisions for explicit sharing of costs are unusual in liability insurance contracts, except possibly on contracts held by large organizations. Some liability insurance for individuals in professions (e.g., medical malpractice liability insurance) has been written with deductibles (e.g., $1000 per claim), but deductibles are not typical on liability insurance contracts held by individuals. Rather, financial incentives to prevent claims (or penalties for creating claims) are provided through surcharges on premiums or, in extreme cases, the implied threat of cancellation. Insurers' concern with retaining control of legal defense may explain their reluctance to share financial responsibility for claims with insureds.

Key Concepts

aggregate liability limits   Limits used in some liability insurance policies that state the most the insurer will pay because of occurrences covered during the policy year regardless of the number of occurrences, claimants, or insureds.

all risk coverage   A contract that covers all perils not specifically excluded.

blanket coverage   Property insurance that applies a single policy limit to many types of property at one location or the same type of property at two or more locations. Blanket coverage permits property to be moved from one covered location to another without changing the amount of protection.

cancellation The termination of an insurance contract by an insurer or an insured prior to the end of the policy term. Insurance contracts usually give insurers and insureds cancellation rights.

chain-of-causation concept A legal doctrine that makes the insurer responsible for losses caused by perils covered under the contract and other perils that the covered perils may set in motion. For example, a fire policy covers fire, smoke, and water damage caused by a fire.

claims-made policy A liability insurance policy that covers claims made during the policy period if the injury or damage occurred on or after some retroactive date.

coinsurance clause A clause that obligates the insurer to pay only the proportion of any loss that the amount of insurance purchased bears to the product of the coinsurance percentage and the value of the insured property at the time of the loss.

contract of indemnity A contract that will indemnify the insured for losses sustained but will not permit the insured to gain from the occurrence of the event insured against. Related concepts are measure of the loss, insurable interest, other insurance, and subrogation.

deductible clause A clause that requires the insured to retain part of the potential losses covered under an insurance contract, such as the first $100 per occurrence.

divided or specific coverage Property insurance that applies separate policy limits to narrowly defined types of property or to the same type of property at different locations.

floater A contract that covers all locations not specifically excluded.

insuring agreement The section of an insurance contract in which the insurer tells what events are covered, subject to the exclusions and conditions sections.

named perils coverage A contract that specifies the perils covered.

reporting form A property insurance form under which the policy limit is adjusted in response to amounts periodically reported by the insured.

single-limit liability insurance Liability insurance that imposes a single policy limit on all claims per occurrence, regardless of the mix of bodily injury and property damage and the number of claims.

455

CHAPTER 17
*Insurance Contract
Analysis: Property
and Liability
Coverage*

Review Questions

1. The provisions in an insurance contract can be classified as (1) declarations, (2) insuring agreements, (3) exclusions, and (4) conditions.
   a. Describe briefly each of these sets of provisions.
   b. Are contract provisions always grouped into these categories?
2. Do contract exclusions ever benefit the insured?
3. Summarize briefly the framework suggested in the text for analyzing insurance contracts with respect to events covered (for both property and liability contracts).
4. Would you prefer a named-perils or an all risks contract? Why?
5. How have insurers changed all risks policies in response to court decisions based on concurrent causation?
6. a. The Smith Manufacturing Company owns a $200,000 building on which the First National Bank holds a $100,000 mortgage. The Smith Manufacturing Company has a $200,000 fire insurance contract covering the building. If the building is vacant for over four months (a breach of a contract condition) when a fire occurs causing $120,000 damage, what is the responsibility of the insurer if the contract:
   (1) Has been assigned to the First National Bank?
   (2) Contains a standard mortgagee clause?

   b. If the Smith Manufacturing Company had not breached a condition in the contract, how would the loss be settled if the contract contains a standard mortgage clause?
7. In analyzing a contract with respect to the losses reimbursed, what questions would you ask if the contract is:
   a. A property insurance contract?
   b. A liability insurance contract?
8. Discuss the cancellation rights of insurers in property and liability insurance.
9. A property insurance contract covers contents located at three different addresses. Is this contract a floater?
10. How does a claims-made liability insurance policy differ from an occurrence policy?
11. Are property and liability insurance contracts contracts of indemnity? Why or why not?
12. A $50,000 building, insured for $40,000, is totally destroyed by a fire caused by the negligent act of a neighbor. The insurer pays $40,000 and the insured and the insurer sue the neighbor jointly. If the recovery is $33,000 net of costs, how much will the insured recover?
13. Under what conditions would a risk manager select each of the following?
   a. Specific coverage
   b. Blanket coverage
   c. A reporting form.
14. An insured suffers an insured loss during a policy period. How will the insured's recovery for this loss affect the policy limits applicable to future losses in:
   a. Property insurance?
   b. Liability insurance?
15. An insured purchases a three-year $90,000 fire insurance contract containing an 80 percent coinsurance clause on a building valued at $100,000. Two years later, when a $40,000 loss occurs, the building is valued at $150,000. How much will the insurer pay? How much would the insurer pay if the loss had been $130,000?

References and Suggestions for Additional Reading

HEAD, GEORGE L.: *Insurance to Value* (Philadelphia: Published for the S. S. Huebner Foundation for Insurance Education by Richard D. Irwin, Inc., 1971).

HORN, R. C.: *Subrogation and Insurance Theory and Practice* (Homewood, Ill.: Richard D. Irwin, Inc., 1964).

KEETON, R. E.: *Basic Text on Insurance Law* (St. Paul, Minn.: West Publishing Company, 1971), chap. 3.

MEHR, ROBERT I.: *Fundamentals of Insurance* (Homewood, Ill.: Richard D. Irwin, Inc., 1983), chap. 7.

———, E. CAMMACK, and T. ROSE: *Principles of Insurance* (8th ed., Homewood, Ill.: Richard D. Irwin, Inc., 1985), chap. 9.

MOWBRAY, A. H., R. H. BLANCHARD, and C. A. WILLIAMS, JR.: *Insurance* (6th ed., New York: McGraw-Hill Book Company, 1969), chaps. 10 and 11.

WILLIAMS, C. A., JR., G. L. HEAD, R. C. HORN, and G. W. GLENDENNING: *Principles of Risk Management and Insurance,* vol. II (2nd ed., Malvern, Pa.: American Institute for Property and Liability Underwriters, Inc., 1981), chaps. 8, 11–13.

CHAPTER 18

Insurance Contract Analysis: Life Insurance

Learning Objectives

After you have completed this chapter, you should be able to:

1. Explain how life insurance coverage can be described as a two-part contract consisting of term insurance and an investment.
2. List the three persons or organizations with an economic or legal interest identified in life insurance contracts.
3. Identify three primary determinants of life insurance prices and explain how each affects the cost of life insurance.
4. Describe dividend options usually available on participating life insurance contracts.
5. Describe the nonforfeiture and settlement options typically found in life insurance contracts.
6. Identify three policyholder characteristics that would affect the attractiveness of investment features found in life insurance and explain how each affects the attractiveness of this type of investment.
7. Explain how the structure of universal life insurance can allocate investment risks on an individual policy basis.
8. Explain how the suicide exclusion, aviation exclusion, and incontestable clauses affect the rights of a holder of life insurance.
9. Explain how the provision for payment of dividends on participating policies can allocate mortality and investment risks across a group of policyholders.
10. Describe riders and optional benefits commonly offered in conjunction with life insurance and describe the benefit provided by each.

INTRODUCTION: PERSPECTIVE FOR ANALYSIS

When compared with property and liability insurance, the structure of most life insurance policies would appear fairly straightforward. Usually, the event triggering the payment of benefits is well-defined, such as the death of the insured person. Also, the amount of the benefit usually is fixed by contract. The typical life insurance policy does not require an analysis of possibly complex contract provisions, such as duplicate coverage provisions, deductibles, and coinsurance clauses, often found in property and liability coverage. Instead, the key to understanding life insurance is recognizing the motives leading to the purchase of coverage.

This chapter focuses on the motives leading to the purchase of life insurance. Because many types of life insurance contracts incorporate investment features, possible investment motives for holding the coverage must be considered. Analysis of investment features represents a significant departure from the patterns of analysis developed in the preceding chapter on property and liability insurance. With few exceptions, explicit consideration of investment motives is not required for the analysis of property and liability insurance coverage. For many types of life insurance, in contrast, investment motives can be the dominant factor leading to the purchase of coverage.

The reasons for holding life insurance can be contrasted with motives leading to the purchase of property and liability insurance. Property and liability exposures usually are fairly obvious; most individuals are aware of the value of objects they own or their exposure to potential liability. The difficult part of property and liability contract analysis is understanding the structure of the coverage and the effect of provisions that may appear obscure or complex. In contrast, the analysis of life insurance almost requires the perspective to be reversed. In life insurance, the structure of the coverage itself tends to be relatively simple; the difficult part is identifying and evaluating motives leading to the purchase of coverage.

Some readers may question whether the analysis of life insurance belongs in a text on risk management for organizations. Most demands for life insurance spring from individuals or families as isolated units, not collectively as a result of being members of organizations. Individual employees and their families bear most of the direct consequences of the event covered by a typical life insurance contract. The absence of a direct effect on the organization might seem to distance the analysis of life insurance coverage from the concerns of an organization's risk manager, especially in large organizations with diverse ownership interests.

As explained in Chapter 7, however, valid reasons exist for risk managers to be concerned with human resource loss exposures faced by employees. As a result of this concern, organizations often provide coverage that employees could purchase for themselves. An understanding of motives that could lead employees to purchase life insurance coverage is essential to designing an effective program of benefits for employees. In addition, organizations often provide their employees access to individual coverage through group-purchasing arrangements, so the risk manager may be asked to evaluate a proposal to offer coverage in this manner. An understanding of life insurance coverage and the motives it serves is essential to fulfilling this part of a risk manager's responsibilities.

Further, life insurance may be used to finance a risk facing the organization itself; an example would be life insurance used to fund a business-purchase agreement for a closely held firm. Instances in which life insurance can be used for this purpose were identified in the discussion of business-discontinuation losses in Chapter 7.

After discussing basic issues related to the structure of life insurance coverage, this chapter shows how the typical life insurance policy is a two-part contract comprised of term insurance and an investment. The investment feature of life insurance arises from the way the coverage is financed (i.e., the schedule of premium payments). A two-part contract requires two distinct types of motives to be considered in the analysis of coverage. The investment element requires the analyst to consider motives leading organizations or individuals to hold investments. At the same time, the insurance element implies that motives leading to the purchase of insurance (e.g., protection against large unforeseen loss) should be considered.

BASIC CONCEPTS RELATED TO THE STRUCTURE OF COVERAGE

The analysis of life insurance coverage can begin using the same framework used for property and liability coverage: determining the *events covered* and the resulting *amount of recovery.* Under life insurance coverage, the covered events are the contingencies leading to the payment of the benefit. While the contingency leading to benefit payment may be complex, in *term insurance* contracts it is simple: the death of the person whose life is insured. Term insurance contracts require that the death occur during the period of coverage (the "*term*") for the benefit to be payable. Under term insurance, death is the singular covered event. Other types of contracts provide narrower coverage, such as death resulting only from specified causes such as accidents. Certain policies, to be identified shortly as whole life insurance, provide benefits under a broad range of circumstances, including events other than death. As a footnote, most individual life insurance coverage contains a *suicide exclusion* denying full benefits for death resulting from suicide during a stated period (by law, not to exceed two years) following the issuance of the contract.

Annuity contracts, by way of comparison, provide a benefit for survival; a *straight life* annuity, for example, provides a periodic income benefit as long as the covered individual survives. Annuity contracts commonly provide additional guarantees. A *life annuity with period certain* guarantees that benefits will continue for the lifetime of the annuitant, but under no circumstances for a shorter time than a "period certain," such as 10 or 20 years. A *refund annuity* guarantees that benefits will continue for the lifetime of the annuitant, but under no circumstances will the benefits total less the purchase price. The refund guarantee can take two forms. If the annuitant dies prior to receiving the guaranteed amount, an *installment refund annuity* continues the periodic installments until the purchase price is refunded; a *cash refund annuity* pays the difference as a lump sum death benefit. Further discussion of annuities in this chapter is limited mainly to their appearance as optional methods for receiving payment of life insurance proceeds. Similar provisions also appear as options in pension plans providing retirement benefits, which are discussed in Chapter 24.

The amount of recovery under life insurance is stated as part of the contract, making life insurance an example of a *valued contract*. For some contracts, the benefit amount depends on covered event, such as an increased benefit if death results from an accident. Even when the benefit amount varies across circumstances, however, life insurance still is a valued contract. The occurrence of the covered event triggers payment of a benefit whose amount does not depend on the size of the loss. In some contracts, the benefit amount is not stated in dollars, as in a *variable life insurance* coverage or *variable annuity*. In these contracts, the benefit may be stated as a share of an investment fund whose dollar value changes daily.

Many types of life insurance coverage can be analyzed as consisting of two parts: term insurance and an investment. Normally, this type of contract provides a benefit payable under any set of circumstances, with a larger benefit payable if the covered event has occurred. For example, a *whole life* insurance policy provides a stated benefit when the insured person dies, with a smaller benefit if the insured person is living when the benefit is paid. This smaller benefit, called the *cash surrender value,* is the amount the holder of the policy can elect to receive by surrendering the contract to the insurer while the insured person is alive.

Policies also offer a set of options for payment of the cash surrender value, called *nonforfeiture options.* These nonforfeiture options have value equivalent to the cash surrender value but differ in form of payment (e.g., an annual income may be provided in lieu of a single payment). Hence, the holder of the policy is not necessarily required to take the surrender value as cash. Optional forms of benefit payment are also offered through *settlement options* stating ways in which death benefits may be paid. The structure of these nonforfeiture options and of other policy options is discussed in a later section of this chapter. In essence, the holder of the contract has a set of options: surrender the contract for its cash surrender value or a benefit of equivalent value, or continue holding the contract in anticipation of a larger benefit when the insured person dies.[1]

If a life insurance policy is a *participating* contract, the holder of the policy is entitled to dividends when they become payable. The dividends arise from favorable experience of the insurer, such as low mortality rates or high earnings from investments. The dividends also may be used to purchase other benefits offered under the policy. When the provision for dividends is absent, the contract is *nonparticipating.* Participating contracts and the options offered under these contracts are discussed later in this chapter.

---

[1] When the contract has an endowment feature, the death benefit and surrender value are identical at the end of the period of coverage. Under most whole life insurance policies, for example, the face value of the policy is payable if the insured survives to age 100. The technical term for this feature is *endowment* at age 100. More generally, an endowment contract provides a stated benefit, payable either as a death benefit if the insured dies prior to a stated age, or as a matured endowment if the insured survives to that age. For example, a 20-year $50,000 endowment issued to an insured age 35 pays $50,000, either as a death benefit if the insured dies prior to age 55 or as a matured endowment if the insured survives to age 55. Changes in the U.S. Tax Code in 1984 were unfavorable to endowments, and many insurers dropped endowments from their portfolio of products. Endowments are popular in other countries where tax provisions are more favorable toward the coverage.

Persons with an Economic or Legal Interest Identified in the Contract

Three persons can affect or be affected by a life insurance contract: the insured, the beneficiary, and the owner. These persons may be living individuals or legal entities, such as a corporation or an individual's estate. The distinctions between these three persons can have important legal and tax implications. The brief discussion below of these persons and their rights with respect to a life insurance policy provides an introduction; interested readers should consult Mehr and Gustavson (1987) or Greider, Crawford, and Beadles (1984) for further information.

In a policy providing a death benefit, the *insured* is the individual upon whose death the benefit is paid. More generally, the insured can be defined as the status upon which the payment of the policy benefit is contingent. For example, the periodic income benefit payable under a straight life annuity contract continues during the lifetime of the insured individual, who usually is referred to as the *annuitant*. In this straight life annuity, the "status" being "insured" is the continued lifetime of the annuitant. In some contracts, the insured status is defined with respect to more than one life. For example, a *joint life* policy insuring two individuals' lives provides a stated death benefit when the first of the two individuals dies. A *joint and survivor annuity* provides a periodic income benefit as long as either one of two individuals (the "survivor") is living, with the benefit amount possibly decreasing at the first death (the ending of their "joint life").

The *beneficiary* is the person or organization to whom the benefit is paid. In the economic sense of the term, the beneficiary is the one whose interest is insured, analogous to the insured in a property insurance contract. A *primary beneficiary* is the one who, if living at the time of the insured's death, receives the death benefit. A *contingent beneficiary* is the one to whom the death benefit is paid if the primary beneficiary is no longer living at the time of the insured's death. A beneficiary designation in a life insurance policy can specify an order of succession: a primary beneficiary, a secondary beneficiary, a tertiary beneficiary, and so on.

The *owner* is the one who controls the policy; the person or organization in whom the rights of ownership are vested. Prior to the death of the insured (or termination of the insured status), the owner has the right to assign or transfer the policy, to change the beneficiary, and to exercise other rights and options provided by the policy. Upon the death of the insured, ownership rights become vested in the beneficiary.

With respect to legal and tax issues, ownership is a key concept. The owner can exercise every right provided by the policy unless he or she has agreed to a restriction. For example, the owner can change the beneficiary unless this right has been given up, in which case, the beneficiary designation is said to be *irrevocable*. Also, any tax liability with respect to the policy generally accrues to the owner; if the owner of the policy is the individual whose life is insured, for example, the policy proceeds are considered part of deceased owner's estate for purposes of estate taxation.

462

PART FOUR
Insurance
Institutions and
Coverages

THE INVESTMENT ELEMENT IN LIFE INSURANCE

The Source of the Investment Element

For life insurance coverage that is a two-part contract comprised of a term insurance element and an investment (e.g., whole life insurance), the investment element arises from the way the contract is financed. This conclusion becomes apparent by considering two aspects of a life insurance policy: its *benefit provision* and its *premium payment, or financing provision.* The benefit provision of the policy is what the insurer promises to do: the circumstances under which a benefit is paid and the amount payable under these circumstances. The analytical framework outlined on the preceding pages—"events covered" and "amount of recovery"—addresses the benefit provision only. The other aspect of the policy—the premium payment provision—is the method for funding the benefits promised under the policy. The premium payment provision states the schedule of premium payments required for the insurer to provide the benefits promised under the policy.

The distinction between the benefit provision and premium payment provision is important to understanding how an investment element arises in a life insurance policy. A given benefit may be financed in several different ways, for example, it is possible to purchase a whole life insurance policy with a single premium payment, although such a financing provision is not chosen commonly. This contract, which is said to be "paid-up at issuance," is called *single premium insurance.* More commonly, whole life insurance is financed using installment premiums payable as long as the insured is living. The latter contract often is called *straight (or ordinary[2])* life insurance, especially if the required installment premium stays level during the insured's life. Whole life insurance contracts with premium payment provisions falling between these two extremes are called *limited-pay* contracts, such as 20-pay or 40-pay contracts. Often these limited-pay contracts are identified by stating the age at which the final premium payment is due, such as life paid-up at age 65 or at age 95. These contracts all are whole life insurance, so they provide the same death benefit using different financing provisions. If the insured dies prior to the time the policy becomes paid-up, the death benefit is not affected; the premium is set at a level that contemplates some insureds dying prior to the policy becoming paid-up.

Annually renewable term insurance (ART) may be considered yet another type of financing arrangement. ART is term insurance, but if ART were renewable for life the insurance coverage would resemble whole life. Under an ART contract, the insurer promises to pay a stated death benefit if the insured dies during the year, with an additional guarantee of the right to renew the contract at the end of the year. Typically, the right to renew expires at an advanced age (such as age 70), although contracts renewable beyond age 90 are offered.

Because ART is term insurance, it does not provide a cash surrender value. The financing provision in ART does not allow the development of surrender

---

[2] This use of the term "ordinary" is misleading. As a class of life insurance, "ordinary insurance" encompasses coverage as diverse as whole life insurance, endowments, and term insurance whose period of coverage exceeds 10 years.

values, while the financing provision in whole life does. Under level-premium whole life insurance, the amount of the installment payments begins at a higher level than ART providing the same amount of coverage but remains level during the payment period. Under ART, the annual premium begins at a lower level but increases with each renewal. The increasing premium reflects mortality rates increasing with age and the tendency of healthier-than-average individuals to discontinue (or *lapse*) the coverage.

Table 18.1 shows, for contracts issued between ages 25 and 75, illustrative premiums charged by one U.S. life insurer for four types of contracts: ART, life paid-up at age 95, life paid-up at age 65, and 20-pay life. Two relationships are apparent from the data in Table 18.1. The annual premium increases with the age of the insured and increases as the premium payment period is shortened. For a given type of coverage, the age-related increase appears as one proceeds down the column listing the annual premiums for that coverage. The effect of shortening the premium payment period appears as one proceeds to the right across the row for a given age. The annual premium increases as one proceeds to the right, with one exception: the figures for paid-up at age 65 and 20-pay life, both issued at age 55. When issued at age 55, life insurance paid-up at age 65 is *10-pay* life insurance, whose premium is higher than for 20-pay insurance. In all other cases for which data is given in Table 18.1, the 20-pay life insurance is the shortest premium payment period, with the highest annual premium.

Another relationship is less apparent from the data in Table 18.1, but critical to understanding how an investment element arises in a life insurance policy. The published rates for ART are rates for the insured's *attained age*, regardless of the age at which the policy was issued. For other types of policies shown in Table 18.1, the rates are *level premiums* that remain constant after the policy is issued. A 25-year-old male who purchases ART pays a premium of $1.63 per $1000 of coverage; at age 65, his rate per $1000 of coverage will have risen to $12.19. If a 25-year-old male purchases life paid-up at age 95, in contrast, the rate

TABLE 18.1. Premium Rates per $1000 of Coverage for a $100,000 Life Insurance Policy, by Age, Sex, and Method of Premium Payment

Age	ART*		Paid-up at 95		Paid-up at 65		20-pay Life	
	Male	Female	Male	Female	Male	Female	Male	Female
25	$ 1.63	$ 1.48	$ 9.90	$ 8.21	$12.05	$10.51	$15.89	$13.76
35	$ 1.65	$ 1.55	$ 15.30	$12.44	$17.55	$15.08	$21.09	$18.13
45	$ 2.73	$ 2.09	$ 26.10	$20.75	$29.08	$24.53	$29.08	$24.53
55	$ 5.64	$ 3.92	$ 40.05	$32.82	$64.49	$54.41	$42.11	$34.23
65	$12.19	$ 8.58	$ 62.57	$52.63	—	—	$66.02	$51.38
75	NA	NA	$116.69	$96.13	—	—	NA†	NA†

Nonsmoker participating rates per $1000 of coverage on a $100,000 policy. In the case of ART, rates are those currently being charged, which may increase to a maximum about 30–40 percent above the current rate.
*Renewable to age 80, but published rates available only up to age 70. Rates for age 70 are: Male, $20.16; Female, $14.14.
†NA, data not available.
Source: Computed from *Best's Flitcraft Compend, Life-Health,* 1991 edition.

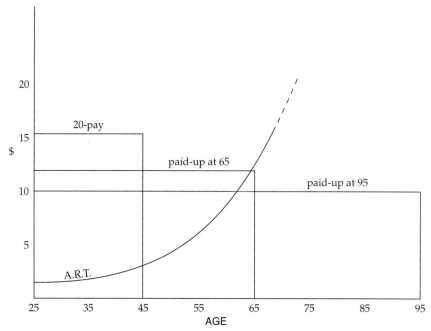

FIGURE 18.1. Annual premium rate per $1000 for $100,000 life insurance contracts issued at age 25.

per $1000 of coverage is $9.90, both at age 25 and at age 65. In other words, the ART rate per $1000 of coverage for an insured who continues to live eventually rises above the rate for life paid-up at age 95. The increase in the rate is especially dramatic at advanced ages. Published ART rates often do not go beyond age 70, as in Table 18.1, although the ART contract for which Table 18.1 provides data is renewable to age 80.

Figure 18.1, which is based on the data in Table 18.1, illustrates the effect of the different financing provisions on a $100,000 contract issued to a male age 25. Technically, the ART contract is not comparable to the whole life policies as it is not renewable for life. For this reason, Figure 18.1 includes a hypothetical projection of the ART rate for the policy if it were renewable beyond age 70. As shown in Figure 18.1, the annual premium on the whole life policies is inversely related to the premium-paying period; life paid-up at 95 has the lowest annual premium, which is payable until age 95. The highest premium is for the 20-pay contract, but this policy becomes paid-up in the shortest period of time.

Also, the whole life policies all require a premium that is larger than the initial cost of the ART policy providing the same amount of coverage. At age 25, for example, the premium for the $100,000 life paid-up at 95 policy is $990.00, as compared with $163.00 for ART. The additional premium of $990.00 − $163.00, or $827.00, finances additional benefits provided by the life paid-up at 95 policy as compared with ART. These additional benefits, which include the right to renew the policy for life at the level premium rate, have the character of an investment. By age 65, when the premium for the $100,000 ART contract has risen to $1,219.00, $229.00 above the $990.00 for the life paid-up at 95 policy, the holder of the policy has begun to experience the return from the accumulated investment.

The investment element in a whole life policy arises from the holder of the policy paying more than the cost of term insurance providing the same death benefit. For life paid-up at 95 as compared with ART, both providing a $100,000 death benefit and issued to males age 25, the additional $827.00 premium for life paid-up at 95 purchases a set of additional rights. In addition to the right to renew the policy for life at the level premium rate, the higher premium finances: (1) a right to surrender the policy for a cash surrender value, (2) the right to use this cash value to purchase other types of benefits at guaranteed rates and terms, (3) the right to borrow against the cash value on terms specified in the contract, and (4) if the policy is a participating contract, entitlement to dividends or the right to use the dividends to purchase other benefits offered under the policy.

The additional benefits provided by whole life as compared with term insurance have the character of an investment because they do not require the insured's death to become available. Of these benefits, the *cash surrender value* is fundamental, as it is the amount the owner of the policy receives if the policy is surrendered for cash. Should the owner of the policy believe that the investment in the policy would be better employed elsewhere, the right to surrender the policy for cash allows the investment to be transferred to the more productive use. If the level of the dividend and the rates and terms provided on other purchase options are not competitive with those available for the same insured currently in the marketplace, the policy owner would be expected to surrender the policy and invest the proceeds in higher-return alternatives.

Table 18.2 illustrates the schedule of cash values on the $100,000 life paid-up at 95 policy issued at age 25. As shown in Table 18.2, the cash surrender value becomes substantial by age 65, being 37.8 percent of the ultimate benefit in the case of females and 45 percent for males. The cash values may appear to discriminate in favor of males, but readers should recall that the premium is

TABLE 18.2. Cash Surrender Values at Selected Ages, $100,000 Life Paid-Up at Age 95, Issued at Age 25.

Age	Cash Values	
	Female	Male
30	$ 1,100	$ 1,500
35	$ 4,700	$ 5,800
40	$ 8,200	$10,200
45	$12,300	$15,500
•	•	•
•	•	•
60	$29,800	$36,500
65	$37,800	$45,000

Source: Computed from *Best's Flitcraft Compend, Life-Health,* 1991 edition.

higher for males (at age 25, $990 for males versus $821 for females). By paying a $990 annual premium, a female could have purchased about $121,000 of coverage, which by age 65 would have a cash surrender value over $45,500.

Because the availability of the investment element in the contract does not depend on whether the insured is alive, the amount of insurance coverage provided by the policy is the difference between the promised death benefit and the cash surrender value. For a male age 45, for example, the amount of insurance is $100,000 − $12,300, or $87,700. The intuition behind dividing the contract into investment and insurance elements is evident, and key to analyzing the motives served by the contract. When the insured reaches age 45, the owner of the life insurance policy holds a $12,300 investment and a decreasing term insurance policy currently providing $87,700 of coverage.

If the insured's health is now poor, the holder of the policy would be expected to continue to coverage as opposed to surrendering the policy for its cash value, because the insured's poor health causes the value of the term insurance element to increase. By way of comparison, the holder of the policy on an insured whose health is excellent has a stronger incentive to surrender the policy, especially if the investment element is not performing favorably compared with other investment alternatives. Appendix 18.1 to this chapter discusses issues in evaluating the investment element in a life insurance policy. Appendix 18.2 extends this discussion by suggesting a procedure for evaluating life insurance coverage at the time of purchase.

RISKS BORNE BY PARTIES TO A LIFE INSURANCE CONTRACT

The concept of life insurance as a two-part contract provides the background for a discussion of risk allocation among three parties: (1) the owner of a life insurance policy, (2) the beneficiary, and (3) the provider of coverage (typically, the provider is an insurer). The beneficiary faces the possibility of financial loss from the insured's death. A policy providing a death benefit alleviates this risk by passing part of the financial consequences to the insurer-provider. This motive for purchasing coverage, often called the "death protection" motive in literature on life insurance, is a primary motive served by a term insurance policy. The death protection motive also may be served by a two-part contract having an investment element, although the presence of the investment element requires analysis of other motives as well. For the two-part life insurance contract described in the preceding section, the magnitude of the term insurance element declines and the magnitude of the investment element increases over time as the policy remains in force.

Allocation of Mortality Risks and Burdens of Adverse Selection

From the viewpoint of the provider of life insurance coverage (such as a life insurance company), the risks associated with providing the death benefit (the term insurance element of the policy) are related to mortality rates in the insured population and, possibly, adverse selection from renewal guarantees provided as part of the coverage. Adverse selection occurs because policyholders would be expected to exercise renewal options on policies covering insureds whose health has deteriorated, while they are less likely to exercise these renewal options on insureds in above-average health.

One method for circumventing this adverse selection problem is to periodically offer policyholders the option to resubmit underwriting information (e.g., a medical screening or physical examination) with a favorable outcome entitling the holder of the contract to lower rates. Policyholders who fail to provide the information or who cannot meet underwriting tests are allowed to continue the coverage, but at a higher price. In effect, this resubmittal arrangement allocates back to policyholders much of the risk related to adverse selection as the insured group ages, while the insurer continues to bear the risk related to unexpected death.

Risk allocation in life insurance is not a new concept, particularly with respect to the mortality risk. The earliest fraternal insurance plans were organized on a full assessment basis (Mehr and Gustavson [1987], p. 605). In its purest form, a full assessment policy divides benefit costs among members of a group. For example, a group of individuals could form a pooling arrangement under which group members agree to share the cost of providing a $100,000 death benefit to the estate of group members who die. If the group consists of 10,000 members, of whom 20 die during the year, the pooling arrangement would lead to an assessment of (20)($100,000/(9,980), or about $200.40, if the benefit payment and assessment are concurrent.

Under this full assessment policy, what risks are borne by the group members? Higher-than-expected mortality rates is an obvious answer. However, a more subtle and, for the persistency of the pooling arrangement, more important issue is the risk associated with mounting benefit costs as the group ages and consequent adverse selection against the group. Without new entrants, the group will age, members will die at an increasing rate, and the increasing cost of benefits will be divided among fewer survivors. Healthier-than-average group members would be expected to drop out of the group in response to increasing costs, further exacerbating the increase in costs. The above-described increase in benefit costs and resulting adverse selection led many fraternal insurers to adopt level-premium financing plans and holding of funds in reserve that are typical features of modern coverage.

Allocation of Investment Risks

Under a two-part contract, investment risks are allocated between the insurer-provider and policyowner. Risks borne by the provider of the coverage depend on guarantees provided in the contract. On nonparticipating contracts, virtually all of the investment risk (and mortality risk) is borne by the insurer. On participating contracts, some or perhaps most of the investment risk is allocated to policyowners as a group.

The preceding sections of this chapter develop the concept of a two-part life insurance policy using a fixed-benefit, participating, "traditional" life insurance coverage. This type of contract provides a fixed schedule of values (including the cash value) for a fixed premium. The owner of the policy "participates" in the experience of the group of policyholders through dividends (or rarely, assessments), as a consequence of which risk is allocated back to policyowners as a group. If death rates are higher than expected or the yield on investments is lower than expected, for example, the dividend declines. Conceptually, the participation resembles the prospective experience rating provision used in property and liability insurance, with the experience rating adjustment applying to an entire group of policyholders. As a method for allocating risk between the insurer and the owner of the policy, the participating contract is quite old.

Traditional and Universal Life Coverage

More recently, many of the "universal" life insurance and retirement funding products developed during the last two decades provide for explicit allocation of risk between the policyowner and the provider of coverage. Especially when the policyowner controls the allocation of funds across investment alternatives, the allocation of investment risk usually is with respect to investments backing the *individual policy*, not averaged across a group of policies. The development of low-cost data processing allowed the policy-specific allocation mechanisms, which would have been impractical using older data recording and storage technologies. Contracts used for the accumulation of funds for retirement often use policy-specific allocation without any special language identifying the allocation mechanism. Conceptually, these policy-specific allocation methods resemble retrospective experience rating in property and liability insurance. The experience of the policyholder can be fairly sensitive to short-run changes in the investment environment and in choices with respect to the policy.

The structure of a typical "universal life" policy or retirement accumulation is illustrated in Figure 18.2. A universal life policy is an investment fund (or "side fund") combined with term insurance. In a retirement accumulation vehicle in which no insurance coverage is provided, the contract consists of an investment fund only. Periodically, the policyowner makes payments that are deposited in the investment fund. The allocation of the fund across investments may be under the control of the policyowner. For example, a universal life coverage may allow the policyowner to choose between several bond funds or stock funds. Earnings on the chosen investments are credited to the policy's investment fund, against which policy costs are assessed. Part of these costs is related to policy issuance and maintenance, such as sales fees, taxes, administrative costs, and investment fees.

On universal life coverage, charges for the required amount of term insurance are assessed against each policy's investment fund. The method for determining the amount of term insurance is stated in the contract. For example, one type of universal life insurance policy provides a fixed death benefit stated in dollars, such as a $100,000 death benefit. In this type of contract, the amount of term insurance is the difference between the stated death benefit and the amount accumulated in the investment fund. When the policy has accumulated an investment fund of $30,000, for example, $70,000 of term insurance is required for a $100,000 death benefit. Another type of policy provides a fixed amount of term insurance. If the policy provides a $100,000 fixed amount of

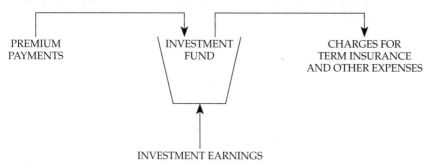

FIGURE 18.2. Structure of universal life coverage or retirement accumulation.

term insurance, for example, a policy that has accumulated an investment fund of $30,000 provides a death benefit of $130,000. For either of these policies, the amount of the benefit paid at death always equals the sum of the term insurance amount plus the accumulation in the investment fund. The difference is in the method used to determine the amount of term insurance: either a fixed amount or the difference between the death benefit and the accumulated investment value.

Typically, term insurance charges under universal life policies are assessed each month. The monthly rates are based on the insured's attained age. The method for determining monthly term insurance charges in universal life insurance allocates the risk of changes in *group* mortality rates (and consequent changes in lapse rates) across a group of policies. The typical contract states guaranteed maximum rates that will apply for each age, but the guaranteed maximums may be as much as triple the rates available on currently issued, underwritten ART policies. Readers may refer back to Table 18.1 for illustrative ART rates on underwritten policies. Because the rates in Table 18.1 are annual rates, the implied monthly rate is about one-twelfth the rate shown in Table 18.1.

The design of most universal life coverage seems oriented toward investment motives for holding the coverage, and guarantees provided by universal life coverage often focus on the investment element in the contract. For example, many providers of universal life coverage offered guaranteed high returns on the investment element during periods of high short-term interest rates. Of course, the return guarantees were patterned after yields then available in bond markets (e.g., an insurer-provider might have offered a guaranteed 8 percent yield for the first three years when three-year bonds were yielding 8.5 percent).

Because the taxation of returns in the investment element can be an important factor affecting the yield to policyholders, most universal life coverage is designed to meet provisions of the U.S. Tax Code defining life insurance. These provisions require a minimum amount of term insurance for a given amount of coverage. Appendix 18.1 to this chapter explains how life insurance cash value increases are either not taxed or taxed favorably relative to other investments.

As compared with "traditional" life insurance coverage, the distinguishing feature of universal life is the explicit identification of a separate investment fund and term insurance coverage. Earlier, "traditional" coverage was characterized as term insurance and an investment element, a concept linking universal and traditional coverage. However, a universal life contract explicitly identifies separate term insurance and investment elements. Frequently universal life contracts are called "unbundled" coverage in that the investment and insurance elements are distinct rather than unified. Because of the unbundled nature of the investment and term insurance elements, a universal life contract has no stated, fixed premium. As long as the accumulated investment is sufficient to support charges for term insurance and other expenses assessed against the policy, the policy remains in force even if premium payments are skipped. Also, the policy owner is free to voluntarily increase the amount of the payment, in which case the investment element builds up at a higher rate. In other words, a universal life contract tends to offer greater budgeting flexibility than a similar traditional contract.

In contrast, a traditional life insurance coverage is a contractual promise to provide a set of benefits and options in return for payment of a stated premium. If the policyholder fails to pay the stated premium, the nature of the benefit promised by the insurer changes. The options that take effect if the premium is not paid, the nonforfeiture options, are discussed in a later section of this chapter. Through the use of these nonforfeiture options, the policyholder can achieve much the same outcomes as under universal life, although these results require actions by the policyholder rather than being automatic.

The number and character of the guarantees provided by most traditional forms of coverage make policy-specific allocation of risk and return more difficult to achieve than is the case with universal life. In some respects, the policy-specific allocation of risk can work against budgeting flexibility in universal life coverage. If interest rates fall below levels used to project required premium payments (or mortality rates increase), the premium required to support the policy may increase. With a traditional policy, these cost-increasing factors may reduce the dividend otherwise payable on a participating policy, but the premium would not increase unless the contract language specifically provides for such increases.

The policy-specific allocation of risk in universal life coverage has been extended to include the determination of the benefit itself in *universal variable* life insurance. Under these contracts, changes in the value of the investments used to support the contract are leveraged through changes in the level of the promised benefit. Hence, the level of the death benefit provided by the coverage depends on the performance of the investments. While this same effect is present in a general sense in universal life products, standard universal life insurance provides either a stated death benefit or a stated amount of term insurance, with amounts stated in dollars. In universal variable life insurance, other policy variables as well as the value of the investments themselves can be influenced by investment performance.

Summary

The alternatives for allocating risk and return under life insurance coverage are illustrated in Table 18.3. The relative placement of each coverage is determined according to investment risk borne by the policyowner. Coverage at the top of

TABLE 18.3. Relative Placement of Life Insurance Coverage, According to Investment Risk Allocated to Policyowner

Greatest Investment Risk	"Universal Variable" Coverage
	Annuity Accumulations
	"Universal" Coverage
	Participating Coverage
Lowest Investment Risk	Nonparticipating Coverage

the list (universal variable life) tends to impose the greatest investment risk (and possible rewards) on the policyowner, while coverage at the bottom of the list tends to impose little if any risk (and consequently offers lower rewards) by providing the greatest number of guarantees.

OPTIONS AND OTHER FEATURES OF LIFE INSURANCE

Although life insurance can be analyzed as a two-part contract consisting of term insurance and an investment, most contracts contain additional features and options. This section offers a brief discussion of these additional features. These features can be grouped into three classes: (1) optional benefits purchased at policy issue; (2) standard contract provisions not requiring any decision by the policyholder, and (3) option clauses, which offer a set of rights or options from which the policyholder can choose.

The features under group 1 appear as riders providing a benefit whose amount is based on the coverage provided by the underlying policy. In concept, these optional benefits can be considered coverage that is separable from the underlying policy, that can be analyzed using the same methods used to analyze the underlying coverage.

Members of groups 2 and 3 usually are not separable but are part of the underlying contract. Many of group 2, the standard contract provisions, are mandated by state law. Options in group 3, while possibly not mandated, are typical. These options usually offer alternative forms for payment of benefits.

Because the beneficiary could elect a cash settlement and use the proceeds in a market transaction to purchase a benefit equivalent in form to the options offered under the contract, the value of the options arises primarily from price guarantees. Presumably, the beneficiary will elect the cash settlement in lieu of some other option unless the price offered under the option is favorable. Some options may become valuable as a result of special circumstances faced by the holder of the policy or because of tax considerations.

While options and other features may contribute to the value of the contract, most of its value is determined by the underlying investment and insurance elements. The options and contract features discussed below form a core set that commonly appears on life insurance coverage offered in the United

States. The variety of options and other features offered in conjunction with life insurance is too great to allow a comprehensive description in a single section of an introductory text, especially if the discussion is extended to encompass countries other than the United States.

The life insurance industry continues to experiment with new options and benefit forms designed to enhance the marketing appeal of its products. As an example of this experimentation, one insurer has offered a product allowing the naming of a new insured in limited circumstances such as marriage. A second example is a policy that allows terms of coverage to be adjusted to meet demands that vary during the life cycle—*"adjustable life"* or "life cycle" insurance. A third example is a recently developed *"living benefits"* option that allows the policyholder who has acquired a terminal illness to make advance withdrawals against the face amount of coverage to meet medical expenses or other final expenses, in effect providing a reduced, premature death benefit. Readers may consult Dorfman and Adelman (1992, ch. 10) for additional information on policy provisions and options.

Riders and Other Optional Benefits Purchased at Policy Issue

The *waiver of premium* provision excuses premium payments if the insured becomes totally disabled before reaching a stated age such as 60 or 65. The policy continues in force just as if the premiums had been paid on time. The benefit may continue during the entire period of disability or may terminate at age 65. In effect, the waiver of premium clause provides a periodic disability income benefit whose amount is the premium required to continue the policy. Waiver of premium may be sold as a policy rider for which an explicit charge is made, although many life insurance policies include waiver of premium as part of the standard contract with no explicit charge.

A *disability income* rider provides a monthly income benefit if the insured becomes totally disabled before a stated age such as 60 or 65, with the monthly income expressed as a percent of the amount of underlying coverage (commonly 1 percent). For example, a 1 percent disability income rider on a $100,000 whole life policy provides a monthly income of $1000 during the period of total disability. Insurers often impose further restrictions on the amount of the monthly income benefit (e.g., no more than $3000 per month or more than 70 percent of monthly earnings prior to disablement).

The cost of a disability income rider is considerably higher than the cost of a waiver of premium clause on the same policy. As a consequence, a disability income rider hardly ever is provided without a specific election by the insured. Waiver of premium, however, often is provided as a standard benefit without an explicit election by the policyowner. When a disability income rider is purchased, waiver of premium nearly always is included.

Guaranteed insurability is another type of benefit sold in conjunction with life insurance. A guaranteed insurability rider provides the right to purchase additional insurance at stated points in time without requiring evidence of insurability (e.g., the insured is not required to take a physical examination). The price at which the coverage can be purchased is stated as part of option and the amount of coverage usually is stated as a multiple of the amount provided by the underlying policy. For example, a guaranteed insurability rider may allow the insured to purchase the same amount as the underlying policy at three-year intervals for a period of 15 years. Because a healthy insured could submit to an underwriting evaluation and be issued additional coverage, the option becomes valuable if the insured's health condition deteriorates. The value of the option depends on the prices guaranteed under the option relative to prices that are expected to prevail at the dates the option can be exercised.

Guaranteed insurability also is provided through a *cost-of-living* rider, which bases the amount of additional coverage on changes in a cost-of-living index. For example, a policy providing $100,000 of coverage with a cost-of-living rider allows the purchase of an additional $20,000 of coverage if the cost-of-living index rises 20 percent relative to the year the contract was issued. Typically, the coverage provided under the cost-of-living rider is term insurance, the option expires at a stated age such as 65, and the option must be kept in force continuously or it expires. In contrast, the coverage offered under the guaranteed insurability option usually is the same type as the underlying policy (e.g., whole life if the underlying policy is whole life), and a guaranteed insurability option may be exercised on the stated date without exercising prior options.

Renewal guarantees also are provided in conjunction with term insurance contracts, although the renewal guarantee usually is part of the contract rather than a separate rider. Term insurance is *renewable* if the policyowner can elect to renew the contract without providing evidence of insurability. The price of coverage stated in the contract is based on the insured's age at renewal. For example, the annual renewable term (ART) contract discussed earlier in this chapter is renewable each year. Some renewable contracts have periods of time longer than one year for which renewal at a stated price is offered.

Term insurance is *convertible* if the policyowner can convert the contract to the same amount of whole life insurance without providing evidence of insurability. Convertible term insurance usually is renewable as well, but renewable term insurance may not be convertible.

A *multiple indemnity* rider increases the policy benefit if death occurs under circumstances described in the rider. For example, a rider may double the death benefit if death is due to accident rather than natural causes. Although multiple indemnity riders have been commonplace at times, their popularity is not easily explained. It is doubtful whether the financial loss resulting from an accidental death is any greater than the loss from death due to other causes. Possibly, a policyowner may perceive that the price for the accidental death rider relative to the probability of accident is favorable when compared with the price of the underlying coverage relative to the probability of death from all causes.

Standard Contract Provisions

Important contract provisions required by the laws of most states include the grace period, reinstatement, incontestable, misstatement of age, and suicide clauses. Certain exclusions, although not required by law, are permitted in most states. These clauses, which can have an important effect on the policyholder's rights, are described briefly below.

The *grace period* clause states a period of time following the premium due date during which payment of the premium will keep the original coverage in force. If the premium is paid after the stated due date but during the grace period, the original coverage remains in effect without any change. The grace period in annual premium contracts is 31 days. Under laws in many states, an insurer could charge for lost interest earnings due to the late premium payment, but this is seldom if ever done. If the insured dies during the grace period, the insurer must pay the policy's stated death benefit after first subtracting the unpaid premium. If the premium remains unpaid after the end of the grace period, the policy lapses. The nonforfeiture options triggered when the policy lapses are discussed in a later section of this chapter.

The *reinstatement clause* states the conditions under which the insurer will allow reinstatement of a policy that has been lapsed for nonpayment of premiums. A typical reinstatement clause provides the right to reinstate a policy that has not been surrendered for cash if the reinstatement is requested with five years of lapsation. Overdue premiums must be paid with interest, and the insured person may be required to present evidence that he or she is insurable.

The *incontestable* clause states that the insurer cannot contest payment of the policy proceeds if the insured dies after a period of time that by law cannot exceed two years. A brief discussion of this noteworthy feature of life insurance appears earlier in Chapter 16. Once the policy becomes incontestable, the insurer cannot deny coverage because of inaccurate or incomplete disclosure of information on the policy application.

The *misstatement of age* clause states an adjustment in coverage that will take place if the insured's age has been misstated. The effect of an age misstatement always is an adjustment in the benefit amount, regardless of when the age misstatement is discovered. In other words, the misstatement of age clause is not affected by the incontestable clause. When an age misstatement is discovered, the benefit payable under the policy is adjusted to the level that could have been purchased with the actual premium paid for the insured's correctly stated age. The adjustment could be upward or downward, depending on whether the insured's age was overstated or understated.

The *suicide clause* allows the insurer to deny a death claim if death results from suicide. In the absence of a suicide clause, adverse selection could occur when a person contemplating suicide takes out a large amount of coverage shortly before committing suicide. The suicide clause makes this type of adverse selection unlikely. The suicide clause cannot be invoked for suicide occurring after the policy has been in force for two years. This two-year limitation is imposed in the belief that a person contemplating suicide would not reasonably be expected to take a large amount of coverage more than two years in advance of the act. Further, invoking a suicide clause after two years could result in hardship for an innocent beneficiary.

Exclusions permitted by many states include provisions applying to private *aviation* (or, more broadly, *hazardous sports*) or to *war*. The aviation exclusion or a related exclusion applying to hazardous activities allows the insurer to deny coverage by merely returning accumulated premiums plus interest if death results from causes identified in the exclusion. The aviation exclusion does not apply to scheduled flights on commercial airlines, but is limited to private aviation. The hazardous sports exclusion applies to activities likely to carry higher-than-average mortality risks, such as hang gliding, scuba diving, and motorcycle racing.

Typically, these exclusions are not incorporated as standard features in life insurance contracts. In the course of gathering information to evaluate factors likely to affect the insured's mortality, an insurer usually will inquire about the insured's participation in hazardous activities. If the insured states that these activities are likely, the insurer may offer a policy without the exclusion but carrying a surcharged rate. If the insured declines the surcharged policy, a policy with the exclusion but carrying a standard rate may be offered. If the insured fails to reveal or misrepresents involvement in the activity and as a consequence induces the insurer to issue a policy without the exclusion carrying a standard rate, coverage may be denied if death occurs prior to the policy becoming incontestable. Once the policy becomes incontestable, however, denial of coverage is very unlikely.

A *war exclusion* permits an insurer to deny a death claim related to war. Some forms of the exclusion apply if death is caused by war while others apply if death occurs while the insured is in the armed forces during wartime. As a practical matter, the war exclusion tends to appear when war is likely or in progress. After the end of the war, the clauses usually are cancelled, perhaps with retroactive payment of claims that were denied as a result of using the exclusion. Thus the war exclusion appears to have limited practical significance.

Option Clauses

The different ways in which the life insurance policy may be used are stated in the option clauses: policy conversions, nonforfeiture options, the loan provision, settlement options, and dividend options.

Standard provisions required by state law usually (1) prescribe minimum nonforfeiture values available as a cash surrender value and at least one option to continue insurance coverage, (2) require a loan provision with the method used to determine the loan interest rate stated as part of the contract, and (3) on participating contracts, require the payment of dividends when the insurer's resources are at a level that allows them to be paid. State statutes also require that tables illustrating amounts available under policy options be incorporated into the contract or otherwise available to policyholders.

A policyholder should realize that the nonforfeiture and settlement options state the minimum amount the insurer is contractually obligated to provide if the option is selected. The person exercising the option is free to elect a lump sum cash payment and use the proceeds to purchase an equivalent benefit elsewhere (unless the owner of the policy has restricted the choice of options). The opportunity to elect a lump sum cash payment imposes the discipline of the market on the insurer at time of policy settlement, and an insurer may be willing to provide a larger benefit than the contractual minimum if allowed to make a new offer. One would expect an insurer to offer an existing policyholder investment returns at least as favorable as returns currently being offered to new applicants in the market.

Policy Conversions. The *policy change* clause permits the insured to convert the policy, without demonstrating evidence of insurability, to some other form requiring a higher premium. The conversion is retroactive, the insured usually making up the deficiency in the premiums already paid by a lump-sum payment equal to the difference in the reserves under the two plans. Conversion to a lower premium plan, if permitted at all, generally requires proof of insurability.

Nonforfeiture Options. As explained earlier in this chapter, the investment element of a life insurance contract is the amount the policyowner could receive if the policy is surrendered to the insurer prior to the insured's death. If the policyowner wishes to continue insurance coverage without continuing premium payments, two options are provided: paid-up insurance and term insurance. These options frequently are called nonforfeiture options. Under the *paid-up insurance* option, the cash value is used to purchase a paid-up insurance policy providing the same form of benefit as the surrendered contract (e.g., whole life if the surrendered contract is whole life) but a smaller benefit amount. Under the *term insurance* option, the amount of coverage provided by the surrendered contract is continued, but the form of coverage is changed to term insurance. The term insurance continues in force for as long a period of time as the cash surrender value will provide. Typically, term insurance rates applying to nonforfeiture options anticipate considerable adverse selection, which would be expected to occur when term insurance is available without underwriting. Table 18.4 lists the nonforfeiture options offered by one nonparticipating insurer per $1000 of coverage on a surrendered policy originally issued to a 35-year old insured.

The Loan Provision. The loan provision permits the policyowner to borrow against the policy's cash surrender value. Methods for determining the upper limit on the borrowed amount vary among policies. A typical loan provision allows the policyowner to borrow an amount which, when accumulated at interest, will not exceed the cash value on the date the next premium is due. Daily interest accrues on the borrowed amount, and the loan may be repaid in whole or in part at any time. In case of death while a policy loan is outstanding, the indebtedness is subtracted from policy proceeds. The policy terminates when total indebtedness exceeds the policy's cash surrender value.

TABLE 18.4. Nonforfeiture Values Per $1000 of Coverage Provided by One Nonparticipating Insurer to an Insured Who Was Age 35 When Policy Was Issued

End of policy year	*Straight life*				*20-payment life*				*Paid-up at 65*			
	Cash value	Paid-up insurance	Term insurance Years	Term insurance Days	Cash value	Paid-up insurance	Term insurance Years	Term insurance Days	Cash value	Paid-up insurance	Term insurance Years	Term insurance Days
5	$ 37	$119	7	279	$ 72	$232	13	106	$ 48	$155	9	283
10	114	306	13	272	186	500	19	228	138	371	15	293
15	200	450	15	151	324	729	22	143	241	542	17	298
20	292	555	15	107	462	Fully paid			355	674	18	41
Age 65	486	745	13	20	629	Fully paid			629	Fully paid		

The method used to determine the interest rate charged on policy loans is stated as part of the contract. A fixed policy loan rate of 4 or 5 percent was common on policies issued prior to 1980. A variable policy loan rate based on an index of market interest rates is more common on policies issued recently.

Some universal life contracts still use a fixed policy loan interest rate, but with an offset. When a low fixed policy loan rate such as 4 or 5 percent is used, the offset reduces the rate of earnings on the contract's investment element when the loan option is exercised. Exercising the loan option results in a portion of the contract's investment element (i.e., the borrowed amount) to earn a rate of interest slightly below the fixed policy loan rate rather than being credited with the rate of return applying to the policy's investment element generally.[3]

Settlement Options. The settlement options state the optional forms of benefit payment available under the contract. Settlement options usually apply to both the death benefit and the cash surrender value. For example, optional forms of settlement usually are available if the policyholder elects to surrender the policy for its cash value. The owner of the policy may restrict the options available to the beneficiary (e.g., direct that the proceeds payable to support minor children be paid in installments). If the owner does not restrict the options, the beneficiary has the right to make the election.

Four types of settlement options are commonly provided on life insurance coverage:

1. *Interest Option.* The insurer retains the policy proceeds, accumulating them at interest. The minimum interest rate paid on the proceeds is guaranteed in the policy. If the beneficiary elects this option, the proceeds and interest may be withdrawn at any time. This option also can be used when the policyholder wishes to defer settlement of the policy for a period of time following the insured's death. If the policyowner is concerned about the possibility of the policy proceeds being paid to a beneficiary who survives the insured for only a short period, for example, the policyowner can require that the policy proceeds be withheld for a period of time and then paid to beneficiaries who survive the time period.

2. *Installment Options.* The policy proceeds are paid as a series of installments. The interest rate used to determine the installment amounts and length of time they will be paid are subject to guaranteed minimums. Tables of installments are incorporated into the contract itself. Typically, fixed installments appear as two separate options: a *specified amount* option and a *specified period* option.

---

[3] An *automatic premium loan* provision is offered on many traditional policies, but only upon request. Often the election is made on the original application for the policy. The provision goes into effect when the premium is unpaid beyond the end of the grace period and the policyowner provides no other specific direction to the insurer (e.g., electing a paid-up insurance option). Under these circumstances, the premium is assumed to be paid by borrowing against the policy's cash value. The automatic premium loan option usually appears as part of the contract's loan provision, but it has the effect of a nonforfeiture option. The original contract stays in force, but an indebtedness is established against the policy. Because any indebtedness is subtracted from the death benefit, the effective amount of coverage declines as the provision remains in force.

3. Life Income Option. The proceeds are used as the purchase price for an annuity at guaranteed rates. The common annuity forms are the straight life annuity, an annuity with a specified number of years certain, a cash refund annuity, and an installment refund annuity. The monthly payments are based on guaranteed interest and mortality rates. Some insurers offer a variable annuity settlement option.

4. Joint and Survivor Option. The policy proceeds are used to purchase an annuity providing a benefit as long as at least one of two covered persons is living. This option might be used by a married couple to provide a retirement income to the household as long as either spouse survives. When the insured is still alive, the settlement option applies to the policy's cash value rather than the death benefit. The cash value is used to purchase a joint and survivor annuity covering both spouses.

Table 18.5 illustrates the monthly incomes per $1000 of policy proceeds offered by one insurer as settlement options. $100,000 of policy proceeds payable to a male beneficiary age 65 could provide $794 for the life of the beneficiary. If life annuity with 10 years certain is chosen, the monthly income decreases to $749. If paid as an installment refund annuity, the monthly income decreases another $10, to $739. The difference between the monthly incomes payable under the life annuity with 10 years certain and the installment refund annuity is small because the guarantees are nearly equivalent for a male age 65. The minimum amount payable under the life annuity with 10 years certain is $749 payable for 120 months, or $89,880. The installment refund annuity increases the guaranteed minimum to $100,000, but the period of time becomes longer: $739 per month implies a guarantee period slightly longer than 135 months, as compared with 120 months (i.e., $739 per month for 135 months totals $99,765).

Settlement options offer guaranteed interest and mortality rates, conversion rights at net cost, freedom from investment worries, and the ability to evaluate a lump-sum payment in terms of the income it replaces. If the policyowner wishes to have the proceeds managed by some third party but wants more flexibility than that provided by the settlement options, a lump-sum payment may

TABLE 18.5. Guaranteed Minimum Monthly Installments per $1,000 of Proceeds Offered by One Insurer as Settlement Options

Minimum Fixed Installments		Minimum Monthly Lifetime Incomes				
Number of Years	Monthly Income	Age of Beneficiary Male	Female	Straight Life	Life with 10 years certain	Installment Refund
1	84.47	55	60	6.45	6.32	6.24
3	28.99	60	65	7.06	6.83	6.73
5	17.91	65	70	7.94	7.49	7.39
10	9.61	70	75	9.20	8.29	8.27
15	6.87	75	80	11.00	9.14	9.46
20	5.51					
30	4.18					

Source: Computed from *Best's Flitcraft Compend, Life-Health,* 1991 edition.

be paid to a trustee under a trust agreement. The return on the trusteed proceeds, however, is not guaranteed; it may be greater or less than if the insurer had retained the proceeds.

Dividend Options. Participating policies allow dividends to policyholders when the assets accumulated under a group of policies exceed the amount required to fund projected benefits payable under the policies. This excess accumulation can arise from favorable experience related to any of the three determinants of life insurance prices: (1) lower than anticipated mortality rates, (2) higher than anticipated investment earnings, and (3) lower than anticipated expenses of servicing the policies. For example, a large proportion of the expenses of servicing policies is incurred when the policies are first put into force. Over time, these costs are amortized against the premium income from the policies. If lapsation of a policy occurs prior to these costs being amortized, the burden on persisting policyholders increases. Hence, lower than expected lapse rates can increase policy dividends. To make payment of dividends likely to occur, premiums for participating policies usually are set higher than for similar nonparticipating policies. The higher premium provides a conservative margin for unfavorable experience.

Dividend options provide optional forms in which the policyholder can elect to receive the dividend payment. Typically the dividend may be received as (1) a cash payment, (2) a reduction in the next premium, (3) paid-up additional life insurance, the additional insurance being purchased by the application of the dividend as a single premium at net rates, (4) a deposit with the insurer accumulating at not less than a guaranteed rate of interest, or (5) one-year term insurance, the dividend being used to purchase a one-year term insurance policy at rates guaranteed in the contract. The amount of additional insurance that could be purchased under the one-year term insurance option can be large, particularly at young ages. If the option were unrestricted as to timing and amount, adverse selection problems would be likely. Some contracts do not offer the option. When the option is offered, typically it must be elected when the contract is first issued and kept in force continually. If the policyowner wishes to elect the option at a later date, evidence of insurability may be required. Also, the amount of coverage available under the option may be limited to the cash value or the amount of coverage provided by the underlying contract.

Option 3, paid-up additional insurance, has the advantage of providing additional coverage that becomes the basis for augmenting the dividend amount. When used over a long period, the compounding effect of this option can substantially increase the amount of coverage and the dividend. Under a closely related option, dividends may be used to decrease the number of premium payments by reducing the time period after which the policy becomes paid-up. For example, whole life paid-up at age 95 could become paid-up at age 94 after the application of one dividend, with further dividends continuing to reduce the premium payment period. Eventually, the dividends might result in the policy becoming paid-up when the insured attains, say, age 59.

Flexibility Provided by Options. The four sets of options discussed in this section make the life insurance contract a highly flexible instrument. An example will serve to summarize the preceding discussion and to demonstrate this flexibility.

A person age 35 purchases a $100,000 straight life insurance contract. At any age, the purchaser may elect to convert this contract to a limited payment contract. He or she may choose to receive dividends according to one of the dividend options. At any age, the insured may elect to borrow on the policy or to surrender the contract and exercise the nonforfeiture options. For example, at age 65, the insured may decide to surrender the contract, have it continued as paid-up insurance of a reduced amount, or have the insurance continued in the same face amount for some limited period. If the insured elects a cash value, he or she may ask to have the proceeds paid out according to one of the settlement options, including a retirement income under an annuity. Finally, in case of death before surrender of the policy for cash, the death proceeds may also be placed under one of the settlement options.

APPENDIX 18.1. EVALUATION OF THE INVESTMENT ELEMENT IN LIFE INSURANCE

Introduction. The evaluation of any investment begins with an identification of objectives for the owner's investment plan. These objectives are used to evaluate the suitability of any particular investment. A full discussion of these issues is beyond the scope of this chapter, belonging instead in a textbook on investments. Instead, this appendix provides a brief overview of the issues involved in evaluating the investment element in life insurance and a general ranking of a typical life insurance coverage with respect to this issue. Readers seeking a deeper evaluation of these issues should consult a modern textbook treatment of investment objectives such as chapter 27 of Bodie, Kane, and Marcus (1993).

Readers should recognize that the opportunity set of investments available to life insurers is not likely to differ dramatically from the opportunity set available to individuals who might purchase coverage. In other words, there is no "magic" that life insurers can work to make their investments consistently outperform those of any other informed, educated investor. Also, the life insurance industry is not legally entitled to print currency, so the funds available to pay death claims and surrender values come from the same sources policyholders would use if they organized their own cooperative investment and claim payment programs. This generalization is qualified in one respect: life insurers are taxed lightly on investment earnings they pass on to policyholders, and in many cases these earnings escape taxation at the policyowner level as well. This light taxation creates a possible advantage of life insurance investment relative to other investments that might be taxed, but the benefits of the light taxation tend to accrue only very gradually and are offset by other transaction costs associated with life insurance. The tax advantages from holding life insurance can become meaningful only if the contract is held a long time.

In evaluating the investment element in life insurance or, for that matter, any investment, an investor usually considers five aspects of the proposed investment: (1) safety or level of risk, (2) the expected rate of return, (3) the degree of liquidity, (4) the tax treatment, and (5) flexibility or options for alternative uses.

Safety or Level of Risk. This aspect of an investment determines the degree of certainty that the investment will achieve a stated objective or provide a given yield. This aspect of an investment is important to risk-averse investors, and is especially important in an investment whose holding period is expected to be a long time. In an insurance product, one would expect risk-aversion to be a major motive driving the purchase of coverage.

The record of the U.S. life insurance industry on this aspect would place it near the "safe" end of the rankings of all investments, although life insurance has not been riskless. The general classification of "safe" has not always applied to specific insurers or specific types of policies. During the 1980s and early 1990s, a number of life insurers defaulted on their life insurance and annuity obligations. In some of these cases, the insurers' investment strategies were based on high-yield risky bonds, and the insurers failed when the market for these bonds performed poorly. In other cases, the performance of real estate investments held by some life insurers was less than expected. Insurers whose investment strategies were oriented toward more secure investments largely escaped these problems. The section of Chapter 15 on life and health insurance guaranty funds discusses some effects of these insolvencies.

In most cases, the obligations of failed life insurers have been assumed by state guaranty funds or by other life insurers. In many of these assumptions, however, policyowners received a lower return than they expected from holding the contract. The above-described defaults involved only a small fraction of the coverage outstanding at the time, which leads to a general conclusion that the record of the life insurance industry appears quite good. The prospective future record may even be more secure, as all states have enacted state-level guarantee funds to cover obligations of life insurers that become insolvent.

In making a prospective evaluation of an investment in life insurance, a policyowner should consider the investment strategy of the insurer issuing the contract (or, if the policy represents a claim against an account segregated from the insurer's other assets, the investment strategy for the account) as well as the performance of the industry generally. When insurers have oriented their investment strategy toward safe investments, such as U.S. Treasury obligations, their record has approached the record of the investments on which their promises are based. When an insurer uses a conservative investment strategy oriented toward secure investments, life insurance can be considered a relatively safe investment, although probably not as safe as U.S. Treasury obligations.

Rate of Return. In a market in which alternative investments, including life insurance, compete for the investment dollars of policyholders, one would expect the return on the investment element in life insurance to be commensurate with its degree of risk. In other words, the level of risk is related to the expected return; one would expect that a high-yield life insurance policy to carry a larger investment risk than a lower-yielding policy. Also, one would not expect yields on life insurance policies to be significantly lower than yields on investments that might compete with life insurance; if they are lower, life insurance will not appeal to investors.

The return on the investment element in life insurance is strongly affected by the length of the holding period, especially if the policy has been in effect only a few years. In most cases, life insurance is a poor short-term investment. Most annual-premium whole life insurance policies do not begin to show a positive cash value until the end of the second or third policy year, which means that the policyholder receives little or nothing in return if the contract is surrendered after only a short holding period. Long holding periods, such as 20 years, are usually required for returns on the investment element in life insurance to approach returns the policyowner could have earned on other investments. Also, long holding periods are required for favorable income tax effects (covered below) to become significant.

Most life insurance policies providing cash values guarantee minimum yields on the cash value. This guarantee may be implicit in the buildup of guaranteed cash values or it may take the form of an explicit guarantee. The guaranteed yield may be related to the holding period, especially if short-term interest rates are higher than long-term rates. For example, the guaranteed yield may be 6 percent for the first five years and 4 percent thereafter. The yield guarantees usually are based on a conservative estimate of the yield the insurer expects to earn on investments.

Liquidity. The term "liquidity" refers to the ease with which an investment can be converted to cash. A passbook savings account, money market account, or actively traded marketable securities would be considered liquid investments, as they can readily be changed into cash. At the other extreme, a partner's legal interest in a business venture might be considered illiquid, as the partnership interest may not be very marketable. Fixed assets such as specialized machinery used in production also tend to be illiquid.

The investment element in life insurance is about as liquid as a short-term certificate of deposit. Life insurance usually would not be considered as liquid as a passbook savings account or a checking account, although the degree of liquidity depends on the circumstances giving rise to demand for payment. Payment of life insurance proceeds requires some form of written notice, with the attendant delay. If payment is demanded as a result of the insured's death, a death certificate is the usual form of notice. If the policy is being surrendered for its cash value, a written request for the cash surrender value usually is required.

Tax Treatment. The tax treatment of life insurance is a matter of the provisions of the U.S. (and state) Tax Code as applied to circumstances in which the life insurance policy is used. The brief description of taxation in typical situations presented below does not offer rules to fit all situations, but will apply to a wide variety of circumstances.

The investment element in life insurance receives favorable income tax treatment. In many cases, earnings on life insurance investments are not taxed or taxed very lightly. The most favorable taxation occurs when a life insurance policy is used to provide a death benefit to a named beneficiary, as a result of three rules. (1) To the extent that investment earnings are passed through to policyholders, a life insurer is not taxed or is taxed very little on the investment earnings used to support life insurance policies. (2) Increases in a life insurance policy's cash value are not considered taxable income to the owner of the policy during the life of the insured, as the owner is not deemed to be in constructive receipt of these increases. (3) The death benefit normally is not considered taxable income to the beneficiary. When a life insurance policy provides a death benefit to a named beneficiary, the investment earnings used to support policy values go largely untaxed. To the extent that investment earnings used to build resources to pay death benefits are derived from taxable investments, otherwise taxable investment earnings escape taxation or are taxed lightly.

A somewhat less favorable treatment applies if the policy is surrendered for its cash value. When the owner surrenders a life insurance policy, the difference between the surrender value and the policy's cost basis is taxable income to the owner. If the owner paid the premium for the policy, the cost basis would be the sum of the premiums less dividends. Even though a tax arises in the case of surrender, the taxation tends to be more favorable than if the increases in cash value had been taxed when they occurred.

Flexibility. Most investments are inflexible in that they must be held in one form or put to a specified use. Even when an investment is liquid, a new use usually requires the investment to be sold and replaced with a new investment suited to the new purpose. An exception would be a multi-purpose asset such as a vehicle that can be used in a variety of circumstances. Life insurance policies often contain features that make them very flexible. These features, which were discussed in the chapter section on options and other features of life insurance, may take the form of options to purchase coverage on favorable terms or to use the policy's cash value in ways deemed useful by a policyowner.

Summary. Is life insurance a good investment? This question cannot be answered independently of circumstances. Certainly the answer must be "no" for an investor whose objectives are focused on the near-term. It may appear that life insurance purchased shortly before the death of the insured is a good investment if it provides a large benefit for a small outlay. Certainly, the purchase of coverage is timely in this case, but the question remains whether the *investment element* was a worthwhile use of funds. Since term insurance would be less expensive than a policy with an investment element, a term insurance policy would have provided a greater amount of coverage for the same expenditure (this statement assumes that the insured would have been eligible to purchase term insurance at the time the coverage was issued).

When life insurance is held for a long period, the return tends to approach and, on an after-tax basis, even may exceed the return the policyowner could have earned on investments carrying the same degree of risk as the investments supporting the policy's values. Also, most life insurance policies relieve the owner of the policy of the burden of making day-to-day decisions on the portfolio of investments, although in some policies the owner is free to allocate the investment element among optional categories of investments.

The balance between these benefits and burdens can be evaluated only in light of the objectives of the policyowner. Life insurance forms the cornerstone of many individuals' investment portfolios. Life insurance is neither a good nor a bad investment, but its characteristics rank it alongside other investments carrying similar degrees of risk and return. In many cases, life insurance is low-yield relative to many other investment opportunities, but its yield is consistent with other investments carrying a similar degree of risk if held for a long time.

APPENDIX 18.2. EVALUATION OF LIFE INSURANCE PRODUCTS

Two themes are developed in this chapter: (1) life insurance coverage other than term insurance is a two-part contract consisting of an insurance and an investment element, and (2) motives served by one element of a typical two-part contract may differ from the motives served by the other element. The motive served by the insurance element often is related to loss of income as a result of an insured's death—the "death protection" motive. Motives served by the investment element can be complex, although the holding of investments can be driven by a motive as straightforward as the desire for an orderly accumulation of financial resources, perhaps to provide a retirement income or a bequest to descendants. It is possible for the two parts to serve multiple interests of different individuals—the investment element offering benefits directed primarily toward the owner of the contract, for example, while the insurance element offering benefits directed primarily towards the beneficiary.

The life insurance industry offers alternatives ranging from "pure" insurance to a "pure" investment. Annually Renewable Term (ART) insurance is an example of a "pure" insurance product, or at least the contract is close enough to pure insurance that the coverage is practically indistinguishable from a contract having only an insurance element.[4] At the other end of the spectrum, a contract for accumulating funds to be used for retirement—often called a "tax-deferred" annuity accumulation—is close enough to a pure investment contract that any insurance element can be ignored. Not until the accumulated funds are converted into an annuity contract (e.g., a joint and survivor benefit) does the retirement contract contain an insurance element. Hence, the contract for accumulating funds for retirement is an example of an investment product sold by the life insurance industry.

The First Step. Most life insurance coverage falls between the extremes illustrated by ART and the retirement accumulation vehicle. When insurance coverage is being evaluated, a logical starting point is identifying the objective toward which the insurance element is directed, that is, the motive driving the holder to seek an insurance product instead of a contract with purely investment features. The least expensive life insurance contract that meets this protection motive often is term insurance. For example, decreasing term insurance

---

[4] From a technical standpoint, the requirement that the premium be paid at the beginning of the year gives rise to a small investment element that dissipates throughout the year. Also, the price of the coverage takes into account the cost of providing a renewal guarantee and the resulting adverse selection. The funding of the renewal guarantee gives rise to an investment element that is small enough to be ignored.

often will be the least expensive contract protecting family members who live at home against loss of income resulting from the death of a family member who works outside the home to provide support. The coverage serving this purpose is decreasing term insurance, for two reasons: (1) normally, the family member who works outside the home plans on retirement, after which time the possible loss of income due to death ceases, (2) as the age of retirement approaches, the amount of insurance required to replace the lost income diminishes, as fewer years of income remain to be lost.

The identification of the least expensive coverage meeting the protection objective considers not only the required amount of coverage at a given point in time but also the evolution of this amount over time, that is, a projection over time of the purpose for which the protection is used. The coverage meeting this objective is not necessarily term insurance; if life insurance were used as the sole means of providing resources for burial and other final expenses, some type of whole life insurance would be required because the resources will be required whenever death occurs. Another example is a joint life insurance policy dedicated to funding a business purchase agreement between two business partners. Again, resources are required at the first death, whenever it occurs. Joint life insurance meets this objective because resources are required only at the first death.

This motive for purchasing coverage, often called the "death protection" motive in literature on life insurance, is a primary motive served by a term insurance policy. The death protection motive also may be served by a two-part contract having an investment element, although the presence of the investment element requires analysis of other motives as well.

The Second Step. After the least expensive contract has been identified, more expensive alternatives may be considered. Additional expense usually arises from the investment features and other options provided as part of the coverage. The issue that remains to be examined is whether these additional features justify the additional expense. For example, a prospective policyowner may consider whole life to provide coverage against loss of income, a purpose for which decreasing term insurance is the least expensive contract. A whole life contract offers a package of options and features that is superior to a decreasing term insurance policy providing the same initial amount of coverage, including: (1) a cash surrender value and other nonforfeiture options, (2) the right to continue coverage beyond the time at which the term insurance expires, a right that may become valuable if new requirements for coverage arise and the insured's health deteriorates, and (3) if the policy is participating, the opportunity to benefit from favorable investment experience. Dividends paid under participating life insurance contracts often comprise a substantial portion of returns to policyholders.

The above sequence may not be appropriate if the reasons for holding life insurance are purely investment-related or driven by the desire for tax avoidance. In this case, only investment or tax-avoidance motives need to be considered. As the term is used in this chapter, however, the annuity accumulation contract is not "life insurance" until it is converted into a life annuity; prior to conversation into an annuity, the contract is only an agreement to hold and invest accumulated funds, so the contract lacks a life insurance element. Examined within the framework developed in this chapter, the annuity accumulation vehicle is an investment product sold by the life insurance industry.

Key Concepts

term insurance Life insurance under which the insurer promises to pay the face amount if the insured dies during the specified term.

whole life insurance Life insurance under which the insurer promises to pay the face amount when the insured dies. Straight life insurance and limited payment life insurance are the two classes of whole life insurance.

annuity A form of insurance under which the insurer promises to pay the insured an income for a specified period or as long as the insured and perhaps a beneficiary are alive.

adjustable life insurance Life insurance under which the insured can change the face amount and the premium each year as his or her needs, capital accumulation objectives, and ability to pay the premium change.

universal life insurance A life insurance contract that identifies explicitly the amount of the term insurance and the investment component included in the policy. The policy owner may be free to allocate the investment component among several investment options.

universal variable life insurance Life insurance under which the amount of coverage and the cash value vary according to the performance of a portfolio of investments.

owner With respect to a life insurance policy, the one who controls the policy; the person or organization in whom the rights of ownership are vested.

beneficiary With respect to a life insurance policy, the one to whom the death benefit is paid.

insured With respect to a life insurance policy, the one whose death causes the benefit to be paid.

nonforfeiture options Ways in which a policyowner can elect to claim the cash value of a nonterm life insurance contract if he or she decides to surrender the contract. The three most common options are cash, paid-up insurance, and extended term insurance.

settlement options Ways in which a policyowner or the beneficiary can elect to have the death proceeds or the cash nonforfeiture value distributed. The most common settlement options are an interest option, an installment time option, an installment amount option, and a life income option.

living benefits An option provided by a life insurance policy that allows the policyholder to receive advance payments against the face amount of coverage to meet medical expenses or other final expenses.

Review Questions

1. Describe the death benefit and financing (i.e., premium payment) provisions in each of the following contracts.
   a. Annually renewable term insurance.
   b. Single premium whole life insurance.
   c. 40-Pay whole life insurance.
   d. Whole life paid-up at age 85, issued at age 35.
   e. 20-Pay 40-year endowment issued at age 25.
2. For an individual age 70, one insurer charges $120,000 per $1000 of monthly income provided by a life annuity with 10 years certain.
   a. Does this information allow you to predict what this insurer would charge for an installment refund annuity issued at age 70?

b. Would you expect the premium per $1000 of monthly income on a life annuity with 20 years certain to be greater or smaller than the above figure?

3. Compare the benefit provided by a guaranteed insurability rider with the benefit provided by a cost of living rider.

4. Compare universal life insurance and participating whole life insurance with respect to
   a. The types of guarantees provided by the contracts, and
   b. The allocation of investment risk between the insurer and the policyowner.

5. Some persons refer to annuities as an upside-down application of life insurance. What are they likely to mean by this reference?

6. Three determinants of life insurance costs were identified in the chapter and their relationship to the level of dividends on a participating life insurance contract was noted. Explain how these same three determinants would affect the level of monthly benefits on a participating annuity.

7. Under what circumstances would a policyowner be likely to choose term insurance as a nonforfeiture option on a whole life insurance policy?

8. Upon reaching retirement at age 65, a married male head of household determines that the coverage provided by a $100,000 whole life policy he has owned since age 25 is less important than it was when he was employed. Identify at least four distinct options available to this policyowner and briefly explain how the attractiveness of these options would be affected by circumstances faced by members of the household.

9. Explain how the temporary discontinuance of premium payments affects policyholder rights under
   a. Universal life insurance
   b. Traditional insurance on which an automatic premium loan provision has been selected, and
   c. Traditional insurance with no automatic premium loan provision.

10. Explain how ownership of life insurance can become an important issue if a married couple becomes divorced.

11. An applicant for life insurance conceals information relative to her plans to become a missionary in an underdeveloped country. Three years after the life insurance is issued, she dies of a fatal disease contracted in her work. Can the beneficiary collect under the life insurance policy? Why or why not?

12. Is investment in life insurance as risk-free as investment in U.S. Treasury obligations? Why or why not?

13. A provision in a life insurance policy entitles a policyholder to a reduced rate if favorable underwriting information (e.g., favorable outcome of a medical examination) is resubmitted. Explain how the provision allocates back to policyholders much of the risk related to adverse selection as the insured group ages.

References and Suggestions for Additional Reading

BLACK, KENNETH, and HAROLD SKIPPER, JR.: *Life Insurance* (12th ed., Englewood Cliffs, N.J.: Prentice-Hall, Inc., 1993).

BODIE, ZVI, ALEX KANE, and ALAN J. MARCUS: *Investments* (2nd ed., Homewood, Ill.: Richard D. Irwin, Inc., 1993).

DORFMAN, MARK S., and SAUL W. ADELMAN: *Life Insurance* (2nd ed., Chicago, Dearborn Financial Publishing, Inc., 1992).

GREIDER, J. E., M. L. CRAWFORD, and W. T. BEADLES: *Law and the Life Insurance Contract* (5th ed., Homewood, Ill.: Richard D. Irwin, Inc., 1984).

MEHR, ROBERT I., and SANDRA G. GUSTAVSON: *Life Insurance: Theory and Practice* (4th ed., Plano, Tex.: Business Publications, Inc., 1987).

CHAPTER 19

Insurance Contract Analysis: Health Insurance

Learning Objectives

After you have completed this chapter, you should be able to:

1. Explain why the typical coverage providing health care benefits is complex.
2. Explain why the definition of disability is an important provision in disability income insurance.
3. State the differences between four different systems for reimbursing providers of health care services: fee-for-service, diagnosis related groups (DRG), resource-based relative value system (RBRVS), and capitation.
4. State how fee schedules are set and explain their importance to insureds.
5. State the differences between service coverage and medical expense reimbursement coverage.
6. Explain the importance of a gatekeeper in a point-of-service exclusive provider organization (EPO) plan and of provider networks in preferred provider organization (PPO) plans of coverage for health care services.
7. State the differences between deductibles, participation percentages and co-payments as they apply to coverage for health care services.

INTRODUCTION

The topics of health insurance and life insurance often appear alongside each other in literature on risk management and insurance, although the two types of coverage share little in common. The problems of health care and its management are almost inseparable from the analysis of health care coverage, while comparable issues hardly ever arise in the analysis of life insurance. Perhaps in one respect, the two types of coverage are similar: most demands for life and health insurance spring from individuals as isolated units, not collectively as a result of their being members of organizations. In other respects, the two types of coverage bear little resemblance to each other.

Chapter 7 of this text provides background data for the assessment of the risks covered by a typical health insurance contract. During the second half of the twentieth century, the burden of providing health care and the coverage to assure access to health care has shifted from individuals and family units to employers and governments. The dramatic rise in the cost of providing health care that accompanied the shifting burden has placed the issues of health care and health insurance coverage at the forefront of organizations' concerns. Further, increasing costs of health care services have been accompanied with a growing belief that entitlement to health care is a basic right of citizens. Such entitlement is envisioned under federally-mandated *universal* health care plans (or national health care programs) currently under consideration.

Growing concerns with access to health care and its cost have created political pressure for shifting the control of health care toward larger and larger organizations and ultimately to governments. The consolidation of health care financing across entities of increasing size has shifted concerns to higher levels of management and government regulation. Along with these trends, the typical coverage for health care services has evolved to the point at which it has become a complex set of financial incentives and administrative restrictions on the delivery and consumption of health care services. Many of these design features were incorporated to make coverage for health care one of the tools for controlling the health care problem.

MORAL HAZARDS AND HEALTH INSURANCE

In many respects, a typical medical expense insurance policy or employer-provided program of health care benefits is more complex than the typical property or liability insurance policy. Health care coverage typically is a contract of indemnity, and contract provisions often are detailed and complex. It is doubtful whether proposed programs of universal coverage (or national health care) will change this aspect of health care coverage, although mandates are likely to make coverage more uniform across different plans. Evidence on this issue is provided by the Medicare and Medicaid programs, which are at least as complex as private health benefit programs. The Medicare and Medicaid programs are social insurance programs providing medical services to, respectively, the elderly and poor. The Medicare and Medicaid programs are discussed further in Chapter 22.

Coverage provisions in health care plans often are designed to create financial incentives or to impose restrictions on the behavior of insured persons and providers of medical services. These provisions are directed toward controlling a problem earlier described as the *moral hazard,* which can be especially strong in the area of health insurance. Of course, moral hazards are present in virtually all lines of insurance. Many insurance contract provisions can be explained as methods to control possible moral hazards (e.g., deductibles on property coverage and the suicide exclusion in life insurance). In health insurance, however, control of moral hazards takes on special importance, in some cases being the primary consideration driving the design of the coverage.

On coverage for health care services, control of the behavior of health care providers and consumers takes on special importance. An important difference that distinguishes this type of coverage from other insurance contracts, including disability income insurance, is the presence of *health care providers,* such as hospitals and physicians. Health care providers interact with consumers of health care and with health care insurers, as illustrated in Figure 19.1. These interactions create the possibility of moral hazards that are complex and difficult to control, as compared with moral hazards arising in other types of coverage in which the only interaction is between the insurer and the insured.

Often, the event triggering coverage is a service from a health care provider to the insured person. Typically, the knowledge and information of health care providers about the insured's state of health, possible effects of the insured's habits on his or her state of health, and alternative methods for discovering and treating health conditions is superior to consumers of health care. This superior information places health care providers in a position to strongly influence the consumption of health care services.

In the absence of insurance for health care services, limits on the consumer's financial resources and his or her willingness to allocate them to the consumption of health care services provide natural restraints against uneconomic usage of health care services. Insurance to provide access to health care can remove these restraints. If the insurance coverage reimburses the health care provider without requiring any payment from the consumer, the coverage removes these restraints while not diminishing any financial incentive for the provider to encourage further consumption of health care services. Even under universal coverage, the effect of coverage provisions on the consumers and providers of medical services is unlikely to disappear as an issue as long as the reimbursement to providers is based on the level of services.

These effects may be especially pronounced for services whose benefits are cosmetic or for conditions whose treatment outcomes are judgmental, such as mental health. Dental benefit programs provided by employers offer a good illustration. When an employer announces its intent to establish a dental benefit program, many employees would be expected to reschedule their next exami-

FIGURE 19.1. Interactions among affected parties, health care insurance as compared with other insurance.

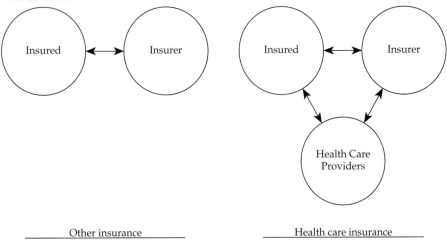

Other insurance   Health care insurance

nation to fall during the period of coverage, thus becoming eligible for reimbursement. Also, the coverage lessens any restraints against performing dental work that has been deferred because of its cost. As a result of these incentive effects, dental plans often have explicit controls or waiting periods for services other than routine examinations and the initial premium anticipates heavy use during the first year.

Also, dental benefit plans typically provide the most favorable reimbursement for routine cleaning and examinations, with the least favorable reimbursement for expensive inlays, crowns, dentures, and orthodontia. This pattern of coverage is the *reverse* of what would be expected if protection against financial consequences of unforeseen loss were the only consideration affecting the design of coverage. The reversal is a response to the effect of the coverage on the providers and consumers of dental benefits. The favorable reimbursement of routine cleaning and examinations creates an incentive for preventive measures, while the increased financial participation of the consumer in the most expensive procedures acts to deter consumption of services whose benefits may be largely cosmetic.

However, the presence of a health care profession is not a requirement for moral hazards to occur. A *disability income insurance* policy providing income replacement benefits if the insured becomes disabled may affect the insured's willingness to continue working. The insured's willingness to work becomes weaker as income replacement benefits from all sources, including the disability income coverage, increase relative to earnings. As a consequence, insurers writing disability income coverage consider benefits from all sources including other disability income policies and Social Security when they underwrite coverage. In addition, disability income policies may include a provision that reduces the benefit when total income replacement benefits from all sources exceeds a stated percentage (e.g., 70 percent) of earnings prior to disablement.

Also, a problem could arise if the condition triggering the benefit (disability) does not have a clear meaning; a hand injury might disable a surgeon but not disable a business executive, for example. The circumstances leading to disability would be expected to vary among individuals and occupations, which creates the possibility of disputes between insurers and their insureds if the conditions triggering the benefit are not defined clearly. Unfortunately, definitions with the clearest meaning often are the most restrictive. Defining disability as "hospital-confined," for example, leaves little room for dispute over the meaning of the term, but the coverage is not very meaningful. Typically, only the most serious medical conditions lead to hospitalization, with the average confinement period being only a few days. Defining disability as "unable to perform the duties of the insured's occupation" provides coverage for a condition more closely related to loss of income, but subjective aspects of the definition increase the likelihood of disputes.

INSURANCE FOR HEALTH CARE SERVICES

The analysis of insurance coverage for health care services can follow the same framework used for property and liability coverage: determining the *events covered* and the resulting *amount of recovery*. In coverage for health care services, the *form of recovery* becomes an important consideration, especially when the coverage is to provide the services in kind rather than reimbursement for the cost of the services. This framework can be used to analyze coverage proposed or mandated under universal programs as well as private programs.

Events Covered

Under coverage for health care services, the event triggering coverage is the delivery of a health care service to a covered person under covered circumstances. The level of benefits also may depend on circumstances giving rise to coverage. Hence the meaning of "covered person" and "covered circumstances" is important. For example, the distinction between work-related injuries and other medical conditions has been important recently because reimbursement of health care services related to work injuries has been more generous than reimbursement of health care services generally. This distinction, which is likely to disappear under universal coverage, is an example of a narrowly defined set of circumstances affecting benefit levels under coverage for health care services.

This type of distinction may continue to affect benefit levels, even under universal coverage. Often coverage for health care services reimburses *accidental injuries* on a more favorable basis than other conditions. The logic behind this distinction is the consumer has less control over the level of medical services provided as a result of an accidental injury than in other circumstances.

Coverage for *illness,* which has a broad range of circumstances triggering benefits, still requires an illness for coverage to apply. Under an illness coverage, a diagnosis of a medical condition is a typical requirement for coverage. For example, an electrocardiogram (an examination of heart rhythm) performed to investigate a suspected heart murmur may be covered by provisions of a policy applying to illness, while the same examination performed as part of a routine physical examination may be covered under less favorable terms unless it reveals an abnormal condition.

The broadest scope of coverage is health care services generally, including *preventive care.* Coverage for preventive care often is detailed and complex, with limits on benefits that vary by category of service and even among specific services. Explicit limits on frequency often appear for services over which the insured and the care provider have some discretion. For example, a policy may impose an age-based limit on frequency of routine physical examinations, such as once every two years prior to age 40 and once a year for persons age 40 and over.

As a general rule, nearly all coverage for health care services has benefits that are affected by circumstances under which medical services are provided. When the scope of coverage is narrow (e.g., accident coverage), the definition of the condition giving rise to benefits places natural limits on covered services. When the scope of coverage is broad (e.g., inclusion of preventive care), greater reliance is placed on explicit controls, such as limits on the frequency of covered services, or limits on the amount payable for services over which the provider and the consumer of medical services have some degree of discretion.

Coverage for health care services often contains *exclusions,* such as elective cosmetic surgery or injury resulting from an attempt at suicide. An exclusion for elective cosmetic surgery could well survive a change to a system of mandated universal coverage, although a suicide exclusion is unlikely to persist. The logic behind suicide exclusions in coverage for health care is not evident, as many of the same policies provide benefits for mental conditions. Only the most severe mental distress would be expected to result in an attempt at suicide, and drawing the line at this point may create perverse incentives. The presence of the exclusion creates an incentive for the health care providers who provide the first level of services following the suicide attempt (e.g., hospital emergency room attendants) to substitute some other diagnosis (e.g., accident) that is not likely to be disputed by the victim.

In some cases, coverage may not apply for services from categories of medical providers (e.g., chiropractors) or for medical procedures that are considered experimental. In lieu of outright exclusions, limits on benefits for these types of services may appear. Outright exclusions can lead to disputes, while limits or other types of financial incentives may be less likely to lead to disputes.

An exclusion for *pre-existing conditions* has been common in health insurance coverage. Typically, this exclusion applies to a medical condition that already was diagnosed prior to commencement of coverage, as exemplified by a chronic illness or an allergy. Often treatment for the pre-existing condition is not covered until the policy has been in force for a period of time, after which time the condition is covered under the same terms as other conditions. This type of exclusion has been developed because insurers and employers do not want to bear the cost of medical conditions that developed prior to coverage and were known to the insured at the time the coverage was issued.

This type of exclusion is likely to disappear under universal coverage. As the burden of financing health care is consolidated across larger and larger groups, the concern with allocating the costs of a specific individual or condition tends to decline in importance. Hence an exclusion for pre-existing conditions is unlikely to be an important issue in coverage offered by health care financing organizations consolidating coverage across large geographic areas.

Form of Recovery

Coverage for health care can be grouped into two broad categories according to the form of recovery: *service contracts,* which provide medical services, and *medical expense reimbursement (or "indemnity") contracts,* which reimburse the cost of medical services. In the United States, Blue Cross and Blue Shield offered service contracts as early forms of coverage for health care. Medical expense insurance, which was developed later, grew in importance from 1950 through 1980. Since 1980, medical expense insurance has diminished in importance relative to service plans. Even under universal coverage, however, medical expense insurance may survive in the form of coverage applying to "gaps" in coverage requiring payments from the covered person. Further, many service contracts are hybrid coverage requiring financial contribution toward the cost of services through deductibles and other cost-sharing provisions.

Under a pure service contract, the insuring organization promises to provide a package of medical services to the subscriber. The consumer of medical services may never become involved in the financial transaction between the insurer and the provider of medical services. Instead, the insurer reimburses the provider directly for medical services provided to the covered person (*"fee-for-service"* reimbursement) or pays an organization of providers a fixed payment per covered individual in return for the provider's promise to render medical services to these individuals (a *"capitation"* arrangement).

Under a medical expense reimbursement contract, the insuring organization promises to reimburse the cost of medical services rather than providing the services in kind. Most coverage applying to health care services is a hybrid of a service contract and an expense reimbursement contract. The hybridization may be a result of the financial participation noted above or by having the coverage reimburse the cost of medical services in some cases and directly pay the provider in others. Some medical expense coverage provides for *assignment* by allowing the policyholder to elect payment of benefits directly to a provider of medical services. Coverage may also be a service contract if the policyholder uses a particular clinic or hospital but become expense reimbursement coverage if the policyholder uses other providers outside the particular clinic or hospital.

Form of Recovery and Types of Insuring Organizations

Although the distinctions between the form of recovery may seem largely semantic, they can have important effects on the recovery for medical services. Often, the insuring organization writing a service contract negotiates with providers of medical services, perhaps receiving discounts from the providers' normal *charges* to the public (and to other insurers) for their services. In return, the insuring organization provides financial incentives to steer subscribers to the *network*, the selected set of providers with whom the insuring organization has contractual agreements.

Generalizations about the effect of the insuring organization on the form and amount of recovery can be misleading because terminology for describing organizational forms is not standard. The extent to which the distinctions noted below will survive the enactment of universal coverage is uncertain. Insurance companies already administer portions of Medicare, for example, and presumably will administer some universal health care programs when they are enacted.

One form of insuring organization is the *health maintenance organization (HMO),* a generic term applied to a collective agreement between a group of medical care providers and subscribers. An *open panel* HMO attempts to include a large proportion of the medical providers in a community, while a *closed panel* plan negotiates with a smaller network of providers. HMOs can be organized by medical providers themselves or by other organizations, such as life and health insurance companies. Insurance companies also sell medical expense reimbursement contracts, and an insurance company may serve as a *third party administrator (TPA)* for health benefit programs sponsored by employers or other organizations. In a program managed by a TPA, the role of the TPA is to administer the plan according to terms set by the plan sponsor (Chapter 10 discusses these administrative service only (ASO) plans). The plan sponsor (e.g., the employer) effectively is the insurer unless the TPA also provides financial guarantees as part of its involvement in the program.

In the area of health insurance and health care financing, *Blue Cross/Blue Shield* organizations deserve special attention because of their size and long history. Blue Cross/Blue Shield plans resemble open-panel HMOs in that Blue Cross/Blue Shield organizations attempt to reach an agreement with most medical providers in an area. Service contracts have always been the dominant type of coverage offered by Blue Cross/Blue Shield plans. Many Blue Cross/Blue Shield organizations were founded in the 1930s as local associations of health care providers, controlled primarily by providers. Initially, Blue Cross was the hospital service association while Blue Shield was the association covering physicians' services.

The Blue Cross/Blue Shield organizations today bear little resemblance to small local associations, as they are neither local nor small. Although the early Blues plans were local, a series of mergers and consolidations had by 1990 led to a single or a few surviving plans for each state. Many Blue Cross/Blue Shield organizations continue to enjoy support from providers of medical services. The organizations continue to offer service contracts, typically reimbursing the provider of medical services directly. Blue Cross/Blue Shield organizations serve as TPAs for plans sponsored by employers and other organizations, and they also administer portions of Medicare. Blue Cross/Blue Shield organizations continue to be an important force affecting the delivery and financing of health care in the United States.

On service contracts, financial incentives to use in-network providers usually take the form of services from network providers being reimbursed more favorably than services provided out-of-network. In an *exclusive provider organization (EPO) plan,* these incentives are quite strong; services from out-of-network providers may receive no reimbursement. A somewhat less severe set of incentives is found in a *preferred provider organization (PPO)* plan, in which services from in-network providers receive favored treatment. For example, services from network providers may be reimbursed at 80 percent of rates that already reflect negotiated discounts, while services from out-of-network providers may be reimbursed at 60 percent of charges.

When the subscriber receives medical services from an out-of-network provider, payment for the uncovered charges usually is the subscriber's responsibility. If an out-of-network medical specialist charges $100 for an office visit for which a PPO plan provides a $60 reimbursement, payment of the $40 difference is the patient's responsibility, and the specialist may be free to *balance-bill* for the $40 difference. The PPO may have negotiated a $60 rate for an office visit to its own in-network specialist, in which case the full cost of the office visit with the network provider is covered.

Service coverage may make further distinctions between in-network providers, often to encourage patterns of medical service utilization within the network itself. For example, a *point-of-service PPO* may provide more favorable reimbursement when the initial contact of the subscriber seeking health care service is with a general practice physician. Later contact with specialists is reimbursed favorably if the contact is the result of a referral by the general practice physician, who serves as *"gatekeeper."* The point-of-service PPO may fully reimburse the cost of an office visit with an in-network general practice physician and pay 90 percent of the cost of a subsequent office visit with an in-network specialist if the visit is ordered by the general practice physician. If the subscriber's initial office visit is with the specialist, the reimbursement may drop to 80 percent for an in-network specialist and to 60 percent for an out-of-network specialist. The rationale for the pattern of reimbursement is to encourage initial contact with in-network general practice physicians, who may be regarded as less expensive than specialists and less likely to order additional expensive testing.

The tradeoff between different types of service coverage often balances price against the subscriber's freedom of choice of medical care providers and control over the delivery of health care services. Historically, plans providing the widest range of choices and fewest restrictions tend to be the most expensive. However, freedom to choose among providers of medical services is an option valued by many consumers of health care. Traditionally, medical expense insurance and Blue Cross/Blue Shield plans have imposed few restrictions on the choice of providers as compared with HMO, PPO, and EPO plans. In some states, however, Blue Cross/Blue Shield organizations have formed HMO plans using smaller networks. These Blue Cross/Blue Shield HMOs are offered to the public alongside coverage imposing fewer restrictions on the subscriber's choice of medical care providers.

Contractual Provisions Affecting Amount of Recovery

Medical expense reimbursement insurance includes contractual provisions, such as policy limits and deductibles, that closely resemble provisions carrying the same names found in property and liability insurance contracts. Service contracts also have many of these same provisions, although they may seem inconsistent with service benefit approach. When these provisions appear in service contracts, the motive for their use is the creation of financial incentives affecting the behavior of consumers and providers of medical services in ways believed to reduce health care costs. For example, a health care policy may impose a $100 deductible for use of a hospital emergency room that does not result in admission to the hospital. Hospital emergency rooms often are expensive to use, and the $100 deductible is likely to deter use of the emergency room for conditions not requiring urgent treatment.

When more than one policy providing health care benefits applies to an episode of health care, a *coordination of benefits (COB)* provision can serve the same function as the "other insurance" clause found in property and liability coverage. The COB provision prevents duplicate recovery for the same set of medical expenses or the same procedure. A COB provision is common in employer-sponsored health care coverage and often is invoked when a husband and wife both work for employers who provide health care coverage. The COB provision determines which of the two policies is primary. With respect to the employees themselves, the policy on the employee is primary and the other policy is secondary. With respect to the working couple's dependent children, the primary policy typically is the coverage on the employee whose birthday falls earliest in the calendar year. The consolidation of health care financing across wide geographic regions envisioned in proposals for universal coverage is likely to eliminate the need for COB provisions.

Policy limit(s) specify a maximum recovery for covered medical expenses during a time period, which may be as long as the lifetime of the covered individual. If a lifetime limit appears, the policy also may include an annual restoration. For example, a policy may contain a $500,000 lifetime limit for covered expenses with a $10,000 annual restoration. If a heart bypass operation for a covered individual results in the payment of a $65,000 benefit, the remaining limit is reduced to $435,000. The next year the limit would be increased to $445,000 if no claims are paid, or to only $440,000 if additional medical expense benefits of $5,000 are paid during that year.

On service contracts, the limit may be stated in service units, such as 120 days in the hospital. This approach has been used in Blue Cross coverage and in Medicare; its appearance in Medicare suggests that limits serve a purpose that is likely to continue under universal coverage. Service contracts also may impose dollar limits rather than limits on service units. Instead of applying to a time period, a policy limit may apply on some other basis, such as to each episode of illness or injury. In this case, the coverage will contain contractual language defining what constitutes a "spell of illness or injury" (see "recurrent disability" provision under insurance for loss of income below). Often, separate limits apply to categories of expense, such as mental health care, in which moral hazard problems are believed especially difficult to manage. For example, a policy with a $500,000 lifetime limit for medical expenses may further impose a $100,000 lifetime limit on in-hospital mental health care, with a further restriction of no more than 30 days' confinement in a single year. Further, more restrictive limits may apply to benefits for mental care provided outside a hospital.

As in property insurance, the *deductible* is an amount subtracted from the covered expense to determine the recovery. If the covered expense is less than the deductible amount, no benefit is paid. The deductible may apply to each spell of illness, to each insured individual, to total expenses incurred in a year, or on some other basis. Often, health insurance coverage provided on members of the same family will impose a per-year deductible for each family member with a larger deductible applying to the family's total expenses during the year. For example, a $100 per-year deductible may apply to each family member with a $300 per-year deductible applying to the entire family. The coverage is triggered when any individual's covered expenses exceed $100 in a year or when the family's covered expenses exceed $300 in a year. For example, if all five members of a family were to each incur $80 of covered expenses, 5($80) − $300, or $100, would be subject to coverage.

The *participation percentage (or "coinsurance")* is a proportionate sharing of medical expenses in excess of any deductible. An 80/20 sharing results in the insurer reimbursing 80 percent of the amount by which the expense exceeds the deductible, with the insured responsible for the remaining 20 percent. The insured's participation rate usually is between 10 and 50 percent, with 20 percent being common.

An *out-of-pocket limit* or *limit on out-of-pocket expenses* is common in policies using deductibles and participation percentages. The limit on out-of-pocket expenses represents an upper limit on payments by the insured as a result of the deductible and participation percentage. For example, a $1000 limit on out-of-

TABLE 19.1. Reimbursement for Selected Levels of Covered Medical Expense from a Medical Expense Insurance Policy Providing $100,000 of Coverage Subject to a $200 Deductible, 20 Percent Participation, and $1000 Limit on Out-of-Pocket Expenses

Covered expense	$175	$750	$2000	$10,000	$65,000	$125,000
Benefit	$0	$440	$1440	$9000	$64,000	$100,000

pocket expenses on a policy with a $100 deductible and 20 percent participation is reached when covered medical expenses reach $4600; $100 + 0.2($4600 − $100) = $1000. Beyond this point, the insurance policy provides coverage for the full amount of any further covered medical expenses. Table 19.1 illustrates the combined effects of a $200 deductible, 20 percent participation, and a $1000 limit on out-of-pocket expenses on a medical expense insurance policy with a $100,000 policy limit. The limit on out-of-pocket expenses is reached at covered expenses of $4200, but the overall policy limit is encountered when covered expenses exceed $101,000.

A *co-payment* is a fee paid by an insured individual to become entitled to a medical service. In health insurance, the term "co-payment" has been used in a generic sense to denote a cost-sharing agreement, such as a deductible or participation percentage, although the meaning of the term gradually evolved to mean a fee imposed before other coverage provisions apply. For example, a health care policy may impose a $10 co-payment for routine visits to physicians' offices in addition to a $100 deductible and a 20 percent participation. Under such a policy, a $25 office visit leading to $175 of fees for laboratory work would result in $15 of the cost for the office visit and $175 of the laboratory fees, a total of $190, being subject to coverage. After the $100 deductible is applied, $90 remains as eligible for reimbursement. The actual reimbursement is (0.8)($90), or $72. Without the copayment, the reimbursement would have been $80; i.e., [(0.8)($100)].

Service contracts often impose co-payments. Co-payment levels often are set to create financial incentives shaping the behavior of covered individuals or providers. For example, the co-payment level for use of a hospital emergency room not followed by admission to the hospital may be set at $50, while the co-payment applying to other urgent care facilities may be $10. The differential co-payment levels create an incentive to use urgent care facilities other than hospital emergency rooms when these other facilities are available. Other urgent care facilities tend to be less expensive than hospital emergency rooms.

A *fee schedule* is a set of limits applying to specific types of services or to diagnoses. The fee schedule sets a limit on the *allowable charge* that will be considered in computing reimbursement for covered medical services, a feature that distinguishes the fee schedule from other types of policy limits. Charges beyond the fee schedule are not considered in determining benefits. For example, if a specialist charges $100 for an office visit and the fee schedule has a $40 limit for an office visit with a specialist, only $40 is considered in computing the benefit. If the policy also uses a $100 deductible, $60 of deductible remains after the visit with the specialist even though the insured person may have paid the full $100 cost of the office visit. The practice of billing the patient for the differences between actual charges and allowable charges is called *"balance billing."*

In coverage in which the insurer has negotiated favorable rates from a network of medical providers, the fee schedule may be set at the level negotiated with the network. When a network of providers is not present, fee schedules may be based on survey data on charges of medical providers for categories of service, such as daily room and board charges by hospitals. The survey data ranks charges of providers, with the insuring organization choosing a cut-off point beyond which charges will not be considered. For example, an insurer may believe that the 80th percentile of charges in a community represents a limit on "reasonable" charges.

Historical patterns of charges by providers in a community also may influence limits on allowable charges, resulting in *"usual, customary, and reasonable" (UCR)* charges. This method of setting limits can create an incentive for health care providers to regularly increase nominal charges for their services, even while the providers, as members of a network, are willing to accept a smaller amount than their full charges. This discrepancy between nominal charges and amount providers are willing to accept as compensation could disappear under a *single-payer* approach, a term applied to a system in which all financing of health benefits is channelled through the same organization, such as a government agency. A single payer system could use more than one source of funds, such as having individuals be responsible for the first $250 of expense during a calendar year. When more than one source of funds is used, presumably the same charge would apply across all categories of consumers and payers, regardless of the ultimate source of funds. Because the same price would apply to all users, a single-payer approach could eliminate problems related to balance-billing.

A precedent for using a single-payer approach in universal coverage exists in the portion of the federal Medicare program applying to physician's services. The coverage of this portion of Medicare prohibits balance-billing for providers who agree to accept assignment of Medicare benefits. In many cases, Medicare completely disallows charges for services it deems unnecessary, leaving the provider who accepts assignment no recourse. Because the methods chosen to regulate fees and charges directly affect the income of medical care providers, this aspect of any proposed system of universal coverage is likely to be controversial.

The foregoing limitations share in common a reliance on a fee-for-service method for determining the level of reimbursement. The *diagnosis-related groups (DRG)* system of reimbursement was adopted in the mid-1980s in lieu of the fee-for-service method under the portion of Medicare applying to hospital reimbursement. The DRG system also has received attention from private health care insurers. The DRG system, which bases the payment to the hospital on a complex system for classifying medical diagnoses, was adopted in the belief that the fee-for-service system was partly responsible for rising hospital costs. Under a fee-for-service system, the hospital is reimbursed for each medical service, so the system offers no financial incentive to control the use of medical services. Under a DRG system, however, the hospital receives no additional payment when additional services are provided, the payment instead being based on the diagnosis.

For example, a hospital would receive the same reimbursement for two patients with identical diagnoses, even though one patient is confined for 10 days while the other is confined for only 5 days. In concept, a provider of medical services under a DRG system has no incentive to encourage the consumption of medical services whose economic value is questionable. By placing the financial burdens of additional services on the provider, the DRG system was designed to encourage providers to order only those medical services that are essential for the treatment of a medical condition.

In 1992, Medicare began reimbursing physicians using a *resource-based relative value scale (RBRVS)*, which assigns a numerical value to the effort of the physician in providing a medical service, and to the expenses of maintaining a medical practice. The reimbursement is determined by applying the numerical value to a standard conversion factor applying to the entire U.S. In concept, RBRVS uses a fee-for-service approach, but reimbursement is determined by a numerical technique rather than set by physicians and insurers in the market. Compared with prevailing levels of fees and charges, RBRVS is designed to increase reimbursement of primary care physicians relative to specialists.

Direct Controls

In addition to financial incentives designed to shape the behavior of providers and consumers of medical services, coverage may impose direct controls on the use of health care services. A *prior notification* requirement, for example, may require a surgeon who plans to perform an elective surgical procedure to first submit a plan to the insurer and await approval before performing the operation. Health benefit plans also use *case management* to control the cost of expensive medical procedures by involving the plan's medical director (who may be a physician) in the day-to-day decisions related to the administration of medical procedures to an insured person whose medical care costs have exceed a threshold. A *second opinion* requirement has been used in medical benefit programs to require a second surgeon to agree that surgery is necessary for a condition not requiring urgent care.

Summary

In the absence of coverage for health care services, market forces and limits on individuals' resources regulate prices and consumption of health care services. Coverage for these services, whether purchased by employers or provided by governments, tends to lessen these natural restraints. As a consequence, other rationing methods, such as financial incentives or direct controls, may be imposed.

The typical coverage for health care services is complex. This complexity is likely to persist after the enactment of universal coverage, although coverage provisions may become more uniform across different plans. The provisions found in health benefit programs evolved in response to problems inherent to coverage for health care services. Unless universal coverage eliminates these problems, mechanisms to control them will survive in some form.

INSURANCE FOR LOSS OF INCOME: BASIC CONCEPTS

Compared with coverage that provides benefits for health care, contracts providing income replacement benefits are relatively simple. The analysis of *disability income* coverage uses the same framework as for other coverage: identify the *situations covered* and evaluate any provisions affecting the *amount of recovery*.

Events Covered

The covered event under disability income insurance is the disablement of the insured person. Normally, only one individual is insured by a disability income insurance contract. The meaning of the term "*disability*" is defined in a separate section of the policy used to define terms, or it may be defined in the insuring agreement itself. Coverage may require "*total disability*" of the insured person to trigger benefits, although some policies also provide benefits for "*partial disability*" (although usually for a shorter period of time).

The definition of disability is an important provision in the contract. The term may be defined in a way that restricts coverage to relatively few situations, or the definition may be broad enough to encompass most cases in which the insured person is unable to work due to a medical condition. An example of a restrictive definition that has been used in some policies promoted to elderly persons, often through mail-order, is "*hospital confined.*" This type of coverage, which was promoted during the 1980s and inaccurately described as "hospital indemnity" coverage, typically promised a benefit such as "$100 a day while you are in the hospital," a very restrictive definition of disability. Other contracts require the disablement to be the result of an accident, possibly with additional restrictions limiting coverage to disablement involving accident as the sole cause. "*Inability to perform the duties of [the insured's] own occupation*" offers an example of a broad definition of disability. Some policies allow for presumptive disability in special cases, such as the loss of the sight of both eyes or the loss of use of both hands or both feet.

Policies often contain language identifying *recurrent disability*: a condition in which a disability is considered a continuation of an already-existing disablement. For example, a recurrent disability may be defined as the recurrence of the same medical condition within a six-month period. If the insured person is disabled but recovers for a period longer than six months, a recurrence of the same medical condition is considered a new disability. Having the condition considered a new disability means that policy provisions (e.g., the policy limit) are renewed for the condition.

Typical *exclusions* in disability income policies include self-inflicted injury (e.g., injuries from a suicide attempt), pre-existing conditions, aircraft other than while a passenger on a regularly scheduled commercial airliner, war, foreign travel, or military duty.

Amount of Recovery

Disability income insurance is a *valued contract*; it provides a stated benefit (a periodic income) if the insured event occurs. Usually this benefit is paid after a *waiting period (or "elimination" period)*, which is analogous to a deductible in property insurance. The periodic benefit is paid until the *policy limit* is exhausted. The policy limit may be stated as a maximum time period during which benefits are paid (e.g., five years) or it may be stated as an age at which benefits cease (e.g., age 65). The applicable policy limit may depend on the cause of disablement, for example, benefits paid for disablement due to an accident may continue for a longer time period than disablement due to illness.

Disability income coverage may include an *"other insurance"* provision limiting the amount of disability income coverage relative to the insured's earnings. For example, a provision may reduce the benefit when the total of income replacement benefits from all sources, including other disability income policies and Social Security, exceeds a stated percentage (e.g., 70 percent) of earnings prior to disablement. Also, insurers writing disability income coverage consider benefits from other sources when they underwrite coverage.

A *waiver of premium* benefit often is provided while the insured person is being paid disability benefits under the coverage. Under a waiver of premium clause, no premium payment is required during the period that benefits are being paid (which, in a policy covering a stated maximum time period, may be shorter than the period of disablement). *Accidental Death and Dismemberment (AD&D)* frequently is offered by insurers as an additional coverage or a rider to a disability income insurance policy. AD&D usually provides stated lump sum benefit amounts for accidental death or specified types of dismemberments due to accident.

Disability income insurance also may be offered by insurers in conjunction with life insurance through *waiver of premium* or *disability income* riders. These riders were discussed in Chapter 18.

Renewal Provisions

In health insurance, the renewal provision states the conditions under which the insured can require the insurer to renew the contract. Renewal provisions are common in disability income coverage; renewal provisions are also found in medical expense insurance, but the renewal guarantees for medical expense insurance tend to be weaker than for disability income coverage. Some contracts do not provide for renewal. Presumably, enactment of mandates for universal coverage will remove the issue of renewal from consideration in health care benefit programs, but renewal provisions will continue on disability income coverage.

The range of renewal provisions is exemplified by four standard renewal options: *optionally renewable, conditionally renewable, guaranteed renewable*, and *noncancellable*. An *optionally renewable* contract is renewable at the option of the insurer. Although this provision does not provide a renewal guarantee, cancellation during the policy period is not permitted. The insurer can refuse to renew the contract at the policy anniversary date, but is not allowed to cancel during the period of coverage.

A *conditionally renewable* contract is renewable as long as the insured meets certain conditions; commonly, these conditions are related to age and occupational status (e.g., "gainfully employed and under age 65"). The insurer cannot refuse to renew the coverage solely because the health of the insured person has deteriorated.

Under guaranteed renewable and noncancellable coverage, the right to renew the contract is guaranteed, often to an advanced age such as age 65. The difference between these two renewal guarantees involves the price at which the renewal takes place. Under *noncancellable* coverage, renewal premiums as well as the renewal right is guaranteed. The renewal premium does not necessarily remain level during the life of the policy; a schedule of renewal premiums may be part of the contract.

Under the *guaranteed renewable* contract, the right to renew but not the renewal price is guaranteed. The insurer is free to change the premium, but only with respect to classes of insureds. Usually classes of insureds are identified with respect to age and occupational characteristics (e.g., office workers between ages 30 and 45). The restriction allowing the insurer to change premiums only for an entire class appears to offer protection to individuals against arbitrary premium increases.

Key Concepts

universal health care A program of health insurance mandated by the federal government in which virtually the entire population becomes entitled to coverage for health care services.

health care provider A person or entity engaged in the business of offering health care services to consumers.

disability income insurance An insurance policy that provides income replacement benefits if the insured becomes disabled.

service contract A type of coverage for health care services that promises to provide services in kind rather than cash benefits.

medical expense reimbursement contract A type of coverage for health care services that promises to reimburse the cost of medical services rather than provide the services themselves. Also called medical expense insurance.

fee-for-service A system for reimbursing health care providers under which payment is made for each medical service provided to the consumer.

capitation A system for reimbursing health care providers under which payment is based on the number of covered lives rather than the level of services.

charge When applied to fees for medical services, the charge is the nominal amount appearing on the billing to the consumer or the insurer. When levels of reimbursement to providers have been negotiated on a group basis, the charge usually exceeds the negotiated reimbursement.

fee schedule A set of limits applying to specific types of services or to diagnoses. Typically the fee schedule sets a limit on the *allowable charge* that will be considered in determining benefit levels.

balance-billing When applied to fees for medical services, balance-billing refers to a provider of medical services billing the consumer for the difference between the charge and the amount considered for possible reimbursement in a health benefit program.

usual, customary, and reasonable (UCR) When applied to a fee schedule, UCR denotes an upper limit to allowable charges determined by considering historical patterns of charges by a particular provider as well as charge levels prevailing in the community.

single-payer An approach for setting reimbursements to providers in which the same charge and reimbursement applies across all categories of consumers and payers.

network A group of medical service providers with whom an insurer or other payer has negotiated favorable rates of reimbursement. Under the plan of coverage offered by the insurer or other payer, coverage for services from network providers reimbursed on more favorable terms than services from out-of-network providers.

health maintenance organization (HMO) A collective agreement between a group of medical care providers and subscribers. An **open panel** HMO reaches agreement with a large proportion of the medical providers in a community, while a **closed panel** HMO reaches agreement with a smaller network of providers.

third party administrator (TPA) An organization or entity that manages health benefit programs offered by employers or other organizations.

exclusive provider organization (EPO) plan A type of health benefit program under which services from out-of-network providers receive no reimbursement or are reimbursed only under limited circumstances.

preferred provider organization (PPO) plan A type of health benefit program under which services from out-of-network providers are reimbursed less favorably than services from in-network providers.

point-of service PPO A type of preferred provider organization plan that offers financial incentives for the consumer's initial contact with providers to be with

a general practice physician, who serves as **gatekeeper.**

coordination of benefits (COB) A provision in a health benefit program that prevents duplicate recovery for the same set of medical expenses or the same procedure.

co-payment A payment required by the covered person to become entitled to a medical service.

participation percentage ("coinsurance") A provision of a health benefit program that imposes proportionate sharing of medical expenses in excess of any deductible. An 80/20 insurer/insured sharing is common.

out-of-pocket limit A contractual limitation on the dollar amount of cost sharing imposed on the insured as a result of a deductible and participation percentage during a time period such as a year.

diagnosis-related groups (DRG) A system of reimbursement in which the reimbursement to the provider is based on a complex system for classifying medical diagnoses, rather than the level of services. A DRG system has been used under the portion of Medicare applying to hospital reimbursement.

resource-based relative value scale (RBRVS) A system of reimbursement used by Medicare to determine physician reimbursement. The system assigns a numerical value to the effort of the physician in providing a medical service, and to the expenses of maintaining a medical practice. The reimbursement is determined by applying the numerical value to a standard conversion factor applying to the entire U.S.

prior notification A provision in a health benefit program requiring a provider of medical services to first seek approval from the payer or the insurer before undertaking a major medical procedure.

case management A method used in health benefit programs to monitor the day-to-day decisions related to the administration of medical procedures to an insured person whose medical care costs have exceeded a threshold.

second opinion A provision in a health

benefit program requiring an independent review and concurring opinion from a second provider of medical services before undertaking a major medical procedure.

recurrent disability In disability income insurance, a condition in which a disability is considered a continuation of a previously existing disablement.

waiting period (or "elimination" period) In disability income insurance, a period of time during which no benefit is paid despite the insured being considered disabled under the terms of coverage.

optionally renewable A type of renewal provision in disability income insurance in which renewal is at the option of the insurer.

conditionally renewable A type of renewal provision in disability income insurance in which the contract is renewable as long as the insured meets certain conditions. Usually, the conditions allowing renewal are related to age and occupational status.

guaranteed renewable A type of renewal provision in disability income insurance in which the contract is renewable until some stated age. The price of coverage at renewal is not guaranteed. The insurer can change premiums only with respect to classes of insureds, not with respect to individuals.

noncancellable A type of renewal provision in disability income insurance in which the contract is renewable until some stated age. The price of coverage at renewal is also guaranteed at the time the contract is issued.

Review Questions

1. Explain why coverage provisions in dental benefit programs provided by employers to employees are almost the reverse of what would be expected if protection against the financial consequences of unforeseen events were the primary consideration driving the design of coverage.

2. Briefly define the following four systems for reimbursing providers of health care services and explain the differences among the systems:
   a. Free-for-service
   b. Diagnosis related groups (DRG)
   c. Resource-based relative value system (RBRVS)
   d. Capitation.

3. Briefly define each of the following terms and explain how it may apply to coverage provided by a health benefit program:
   a. Deductible
   b. Participation percentage (coinsurance)
   c. Co-payment.

4. Explain how usual, customary, and reasonable (UCR) fee schedules are set and why the existence of a fee schedule may result in a consumer of medical services being required to pay amounts beyond the deductible, participation percentage, and co-payments imposed by a health benefit program.

5. State the differences between service coverage and medical expense reimbursement insurance contracts as used to finance health benefit programs.

6. Explain the role of a gatekeeper in a point-of-service exclusive provider organization (EPO) plan. What are the consequences of a covered individual bypassing the gatekeeper in such a plan?

7. State the importance of provider networks in preferred provider organization (PPO) plans of coverage for health care services. What are the consequences of a covered individual using out-of-network providers in such a plan?

8. Explain why the definition of disability is an important provision of a disability income insurance contract.

9. Briefly define each of the following terms and explain how it may apply to disability income insurance:
   a. Waiting period (or elimination period)
   b. Recurrent disability
   c. Guaranteed renewable
   d. Noncancellable.

References and Suggestions for Additional Reading

BEAM, BURTON T., and JOHN J. MCFADDEN: *Employee Benefits* (3rd ed., Chicago, Dearborn Financial Publishing, Inc., 1992).

LEVIT, KATHARINE R., and CATHY A. COWAN: "The Burden of Health Care Costs: Business, Households, and Governments," *Health Care Financing Review* (vol. 12, no. 2, Winter 1990), pp. 127–137.

MCCAFFERY, ROBERT M.: *Employee Benefit Programs: A Total Compensation Perspective.* (Boston: PWS-Kent Publishing Company, 1988).

Source Book of Health Insurance Data. (Washington: Health Insurance Association of America, annual).

PART FIVE

Topics in Risk Management Administration

Part 5 provides readers with an exposure to several special topics of importance to risk managers. Chapter 20 provides a detailed discussion of administrative issues surrounding the practice of risk management. Practical issues such as policy statements, cost allocation systems, and broker selection techniques are addressed in this chapter. Chapter 21 presents readers with an overview discussion of the types of property and liability insurance contracts that a typical risk manager might purchase. Important contracts, such as the commercial general liability policy, are given particular emphasis.

Chapters 22 and 23 introduce and discuss social insurance. Chapter 22 is structured to present an overview of social insurance in theory and practice. Readers will be introduced to old-age, survivors, disability and health insurance, and unemployment insurance. A special social insurance topic, workers' compensation, is of such importance that it is the sole subject of Chapter 23. In addition to covering the history and present structure of workers' compensation, Chapter 23 will also discuss risk management and workers' compensation—including a presentation of risk control tools that can assist risk managers. Chapters 24 and 25 discuss the important subject of employee benefits. Chapter 24 introduces such plans, and describes the nature of the benefits provided. Chapter 25 focuses on the administrative issues associated with offering an employee benefit plan. A discussion of pension and pension management issues is also provided.

Each of these chapters builds on information presented earlier in the textbook. Many instructors may wish to "drop in" these chapters earlier in their course. For instance, Chapter 20 might be discussed easily after Chapter 10 or Chapter 12. Chapters 21 through 25 might be read immediately following their corresponding introduction chapters (Chapters 17 through 19). With these thoughts in mind, the authors have designed each of these six chapters to stand alone so that they may be used to provide more detail for instructors seeking such detail—at the same time permitting instructors not seeking such institutional detail to omit the chapters without disrupting the flow of the book.

CHAPTER 20

An Overview of Risk Management Administration

Learning Objectives

After completing this chapter, you should be able to:

1. Explain the differences between a policy statement and a policy manual.
2. Identify issues related to the organizational structure of a risk management program.
3. Briefly explain the historical justification of the risk management function.
4. Define and explain risk communication.
5. Identify the basic issues surrounding the use of risk management information systems (RMIS).
6. Discuss several alternatives for designing a cost allocation system.
7. Explain the issues arising from the use of agents and brokers.
8. Identify the pros and cons of bidding for contracted services.
9. Briefly explain the purpose of a certificate of insurance.
10. Explain why letters of credit may be used by risk managers.
11. Identify the issues arising from program audits.

INTRODUCTION

Risk management is a *management* function. Although this statement seems self-evident, it is important to remember that the technical aspects of the discipline must be integrated and applied in an organizational setting: risk must be "managed." No single person can become expert in *all* the technical matters related to risk management. Because this is so, the risk manager must rely on his or her managerial abilities to coordinate, direct, organize, motivate, facilitate, and otherwise move the organization toward an integrated and rational plan for managing risks.

Risk managers—at least the best ones—understand management. They understand that an organization is a living system that must discipline itself to move efficiently and effectively toward its mission. They know that their organization has strengths and weaknesses that influence its ability to confront threats as well as opportunities. And, they understand that it is of little use for a risk manager to possess an extraordinary depth of knowledge about, say, insurance claims management, if he or she cannot work within the parameters and constraints of his or her organization to design an effective claims management program.

Risk managers are not just generalist managers, however. They do have specialized knowledge. Notably, risk managers understand risk. They understand how to quantify risk and how to classify risk. They also understand the psychology of risk and its social, political, ethical, and economic dimensions. They understand how risk manifests itself through the physical environment, the political environment, the operational, economic, and cognitive environments. Risk managers also understand uncertainty, and the costs it exacts on organizations. Because risk managers understand risk, they have related technical competencies: they are insurance and risk financing experts, they understand the law, they are conversant in safety engineering principles, and they understand the structural and operational nature of their organization. Good risk managers have significant technical expertise.

An introduction to general management principles would be a dramatic expansion of this textbook. Because most readers are likely to have been exposed to a general management course, this chapter focuses on five critical administrative, or managerial, issues that risk managers face: (1) the challenge of establishing risk management policies and procedures, (2) organizational and interpersonal "risk" communications, (3) the management of contracts and contract portfolios, (4) claims supervision, and (5) the process of reviewing, monitoring, and evaluating the risk management program. In the course of discussing these topics, the text provides the reader with a sense of broader managerial challenges confronting the risk manager.

POLICIES AND PROCEDURES

Although a great many risk management activities must be dispersed throughout an organization, a lack of coordination can lead to loss of program cohesion. Resolution of the tension between centralized control/cohesion and decentralized operation is a key policy issue for risk managers. However the balance is struck, the risk manager must formalize the approach through a statement of policies and procedure. The formal statement should outline the function's organizational structure and define the activities that constitute the function.

Risk management policy statements vary among organizations according to their respective missions. The process of establishing risk management policy begins with the organization's mission statement, as the risk management policy statement is embedded in the framework of the organization's mission. Since risk management's challenge is to help the organization achieve its mission in the most effective and efficient way possible, the risk management policy statement must flow from the overall organization's mission.

Risk Management Policy Statement

A policy statement establishes an organization's risk management goals and objectives. The purpose of a policy statement is to affirm what the organization hopes to accomplish or views as important. It does *not*, as a general rule, describe how the policies of the organization are made operational. The policy manual serves that function, making the policy statement operational.

Tables 20.1 and 20.2 show policy statements of two large organizations, one public and one private. They reveal some common policies, but they also reveal the fundamental differences in organization missions. General Mills is a publicly-held corporation, which seeks to maximize its shareholders' wealth, while the State of Minnesota's mission is more difficult to summarize. The state's mis-

TABLE 20.1. General Mills, Inc., Risk Management Policy Statement

Activities of the Risk Management Department are influenced by the Company's general insurance philosophy which can be summarized as follows:
1. Eliminate or reduce as far as practicable the conditions and practices which cause insurable losses.
2. When risk cannot be eliminated or reduced to workable levels:
   a. Purchase commercial insurance that will provide indemnity for catastrophic losses,
   b. Either insure or assume, whichever judgment indicates to be in the Company's best interest, those risks not considered to be of major importance individually to the operating or financial position of the Company.

But, in any event, to retain whatever portion of the risk for General Mills' account that premium reductions make economically attractive.

The Risk Management Department's responsibility for implementing this policy includes:
1. Assisting divisions and subsidiaries to design and operate fire control and loss prevention programs.
2. Reviewing new construction and facility alteration plans to assure risk control features and insurance acceptability.
3. Developing insurance coverage policies and programs and keeping them up to date to assure their effectiveness.
4. Negotiating and placing (or otherwise approving) all insurance contracts and bonds to assure conformity with established programs.
5. Reviewing foreign insurance programs.
6. Approving insurance provisions of leases and contracts prior to execution.
7. Reporting and adjusting all insurance claims.
8. Serving in an advisory capacity to the Corporate Accounting Department and subsidiaries to determine insurable values.
9. Administering and operating GMI's insurance subsidiary, Gold Medal Insurance Co.

In carrying out these responsibilities, the Risk Management Department requires the cooperation of people throughout the subsidiaries, divisions, and departments for information, risk identification and analysis, and coordinated implementation.

TABLE 20.2. State of Minnesota Policy Statement on Risk Management

The State of Minnesota will apply to the risk of accidental and fortuitous loss the risk management process which includes a systematic and regular identification of loss exposures, the analysis of these loss exposures, the application of sound risk control procedures, and the financing of risk consistent with the state's financial resources.

The state, in accordance with its statutes and laws, is to be protected against accidental loss or losses which in the aggregate during any financial period would significantly affect the budget or the ability of the state to continue to fulfill its responsibilities to taxpayers and the public. Loss prevention and contract activities are of paramount importance to the state.

The administration of the State of Minnesota Risk Management Program is assigned to the Director of Risk Management, reporting to the Assistant Commissioner, Department of Administration.

Risk Management Purposes
1. Objectives:
   a. The State of Minnesota with respect to the management of all risks of accidental loss shall have as its objectives:
      (1) The protection of the state against the financial consequences of accidental losses which are catastrophic in nature.
      (2) The minimization of the total long-term cost to the state of all activities related to the identification, prevention, and control of accidental losses and their consequences.
      (3) The creation of a system of internal procedures providing a periodic assessment of fluctuating exposure to loss, loss bearing capacity and available financial resources, including insurance.
      (4) The establishment to the extent possible of an exposure-free work and service environment in which the state employees as well as the public can enjoy safety and security in the course of their daily pursuits.
2. Risk Management Functions:
   a. The Director of Risk Management shall have authority for:
      (1) Identification and measurement of risks of accidental loss.
      (2) Selection of appropriate Risk Management techniques for resolving exposure problems: i. Risk Assumption, ii. Risk Reduction, iii. Risk Retention, iv. Risk Transfer, v. Other systems, as appropriate, including the purchase of insurance.
      (3) Development and Maintenance of a Risk Information System in coordination with existing systems for the timely and accurate recording of losses, claims, premiums and other risk-related costs and information.
      (4) Allocation of insurance premiums, uninsured losses and other risk costs and information.
      (5) Risk Management Consultation to the state, its agencies, departments and commissions.
3. Risk Retention
   a. With regard to risks of accidental loss it shall be the state's policy to self insure all losses:
      (1) which occur with predictable frequency, and
      (2) which will not have a significant impact on the state's financial position, and
      (3) will be in compliance with the laws and statutes of the State of Minnesota.

b. The intention of the state as a general guideline is to self insure aggressively and to maintain high standards of claims handling and risk management capabilities. Exceptions to these guidelines should be allowed:

    (1) Whenever certain necessary services can be obtained only through the purchase of insurance.

    (2) When the state is obligated by contract or law to purchase insurance and no alternate method is available.

    (3) When deductibles, non-insurance and self insurance do not result in long-term economies.

4. Purchase of Insurance

    a. The procurement of all property/casualty insurance in the state will be coordinated through the Division of Risk Management.

    b. Insurance shall be purchased from any source determined to be in the best interest of the state.

    c. Whenever possible, the remuneration of agents and brokers providing services to the state shall be made on a fee basis.

sion includes providing for security and infrastructure, the regulation of commerce, the provision of certain services, the protection of individual rights, and the enforcement of the law.

A clear policy statement can have at least four specific benefits. First, the creation of a policy statement forces upper level managers to focus their attention on the function of risk management. The creation of a policy statement requires managers to clearly enumerate preferences, values, and attitudes that are incorporated into the document and, thus, communicated to the entire organization. Creation of the statement also requires managers to commit to risk management.

Second, the policy statement can provide guidance for the development of an operational and organizational plan. What activities are required to accomplish our policies, and how do those efforts relate to one another? Where does the risk management function (and/or department) fit into the organizational chart? How does risk management relate to the other managerial functions within the organization?

Third, the policy statement defines duties and responsibilities. Allocation of responsibility is essential in risk management because the actual practice of risk management requires participation from every employee in the organization. The statement brings discipline to a potentially uncontrollable function.

Fourth, the statement facilitates communication. The preparation of the statement provides an opportunity for the risk manager to interact with all areas of the organization, and to market the risk management program. The process also creates awareness of the need for an integrated information management system, one in which information flows can be formalized to assure that all managers are receiving relevant information in a timely manner.

The policy statement is developed by managers throughout the organization, but it becomes credible only if the highest level of management authorizes its adoption. This point, while seemingly obvious, sometimes is overlooked by organizations—with unfortunate consequences. In the long run, lack of support or awareness from higher management levels can lead to risk management program failure, since without their support, few managers in an organization are likely to take the risk manager seriously.

Organization

In Chapter 2, risk management was identified as a general management function, but this view is not widely applied in organizations today. Because most organizations still remain hierarchical and bureaucratic, the risk management function is usually placed in a dedicated department or office that has administrative responsibilities for the risk management function. This traditional view of risk management is reflected in the Institute of Management Accountants (IMA, 1993) publication on the classification of risk management costs for internal accounting purposes, and interested readers are encouraged to obtain and examine this document.

In the traditional view, risk management is one of six general management functions. This concept arises from the writings of Henri Fayol, a famous early French management theorist. Fayol (1949) defined management as follows:

> To manage is to forecast and plan, to organize, to command, to coordinate and to control. To foresee and plan means examining the future and drawing up the plan of action. To organize means building up the dual structure, material and human, of the undertaking. To command means maintaining activity among the personnel. To coordinate means binding together, unifying and harmonizing all activity and effort. To control means seeing that everything occurs in conformity with established rule and expressed command.

Fayol also suggested that all activities in organizations can be divided into six basic functions:

1. Technical activities (production, manufacture, adaptation)
2. Commercial activities (buying, selling, exchange)
3. Financial activities (search for an optimum use of capital)
4. Security activities (protection of property and persons)
5. Accounting activities (stock taking, financial statements, costs, statistics)
6. Managerial activities (planning, organization, command, coordination, control).

Thus, at an early date, Fayol identified risk management (i.e., the security function) as one of the prime functions of management, even though at that time the security function was much more limited in its scope than it is today. According to Fayol,

> The object of this (security activity) is to safeguard property and persons against theft, fire and flood, to ward off strikes and felonies and broadly all social disturbances or natural disturbances liable to endanger the progress and even the life of the business. It is the master's eye, the watchdog of the one-man business, the policy or the army in the case of the State. *It is, generally speaking, all measures conferring security upon the undertaking and requisite peace of mind upon the personnel.* (Emphasis added by the authors.)

Except for the last sentence, Fayol appears to be emphasizing the loss-control aspects of the traditional risk management function; the security function would be more broadly conceived today.

Like other management functions, the security function is handled differently in large, medium, and small firms. Table 20.3, adapted from information presented in the 1991 *Cost of Risk Survey* (Tillinghast/RIMS, 1992), shows the varying sizes of risk management departments for organizations classified by annual revenue.

The *Cost of Risk Survey* found that the average risk management department size was 4.67 employees (essentially, 3 "professional" employees and 1+ "clerical" employees), though wide variation was evident. A small staff of three typically includes the risk manager, an assistant, and a secretary; or the risk manager, a property and liability specialist, and an employee benefits specialist. Larger staffs may include, in addition to the risk manager and a secretary, a property and liability insurance manager, a loss control manager, and an employee benefits manager. The property and liability risk manager may have a staff of specialists in various lines of insurance. The employee benefits specialists may have subordinates specializing in pensions, death benefits, disability income benefits, medical expense benefits, and unemployment benefits. The loss-control manager may supervise specialists in controlling fire and related losses, crime losses, industrial injury and diseases, and liability losses. Still larger staffs may include subspecialties in each of these areas.

Large, diversified firms must decide whether to have a centralized or decentralized operation. Under a centralized operation, the risk manager supervises a staff operating for the most part out of the home office. Under a centralized operation, the same philosophy and objectives are likely to pervade all risk management decisions. The staff is likely to be smaller, more experienced, and better able to handle unusual problems. Centralization also makes possible some savings through quantity discounts and the use of blanket policies. Under a decentralized operation, each subsidiary, division, branch, or plant has a risk manager, each of whom reports to the corporate risk manager. Having a risk management department at each subsidiary may provide more informed, prompt, personal attention to the problems arising at that level. The more geo-

TABLE 20.3. Risk Management Department Size, by 1990 Revenue Level

Revenues	*Department Size (Percentages reporting . . .)*			
	0–1	2–6	5–10	over 10
Less than $30M	27.5%	56.9%	7.8%	7.8%
$30 to $100M	29.8%	58.5%	8.5%	3.2%
$100 to $300M	26.2%	59.2%	12.2%	2.4%
$300M to $1B	18.1%	65.0%	10.1%	6.8%
$1B to $3B	4.2%	68.9%	16.2%	10.8%
$3B and higher	2.1%	36.9%	31.6%	9.1%

Source: 1991 Cost of Risk Survey: Tillinghast/RIMS.

graphically dispersed and the greater the diversity in the organization's operations, the stronger the case for decentralization. An intermediate approach is a centralized operation except that loss control and foreign operations are handled by local people.

The organization risk management (ORM) view of risk management that was explained in Chapter 2 is at the opposite end of the spectrum. In Chapter 2, risk management was defined as all activities and actions that address risk and uncertainty. This definition takes the broadest possible view of the risk management function, in that all risks are considered as subjects for possible treatment. Speculative risks have features that may distinguish them from pure risks, but the differences do not disqualify—conceptually—the risk manager from involvement. Rather, pure and speculative risks are both examples of risk, regardless of their specific elements, and any activity that seeks to control or otherwise manage risk is "risk management."

The ORM view, almost by definition, is not suited to the traditional "risk management department" approach. Rather, risk management is a function that is undertaken by every person in an organization, indeed, *must* be undertaken by every person in the organization. The point of contact for most risk management techniques is at the level of the exposure unit: training of employees, creation and employment of safety standards, maintenance and housekeeping, security, adherence to policies and procedures, personal health habits and behaviors, emergency response protocols, and so on. Instead of confining the activity to a designated risk management department, the ORM approach would imply that risk management responsibilities be written into the formal job description of each employee of the organization.

If risk management is to be an integrated and rational function, then the ORM view would suggest that supervision and coordination take place at the executive level. The placement in the organization is important. If risk management is a general function, then placement of the function below the executive level imposes constraints. Risk management is not just a financial matter, or a safety matter, or a legal matter; it is a general management matter. Centralized coordination at the executive level also allows the organization to reap economies of scale, particularly in the area of risk financing.

The idea of an executive-level risk manager with responsibilities for a function that is diffused throughout the organization's activities accommodates a wide variety of observed phenomena, most notably, the recent appearance of many different types of risk management (such as immunization of pension funds against interest rate risk). The ORM view recognizes that these activities are the practice of risk management, in the context of particular areas of responsibility. Under the ORM view, an executive risk manager coordinates the pension fund manager's risk management activities with risk management activities of other employees within the organization.

Manuals

Risk management manuals are important in making the risk management policy statement operational. Specifically they delineate the procedures, methods, and activities that allow the organization to accomplish its risk management goals and objectives. Quite apart from this purpose, the manual also provides a tool for communicating and promoting risk management within the organization. The manual allows the risk manager to market the risk management program to management and employees within the organization. A number of different forms for a risk management manual are possible. One type of manual is oriented toward upper management only. This form would be almost an executive summary manual, providing only broad and generalized information on the policies and procedures of the organization. A second type of manual is oriented toward employees at the operational level. This manual provides detailed information, guidance, and instruction on risk management duties, while providing only general information on aspects of the risk management program that are not directly relevant to that particular operational unit. A third manual type is comprehensive, containing all information relevant to the entire organization in a single document. The strength of this approach is that the manual documents every element of the risk management program. The obvious limitation of such an approach is that the manual could become unwieldy. Appendix 20.1 at the end of the chapter provides an example outline for a risk management manual.

INFORMATION MANAGEMENT

Information management is more than administrative duty. It is a risk management tool. As discussed in Chapter 8, risk control includes "information management" activities. Information reduces uncertainty. Since uncertainty is defined as doubt concerning the ability to predict, information (of course, appropriate information) can lessen doubt.

Since information is an important risk management tool, the management of information is a concern for risk managers. The nature of the information and the structure of the system for managing that information will depend on how the risk manager responds to the following questions:

1. What information is necessary for me to perform my job?
2. From where may this information or data be retrieved?
3. When must I have this information, and what sequence to the ordering of this information is logical?
4. By what means and path is that information most efficiently and effectively moved to me?
5. What will I do with this information?
6. What is the appropriate means for storing, processing, or analyzing this information?
7. Who needs information from me, and in what form should it appear?
8. When and how must these others receive this information?
9. How do I identify and eliminate impediments and filters to the flow of information, and what are those impediments?
10. What institutional characteristics of the organization influence the nature of the information system and influence form in which information is communicated? How must these influences be treated?

The management of information could serve as the basis for an entire textbook that would parallel a number of organizational communications publications. In the interest of maintaining risk management focus, the discussion of information management is limited to four issues: (1) risk communication—the nature of the information flowing to and from the risk manager, (2) risk management information systems—current computing technologies that may assist the process of managing information, (3) risk management reporting—the form and content of formal reports to management and others, and (4) cost allocation systems—a budgeting mechanism that can create an important incentive for units within an organization.

Risk Communication

As an emerging subject of study in the field of risk management, risk communication refers to the processes used to transmit information concerning the consequences and treatment of risk and uncertainty. Risk communication, like all communication, has fundamental elements—a communicator, a recipient, a message, and a medium of communication. Closer examination reveals five distinctive features of risk communication: (1) the typical "audience" usually is not knowledgeable about risk management concepts and principles, (2) many aspects of risk management, even when introduced, are not easily understood or are complex, (3) issues addressed by risk management often require specialized knowledge that is challenging for the typical manager, (4) attitudes toward risk are subjective, and (5) individuals often underestimate the importance of risk management. To be effective, the content and structure of communication from a risk manager should be adapted to reflect these special characteristics. A brief discussion of these features appears below.

First, since risk management is a relatively new field, many managers may not be familiar with its principles and concepts. Lacking knowledge of the area, these managers are quite unlikely to include risk management considerations in their decision making. Therefore, at least initially, much of the risk manager's communication should focus on education. This does not mean necessarily "vocational-level" information. Commonly, this education would expose managers to the concepts of risk management and an understanding of its principles, providing them with the background to integrate risk management perspectives into daily activities.

Second, many important risk management concepts are not easily explained to managers in other areas. For instance, few beyond the risk management profession are likely to appreciate the incentives and level of responsibility created by an organization's aggressive retention program. Principles of probability or the relationship between information and uncertainty may be challenging concepts to many. Finally, risk management frequently requires a different orientation toward time. While many managerial functions use quarterly or yearly time horizons, risk management activities often are not well-suited to these short-term frames of reference. Of course, a risk manager's policies should conform to the short- and long-term goals of the employer, but short-term goals often do not fit the time horizon required to evaluate risk management efforts.

Third, many important risk management issues require scientific knowledge on the part of the audience (and the communicator) to fully appreciate the nature of the exposure to risk. Environmental impairment is a good example of this point. Most managers recognize that environmental impairment can be a problem, with some possible scenarios that are frightening. However, when the specifics of a particular environmental hazard are examined, say, controlling the release of chlorofluorocarbons, a manager may need knowledge of technical subject matter such as chemistry, biology, and environmental sciences. A survey of important sources of risk discussed in this textbook—such as workplace safety, political risk, health care delivery, and financing—reveals that many subjects involve highly technical issues.

Fourth, attitudes toward risk are influenced by personal factors that may be unique to the individual. Consequently, the risk manager faces the challenge of communicating information that may be interpreted in different ways. Although subjective assessment of information is not unique to risk management, it is a particular problem for risk communication since the subject matter—risk of injury or loss—can elicit widely ranging reactions.

Fifth, the issues to be addressed are frequently of great significance to the organization: group health care costs, workers' compensation, environmental impairment, product liability, fiduciary liability. For many organizations, these issues are urgent and important. Communicating their importance is a key purpose of risk communication.

Risk Management Information Systems

Advancing computer technology and sophisticated software have enabled risk managers to organize and manage large amounts of information. Risk management information systems (RMIS) have become increasingly sophisticated in the past 10 years, now including programs ranging from a fairly simple "spreadsheet" for organizing records and files to a more complex package of integrated programs that allow simulation and evaluation of organizational risks. Today, RMIS are likely to include capabilities for tracking claims, for analyzing and understanding losses, for loss forecasting, for budgeting, cost allocation, and other types of financial and statistical analysis, for maintaining information on insurance policies, for word processing and report generation, and for maintaining an integrated risk management calendar (Leverett, 1992).

The reasons for wanting to automate information management may seem simple. Who does not want to have a more efficient and effective use of information? However, several issues need to be considered in this decision. First, the organization must clearly identify what information it needs, the form in which this information is to be presented, the timing of information needs, and uses of information. Despite the fact that identifying needs seems self-evident, it is not unusual for an organization to purchase a data processing system *and then* attempt to decide the uses to which the system will be put. Such an approach fails to make use of options and flexibility in markets for RMIS products. Technology today permits sufficient flexibility to allow risk managers to identify needs and then approach the market to have a system designed to those particular needs. "Off the shelf" RMIS is no longer the risk manager's only choice.

Apart from the question of the RMIS structure, one of the key decisions to be made is whether the system should be "stand-alone" or "on-line." That is, should the RMIS be self-contained within the risk management department (desktop) or should it tie into the organization's mainframe or network? Traditionally, the focus of the decision was capacity and speed versus flexibility, with mainframes having higher capacity and speed, and stand-alone systems being more flexible. Though that distinction still exists, changing technology has enabled mainframe systems to become more adaptable and accessible, while stand-alone systems have grown in speed and capacity. Local area networks (LAN) have greatly expanded the capabilities of stand-alone units.

Reporting

Risk communication creates special challenges for the risk manager, particularly in the preparation of reports used within the organization (and to a lesser degree, for outsiders). First, risk management reports generally address two areas: (1) financial performance and (2) operational performance. Financial performance focuses on loss costs, insurance premiums, risk management program costs, legal fees, reserves, subrogation recoveries, and so on. Operational information usually identifies program structures, procedures, management policies and activities, loss control results, and similar subjects.

Second, a risk manager commonly will produce four types of reports in a given budget period (Leverett, 1992). First is the annual report, which provides financial and operational information for a one-year period. The second type is a loss analysis report, which details causes of loss, types of loss, and consequences of those losses. The third type of report is a project request report, in which a specific new program or activity is proposed. For instance, the risk manager may present a request to self-insure the auto liability and property damage exposures of the organization's fleet of vehicles. Detail on such a move, including the financial and operational consequences of self-insuring, would be central aspects of such a report. Finally, if ongoing risk management activities require funding or executive action, the risk manager will produce a specific report to request the action or funding. For example, a safety training program may require periodic reauthorization. The report would present a financial and operational assessment required to decide on continued funding of the program.

Allocation Systems

Cost allocation systems serve two purposes: (1) setting budgets and (2) communicating the relationship between risk-creating activities and the cost of risk. A well-designed system creates financial incentives in favor of activities leading to reduced cost of risk for the organization. A well-designed system also is perceived as fair by managers in areas other than risk management.

Cost allocation systems essentially are cost accounting systems. In concept, these methods allocate the cost of risk to operating units within the organization. Under a cost allocation system, the risk manager does not have a budget per se but has a claim to the budgets of operating units. One type of system allocates costs proportionately; if one operating unit is responsible for 15 percent of the total cost of risk, it will finance 15 percent of the risk manager's budget. Such direct allocation can lead to problems within an organization, and these problems are noted below. However, these problems can be overcome by careful attention to the design of the system.

A major benefit of cost allocation systems *to the risk manager and to the organization* is that the operating units are made aware of their contribution to the organization's cost of risk. This awareness can serve to motivate the unit to participate meaningfully in aggressive risk control activities. A well-designed cost allocation system creates incentives for operating units to reduce losses and other costs of risk, which reduces the risk manager's claim on their budget. Unfortunately, risk managers frequently meet resistance when attempting to introduce a cost allocation system. Rewards under the system often accrue only in the long run, while the cost and inconvenience of change is immediate. Operating units commonly are evaluated on short-term financial performance, so unless upper management demonstrates support for a long-term orientation in evaluating operational performance, managers are likely to perceive conflicting incentives. Also, compensation of a unit manager often is based on the unit's financial performance, which creates a direct incentive for the manager to resist efforts to allocate costs to the unit.

A second problem for cost allocation systems is that loss experience for any given unit may be erratic, and sometimes influenced by events that are beyond the control of that unit. For instance, a small operating unit with five vehicles may have no accidents for seven years, then suddenly have three of its vehicles involved in accidents in a single year. A small exposure base makes "budgeting" for such losses difficult. A different, but equally problematic, example is the operating unit experiencing a disastrous property loss because of a tornado. The benefit to the organization of a system that allocates the full cost of a weather-related loss that was random and largely uncontrollable is not at all clear.

A third problem lies in identifying the "cost" to be allocated. Chapter 3 of the text presented evidence that indirect or consequential losses are broad and lingering, perhaps exceeding the direct cost by a significant amount. The cost allocation system must specify what part of the cost of a particular loss is allocated to the operating unit.

A fourth issue is the level at which the motivational effect is felt. While it is true that the manager of an operating unit is responsible for activities within that unit, allocating the full economic impact of losses to the unit managers still may insulate the persons in the best position to control the loss. Allocating the full burden to the manager may leave employees within an operating unit unable to see the connection between their behavior and the cost of risk, even though they may be the individuals within the organization with the best opportunity to control risks and losses. However, extending the motivational effect of the cost allocation system to lower levels is difficult.

Finally, the timing of cost allocations can be a problem. The setting of a budget and provision of requested amounts occur at regular, fixed intervals, while the timing of losses is random. Questions can arise about the meaningfulness of assessing a unit for a large loss at, say, the beginning of a budget period and totally depleting that unit's budget for the ensuing fiscal year. Also, if the loss is "long-tailed," the unit should be assessed for the loss at the time it occurs even though the loss is paid in increments over time.

Despite these potential problems, many organizations have adopted successful cost allocation systems. Most of these systems strive to allocate all of the costs of risk (insurance premiums, administration costs, uninsured loss costs, loss control costs) to operating units—at least in principle. Successful systems are both *simple* to understand and *equitable* in application, two objects that may be in conflict when the system is designed. Practical experience indicates that complex systems rarely work, even if they are "fair." Alternatively, if the cost allocation system is too simple, equity and fairness objectives may not be met, which tends to undermine support for the program. The cost allocation system must strike a balance—and apparently a number of organizations have found such a balance.

Leverett (1992) identifies five types of allocation systems: (1) the pay your own losses approach, (2) the pro rata share system, (3) the manual rate approach, (4) the mini-retro plan, and (5) the risk matrix approach.

Under the *pay your own losses* approach, the cost of losses are charged back fully to the operating unit where the loss originates. This approach is equitable and simple to apply, but it can create budget instability for the operating unit when losses cannot be forecast with reasonable accuracy.

Under the *pro rata share* approach, according to Leverett (p. 41-10), ". . . the subsidiaries would pay their portion of the premium in the same proportion that their losses bear to the corporate losses. For example, assume that the corporate losses were $100,000 and one operating division had losses of $10,000. Assume further than the total corporate premium was $200,000. In this event the subsidiary would pay 10 percent of the $200,000 premium or $20,000. Therefore, the unit has paid their premium in the same proportion as their losses bore to the total corporate losses." The pro rata system is simple and understandable, but can be inequitable when losses are influenced by factors beyond the unit's control. Further, like the pay your own losses approach, it may contribute to significant budget instability for the operating unit.

The *manual rate* approach relies upon the methodology used in insurance ratemaking. For instance, in workers' compensation ratemaking the premium is based upon unit exposure rates, that is, a truck driver's rate may be $40 per $100 of payroll, while a clerical worker's rate may be 70 cents per $100 of payroll. A company consisting solely of truck drivers and clerical workers would have a premium built from the total payroll for each type of employment. The charge-back to the operating unit would be based on the composition of the unit's workforce and its payroll.

For other types of insurance, such as product liability, the rating basis is gross sales, revenues, or some other figure. Costs could be allocated based upon an operating unit's contribution to those figures. The strength of this system is simplicity and ease of administration. Its major shortcoming is the total lack of responsiveness to the unit's loss control efforts. It also fails to reflect other indirect costs of risk.

Mini-retro plans function on the same principle as retrospectively rated plans discussed in Chapter 14. In essence, each operating unit is responsible for an initial deposit, which is based in part on that unit's past loss experience. The unit is then debited or credited depending upon the actual loss experience in a given year. Investment income may also be credited to the operating unit's "account." Unlike the previously discussed systems, this approach is complex and may be difficult for the average manager to understand. However, the system is responsive to loss control efforts, is potentially equitable, and can mitigate destabilizing effects of random losses.

Finally, the *risk matrix* approach bases the charge-back on a mixture of actual loss experience plus an "exposure charge," which reflects the loss-generating potential of the unit. Leverett (1992) offers an example (pp. 41-12, 41-13) in which roughly 70 percent of the charge is based upon the unit's loss experience for the past five years, while the remaining 30 percent reflects a general exposure base such as payroll, gross sales, or property value. This approach seeks to balance simplicity against fairness and responsiveness. A limitation of this approach is that volatile loss experience could lead to unstable budgets. Instability can be partially controlled by reducing the loss component of the charge (from, say, 70 percent to 50 percent), or by including more than five years loss experience in the charge back formulation.

Another possible way to stabilize a unit's charges would be to limit the amount of any given claim that is reflected in the charge formula. For instance, the risk manager might choose to cap the size of any claim at $10,000. If a unit had a $15,000 loss, only $10,000 of that loss would be counted in the charge-back computation. The excess $5000 would be borne by the organization as a whole. Indeed, this approach can be applied to any loss-sensitive cost allocation methods in the form of a deductible or a retention limit. Under such an arrangement, the cost allocation system imposes the financial consequences on the operating units up to a point, with the consequences of loss beyond that point "transferred" to the organization as a whole.

CONTRACTED SERVICE MANAGEMENT

Conceivably, one person could administer a large risk management operation by contracting with third party providers for virtually all necessary services. One-person risk management programs have become possible because of the emergence of third party administrators specializing in almost all aspects of risk management, and because of the insurance industry practice of "unbundling" of services. Unbundling refers to an insurance company providing selected administrative or financing services that also are available as part of an insurance coverage. For instance, a risk manager might purchase claims administration services from a large insurance company, loss control services from another, and excess loss insurance from yet another carrier.

Very few organizations rely entirely on outside providers of services. However, for those services provided by outside suppliers, the risk manager holds and manages a portfolio of contracts. The management of these contracts entails at least four activities under the control of the risk manager: (1) managing relationships with insurance agents and brokers, (2) bidding for third party services, (3) requiring certificates of insurance, and (4) securing nontraditional risk financing arrangements with third party providers.

Management of Agents/Brokers

Perhaps the most important contracted service relationship the risk manager can have will be with an insurance broker or agent. Brokers and agents are insurance market intermediaries, though legally they have distinct differences. Agents, despite the fact that they are often independent business people, are construed legally to be "agents" of the insurance company (companies) they represent. Brokers, in contrast, legally are the agents of the consumer; although the exact nature of the relationship is a matter of state law. In either case—agents or brokers—the standard arrangement finds the intermediary receiving a commission from the insurance company.

The function and legal authority of agents and brokers as intermediaries in insurance markets was explained in Chapter 13. However, it would be inaccurate to consider brokers and agents as just intermediaries. Due to a long-term trend toward diversification, large agencies and brokerage houses now provide a wide range of risk management services, such as:

1. Risk management audits and consulting
2. Underwriting and claims management services
3. Risk management information services
4. Actuarial services
5. Non-insurance financing arrangements
6. Captive management
7. Marketing services
8. Training and educational services.

This diversification is a response to growing sophistication of risk managers, who have shifted away from reliance on traditional insurance, replacing it with other techniques.

For organizations that are too small to consider sophisticated risk management activities, capabilities in accessing insurance markets may be the single most important criterion in selecting a broker or agent. Identifying a broker who understands the client's risks and the insurance markets appropriate to those risks may be as much as many small organizations can do. For larger organizations whose demands are more complex, the selection criteria often include: (1) marketing competence, (2) consultation expertise, (3) administrative competence, and (4) basis of remuneration.

Marketing competence refers to the broker's (or agent's) knowledge of the insurance markets that possibly can provide the desired coverage. Due to the complexity of the insurance marketplace, this competence need not necessarily be for all types of risk. Rather, it is often important for risk managers to locate brokers with highly specialized areas of market expertise, such as insurance for offshore oil drilling rigs, or insurance for motion picture production.

Consultation expertise refers to the broker's or agent's capacity for providing a possibly wide range of risk management consultative services, such as risk audits, actuarial studies, development of loss control programs, development of alternative risk financing mechanisms, program audits/report development, and risk management information systems. Through these consultative services of the broker or agent, a risk manager can extend the risk management function for his or her organization.

Administrative competence refers to specific administrative services sought by a risk manager: including underwriting services, claims management services, captive management, or financial management services. Evaluating the broker's competence in these areas is required to determine whether these services should be purchased.

Finally with respect to remuneration, two methods are used to compensate brokers: (1) commissions, the most common approach, and (2) fee-for-service, in which the client directly pays the broker for the services provided. Agents are almost invariably compensated through commissions. Most brokers prefer to be compensated on a commission basis because commissions commonly are higher than fees and the level of the broker's compensation is not easily identified by the client. Risk managers tend to prefer the fee-for-service approach because fees generally are lower than commissions, and the broker's compensation is not tied directly to the writing of insurance. When a broker is compensated through commission, the broker arguably has a financial incentive to use insurance when other creative solutions may be better.

Bidding

For many years, bidding has been part of the process for selecting brokers and agents and the procurement of insurance and insurance-related services, especially in public entities. However, with the growing reliance on third party providers for a wide array of services, the bidding process has been applied to a wider range of activities. The proliferation of markets for sophisticated risk management services makes it essential for risk managers to understand the practice of selecting service suppliers through a managed bid process. The discussion that follows uses the selection of a brokerage firm as an illustration, but the procedure is applicable to selecting any kind of service or product.

Why "Bid" for Services? Bidding formalizes the process of selecting a particular service or product. In formalizing the selection process and criteria, the risk manager may identify explicitly the goals, objectives, values, and other factors that are important to the organization. The process offers evidence to stakeholders that their interests are followed when selecting such services, and it reminds service providers of the nature of their responsibilities.

It is not unusual for small local governments to select insurance brokers and agents through an informal approach, as selecting insurance agents is often outside the rules that dictate bidding for other services. The "mayor's brother" holding a lifetime tenure as a town's insurance agent of record is a piece of governmental folklore that is, unfortunately, often grounded in reality. Maintaining a long-term relationship with service suppliers is not necessarily a bad idea. Indeed, modern Japanese management principles emphasize the value of developing near-permanent relationships with product and service providers—presuming that a rigorous selection process precedes the relationship. Formal bidding (or some other rigorous process) provides assurance that the services provided are priced reasonably when compared with alternatives. Periodic re-bidding offers an opportunity to scan the market for possibly better quality products or services or lower prices.

The ideal duration of time between bidding and re-bidding for products and services is open to debate, and is influenced by the specific nature of the product or service provided. Bidding too *frequently* can be as great a problem as bidding too *infrequently.* Conducting the bidding process too often affords little opportunity for continuity, little chance for economies related to experience to emerge, and entails significant administrative costs associated with the bidding process itself. In the public sector, a requirement that some organizations bid for all services on a yearly or biyearly basis is acknowledged widely to be an important reason for the insurance industry having such a brittle relationship with governmental entities.

Bid selection often is based on the lowest cost bid. Basing the decision on a single criterion, such as cost, can lead to four types of problems in risk management, especially with frequent re-bidding. First, when purchasing insurance or other risk transfer products, the long-term financial security of the risk-bearing party may be of greater importance than the price. Second, poor quality broker or agent services can lead to long-term problems or possibly a catastrophe resulting from incompetent risk management advising, ineffective structure and arrangement of risk financing products, or incompetent claims settlement practices. "Buying cheap" is no more logical for brokerage services than it is for legal counsel or financial management services. Third, the scope of *respondeat superior* suggests that service suppliers can create important vicarious liability exposures for organizations, so basing selection on price alone is probably not in the organization's best interest. Fourth, a successful insurance program often is built on mutual knowledge and trust, neither of which are established in the short term.

What Is the Bidding Process? A bidding process can take one of two forms—opened or closed—though variations of each form are possible. Open bidding is commonly seen in the public sector, and often is required by law. Open bidding consists of a publicly announced intention to accept bids from anyone who meets general qualifications set forward in the bid specification statement (sometimes called the request for proposal, or RFP).

Closed bidding, in contrast, is a less public process in which the organization preselects a limited pool of candidates from whom a bid is invited. Although one normally expects more responses to be preferred to fewer, open bidding can be of little value in some situations, such as when the risk manager knows that only three vendors can provide a particular type of service, when a limited time is available to review and evaluate a large number of responses, or when the nature of the bid requires disclosure of sensitive proprietary information.

The bidding process can be outlined briefly using broker selection as an illustration. Broker selection presumes that risk assessment has been complete and thorough. For organizations without a risk manager, risk assessment may entail the formation of a bid committee that evaluates the risks of the organization and identifies insurance and risk management service needs. Frequently, such organizations hire a risk management consultant to assist in risk assessment and in evaluating potential brokers. In either case, the end product of the risk assessment phase is a bid specifications form (the RFP).

The bid specifications form contains general information on contract dates, times, and amounts, contractual conditions, specific requests for certain products or services, loss information, and other descriptive information that will be useful to underwriters, and a questionnaire. The questionnaire asks for information on the broker's level of competence in areas required to manage the organization's account.

For some organizations, the broker selection process is distinct from insurance program placement. The risk manager selects a broker based upon level of competence and access to markets, then works with the broker to develop an insurance program. More commonly, the risk manager selects the broker and the risk financing program as a package. The package approach can lead to problems if competing brokers are permitted to approach any insurance companies for price quotations. This problem can be overcome by assigning brokers to segments of the insurance market. Generally, insurance company underwriters are reluctant to deal with several brokers requesting a quotation on the same account. However, segmenting the insurance market can create fairness issues, and may require a knowledge of the insurance marketplace that a risk manager does not possess.

Certificates of Insurance

For an organization that uses other parties, such as contractors, to provide goods and services, possible vicarious liability can be a concern. As a general proposition, a risk manager would want these vendors to offer evidence that they can respond financially to any losses they create *and* that they can cover the organization's liability arising from vendor negligence. This "assurance" can take several forms: (1) a hold-harmless agreement, (2) a requirement that the third party vendor name the principal-organization as an "additional insured" on liability insurance coverages, or (3) a verification of insurance coverage, that is, a certificate of insurance. As an alternative the principal-organization might insure or retain the risk itself.

The certificate of insurance provides information on the presence and content of a vendor's insurance coverages. Many insurance companies have their own certificate of insurance form, but variations among these forms can be a problem for a risk manager who must monitor many certificates. Fortunately, the Independent Insurance Agents of America and the Professional Insurance Agents of America have led a group of associations and insurers in standardizing certificate language through the ACORD (Agency Company Operations Research and Development) project. The standard form provides the following information:

1. The insurance company underwriting the risk
2. The named insured(s)
3. The named insured(s) address

4. Coverage descriptions
5. Coverage limits, coverage periods, cancellation provisions
6. Nature of liability coverage, if applicable (claims made vs. occurrence)
7. Location and description of operations.

Several problems can arise for a risk manager who relies on certificates of insurance. First, the certificate is not an insurance contract. Laws of most states do not permit certificates to be construed as expanding coverage of the policy (i.e., promising something that is not part of the insurance contract itself). Second, a certificate may *promise* to notify the certificate holder of cancellations, but it does not provide a *guarantee* that notification will occur. The rights of the certificate holder, relative to the insured, usually are limited. Third, the wording of the contract may negatively influence the assurance in the certificate. For instance, a principal organization may be named as an "other insured," but find after a loss that an "other insurance" clause in the insurance contract makes the contract secondary to "other insurance" available to pay the claim. Finally, monitoring certificates can be a very time-consuming task when these legal issues are evaluated and reevaluated.

Security for Risk Financing Programs

As explained in Chapter 15, a state-level system of financial regulation monitors the ability of insurers to meet their obligations. In the event of failure, a system of guaranty associations compensates insureds for unmet obligations. These systems have worked well, particularly for individuals and small organizations. However, non-insurance risk financing arrangements have proliferated and the regulatory environment for assuring financial security of these arrangements is not as well developed. Many types of risk financing arrangements operate without any kind of oversight, which can be a concern for risk managers.

Commercial banks are becoming increasingly involved in providing financial assurance in risk financing arrangements. Collection systems and letters of credit serve to illustrate the type of risk financing services available through commercial banks.

A collection system is an arrangement in which a bank facilitates the transaction of business through the processing of transaction documents, such as bills of lading, sight-time drafts, invoices, certificates of origination, and certificates of insurance. The importance of collection (or processing) services has increased as business has become global. Sizable risks arise when business transactions become international. Will a government in a developing nation allow expeditious payment for goods purchased? Does the transaction leave the business exposed to significant currency exchange risks? If a risk manager is unable or unwilling to manage the risks arising from foreign transactions, large commercial banks may provide these important risk management services.

Letters of credit are another important tool used in business and government (see Leverett, Chapter 32, 1992). Similar in nature to a surety bond or a promissory note, a letter of credit (LOC) serves as a banking mechanism for securing payment of an obligation, such as a risk financing commitment. An LOC

is the bank's assurance that the promisor can pay. LOCs can fall into several categories: revocable or irrevocable, standby, confirmed or unconfirmed, straight
or negotiable, domestic or international. A revocable LOC allows the issuing
bank the right to cancel or modify the terms of the LOC without beneficiary consent. An irrevocable LOC represents a secured promise to pay or accept a draft
drawn on the letter of credit. A standby LOC is an unfunded line of credit. A
confirmed LOC requires a second bank to secure or "confirm" the solidity of the
LOC, while an unconfirmed LOC does not. A straight LOC honors drafts from
the beneficiary alone, while a negotiable LOC may permit drafts originating
from other designated parties. Finally, domestic LOCs are used within the
United States, are subject to the Uniform Commercial Code, and may fall under
state regulations, while an international LOC is used in international transactions.

Letters of Credit have been used to secure a variety of non-insurance risk financing arrangements. LOCs have been used to support captive insurer capi-
talization, to secure loss and unearned premium reserves, to capitalize risk financing pools, to assure payment of large or catastrophic losses, to anchor
reinsurance and "finite risk" insurance programs, to support fronting arrangements, and to secure retrospectively rated insurance plans.

CLAIMS SUPERVISION

A risk manager is likely to be involved in overseeing claims, regardless of
whether the risk is self-insured or fully insured. Important organizational interests attach to the resolution of a claim against that organization. Even if an insurance company claims manager is responsible for the administration and
management of an insured's claim, the risk manager will have incentives to be
an active participant. The claims function of an insurer has been discussed in the
earlier chapters covering insurance, so there is no necessity to revisit the issue.
However, the risk manager's role in claims management—especially claims in
which primary administrative responsibility lies with an insurer or a third party
administrator—has not been discussed, and that is the subject of this section.

Property Claims

When an organization incurs a property loss claim, the risk manager is responsible for negotiating with an insurer's claims representative and assembling information pertinent to the claim. Proof-of-loss requirements in insurance contracts will direct the risk manager to develop an itemized listing of property,
property values, demonstrations of insurable interest, and other possible evidence. The nature of this particular activity will, of course, vary with the type of
loss that has occurred. One particularly challenging property loss is the time element loss. For reasons discussed in Chapters 5 and 21, the determination of the
value of time element losses can be challenging.

Occasionally, the risk manager and the claims manager will disagree on
some aspect of the claim: its compensability, the value of the loss, the extent of

the loss, or the insured's interest in the loss. Insurance coverages commonly state a procedure for arbitrating differences in which claims are resolved through a formal mediation process. On rare occasions, mediation and arbitration are unsuccessful and the insurer and insured resolve the claim through litigation. Whether litigated or arbitrated, a good deal of a risk manager's time will be consumed in supervising such claims to resolution.

Third Party or Liability Claims

Frequently, a third party claim will be paid with little in the way of formal legal action. For example, "slip and fall" claims (e.g., a customer falls on an icy parking lot) often can be resolved through a payment to the claimant for medical expenses. Other types of claims involve more time but still avoid formal legal proceeding, through mutual agreement. Some claims are resolved through a formal legal process that is outside a courtroom—alternative dispute resolution (ADR) plans being notable examples.

When an organization is involved in a claim that leads to litigation, the risk manager will act closely with the insurer to develop and pursue a plan of claim resolution. This effort involves considerable time when the risk manager is responsible for gathering information necessary for defending the claim, is asked to participate in investigative activity, and, perhaps, is asked to be involved in negotiation before or during the trial.

One important issue in liability claims management is the contractual power of the risk manager in resolving claims. In many commercial liability contracts, the insured is encouraged to participate in claims resolution but is not empowered to determine claims strategy. In these contracts, the insurer retains the right to decide whether a claim will be settled or litigated. In many cases, the particular litigation strategy adopted is outside the insured's control. Interestingly, although the insurer has clear incentives to act in the insured's best interest, conflicts of interest do arise. For this reason, risk managers commonly insist on being actively involved in meetings in which claims strategy and tactics are discussed. A related problem can arise under administrative services only (ASO) agreements when the servicing organization's compensation is based on claims volume. Failure to use proper controls on this type of arrangement can lead to excessive claims payments. In the few situations in which the risk manager believes that the insurer's failure to represent the insured's interests is egregious, a "bad faith" claim may be filed by the insured against the insurer. In other contracts, such as professional liability coverages, the insured retains strong influence in litigation management decisions.

Human Resource Claims

When risk managers have responsibility for employee benefits, they will find themselves in a somewhat different claims management environment. While the handling of premature death claims is fairly straightforward and involves little supervisory time (other than to assure that payments are expedited), disability and health claims can be very time-consuming and complex.

The nature of poor health and coverages that address risks of poor health are discussed in Chapters 7, 18, 19, 24, and 25, so an elaboration of the risks and coverages is inappropriate here. Forces influencing the management of these claims differ from those at work on third-party claims, since the claims typically involve a fellow employee. Multiple internal interests are served in resolving these claims. The employer has an interest in assisting the employee, and also in controlling the cost of the claim and mitigating against any moral hazard problems. The employee, of course, wants an improved health condition. Health care providers have multiple incentives as well; some of them obvious (making a profit) and some of them not so obvious (ethical and moral objectives). Balancing these competing interests can increase the inherent technical complexity of health care claims management.

Discussion

Since claims management requires specialized knowledge, few risk managers retain total responsibility for investigating, negotiating, litigating, and resolving claims. If an insurer is not involved, the risk manager is likely to have one or more third-party administrators involved in the day-to-day activities of claims management. However, use of third party administrators does not alleviate the risk manager of the general responsibility of setting the claims policy, monitoring and evaluating the administrator, and providing decision-making guidance. No matter how claims management is done, a significant amount of the risk manager's time is devoted to claims and claims-related activities.

PROGRAM REVIEW AND MONITORING

How do you convince your superiors that your mighty efforts have produced nothing—no accidents, no deaths or injuries, no liability suits? And more importantly, how do you convince your superiors that you should be rewarded for these "nothings" happening? Those two questions—though overly simplistic and rhetorical—underscore the central problem in evaluating the success of risk management activities. Traditional risk management does not produce a tangible product. Rather, it prevents unwanted events from happening and reduces their impact when they occur or it improves the likelihood of positive outcomes—but it is not generally perceived as producing the positive outcome. The measurement of risk management effectiveness requires the evaluator to overcome questions such as, How do you know that some effort prevented a particular loss from occurring, and how do you measure the economic impact of its "non-occurrence"?

A second evaluation problem arises from the long-term nature of many risk management efforts. Risk financing plans may require a long period of time for evaluation if random loss fluctuations can dramatically influence performance in a single year. Loss control programs may require many years before the return on investment becomes apparent. For instance, a smoking cessation program may require five or more years before benefits such as reduced medical costs for respiratory illness and other related health problems can be seen. The long-term orientation of many risk management efforts may be difficult to justify in an organization in which managers are evaluated on short-term performance. To overcome this problem, the risk manager may need to persuade other managers to adopt longer planning horizons and convince them that some benefits of risk management may not be measurable directly.

Ongoing Monitoring

Evaluation of risk management programs by higher levels of management usually is accomplished through periodic reports. The risk manager, however, usually monitors program performance on a continuous basis. The capability to continuously monitor the performance of risk management programs is one advantage of a well-designed risk management information system.

A popular basis for evaluation (discussed in Chapter 1) is the "cost of risk." The Risk and Insurance Management Society, Inc. (RIMS) publishes a periodic survey of the cost of risk in North American organizations, the *Cost of Risk Survey*. The costs included in the survey are (1) premiums, (2) unreimbursed losses, (3) costs of operating captive insurers, (4) costs of outside services, and (5) other department costs.

A risk manager may consider the *Cost of Risk Survey* data as a benchmark, but not the sole basis for evaluation. Two categories of cost are unlikely to appear in the survey data: risk control expenditures and the "worry costs" identified in Chapter 12. Further, some elements of the cost of risk are completely beyond the control of the risk manager—the competitiveness of the insurance market, for example. This textbook has asserted in Chapter 1 that the cost of risk must include all costs exacted from an organization because of the presence of risk and uncertainty. This definition not only includes directly measurable costs, such as the cost of losses that occur, but also includes indirect costs, such as increased charges required by lenders who perceive the borrowing organization to be vulnerable to risks that could be managed. This interpretation of the cost of risk includes intangible benefits and costs. The use of narrower definitions may portray the impact of risk inaccurately and distort the impact of the risk manager's efforts on the organization.

Program Audits

An audit verifies whether a monitoring system or a periodic report accurately reflects program performance. Monitoring occurs internally. Audits also may be conducted internally, but most audits are performed externally. Risk management consulting firms can provide this kind of evaluation, which may take the form of an actuarial, financial, or a performance audit.

The audit serves the purpose of evaluating the risk manager and the risk management function, and it also can provide objective feedback for program development. Reputable consulting groups can analyze the full range of risk management activities and provide recommendations and suggestions for enhanced performance. Good consultants also can assist the risk manager in designing and implementing changes to existing programs.

APPENDIX 20.1. ONE SUGGESTED OUTLINE FOR A RISK MANAGEMENT MANUAL

I. Risk Management Policies and Procedures
   A. Risk management policy statement
   B. Statement of policy affirmation by chief executive officer
   C. Organizational policies affecting risk management
   D. Risk management administration
      1. Organization
      2. Reporting requirements
      3. Relationships
      4. Cost allocation procedures

II. Risk Assessment
   A. Assessment procedures, policies, documents
   B. Property exposures
   C. Time element exposures
   D. Liability exposures
   E. Human resource exposures
   F. Risk, claims, loss information

III. Risk Control
   A. Loss prevention program statement
   B. Claim reporting procedures, policies, documents
   C. Property loss control programs
   D. Liability loss control programs
   E. Human resource loss control programs

IV. Risk Financing
   A. Policy on retention
   B. Policy on assumption
   C. Statement on use of deductibles, retention limits
   D. Captive documentation
   E. Insurance contract catalog
   F. Leases, contracts, and noninsurance transfers
   G. Financial structure of risk management function, and explanation of cost allocation system

V. Statement on Risk Management Program Audit and Review Programs and Procedures

VI. Appendices
   A. Insurance schedules
   B. Exposure inspection checklists
   C. Return-to-work program guidelines
   D. Frequently asked questions
   E. Catastrophe management plan policies and procedures

Key Concepts

risk management policy statement A document that establishes an organization's risk management goals and objectives.

risk management manual An organizational document that delineates the procedures, methods, and responsibilities that allow the organization to accomplish its risk management goals and objectives.

risk communication The processes by which information concerning risk, uncertainty, their consequences, and their treatment are transmitted from one party to another.

cost allocation systems A financial accounting tool that permits the risk manager to allocate the costs of risk across the organization according to some agreed upon formula.

request for proposal (RFP) A document/questionnaire which is used to solicit bids from vendors for various services.

certificates of insurance A document that provides information regarding the presence of and content of a third party's insurance coverages.

letter of credit A banking arrangement that permits an organization access to a specified amount of credit, with terms of the arrangement established contractually.

Review Questions

1. Illustrations 20.1 and 20.2 show the risk management policy statements of a private and a public organization. What similarities do you find in their statements? What differences? What explains the differences?
2. What are the benefits of a written policy statement?
3. The implication of the ORM view of risk management is that program administration be centralized, while the actual management of risks is dispersed throughout the organization. Why?
4. Risk management–like activities were identified by Henri Fayol earlier this century. What are Fayol's six basic management functions, and which one corresponds most closely with risk management? Do any of the others have a relationship to risk management? Which ones?
5. Imagine you are a risk manager who is new to an organization. How would you go about identifying the nature of the information and the structure of the system for managing that information?
6. What are the characteristic elements of risk communication? Explain this in the context of an example (such as environmental impairment liability, or work-related injuries).
7. What considerations are most important in selecting a RMIS for your organization?
8. What are the costs and benefits of instituting a cost allocation program?
9. Briefly explain three different approaches to cost allocation.
10. Explain the difference between compensating a broker on a commission basis versus a fee-for-service basis. Is one preferred by risk managers? Why or why not?
11. Explain the typical bidding process for contracted services.
12. What is the purpose (or purported benefit) of bidding for services?
13. Why do risk managers rely on certificates of insurance? What is the potential problem with too great a reliance on certificates?
14. What is a banking collection system, and why might it be a risk management tool?
15. What roles may letters of credit play in the world of risk management?
16. What is the distinction between ongoing monitoring of a risk management program and a risk management audit?

References and Suggestions for Additional Reading

AMERICAN SOCIETY FOR HEALTHCARE RISK MANAGEMENT: *Journal of Healthcare Risk Management* (Chicago: American Hospital Association, published quarterly).

FAYOL, HENRI: *General and Industrial Management* (New York: Pitman Publishing Corporation, 1949).

GREENE, M. R., and O. N. SERBEIN: *Risk Management: Text and Cases* (2nd ed., Reston, Va.: Reston Publishing Co., Inc., 1983).

HEAD, G. L., and STEPHEN HORN, II: *Essentials of the Risk Management Process,* Vols. I and II. (Malvern, Pa.: Insurance Institute of America, 1985).

INSTITUTE OF MANAGEMENT ACCOUNTANTS: *Internal Accounting and Classification of Risk Management Costs.* Statements on Management Accounting, Statement Number 45, June 30, 1993. (Montvale, N.J.: IMA Publication Number 93287).

LEVERETT, E. J., JR.: *Risk Management* (Athens, Ga.: University of Georgia, 1992).

MEHR, R. I., and B. A. HEDGES: *Risk Management: Concepts and Applications* (Homewood, Ill.: Richard D. Irwin, Inc., 1974).

PUBLIC RISK MANAGEMENT ASSOCIATION: *Public Risk* (Arlington, Va.: published monthly).

The Risk and Benefits Journal (Marina del Rey, Calif.: Curant Communications, Inc., published bimonthly).

RISK AND INSURANCE MANAGEMENT SOCIETY, INC.: *Risk Management* (New York: Risk and Insurance Management Publishing, Inc., published monthly).

TILLINGHAST/RIMS: *1991 Cost of Risk Survey* (published by Tillinghast, a Towers Perrin Company, and by the Risk and Insurance Management Society, Inc.), April 1992.

CHAPTER 21

Property and Liability Insurance Contracts

Learning Objectives

After you have completed this chapter, you should be able to:

1. Briefly discuss the ISO commercial lines program.
2. Explain the general purposes of coverages provided in the commercial property coverage part.
3. Explain the basic protection provided for under a business income coverage form.
4. Identify why an organization might wish to purchase differences-in-conditions insurance.
5. Briefly discuss the ways in which an organization can insure against theft and employee dishonesty losses.
6. Explain the difference between inland and ocean marine insurance.
7. Describe the major types of surety bonds and their uses.
8. Summarize the protection provided by the boiler and machinery coverage part.
9. Describe the coverages provided for under the commercial general liability coverage part.
10. Distinguish between occurrence and claims-made liability insurance policies.
11. Explain the purposes of and differences between professional liability insurance, errors and omissions insurance, and umbrella liability insurance.
12. Summarize the major provisions of the business auto policy.
13. Summarize briefly the businessowners' program.

INTRODUCTION

Summarization of commercial property and liability contracts is difficult. Historically, many insurers have developed their own policies and these policies can be quite varied in form and content. Further, the needs of commercial customers tend to be more complex than are an individual's insuring needs, so commercial property and liability coverages are not only numerous—they can be difficult to understand.

While the variety and multiplicity of commercial property and liability contracts is something of a deterrent to study, students of risk management must strive to develop a working knowledge of insurance contracts. Insurance remains an important risk financing mechanism—discussions in Chapters 9 and 10 notwithstanding—and for the vast majority of small and medium-sized organizations, risk financing activities center on insurance contract acquisition and management.

The purpose of this chapter is to introduce readers to the property and liability insurance contracts that are most important to the typical risk manager. "Representativeness," rather than "comprehensiveness," is the goal of this chapter—as is "simplification." To these ends, the authors have chosen to present a portfolio of contracts that a risk manager might assemble; a portfolio that centers on contracts promulgated by the Insurance Services Office (ISO). While many insurance companies do not use ISO contracts, ISO's influence on the form and content of property and liability contracts is significant. Further, ISO's commercial lines series provides one useful way to present the variety of contracts available to the risk manager.

Chapter 21 begins with a discussion of six important types of property and liability insurance contracts: commercial property coverages, crime insurance, boiler and machinery insurance, ocean marine and inland marine insurance, commercial general liability insurance, and automobile insurance. The chapter then discusses several special coverages—businessowners' package policies, professional liability insurance, differences-in-conditions coverage, surety bonds, among others. Notably, workers' compensation insurance is omitted from this discussion. Due to its many unique aspects, workers' compensation is now the subject of a separate chapter (Chapter 23).

PROPERTY AND LIABILITY COVERAGES

In 1986 and 1987 the Insurance Services Office (ISO) introduced a new commercial lines program that replaced many of the contracts discussed in previous editions of this textbook. ISO is a trade association of insurers. ISO develops standard policies and advisory rates for most property and liability insurance lines. Not all property and liability insurers use ISO standard policies, but a large proportion of the policies in force, especially commercial lines policies, were developed by ISO. Furthermore, the protection provided by nonstandard policies is usually very close to that provided by ISO standard policies. Under the ISO commercial lines program, the insured can purchase a policy that contains one or more of the following coverage parts:

1. Commercial property
2. Commercial crime
3. Commercial boiler and machinery

4. Commercial inland marine
5. Commercial general liability
6. Commercial automobile.

Other coverage parts can be added, but the six coverage parts named above are the most important.

To qualify as a *commercial package policy (CPP),* a policy must include two or more of the six listed coverage parts. If the CPP includes at least (1) the coverage part covering the insured's general business property against direct physical losses caused by fire and other perils, and (2) the coverage part covering the insured's legal liability for claims arising out of the insured's premises and operations, the total premium that would otherwise be paid is reduced by a premium modification factor. In addition to these coverage parts, the CPP consists of common policy declarations that indicate which of the coverage parts are included and the premiums charged, common policy conditions applicable to all coverage parts, and, if necessary, endorsements modifying the rest of the policy.

The common policy conditions deal with such matters as cancellation of the contract; concealment, misrepresentation, or fraud; the right of the insurer to examine the insured's books and records and to inspect the insured's property and operations; and restrictions on transfer of the insured's rights and duties under the policy.

What follows is an introduction to each of these six parts of the ISO commercial lines program plus discussion of several other non-ISO coverages that play an important role in rounding out the typical property and liability insurance portfolio.

The Commercial Property Coverage

The commercial property coverage part includes (1) commercial property declarations which, among other items, list the name of the insured, the location of the property, the coverages purchased, and the policy limits, (2) a commercial property conditions form, (3) one or more coverage forms (the major possibilities being a building and personal property coverage form and a business income coverage form), and (4) at least one of the four possible causes-of-loss forms (a basic form, a broad form, a special form, and an earthquake form).

The Building and Personal Property Coverage Form. The perils covered under this contract are determined by whether a *basic, broad,* or *special* causes-of-loss form is attached. If the contract is a *basic* form the covered perils are:

1. Fire
2. Lightning
3. Explosion
4. Windstorm or hail
5. Smoke
6. Physical contact by vehicle, aircraft, missile, or other object
7. Riot or civil commotion
8. Vandalism

9. Sprinkler leakage or accidental discharge
10. Sudden sinking of land
11. Lateral or vertical movement of land
12. Volcanic eruption.

If the contract contains the *broad* form instead of the basic form, the perils covered include those listed above plus:

13. Breakage of glass
14. Falling objects
15. Weight of ice or snow
16. Accidental discharge/leakage of water/steam
17. Collapse of part or all of the building.

If the contract includes a *special* form, the broadest of the three possibilities, the policy covers all perils not specifically excluded. Some major exclusions are earth movements other than sinkhole collapse or mine subsidence; volcanic eruption, artificially generated currents, governmental seizure or destruction; mechanical breakdown, nuclear reactions or contamination; war; and floods, surface water, tidal waves, mudslides, backups of sewers and drains, and seeping underground waters; among others.

Because earthquake is not a covered peril under any of the three cause-of-loss forms, an insured who wishes this coverage must have an "earthquake form" included in the commercial property coverage part. This form includes among the covered perils (1) earthquakes and (2) volcanic eruptions, explosions, or effusions. All shocks or eruptions within a 72-hour period are considered to be a single event.

The property covered under the building and personal property coverage form may include (1) buildings, (2) the insured's business personal property, and (3) personal property of others in the insured's care, custody, or control. The declarations indicate which of these three coverages apply and describe the specific buildings or personal property to which they apply. The "building coverage" may include:

1. Completed additions
2. Permanently installed fixtures and equipment
3. Outdoor fixtures
4. Personal property owned by the insured used to service the building or its premises
5. Additions under construction, alterations, repairs.

An organization must be mindful as to whether it is responsible for losses to telephone switching equipment, power transformers, or vending machines owned by others, for while they may be covered under the policy, that coverage must be explicitly requested.

The "personal property coverage" includes all the following:

1. Furniture and fixtures
2. Machinery and equipment
3. Stock
4. All other personal property owned by insured

5. Labor, materials, or services furnished or arranged by the insured on the personal property of others.

This personal property must be located in or on the building described in the declarations or in the open within 100 feet of the described premises.

The "personal property of others coverage" is subject to the same location restriction mentioned above. Unlike the other two coverages, this coverage protects persons other than the insured. The named insured may purchase this coverage to avoid liability claims, as a goodwill gesture, or as part of an agreement for which the others pay a fee to the named insured.

None of these three coverages provides coverage for:

1. Accounts, bills, currency, evidence of debt, money, notes, securities
2. Bridges, roadways, walks, patios
3. Cost of excavation, grading, filling
4. Building foundations
5. Growing crops or lawns
6. Pilings
7. Personal property while waterborne
8. Property covered elsewhere
9. Retaining walls
10. Underground pipes, flues, or drains
11. Valuable papers and records
12. Self-propelled vehicles
13. Animals, aircraft, and watercraft.

This coverage part provides protection against direct and (to a lesser degree) indirect losses—but does not protect against net income or time element losses. Two additional coverages provided under the contract obligate the insurer to pay the cost of removing debris for covered property caused by a covered peril and pay the insured's liability for fire department charges assumed under a preloss agreement or required under a local ordinance.

Under ordinary circumstances, this coverage agrees to pay the *actual cash value* of most lost or damaged property. However, if the property is merchandise or finished goods that have been sold but not delivered, the insurer will pay the selling price less discounts and expenses the insured otherwise would have granted or incurred. Also, if the property is glass, the insurer pays the cost to replace the damaged property with safety glazing material if required by law. Finally, if the contract contains a coinsurance condition and the amount of insurance is equal to or greater than the coinsurance requirement, the insured will pay the full cost of building repairs or replacement up to $1000.

Separate policy limits that state the maximum payment per occurrence apply to each of the three types of property: buildings, business personal property, and personal property of others. Each of these three types of property can be insured on either a specific-location or blanket-at-all-specified-locations basis. In addition to the general policy limits, there are several internal limits that warrant a mention. Theft losses, for instance, are subject to such internal limits: $2500 for furs; $2500 for jewelry, watches, and precious stones; $2500 for patterns, dies, molds, and forms; $2500 for stamps, tickets, and letters of credit. Nonconformance with coinsurance conditions (should such a clause be included) may further limit coverage, and—of course—the presence of a deductible will influence the amount an insured will recover under the coverage.

Finally, three optional coverages that affect the amount of recovery apply if they are entered into the declarations. First, for each of the items to which an agreed value coverage applies, the coinsurance provision does not apply. Instead, the insurer pays a fraction of the loss determined by the ratio of the insurance amount to the agreed amount. Second, under an inflation guard coverage, the limits of insurance to which this coverage applies automatically increase by a pro rata portion of the annual increase percentage shown in the declarations. Third, under replacement cost coverage, the insurer promises to pay the replacement cost without any deduction for depreciation instead of the actual cash value of lost or damaged property. The insurer, however, will not pay for any loss or damage on a replacement cost basis (1) until the lost or damaged property is actually repaired or replaced, and (2) unless the repairs or replacement are made as soon as reasonably possible.

Business Income Coverage Form. Instead of or in addition to a building and personal property coverage form, the commercial property coverage part may include a business income coverage form. Under the business income coverage form, the insurer pays for the actual and necessary loss of income the insured organization sustains if its operations are suspended because a covered peril causes direct physical loss of or damage to the insured property. The covered perils depend upon which of the four causes-of-loss forms (mentioned previously) is attached.

"Business income" is defined to mean (1) the net income (net profit before income taxes) that would have been earned, plus (2) the normal operating expenses, including payroll, that continue during the suspension. The suspension period that is covered starts with the date of the physical loss or damage to the property and ends on the date when that property should be repaired, rebuilt, or replaced if the insured acts with reasonable speed to obtain similar quality. The covered period does not include any additional time required because of any law that regulates the construction, use, or repair, or requiring the tearing down of any property.

Four additional coverages provided by the form are (1) alterations and new buildings, (2) civil authority, (3) extra expenses, and (4) extended business income. Under the first of these four additional coverages, the insurer promises to pay business income losses sustained because of physical loss or damage to new buildings or structures, whether complete or under construction, or to alterations or additions to existing buildings or structures.

Under the second additional coverage, if civil authorities prohibit access to described premises because of physical loss or damage to property that is not on the described premises, the insurer will pay any resulting business income loss for up to two weeks.

Under the third coverage, the insurer will pay any expenses exceeding normal expenses that the insured incurs to avoid or minimize the suspension of business income by continuing operations at the described premises or at replacement locations, which may be temporary. If the insured continues operations at replacement locations, the insurer will pay relocation expenses and costs to equip and operate the replacement locations.

Under the fourth coverage, the insurer will pay the loss of business income that the insured incurs during the period that starts on the date the property is actually repaired or replaced and operations are resumed and ends 30 days later, or if earlier, on the date the insured could restore the business to its pre-loss level if it acted with reasonable speed. This coverage recognizes that the insured may need some time after operations are resumed to restore its business to its former sales or production volume and profit level.

Other Forms and Endorsements. The building and personal property coverage form and the business income coverage form are only two of the coverage forms that may be included in the commercial property coverage part. Furthermore, each of these coverage forms and the causes-of-loss forms can be endorsed in various ways. Among the other forms are (1) a builder's risk coverage form, (2) a value reporting form, (3) your business personal property—separation of coverage form, (4) a legal liability coverage form, (5) a leasehold interest coverage form, (6) a glass coverage form, and (7) a business income from dependent properties coverage form.

The *builder's risk coverage form* is used for buildings under construction to protect the named insured builder against loss of or damage to buildings described in the declarations while in the course of construction. The *value reporting form* modifies insurance provided under the building and personal property coverage form. Under this form, the insured pays an advance premium based upon the policy limit and an estimate of the average value to be exposed during the term. This coverage is ideally suited for exposures such as inventory, in which the value may vary widely throughout a business year. Under the *your business personal property—separation of coverage form,* the insured may exclude certain types of personal property or cover them under separate policy limits.

Under the *legal liability coverage form,* the insurer promises to protect the insured against liability the insured may have for damages sustained because of direct physical loss or the loss of use of tangible property of others in the care, custody, or control, of the insured. A *leasehold interest coverage form* covers those types of losses that an insured tenant may suffer because a lease is canceled following damage caused by a covered peril. The coverage is not restricted to leases that are canceled because of a clause that gives the landlord the right to cancel the lease if fire damages the property by more than a stated percent of its value. A *glass coverage form* is unique in that it specifies the peril covered in addition to the property covered. The form covers damage to glass and to any lettering or ornamentation caused by breakage of glass or by chemicals accidentally or maliciously applied. A *business income from dependent properties coverage form* protects the named insured against business interruptions or extra expense incurred to continue operations that are caused by damage to the property of a supplier or a customer.

"Endorsements" can be added to increase or decrease the coverage under the building and personal property, business income, or other forms. For example, coverage may be increased by adding to the covered property outdoor trees, shrubs, and plants; outdoor signs; or radio or television antennas. A building ordinance coverage endorsement removes the building ordinance exclusion.

Two endorsements are specifically directed toward the business income form. Under an ordinary payroll limitation endorsement, the business income loss that is covered does not include ordinary payroll expense that is incurred after the number of days shown in a schedule. Under a manufacturer's selling price endorsement, the insured is covered against the loss of potential profits on finished goods that are not being held for sale at any retail outlet.

Crime Insurance

Crime insurance includes protection against (1) thefts of various types by outsiders and (2) dishonest acts by employees, plus, for money and securities, coverage against all other causes of loss not specifically excluded. If a building owner has named-perils coverage on a building or its contents, he or she should seriously consider crime insurance as a way of protecting the business against this exposure, which is not covered under either the basic or broad causes-of-loss forms described earlier. Theft by outsiders is generally one of the perils covered under all the risks policies (like the "special form" discussed earlier, dishonest acts of employees is not). Furthermore, under these policies, certain types of property, such as money, that are highly susceptible to theft losses are usually excluded or subject to some small internal limits. Crime insurance is one of the lines included in the new ISO commercial lines program.

The commercial crime coverage includes one of a number of possible policy forms (A through J), which are described briefly below. The general provisions of the crime policy deal with such matters as (1) the exclusion of losses resulting from dishonest or criminal acts committed by the insured or any partners, whether acting alone or in collusion with others, (2) the limitations of coverage to losses discovered no later than one year from the end of the policy period, (3) the duties of the insured following a loss, (4) the noncumulation of the limit of insurance from year to year or policy period to policy period, (5) loss sustained that would have been covered under prior insurance except for the discovery period limitation, (6) the territory covered, and (7) a requirement that the insured keep records of all covered property as an aid to verifying the loss.

Coverage Form A—Employee Dishonesty. Coverage Form A is an employee dishonesty (or fidelity bond) coverage. Under each of the other forms (B through J) dishonest acts of employees are not covered. Coverage A is a fidelity bond under the jurisdiction of the Surety Association of America, not ISO. The peril covered is any fraudulent or dishonest act of an employee. This insurance covers any type of property; it is not limited to money or securities. The insured property may be owned by the insured, held by the insured in any capacity, or property for which the insured is liable. Only direct losses are covered, not net income losses. The coverage is a "floater policy" covering any location within the territory specified in the crime general provisions.

Coverage Form B—Forgery and Alteration. Coverage Form B is the only other crime coverage form developed by the Surety Association of America.

Forgery and alteration includes either a fictitious payee, impersonation of a real payee, or alteration of the amount of an otherwise valid instrument. Only outgoing instruments are covered. Outgoing instruments include checks, drafts, promissory notes, bills of exchange, or similar promises made or allegedly made by the insured.

Coverage Form C—Theft, Disappearance and Destruction. Coverage Form C contains two sections. Under Section 1, money and securities inside that portion of any building occupied by the named insured's business or a banking institution or similar safe depository are covered against theft, disappearance or destruction. Section 2 provides the same type of protection if the loss occurs outside the premises while the money and securities are in the care and custody of the named insured, any partners or any employee. This coverage is extended to cover property outside the premises while in the care and custody of an armored motor vehicle company.

Coverage Form D—Robbery and Safe Burglary. Section 1 of Coverage Form D covers actual or attempted robbery of property other than money and securities inside the premises in the care and custody of a custodian (the named insured). Section 2 covers robbery losses of property other than money or securities outside the premises while in the care and custody of a manager, including an armored motor vehicle company.

Coverage Form E—Premises Burglary. Coverage Form E covers actual or attempted robbery of a watchperson, or burglary of property other than money or securities inside the premises.

Coverage Form F—Computer Fraud. This form covers for losses due to theft through fraudulent transfer by computers of money and securities or other property.

Coverage Form G—Extortion. Under this form the insured is covered for the surrender of property away from the premises as a result of a threat of bodily harm to the named insured, an employee, or relatives of either who is, or allegedly is, being held captive.

Coverage Form H—Premises Theft and Robbery Outside the Premises. This coverage essentially combines and extends coverage forms D and E.

Coverage Form I—Safe Deposit Box Coverage. This form covers for the theft, destruction, or disappearance of money and securities in safe deposit boxes, plus burglary and robber of other property.

Coverage Form J—Securities Deposited with Others. This form covers for losses to securities that have been deposited with parties other than the named insured.

Commercial Boiler and Machinery Coverage

One of the major gaps in the commercial property coverage part is protection against the bursting of steam boilers. This coverage is provided by a separate commercial boiler and machinery coverage part under the ISO commercial lines program, because, as will become apparent shortly, boiler and machinery risks have some unique characteristics.

Boiler and machinery insurance is not limited to steam boilers but also covers similar equipment subject to internal pressure such as air tanks, compressors, devulcanizers, furnaces, kettles, mangle rolls, refrigerating systems, and steam pipe lines. Damage caused by accidents involving flywheels, electrical machinery, and turbines can also be included in this insurance.

The boiler and machinery coverage part includes (1) declarations, stating the name of the insured, the objects covered, the policy limits, the deductible amount, if any, and what endorsements are included, (2) one coverage form (a boiler and machinery coverage form or a special form designed for small businesses), and (3) endorsements.

The insurer promises to pay the cost of repairing or replacing the named insured's property without any deduction for physical depreciation or economic obsolescence. The losses, property, and persons covered are direct (not time element) losses to the named insured's property, plus the insured's liability for damage to property in the insured's care, custody, or control. With respect to this liability, the insurer promises to defend the insured and pay all defense costs.

There are several possible endorsements. One endorsement covers actual losses sustained in a manner similar to the business income coverage form discussed earlier. A second endorsement pays a specified amount per hour or per day the object cannot be used. A third endorsement provides medical expense insurance. A fourth covers the financial loss that the insured suffers because an accident that interrupts power, light, refrigeration, steam, or heat causes insured property to spoil. A fifth extends the liability coverage for property damage to property of others beyond property in the care, custody, or control of the insured. A sixth adds bodily injury liability coverage.

One notable characteristic of boiler and machinery coverage is the emphasis on loss control. The insurer typically invests a good deal of time in inspecting and examining property in the interest of preventing losses from occurring. For some insurers, fully one-quarter to one-third of the premium is dedicated to this function.

Marine Insurance

Contracts concerned primarily with water transportation are considered to be *ocean marine* insurance. Ocean marine insurance—which is not part of the ISO commercial lines series—includes (1) hull insurance, (2) cargo insurance, and (3) protection and indemnity insurance, a form of liability insurance.

For a considerable time, ocean marine insurance was the only kind of modern insurance. Prior to the fourteenth century it was customary for moneylenders to make *respondentia* loans under which they agreed that if the cargo failed to arrive at its destination, the loan was canceled and no repayment was necessary. Modern ocean marine insurance was born in the Mediterranean area when the twin functions of lending and insuring were separated and a separate insurance contract was issued. Until the seventeenth century, people were not generally insurance-conscious because of the feudal system and the modest accumulations of most families. There was also a strong religious sentiment against thwarting the "will of God." Merchants, however, were risking substantial sums at sea, and they feared the perils of the sea. It took the London fire of 1666 to create a similar awareness of the fire peril and to inspire the formation of the first fire insurers.

Inland marine insurance grew from ocean marine, and its name reflects part of its history. As the use of insurance extended in the seventeenth and eighteenth centuries, merchants and insurers adapted the ocean marine contracts to meet the particular needs of waterborne vessels (and cargo) on inland waterways. As modes of transportation have evolved since the eighteenth century, inland marine insurance has expanded to meet new circumstances, but the term "inland marine" has remained. Today, inland marine insurance includes several types of insurance that would be important for many businesses. The two most likely categories are (1) cargo insurance and (2) floaters.

Some of this coverage is provided under the commercial inland marine coverage part of the ISO commercial lines program, but most is not. Of the cargo insurance policies, only those covering mail shipments are part of the program. None of the floaters are ISO policies but some businesses, such as jewelers, equipment dealers, and musical instrument dealers, can secure all necessary insurance on their stock of merchandise under ISO forms. An ISO accounts receivable policy, for instance, covers the value of accounts that cannot be collected because the insured's records are destroyed by a peril that is not excluded. Valuable papers insurance, another ISO form, covers the cost of reproducing records, drawings, blueprints, tax data, and other valuable papers destroyed by a peril that is not excluded.

Cargo Insurance. Cargo insurance covers shipments primarily by land or by air. Although the trucker, railroad, or airline may be a common carrier with extensive liability, the shipper may still be interested in cargo insurance because:

1. It is usually more convenient to collect from an insurer than a carrier.
2. A common carrier is not responsible for perils such as acts of God, an act of war, exercise of public authority, or inherent defects in the cargo.
3. The carrier may have issued a released bill of lading limiting the dollar amount of its liability.

Unless the insured makes only a few shipments each year, it is generally less expensive to buy cargo insurance than to increase the limits under the bill of lading.

Floaters. Four important types of business floaters are (1) equipment floaters, (2) merchandise or stock floaters, (3) installation floaters, (4) bailee's customers' contracts. Equipment floaters cover movable property that is being used by the insured in his or her business, but they exclude merchandise on sale or consignment or in the course of manufacturer. Stock floaters are used when a business may have placed its property in the hands of others, and this property is subject to transportation perils. Installation floaters are used when the sale of equipment (typically, heavy machinery, air conditioning systems, etc.) involves installation. During this installation period, the title of the property or the responsibility for any losses remains in the hands of the seller. Finally, bailee liability insurance protects a bailee against liability for damage to property in his or her care, custody, or control.

Commercial General Liability Coverage

General liability insurance protects insureds against liability arising out of their premises or their operations on or off the premises. The commercial general liability (CGL) coverage part may be written separately or in conjunction with one or more of the other coverage parts listed previously.

The CGL coverage part includes the following. First, CGL declarations will list, among other things, the name of the insured, the policy period, and the policy limits. Second, a CGL coverage form will describe the three possible coverages (coverage A, bodily injury and property damage liability; coverage B, personal and advertising injury liability; and coverage C, medical payments), the insurance limits, and some special conditions and definitions. As will be explained shortly, this coverage form is written on either an "occurrence" or a "claims-made" basis. Third, the contract will contain the common policy conditions form described earlier and may contain some endorsements modifying the basic contract.

Occurrence or Claims-Made Forms. An insured often can choose one of two commercial general liability forms: an "occurrence" form or a "claims-made" form. Under Coverage A (discussed shortly), the occurrence form covers bodily injuries or property damage that occur during the policy period. Often the claim is made during the same year the injury or damage occurs, but the claim may be made much later. The resulting claims are covered no matter when they are made, even if many years elapse between the occurrence of the injury or the damage and the filing of the claim. Consequently, if the contract is canceled or not renewed, the insurer remains responsible for claims made in the future for injuries or damages that occurred when the policy was in effect.

Under the CGL contract previously in effect only the occurrence form was available. Insurers encountered many problems with this form. Determining when the injury or damage occurred was often difficult, especially in the case of latent bodily injuries and long-term exposures involving such substances as asbestos. Insureds sometimes found that because of inflation and more liberal juries, the maximum amount the insurer was obligated to pay under the policy in effect when the injury or damage occurred was too small to handle current claims based upon that injury or damage.

The claims-made form is the insurer's answer to these problems (and others), but for most kinds of organizations they continue to offer the occurrence form for those who prefer it. Under the claims-made form the insurer is responsible for claims made during the policy period, even if the injury or damage occurred earlier. However, this injury or damage must not have occurred prior to a "retroactive date" specified in the declarations page. Usually this retroactive date will be the date the insured bought its first claims-made policy.

If the claims-made contract is canceled or not renewed, a basic extended reporting period begins when the policy ends. For 60 days the insurer will pay claims that are made because of occurrences between the retroactive date and the end of the policy period, even though the policy period has expired. For five years the insurer will also pay claims that are made after 60 days because of occurrences (not claims) between the retroactive date and the end of the policy period that insured reports to the insurer within 60 days after the policy termination. During those 60 days, the insured also has the option to purchase a supplemental extended reporting period endorsement (often called a "tail"). Under this tail, the insured promises to pay claims first made after the cancellation or nonrenewal for injuries or damage that occurred between the retroactive date and the cancellation or nonrenewal date and not covered by the basic extended reporting period.

CGL Coverage. The Commercial General Liability coverage part consists of three sections: Coverages A, B, and C. Under Coverage A, an organization is covered for liability arising from the nonintentional bodily injury or property damage for which the organization may be held responsible. This liability may arise from the premises or the operations of the organization. To put it slightly differently, Coverage A responds if the insured is held liable for physical injury or property damage to others if those losses arise from (1) the insured's premises (a customer slips and falls on an icy sidewalk, (2) the insured's operations (a construction crew negligently damages property on a neighboring lot), or (3) defective products or services of the insured.

Notably, Coverage A has several exclusions. Liability assumed by contract is commonly not covered. Bodily injury to employees arising out of their employment is excluded. Perhaps most important of all, the CGL has now virtually eliminated coverage for environmental pollution liability. Formerly, sudden and accidental discharges, dispersals, releases, and escapes of pollutants were covered, but some courts interpreted this exception to the pollution liability exclusions so broadly that insurers were exposed to far more claims than they expected. Furthermore, under the occurrence form, determining when latent bodily injuries or property damage occur is especially difficult, and pollution-related injury or damage is often latent.

Even under the new forms, pollution coverage may still be available in a limited form. For instance, off-site emissions, both gradual and sudden, are covered unless the pollutants are waste or unless the pollutants are brought to a job site in connection with the operations of the name insured. However, not covered in any case are the costs or liabilities arising out of cleanup or monitoring operations performed at the request or direction of the government.

Although there are other exclusions in Coverage A, only one other illustration will be provided. Under product liability coverage afforded in Coverage A, the insured is not protected against the associated costs of replacing or repairing defective products, nor is there coverage for the costs of a product recall.

Coverage B adds to the contract protection against liability for (1) "personal injury" if caused by an offense arising out of the conduct of the named insured's organization, excluding advertising, publishing, broadcasting, or telecasting, and (2) "advertising injury" if caused by an offense committed in the course of advertising the named insured's goods, products, or services. "Personal injury" is defined as injury, other than bodily injury, arising out of false arrest, detention, or imprisonment; malicious prosecution; wrongful entry into or eviction of a person from the premises occupied by the person; libel or slander; and oral or written publications that violate a person's privacy. "Advertising liability" means injury arising out of publications that slander or libel a person or organization or disparage their goods, products, or services; oral or written materials that violate a person's privacy; misappropriation of another's advertising ideas or business style; or infringement of a copyright, title, or slogan.

Under Coverage C the insurer agrees to pay, regardless of fault, medical expenses incurred because of an accident (1) on premises owned or rented by the named insured, (2) on ways next to those premises, or (3) arising out of the named insured's operations. The expenses include first aid at the time of the accident; medical and dental services, including prosthetic devices; and funeral expenses. The expenses must be incurred within one year of the accident.

The amount the insurer will pay because of events covered under the CGL is determined by (1) two aggregate limits, (2) one per occurrence limit, and (3) three sublimits. One of the two aggregate limits states the most the insurer will pay under the policy for damages under coverages A, B, and C combined, except for damages resulting from the products-completed operations hazard. The second aggregate limit states the most the insurer will pay under coverage A for damages arising out of the products-completed operations hazard. The per occurrence limit states the most the insurer will pay per occurrence for damages under coverage A and coverage C combined. One sublimit states the most the insurer will pay under coverage B for injuries sustained by one person or organization. A second sublimit limits the insurer's responsibility under the coverage A fire legal liability insurance (not mentioned above) to a specified amount per fire. The third limits medical payments under coverage C to a specified amount per person. Defense costs and other supplementary benefits are not subject to any policy limits, that is, the insurer's duty to defend the insured is separate from its duty to indemnify the insured.

Automobile Insurance

Most automobile insurance contracts are schedule contracts that permit the insured to purchase both property and liability insurance under one policy. The contract can be divided, however, into two separate contracts—one providing insurance against physical damage to automobiles, and the other protecting against potential liability arising out of the ownership, maintenance, or use of an automobile. Some automobile insurance contracts, notably those issued by insurers associated with automobile finance companies, cover only physical damage insurance.

Types of Contracts. By voluntary agreement, many automobile insurers use the same standard contracts, but others, including the four largest writers of automobile insurance, have designed their own. All automobile insurance contracts, however, are so similar that an analysis of the standard contracts will enable the reader to understand the most important provisions in most, if not all, automobile insurance contracts.

Two standard automobile insurance contracts can be used by businesses. The first is the business auto policy (BAP), designed for corporations and partnerships insuring any type of automobile (for example, private passenger automobiles, trucks, or taxis) or for sole proprietors insuring any automobile other than a private passenger automobile. Under the ISO commercial lines program, the BAP has become the commercial automobile coverage part that consists of (1) business automobile coverage form declarations and (2) a business automobile coverage form. The BAP can be written as the only coverage part in the policy or as one of two or more parts of a commercial package policy (the CPP discussed earlier).

The second contract is the personal auto policy (PAP), designed primarily for nonbusiness automobiles, but which sole proprietors can purchase to insure private passenger automobiles used in their businesses. Both of these policies are written in more simplified and readable language than the standard contracts they replaced in the 1970s. In the interest of brevity, only the BAP is discussed below.

The Business Auto Policy (BAP). The BAP permits the insured to purchase five kinds of protection:

1. Physical damage or property insurance
2. Liability insurance
3. Medical payments insurance
4. Uninsured motorist insurance
5. Personal injury protection, required in those states with no-fault statutes.

Property Insurance. Under the property insurance section of the BAP, the insured may choose the perils against which the organization wishes to be insured. The choices are a "specified perils" policy, a "comprehensive perils" policy, and/or a "collision" policy. If the insured wishes, it can pay an additional premium to cover towing and labor costs incurred at the place of disablement. The insured may also select what property, in this case what automobiles and their equipment, are to be insured. The choices are (1) only owned automobiles, (2) only owned private passenger automobiles, (3) only owned automobiles other than private passenger vehicles, (4) only owned automobiles that are specifically described, and/or (5) only automobiles that are leased, hired, rented, or borrowed. Notably, personal property carried in the automobiles is not covered.

The protection is limited to direct property losses with one exception—extra transportation costs incurred because of the theft of a private passenger auto insured under the policy. Several conditions affect the amount of the recovery. Unless the policy is endorsed to provide coverage on a stated amount basis, the insurer promises to pay the smaller of two amounts (less, of course, a deductible, if applicable):

1. The actual cash value of the damaged or stolen property at the time of the loss, or

2. The cost of repairing or replacing the damaged or stolen property with another of like kind and quality.

Liability Insurance. Under the liability insurance part of the BAP, the peril covered is an accident for which the insured is legally liable. "Accident" is defined to include, but is not limited to, continuous or repeated exposure to the same conditions, resulting in bodily injury or property damage which is neither expected nor intended. The source of the liability covered is the "ownership, maintenance, or use of a covered automobile." As with the property coverage, the insured may select which automobiles it wishes to have covered. The choices are identical to those cited previously, but the liability coverage may be extended to non-owned autos other than those leased, hired, rented, or borrowed. This extension would cover employee autos driven in the course of business.

The named insured is an insured person for any covered automobile. With two exceptions, anyone else using a covered automobile owned, hired, or borrowed by the named insured is an insured person if he or she is using the auto with the permission of the named insured. The two exceptions are (1) someone else using an automobile the named insured borrows from any employee or a member of the employee's household, and (2) someone else using a covered auto while working in a business of selling, servicing, repairing, or parking automobiles.

The amount of recovery is determined by several provisions. A single limit per accident applies to all court awards or settlements. Separate limits for bodily injury and property damage losses are available by endorsement. Defense and investigation costs are not subject to this limit, but payment of this amount toward an award or a settlement ends the insurer's obligation to defend the suit.

Medical Payments Insurance. Medical payments insurance, covering expenses for medical services, is a form of health insurance added by endorsement to the BAP. The legal liability of the insured for these expenses is not an issue. The insurer promises to pay all reasonable medical and funeral expenses incurred within three years following an accident incurred while a person is entering, occupying, or leaving a covered automobile. The insured, again, may determine what is a "covered automobile."

Medical expenses paid under this endorsement do not reduce the insurer's responsibility under liability insurance. Thus, if an insured is legally responsible for medical expenses incurred by a passenger, that passenger could collect twice from the insurer for the same medical expenses. Because the usual occupants of covered automobiles are employees, this coverage is a much less frequent part of the BAP than of the personal auto policy (because workers' compensation would respond). Furthermore, only for sole proprietors are the benefits extended to cover the named insured.

Uninsured/Underinsured Motorist Insurance. In order to provide protection against uninsured motorists and against hit-and-run drivers, insurers have developed uninsured motorist insurance, which can be added by endorsement to the BAP. Under this endorsement, any person injured while occupying the insured auto can submit a claim to the insurer issuing the endorsement which will act as if it represented the negligent "uninsured" driver or hit-and-run driver.

A vehicle is considered to be "uninsured" if it is insured for less than the minimum amount specified under the financial responsibility law of the state in which the covered auto is principally garaged. Under an "underinsured motorist" endorsement, the auto is underinsured if it is insured for less than the limit of the insured's underinsured motorist coverage.

It should be noted that the insured victim cannot collect under this coverage unless the uninsured or underinsured motorist was negligent. On the other hand, it is not necessary for the insured to obtain a judgment before seeking or obtaining reimbursement from the insurer. Instead, the insured and the insurer must decide through negotiations whether the uninsured or underinsured motorist was negligent.

Personal Injury Protection. In states that have passed no-fault laws, the BAP coverage on the named insured's owned automobiles must provide the benefits specified in the statute. A personal injury protection endorsement (frequently referred to as the PIP endorsement) adds these benefits.

As explained in Chapter 6, all no-fault laws permit tort liability actions under certain conditions. Most bodily injuries, and in some states property damage, will—it is hoped—involve only the no-fault endorsements and the physical damage coverages. In more serious cases, however, the liability coverages are still needed.

Other Property and Liability Insurance

Private and public insurers issue many kinds of insurance in addition to those described to this point. An illustration of the variety of coverages is presented below.

Businessowners' Policy. Instead of purchasing a commercial package policy or some monoline contracts, many insureds—especially small and medium-sized businesses—prefer to purchase a package contract designed to meet their particular needs. The ISO contract developed for these insureds is the "businessowners' policy." This policy was revised in 1987 to reflect the introduction of the commercial lines program discussed earlier.

The businessowners' policy consists of three forms plus any endorsements that insured may elect to purchase. The three forms are (1) a common conditions form, (2) either a standard property coverage form or a special property coverage form, and (3) a liability coverage form. The standard form covers essentially the perils listed in the ISO basic causes-of-loss form. The special form, like the special ISO causes-of-loss form, provides all risks coverage. Otherwise, the two property forms are almost the same. The liability coverage form is very similar to the CGL discussed earlier.

Professional Liability Insurance. Professional liability is usually excluded by endorsement under the CGL policy. To fill the gap, a wide variety of professional liability policies, sometimes called "errors and omissions" insurance, has been developed. Illustrative of these contracts are policies issued to druggists, hospitals, physicians, surgeons, dentists, lawyers, accountants, building managers, members of boards of directors, and insurance agents and brokers. Under these policies the insurer agrees to pay all sums that the insured becomes legally obligated to pay because of damages arising out of malpractice, error, or mistakes in rendering or failing to render the appropriate professional services. A close examination of these contracts would reveal significant differences, differences that need not be covered in this textbook. However, two characteristics that should be noted are: (1) most professional liability policies are now written on a claims-made basis, and (2) under many of these policies, the insurer does not have the right to settle a claim in the manner it deems most expedient (a feature of almost all CGL policies). Because the insured's professional reputation and livelihood may be at stake, the insurer may not be permitted to negotiate a settlement with the plaintiff without the insured's consent.

Surety Bonds. The central purpose of surety bonds is to guarantee the fulfillment of expressed obligations. Although any expressed obligation could be the subject of a surety bond and new types of surety bonds are constantly being written, the more common surety bonds can be grouped into the following classes: (1) contract bonds, (2) court bonds, and (3) license and permit bonds.

Under *contract bonds* the surety guarantees the promise the principal has made to the obligee under some contract. Usually the contract covers construction, supply, or maintenance. Some of these bonds promise that the surety will carry out the contract if the principal fails to do so; others promise to pay damages.

Court bonds include all those bonds that may be filed in connection with judicial proceedings. They fall into two general classes, litigation bonds and fiduciary bonds. Litigation bonds may be required by the court whenever the plaintiff or the defendant asks the court to take some action on his or her behalf that may injure the other party to the suit. Perhaps the best-known court bond is a "bail bond," which stipulates a penalty to be paid if a defendant does not appear in court at the time of the trial. Fiduciary bonds guarantee that persons entrusted through court order with the management of property for the benefit of some other person will perform their duties honesty and capably. Principals in such cases might include executors or administrators of estates, guardians of minors, receivers or trustees of a bankrupt business, or assignees for the benefit of creditors.

License and permit bonds are often required by federal, state, or local law when a person applies for a license to engage in a particular occupation or business, or for a permit to engage in a specific activity. These bonds can be divided into two major classes: (1) those that guarantee the licensing authority that the licensee will be responsible for losses to the government or to the public caused by violations of certain regulations or in some cases from the activity itself, and (2) those that guarantee the payment of certain taxes on products processed or sold.

Some of the bonds in the first group give injured third parties the right to proceed directly against the surety, while others protect only the public authority against damage to its own property or suits by private persons. Some of these bonds, which could be considered to constitute a third category, also provide for the forfeiture of the bond penalty if the licensee violates certain regulations, even if no damage results.

Differences-in-Conditions Insurance. Even when all of the previously mentioned property coverages are considered, a risk manager could find gaps or limitations in the portfolio of policies. Ideally, the risk manager would like to fill the gaps and tailor-make the portfolio to meet the specific property coverage needs of his or her organization. One practical solution is the differences-in-conditions insurance coverage, a coverage that is not part of the ISO commercial lines program.

Differences-in-conditions insurance (DIC) supplements a basic property insurance contract with one that covers additional perils. DIC is not "excess insurance"; it covers losses not covered by the basic insurance coverage. DIC can be customized to meet the needs of the insured. Typically, it provides all risks protection (like the special causes-of-loss form discussed earlier) subject to certain exclusions that include fire other perils covered under the basic insurance coverage. A major attraction of DIC is that the insured has more flexibility in establishing the policy limit because the contract does not usually contain a coinsurance clause.

Umbrella Liability Insurance. "Umbrella" liability insurance, which is not standardized and varies greatly depending upon the insurer, provides two types of protection. First, umbrella insurance is excess insurance over the insured's traditional liability insurance policies of all sorts—general liability, workers' compensation, automobile liability, aviation liability, and others. Second, umbrella insurance covers sources of liability not covered under the insured's other policies, subject to a minimum deductible of some large amount (say, $25,000 per occurrence). Illustrations might be contractual liability not covered under the primary CGL policy, or liability for invasion of privacy in advertisement. The maximum limit of liability under the umbrella policy is usually at least $1 million per occurrence and may range as high as $25 million or more per occurrence.

Credit Insurance. Credit insurance protects the insured business against abnormal losses on accounts receivable. Credit insurance differs from accounts receivable insurance, which covers abnormal bad debt losses suffered by an insured because records are damaged or destroyed by any peril not specifically excluded. Credit insurance applies when the records are not destroyed, but one or more debtors for some reason fail to pay what they owe by the due date. Only firms such as manufacturers and wholesalers that sell to other businesses are eligible for this insurance.

Export Credit Insurance. Export credit insurance protects exporters against credit risks (insolvency of the buyer) and political risks (inconvertibility of foreign currency to dollars and cancellation or restriction of export or import licenses) on sales to buyers in friendly foreign countries. The Foreign Credit Insurance Association, an uncorporated association of private insurers, issues this insurance in cooperation with the Export-Import Bank of the United States, a government agency. The Export-Import Bank insures the political risks and reinsures the credit risks under all the policies written.

Title Insurance. Title insurance reimburses the insured for any losses that may be incurred if the insured's title to real estate proves to be defective. Title insurers search records in their own offices and other sources and protect the insured against existing defects that they fail to discover. Only one premium is paid at the commencement of the insurance, which continues until the insured's interest in the property ceases. Some states and counties operate a *Torrens system,* under which a hearing is held in order to discover defects. If no defects are discovered, the title is registered, and the owner is, except under certain circumstances, assured of a clear title. The registration fee includes a contribution to a fund that is used to indemnify persons who can prove later that they have some right that existed prior to the registration.

Aviation Insurance. Aviation insurance, a rapidly growing field, includes a wide variety of contracts. Like automobile insurance, aviation insurance includes both property and liability insurance on the aircraft.

Nuclear Energy Insurance. Nuclear energy insurance also includes both property and liability insurance. Nuclear energy property insurance protects the operator of a nuclear reactor against damage to the reactor itself and other property on the described premises as the result of a nuclear explosion or any other peril not specifically excluded. Because of the large values exposed to loss and the catastrophic possibilities, this insurance is underwritten only by a stock insurer pool and a mutual insurer pool. Individual insurers write radioactive contamination insurance for organizations with nuclear hazards less than those faced by organizations eligible for nuclear energy insurance. Nuclear energy insurance protects the insured and any other person who may be held liable for loss against liability arising out of a nuclear incident.

The two pools mentioned above have gradually increased the limits of their liability coverage. Under the 1957 Price-Anderson Act, the maximum liability of each operator was limited to $560 million per incident. The Nuclear Regulatory Commission promises to indemnify operators for losses up to this limit less the private protection required by law. This private protection includes the private pool insurance plus, if necessary, a retroactive assessment on the entire nuclear power industry that currently would satisfy the Price-Anderson limit. However, the 1979 incident at the Three Mile Island facility in Pennsylvania, and the 1986 accident at Chernobyl intensified interest in whether the $560 million limit under the Price-Anderson Act was adequate. On August 1, 1987 the Price-Anderson Act officially expired.

A modified and expanded Price-Anderson Act came into being in 1988, and the modifications were significant. The members of the nuclear power industry are required to purchase insurance from the commercial pools in amounts that vary with the market: in 1993 that amount was $200 million. For losses above $200 million, Price-Anderson has created an assessment mechanism, whereby each *facility* (not each power company) may be assessed up to $66.15 million to cover additional losses. Given the fact that there are roughly 115 participating facilities in the U.S., the maximum total possible assessment would be about $7.6 billion—a considerable sum when compared with the prior limits of $560 million.

Crop Insurance. Crop insurance is sold by private insurers and by the Federal Crop Insurance Corporation. Three major classes of private insurance exist: (1) crop-hail insurance, whose name suggests its function, (2) insurance on fruit and vegetable crops against frosts and freezes, and (3) insurance covering hail, drought, excessive heat, flood, excessive moisture, and many other perils. The federal program covers all natural perils. Both the federal coverage and the broad private form are written only in selected areas.

Electronic Data Processing Insurance. "EDP" insurance has become increasingly important with the widespread adoption of computers. Under this insurance "all risks" coverage is provided on a variety of EDP exposures, including the computer hardware; tapes, discs, and cards on which information has been stored; and valuable papers and records, including documentation materials or information that has not been stored on tapes, discs, or cards. The coverage on the tapes, discs and cards and the valuable papers or records covers the cost of research and other expenses required to reproduce this information. Other expenses that can be insured include the inability to collect on accounts receivable if the records of accounts receivable are destroyed before or after storage; extra expenses incurred to hand process information until the computer is restored to normal, to rent substitute equipment, or to speed up repairs; and business interruption caused by damage or destruction of the EDP equipment.

Motortruck Cargo Legal Liability Insurance. This insurance obligates the insurer to pay any loss to cargo for which the trucking concern, as a common carrier, is liable—if the cause of the loss is one of a stated number of perils. As a common carrier, the trucker has the responsibility discussed in Chapter 6, and the Interstate Commerce Commission requires motor carriers engaged in interstate commerce to purchase this insurance unless they can demonstrate their ability to self-insure this obligation. Under the contract the insurer does not pay unless the carrier is legally responsible for the loss, but the carrier can be legally responsible without the insurer incurring any liability because the cause is not one of the specified perils.

Key Concepts

commercial lines program A program of coverages developed by the Insurance Services Office that includes most forms of property and liability insurance.

commercial property coverage part The commercial lines program coverage part that provides basic property insurance protection needed by organizations. This part includes commercial property declarations, commercial property con-

ditions, one or more coverage forms, and at least one causes-of-loss form.

differences-in-conditions insurance Supplementary insurance that covers perils not covered under basic property insurance policies. An alternative to including the special causes-of-loss form.

commercial crime coverage part The commercial lines coverage part that, depending upon the coverage form included, protects the insured against (1) thefts of various types by outsiders, (2) dishonest acts of employees, plus (3) money and securities, coverage against all other causes not specifically excluded.

commercial boiler and machinery coverage part The commercial lines coverage part that protects an insured against losses to the insured's property and liability for damage to the property of others in the insured's care, custody or control caused by sudden and accidental breakdown of a boiler or some other scheduled machinery.

cargo insurance An ocean or inland marine insurance contract that protects the insured against the loss of or damage to shipments.

inland marine insurance floaters Inland marine insurance contracts that cover movable property that is subject to transportation risks as well as other perils.

contract bond A surety bond under which the surety guarantees the performance of the principal under some contract.

commercial general liability coverage part The commercial lines coverage part that promises to defend the insured and pay claims for which the insured may be legally liable caused by accident and arising out of a source of liability not excluded under the contract.

errors and omissions or professional liability insurance Insurance that protects insured professionals against negligent acts in their business pursuits.

business auto policy The standard automobile policy designed for corporations and partnerships and for sole proprietorships insuring vehicles other than private passenger vehicles.

umbrella liability insurance Insurance that provides excess protection against perils covered under basic liability policies plus coverage, subject to a deductible, against some events not covered under the basic contracts.

businessowners' policy A package property and liability insurance program designed for small and medium-sized organizations.

Review Questions

1. What is ISO?
2. List the six coverage parts included under the ISO commercial lines program.
3. What is a commercial package policy?
4. Describe the difference in coverage between the building and personal property form and the business income coverage form.
5. What must an organization do to assure that earthquake coverage is provided under the commercial property coverage part?
6. What is differences-in-conditions insurance?
7. If an organization has a commercial property coverage part, why might it still need a commercial crime coverage part?
8. What does the employee dishonesty coverage form cover?
9. Summarize the protection provided by the boiler and machinery coverage part.
10. How are ocean marine and inland marine insurance alike? What distinguishes them from one another?
11. What is the difference between cargo insurance and inland marine floaters?
12. A school district asks for bids on the construction of a new school. What types of bonds might be used in connection with this construction project? For each bond, identify the obligee, the principal, and the expressed obligation.
13. Which of the commercial general liability forms would you prefer—the occurrence form or the claims-made form? Explain how each works and the reason for your preference.
14. Summarize the coverage available to an insured under the commercial general liability coverage part.

15. How does professional liability insurance differ from commercial general liability contracts?
16. Identify and briefly explain the parts of the business auto policy.
17. How does umbrella liability supplement basic liability insurance?
18. Describe briefly the coverages a small business can obtain under a businessowners' policy.
19. Describe the coverage provided under electronic data processing equipment insurance.

References and Suggestions for Additional Reading

BICKELHAUPT, D. L.: *General Insurance* (11th ed., Homewood, Ill.: Richard D. Irwin, Inc., 1983), chaps. 23 and 25.

Commercial Package Policy Guide (1986 edition, Indianapolis: The Rough Notes Company, 1987).

Fire, Casualty, and Surety Bulletins (Cincinnati: The National Underwriter Company, updated monthly).

GORDIS, P., and E. A. CHLANDA: *Property and Casualty Insurance* (Indianapolis: the Rough Notes Company, revised annually).

HUEBNER, S. S., K. BLACK, and R. CLINE: *Property and Liability Insurance* (3rd ed., Englewood Cliffs, N.J.: Prentice-Hall, Inc. 1982) chaps. 12–16, 19, 24, 25, 27, 28, and 32–35.

MALECKI, D. S., R. C. HORN, E. A. WIENING, and J. H. DONALDSON: *Commercial Liability Risk Management and Insurance,* vols. I and II (2nd ed., Malvern, Pa.: American Institute for Property and Liability Underwriters, 1986).

RODDA, W. H., J. S. TRIESCHMANN, E. A. WIENING, and B. A. HEDGES: *Commercial Property Risk Management and Insurance,* vols. I and II (2nd ed., Malvern, Pa.: American Institute for Property and Liability Underwriters, 1983).

CHAPTER 22

Social Insurance

Learning Objectives

After you have completed this chapter, you should be able to:

1. Define social insurance and distinguish social insurance from social security and most private insurance.
2. Determine whether a person is eligible for retirement, death, or disability benefits under OASDI and calculate the benefit amounts.
3. Explain the eligibility requirements and benefits provided by the two parts of Medicare.
4. Describe how the four components of OASDHI are funded and comment on their actuarial soundness.
5. Explain, for a typical state, who is eligible for unemployment insurance benefits and the amount and duration of the benefits provided.
6. Comment on the funding of state unemployment insurance benefits.

INTRODUCTION

Since the late nineteenth century, most industrialized nations have developed arrangements for providing some measure of economic security for their citizens. These programs have a profound impact upon organizational risk management because they address (principally) the human resource loss exposure area discussed in Chapter 7. Social insurance programs are important for other reasons as well. In most developed nations, employers are expected to contribute directly or indirectly to the financing of such programs, so organizations carry an externally imposed financial obligation that can be significant. Another reason for interest is the relationship between social insurance programs and employee benefit programs. The management of employee benefits requires an awareness of social insurance programs, because there are significant integration issues involved.

This chapter begins with a discussion of the concepts that underlie social insurance. What is it? How does it differ from private insurance and public assistance? What is its purpose? Then, the chapter turns to a presentation of three major social insurance programs in the United States. Some attention will be paid to programs in other nations, but the main purpose here is to illustrate social insurance in practice through a discussion of the Old-Age, Survivors, and Disability Insurance (OASDI) program, Medicare, and Unemployment Insurance. Workers' compensation, one of the most significant social insurance programs in most developed nations, is only mentioned briefly here. Workers' compensation has many unique properties and numerous specific issues and problems, and it is discussed separately in Chapter 23.

As this edition is going to print, the United States government is considering a major restructuring of health care financing and delivery, so readers and instructors using this book are cautioned to proceed carefully in the presentation of Medicare material. The authors have included some discussion of the issues likely to influence the Clinton administration's plan, but they expect that at present this discussion can be only general in approach.

WHAT IS SOCIAL INSURANCE?

The American Risk and Insurance Association (ARIA, the principal professional association of professors of risk management and insurance) has defined "social insurance" to include all insurance required by law for substantial numbers of the general population, administered or closely supervised by the government, and supported primarily by earmarked contributions, with a benefit structure that usually redistributes income to achieve some social objective, not private equity. Several features of this definition are worthy of a brief comment.

First, although all current social insurance programs deal with human resource risks, the concept could be extended in the future to property and liability risks. Indeed, some scholars would argue that no-fault automobile insurance is an existent illustration of social property and liability insurance. The national flood insurance and crime insurance programs in the United States and some other public property and liability insurance programs might also be identified as having some of the characteristics of social insurance. Social insurance programs historically have emphasized human resource risks because all members of society are likely to incur important economic losses occasioned by death, old age, poor health, or unemployment.

Second, the term "social insurance" is reserved for programs that apply to large segments of the general population and that are compulsory for most eligible persons. Plans established by the government solely for its present or former employees, such as the Civil Service Retirement System, are not considered social insurance. Federal government life insurance programs for veterans are omitted for the same reasons and because they are voluntary.

Third, although some government agency is commonly the insurer, the level of direct supervision by the government may be limited to the settlement of contested cases or checking compliance with insurance requirements, most of the daily operations being conducted by private insurers.

Fourth, although the definition does not rule out some financial support from general government funds, most of the financing comes from contributions made specifically for this purpose. Although others may sometimes make these contributions, usually they are paid for by employees or their employers.

Fifth, like all insurance, social insurance pools the risks associated with covered perils, such as death, poor health, and unemployment. In addition, social insurance benefit structures usually stress "social adequacy" rather than "private equity." Instead of relating the benefits for any individual directly to the contributions made by that person or by others in his or her behalf, the system usually favors some groups whom it is considered socially desirable to help. For example, the program may favor persons with low prior wages or a large number of dependents. As will be demonstrated, however, the United States has been reluctant to ignore completely private equity considerations.

SOCIAL SECURITY, SOCIAL INSURANCE, AND PUBLIC ASSISTANCE

Social insurance is part of a social security system. A "social security" system includes all government measures designed to protect its citizens against (1) perils such as death, poor health, unemployment, and superannuation, and (2) poverty and substandard wages, hours, or conditions of employment. A social security system includes loss-control measures (e.g., safety regulations, "full" employment measures, and public health activities) and transfers, of which social insurance is the principal example. The other major transfers included in the system are "public assistance" and "income supplements."

The major distinction between social insurance and public assistance is that public assistance benefits are paid, in principle, only to those persons who can demonstrate their individual need, and then only to the extent of that need. Public assistance programs are usually financed out of general revenues. Social insurance benefits, in contrast, do not require the demonstration of individual need and are usually related in some way, however imprecise, to contributions made by the beneficiary or made in his or her behalf. The two most important public assistance programs are (1) Aid to Families with Dependent Children (AFDC), a federal-state program that provides cash benefits to certain needy families with children; and (2) Medicaid, which provides important medical services to certain needy persons.

Income supplements are closely related to public assistance. Payments are based on need, but need is determined not through a demonstration of individual needs but by the difference between some guaranteed minimum income and the family's actual income. For example, under the Federal Supplemental Security Income program, aged, blind, and disabled persons are guaranteed a specified monthly income. The SSI payment is the difference between this amount and other income excluding (1) the first $20 of OASDHI or other income, and (2) the first $65 of earned monthly income plus one-half of any excess. In 1994 the guaranteed income is about $446 for an individual maintaining his or her own household, and $669 for a couple. SSI differs from a pure income supplement plan in that the recipients must also not have other resources, such as savings accounts, in excess of a specified amount.

IS SOCIAL INSURANCE "INSURANCE"?

One question that has generated considerable debate for many years is whether social insurance is "insurance." Many observers believe that the answer is clearly "no" with respect to many social insurance programs. They point to the emphasis upon social adequacy, the absence of a legal contract, and the method of financing, which often defers many of the costs to future generations. They believe that the benefits are better described as transfer payments from one sector of the population to another. They believe that public acceptance of social insurance programs is often influenced by the "halo effect" of the insurance label and that unfair comparisons are often drawn between the relative performance and efficiency of social insurance and of private insurance.

The answer to the question depends upon how one defines insurance. If an insurance program must possess all the characteristics typical of private insurance, social insurance is clearly not insurance, as will be demonstrated below. However, social insurance is a device for pooling and sharing the risks of death, old age, unemployment, and poor health. Consequently, it possesses the only necessary conditions for insurance specified in the definition given in Chapter 16.

Most private insurance, however, differs from social insurance in several important respects:

1. Each individual decides how much, if any, private insurance he or she wants to purchase. Employees, it is true, may have no choice under employee benefit plans, but the decision is made voluntarily by someone other than the insurer, for example, the employer or the union.
2. Benefits and premium rates are prescribed by a contract that cannot be changed except by mutual consent.
3. The benefits are related on an actuarial basis to the contributions paid, that is, private equity is an important goal of private insurance pricing.
4. Numerous insurers compete with one another for business.

Social insurance programs are compulsory for most people; benefits and contribution rates are prescribed by law but are subject to change; social adequacy is usually stressed; and although numerous private insurers may be involved, the program is often administered by a single government insurer.

Certain characteristics of social insurance enable it to encompass some risks, such as unemployment, that private insurers have been reluctant to write. The compulsory feature avoids adverse selection; the flexibility in benefits and contribution rates plus the compulsory feature enables the program to be adapted to changing conditions without losing any insureds.

REASONS FOR SOCIAL INSURANCE

The first major social insurance program in the United States, workers' compensation, is about 80 years old, but it was not until the Social Security Act of 1935 that the United States began to adopt an extensive social insurance system. The reasons for the various social insurance programs are not the same, but certain basic changes in the economy explain the increasing interest in the general concept of social security.

In a predominantly agricultural society, families were fairly self-sufficient, and were bound together by common interests. It was not too much of a burden for the family to maintain disabled, aged, widowed, orphaned, or unemployed family members. Because their needs were modest, they could perform some of the family household tasks, and there was usually ample space.

With increasing industrialization and urbanization, the picture changed. First, continued employment depended upon the ability of the employer to provide a job, and this ability, in turn, depended upon the functioning of a complex interdependent economy. Second, it created new occupational accidents and injuries, particularly around the turn of the century. Third, families became less self-sufficient. More and more household products and services were purchased from outsiders. An extra hand became less useful unless he or she added cash to the family budget. What is more important, the loss of the breadwinner's wage became a financial catastrophe. Fourth, families became more widely separated geographically (particularly in the United States, but also in Europe), and this separation, together with a divergence in interests among generations, tended to weaken family ties. Fifth, assisting an unfortunate family member became more burdensome because of smaller living quarters, increased obligations to children, and a desire to maintain or improve the standard of living of the immediate family.

Since it was less easy to turn to relatives in time of need, more families had to handle their risks themselves or turn to outsiders for assistance. Few families could accumulate enough assets in advance to meet the losses caused by death, poor health, unemployment, or superannuation. Private charities, churches, labor unions, fraternal organizations, and the like provided valuable but limited assistance. Private life insurance had been developing steadily in Europe since the early 1800s and in the United States since the American Civil War, but by the time of the Great Depression of the 1930s, most of the populations in developed nations had very limited coverage at best. The insurance protection against poor health and old age was even less effective; unemployment insurance was limited to some trade union plans and a few employer plans. Some persons could not afford private insurance protection; others were ineligible because of poor health; and still others did not appreciate their need for insurance. Government assistance during the nineteenth century and the early twentieth century took the form of poorhouses or "outdoor" relief for needy persons. The relief was either an outright grant in cash or services or was given in exchange for some services such as work on a public project. This meager assistance was usually provided by state or local governments.

By the close of the nineteenth century, the inability of many individual families to provide a minimum "floor of protection" for themselves and the dissatisfaction with the stigma associated with accepting relief caused Germany to adopt a fairly complete social insurance system. Great Britain acted during the first two decades of the present century. Other countries followed the lead of these two nations. The United States, however, did not adopt a comprehensive program until 1935.

The United States was slower to act for several reasons. First, the population enjoyed a more favorable economic status than did most developing and developed nations. Second, the United States stressed the freedom and responsibility of the individual for his or her own future. Third, the life insurance industry, although limited by today's standards, was more fully developed. Fourth, it was not clear whether the states or the national government should take the lead in developing social insurance. Fifth, states varied in their need for, and attitude toward, social insurance programs. Sixth, states feared that some businesses would leave or not enter their state if their taxes were higher than those of other states. The Great Depression, however, shook America's confidence in individual responsibility, made Americans more aware of the risks facing the population, and caused more people to turn to the federal government for assistance. Further industrialization and improved education also increased Americans' social conscience.

The Social Security Act of 1935 was a response to this important change in Americans' attitudes, but, as will become apparent in the discussion of the social insurance system, the circumstances that retarded the development of any social insurance system influenced the nature of the programs adopted. Since 1935, the factors favoring an extensive social insurance system have become more important. Until recently, as the economy prospered, Americans revised their standards for social insurance upward because the concept of a minimum floor of protection changed, and the ability to bear the taxes involved improved. During the past decade, as concern about the costs and financial solvency of the system increased, benefits in some component programs have been reduced. Social insurance, however, still provides an extremely important part of the average family's total insurance protection.

Although the preceding paragraphs offer a sufficient explanation for the passage of the Social Security Act, other reasons must be cited for the adoption of other social insurance programs. Workers' compensation, for example, arose out of dissatisfaction with the employers' liability method of handling industrial injuries and diseases. The Medicare program, established in 1965 (thus making OASDI the OASDHI program), reflected dissatisfaction in many quarters with the efforts of private health insurers to provide medical expense coverage for the aged.

SOCIAL INSURANCE SYSTEM OF THE UNITED STATES

A summary view of the social insurance system of the United States will help the reader to view each individual program in its proper perspective. The major social insurance programs providing protection for large segments of the general public against each of the four human resource perils included under these programs are as follows:

    I. Death
        A. Old-Age, Survivors and Disability Insurance (OASDI)
        B. Federal and state workers' compensation legislation (occupational death only)

II. Old Age
   A. Old-Age, Survivors and Disability Insurance
III. Poor Health
   A. Disability income benefits
      1. Old-Age, Survivors and Disability Insurance
      2. Federal and state workers' compensation legislation (occupational illness only)
      3. Temporary nonoccupational disability insurance legislation in Rhode Island, California, New Jersey, New York, and Hawaii
   B. Medical expense benefits
      1. Medicare—Hospital Insurance and Supplementary Medical Insurance
      2. Federal and state workers' compensation legislation (occupational illnesses only)
      3. Medical expense insurance plans in several states
IV. Unemployment
   A. State unemployment insurance

For purposes of simplification, only OASDI, Medicare, and Unemployment Insurance will be discussed here. As has been noted, workers' compensation is discussed in Chapter 23.

The Social Security Administration estimates that nearly 41 million Americans received benefits under the OASDI program in 1991. These individuals were paid $222.98 billion in benefits during that year, with average monthly benefits ranging from $583 for survivorship benefits to $629 for retirees. Medicare paid out over $118 billion in benefits during 1991, while total benefit payments for Unemployment Insurance were estimated at just over $20 billion. Workers' compensation, the only program of the four that is exclusively state-administered, paid over $37 billion in that same year.

These numbers do little to reveal the dynamic growth in expenditures since 1960. Table 22.1 indicates the dramatic expansion in expenditures (which includes administrative costs as well as benefit payments) that has occurred in OASDI, Medicare, Unemployment Insurance, and workers' compensation.

OLD-AGE, SURVIVORS AND DISABILITY INSURANCE

Old-Age, Survivors and Disability Insurance (OASDI), which technically consists of two programs—Old-Age and Survivors Insurance, and Disability Insurance—is one of the three components of Old-Age, Survivors, Disability, and Health Insurance (OASDHI). The other two parts are Hospital Insurance and Supplementary Medical Insurance—popularly known as Medicare. OASDHI was established under the Social Security Act of 1935 and its amendments. This act, which was a landmark in social legislation, also introduced a federal-state program of unemployment compensation; federal-state programs of public assistance to the needy aged, blind, disabled, and dependent children; and federal-state programs creating and extending public health services, health and welfare services for children, and vocational rehabilitation services. Although

TABLE 22.1. Expenditures for Selected Social Insurance Programs, 1960–1990 (in millions)

Programs	1960	1970	1980	1990
OASDI	11,032.3	29,686.2	117,118.9	245,555.5
Medicare	—	7,149.2	34,991.5	106,806.3
Unemployment Insurance	2,829.6	3,819.5	18,326.4	19,971.3
Workers' Compensation	1,308.5	2,950.4	13,457.2	37,358.9

Source: Social Security Administration, 1992.

these other programs are extremely important, OASDHI is by far the largest in scope.

OASDHI, which is frequently—thought incorrectly—referred to as "Social Security," has been amended numerous times since 1935. Originally the system was designed primarily to provide retirement benefits, but OASDHI today also provides death benefits (added in 1939), disability benefits (added in 1956) and hospital and health care benefits (added in 1965). The following discussion presents a general outline of the OASDHI system. Readers seeking greater detail are encouraged to examine books by George E. Rejda and Robert J. Myers (Rejda, 1991; Myers, 1985).

Eligibility Requirements

In order to receive benefits, a worker must have qualified by working in covered employment for a specified period of time. Over nine out of ten types of employment are covered on a compulsory basis. Student workers in institutions of learning, hospitals, college clubs, fraternities, or sororities are excluded. Railroad workers are protected by a separate federally operated Railroad Retirement System, but under some circumstances they may receive OASDI benefits in addition to or in lieu of the railroad retirement benefits. Ministers and members of religious orders and employees of state and local governments may be covered under the system under certain conditions. Self-employed persons, domestic workers, and farm laborers are covered on a compulsory basis if they earn at least some small specified amount.

To receive OASDI benefits, the worker usually must be "fully insured." To receive some death benefits, however, it is sufficient to be "currently insured." In order to explain the requirements of fully or currently insured status, the term "a quarter of coverage" must be defined. In 1994 a worker receives credit for one quarter of coverage for each $620 of annual earnings in covered employment. Each year the amount one must earn to receive credit for one quarter is increased to reflect changes in average national earnings. Not more than four quarters may be earned in any one year.

To be fully insured, a worker must have quarters of coverage equal to at least the number of years elapsing since 1950 or, if later, since the end of the year in which the worker was 21. However, the worker never needs more than 40 quarters of coverage and must have at least 6 quarters. For example, a worker aged 38 on January 7, 1993 is fully insured in 1993 if he or she has at least 16 quarters of coverage. To be currently insured, a worker must have at least 6 quarters of coverage among the last 13 quarters, including the current quarter.

To receive disability benefits a worker must, in addition to being fully insured, have at least 20 quarters of coverage in the 40 calendar quarters prior to his or her disability. Blind persons and workers disabled before age 31 can qualify with less than 20 quarters of coverage.

Benefits

Benefits are paid if the worker (1) retires, (2) dies, or (3) is totally disabled for a long period (HI, Medicare, will be discussed shortly).

Retirement. The basic benefit is a monthly retirement income for life to a worker age 65 or over. The worker may elect to retire as early as age 62, but the benefit is reduced. The retirement income is equal to the worker's primary insurance amount (PIA), which usually depends upon the worker's average indexed monthly earnings (AIME) during the period beginning with 1956 or the year in which he or she became 27, if later, and ending with the year before he or she becomes (or would have become) age 62, dies, or becomes disabled, whichever happens first. The earnings counted in computing this average are unlikely to be the worker's actual earnings over this period for several reasons. First, the earnings each year are limited to the amount subject to an OASDI tax over the period. For instance, in 1994 the wage base is $60,600 (as a point of reference, the wage base was $3600 in 1954, $4800 in 1965, $14,100 in 1975, and $39,600 in 1985). Each year the wage base is adjusted with changes in average national earnings.

Second, the earnings each year (limited to the wage base) are indexed or adjusted to reflect changes in average national earnings from that year to the second last year of the base period. To illustrate, if average earnings that year had increased by 50 percent over that time span, the worker's earnings that year will be increased 50 percent. The earnings during the last year of the base period are not adjusted. Third, the worker can substitute years before or after the base period for years within the period if he or she would benefit from the change.

For workers who were age 62 prior to 1979, a method that is being phased out is used to calculate the primary insurance amount. For workers age 62 in 1984 or later a decoupled formula method is used. For workers who reached age 62 during 1979 to 1983 inclusive, a transitional guarantee method is used that gives the worker the higher of two benefits—one determined using the decoupled formula and the other using a modification of the old formula. Only the decoupled formula method will be discussed here.

Under this method, the PIA formula used to calculate retirement benefits depends upon the year in which the worker was age 62. For example, for workers who reached age 62 in 1991, the PIA formula used if they retired at age 65 in 1994 would be as follows:

90 percent of the first $422 of the AIME plus
32 percent of the next $2123 plus
15 percent of the excess

multiplied by a factor that represents the cumulative increases in the Consumer Price Index (CPI) from 1990 to 1993. For example, if this factor is 1.15 and the AIME is $1000, the PIA will be 1.15 times $565 (rounded up from $564.76), or $650 ($649.75). The PIA is computed: $[(0.9)(\$422) + (0.32)(\$578)]$. In December of 1994, the benefit is increased automatically to match the increase in the CPI from the third quarter of 1993 to the third quarter of 1994. Each December thereafter these workers will receive similar automatic adjustments for changes in the CPI.

The PIA increases, but not proportionately, with the AIME. This feature of the OASDI benefit formula is widely misunderstood, so an illustration is useful. Imagine two workers (age 62 in 1991) who are identical in every respect except that worker A has an AIME of $2000 while worker B has an AIME of $1000. Their benefits are computed as follows:

Worker A benefit $= [(0.9)(\$422) + (0.32)(\$1578)] = \$884.76$

Worker B benefit $= [(0.9)(\$422) + (0.32)(\$578)] = \$564.76$

Each figure is then multiplied by the CPI adjustment (1.15; see above) resulting in a benefit of $1017.47 for Worker A and $649.75 for Worker B.

A's benefit is larger in real terms, but as a percentage of the AIME, A's benefit is smaller.

Worker A's benefit as a percentage of AIME $= \$1017.47 / \$2000 = 50.87$ percent

Worker B's benefit as a percentage of AIME $= \$649.75 / \$1000 = 64.98$ percent

The PIA benefit formula represents a compromise between the desire to provide socially adequate benefits for all workers and the wish to preserve some elements of private equity. This formula changes every year. The PIA "bend points" (90, 32, and 15 percent) do not change, but the dollar amounts are adjusted to match increases in average national earnings. The CPI multiplication factor is also updated.

As was noted, workers may choose to retire earlier than age 65 (as early as 62) but their benefit is adjusted downward. For each month the worker retires prior to age 65, the PIA is reduced 5/9 of 1 percent. Thus, if the worker retires at age 62, the reduction is 20 percent. If the worker retires after age 65, the PIA is increased. Until recently, that increase was a maximum of 3 percent per year (more on this shortly).

Under certain conditions, the spouse and children of retired workers are eligible for dependents' benefits. These benefits, which are expressed as a percentage of the PIA, are summarized in Table 22.2. The total monthly benefits paid to one family are limited to a specified maximum that is a function of the PIA. This maximum varies between 150 percent and 188 percent of the PIA.

The family of a retired worker, age 65 or over, will lose in benefits one-half the amount that the worker earns after retirement in excess of a specified amount ($11,160 in 1994). However, no reduction in benefits is made if the worker is age 70 or over. If other members of the family earn more than the threshold earnings amount, only their own benefits are reduced. However, for beneficiaries under age 65 the limit is less—$8040 in 1994.

Until 1984, OASDI benefits were not subject to federal income taxes. Now

TABLE 22.2. OASDI Dependents' Retirement Benefits

Type of benefit	Amount expressed as a percentage of the worker's PIA
Monthly life income for spouse age 62 or over	50, reduced by 25/36 of 1% for each month benefit starts before 65th birthday
Monthly income for dependent children to age 18	50 for each child
Monthly income for spouse until youngest dependent child is age 16	50

half of the OASDI benefit is taxable unless it is more than half of the amount by which the adjusted gross income (including for this purpose interest on tax-free municipal bonds) plus one-half the OASDI benefit exceeds a specified base amount. For individuals, this base amount is $25,000; for married couples filing joint returns the base amount is $32,000. If half the OASDI benefit is more than half of the excess amount, only half of this excess amount is taxable. For many persons, therefore, none of the benefits are taxed. The income taxes collected on these benefits are earmarked for transfer to the OASDI trust funds.

Death. The survivorship benefits that are payable in case the insured worker dies are presented in Table 22.3. The worker's PIA is computed using the AIME up to the year the worker died and the PIA formula in effect that year. The family maximum discussed in connection with the retirement benefits also applies here, as does the earnings test. Two points that deserve special emphasis are (1) the magnitude of the survivorship benefits for a young person with a large family, and (2) the gap that exists in the protection between the times when the youngest child attains age 18 and the surviving spouse reaches age 60.

TABLE 22.3. OASDI Survivorship Benefits

Type of benefit	Amount expressed as a percentage of the worker's PIA
Monthly life income for surviving spouse age 60 or over	100, reduced by 19/40 of 1% for each month benefit starts prior to spouse's 65th birthday
Monthly income for dependent children to age 18	75 for each child
Monthly income for surviving spouse until youngest dependent child is age 16	75
Monthly life income for dependent parent age 62 or over	75 for each parent; 82.5 if only one parent
Lump-sum payment to surviving spouse or to person who paid burial expenses	$225

Disability. The major disability benefits are a disability "freeze" and disability income payments. To receive these two benefits, the worker must be unable to engage in any substantially gainful activity, the disability must have lasted at least 5 months, and the condition must be expected to result in death or to continue for at least 12 calendar months. Readers should note that this is a much more restrictive definition of disability than would be seen in most individual or group disability insurance policies—indeed, is more restrictive than most workers' compensation definitions as well.

The first benefit freezes the workers' earnings record as of the date of disability. In other words, the worker's insured status for retirement and survivor's benefits and the average monthly wage are determined by ignoring the time during which the worker was disabled.

The second benefit provides an income for the disabled worker, dependent children, and the worker's spouse (until the youngest dependent child is aged 16) beginning after the worker has completed five months of disability. The benefit amounts are usually determined in the same way as the retirement benefit amounts except that the maximum family benefit may be less and no adjustment is made for early retirement. The worker receives the PIA. The benefit for each child is 50 percent of this amount and the spouse's benefit is another 50 percent. At age 65, the disability payments cease and the retirement payments begin.

Future Changes and Changes Already Enacted

The Social Security amendments of 1983 introduced several benefit changes that have occurred since that date or will occur in the future. Some of the more important changes arising from the 1983 amendments are:

1. For persons reaching age 62 during 2000 to 2005, the retirement age at which full benefits will be paid will be increased by two months a year until it reaches age 66, at which age it will remain for persons reaching age 62 during 2006 to 2016. For those persons reaching age 62 during 2017 to 2022, the retirement age will again be increased two months a year until it reaches age 67, at which age it will remain for future retirees.
2. Early retirement will still be permitted as early as age 62 but, when the normal retirement age rises above age 65, the percentage reduction for retirement that early will be larger.
3. Since 1990, the delayed retirement benefit has begun gradually increasing at a rate which will, in the year 2008, mean that the pre-1990 annual benefit increase of 3 percent will then be 8 percent.
4. If, at the beginning of the year, the balance of the OASDI Trust Funds is less than 20 percent of the expected disbursements that year, the annual automatic benefit adjustment will be the lower of (1) the increase in the Consumer Price Index or (2) the increase in average national earnings.
5. Since 1990, the earnings test for beneficiaries ages 65 to 69 has been revised so that OASDI benefits will be decreased by $1 for each $3 earned above the specified dollar limits instead of each $2.

Taxes

Employees and their employers contribute equally to the cost of OASDI. A self-employed person pays both the employer and the employee contributions. The employer contribution is deductible as a business expense. The present tax rate is 6.2 percent from both the employer and the employee for a combined contribution rate of 12.2 percent (this does not include taxes for Medicare, which is discussed below).

These taxes are not levied on all income, but rather on income only up to the maximum taxable wage base, which changes each year with changes in average national wages. As was noted earlier, in 1994 all wages up to $60,600 are subject to the OASDI tax.

Funding

Congress has expressed its intent to maintain OASDI on a self-supporting basis. The tax schedule is designed to achieve this result for at least the next 75 years, if many underlying assumptions regarding mortality, interest rates, total employment, and the like are satisfied.

The taxes deemed necessary to meet the administrative expenses and the costs of the retirement benefits, the death benefits, and some disability benefits such as the "freeze" are placed in the Old-Age and Survivors Insurance Trust Fund. The remainder is placed in the Disability Insurance Trust Fund. Most of the assets remaining after current expenditures are invested in interest-bearing government securities.

The program is not "fully funded," a term used in pension management (see Chapters 24 and 25) to reflect a plan in which funds sufficient to pay for all future obligations already incurred are held in reserve. If OASDI were to cease operations today, the money in the trust funds would not be enough to support the continued benefits to those already receiving them and to return a "fair" amount to other contributors. In fact, if the program were to be terminated today, payments to persons already receiving benefits could not be continued for more than a year or two. Historically, the intent was to maintain the program on a "pay-as-you-go" basis with a small trust fund. So long as the system operates indefinitely, a "full reserve" is not required for the plan to meet its obligations on a self-supporting basis. In fact, it can be argued that a full reserve would be unwise for various reasons, one of which would be the excuse it would offer for unwarranted liberalization of benefits. However, as is noted below, the 1983 amendments produced rapidly growing trust fund balances (surplus over outgo), which has moved OASDI away somewhat from the pay-as-you-go concept—with, it might be added, interesting effects.

Issues

Only a sample of the many issues surrounding OASDI can be discussed here. These issues are categorized according to whether they affect coverage, benefits, or financing.

Because most employments are now covered under OASDI, much less pressure exists than in the past for the inclusion of new occupations. The Social Security Act amendments of 1983 added newly hired federal civilian employees and the employees of nonprofit organizations. The only major group still not included on a compulsory basis is state and local government employees.

Several features of the benefit structure are highly controversial. First, the balance between social adequacy and private equity implicit in the present benefit structure is not acceptable to many. One proposal, not seriously considered at this time, is that all beneficiaries receive the same benefit, regardless of their past earnings. At the other extreme, a few critics argue that benefits should be related proportionately to average monthly earnings. Between these two extremes there are numerous possible positions. The desired relationship between benefits and contributions depends, among other things, on one's preferred balance between public and private responsibility for protection above the minimum benefit level, one's concept of a fair redistribution of income, and one's degree of concern about possible adverse effects upon the private insurance business.

Second, the earnings test that causes beneficiaries earning more than a certain amount a year to lose benefits or to receive reduced benefits has been attacked on the ground that it forces some able aged persons out of the labor force or prevents them from obtaining benefits to which they are allegedly entitled because they have paid for them through contributions to the program. The test is also considered unfair because it considers only wages and salaries, not interest and dividends. Removing the test, however, would increase the cost of the program to meet what many consider to be a relatively unimportant need.

Third, although most of the differences in treatment of men and women have been removed, several additional changes have been proposed. For example, homemakers (usually women), it is often argued, should be permitted to pay OASDI taxes on the imputed value of their services. Another suggestion would give the homemaker credit for one-half the spouse's earnings, the other one-half being credited to the spouse. Each member of a two-wage-earner couple would receive credits based on one-half their combined earnings.

One important financing issue is whether contributions should be increased by raising the earnings base or the contribution rate. In deciding between these two alternatives, a major consideration is the relative impact upon high- and low-paid workers. It is also argued that a high earnings base would permit the program to capture more contributions in periods of economic prosperity and to reduce contributions in periods of economic decline. The most controversial proposal is the use of general revenues to pay part of the cost of the system. Because of the windfall benefits provided many aged persons during the early years of the program, and the emphasis upon socially adequate benefits for workers with low earnings or many dependents, the contributions paid by many young workers and their employers have reached the level at which they could be used to obtain superior benefits from private insurers, assuming no further liberalizations in the benefits. To correct this situation and to make possible some benefit increases and other liberalizations, it has been suggested that some specific fraction of the cost of the benefits be financed out of general revenues. The fundamental principle of contribution-related benefits would be retained and benefit liberalization would require increased contributions. In opposition, it has been argued that employer contributions are not made in behalf of their own employees but as their share of the cost of the entire program, that it is unfair to shift the burden of OASDI benefits to general revenues, that benefits will be unduly liberalized when the new funds are made available, and that the role of general revenues will be expanded beyond the proposed one-third. As indicated earlier, the 1983 amendments introduced an earmarked federal income tax on benefits which generates some indirect general revenue financing.

Changing demographic and economic trends resulted in what was termed the Social Security financing crisis during the early 1970s. The system faced a serious cash flow during the remainder of the decade and a predicted deficit on the average over the next 75 years. The Social Security amendments of 1983 raised taxes and lowered some benefits to deal with this problem.

Ironically, the measures taken to resolve the solvency problems have created several new issues for the OASDI program. First, the raising of taxes was undertaken in part to "prefund" some of the benefits that would be paid when "baby boomers" begin retiring after the year 2010. While OASDI has typically had a surplus, this adjustment has created a very large surplus in a short period of time. For instance, between 1984 and September of 1993 the OASDI Trust Fund balances have grown from $27.1 billion (OASI) and $3.9 billion (DI) to $355.6 billion (OASI) and $10.3 billion (DI) (Social Security Administration, 1994). Although this change can be justified in political and actuarial terms, it has moved OASDI away from its pay-as-you-go philosophy.

Second, since surpluses are "invested" in government paper, the profound growth of these fund balances has influenced both overall government spending and the overall tax burden on citizens. Essentially, trust fund surpluses have been used to finance general federal government spending, which some argue has promoted an expansion of government programs. Further, since income tax rates declined in the 1980s, it is argued that Social Security taxes (which increased during that time period), have, in effect, replaced income tax revenues as a general government funding source. Since upper income tax rates were most dramatically reduced, there is a resultant tax burden shift away from higher-income Americans to lower-income Americans (since the OASDI tax is only levied on incomes below the tax base).

Third, at a time of severe budgetary crisis in the federal government, the presence of large surpluses has muddied the debate over budgetary reform. As a result, some observers argue that OASDI should return to its original pay-as-you-go approach, with future generations paying higher rates during the baby boom retirement years. Some others argue that the trust funds should be invested in the private sector. Regardless of the argument for or against the surpluses, they are a temporary phenomenon, for they will begin to disappear after 2010 as the funds will be used to finance the benefits payable at that time.

MEDICARE

Medicare consists of two components: Hospital Insurance (HI), also known as Medicare Part A, and Supplementary Medical Insurance, also known as

Medicare Part B. Medicare was established under a 1965 amendment to the Social Security Act.

Hospital Insurance

All employments covered under OASDI plus railroad employment are covered under the HI program. Benefits are paid to aged and disabled persons meeting certain requirements. OASDI and Railroad Retirement System beneficiaries, age 65 or over, are eligible for HI benefits. Also eligible are those aged persons who would be receiving OASDI benefits except for the fact that their current earnings cause them to lose their benefits. As a transitional feature, benefits are also paid to most other persons age 65 or over before 1968. Persons age 65 after 1967 but before 1973 (1971 for women) must have some quarters of coverage but they need not be fully or currently insured. Aged persons who do not otherwise qualify can enroll voluntarily by paying the full cost of their coverage.

Disabled OASDI and Railroad Retirement System beneficiaries become eligible for these benefits after they have been entitled to disability benefits for at least 24 months. The OASDI beneficiaries include disabled workers, disabled widows or widowers, and disabled child beneficiaries. Fully or currently insured persons and their dependents with chronic kidney disease who need dialysis or transplants are also covered.

The program provides (1) hospital benefits, (2) skilled nursing facility benefits, (3) home health services benefits, and (4) hospice care. The hospital benefits include such items as room and board in a semi-private room, general nursing services, operating room, laboratory tests and x-rays, drugs, dressings, and the services of interns and residents in training. The maximum duration is 90 days in a single "spell of illness," which begins on the first day that the person receives hospital or skilled nursing facility services and ends when a person has not been in any hospital or skilled nursing facility for 60 consecutive days. Each person also has a "lifetime reserve" of 60 additional benefit days, which can be used to supplement the 90 days provided for each spell of illness. However, those days are not replenished with each new spell of illness. Thus, if during a particular spell of illness a person draws on 5 days from the lifetime reserve, that person will have only 55 reserve days available for future spells of illness.

HI imposes cost-sharing provisions on beneficiaries in the form of deductibles and a type of copayment (Medicare refers to all cost sharing provisions as "deductibles"). These deductibles and copayments are based upon the average cost of a single day's stay in a hospital, and, consequently, are changed each year to reflect the changing average. For instance, a deductible equal to that single day average cost is required for each spell of illness requiring hospitalization. In 1994 that deductible is $696. If hospitalization extends beyond 60 days (that is, extends into days 61 to 90) a per day copayment set at one-fourth of the deductible is required of the beneficiary. In 1994, that per day copayment was $174. If lifetime reserve days are used, a per day copayment equal to one-half the deductible is imposed ($348 in 1994).

Similar services are covered in a skilled nursing facility after the person has been in the hospital for at least three days (thus incurring the initial deductible) and, although not well, no longer needs intensive hospital care. The maximum duration is 100 days in a spell of illness. If the stay extends beyond day 20 (that is, into days 21 to 100) there is a per day copayment equal to one-eight of the deductible ($87 in 1994).

Home health services following hospitalization include such items as part-time visiting nursing care and use of medical appliances but not full-time nursing care or drugs. No limit is placed on the number of home health visits.

Hospice care services are provided for terminally ill beneficiaries. The coverage consists of two 90-day benefit periods, a subsequent 30-day extension, and the potential for an unlimited further extension.

The transitional benefits for aged persons not covered under OASDI are financed through general revenues, but most HI benefits are financed through a contribution rate levied on wages. The contribution rates are scheduled to remain at 1.45 percent for employees, 1.45 percent for employers, and 2.90 percent for self-employed persons. Notably the maximum taxable wage base for HI is not the same as it is for OASDI ($60,600 in 1994). Rather, in 1994 and thereafter, there is no maximum—all wages are subject to the HI tax. These contributions are appropriated to a Hospital Insurance Trust Fund from which benefits and expenses are paid.

An unusual feature of this program is the involvement of private insurers in the administration of the program. Each hospital or other provider or services can deal directly with the federal government, but most have elected to receive their payments through a fiscal intermediary approved by the federal government—usually a Blue Cross association. These fiscal intermediaries are reimbursed for their reasonable costs of administration. The experience of these agencies in dealing with overutilization of services and excessive charges was partially responsible for involving them in the program. Hospitals and other agencies are themselves required to meet certain standards and to take steps to discourage overutilization of their services. Professional standards review organizations (PSRO), composed of practicing physicians in the local area, are responsible for a comprehensive, ongoing review of the services provided under both parts of Medicare.

Until the Social Security amendments of 1983, hospitals and other providers of services were reimbursed on the basis of the "reasonable cost" of providing those services, not their charges, unless these charges were less. The 1983 amendments introduced a prospective payments plan that establishes standard payment amounts for 467 categories of hospital treatment. Under this approach hospitals have a strong incentive to provide these services for less than the standard payment amounts.

Supplementary Medical Insurance

Unlike the other OASDHI programs, Supplementary Medical Insurance (SMI) is voluntary. Subject to certain exceptions, all aged persons are eligible to participate. However, in order to avoid adverse selection against the program, persons wishing to participate must elect coverage during specified enrollment periods. Also eligible are the OASDI and Railroad Retirement System disability beneficiaries and persons needing kidney transplantation or dialysis who qualify for hospital insurance.

The benefits include doctors' services, certain medical services and supplies, such as artificial limbs and ambulance services, and the home health services covered under HI, but the patient need not be hospitalized first to receive these services. Except for a special limit on the treatment of mental disorders, no limit is placed on the protection afforded. However, there is a deductible equal to the first $100 of expenses incurred in a calendar year plus 20 percent of the excess.

In 1994, participants pay a $41.10 monthly premium, which is much more than matched by the federal government out of general revenues. These moneys are appropriated to a Supplementary Medical Insurance Trust Fund. Because these premiums are based upon short-range cost estimates, they are subject to annual change.

Like HI, SMI involves private agencies in its administration, commonly a commercial insurer. However, unlike HI, SMI provides two methods for paying doctors' bills. The doctor, like the hospitals under HI, may submit the claim directly to the fiscal agency, in which case he or she must accept the SMI payment as the total fee. The SMI payment is limited to the charges made by most physicians in the locality for such services. If the doctor refuses to submit his or her bill to the administering agency or the patient prefers this approach, the patient can submit an itemized bill, paid or unpaid, for reimbursement. If the doctor's charges exceed the SMI payment, the patient is responsible for the excess.

NATIONAL HEALTH INSURANCE PROPOSALS

Interest in a national health insurance scheme has ebbed and flowed since at least the 1930s. The presidential election of 1992 provided a forum for a renewed interest in a solution to the numerous problems associated with the health care delivery and financing systems, and Governor Bill Clinton's election signaled the beginning of an active federal government effort to attack the "health care crisis." "Crisis" is, perhaps, an overused word, but most Americans agree that there is a problem with health care in the United States. Often cited evidence of the problems include:

1. An inflation rate for health care services that is consistently at least twice the overall inflation rate for the economy.
2. An estimated 12.5 to 13 percent of the nation's GNP finances health care consumption; a figure that is considerably larger than any other developed nation (European nations with national health care schemes spend anywhere from 6.5 to 9.5 percent of GNP).
3. An estimated 33 to 37 million Americans who are uninsured at any given time, and at least that many more who are "underinsured."
4. A failure of American health care to meet international standards of performance in baseline health care outcomes: life expectancy, infant mortality, childhood immunization penetration, and so on.

5. Apparent inefficiencies in a system that is partly socialized, partly private, and that often involves complex financing arrangements to pay for services consumed.

Various proposals have been given for restructuring health care in America. Some have proposed national health care schemes similar to those in Great Britain and Sweden, in which the national government is the provider of health care services. Some have suggested that Canada's system, which combines public and private delivery and financing, is more appropriate. Some believe that the government should be almost entirely outside the health care system.

Health care reform is likely to take a distinctively American form, which is to say that it will reflect the federal nature of the political system, the geographic spread of the nation, the emphasis on private sector solutions, and the demographic diversity of the population.

UNEMPLOYMENT INSURANCE

As was stated earlier, the Social Security Act of 1935 introduced a system of grants to states that had unemployment insurance programs. Wisconsin and New York were the only states with programs at the time the act was passed, although a few other states had legislation that was not yet effective. This situation soon changed because of the nature of the federal legislation. By 1937, all states had unemployment insurance systems.

The Role of the Federal Government

The Social Security Act levied a 3 percent payroll tax on all employers of eight or more persons, but the legislation did not apply to certain types of employment, such as domestic service, agricultural work, casual labor, work for most nonprofit organizations, and government employment. The employer could credit against this tax his or her contributions to an approved state program (including any reduction in these contributions as a result of experience rating), but the credit could not exceed 90 percent of the federal tax. For example, if the state tax was 2.7 percent, the effective federal tax was only 0.3 percent. If the state had no unemployment insurance program, the federal tax would be 3 percent. Essentially, the same rules apply today, except that as a result of several amendments, the tax is now levied on employers of one or more workers in each of 20 days in a year or who have a payroll of $1500 in a calendar quarter. Agricultural workers and domestic servants are now covered subject to some special wage requirements. The federal tax still does not apply to nonprofit organizations or services for a state or local government, but the federal tax rate is not reduced by the state tax unless the state plan covers most employees in these two categories. The federal tax rate is 6.2 percent applied to the first $7000 of an employee's wages. The maximum offset for contributions to an approved state program is 5.4 percent. The present effective federal tax then is 0.8 percent. The federal tax rate will be reduced to 6.0 percent (and effective federal tax of 0.6 percent) when the federal account has repaid moneys it borrowed from the

United States Treasury in the mid-1970s to pay temporary extended benefits in addition to the permanent program described below.

The incentive to establish a state unemployment program was further strengthened by the fact that the federal government uses its tax income to defray the administration costs of the state systems. The remainder is used to establish a fund from which states may, under certain conditions, obtain loans and to pay its share of the extended benefits described below.

The federal government does not prescribe any eligibility requirements or benefit levels for approved plans, but it does require that benefits shall not be denied to any person who refuses employment that (1) is available because of a labor dispute, (2) requires or prohibits union membership, or (3) is subject to substandard conditions. Benefits must be paid through public employment offices. In periods when state insured unemployment rates exceed specified amounts (6 percent or 5 percent and at least 1.2 times the rate in the two preceding calendar years), states must increase the maximum number of weeks an unemployed worker will receive benefits by 50 percent. The maximum extension required is 13 weeks; the combined regular and extended benefit period, however, need not exceed 39 weeks. The federal government reimburses the states for one-half the cost of benefits in excess of 26 weeks (up to a maximum of 13 weeks) for benefits paid during an extended benefit period.

Another important requirement is that the state taxes be placed in an unemployment trust fund maintained by the federal government but in which a separate account is established for each state. Withdrawals from the fund are to be used almost exclusively for unemployment benefits to insureds. Under some conditions, some of the state moneys may be used to pay administrative expenses, but the bulk of these expenses are met by the federal grants.

States can experience-rate employers under plans meeting minimum federal standards.

State Programs

State unemployment insurance programs vary greatly with respect to coverage, qualifying requirements, benefit levels, and financing. Only a brief summary of the major provisions is presented here.

Coverage. State plans must cover the employees subject to the federal tax plus those that must be covered for federal approval. In addition, many states reduce the 20-day or $1500 payroll required. They may also cover additional types of employment.

Eligibility for Benefits. To be eligible for benefits, a worker must first demonstrate an attachment to the labor force. In most states, this attachment is demonstrated by having earned certain minimum wages (usually some multiple such as 1.5 times the high-quarter earnings) during a base period, which is generally the first four of the last five completed calendar quarters prior to the date a claim is filed. In addition, the worker must be unemployed (or working less than full time and earning less than some specified amount), must (except in a few states) be physically able to work, and must be available for work, that is, must be willing and able to take any suitable employment. In many states, the worker must, in addition, be actively seeking work. In all states, the worker must register for work with the state employment service. The benefits may be postponed or reduced if the worker leaves a job voluntarily without good cause, is fired because of misconduct, refuses suitable work, is idle because of a labor dispute, misrepresents the facts to receive benefits to which he or she is not entitled, or receives other forms of income, such as wages in lieu of notice, dismissal payments, workers' compensation benefits, OASDI benefits, or a pension. Benefits are postponed in many states for some of these causes instead of being canceled for the duration of the workers' unemployment on the theory that after the passage of the postponement period, the person's unemployment is not attributable to the reason for which he or she was disqualified. The most severe penalty is cancellation of the worker's wage credits during the base period, which might prevent the worker from collecting benefits from a second spell of unemployment because he or she would not be able to demonstrate attachment to the labor force.

Benefits. Most states require that an unemployed person be unemployed for one week before benefits are payable. However, once a person has satisfied this waiting period requirement, he or she need not satisfy it again with respect to future spells of unemployment during a "benefit year." A benefit year is usually the year beginning with the date the person files an unemployment claim.

About two-thirds of the states relate the worker's benefit during a benefit year to his or her earnings during that calendar quarter of the worker's base period in which he or she had the highest earnings. About one-third of these states multiply these high-quarter earnings by 1/26, which would give a worker with 13 full weeks of employment about 50 percent of his or her average weekly wage as a benefit. About half the states basing benefits on high-quarter earnings use larger fractions to allow for some periods of unemployment during the base quarter. All but one of the remaining high-quarter-earnings states use a lower fraction for persons with high earnings than for those with low earnings. The remaining state pays half of the full-time average weekly wage in the high-earnings quarter. The other jurisdictions relate their benefit to the workers' earnings during the entire base period. Thirteen states pay additional weekly allowances for dependents.

The benefits developed by these formulas are subject to both minimum and maximum limits. More than two-thirds of the states have maximums ranging from 48 to 70 percent of the statewide average weekly wage.

Some jurisdictions pay benefits for a uniform period, usually 26 weeks, during a benefit year to all unemployed workers. The remainder limit the maximum duration in two ways. First, they specify some maximum period, usually 26 weeks. Second, if this would produce a shorter period, they either limit (1) the maximum dollar payout to some fraction, such as one-third or a fraction that declines as the earnings increase, of the base-period wages, or (2) the maximum number of weeks to some fraction, such as three-fourths of the number of weeks of employment in the base period. As required by federal law, all jurisdictions provide for extended benefits, usually by 50 percent up to a maximum of 39 weeks, when unemployment in the state reaches a specified level.

Some states impose special requirements on seasonal workers. For example, wage credits earned in seasonal employment may be counted only in connection with unemployment during the operating season. Unlike workers' compensation benefits, unemployment benefits are subject to federal income tax.

Financing. In all but three states, employers pay the entire cost of the program. In some states, the taxable wage base is higher than the $7000 federal base. In a few cases, this base is tied to the state average wage. Most states have a standard tax rate of 5.4 percent, but in all states, the rates paid by employers depend upon their experience and the status of the state unemployment trust fund. When the state fund is in its most favorable condition, the minimum rates range as low as 0 percent in several states to 1.2 percent. Under the least favorable state fund condition, maximum state rates range as high as 10.5 percent in one state. Some states have substantial balances in the Unemployment Trust Fund; others have less than the maximum amount they have paid in a 12-month period. Some states currently have a deficit account because of moneys they borrowed earlier from the fund. In states that run a deficit for two years in a row, the federal unemployment tax is higher than the 0.8 percent collected in other states.

Some Important Issues

Unemployment compensation plans have been subjected to much criticism in recent years. Some of the major issues are described briefly here.

Since unemployment is in many respects a national problem, it is argued that one federal system should replace the heterogeneous state plans. A radical suggestion is that state plans be required to meet certain federal standards. In opposition to these arguments, it is claimed that the state plans have performed satisfactorily and that federal intervention would ignore local conditions and needs and violate states' rights.

State plans have been criticized for basing eligibility on work during too distant a base period and for setting too high a requirement. The maximum weekly benefits are said to be too low, forcing too many workers to receive less than 50 percent of their lost wages. Basing maximum duration on wages earned during the base period has, it is alleged, resulted in inadequate benefits for many workers, particularly low-income workers. On the other hand, the plans may be too liberal with respect to part-time workers and similar groups who may obtain the benefits designed for low-income full-time workers. The 50 percent goal itself has been questioned as being over generous because it was established at a time when income tax rates were much lower, but this criticism preceded the income taxation of unemployment insurance benefits.

Because the program must be administered with discretion, the state administrations have been called too restrictive by some and too lax by others.

The financing of the plans has been a prime target for criticism. The financial status of the plans as a result of low tax rates and some recent recessions is a matter of universal concern. The logic behind a taxable wage base that is much lower than the OASDI wage base has been questioned. The merits of experience rating have been debated at length. Critics argue that (1) a single employer has little control over his or her unemployment rate, (2) some employers fire employees before they become eligible for benefits in order to cut their losses or deny claims of eligible employees, and (3) experience rating feeds inflation and deepens depressions by producing low rates during boom periods and high rates during recessions. Several technical questions have been raised concerning the application of experience rating. The principle pro arguments are that experience rating provides an incentive for employers to stabilize employment and penalizes employers who contribute to unemployment. Indeed, it is sometimes argued that rates should be even higher for those with high unemployment.

Key Concepts

social insurance All insurance required by law for substantial numbers of the general population, administered or closely supervised by the government, and supported primarily by earmarked contributions, with a benefit structure that usually redistributes income to achieve some social objective, not private equity.

social security system All government measures designed to protect its citizens against (1) human resource risks and (2) poverty and substandard conditions. Social insurance is one part of a social security system.

Old-Age, Survivors, Disability, and Health Insurance (OASDHI) The major social insurance program of the United States established by the Social Security Act of 1935 and greatly expanded since that time. The program has four components with separate trust funds—Old Age and Survivors Insurance, Disability Insurance, Hospital Insurance (Medicare Part A) and Supplementary Medical Insurance (Medicare Part B).

unemployment insurance In the United States, a joint federal-state program that provides certain benefits for individuals experiencing periods of unemployment. Like OASDHI, the statutory roots of Unemployment Insurance is the Social Security Act of 1935.

Review Questions

1. Is social insurance "insurance?" Explain your reasoning.
2. Distinguish among social insurance, social security, and public assistance.
3. Social insurance programs have often been criticized on the ground that they are not actuarially fair. Explain this criticism.
4. How would you determine whether a person was fully insured under OASDI? currently insured?
5. Is OASDI "actuarially sound"?
6. Identify some of the leading current issues with respect to OASDI, and discuss the arguments presented in connection with each issue.
7. Compare Hospital Insurance and Supplementary Medical Insurance with respect to
   a. eligibility requirements
   b. benefits
   c. financing.
8. What is the role of the federal government with respect to unemployment insurance?
9. Comment on each of the following criticisms of state unemployment insurance programs:
   a. The eligibility and benefit provisions favor secondary wage earners, such as part-time and seasonal workers.

b. The maximum weekly benefits are too low.

c. The system encourages strikes and quitting without good cause.

d. The system does not protect the worker against long-term unemployment.

References and Suggestions for Additional Reading

MYERS, R. J.: *Social Security* (3rd ed., Homewood, Ill.: Richard D. Irwin, Inc., 1985).

REJDA, G. E.: *Social Insurance and Economic Security* (4th ed., Englewood Cliffs, N.J.: Prentice-Hall, Inc., 1991).

Report of the National Commission on Social Security Reform (Washington, D.C., January, 1983).

SOCIAL SECURITY ADMINISTRATION: *Social Security Bulletin* (Washington, D.C., published quarterly).

SOCIAL SECURITY ADMINISTRATION: *Social Security Bulletin: Annual Statistical Supplement* (Washington, D.C., January, 1993).

SOCIAL SECURITY ADMINISTRATION: "Social Security Programs in the United States" *Social Security Bulletin* (Washington, D.C., Winter, 1993), pp. 3–84.

WILLIAMS, C. A., J. G. TURNBULL, and E. F. CHEIT: *Economic and Social Security* (5th ed., New York: John Wiley & Sons, Inc., 1982).

CHAPTER 23

Workers' Compensation and Workplace Safety

Learning Objectives

After completing this chapter, you should be able to:

1. Describe the legal conditions of workers prior to the adoption of workers' compensation laws.
2. Explain the meaning and purpose of employer liability laws.
3. Identify and discuss the various theoretical foundations of workers' compensation.
4. Explain the coverage provided under workers' compensation laws.
5. Describe the benefits provided under workers' compensation laws.
6. Explain state differences in financing arrangements for workers' compensation.
7. Identify and discuss principal issues and problems associated with workers' compensation.
8. Discuss the administration issues associated with the management of work-related injuries and illnesses within an organization.
9. Explain the meaning and purpose of a "return-to-work" program.

INTRODUCTION

Chapter 7 introduced the subject of human resource exposures, noting that employees are valuable organizational assets. Safeguarding these assets is an essential component of risk management. Efforts to protect human resources address safety, health, and economic concerns arising from work, from personal health habits, as well as from risks entirely outside the employment setting. Perhaps the most important program for dealing with worker safety and health *in an employment setting* is workers' compensation.

Workers' compensation is a statutory program mandating benefits for employee injury, illness, or death as the result of compensable work-related activity. All states, the District of Columbia, Puerto Rico, the U.S. protectorates, and the federal government, have a workers' compensation program, and in many regards each program is unique. Such variety can make summarization difficult, but it is possible to present a general explanation of workers' compensation. This explanation then can serve as a blueprint for students wishing to investigate the workers' compensation law of a particular state.

This chapter begins with a description of the legal environment that existed prior to the adoption of workers' compensation laws in the United States. Of particular interest will be a discussion of employer liability statutes, which were adopted by most states but were superseded ultimately by workers' compensation laws. The chapter then provides an explanation of the historical and theoretical foundations of modern workers' compensation laws. When the history and foundations of workers' compensation have been established, the discussion turns to the essential characteristics of the various workers' compensation systems. Particular attention will be paid to coverage, benefits, and security arrangements.

The chapter then focuses on workers' compensation on the international stage. The emphasis will be on presenting a representative sample of workers' compensation practices, rather than on a comprehensive assessment of workers' compensation today. Following the discussion of international issues, attention shifts back to the United States. Problems and issues with workers' compensation are identified and explained, and some future possible directions are discussed. Finally, the discussion of workers' compensation moves to a risk management orientation. Particular emphasis is placed on explaining the relationships between loss control and workers' compensation, claims management and workers' compensation, and on the issues surrounding the decision to self-insure workers' compensation. Readers will also be introduced to a particular loss reduction technique, return-to-work programs, and will be given an illustration of the possible costs and benefits of such a program.

COMMON LAW LIABILITY FOR EMPLOYERS

The benefits of the Industrial Revolution have been acknowledged widely. However, industrialization also brought with it profound problems. At the social level, it dramatically shook up family life and work life. Preindustrial society was based largely upon agricultural and cottage work. Often, the business organization was the family unit, and workers lived where they worked. Industrialization changed dramatically this social structure. Workers, in increasing numbers, left home to find employment in large manufacturing organizations located in rapidly swelling towns and cities, and the nature of the work they found was different from anything most of them had ever experienced.

The development of this story is important, but is best left to the social historian. Nevertheless, it is essential to note that industrialization brought with it a significant increase in the awareness of worker injury and death, and by the late nineteenth century most industrialized nations had identified workplace safety as an important problem.

In and of itself, the rising awareness of workplace safety may not have been sufficient to warrant government intervention. However, civil law exacerbated the perceived problem because it had not kept pace with the social changes wrought by industrialization. Indeed, in many respects the law consciously chose to ignore workers' rights with respect to injury and death, arguing that to insert the law into work life was to violate important legal and political principles that protected the sanctity of the family; a view that by the latter half of the nineteenth century was—to say the least—a curious relic of a bygone, preindustrial world.

This is not to say that the law was absolutely static during the nineteenth century. As will be noted, the law did move slowly toward the general notion of affording workers some rights vis-à-vis the employer. However, the evolution to a workers' compensation system was facilitated ultimately by legislative, rather than court, activity. Therefore, a brief *legal* history of this period is useful.

There is very little evidence of workers suing employers for industrial injury prior to the 1830s; a phenomenon largely explained by the characteristics of preindustrial society and law mentioned previously. One of the earliest glimpses of the legal environment for injured workers is found in a famous English case, *Priestly v. Fowler* (1837). In that case, the judge made it clear that an employee would find it more difficult to collect from the employer under the law of negligence than would a complete stranger. This inferior position of the employee reflected in part the laissez faire attitude of the industrial revolution. The employee, like the stranger, was forced to prove negligence on the part of the employer, had to share the recovery with his or her legal counsel, and often was forced to wait many years for recovery because of crowded court calendars, delaying tactics, and difficulties of proof. The employee, like the stranger, lost the right to recover if he or she was guilty of contributory negligence, a common law defense explained in Chapter 6. Actions also expired upon the employee's death. Verdicts often bore little relationship to the merits of the employee's case.

The employee's plight was worse than that of the stranger, however, because the person being sued was his or her employer who might penalize the employee in other ways. Fellow employees, who might otherwise strongly support the worker's case, were also often unwilling to testify for fear of losing their jobs. In addition, the law allowed the employer to plead certain special defenses to these actions that were quite effective in defeating the worker's claim. These defenses were:

1. *The fellow servant rule,* which relieved the employer from liability if it could be shown that an injury was caused by the negligence of a fellow worker
2. *The assumption of risk defense*, which said that in the absence of statutory rules or provisions in the employment contract, the employer was not liable for injury caused by unsafe conditions of work if the worker knew of such conditions and voluntarily entered or continued in the employment.

Over time, however, courts began to recognize a special duty owed to the "servant" by the "master," distinct from those owed to the general public. While they held that the master was not an insurer of a servant's safety, they came to maintain that the master owed a duty to provide working conditions that were reasonably safe, considering the nature of the employment, and to warn the servant of unsafe conditions that the servant might not discover by the exercise of due care. This duty was gradually extended to include inspection, maintenance, and repair of the premises within the master's control and to the safety of the tools that the worker used. If an injury was due to the employer's violation of these duties, the employee could bring action for recovery of damages sustained. In addition, the courts began to chip away at the employer's defenses. For example, the employer could not plead the fellow-servant rule if the negligent employee was a supervisor or one with whom the injured employee normally had little contact. Some courts substituted a comparative negligence doctrine for contributory negligence.

By the early 1900s, employers' liability statutes had been enacted in most jurisdictions, which had accelerated the evolutionary process. The federal government had enacted the Federal Employers' Liability Act, applying to interstate railroad employees, and the Jones Act, applying to the crews of merchant ships. These laws, like the courts, tended to modify and limit the employer's use of the fellow-servant rule, assumption of risk, and contributory negligence defenses. Specific safety statutes were enacted to prescribe minimum safety standards and working conditions, making it easier for the worker to show negligence of the employer by violation of the law.

Employer liability statutes were not, however, free from criticism. The basic defects of a system still dependent upon negligence claims (difficulties in proving negligence, adverse employer reactions, delays, legal costs, and awards that were often not related to the worker's loss) remained, and so the early 1900s were years of social agitation and reform. As a result, workers' (formerly "workmen's") compensation laws were enacted that completely changed, for most employers and employees, the concepts of employer responsibility for injuries "arising out of and in the course of employment."

Under workers' compensation a covered employer became absolutely responsible for the economic losses suffered by his or her employees because of job-related injuries and diseases. Who was at fault did not affect this responsibility. However, the employee gave up the right to sue the employer because of such losses and accepted specified compensation for economic losses only. Workers' compensation became the "exclusive remedy" of the employee against the employer *in situations in which the law applied.*

The italicized qualification above is important because employers' liability remains the legal redress for (1) employees not covered under the workers' compensation law, (2) those disabled by a possibly job-related disease not covered under the law, and (3) those permitted by law before or after an accident to elect not to come under workers' compensation. In addition, some workers' compensation laws permit employees to sue fellow employees who are responsible for their injuries, and employers may elect to assume such claims. In a few instances, spouses of injured employees have been permitted to sue the employer for loss of consortium. In some other cases, the injured employee may sue a third party, such as a railroad, which through a hold-harmless agreement is able to transfer its common law liability to the employer. Finally, during the past few years, the concept that workers' compensation is the exclusive remedy of the employee against the employer has been subjected to a new challenge through the "dual capacity" theory. The dual capacity theory argues that when a worker is injured on the job by a product or by equipment made by the employer, the employee may choose between collecting benefits under workers' compensation or pursuing a civil action under product liability.

Since workers' compensation is not comprehensive, the workers' compensation insurance policy typically purchased has a supplemental "employers' liability" coverage section. This part of the policy would provide an employer coverage for claims like those identified in the preceding paragraph. Although employers' liability coverage can be very important, the chapter focuses on the workers' compensation side of the policy.

WORKERS' COMPENSATION THEORY AND PRACTICE: 1911 TO PRESENT

Workers' compensation introduced the following revolutionary changes:

1. As stated above, the concept of negligence and fault on the part of the worker or the employer was abandoned as the basis of financial responsibility. Rather, all accidents or injuries related to "industrial causation" or arising out of the employment were to be compensated. The cost of injuries was determined to be a cost of manufacture and therefore passed on to the consumer through higher prices. In other words, a no-fault concept was adopted.
2. The benefit amounts were scheduled by statute rather than awarded by juries. The injured worker was to be compensated only for economic losses, not for pain and suffering.
3. Administration was, in most cases, given to an administrative agency of the state, which had authority to make rules and regulations concerning interpretations of the law, subject to judicial review.

Workers' compensation laws were enacted as early as 1902, but it was not until 1911 that Wisconsin passed the first state law to become effective that was not later declared unconstitutional (courts had argued such laws were a violation of due process in the taking of employer "property"). Nine other states acted later that year. By 1920, all but six states and the District of Columbia had passed such legislation. In addition, the federal government, in 1908, had enacted a law covering civilian federal employees. In 1948, Mississippi became the last state to adopt the workers' compensation approach to industrial injuries and diseases.

National Commission on State Workers' Compensation Laws

Because of its dissatisfaction with the performance of state workers' compensation laws, in 1970 Congress established as part of the Occupational Safety and Health Act a national commission to evaluate state workers' compensation laws. In its July, 1972 report, the National Commission on State Workmen's

Compensation Laws supported the basic concept of workers' compensation, but emphasized what it considered serious deficiencies in existing programs. The Commission recommended many standards for an effective program, 19 of which were deemed essential. The Commission urged all states to meet these standards by July 1, 1975. It recommended that Congress check the degree of compliance as of that date and, if necessary, with no further delay, act to guarantee compliance with these recommendations. Congress has never acted on the Commission report but, for several years following that report, it seriously considered bills that would establish federal standards which, if not satisfied within a state by a specified date, would apply to occupational injuries and diseases in that state. States, however, have taken many steps. Although no state has satisfied all the Commission recommendations, state workers' compensation programs are much closer to meeting these recommendations today than in 1972. Also, many states have adopted several important Commission recommendations not included among the 19 essential recommendations.

In compliance with another recommendation of the Commission, an Interdepartmental Policy Group, including the Secretaries of Labor, Commerce, and Health, Education and Welfare (now Health and Human Services), plus the Federal Insurance Administration, was appointed to encourage and assist the states in administering workers' compensation, and to examine certain areas more closely. In 1974, an Interdepartmental Task Force was formed to conduct further research. In 1977, the Policy Group, using the Task Force's findings, recommended that the states be granted more time to meet the National Commissions essential recommendations, but that they be encouraged to go beyond the 19 essential recommendations. The Policy Group modified some of the Commission's recommendations and added some of their own. The Policy Group reports have also stimulated program changes at the state level.

Beginning in the 1980s, most states began to experience financial difficulties with their workers' compensation systems. The reasons for difficulty were not always the same, but the result has been that almost every state legislature has been compelled to address workers' compensation in almost every legislative session since 1983. In the early 1990s, momentum for legislative activity is even more intense, due to continuing poor financial performance and important political difficulties. These problems are addressed later.

The Theory of Workers' Compensation

Various economic theories have been offered over the past 80 years to explain or justify workers' compensation. Generally, these theories can be said to either (1) justify the no-fault idea that is the foundation of workers' compensation, or (2) seek to define the extent of an employer's obligation to an injured worker.

Prior to the adoption of workers' compensation laws, the basic justification for the liability environment and the employer liability statutes was that the inherent risks of an occupation were reflected in the wage of that occupation. That is, the employee would demand and receive a wage that reflected the relative risk of the occupation, for example, lumberjacks would receive a risk-adjustment in their wages to reflect the occupational hazards of the job. Interestingly, modern economists use a methodology known as the "hedonic wage equation" to determine such a risk-adjusted wage, and the literature on the risk-wage tradeoff is fairly extensive (Viscusi, 1993).

In at least one way, workers' compensation embodies a contrary view of risk and wages. Workers' compensation implies, at least, the failure of workers to obtain a risk-adjustment to their wages. Early supporters of workers' compensation noted that often workers in the most hazardous industries were subject to forces (competition for jobs, racism, inequalities in the bargaining positions of employees and employers) that prevented such workers from commanding a risk-adjusted wage. Perhaps surprisingly, however, opponents of the risk-adjusted wage view sometimes employed exactly that concept in justifying workers' compensation. For instance, it was occasionally said that the cost to employers of workers' compensation insurance represented the risk-adjustment that employees were unable to demand from employers.

The two early economic theories that focused exclusively on the no-fault idea were the *theory of occupational risk* and the *theory of least social cost. Occupational risk* theorists argued that a worker's injury was part of the cost of production, and should be reflected in the price of the product or service sold. A leading British politician of the day, David Lloyd George, immortalized the occupational risk view of workers' compensation when he argued that ". . . the cost of the product should bear the blood of the working man."

In its purest form, this theory argued that employers would factor the cost of worker injuries into the price of the product they produced and that consumers would then bear the cost of these injuries. Cost spreading to the portion of society that enjoys the product was argued to be a logical and fair process for financially supporting injured workers. Economic theory would suggest that the merit of the occupational risk idea depends on elasticity of demand, meaning that consumers will purchase a product regardless of its cost. Logic would dictate that this is not always true; the consumer might choose to purchase from another company, might choose not to purchase at all, or might seek out a substitute product. The consumer's unwillingness to absorb the cost of injuries means that the ultimate burden could fall on the workers (through lower wages), the employer (through lower profits), or on others (perhaps creditors of the employer). Because the burden may not fall on those who enjoy the fruits of the worker's labor, the occupational risk theory has lost some of its appeal.

In the 1920s, the *theory of least social cost* emerged. This theory was based in part on the occupational risk view of workers' compensation, in that it did argue that part of the cost of losses was transferable to consumers. However, least social cost theory did not make the argument that "markets" could solve the problem of apportioning the economic burden of worker injuries. Indeed, least social cost theorists believed that efficient allocation of costs was not possible, given the political, economic, and social pressures on such a system. They believed that the workers' compensation system is simply the best, least costly method for handling worker injuries given the practical constraints that prevent an "ideal" solution from being adopted.

A famous social insurance scholar, Edwin E. Witte, refined the least social cost theory in the late 1920s. In Witte's view, workers' compensation does not place the cost of injuries fully on the employer, the employee, or the consumer. Rather, it provides for a sharing of the cost of losses on a predetermined basis, without regard to fault. Witte underscored the compromise nature of workers' compensation and acknowledged that costs to employers and competitive conditions are as much part of the equation as are the needs of an injured worker. As he explained, "The test of the system is not whether employers are made responsible or whether exact justice is achieved, but what arrangements on balance result in the least cost to society" (cited in: National Commission on State Workmen's Compensation Laws, 1973).

A very different strain of workers' compensation theory focuses upon the nature of the obligation of the employer to the employee. Two important theories that characterize the competing views of this area are the *earning capacity theory* and the *whole-person theory.* The *earning capacity* view argues that the system is responsible for restoring as much of the worker's earning capacity as is possible. The *whole-person* approach states that the purpose of workers' compensation is not just the restoration of earning ability but rather the restoration of an injured worker to a "whole person." Under this second view, awards should not be based solely on loss of earnings but on the physical (or mental) impairment. The much-discussed shortcoming of the whole-person approach is the difficulty in accurately assessing the economic value of many types of impairments, such as the inability of an injured worker to procreate as the result of work-related event. Supporters of the whole-person view argue that the fact that such losses are difficult to assess does not mean they should be ignored.

It should be noted that legal scholars have also contributed to the development of theory regarding the no-fault idea. As an example, the *social compromise theory* argues that both employers and employees gave up important legal rights and protections by entering into the workers' compensation contract. Employers promise to assume responsibility for work-related injuries, regardless of fault, while employees relinquish their right to sue the employer for injuries arising out of and in the course of employment. A second legal theory is commonly known as the *status theory.* According to this argument, the employer's responsibility to the injured worker arises, not from any action or omission of the employer, but from the existence of the relationship which the employer bears to the employment because of and in the course of which the worker has been injured.

WORKERS' COMPENSATION TODAY

The following discussion focuses on a general summary of workers' compensation programs as they exist in 1994: their covered employments, covered injuries and diseases, benefits, and funding requirements.

Employments Covered

Workers' compensation laws cover all employments that are not specifically excluded. The most commonly excluded employments are domestic service, casual work, and agricultural employment. Railroad workers engaged in interstate commerce are excluded under all state laws because they are covered under the Federal Employers' Liability Act. About one-fourth of the states exclude employers with less than a certain number (three, four, or five) of employees. Until recently, many states permitted employers to determine whether they would bring their employees under the law. However, if they elected not to be covered, they lost the assumption of risk, fellow-servant, and contributory negligence defenses in any employer's liability suits. Only three such elective laws remain.

Accidents and Diseases Covered

All laws cover injuries "arising out of and in the course of employment." They also cover occupational diseases. The laws are fairly uniform in language but have been interpreted differently as to what injuries "arise out of" and are "in the course of" employment. These two phrases suggest that the injury must occur in the course of the employee performing the job, and that the injury must arise out of the activities of the job. If those "tests" are met, the injury is compensable, and the employer's only possible defenses are that the injury was intentionally inflicted or that, subject to certain exceptions, the employee was intoxicated at the time of the injury. Examples of some troublesome claims are back injuries, which may have been caused by some nonwork activity, heart attacks on the job, injuries suffered during a coffee break, injuries suffered on the way to and from work, and injuries resulting from horseplay. Determining what diseases, as opposed to injuries, should be attributed to the workers' occupation has proved to be especially difficult because (1) the disease may not manifest itself until years after the employee was first exposed to the disease, and (2) the disease may have some mixture of occupational and nonoccupational causes.

Benefits

The laws provide four types of benefits: (1) medical benefits, (2) disability income benefits, (3) death benefits, and (4) rehabilitation benefits.

Medical Benefits. Each jurisdiction makes its most generous benefit promise in the area of medical benefits. Essentially, all medical expenses arising out of the compensable injury or disease are covered. However, because of rising medical costs, a number of states have begun to impose some indirect and direct restrictions. For instance, the state of North Dakota has imposed a $250 statutory deductible on employers for each medical claim. Other states have introduced fee schedules that specify the amounts to be paid for scheduled services. More recently, some states have introduced managed medical care programs, which include peer review, second opinion surgery, case management, utilization review, and service networks, as well as other health care management techniques. Subsequent discussion on problems and issues will examine the challenge of medical benefit cost inflation.

Disability Income Benefits. The disability income benefits are related to the worker's wage at the time of the disability. Most of the disability claims involve *temporary total disability,* for which a typical benefit is two-thirds of the weekly pre-injury wage, but in no cases more than a specified maximum amount per week nor less than a specified minimum, beginning with the fourth or eighth day of disability and continuing until the claimant has recovered, or until a stated period—such as 360 weeks—has expired. If the disability lasts longer than, say, two or three weeks, the worker is also compensated retroactively for the four- to eight-day waiting period. The maximum weekly benefit is usually less than the state average weekly wage. All but nine states adjust the maximum annually as the state average weekly wage increase. Eight states pay higher benefits when the worker has dependents.

Permanent total disability benefits are determined in the same way as temporary total disability benefits, except that in some states the maximum or minimum weekly benefit is different. In most states, these weekly benefits are continued for the lifetime of the worker, but 11 states limit the benefit to a stated number of years or an aggregate dollar amount. In 11 states plus the District of Columbia, permanent total disability benefits awarded previously are adjusted annually to maintain either the disabled worker's standard of living or purchasing power.

Permanent partial disability benefits is the most controversial category of benefits. Generally, permanent partial disability benefits follow a period of temporary total disability. The worker is not eligible for permanent total disability benefits, but either is found or presumed to have suffered some permanent partial reduction in income because of a permanent physical or mental handicap. Benefits are either scheduled or unscheduled. Scheduled benefits are paid to workers with specified impairments. The benefit is usually the weekly temporary total disability benefit amount times the number of weeks prescribed for the specified impairment. The benefit may be paid in installments or in a lump sum. For example, in one jurisdiction, the prescribed number of weeks is 288 for the loss of (or loss of use of) a leg, 160 weeks for one eye, 312 weeks for an arm, 75 weeks for a thumb, and 15 weeks for a little finger. The schedules vary among the states as to the impairments that are scheduled, whether partial loss of use of a member is included, and if so, on what basis, and the number of weeks the benefit is paid for each disability. A few states reduce the number of weeks for older workers. This benefit is continued even if the employee returns to work. The most common explanation of this approach is that the benefit represents the average loss in earning capacity associated with specified impairments. Basing the benefit on the person's physical and mental capacity instead of the employee's actual wage loss following maximum medical improvement (MMI) removes an important disincentive to the employee's return to work and avoids the often difficult question of the extent to which the employee's failure to return to work or return at a lesser wage is caused by the impairment. This approach has been criticized because the actual economic loss for each impairment differs among occupations (for instance, an accountant who loses a leg may as a result lose little or no income while a truck driver may lose considerable income) and if the award is at least in part merely an award for the impairment, it should not be tied to prior earnings. Furthermore, if the schedule includes partial loss of use and impairments other than the loss of eyesight, hearing, or a body member (for example, a back impairment), disability determinations can be extremely difficult.

For unscheduled impairments (that is, impairments not identified in statutory schedules), the benefit is also commonly based on the presumed loss of earning capacity, not the actual wage loss. For example, the effect of the impairment may be expressed as a percent of the loss of the "whole person." The worker may receive, say, 66²/₃ percent of his or her earnings, subject to minimum and maximum weekly benefits amounts, for a number of weeks equal to the impairment percentage times the number of weeks stated in the law for loss of the "whole person." Alternatively, the worker may receive, say, 66²/₃ percent of the wage loss times the impairment percentage for the number of weeks specified for loss of the "whole person." In some states, the specified benefit is 66²/₃ percent of the actual reduction in wages caused by the impairment. In practice, however, in most of these states, the cases are settled under compromise and release settlements for lump sums based presumably on loss of earning capacity.

Florida has adopted a modified wage loss approach to all permanent partial disability cases. For example, Florida provides two benefits. The first is a small impairment benefit that is not related to the worker's earnings. The benefit is $50 for each percentage point of impairment up to 50 percent and $100 for each higher percentage point up to 100 percent. The second is a wage loss benefit payable for up to 525 weeks of payments equal to the difference between 85 percent of the worker's prior earnings and the worker's earnings after the healing period, subject to a maximum weekly benefit.

In 1983, Minnesota made the permanent partial disability benefit depend upon whether the employer made a bona fide job offer to the worker or convinced some other employer to make such an offer. If the employee receives such an offer, the benefit will be a lump sum tied to the impairment but not the wage. If the employee does not receive such an offer, the benefit is weekly compensation tied to the worker's wage payable for a number of weeks that varies with the nature of the impairment. This economic recovery compensation is larger than the special impairment award.

Death Benefits. Death benefits include (1) a funeral expense allowance and (2) an income-related benefit for survivors. The funeral expense allowance is a lump sum, usually between $1000 and $3000. The income-related benefit, limited to family dependents, is a weekly benefit that may or may not depend upon the number of survivors. For example, in some states, the wage replacement rate may be 50 percent for a surviving spouse with or without children. In all states, the weekly benefit is limited to a maximum amount. The spouse's benefit may be continued until the spouse dies or remarries, but almost half of the states limit the benefit to a stated number of years, a specified dollar amount, or both.

Rehabilitation Benefits. Five jurisdictions operate their own rehabilitation centers. About two-thirds of the jurisdictions provide some maintenance benefits for persons undergoing rehabilitation. Many disabled workers receive benefits under a federal-state vocational rehabilitation program, which serves persons with all types of occupational and nonoccupational disabilities.

Second Injury Fund. Another measure designed to help handicapped workers is a second injury fund, found in almost all states (though some states are considering discontinuing it and Minnesota has recently done so). This fund is designed to encourage the employment of handicapped workers by transferring to the fund, which is administered by the state, all responsibility for the extra workers' compensation benefits, if any, associated with the disability. For example, if a worker with one eye loses the sight of the other eye, the worker is compensated for blindness. The employer is responsible only for the benefit payable in case the worker had lost one eye; the second injury fund pays the difference. A second approach limits the employer's responsibility to the first 52 or 104 weeks of disability payments plus a portion of the medical expenses. Some states have broad funds covering most prior disabilities, but most states limit their fund either to a few serious disabilities—generally the loss of a hand, arm, foot, leg, or eye—or to second injuries that, combined with the previous disability, produce permanent total disability. Many methods are used to finance these funds, the most common being special payments in death cases when there are no dependents to receive compensation benefits or assessments expressed as a percentage of the insurance premium paid, or, in the case of self-insurers, the premium that would have been paid if they had not been self-insured. Four states finance their funds in whole or in part from general revenues. The advent of the Americans with Disabilities Act (ADA) is expected to have some effect on the presence of second injury funds, although it is not clear whether ADA will nudge such funds toward extinction, or whether they may become a more important source of financing for employers of disabled workers. The ADA is discussed later in this chapter.

Security Arrangements

In addition to prescribing the benefits to be paid, legislators have been concerned, from the beginning of workers' compensation legislation, about the ability of employers to make these payments when the occasion arises. Today, six states—Nevada, North Dakota, Ohio, Washington, West Virginia, and Wyoming—operate a monopolistic state fund. That is, these six states require employers to purchase coverage from a state agency (though two of the six do permit some larger employers to self-insure). The 44 remaining states and the District of Columbia rely entirely or in part on commercial insurers to provide workers' compensation coverage for employers. Of those 45 jurisdictions, 16 operate competitive state funds. Competitive state funds are similar to monopolistic state funds except that they compete directly with commercial insurers. In addition, 44 of those 45 jurisdictions also permit self-insurance under certain conditions.

Although workers' compensation is clearly social legislation, most states have not established state funds. The heavy reliance on private insurers can be explained by the facts that when workers' compensation was introduced, private insurers were already experienced writers of employers' liability insurance and workers' collective insurance (a form of health insurance); the British had adopted this approach; "government in business" was opposed by many; and competition among insurers was considered necessary to stimulate the loss-prevention and reduction activities, which at that time were sorely needed. The principal counterarguments in favor of state funds were that workers' compensation insurance, being social insurance, should be written by nonprofit public insurers; private insurers were unwilling to insure all employers needed protection; public insurers should be able to operate with lower expense loadings; and competitive state funds provide a yardstick for measuring the performance of private insurers.

WORKERS' COMPENSATION OUTSIDE THE UNITED STATES

This chapter has noted the difficulties in summarizing American workers' compensation laws. Those difficulties are significantly greater when attempting the same thing on an international scale. The variations in approach are as great as could be possibly imagined: from total nonexistence in underdeveloped nations to highly centralized and comprehensive programs in many developed nations. Nevertheless, for risk managers operating in an international environment, understanding the characteristics of different systems is essential.

It is important to note that most of the schemes for dealing with work-related injury are variations of the approaches devised by Germany and Great Britain in the late nineteenth century. Though those two systems have changed markedly from their early days, a brief history of the systems helps the reader understand the fundamentals of workers' compensation systems around the world.

Work Injury Compensation in Germany and Great Britain

Germany's "workers' compensation" law was established in 1884, and was further evidence of Bismarck's commitment to social insurance remedies (a health insurance program had been created the previous year). This law was conceived to be an (essentially) exclusive remedy for work-related injuries. A worker might be able to collect additional amounts if the employer could be shown to have acted with criminal intent or gross negligence, but basically the German law was a "no-fault" system.

The British law was enacted in 1897, and differed from the German system in a number of respects. Notably, the employer's civil liability was not replaced. Rather, an injured worker had a choice between pursuing relief through the statutory law or through the civil courts. The selection of the statutory remedy barred the worker from pursuing relief under civil law and vice versa, except that the civil courts retained the ability to award some statutory benefits (less the already incurred legal expenses) if the worker were to lose a civil action. Although the British law was essentially elective, it did serve the important function of casting into statutory law the evolving principle of strict liability.

The differences in the two systems resulted in a number of distinct characteristics. For instance, the German approach tended to lead nations toward the idea of a centrally administered system, with active governmental involvement—what might be called a "conventional" social insurance approach. The British approach seemed to lead to systems that permitted a more decentralized and even private-sector flavor. In truth, the fairly well developed insurance industry in Britain was influential in that nation's use of private insurance, but arguably the nature of the statute lent itself to a less conventional social insurance system. Readers should note, however, that the present system in Britain differs in significant ways from its predecessor system; most importantly, it is no longer an elective system.

Current Systems Around the World

Virtually every nation with an industrial injury system today has adopted the essence of the German approach, that is, most countries view the idea of strict liability as fundamental (not elective) to their system. However, the systems differ in the burden of liability. The British approach has led to a number of nations using an employer burden of liability (i.e., the employer buys insurance for or self-insures this liability), whereas the German approach has influenced a more collectivist model (the government finances the program through general revenues).

In recent years, many nations have begun to examine the logic of a separate system for dealing with work-related injuries. The notion of the distinctiveness of industrial injury has lost its appeal as other sources of injury and death have emerged (motor vehicle accidents, for instance). Over the past 30 years, there has been some movement to fold workers' compensation systems, at least loosely, into other social insurance programs. Paradoxically, at the same time there has been this trend toward greater collectivization of this risk, many of the collectivist systems have begun to shift some of the obligation to employers.

Readers interested in investigating workers' compensation systems around the world would find C. Arthur Williams, Jr.'s *An International Comparison of Workers' Compensation* (Williams, 1991) to be a particularly comprehensive introduction to the subject.

CURRENT ISSUES AND PROBLEMS WITH WORKERS' COMPENSATION

For 1993, the cost of workers' compensation in the United States was estimated to be over $60 billion. This represents an increase of almost 50 percent since 1988 (Burton, May/June 1992). In virtually every state, the rising cost of workers' compensation has captured the attention of legislators. A significant volume of legislation has been enacted since 1983 to attack the problem of rising workers' compensation costs. Indeed, the high intensity of legislative activity has proven itself to be an issue. The virtually constant "tinkering" that has occurred in some states has made it very difficult to identify and measure the effects of legislative enactments.

As with many topics in this textbook, workers' compensation issues and problems cannot be summarized easily. Each jurisdiction's system is different; each jurisdiction is unique. However, there do appear to be several common problems and issues that transcend individual jurisdictions. It is these general problems to which discussion now turns. Readers should be mindful that other problems not discussed here may be important in a particular state.

Rising Medical Costs

The rapidly rising cost of health care is one of the more challenging public policy issues in the United States. The average annual rate of inflation for health care services has been roughly 11 percent over the past decade. Naturally, when a program such as workers' compensation statutorily promises to provide for all medical expenses arising from a compensable injury, it is making an expensive commitment.

However, general medication cost inflation is compounded in workers' compensation by the relatively meager efforts that have to be expended to manage workers' compensation medical expenses. Virtually all other third-party payers in health care (commercial insurers, Blue Cross/Blue Shield, self-insured employers, Medicare, Medicaid) have introduced aggressive measures to manage the cost of health care: fee schedules, utilization reviews, bill audits, second opinion surgery, deductibles and copayments, health care networks, and so on. Workers' compensation systems have lagged behind other payers, meaning that in many states workers' compensation is the only "first dollar, every dollar" plan in existence. Not surprisingly, there is some evidence to suggest that health care providers are shifting costs (unrecoverable from other payers) to the workers' compensation system.

Further evidence of the growing importance of medical expenses in workers' compensation can be found by looking at the proportion of total workers' compensation dollars committed to medical expenses. Historically, medical expenses have represented 20 to 30 percent of total dollars. In the 1990s, several states now report that medical expenses are approaching or exceeding 50 percent of total expenditures.

Some states have begun to introduce managed medical care programs into workers' compensation, but they have not existed long enough to provide insight into their effect. Many risk managers are skeptical as to whether managed care can do much more than slow the growth rate. Few, at present, believe costs could actually be reduced through managed medical care. Indeed, since workers' compensation medical expenses remain such a small part of the bigger health care picture (far less than 5 percent of total national expenditures), a meaningful global attack on workers' compensation medical costs will probably only occur when the entire national health care system is reformed.

Loss Control and Workers' Compensation

Early twentieth century social insurance scholars such as Edwin Witte argued that loss prevention and safety were explicit objectives of workers' compensation laws. Workers' compensation was envisioned as extending beyond merely addressing injuries that occurred, and focusing upon the issue of injury and illness prevention. Preventing losses is almost invariably a more effective way to address the impact of occupational safety and health risks, and it is typically much less expensive than financing the costs of losses that occur.

Although there has been a strong undercurrent of loss control in workers' compensation since such laws were adopted, loss financing has been the dominant focus of most programs. The evidence of this fact is perhaps best summarized in the following example. Workers' compensation professionals note that employers should be sensitive to loss prevention because the premiums they pay are linked (recall the discussion of rating in Chapter 14) to the employer's loss experience. This experience rating should promote active loss prevention because good accident experience is rewarded; bad experience is penalized. However, little active loss prevention actually occurs in many organizations, because the connection is only infrequently made. In fact, it is quite common for employers to explain that workers' compensation is a useful way to get rid of undesirable employees. If they are collecting benefits, the argument goes, the injured worker is no longer the employer's problem.

This phenomenon, the inability of many employers to see the relationship between "risk and rate," is exacerbated by class rating for small employers and by residual markets and rate restrictions for larger employers. The influence of class rating is probably unavoidable. As discussed in Chapter 14, small risks with limited loss experience are not good candidates for experience rating because that limited experience (or exposure base) is statistically unreliable. Therefore, such risks are subject to a classification rate that reflects loss experience of a similar class of organizations. In principal, the "good risks" in the class pay the same as the "bad risks." While class rating is appropriate for purposes of premium stabilizations, it must be acknowledged that such a system mutes the economic incentives to practice loss control.

While class rating may not be avoidable, the effects of residual markets and rate regulation may be. In most states, insurers are not completely free to establish rates, which means that there is a politicization of the rate setting process. Almost invariably, the allowable rates are inadequate from an actuarial perspective. Essentially, this creates a pricing environment in which low risk/low loss employers may be rewarded, but high risk/high loss employers may not be penalized. Over time, this reduces incentives for loss control, and also creates incentives for commercial insurers to refuse to underwrite the high risk/high loss employers. The residual market insures such employers, but because the insurance must be available to employers, this market must also suppress rates. The result is that financial incentives to practice loss control are muted for commercially insurable employers (who indirectly subsidize the residual market), and they almost completely disappear for employers in the residual market.

The Expanding Definition of Compensability

Workers' compensation laws are virtually uniform in stating that compensability is based upon injuries and illnesses "arising out of and in the course of employment." While this phase appears to be unequivocal, there has been a fairly dramatic expansion in its application over time. Early in the twentieth century, the general thought was that compensable losses were tangible injuries to the musculoskeletal structure of the human body (broken legs, severed fingers). Over time, this more discrete notion of covered injuries has grown to include neurological problems, diminishment of mental capacity, inability to procreate, cardiovascular conditions, as well as a host of industrial diseases. The reasons for this expansion are more complex than might first be imagined.

First and foremost, the growing capability of medical science to diagnose, treat, and understand the pathology of health problems has dramatically influenced the nature of compensability. Initially, growing medical capability was felt in the expanding survival rate of workers who suffered industrial accidents. A worker may be nursed through the "structural" injury, only to face psychological, neurological, and other event-related problems. To put it more simply, medical technology saved injured workers from death, but imposed new health problems on the workers' compensation systems. Additionally, the increasing sophistication of medical science allowed a firmer understanding of the relationship between health cause and effect, a particularly influential factor when one considers the important area of industrial disease (such as asbestosis and other diseases with a long latency period). Health problems previously unrelatable to work conditions were now *at least arguably* connected to work. Finally, linkages that have been established between physical and mental health have expanded the understanding of the psychological effects of physical injury or poor health.

Second, the definition of compensability lends itself to gradual expansion. If taken literally, "arising out of and in the course of employment" is a very broad definition. Essentially, the phrase states, if the condition can be linked to work—it is compensable.

Third, there has been some exploitation of the system, which has allowed for unwarranted expansion, that is, there is some evidence that compensability determinations may sometimes be based upon considerations other than job-relatedness. For instance, workers' compensation is sometimes looked upon by attorneys, workers, employers, and courts as a type of welfare system. Judgments for compensability are occasionally given when the facts of the injury do not merit such a finding (for instance, the worker may be suffering a noncompensable injury, but the financial circumstances of the worker's family may be sufficiently dire to evoke a humanitarian—but not strictly "correct"—interpretation).

Fraud and System Abuse

There is evidence that fraud is an important contributing factor to the growing cost of workers' compensation, with some estimates suggesting that 30 to 40 percent of all costs go to fraudulent claims. Certainly, workers' compensation fraud is a "sensational" topic, and is frequently a subject of news media attention.

Noted authority, John Burton, urges caution in overestimating the role of fraud in the escalating costs of workers' compensation (Burton, 1992). He notes that there is very little empirical evidence to suggest that fraud is actually a major problem when compared with the aggregate costs of the systems. Burton does not dismiss the potential importance of fraud (that is, if left unchecked it could become a significant issue), but does suggest that what is often called fraud is really "systems failure." For instance, physicians are sometimes accused of defrauding workers' compensation by ordering additional tests for injured workers. However, the value of additional tests is not a black and white issue, so though the tests might be unnecessary by some standards, they are not fraudulent. Rather, as many argue, the phenomenon of unnecessary tests suggests an improper management of medical care by the workers' compensation system.

Workers' compensation fraud is commonly associated with illegal behavior of workers, but fraud may be perpetrated by many different groups. Attorneys, physicians, chiropractors, rehabilitation specialists, management consultants, and others have all been among those convicted of illegal activity in the area of workers' compensation. Further, though it is rarely noted, employer abuse of the system is probably as significant as that of any other group, in that employees are frequently misinformed or misled as to their rights under workers' compensation law.

WORKERS' COMPENSATION AND RISK MANAGEMENT

For many organizations, workers' compensation is one of the top three expense items *and* problem areas (a related issue, group health insurance, is probably also in that list). Not surprisingly, the challenge of managing the risk of work-related injury and illness is foremost in the typical risk manager's mind. This section focuses upon several risk management aspects of workers' compensation: the importance of loss control, the relationship of workers' compensation to the Americans with Disabilities Act and the Occupational Safety and Health Administration, workers' compensation claims management, the concept of 24-hour coverage, and return-to-work programs.

Loss Control

The point has been made earlier that preventing and controlling worker accidents is an appropriate objective of workers' compensation, though it is often given limited attention. However, many risk managers believe that loss control is probably the only systematic way to actually *reduce* the net cost of worker injuries.

One of the significant challenges of workers' compensation systems is to help employers understand the relationship between injury frequency and severity and the cost of workers' compensation insurance. As was noted, though this relationship may seem obvious to the reader, there is evidence that this insight is not experienced widely. For the risk manager of an organization, there is an equally challenging second layer to this problem. Within a single organization there may be difficulty in conveying the relationship between "risk and rate" to the line managers. The employer may be a distant presence for the unit manager, who experiences no direct pain when the employer's insurance rates rise. Cost allocation systems, discussed in Chapter 20, are one effort to enhance manager awareness of the link between worker safety and workers' compensation costs.

The Americans with Disabilities Act and the Occupational Safety and Health Administration

Workers' compensation does not exist in a vacuum. Whether intentional or not, workers' compensation relates to and overlaps with several other governmental initiatives. Two of these initiatives, the Americans with Disabilities Act and the Occupational Safety and Health Administration, are cited here for illustrative purposes.

The Americans with Disabilities Act (ADA) is a federal law that was phased in between 1992 and 1994. Essentially, the law requires applicable organizations to provide reasonable access for individuals with disabilities, and it also forbids discrimination on the basis of disability—as long as the disability can be reasonably accommodated by the employer. The ADA is likely to have an impact upon workers' compensation, although that impact is not entirely clear at present. Possible impact points could be:

1. The impact on workers' compensation claims frequency and severity, when large numbers of disabled workers enter the workforce
2. The effect of ADA on second injury funds
3. The effect on return-to-work programs
4. The impact upon the exclusive remedy rule (that is, does ADA allow for a path to a civil law remedy?)
5. Changes in the types of injuries and accidents that occur
6. Changes in standards of care and burdens of proof.

The Occupational Safety and Health Administration (OSHA) is a well-known federal (and/or state) agency that has responsibilities for promulgating and enforcing workplace safety standards. The conceptual relationship between OSHA and workers' compensation is quite apparent, which might lead one to assume that there would be a coordination of efforts between the programs. Unfortunately, this rarely occurs, and the lack of coordination must be viewed as a risk management problem. OSHA is, for all intents and purposes, a social loss control program that focuses upon preventing and controlling workplace injury, disease, and death. Logically, OSHA's ability to fulfill its mission should be of keen interest to workers' compensation systems. Likewise, workers' compensation's method for structuring the financial burden of worker injuries should be of interest to state and federal OSHA programs.

Workers' Compensation Claims Management

Elsewhere in this textbook, the subject of self-financing risks has been discussed in detail. In those discussions, the issue of administrative services has been identified as important. Specific to that issue is the question of whether those services should be provided for internally or externally.

In earlier times, the question was moot because a large self-insuring entity had virtually no external options. The employer had to conduct all the administrative activities "in-house." More recently, the emergence of a vigorous third-party administrator (TPA) market has allowed risk managers to consider the question more fully: Is it better for me to administer our workers' compensation program internally, or are there advantages to selected—if not complete—contracting for administrative services? Possibly the most developed TPA market in workers' compensation is the market for claims management services. There is a wide array of organizations, including insurance companies, that can provide this particular service.

Chapter 12 presented decision-making models that might help a risk manager to think through the in-house versus TPA question, but it is useful here to discuss briefly some of the claims management issues of particular importance in workers' compensation.

The first principle of claims management is early intervention/involvement. The more quickly a claims manager becomes involved in a claim, the greater the likelihood that the claim can be resolved equitably, efficiently, and effectively. In one sense, claims management begins *before* an accident, and this occurs through informing workers and employers about the procedural aspects of claim filing. If all involved parties know what to do when an accident occurs, then the "intervention" has begun. In workers' compensation, the principle of early intervention is complicated by the fact that there are at least three parties who must be contacted early in the process: the injured worker, the employer, and the treating medical professional. Each of these parties has a great stake in, and influence on, the outcome of a claim, so involving all of them as a team is the claims manager's objective. In the case of a self-insured workers' compensation plan, the risk manager is the employer, so the process is somewhat streamlined. However, the risk manager is likely to need to keep informed key individuals in the organization (the owner, the unit manager).

Second, there is a general recognition among workers' compensation claims managers that claims have a somewhat limited window of opportunity with respect to cost control and resolution—if the worker has not returned to work within six months of the date of injury it is more likely that the worker will not return or that the claim will become increasingly complicated and expensive.

Third, cost reduction techniques are important in workers' compensation, as they are in any insured or self-insured plan. One of the key reduction techniques is subrogation. Subrogation is the legal transfer of a right to pursue a civil cause of action against a negligent party. In insurance settings, subrogation means that when an insured is indemnified by his or her insurer, that insurer obtains the right to pursue legal redress from any negligent third party. In workers' compensation, subrogation is—conceptually, at least—a significant cost reduction technique since many claims involve the negligence of third parties (excluding fellow employees, who are largely immune under workers' compensation laws). Motor vehicle accidents, defective equipment, negligent provision of outside services—each of these examples underscores the fact that third party negligence could play an important part of workers' compensation costs. A cautionary word is necessary, however, because many states statutorily restrict the right of subrogation in workers' compensation. For instance, Wyoming permits the injured worker to collect workers' compensation benefits *and* to pursue a third-party action against a negligent party (including, due to a recent court decision, fellow employees). The injured worker is obliged under the law to reimburse the state fund if monies are collected through the civil action. Another potential problem is that a third party might cross-claim the employer (or counter sue) to minimize its liability. This would be a circumstance in which the employer liability section of the workers' compensation policy would come into play.

Fourth, the process of managing claims (whether in-house or through a TPA) will involve the establishment of reserves for claims. Reserving, that is, the recognition of liabilities incurred because of a claim, is an activity that is both art and science. It is a science in the sense that statistical analysis of claims can guide risk managers or claim managers in estimating the ultimate cost of claims. It is an art because workers' compensation claims are subject to numerous exogenous factors that cannot be fully anticipated—the sudden change of treating physicians, the appearance of an attorney, inflation, unexpected complications arising from the compensable injury, and so on. The responsibility for reporting incurred losses has heightened in recent years as both the Financial Accounting Standards Board (FASB) and the Governmental Accounting Standards Board (GASB) have issued statements that direct organizations to adopt actuarially sound reporting procedures for self-insured programs.

Finally, managing workers' compensation claims internally or externally poses purely qualitative challenges. Workers' compensation law can be difficult to comprehend in the best of circumstances, but unfortunately, most workers are thrust into the position of learning about it in the first few days following a traumatic event. There can be little wonder that workers might be suspicious of employers and insurers in such a situation. The issues involved in workers' compensation are emotionally charged, almost by definition. Therefore, managing claims requires a high degree of sensitivity to a fundamental goal of workers' compensation, which is to respond to the basic needs of injured human beings.

24-Hour Coverage

In recent years, the growing costs of workers compensation have fostered a significant amount of thinking about possible remedies. One largely untested proposal is the concept of 24-hour coverage. Although there are numerous variations of this idea, the essential notion of 24-hour coverage is that employers would merge workers compensation with group health and disability plans. In that way workers would be protected against the costs of injuries regardless of when or where they occurred.

The purported benefits of round-the-clock coverage are (1) it almost completely eliminates the need for litigation over compensability—everything is covered, (2) it allows for coordination of medical care management, (3) it allows for possible economies of scale in meeting certain medical service needs, and (4) it aligns with the international trend of merging industrial injury programs with other health and disability programs.

The costs of or problems for such an innovation are not entirely clear at present. One fairly apparent difficulty would be the harmonizing of group health and disability plans with workers' compensation statutes. Most group plans are beholden to federal requirements established under the Employee Retirement and Income Security Act (ERISA), and it may not be legal for employers to change their health and disability plans to conform with state workers' compensation law. Additionally, under present law, such a scheme could only be implemented on a voluntary employer-by-employer basis since it is unlikely that the federal government would mandate employers to provide comprehensive health and disability benefits for employees. These points should not necessarily lead the reader to believe that such a system could not come to pass. However, it is likely to be many years before such a scheme would be available on a large scale.

Return-to-Work Programs

Risk managers realize that temporary total disability benefits can present a substantial cost to an employer. This benefit, commonly two-thirds of the worker's pre-injury wage, subject to statewide minimums and maximums, may be paid for several years in some states, and poses interesting challenges for risk managers. Most importantly, the benefit—in and of itself—provides very little incentive for workers to return to work as early as is reasonably possible. This is because the benefit is related to gross wage, and it is frequently subject to a minimum benefit restriction, which means that a lower-paid worker may actually take home more money in benefits than that worker was bringing home in after-tax wages.

A formal return-to-work program typically consists of some variation of the following activities:

1. *Job Analysis.* The employer conducts an analysis of the injured worker's position. This analysis outlines the physical demands and characteristics of the job (an activity that will become increasingly prevalent under the Americans with Disabilities Act).
2. *Functional Capacities Evaluation.* The employer analyzes the physical abilities of the worker following an injury. Commonly, the attending physician will participate in, if not lead, this evaluation.
3. *Job/Capacity Matching.* The job analysis and the functional capacities evaluation are compared and matched to understand the potential for returning the worker to some form of his or her pre-injury position. The detail of this matching process forms the basis for the design of the return-to-work program.
4. *Program Design.* A return-to-work program is designed that will include a description of the work that may be done, as well as schedules and overall objectives.
5. *Work Hardening.* Essentially a component of item 4, work hardening consists of those activities in a return-to-work program that move the worker toward a resumption of the job on a full-time, unrestricted basis (this could include such things as physical and occupational rehabilitation).
6. *Internal Transfer.* Also a component of item 4, internal transfer can become part of the process if the worker cannot be returned to full-time employment in his or her job. Other work within the organization (or even in another organization) is found for the worker.

Under a return-to-work program, the presumed cost savings are achieved because (1) the duration of the claim is reduced, (2) the claim becomes a temporary partial, rather than temporary total claim, (3) if properly structured, such plans can project a sense of employer concern for workers, (4) if properly structured, such plans can help employees feel productive and useful, and (5) the employer can reduce the indirect costs associated with worker injuries (for instance, hiring temporary help).

There are dangers with return-to-work programs. Perhaps most notably, rushing the worker back to work might lead to re-injury or more serious complications. Additionally, if not properly designed, healthy employees may look at a return-to-work program as "freeloading." Finally, return-to-work programs are probably of limited value if the employee simply does not want to return to work; a not uncommon situation when the nature of the work is uninteresting or the employer-employee relationship is unpleasant.

Key Concepts

workers' compensation The program created by statute that makes the employer, regardless of fault, responsible for most job-related injuries or diseases.

employers' liability The common law or special statutory responsibility of employers for job-related injuries and diseases caused by their negligence but not covered under workers' compensation.

exclusive remedy The term commonly used to indicate the no-fault nature of workers' compensation, as in "workers' compensation is the exclusive remedy of the injured worker against the employer."

the theory of least social cost The prevalent theory of workers' compensation, least social cost theory argues that workers' compensation is a social compromise that balances the interests of employees, employers, and society as a whole. It is argued to be the approach that exacts the "least cost" to society, when compared with other possible approaches.

Review Questions

1. What defects in employers' liability led to the passage of workers' compensation statutes?
2. In what sense is workers' compensation a no-fault program?
3. What workers are covered under workers' compensation?
4. What is the significance of the phrase ". . . arising out of and in the course of employment?" What does it mean?
5. What benefits are provided for in the typical state plan?
6. Differentiate between permanent total, permanent partial, temporary total, and temporary partial benefits.
7. How do employers meet their obligation for financing the costs of workers' injuries?
8. Why are Germany and Great Britain influential in the development of workers' compensation programs around the globe? What are the principal characteristics of their early systems?
9. Why is medical care inflation particularly problematic in workers' compensation?
10. Why is the expanding definition of compensability perceived to be a contributing factor to the growing cost of workers' compensation?
11. What possible effects might the Americans with Disabilities Act have on workers' compensation?
12. What is 24-hour coverage?
13. Why is it important for risk managers to understand the relationship between loss control and the cost of workers' compensation?

14. Why is early intervention important in workers' compensation claims management?
15. What are the basic elements of a return-to-work program?

References and Suggestions for Additional Reading

BARTH, P. S., and H. A. Hunt: *Workers' Compensation and Work-Related Illnesses and Diseases* (Cambridge, Mass.: MIT Press, 1980).

BERKOWITZ, M., and J. F. BURTON, JR.: *Permanent Disability Benefits in Workers' Compensation* (Kalamazoo, Mich.: W. E. Upjohn Institute for Employment Research, 1987).

BURTON, J. F., JR.: *Workers' Compensation Monitor* (Horsham, Pa.: LRP Publications, published bimonthly).

CHELIUS, JAMES (ed): *Current Issues in Workers' Compensation* (Kalamazoo, Mich.: W. E. Upjohn Institute for Employment Research, 1986).

MYERS, R. J.: *Social Security* (3rd ed., Homewood, Ill.: Richard D. Irwin, Inc., 1985).

National Commission on State Workmen's Compensation Laws, Report of the (Washington, D.C.: U.S. Government Printing Office, 1973).

————: *Compendium on Workmen's Compensation* (Washington, D.C.: U.S. Government Printing Office, 1973).

————: *Supplemental Studies for the National Commission on State Workmen's Compensation Laws*, vols. I–III (Washington, D.C.: U.S. Government Printing Office, 1973).

NATIONAL COUNCIL ON COMPENSATION INSURANCE: *Issues Report: A Summary of Issues Influencing Workers' Compensation* (New York, published annually).

REJDA, G. E.: *Social Insurance and Economic Security* (4th ed., Englewood Cliffs, N.J.: Prentice-Hall, Inc., 1991).

VISCUSI, W. Kip: "The Value of Risks to Life and Health." *Journal of Economic Literature* (vol. XXXI, no. 4, Dec. 1993), pp. 1912–1946.

WILLIAMS, C. A., JR.: *An International Comparison of Workers' Compensation* (Boston, Mass.: Kluwer Academic Publishing, 1991).

————, J. G. TURNBULL, and E. F. CHEIT: *Economic and Social Security* (5th ed., New York: John Wiley & Sons, Inc., 1982).

WORRAL, J. D. (ed.): *Safety and the Workforce: Incentives and Disincentives in Workers' Compensation* (Ithaca, N.Y.: ILR Press, Cornell University, 1983).

————, and D. APPEL (eds.): *Workers' Compensation Benefits: Adequacy, Equity, and Efficiency* (Ithaca, N.Y.: ILR Press, Cornell University, 1985).

CHAPTER 24

Employee Benefit Plans

Learning Objectives

After you have completed this chapter, you should be able to:

1. Distinguish between life insurance benefit programs that use yearly renewable term insurance, group paid-up life insurance, and programs that provide other types of survivor benefits.
2. Explain how tax incentives encourage employers to provide up to $50,000 of term life insurance on individual employees.
3. Describe provisions typically appearing in dental care and vision care benefit programs.
4. Describe the different plans that typically are used to provide disability income coverage as an employee benefit.
5. Distinguish between defined benefit pension plans, defined contribution pension plans, and profit-sharing plans.
6. Explain the importance of vesting and funding provisions in pension plans.
7. Explain how the normal retirement age and the form of the annuity affect the monthly benefit payable under a pension plan.
8. Explain how PBGC insurance and ERISA affect pension plans.
9. Describe the structure of 401(k), 403(b), and other salary-reduction plans.
10. Describe the structure of a typical flexible benefits program and flexible spending account.
11. Explain the concept of group underwriting.
12. Describe the conversion privilege in group life and health insurance.

INTRODUCTION

Benefits other than direct cash payment are an important component of compensation to most working individuals. Whether financed by an employer or by the employee, benefit programs can be an important condition of employment. As explained in Chapter 7 on the assessment of human resource exposures to risk, valid reasons exist for risk managers to be concerned with human resource exposures of individual employees and to design programs to alleviate these exposures. Employee benefits often take the form of protection against events whose possible occurrence could distract the employee and reduce productivity: poor health, interruption of household income, or retirement. In the absence of these programs, employees could obtain similar benefits using their own resources. However, programs that are designed, financed and managed by employers can be more cost-efficient than having employees obtain similar benefits with their own resources.

This chapter describes typical features of benefit programs designed to comply with federal requirements. These programs, called *qualified* plans, receive tax-favored treatment compared with employees obtaining the same coverage using their own resources. In exchange for tax-favored treatment, a benefit program is required to comply with a complex web of restrictions and mandates designed to serve social objectives. Some of these restrictions are discussed in this chapter, while the tax treatment of qualified plans and the merits of qualifying a plan are examined in Chapter 25. Together, Chapters 24 and 25 suggest reasons for qualifying a plan and describe some but not all of the significant regulations applying to qualified plans. Regulations applying to benefit programs is a subject that easily can occupy an entire text. Beam and McFadden's (1992) text on benefit programs offers additional detail on these regulations, which change frequently enough that access to an on-line information retrieval system or data service may be required to design benefit plans in compliance with current restrictions.

Private employee benefit plans have become an important condition of employment for most employees. Through these plans, some employees secure protection that they could not purchase at all or at reasonable cost on their own, while most secure protection at a lower after-tax cost. Employers use these plans for a variety of reasons—for example, to attract and retain high-quality employees, to free employees from certain worries, to provide incentives for improved performance, to achieve certain tax savings, or to match the plans of competitors.

Employee benefits can be provided through pensions, savings plans, life and health insurance programs, property and liability insurance plans, and flexible benefits programs. This chapter describes the types of benefits provided under these programs and standard provisions typical for these plans. Programs that do not address human resource risk exposures, such as paid vacation and holidays, leaves of absence, child care services, and discounts on goods and services, receive little if any attention. Although the benefits offered under these programs can be important, the design of these plans usually does not involve risk management issues.

SCOPE AND IMPORTANCE

Employee benefits can be defined broadly to include all forms of compensation other than direct wages and salaries. Under this broad definition, employee benefits include pensions, death benefits, sick pay, health care, unemployment benefits, paid vacation and holidays, employer-provided vehicles, and purchase discounts on products. Survey data collected by the U.S. Chamber of Commerce in 1992 show that the value of these broadly defined benefits is 39.1 percent of payroll in the United States. This chapter focuses on a narrower category of benefits: ones that constitute a direct outlay by the employer and address human resource risk exposures of employees.

Using the narrower definition, the cost of employer-provided benefits still is a major outlay for employers. Table 24.1, which is based on 1992 U.S. Chamber of Commerce survey data, provides an estimate of the cost of benefits relative to payroll in 1992, with a comparison to 1929. Relative to payroll, the cost of these programs has grown more than 20-fold since 1929. Growth in mandated social insurance coverage explains part of the increase, and social insurance contributions such as OASDHI payroll tax are mandated by law for most employers. However, the most rapid growth has been in the cost of life and health coverage (principally health care), which for the most part has been voluntary. Even if health care coverage becomes mandated as envisioned under current proposed legislation, much of the growth in this category will have occurred while coverage was voluntary.

The rate of participation in benefit programs is a second measure of importance. Annual surveys conducted by the U.S. Department of Labor offer data on the percent of full-time employees who participate in selected categories of benefit programs. A portion of the survey data appears in Table 24.2 for all types of employees of large private organizations, small private organizations, and state and local governments. The Department of Labor survey offers additional detail, such as participation rates classified by type of employee, so a risk manager could use the data as a set of national benchmarks.

LIFE INSURANCE AND SURVIVOR BENEFIT PROGRAMS

The first known group life insurance contract was written in 1912 on the employees of Montgomery Ward & Company, making life insurance one of the earliest known employee benefit programs in the United States. The coverage in the Montgomery Ward plan took into account family conditions and salary status, so it resembled survivor income benefit programs more closely than the

TABLE 24.1. Employer's Cost of Selected Categories of Employee Benefits as a Percent of Wages and Salaries, 1929 and 1992

Type of Benefit	1929	1992
Legally Required (OASDHI, Workers' Compensation, Unemployment	0.8	12.1
Pensions	0.2	5.3
Insurance Coverage	0.1	7.2
TOTAL	1.1	24.6

Data Source: Employee Benefits, 1993 edition. Washington, D.C., U.S. Chamber of Commerce, annual.

TABLE 24.2. Percent of Full-Time Employees Participating in Selected Categories of Employee Benefit Programs

Type of Benefit	*Percent Participating*		
	Medium and Large Private Establishments (1991)	Small Private Establishments (1990)	State and Local Governments (1990)
Medical Care	83	69	93
Long-Term Disability Income Insurance	40	19	27
Dental Care	60	30	62
Life Insurance	94	64	88
Retirement Income	78	42	96
Flexible Benefits Programs	10	1	5
Reimbursement Accounts	36	8	31
Paid Vacations	96	88	67
Paid Maternity Leave	2	2	1
Paid Paternity Leave	1	nil	1
Unpaid Maternity Leave	37	17	51
Unpaid Paternity Leave	26	8	33

Sources: U.S. Department of Labor, Bureau of Labor Statistics: *Employee Benefits in Medium and Large Private Establishments, 1991, Employee Benefits in Small Private Establishments, 1990, Employee Benefits in State and Local Governments, 1990.* Washington, D.C., U.S. Government Printing Office, issued in alternate years.

typical life insurance program offered today. Most group life insurance offered today is yearly renewable term insurance. The plan provides a stated death benefit if the employee dies during the period of coverage, with no cash value or other savings provided to an employee who withdraws from the plan. Some employers also offer survivor income benefit programs whose benefits depend on the number and type of the employee's dependents. A few employers offer group paid-up life or group universal life plans, although some of these plans are only mass merchandising programs with employees paying most or all of the program's cost.

Yearly Renewable Term Insurance

Under group yearly renewable term insurance, a one-year term insurance policy is purchased on each group member. The amount of coverage often is a multiple of earnings. Less common are plans providing the same amount on all employees or an amount of coverage that depends on the occupation of the employee. Some plans offer elective additional coverage on dependents or employees, with employees paying part or all of the cost.

Because the cost per $1000 of term insurance coverage increases as a group member ages, the value of the benefit tends to increase as an employee becomes older. Some plans reduce the amount of coverage on the employee after the employee passes a threshold age. For example, a plan providing coverage of two times annual earnings reduced by 5 percent per year beyond age 55 would provide 185 percent of annual earnings to an employee age 58. The reduction in coverage after a threshold age tends to offset the effect of the age-based rate increase.

If an employer-provided life insurance plan qualifies for favorable tax treatment, the employee is not required to report the premium for the first $50,000 of term life insurance as part of taxable income. The employer is allowed to deduct the cost of coverage from its taxable income, the same as other compensation to employees. Similar tax treatment applies to employer contributions to fund term life insurance benefits after retirement under *retired lives reserves*; the employer is allowed to deduct contributions that are not included in employees' taxable income. The net effect of this favorable tax treatment is to allow the cost of the first $50,000 of coverage to be received by employees as a tax-free benefit. The cost of coverage in excess of $50,000 is imputed as income to the employee (the employer is allowed to deduct the cost of all coverage).

The amount of imputed income is calculated using an IRS table of group term insurance rates, not the actual cost of coverage to the employer. The $50,000 limit on the amount of coverage that can be provided tax-free has applied for decades, having not been indexed for price increases. During the mid-1960s, $50,000 was at least six times earnings for a typical new college graduate. In 1994, $50,000 is about twice the annual earnings of the new college graduate. Over time, the effect of failing to increase the limit is to sweep an increasing proportion of group life insurance benefits out of the tax-favored category.

The favorable tax treatment applies only to insurance, not death benefits paid directly by the employer. If the employer provides a death benefit directly, the amount in excess of $5000 is considered part of the employee's taxable income. The strong tax incentive favoring insurance applies when insurance plans use retrospective premium adjustments and dividends, financing plans that can closely resemble self-insurance. Chapter 10 offers additional information on risk financing plans that employ services of insurers. As a consequence of the tax incentive to provide death benefits through insurance, almost all group plans providing death benefits are funded using insurance or a 501(c)(9) trust, sometimes called a VEBA (Voluntary Employees' Beneficiary Association).

Survivor Income Benefits

Survivor income benefit insurance differs from the usual form of yearly renewable term insurance in that generally (1) the death benefit is payable only if there is a qualified survivor such as a spouse or dependent child, (2) the benefit is a monthly income that is related to the deceased employee's earnings, and (3) the benefits stop if the survivor dies before the maximum number of payments have been made. To illustrate, one plan pays a surviving spouse 25 percent of the deceased's monthly earnings and each of the surviving children 15 percent, subject to a family maximum of 40 percent. The spouse receives his or her benefit to age 62 unless he or she dies or remarries earlier. Instead of basing the benefit on the deceased's employee's earnings, some plans provide flat monthly benefits; others vary the benefit according to the employee's position. The family maximum benefits also vary. For example, some plans will pay a surviving spouse a lifetime income if he or she does not remarry. Some permit the employee to designate a beneficiary other than a spouse or children, but in this case, the benefit is paid only for a specified period. Finally, the insurer may pay a lump-sum benefit if the spouse remarries. Survivor income benefit insurance is seldom the only group life insurance benefit. Instead, it usually supplements a multiple-of-earnings plan with the employee paying all or part of the cost.

Group Paid-up Life or Group Universal Life Insurance

Whole life or universal life insurance is offered under group benefit programs, although not as commonly as term insurance. Under group paid-up or universal life plans, the employee is entitled to a cash surrender value or other nonforfeiture values upon withdrawing from the plan. Typically, employee contributions are used to fund the investment portion of the policy, with the employer funding the term insurance portion (see Chapter 18 for a description of the investment and term insurance portions of life insurance).

For example, a plan may offer the same amount of coverage to all employees. Employee contributions may be used to purchase single-premium life insurance whose amount accumulates as the employee continues to remain in the plan. Employer contributions are used to fund term insurance providing the balance of the promised benefit. Under such a plan, the employer funds a decreasing term policy while the employee funds an increasing investment. None of the employer contribution can be used to fund the investment portion of the policy without creating taxable income for the employee. Employer contributions used to fund term insurance are accorded the same tax treatment as employer contributions to yearly renewable term coverage.

In some cases, plans offering whole life or universal life insurance are only mass merchandising arrangements with employees paying most or all of the plan's cost. Mass merchandising methods and payroll deduction financing may reduce distribution costs of the insurance sold under these plans, allowing the insurer to offer rates that may be lower than for comparable individual coverage. Although an employer may view such a plan as involving no direct costs, the time and effort of the employer's staff (e.g., in administering payroll deduction) and time of employees spent during marketing solicitation efforts by the insurer are factors to weigh in considering such plans.

Other Life Insurance Benefits

A variety of other life insurance benefits are offered through employer-sponsored benefit programs, although the amounts of coverage tend to be less significant than coverage under plans discussed above. For example, many employers offer dependent life insurance coverage, with employees paying most or all of the cost of coverage. Many of these plans offer an amount of coverage on dependent children that is small enough to suggest usage as a funeral expense benefit. Some employers provide self-insured benefits to employees, although the previously noted $5000 limit on death benefits that can be provided tax-free by an employer is a restraint on these plans.

Death benefits often are provided as part of a pension plan (e.g., a death benefit to a surviving spouse if the employee dies prior to retirement). Federal regulations require that pension plans provide survivor benefits that closely resemble life insurance and in some circumstances are funded through the purchase of insurance (e.g., a surviving spouse being entitled to a monthly income that is at least as large as the benefit that would have been paid if a joint and survivor annuity providing 50 percent to the survivor had been selected as the retirement income option). As a general rule, providing death benefits through a pension plan is not likely to jeopardize the tax status of the plan as long as the cost of death benefits beyond the minimum required by federal regulation is not a substantial fraction of the total cost of the plan. Beam and McFadden (1992, ch. 21) offer information on regulations applying to incidental benefits provided as part of a retirement program.

HEALTH BENEFIT PROGRAMS, INCLUDING DISABILITY INCOME

Coverage offered under employer-sponsored health benefit programs can be classified into two categories: (1) programs offering medical care service or reimbursement of medical expenses, and (2) disability income coverage. Of the two areas, medical expense insurance has become identified as a more controversial economic and social problem. The topics of health care and coverage for health care services are important enough to merit an entire chapter, Chapter 19. Methods used by employers to finance coverage for health care services have been discussed in Chapter 10.

Discussion of benefit provisions in coverage for health care services and in disability income insurance appeared in Chapter 19 and will not be repeated here. Rather, two areas of coverage for health care services that were not discussed extensively will be reviewed: dental benefit programs and vision care plans. Although these programs often provide benefits related to health care, typically they are not covered by the broader health insurance coverage because cost-efficient specialty payers and providers have evolved.

More precisely, group health insurance plans usually apply to vision or dental problems related to a broader health condition (e.g., vision problems related to diabetes or dental care required after injuries in an automobile accident). However, routine services, such as eye examinations and corrective lenses or dental cleaning and fillings, usually require specific coverage. In addition, many employer-sponsored benefit programs offer special coverage for prescription drugs.

Dental, Vision Care, and Prescription Drug Benefit Programs

For most individuals, dental, vision care, and prescription drugs comprise only a minor share of the total cost of medical services generally, although employees often regard coverage for these areas as important. Employers that offer coverage for medical services frequently include coverage for dental and vision care. Earlier, Table 24.2 showed that 60 percent of the employees of medium-sized and large employers report that they participate in a dental benefit program. Typically, dental benefit plans are written by insurers that specialize in this type of coverage or health insurers writing broader coverage that have a department specializing in the dental benefit area. Dental benefit programs tend to rely on explicit controls, such as limits on frequency of covered services, requirements for predetermination of benefits by the insurer in advance of expensive procedures, and limits on the use of precious metals.

The typical dental benefit plan provides fairly full coverage for services such as diagnosis and routine cleaning, with limits on frequency. A 20 percent participation may be imposed on the cost of basic restorative services such as fillings, root canal, and gum treatment, often after a deductible. Fee schedules also may impose limits on charges considered for these services, subject to a further limit on benefits during a calendar year. The most expensive procedures, such as prosthodontia, orthodontics, and inlays employing precious metals, require a 50 percent participation. Reimbursement for orthodontic procedures often is limited to dependent minors and is subject to a relatively low lifetime limit such as $750.

As a general rule, the more expensive procedures receive only limited coverage, while routine cleaning and examinations are more fully covered, subject to limits on frequency of usage. The pattern of coverage in these plans is nearly the reverse of what would be expected if protection against large, unpredictable outlays were the major concern driving the design of the plan. Concern with possible effects of the plan on providers and users of dental services weighs heavily in the design of these plans.

Provisions of group vision care plans tend to mirror those in dental benefit programs. Plans tend to be administered by organizations that specialize in this type of coverage. Strict limits are common on frequency of services and on reimbursement of items in which fashion and appearance can be important. For example, a plan may allow one vision examination and one pair of corrective lenses every two years. The full cost of the examination and corrective lenses may be covered, but reimbursement for frames may be based on the lowest-cost (and least attractive in appearance) option offered by a manufacturer.

Coverage for prescription drugs is provided under most group health benefit plans, but the area often is identified for special coverage or financial incentives are used to steer usage toward low-cost providers or to use generic drugs. For drugs taken over extended periods, some plans waive copayments for drugs provided through a mail-order pharmacy in order to provide a financial incentive to use a low-cost source of prescription drugs.

Temporary Disability Income Insurance

Group temporary disability income insurance, often referred to as group accident and health insurance, provides a specified weekly benefit for a totally disabled person for a maximum duration of 13 or 26 weeks, or less commonly, 52 or 104 weeks. No distinction is made between disabilities caused by accident or sickness except that no benefits are usually payable for at least the first seven days of sickness-incurred disability, whereas a shorter waiting period or none at all may apply to disabilities caused by accidents. The weekly benefit is usually two-thirds of weekly earnings, subject to some maximum weekly amount.

Occupational injuries and diseases are commonly excluded under the contract. Temporary disability income benefits, however, sometimes exceed the statutory workers' compensation payments. Consequently, some employers prefer to cover occupational injuries as well, but deduct workers' compensation payments from the group insurance benefit.

If an employee terminates employment, his or her insurance automatically terminates except that an employee who is absent on account of injury or sickness continues to be covered until premium payments are discontinued or, if earlier, until maximum benefits have been paid for any one disability.

Long-Term Disability Insurance

Starting in the 1960s long-term disability (LTD) insurance began to attract considerable interest and attention. Initially these plans were limited to the organization's higher-paid management employees. Many plans are still so limited, but most cover a broader class of employees.

LTD plans typically pay a totally disabled employee a monthly income for some long-term period after the completion of a waiting period. Payments are usually continued to age 65 or 70, but some plans limit payments to five or ten years. Typically, the employee is considered disabled the first two or five years if he or she cannot perform the duties of his or her own occupation. To receive benefits after the first two or five years, the worker must be unable to engage in any occupation for which he or she is reasonably fitted by education, training, or experience. Some insurers, however, use the "own occupation" standard for much longer periods, for example, to age 65 or 70. Disability benefits are not paid if the disablement is caused by self-inflicted injuries, war, and injuries sustained by the insured while committing a felony.

The waiting period is usually five or six months, which restricts benefit payments to seriously disabled workers and lessens the chance of overlaps with TDI or paid sick-leave plans. If the organization has no short-term disability plan, the waiting period may be only 60 or 90 days.

The monthly income payment is usually some percentage, such as 60 percent, of the worker's most recent base wage, subject to some maximum dollar amount. Benefits are usually reduced by any Old-Age, Survivor, Disability, and Health Insurance; workers' compensation; other public programs; or private pension benefits. For example, a plan may state that the benefit is 60 percent of the worker's prior earnings less the worker's OASDI benefit. Under a second plan the benefit may be 70 percent of the worker's prior earnings less the worker's and his or her dependents' OASDI benefits. A third example is 50 percent of the worker's prior earnings but no more than 70 percent of the prior earnings less the worker's and dependents' OASDI benefits.

Because the OASDI definition of total disability—inability to engage in any substantially gainful activity—tends to be more restrictive than LTD definitions, many disabled workers would receive LTD benefits without any OASDI offset.

Some LTD plans provide for periodic adjustments in the benefits being paid to disabled workers as price levels change. The adjustment is usually limited to 3 percent, but the benefit cannot drop below the original benefit amount. A more common approach simply ignores the cost of living increase in OASDI benefits in determining the OASDI offset to LTD benefits.

Many plans provide partial disability benefits that are designed to provide incentives for a person receiving total disability benefits to return to work. One approach reduces the total disability benefit by less than 100 percent of the amount earned by the partially disabled worker. Others do not promise to pay partial disability benefits but do so as part of a rehabilitation process. At least one plan has experimented with partial disability benefits based on reduction of earnings, but does not require that the initial disablement be total.

Another feature of some LTD plans is a pension accrual benefit that either continues contributions to the organization's pension plan on behalf of the disabled employee or supplements the employee's pension after he or she reaches retirement age.

The rates for LTD coverage depend primarily upon the age and sex composition of the group. Experience rating and retrospective rate adjustments also affect the rates.

Disability Provisions in Group Life Insurance Plans

Most group life insurance contracts being issued today waive future premiums for a totally and permanently disabled employee. Some provide for the payment of the face amount if the employee either dies or becomes totally and permanently disabled. A one-year waiver of premiums, called *extended death benefit*, also is found in some contracts.

Disability Provisions in Pension Plans

Pension plans have early retirement and withdrawal benefits that are available to totally and permanently disabled persons as well as to others, but the use of these options reduces or eliminates the retirement benefit. Sometimes early retirement is possible only if the employee is totally and permanently disabled. Another approach in such cases is to liberalize the vesting conditions. The most liberal benefits, found in few plans, provide for the waiver of future contributions toward the pension plan, the payment of a total and permanent disability income, or both.

Sick-Leave Plans

Sick-leave plans are underwritten exclusively by the employer. These plans usually continue the wages or salary of the disabled worker in full for a specified period, which may be graduated by length of service. Under most plans, sick leave is not cumulative. Many sick-leave plans supplement in some way an insured program providing benefits in case of temporary disability, for example, by payments during the first two weeks, after which the insurance program takes over. Some workers collecting temporary disability insurance or workers' compensation benefits receive additional amounts under the sick-leave plan.

The sick-leave risk is retained because the loss can be predicted with a fair degree of accuracy, the loss severity is small, and, many claim, employees are less likely to feign illness if they are accountable to their employer. In addition, insurers are reluctant to provide benefits equal to the full wage. Sick-leave payments are usually made out of current operating income.

An objective for a retirement income program can be stated simply: to provide post-retirement income that maintains the employee's life style prior to retirement. Underneath this apparent simplicity, retirement income programs often include features whose complexity rivals the regulations applying to all other benefit programs combined. The level of resources required is one reason for the complexity. Retirement tends to be an expensive proposition. A single-life annuity providing an annual benefit of $35,000 at age 65 requires a premium of approximately $400,000. Allocating the responsibility for accumulating a fund this large and accounting for the consequences can give rise to complex technical issues.

This section describes basic features of retirement income programs and explains their relationship to the objective stated above. It does not cover all types of programs, and it is not a guide to taxation of retirement income programs or to meeting qualification requirements. Additional information on retirement programs appears in Beam and McFadden (1992) and in other references appearing at the end of this chapter. The most current information is available from on-line information retrieval systems and data services.

Profit-Sharing Plans Contrasted with Pensions

The distinction between profit-sharing plans and pension programs is basic. A profit-sharing plan is a promise by an employer to share profits with employees. The employer, usually a business firm, agrees to contribute a share of profits to a fund for the benefit of employees. The profit-sharing plan may distribute these contributions immediately or on a schedule of payouts. Under a deferred profit-sharing plan, the distribution of funds to an employee occurs only on the occurrence of specified events, such as the employee's death, disablement, retirement, or termination of employment.

As a retirement income program, a profit-sharing plan suffers from several shortcomings: (1) the level of retirement income cannot be predicted accurately because the level of future employer contributions is not known, (2) the plan cannot guarantee a lifetime income to a retired employee unless the employee's accumulation is used to purchase an annuity at retirement, and (3) adequate recognition of service provided by older employees prior to the date the plan was established is impossible if the plan is to be qualified under the Internal Revenue Code.

From the employer's point of view, a profit-sharing plan is subject to fewer regulations because the plan does not promise a pension benefit. The profit-sharing plan also offers the employer the advantage of relating contributions to profits. Some employers may argue that a profit-sharing plan creates a financial incentive for employees to improve the employer's profitability. However, the contribution of an individual employee to an employer's overall profitability is likely to be small, making this incentive weak.

As contrasted with profit-sharing plans, a pension plan offers stronger guarantees. The employer guarantees either a specified benefit at retirement (under a *defined benefit* plan) or guarantees a contribution to a fund available to the employee at retirement (under a *defined contribution* plan). Pension plans also are subject to heavier regulation, particularly defined benefit plans. The nature of the guarantees and the regulations that apply to pension plans comprises a substantial portion of this chapter.

Defined Benefit Plans Contrasted with Defined Contribution Plans

With respect to pension plans, the distinction between defined benefit and defined contribution plans is basic. In a *defined benefit* plan, the benefit to which a retiring employee is entitled is stated in the plan description. A defined benefit plan uses a formula, usually based on the employee's compensation near retirement and length of service, to determine the pension benefit to which the retiring employee is entitled. Final average salary (FAS) formulas have been popular in defined-benefit plans. The FAS formula is used to determine average salary during years near retirement, which then is weighted by the employee's length of service under the plan. For example, a final average salary plan might provide 2 percent of final average salary for each year of service, where final average is the average salary during the employee's 3 years of highest earnings. If final average salary is $30,000 and the employee has 25 years of service, this plan would provide a pension of (0.02)(25)($30,000), or $15,000 a year. Defined benefit plans also have used formulas that base the benefit solely on the number of years of service, or on a flat percentage of compensation at retirement.

Under a *defined contribution* plan, the employer contributes a stated amount to an account for each employee. Typically, the employee has control over the investment of funds in the account. From the employer's point of view, the defined contribution plan has the advantage of a known current cost. From the employee's point of view, this advantage for the employer translates into a disadvantage for the employee: the ultimate benefit is unknown, depending in part on investment earnings on the employee's account.

Under a defined contribution plan, the investment risk is borne by the employee. If investment earnings under a defined contribution plan are lower than expected, the reduced earnings translate into lower benefits for the retired employee. For this reason, a defined contribution plan may be called a *money purchase* plan: the retirement benefit for the employee is whatever the account will purchase. Under a defined benefit plan, however, the investment risk is borne by the employer. If investment earnings under a defined benefit plan are less than projected levels, additional funding contributions may be required of the employer.

Defined benefit plans differ from defined contribution plans in another important way: defined contribution plans are subject to fewer regulations. The complexity of defined benefit plans is one reason for heavier regulation of these plans. In a defined benefit plan, an employer promises to pay a retirement benefit whose amount is stated in plan documents. The long interval between the making of the promise and the actual delivery of the benefit creates a public interest in monitoring the performance of the defined benefit plan. Under a defined contribution plan, in contrast, an employer promises to set aside a stated amount in an employee's account. The interval between the making of the promise and actual delivery is much shorter, so less monitoring is required.[1]

Plans have been developed that may be considered hybrids of the defined benefit and defined contribution approaches. For example, a target-benefit plan is a defined contribution plan in which contributions have been set to produce a specified or "target" benefit at retirement. Another type of plan, known as a cash balance plan, is a defined contribution plan in which employees' accounts are credited with a guaranteed return. The cash balance plan thus relieves the employee of a portion of the investment risk present in the typical defined contribution plan.

Other Factors Affecting Benefit Amounts

In a defined contribution plan, the benefit becomes whatever the retiring employee's account is able to purchase. For example, if the cost of a straight life annuity providing $1000 a month for life is $130,000 at age 65, an employee who has accumulated $300,000 is able to purchase a monthly benefit of $2307.69. As an alternative, the employee may take the $300,000 as a lump sum, invest the proceeds and use the investment income for living expenses.

The determination of the benefit amount under a defined benefit plan is more complicated. Under a final average salary plan, for example, the formula benefit (e.g., 2 percent of FAS per year of service) presumes a given age at the time of retirement. This age, called the *normal retirement age,* customarily has been age 65 but a plan could be designed with some other normal retirement age. Ordinarily, retiring before the normal retirement age would be expected to reduce the monthly benefit, while late retirement would be expected to increase the benefit.

These benefit changes are required to maintain actuarial equivalence between benefits paid to employees retiring at different ages. Three factors influence the level of benefits provided: (1) the amount of contributions, (2) the length of time these amounts have been on deposit to earn investment income, and (3) the length of time over which benefits will be paid. If an employee retires prior to the normal retirement age, for example, fewer contributions have been made on the employee's behalf and these deposits have been invested for a shorter period of time. In addition, the early retirement allows the employee to collect benefits over a longer period of time prior to death. In cases in which an employer wants to create *early retirement incentives,* benefits paid to employees who retire early are increased over the amount indicated by actuarial formulas.

The benefit amount also is affected by the *annuity form.* The stated benefit payable at normal retirement age usually is based on a straight life annuity on a single life. Other annuity forms are available as options, but selecting one of these other options usually reduces the benefit amount. For example, a retiring

---

[1] Effective in 1994, both defined benefit and defined contribution are subject to a common restriction: the largest amount of annual compensation that can be considered (in determining either the benefit under a defined benefit plan or the contribution under a defined contribution plan) is $150,000. A limit of $200,000 applied during 1989 to 1993.

employee and spouse may elect an annuity form that provides $3000 a month while both are living, with the benefit reducing to $2000 a month after the first death (a "two-thirds to survivor" annuity). Election of a benefit payable in this "joint and survivor" form typically reduces the benefit below the level payable under the single life annuity option. Other annuity forms typically are offered under retirement plans, such as life annuity with 10 years certain and life annuity with 20 years certain. These annuity forms, which were described in Chapter 18, reduce the benefit below the level that otherwise would be payable as a straight life annuity.

Integration with OASI

Retirement benefit programs can be designed to maintain a stated percentage (e.g., 60 percent) of the employee's income prior to retirement. Because OASDI benefits are another important source of income for most retired employees, the income-maintenance objective usually attempts to integrate the pension with OASDI benefits. Methods used to integrate pension benefits with OASDI can be complicated, in part because federal law restricts the type of formula that can be used. One approach is to offset the retiring employee's initial benefit by a percentage of the OASDI benefit, so that the total OASDI and pension benefit approximate the desired relationship with pre-retirement earnings. Another approach is to integrate the employer's contribution to the pension plan with the contribution to OASDI payroll taxes, stepping up the contribution rate on earnings in excess of the OASDI taxable wage base. However, federal law does not allow pension benefits to be reduced to reflect increases in OASDI benefits that are based on changes in the cost of living after retirement. Only the initial pension benefit can be adjusted to reflect benefits payable under OASDI.

Cost-of-Living Adjustment

Over long periods of time, price increases can dramatically reduce the purchasing power of a fixed pension benefit. Concern with possible effects of price increases may lead to a cost-of-living (COLA) provision in a retirement benefit program. Chapter 22 explained how OASDI benefits are indexed to changes in the price levels reflected in the CPI. Also, employees covered by a final average salary plan enjoy some degree of protection against price increases prior to retirement because salaries tend to be linked to price levels. However, few private pension plans provide for automatic benefit increases linked to price levels. Instead, some private plans make ad hoc benefit adjustments to reflect increased price levels. The few plans having COLA formulas are likely to place a limit, such as 3 percent, on benefit increases due to higher price levels.

Eligibility Requirements

Although pension plans may be designed to cover all employees, normally some eligibility requirements are established. These requirements are commonly higher for pension plans than for other employee benefit plans. Three types of requirements are in common use, either singly or in some combination: (1) Employees may be required to have worked for the employer some minimum period. The purpose here is to reduce the administrative costs associated with rapid turnover. (2) A minimum-age requirement may be established in order to reduce turnover costs related to age. Persons hired near or after the normal retirement age cannot be excluded, but within limits the beginning of their pension can be delayed beyond the normal retirement age. (3) The type of employment may determine whether the employee is eligible. For example, the plan may be limited to full-time employees, salaried employees, union employees, or the employees of one particular plant.

Under federal regulation the maximum service-age eligibility requirement is the later of one year service or age 21. However, a plan that provides immediate full vesting (see below) may require two years of service. The type of employment requirement must not discriminate in favor of highly compensated employees.

Vesting Provisions

The vesting provisions in a pension determine the employee's rights with respect to funds set aside in the plan. If the employee's rights are vested, they are nonforfeitable. If an employee ceases to serve the employer, vested rights under the pension plan belong to the employee. If they are not vested, the employee loses the right to a benefit under the plan. Vesting can be proportional; if an employee terminates participation in a pension plan when a benefit is 60 percent vested, the employee has a legal right to 60 percent of the benefit.

Employee contributions to a pension plan are vested. An employee who terminates employment is entitled to a return of his or her contributions. Also, benefits must become fully vested at the normal retirement age. Prior to the normal retirement age, however, employer contributions may not be fully vested until the employee has completed a minimum length of service. Vesting provisions in pension plans are an important public policy issue because of their effect on the mobility of employees. A very restrictive vesting provision (e.g., vesting only at retirement) would deter employees with substantial service under a pension plan from moving to another employer, because the move would result in losing entitlement to the pension benefit.

Funding Levels

The objective of a pension plan is to accumulate resources that will be used to provide income benefits after retirement. In concept, the level of funding measures the extent to which assets set aside in a pension plan meet this objective. The objective of maintaining a given level of income after retirement (e.g., 60 percent of pre-retirement earnings) can be viewed as setting a target (see the earlier discussion of target-benefit plans). The degree of funding measures how closely the target level has been met. From the viewpoint of an employee covered by a pension plan, the funding level is an important measure of security. The funding level becomes especially important if the employer encounters financial problems that make continued contributions to the pension plan impossible. To the extent that the plan is funded, the benefits promised under the plan are secure despite the employer's inability to continue contributions.

Although the concept of funding is simple, actual measurement of funding may involve accounting and actuarial techniques that are far from simple. The simplest case to consider is a defined contribution plan in which the employer agrees to set aside a percent of an employee's salary (e.g., 5 percent) in an account that belongs to the employee. When delivery of the required contribution is made, the employer has met its promise and the contribution is funded.

Actuarial Cost Estimates. Measurement of funding levels in defined benefit plans can be complex. One problem is that the required level of contributions is uncertain. Even in a final average salary plan, the payments that will be made to employees who retire in the future are not known exactly. Estimates of these payments (or their present value) require assumptions about evolution of future salary levels (since benefits depend directly on salaries), mortality rates prior to and after retirement, turnover rates among covered employees (at least prior to the point at which benefits are vested), retirement rates at the ages when employees are eligible to retire, and levels of future investment returns.

In addition, more than one accounting method is available to measure an employer's obligation with respect to the pension plan. For the purpose of illustration, assume that an employer has established a pension plan providing 2 percent of final average salary per year of service. Possible effects of mortality or turnover are not considered in the illustration. An employee, currently age 51, has just completed 16 years of service, earning a salary of $30,000 during the year. In another 14 years, the employee will have reached the normal retirement age of 65 and be eligible for retirement after completing 30 years of service. The employee's final average salary at retirement is estimated to be $45,000. Based on these assumptions, the estimated annual benefit the employee will receive is (0.02)(30)($45,000), or $27,000.

One year ago, the employee had 15 years of service. By completing the sixteenth year of service, the employee became entitled to an additional 2 percent of final average salary, or $900. The cost of funding benefits attributable to the current year of service is called the *normal cost*. One method for estimating the normal cost for this employee is to calculate the present value of the benefit attributable to the recently completed year of service, in this case the present value of an annuity that pays a benefit of $900 a year with payments commencing in 14 years. A notable feature of this method, called the *accrued benefit* method, is a pattern of funding costs that tends to increase as the employee becomes older. Even if the assumed salary in the last year of service remains at $45,000, the funding cost increases over time because fewer years remain until retirement. At the end of this employee's thirtieth year of service, for example, the normal cost for this employee is the present value of a $900 annuity with payments commencing immediately.

Another approach to estimating normal cost, called the *projected benefit* method, calculates the level annual contribution required to fund the benefit that will be paid when the employee retires. In the above illustration, the cost of providing $45,000 per year at the date of the employee's retirement is amortized over the period of service, but as level annual amounts. If the assumptions used in the original projection remain unchanged, the normal costs for an individual employee remain level over the employee's period of service rather than increasing as the date of retirement draws closer.

The normal cost of a pension plan measures only the employer's obligation arising from the current year's service, which may not be the total amount. An obligation to the pension plan can arise in other ways. A benefit formula under a pension plan may include service that was provided by employees prior to the date the plan was established. In the above illustration, the pension plan may have been established only one year ago, when the employee was age 50 and had 15 years of service. If the pension plan provides credit for this prior service, the benefit upon retirement will be based partly on service for which no contributions were made. This liability, called the *past service liability*, measures the employer's obligation arising from service provided by employees prior to the date the plan was established. Over time, a past service liability tends to grow as the date of retirement draws closer because the present value of each dollar of retirement benefit increases.

An employer's obligation to a pension plan may change in other ways. Changes in benefit formulas, cost-of-living adjustments, or deviation in plan experience from earlier projections may cause the estimated liability to change over time. The total liability arising from past service as well as from these changes in plan experience is called a *supplemental liability*.

Funding the Liability. Once the level of the employer's obligation to the pension has been estimated, the employer's response to that obligation determines the degree of funding. If the degree of funding is portrayed as a continuum, *pay-as-you-go* is at one extreme—the plan is not funded. Under a pay-as-you-go method, the employer contributes only the amount required to pay benefits to currently retired employees. If an unfunded pension plan is terminated, all benefits cease immediately.

Most pension plans use advance funding in that assets are set aside in advance of employees' actual retirement. Typically, assets are transferred to a trustee or an insurance company that administers the plan. A *fully funded* plan holds title to assets whose current value equals the total liabilities of the plan. In concept, a fully funded plan owns assets whose value is large enough to fund all benefits that have been promised for service provided to date. For a pension plan to become fully funded, the amounts contributed to the plan must cover the plan's normal cost plus an additional contribution to amortize the supplemental liability. After the plan becomes fully funded, contributions equal to the plan's normal cost allow it to remain fully funded unless the plan's experience deviates from levels assumed in funding estimates.

However, two pension plans that have identical benefit formulas and are fully funded still may own asset portfolios whose values are not identical. The type of actuarial cost technique employed by the pension plan determines the level of assets required to be fully funded and the pattern of contributions required to remain fully funded.

In particular, the accrued benefit method implies a pattern of increasing costs as an employee becomes older, while under the projected benefit method the cost accruals are level. In concept, liability with respect to an individual employee is identical under either method by the time the employee reaches normal retirement age. However, the pattern of accruals is increasing over time under an accrued benefit method and level under a projected benefit method.

This difference could become important if a pension plan is terminated. At a given point in time, the liability of a plan sponsor tends to be smaller under an accrued benefit method because a larger portion of the cost accruals have yet to take place. If a plan sponsor were to terminate a fully funded pension plan and purchase annuities from an insurance company to fulfill its obligation for benefits accrued to date, the value of the annuities is smaller under the accrued benefit method.

Also, a final average salary plan that is terminated is likely to base an employee's benefit on final average salary during the time the plan was active, not the salary that would have been used to determine the benefit if the plan had remained in force. An employee who is age 55 and currently earns $30,000 a year may expect to have a final average salary of $40,000 by normal retirement age of 65. If the plan is terminated when the employee is 55, the plan sponsor's obligation may be assessed using a salary of $30,000 rather than the $40,000 that would have been used if the plan had not been terminated.

Pension Plan Administration

The assets of qualified pension plans must be held by a *funding agency,* such as a trustee or an insurance company. A trustee, such as the trust department of a bank, is the most common type of funding agency. The duties of the trustee are set out in a formal trust agreement. The trustee, as a fiduciary for the pension plan, is obligated to invest the plan assets prudently and to distribute benefits according to directions from the employer. In discharging these duties, the trustee is required to act solely in the interest of employees covered by the pension plan. Typically, the trustee makes no guarantees with respect to pension plan benefits other than to invest the plan assets prudently and to manage the plan in accordance with terms of the agreement with the employer.

Plans using an insurance company as funding agency are less common than trusteed plans. Under insured plans, an insurer may back up promises of the employer. *Group deferred annuities, deposit administration contracts* and *separate account plans* are examples of pension plans that use an insurance company as funding agency. Under a group deferred annuity plan, employer contributions are used to purchase a deferred annuity providing the promised benefit. Because of inflexibility with respect to funding patterns and benefit formulas, group deferred annuity plans are not common.

Deposit administration contracts are more flexible than group deferred annuity contracts, but they also include fewer guarantees by the insurer. Contributions to the plan are paid into a fund that accumulates interest. Unlike the group deferred annuity plan, the fund is undivided, that is, there are no accounts for individual employees. At retirement, an annuity may be purchased on the retiring employee. In some cases, the annuity may be purchased when benefits become vested. The insurer may provide guarantees with respect to annuity purchase rates or a minimum rate of return on investment.

A separate account plan is a type of deposit administration plan in which the employer's contributions are deposited in a separate account that is not commingled with the insurer's other assets. The separate account is not subject to the usual restrictions applying to insurers. For example, a large portion of the separate account may be invested in common stock, which allows the separate account to offer a higher expected return but fewer guarantees than a deposit administration plan not using a separate account.

The Employee Retirement Income Security Act of 1974

The Employee Retirement Income Security Act of 1974 (ERISA), together with the amendments and administrative rulings to interpret the Act, is the most important federal legislation affecting private retirement income programs in the United States during the twentieth century. The Act applies to pension plans except government plans, church plans, union plans to which employers do not contribute, and certain nonqualified plans maintained for the benefit of managers or other highly compensated employees. ERISA places important constraints on the design and management of a pension plan, a few of which are presented below.

ERISA does not apply to all retirement income plans, and it does not require an employer to establish such a plan. The most stringent regulations apply to defined benefit plans, a factor that may have contributed to recent growth in defined contribution relative to defined benefit plans. ERISA also established the *Pension Benefit Guaranty Corporation* (PBGC), a government corporation that administers a federal insurance program to guarantee benefits promised under private defined benefit pension plans. Compared with defined benefit plans, defined contribution plans enjoy relative simplicity, lower levels of regulation, and absence of premiums for PBGC insurance, features that are attractive to employers.

ERISA imposes minimum *vesting standards* for all private pension plans. The vesting schedule must be at least as favorable to the employee as one of the following.

1. 100 percent vesting after five years of service
2. 20 percent vesting after three years of service increasing by 20 percent for each of the next four years. Under this schedule initially benefits will vest faster than under schedule 1 but 100 percent vesting will not be achieved until after seven years of service.

Many plans contain vesting provisions that are more favorable to employees, the most liberal being full immediate vesting. Even these pans, however, usually require the employee to wait until retirement age to receive the vested benefits.

Plans that are considered "top heavy" are required to establish a faster vesting schedule. A plan is top heavy if key employees account for more than 60 percent of total account balances under the plan.

ERISA also requires defined benefit pension plans to meet minimum *funding standards*. For reasons that are obvious, a pay-as-you-go approach does not meet ERISA standards. The basic standard under ERISA is full funding, although a plan generally has a period of 10 to 30 years to achieve full funding. To meet this standard requires contributions equal to the plan's normal cost plus an additional contribution to amortize the supplemental liability over a 10- to 30-year period.

ERISA regulates *annuity forms* provided as options for payment of retirement income. For an employee whose spouse is surviving and has been married to the employee for at least one year at the time of retirement, ERISA requires the plan to continue at least 50 percent of the original benefit to the survivor after the first of the two deaths (i.e., a "50 percent to survivor" benefit). This "joint and survivor" benefit must be provided unless the employee directs otherwise and the spouse consents.

Finally, ERISA imposes minimum standards on *benefit accrual,* the rate at which benefits accrue under defined benefit plans. These standards prevent an employer from circumventing vesting rules by accruing benefits rapidly in the years near retirement. For example, a pension plan could not use a rule in which an employee becomes entitled to 50 percent of final salary only after completing 25 years of service.

Pension Benefit Guaranty Insurance

With the enactment of ERISA in 1974, defined benefit pension plans became covered by a program of plan termination insurance. This insurance program is administered by the Pension Benefit Guaranty Corporation (PBGC), an agency of the U.S. Labor Department. The PBGC insurance program insures *vested* pension benefits of employees covered by a *defined benefit* pension that is terminated, subject to a limit that is indexed over time. The limit, which was $750 per month in 1975, exceeded $2200 in 1991. If the PBGC pays any pension benefit under a terminated plan, the employer remains liable for the unfunded amount and the PBGC is a preferred creditor for up to 30 percent of the employer's net worth.

PBGC insurance does not apply to defined contribution plans, nor does it apply to government plans, church plans, plans favoring highly compensated executives, and other plans not covered by ERISA. PBGC insurance also does not apply to benefits guaranteed by an insurer. For example, if an employer terminates a pension plan and purchases annuity contracts providing the promised benefits from an insurance company, benefit recipients would seek recourse from state insurance guaranty funds if the insurer becomes insolvent.

The PBGC insurance is funded from premiums paid by employers. The premium for single-employer plans, which began at $1 per employee-year in 1975, recently became $16 per employee-year with a possible additional assessment of up to $34 per employee-year for a plan in which unfunded vested benefits are at a high level. Coverage and cost provisions applying to multi-employer plans are more complex than those applying to single-employer plans.

401(k), 403(b), IRA, SEP, and Other Salary-Reduction Plans

The U.S. Tax Code offers tax incentives for individuals and their employers to set aside funds in retirement income programs. The plans discussed in this section provide tax incentives for individuals to set aside a portion of current salary in a retirement account. Because these plans result in an individual's current taxable salary being reduced, they are called salary-reduction or deferred-compensation plans. Often, these plans are set up to supplement another employer-provided retirement income program. Some of these plans also allow employer contributions to the employee's account. They are all defined contribution plans. Often, these plans are identified by the section of the U.S. Internal Revenue Code that permits the program, as in the 401(k) and 403(b) plans. If the plan qualifies by meeting Code requirements related to nondiscrimination and limits on allowable contributions, amounts set aside by employees do not constitute part of their current taxable income.

Although specific Code restrictions apply to each type of plan, a major difference among these plans is the category of individual who is eligible to participate in the plan. Section 401(k) plans apply to employees of for-profit employers. Section 403(b) plans apply to employees of nonprofit employers, such as charitable and educational institutions. Individual retirement account (IRA) plans apply to low- and middle-income employees who are not covered by qualified pension plans. Simplified employee pension (SEP) plans resemble IRA plans in that individual accounts are maintained for each employee, but the plan is established by the employer.

All these plans allow employees to defer taxation of salary set aside to fund retirement benefits. For example, an eligible employee who currently receives a salary of $30,000 may set aside $1500 for retirement and report $28,500 as federal taxable income. Investment earnings on the employee's account are not currently taxable to either the account or the employee. After the employee retires and begins to receive income from the account, the benefits become part of the employee's taxable income. Employer contributions to 401(k), 403(b) and SEP plans are allowed (but not required) as long as the plan meets tests designed to discourage discrimination in favor of highly compensated employees. Under qualified plans, employers are allowed to deduct these contributions from their taxable income, but employees are not required to include these amounts in their taxable income at the time the employer makes the contribution.

FLEXIBLE OR "CAFETERIA" BENEFIT PROGRAMS

Flexible benefits programs allow employees to choose the composition of their program of benefits. For example, an employee with no dependents may be able to reduce the amount of life insurance and allocate the resulting savings to a health care plan that includes a physical fitness program. In a typical flexible benefits program, an employer budgets a fixed amount to an employee's benefits account, which the employee allocates to optional packages of benefits. Employees usually are offered the option to supplement the employer's contribution to the plan by reducing their salary.

Flexible benefits programs were rare before 1980. Uncertainty was present about possible taxation of flexible benefits programs until these issues were resolved by regulations issued during the 1980s. After the clarifying regulations, flexible benefits programs became popular. In general, the kind of benefits that can be included in flexible benefits programs are those that would not be taxable if the employer provided them directly. Parking is an exception, and so is any benefit that defers compensation, such as retirement income. For example, a flexible benefits program can offer life insurance as an option, but the premium for amounts in excess of $50,000 is imputed to the employee's taxable income.

The regulations permitting flexible benefits programs also provide the option to create *flexible spending accounts.* These accounts are not required to be part of a flexible benefits program but may be established in conjunction with a fixed program of benefits. Contributions to these accounts, which may be derived from any combination of employer contributions and salary reduction by employees, may be used to reimburse expenses that could be reimbursed directly by the employer without affecting the employee's taxable income. For example, a flexible spending account could be used to cover the deductible or co-payments required in a medical benefits program.

Employee salary reductions used to fund flexible spending accounts must be elected at the beginning of a plan year as a payroll deduction. The payroll deduction amount cannot be changed during the plan year except under stated circumstances, such as a change in family status. Two types of reimbursement accounts are allowed: health care spending accounts and dependent care accounts. The two accounts must be kept separate. At the end of a plan year, any amounts remaining in either spending account are forfeited by the employee (a "use it or lose it" rule).

With regard to health care spending accounts, the employer must make the full amount available immediately to the employee. If an employee elects to set aside $75 a month but incurs $500 of unreimbursed medical expenses during the first month, the employer is required to reimburse the full $500, in effect advancing a $425 interest-free loan to be repaid by forthcoming payroll deductions.

If an employee has the option to take any benefit under a flexible benefit program as cash (or a benefit that is close to cash such as deferred compensation), the cost of the benefit becomes part of the employee's taxable income. For example, unused contributions to a health care spending account cannot be rolled over into a 401(k) plan without the entire account becoming taxable.

Although these rules on flexible spending accounts may seem harsh in their possible effects, they allow flexible spending accounts to work much as if the employer had provided the in-kind benefits directly to the employee as part of the benefit program. For example, an employer that offers dental benefits to an employee cannot offer the option to take cash in lieu of the benefit without making it taxable. Also, if the employee has extensive dental work that is covered under the plan, the employer is obligated to pay for the dental work under terms offered to all employees, some of whom may have received no dental services during the period.

Flexible benefits plans are popular with employees because they provide choices not available in fixed benefits programs. Despite the administrative complexity and additional recordkeeping burdens, many employers are pleased with flexible benefits programs because they allow budgets for benefits to be determined more accurately. From the viewpoint of employees, however, greater certainty for the employer's share of the benefits cost means that the burden of cost increases has been shifted to employees.

For example, under a fixed benefits program in which the employer pays the full cost of health care benefits, the full burden of cost increases falls on the employer. Under a flexible benefits program in which the employer allocates a fixed amount to each employee's benefit account, increases in the cost of health care coverage become the employee's problem. An increase in the cost of health care coverage forces the employee to either trim back other coverage or increase the amount of salary contributed to fund the program.

Because employees tend to choose benefit options that they believe they are likely to use, the options under flexible benefits programs tend to be more expensive than the same benefits offered under fixed programs in which all employees are provided the same benefits. This tendency toward "adverse selection" can be reduced by plan design. One common design is to offer a common "core" of benefits to all employees, with employees selecting optional benefits beyond the core. Another design is to offer packages or "modules" that combine benefits in ways designed to reduce adverse selection.

TYPICAL FEATURES OF GROUP BENEFIT PROGRAMS

The Concept of Group Underwriting

In group benefit programs, *group underwriting* replaces individual underwriting used on individually issued insurance contracts. In Chapter 13, underwriting was identified as the process that is used by an insurer to determine whether an individual applicant is eligible for insurance coverage. An insurer normally rejects some applicants for individual coverage and accepts others. When coverage is proposed for a group, however, the underwriting decision typically considers the entire group as an entity rather than individual group members. As a result of group underwriting, an individual who becomes a member of the group is eligible for coverage on the same terms as other members of the group. Typically, the outcome of a group underwriting effort would not be the outright rejection of a group, but the plan of coverage might be customized to suit characteristics of the group.

In a benefit program for a group of employees, conditions for eligibility often serve a purpose that is similar to underwriting requirements for insurance issued to individual applicants. These conditions, which are a basic consideration in the design of a benefit program, are discussed in Chapter 25.

Many types of group coverage do not use a formal contract of insurance even though the program of benefits closely resembles insurance coverage the group members might purchase as individuals. An insurance contract, if one is present, is with the plan's sponsor (e.g., the employer). Employees often receive a brochure describing coverage in nontechnical language, but the brochure is not a contract of insurance. Insurers often administer group benefit programs, but under administrative service only (ASO) plans their role is to administer the program following directions of the employer (see Chapter 10 for information on ASO and related plans). Even under fully-insured group benefit plans (student health insurance plans often are fully insured), the provisions of coverage, including restrictions on eligibility, are chosen by the plan sponsor (in the case of student health insurance, the educational institution).

When a fully insured plan is proposed, an insurer may consider some groups ineligible for coverage. Tests that are applied to determine whether coverage is feasible for a group include:

1. The insurance should be incidental to the formation of the group. This requirement means that the primary reason for the group's formation should be for some purpose other than obtaining the insurance. Most employee groups would meet this requirement.
2. The number of group members should exceed a stated minimum, such as 25 or 50. As a practical matter, administrative cost savings are not likely to appear except in large groups, and an underwriting decision on a small group (e.g., one with four members) is likely to consider information on individual group members.
3. When participation in the plan is voluntary for group members, a substantial percentage of the eligible group members should elect coverage.
4. Benefits under the program should be determined by formula or by some other method that precludes individual group members choosing their own benefit amounts.

These requirements are safeguards against possible adverse selection problems. The requirements are not strictly followed in practice, but instead represent guidelines. Programs of coverage can be customized by adding features to control adverse selection problems that otherwise might occur. The earlier example of flexible benefits programs restricting choice options in an effort to reduce adverse selection problems illustrates how plan design can control these problems.

Benefit plan administrators and the insurance industry continue to experiment with different forms for relaxing plan restrictions to make programs more attractive. The knowledge gained from these experiments is used in the design of new programs. For example, a health insurer may be willing to write an elective student health insurance plan in which only about 30 percent of eligible students elect coverage. Although the low participation rate may be a cause for concern, at one time such low participation could have grounds for many insurers refusing to write the plan.

Advantages and Disadvantages of Group Coverage

Group benefit programs offer a distinct advantage over the same coverage purchased as individual insurance: low cost. Particularly for large groups, economies of scale in underwriting and sales efforts can result in substantial cost reductions. Group insurance rates often are between one-third and two-thirds the cost of comparable individual coverage, especially for coverage in which significant adverse selection problems are present. Favorable tax treatment of group plans tends to further reduce costs below the level for individual coverage.

Additionally, group coverage offers a means of providing benefits to individuals who otherwise might be uninsurable. Two features of group coverage allow it to serve in this role. The conditions for eligibility that are part of a group benefit program can safeguard against adverse selection that might be present under individual coverage. Even the condition of being employed provides some information about an individual's health condition. Also, financing arrangements such as ASO plans result in the employer shouldering the full burden of benefits paid to otherwise uninsurable employees. As a consequence, an insurer that administers a large group plan typically is less concerned with adverse selection than on individual coverage. In the design of large group plans, the employer and plan administrator typically focus on the suitability of the plan for the particular group rather than the possibility of individual group members selecting against the plan.

The main disadvantage of group benefit programs is the lack of flexibility with respect to tailoring coverage to individuals' desires. This disadvantage is a direct consequence of the "one size fits all" approach often required in large group benefit programs. Flexible benefits programs can partly overcome this disadvantage, but even these programs restrict options offered to group members. Further, the tendency of group members to select the flexible benefits options that they expect to use drives the cost of the options above the level that would prevail if only a single plan of coverage were offered.

The Conversion Privilege

Under group life insurance programs, an individual who withdraws from group membership is offered the opportunity to continue the same amount of coverage by purchasing an individual life insurance policy, usually whole life. Purchasing the policy does not require the individual to offer any evidence of insurability. The same type of option may be offered if the insurer or employer terminates the plan, with the amount of coverage typically limited to $2000 and the option restricted to employees with more than five years of service. The cost of the converted coverage, which is paid by the individual, is the insurer's standard rate for the age and occupation of the individual at the time he or she withdraws from the group. Because the issuance of coverage is guaranteed, adverse selection would be expected under the conversion privilege (e.g., an individual whose health is poor would be more likely to exercise the option to convert than someone in good health). Insurers may cover the cost of this adverse selection by assessing conversion charges against an employer when an employee exercises the conversion privilege.

A more extensive conversion feature is required in health benefit plans under federal legislation. The Consolidated Omnibus Budget Reconciliation Act of 1985 (COBRA) requires all group health benefit plans (except for some government and church plans) to extend a conversion privilege to any individual who *loses eligibility for coverage* under the plan. Because health benefit plans typically cover a spouse and other dependents, the option to convert must be offered to dependents as well as to the employee who withdraws from the group. For example, many health benefit plans provide coverage to dependent children only until age 22. Under COBRA, the conversion privilege must be offered to the dependent child at the time he or she attains the age at which eligibility for coverage is lost. Other possible reasons for loss of eligibility are divorce, legal separation, or retirement of the employee.

The period of coverage that must be offered to the employee who withdraws from the group is 18 months. For covered spouses and dependent children, the period of coverage that must be offered generally is 36 months. The highest rate that the employer can charge for the converted coverage is 102 percent of the employer's regular group rate. As in the case of the conversion privilege offered in group life insurance, adverse selection would be expected to occur as a result of the guarantee of coverage. The adverse selection could be illustrated by an employee who has developed a medical condition that is excluded as a pre-existing condition under another employer's coverage. Under such conditions, the employee who accepts a position with a new employer might elect to convert coverage for the period of time during which the pre-existing condition exclusion applies.

Key Concepts

qualified plan   A benefit program meeting standards required for tax-favored treatment.

yearly renewable term insurance   In benefit programs, a life insurance plan offering one-year term insurance on each employee with a right to renew.

retired lives reserves   A method of funding post-retirement term insurance on employees by accumulating assets in advance of retirement.

group paid-up life   A type of benefit program that provides paid-up life insurance on employees. Typically, the employer funds the term insurance portion of coverage while employees fund the investment portion.

profit-sharing plan   A type of benefit program in which an employer agrees to share profits with employees.

pension plan   A type of retirement income plan in which an employer agrees to provide a stated benefit after retirement or a specified contribution to an employee's account.

defined benefit plan   A type of pension plan in which the benefit to which a retired employee becomes entitled is stated (usually by formula) in the pension plan documents.

final average salary plan   A type of defined benefit plan in which the amount paid to a retired employee is stated as a percentage of average salary near retirement, usually weighted by the employee's length of service.

defined contribution plan   A type of pension plan in which the employer makes a stated contribution (e.g., a specified percentage of salary) to an employee's account.

normal retirement age   In defined benefit pension plans, the age at which an employee becomes entitled to the full benefit provided in the plan. The normal retirement age often is 65.

annuity form   The provision in a pension plan that states conditions under which monthly income is payable, such as single life annuity or joint and survivor annuity.

cost-of-living adjustment (COLA)   A provision in a defined benefit pension plan allowing for changes in the pension benefit to reflect changes in some measure of price levels.

vesting   The provision in a pension plan stating when the employee acquires a legal right to benefits that become payable in the future.

actuarial cost method   The method employed to recognize an obligation (i.e., the liability) to pay future retirement benefits promised under a pension plan.

funding   The extent to which the liabilities of a pension plan are backed by assets owned by the plan.

normal cost   In a defined benefit pension plan, the cost of funding benefits attributable to the current year of service.

accrued benefit method   A method that measures the normal cost of a defined benefit pension plan by estimating the present value of the benefit that can be attributed to the current year of service.

projected benefit method A method that measures the normal cost of a defined benefit pension plan by estimating the level annual contribution required to fund the benefit that will be paid when the employee retires.

past service liability In a defined benefit pension plan, the obligation arising from service provided by employees prior to the date the plan was established.

supplemental liability In a pension plan, the liability arising from past service and from deviations in plan experience from initial projections.

fully funded A condition in which a pension plan holds title to assets whose current value equals the total liabilities of the plan. In concept, a fully funded plan owns assets whose value is large enough to fund all benefits that have been promised for service provided to date.

funding agency A fiduciary, such as a trustee or an insurance company, that holds and manages assets of a pension plan.

ERISA The Employee Retirement Security Act of 1974. An important federal law setting standards for pension plans.

PBGC The Pension Benefit Guaranty Corporation, an agency of the U.S. Labor Department that insures vested pension benefits of employees covered by defined benefit plans.

salary reduction plan Pension plans using individual accounts such as allowed under sections 401(k) or 403(b) of the Internal Revenue Code. Such plans allow an individual to reduce currently taxable salary if the amount is set aside in a retirement account.

flexible benefit plan A benefit program allowing employees to allocate resources among optional benefit forms.

flexible spending account An account that can be used to reimburse the cost of services an employer could have provided the employee on a tax-favored basis.

group underwriting The process used to determine groups that are eligible for coverage. Typically, group underwriting focuses on the suitability of the coverage for the group rather than the insurability of individual group members.

conversion privilege A provision in a group benefit plan that guarantees the right to purchase an individual insurance policy whose benefits are similar to the group insurance, without the individual being required to offer any evidence of insurability.

COBRA The Consolidated Omnibus Budget Reconciliation Act of 1985. A provision of the Act requires all group health benefit plans (except for some government and church plans) to extend a conversion privilege to any individual who loses eligibility for coverage under the plan.

Review Questions

1. Identify the difference among the following programs providing death benefits on a group basis:
   a. Yearly renewable term insurance
   b. Group paid-up life insurance
   c. A program providing survivor benefits whose amount is based on the number of dependents.
2. If an employer provides $100,000 of term life insurance to an employee, are there any tax consequences? If so, who is taxed and on what basis?
3. Explain why death benefits provided under group programs typically are not provided directly by the employer.

4. Describe different methods that are used to provide disability income coverage as an employee benefit.

5. An employee participated for 30 years under the ABC Manufacturing Corporation pension plan. His annual salary the first year he participated was $20,000. This salary increased $1000 each year until he retired. What would be his monthly pension if the ABC pension plan provides for each year of service 1-1/2 percent of his average career salary? of his "final" (last five years) salary?

6. Under the normal straight life annuity form a pension plan would provide a retiring employee $2000 per month for the rest of his or her life. What provision must be made if the employee wishes to provide some income for a surviving spouse?

7. Are pension plans inflation-proof? Explain.

8. Describe the two minimum vesting schedules required by ERISA.

9. Explain the differences among the following retirement income plans:
   a. A deferred profit-sharing plan
   b. A final average salary pension plan
   c. A defined contribution plan

10. What constraints does ERISA place on eligibility restrictions used in qualified pension plans?

11. Define the terms vesting and funding as they apply to pension plans and explain their importance.

12. If a private pension plan is discontinued because of financial difficulties, how will ERISA affect:
   a. The rights of employees?
   b. The responsibility of the employer?

13. Deferred compensation and salary reduction programs such as 401(k) plans have been increasing in popularity. Why?

14. A flexible spending account allows an employee to reduce her taxable salary and use the amount set aside to purchase medical care on a tax-favored basis. Given the tax advantage, why would she not always elect to set aside the maximum amount allowed by law?

15. An employee who is covered by a defined benefit pension plan wishes to retire upon reaching age 60. Explain how this employee's retirement benefit is affected by the following provisions in the pension plan:
   a. Normal retirement age
   b. The election by the employee of a joint and survivor annuity form

16. Explain how the actuarial cost technique can affect the amount of a plan sponsor's liability when a pension plan is terminated.

17. Explain the concept of group underwriting.

18. Describe the conversion privilege in group life insurance.

19. Describe the conversion options required under COBRA for employers providing group health benefit programs.

References and Suggestions for Additional Reading

AMERICAN COUNCIL OF LIFE INSURANCE: *Life Insurance Fact Book.* (Washington, D.C.: American Council of Life Insurance, 1992 [annual]).

BEAM, BURTON G., Jr., and JOHN J. McFADDEN: *Employee Benefits* (3rd ed., Chicago: Dearborn Financial Publishing, Inc., 1992).

McCAFFERY, ROBERT M.: *Employee Benefit Programs: A Total Compensation Perspective* (Boston: PWS-Kent Publishing Company, 1988).

Pension Plan Guide (Chicago: Commerce Clearing House, Inc., multivolume looseleaf service).

Pension and Profit Sharing (Englewood Cliffs, N.J.: Prentice-Hall, Inc., multivolume loose-leaf service).

PIACENTINI, JOSEPH S., and JILL D. FOLEY: *EBRI Databook on Employee Benefits* (Washington, D.C.: Employee Benefit Research Institute, 1992 [annual]).

U.S. CHAMBER OF COMMERCE: *Employee Benefits* (Washington, D.C.: United States Chamber of Commerce, 1993 [annual]).

U.S. DEPARTMENT OF LABOR, BUREAU OF LABOR STATISTICS: *Employee Benefits in Medium and Large Private Establishments, 1991, Employee Benefits in Small Private Establishments, 1990, Employee Benefits in State and Local Governments, 1990.* (Washington, D.C.: U.S. Government Printing Office, issued in alternate years).

THE WYATT COMPANY: *Comparison* (Washington, D.C.: The Wyatt Company, published periodically).

CHAPTER 25

Design Issues in Employee Benefit Plans

Learning Objectives

After you have completed this chapter, you should be able to:

1. Describe the attributes of an efficient compensation package comprised of salary and benefits.
2. State three requirements for an employee group to prefer coverage against a human resource risk exposure in lieu of direct cash payments and explain why each requirement is important.
3. Explain why provisions typically found in dental care and vision care benefit programs almost reverse the pattern that would be expected if protection against large loss were the primary motive driving the design of the coverage.
4. Explain how social insurance programs can affect the design of an employee benefit program.
5. State three legislative objectives that are reflected in regulations applying to the design of benefit programs.
6. Describe the tax-favored treatment given to qualified medical benefits programs, life insurance programs, pension plans, and disability income programs.
7. Explain how an organization's mission can affect the design of an employee benefit program.
8. Explain how restrictions on eligibility for benefits can serve mutual interests of employees and their employer.
9. Identify advantages and disadvantages of self-funding an employee benefit program.
10. Identify issues involved in determining the financing and administration of an employee benefit program.
11. Identify the factors affecting the design of information and communication systems in benefit programs.

12. Explain how a nonqualified retirement or deferred compensation plan may still serve mutual employer-employee interests despite the absence of tax-favored treatment.

INTRODUCTION

This chapter discusses the design of employee benefit programs. Program design balances four forces: (1) the desires of employees, (2) possible effects of plan design on behavior of employees and service providers, (3) the regulatory and tax environment, including social insurance programs, and (4) the organization's mission. The interaction among these forces shapes the structure of an ideal program of benefits for a group of employees. To the extent that these forces change over time, the ideal benefit structure for an organization is likely to change as well. Changes in regulation, for example, can impose significant restrictions on the design of benefit programs.

An employer's salary policy and the structure of its benefit program determine the mix of employees' compensation between salary and noncash benefits. The structure of a benefit program is reflected in plan provisions such as: (1) the types of benefits provided, (2) conditions leading to eligibility for each type of benefit, (3) the financing method, including the determination of whether employees will be required to pay at least part of the plan's cost, and (4) the determination of whether the organization itself or a third party, such as an insurer, will be responsible for the day-to-day administration of the plan.

FORCES AFFECTING PROGRAM DESIGN

A well-designed program of benefits serves the mutual interests of an employer and its employees. The concept adopted in Chapter 11 of an organization as a set of agreements between stakeholders is useful in understanding how benefit programs can simultaneously serve employer and employee interests. Employees provide services to organizations, whose managers use these services to accomplish the organization's mission. In return for these services, the organization's managers make commitments to compensate employees.

Most of the compensation is in the form of (1) direct cash payments, (2) in-kind services and benefits, such as medical care, or (3) a promise to provide future cash payments, or in-kind services and benefits, such as retirement income or medical services. The design of employee benefit programs determines the composition of employee compensation among these three categories. Once set by the employer, the composition becomes difficult to alter except by employees electing to contribute part of their own cash to the two categories of benefits.

Even under flexible benefits programs, regulations discourage transfers between categories other than the conversion of cash into in-kind services or retirement income. For example, an employee can elect to contribute a portion of salary to a medical benefits or retirement income program, but not the other way around. If an employee has the option to receive cash in lieu of medical benefits, for example, the tax-favored status of the medical benefit is lost. Similarly, withdrawal of funds from a retirement account is likely to trigger tax penalties. Under exceptional circumstances, such as a large unreimbursed medical expense, funds may be withdrawn from a retirement account. However, this exception serves to illustrate the general rule, which discourages transfers between category 3, retirement funds and category 2, in-kind benefits, such as health care, or from either category 3 or 2 into cash.

As stated in the chapter introduction, program design balances four forces: (1) the desires of employees, (2) possible effects of plan design on behavior of employees and service providers, (3) the regulatory and tax environment, including social insurance programs, and (4) the organization's mission. The influence of these forces on program design is described in four sections below.

Desires of Employees

An efficient compensation package combines the three categories of compensation to maximize employee welfare at a given level of total compensation. An efficient allocation of compensation among these three categories implies that no other allocation is preferred by employees. Managers have an incentive to allocate compensation among these three categories efficiently because doing so reduces the organization's costs. For example, if the portion of compensation allocated to health care benefits is too large, employees would prefer direct cash payments in lieu of medical care. By reducing health care benefits and redirecting a portion of the savings into direct cash payments, the organization's managers can reduce costs while leaving employee welfare unchanged.

A given benefit program may be ideal for one category of employee but a poor choice for another. The demographics of an employee group (distribution of age and sex, income levels, number of dependents, etc.) can strongly influence the characteristics of an ideal benefit program, so changes in group composition over time can necessitate changes in program design.

Fortunately, substitution by households creates the possibility of a number of benefit program designs being efficient. For example, employee households would be expected to adjust their own savings levels in response to retirement benefit programs provided by employers. Whether household adjustments are possible depends on the nature of the benefit, the level of households' desires, and the effect of bargaining power. Retirement programs are likely to be a close substitute for household savings, for example, and advantages of employers in negotiating for retirement benefits are not likely to be strong relative to households.

In contrast, coverage for medical care is less likely to induce direct substitution. Households' access to coverage for medical care tends to be poor relative to access by large employers, which implies that shortcomings in an employer's health care benefit program are unlikely to induce households to substitute private health insurance unless the shortcomings are perceived as serious. Minor shortcomings may be met by households' direct payments to medical providers, but households will not enjoy the favorable access to medical care of an employer who has actively negotiated with medical providers. Particularly in the area of health care, program design weighs scale economies of negotiation against the possibility of providing benefits that are not perceived as valuable by all employees.

Also, households cannot adjust the allocation to most benefit areas below zero. If an employer provides a household with more life insurance coverage than the household would select if it had the employer's bargaining power vis-à-vis coverage providers, downward adjustment of the household's allocation is not possible. To the extent that households are free to take on debt, however, downward adjustment of savings in response to retirement income benefits can be accomplished through household transactions.

In the absence of taxes and transaction costs, no specific demand for benefits would arise because employees could design their own benefit programs at the employer's cost. If an employer were to offer a benefit costing $300 a month, for example, the reservation wage of employees who would have purchased the benefit using their own resources would decline by $300, the nonwage benefit being a direct substitute for cash compensation. In fact, a program providing identical benefits to a group of employees could be detrimental to mutual employer-employee interests if demands for benefits vary across employees. In the absence of taxes and transaction costs, a program of uniform benefits would not serve mutual employer-employee interests unless every employee would have purchased at least the uniform package of benefits in the absence of the program.

Clearly, assumptions leading to efficient markets that were discussed in Chapter 11 are unlikely to accommodate benefit programs, particularly ones providing uniform benefits across groups of employees whose demands for coverage are not identical. A rationale for such programs requires a belief that the employer is able to secure coverage on more favorable terms than available to employees acting on their own. When coverage is available to the employer on favorable terms, the welfare of the group is improved if the amount of coverage is no larger than the amount employees would have purchased on their own if they had access to the employer's price.

Providing uniform benefits larger than this minimum level creates the possibility of some employees preferring compensation in the form of cash. The greater the bargaining power of the employer relative to the group members individually, the higher benefit levels can become without some employees preferring direct compensation in the form of cash. In general, one would not expect employee demands for coverage to be high unless the covered risk is significant and other means of managing the risk are expensive or inadequate.

The foregoing analysis suggests three requirements for an employee group to prefer coverage against a human resource risk exposure in lieu of direct cash payments: (1) nearly all members of the group individually face a substantial exposure to the risk, (2) methods available to individuals for managing the risk are expensive, technically complicated, or inadequate, and (3) the employer has relative advantage in securing coverage. Medical care offers an example of a benefit meeting these requirements for many groups.

Possible Effects on Behavior of Employees and Service Providers

These three requirements identify the types of risk exposures likely to become candidates for employee benefit programs, but the management of an exposure meeting one or more of the tests does not automatically become more efficient if covered under such a program. Possible effects of the program on the behavior of covered employees and on providers of covered services strongly influence provisions of many types of programs. This issue is a major influence in the design of coverage for medical care services; much of Chapter 19 focused on coverage provisions designed to shape the behavior of service providers and covered persons.

Coverage for dental care offers an illustration. As noted in Chapter 19 and 24, the pattern of coverage in these plans is nearly the reverse of what would be expected if protection against large, unpredictable outlays were the major concern driving the design of the plan. The typical plan provides fairly full coverage for services such as diagnosis and routine cleaning, with limits on frequency. The most expensive procedures, such as prosthodontia, orthodontics, and inlays employing precious metals receive the least favorable reimbursement. This pattern of coverage may appear puzzling until two characteristics of dental procedures are recognized: (1) often, dental procedures can be postponed, and (2) the type of procedure performed can be influenced by cosmetic considerations. Coverage for dental care lessens any restraints against performing dental work whose cost has been a substantial deterrent. The design of coverage takes these characteristics into account. Full reimbursement of routine cleaning and examinations creates an incentive for preventive measures, while reduced benefits for the most expensive procedures act to deter consumption of services whose benefits may be largely cosmetic.

Disability income coverage offers another example. Workers' compensation programs replace income of employees who become disabled in work-related accidents, while Social Security provides disability income benefits to workers who are so severely disabled as to meet the stringent OASDI disability tests. Both programs, which are mandatory for employers, provide benefits that contribute to the income of a disabled employee. An employer-provided program of disability income benefits often is designed as a supplement to mandatory coverage, with benefits from all sources limited to a fraction (e.g., 50 percent) of the employee's income prior to disablement. The structure of the program reflects the tendency of income replacement benefits to weaken the employee's willingness to return to work. This effect becomes stronger as proportion of income replaced by benefits from all sources becomes higher.

As a final example, a retirement program whose benefits have limited portability if an employee moves to another employer can limit the mobility of employees, particularly ones nearing retirement. The same type of effect can occur if the formula for determining retirement benefits is weighted to favor years near retirement. An employer whose plan provides limited portability might take advantage of this effect by limiting salary increases for employees nearing retirement. In contrast, a savings plan or other retirement program with full portability would be expected to have no effect on mobility of covered employees.

Regulatory and Tax Environment

The structure of benefit programs is strongly influenced by government, either through regulation or through benefits provided under social insurance programs. As shown in the above example of disability benefits, one effect of social insurance programs may be to encourage provisions in employee benefit programs allowing them to supplement social insurance. However, the ultimate effect from changes in regulation may be quite different. For example, medical benefit programs initially designed to supplement Medicare later became primary coverage through a change in regulations.

Much of the regulation applying to benefit programs is embodied in administrative rulings promulgated by government agencies responsible for enforcing legislative objectives. In addition, legislative objectives themselves are subject to periodic revision as new social objectives become prominent. The complexity of the body of rules and regulations applying to benefit programs and its continuous evolution make a full discussion impractical in a single text chapter.

The laws underlying these regulations are exemplified by acronyms, such as ERISA (Employee Retirement Income Security Act of 1974), which established vesting and funding standards for retirement income programs; ADEA (Age Discrimination in Employment Act of 1985), which prohibits discrimination against older employees in benefit programs; and COBRA (Consolidated Omnibus Budget Reconciliation Act of 1985), which mandates that the option to continue health care coverage be offered to persons whose coverage becomes terminated because of a change in family status or employment. Regulations applying to retirement income programs are especially complex. Beam and McFadden (1992) offer considerable information on regulations applying to benefit programs.

Many regulations applying to benefit programs reflect three legislative objectives: (1) preventing benefit programs from favoring select groups of employees, especially highly compensated employee groups, (2) ensuring that programs provide at least a minimum benefit level through means such as mandated minimum benefits, and (3) increasing the level of security associated with the program. The long-term nature of the promises made under pension plans makes the level of security an especially important public policy issue shaping pension regulations.

In many instances, regulations do not outlaw the adoption of a certain type of provision by a plan, but instead require plans to conform to specified standards for benefits to receive favorable income tax treatment. Regulations may specifically identify a type of benefit that does not qualify for favorable income tax treatment (e.g., parking fees paid from a reimbursement account or term life insurance in excess of $50,000), but regulations usually take the form of requirements applying to a category of program. Plans meeting these requirements, called *qualified* plans, receive favorable tax treatment described below. The income tax treatment of plans not meeting these tests, called *nonqualified* plans, is less favorable.[1]

The favorable income tax treatment accorded a qualified plan results in the covered employee receiving a tax-free or tax-deferred benefit. For example, an employee is not required to report the cost of a qualified medical benefit pro-

---

[1] In the risk management and insurance literature, the terms *qualified* and *nonqualified* often are applied to retirement income programs. The concept of qualification as it applies to income tax treatment can be extended easily to benefits other than retirement income.

gram (or the benefits provided under the program) as part of his or her taxable income. In the case of retirement income benefits, the employee is not required to report employer contributions to the plan at the time the employer funds the benefits. Typically, no tax is paid until the employee actually receives benefits in the form of cash. Further, investment income on assets held for the purpose of providing these benefits generally is not subject to income tax when earned.

The taxation of qualified disability income benefit programs is similar. Employer contributions to fund the benefit program do not constitute part of the employee's taxable income, but benefits paid under the program are taxable income. If disability is so severe that it meets the stringent OASDI test of disability, tax credits are allowed.

The income tax implications of the benefit program *for the employer* are the same as if the amount contributed to the program had been paid to the employee as cash. When the employer funds the program, the employer is allowed to deduct the amount contributed, the same as if the amount had been paid directly as compensation to the employee. The net effect of this treatment in a qualified medical benefit program is to provide a tax-free benefit to the employee while still allowing the employer to deduct the cost of the program from taxable income. In a qualified retirement income plan, the net effect is tax deferral, in some cases for a substantial time period (e.g., 30 years). The employer is allowed to deduct contributions to a qualified retirement income program as the contributions are made, while the employee is not required to report income until the benefits are received by the employee as cash.[2]

The same tax advantage would be present under individual coverage if individuals could deduct from taxable income their own payments toward coverage that could be provided by employers. For example, no special tax advantage would be present in offering health benefit programs on a group basis if individuals could deduct the cost of this coverage from their taxable income. In many cases, however, tax rules are structured to provide distinct tax advantages to coverage offered as a condition of employment; at the time of writing, health insurance is a specific example. Unless the sum of an individual's health insurance premiums and unreimbursed health care expenses exceed a significant share of taxable income, they are not deductible for individuals. If provided as a condition of employment, the entire amount of these expenses receives favorable tax treatment.

In many employer-sponsored programs (including but not limited to flexible benefits plans), favorable tax treatment has been extended to employee contributions toward funding the cost of a benefit program. Employee contributions used to fund qualifying benefits are not considered part of the employee's taxable income. If an employee earns $35,000 gross income in a year, $500 of which is contributed to funding the cost of qualifying benefits, $34,500 is re-

---

[2] The description of the tax treatment of qualified benefit programs is not a legal guide. It outlines basic features of tax rules applying to these programs to provide an understanding of how taxation affects the design of benefit programs. Beam and McFadden (1992) offer additional technical information on this issue as well as on regulations for qualification, although their text is not designed as a legal guide either. The most current information is available from on-line information retrieval systems and data services.

ported as taxable income. In this example, the net effect is the same as if the employer had paid the employee $34,500 and directly contributed $500 toward the cost of the benefit program.

The tax treatment of qualified benefit programs creates an absolute advantage to employer-sponsored benefit programs, even in the absence of any other employer advantages, such as the bargaining power noted earlier. Without the qualified benefit program, an employee pays income taxes on compensation used to purchase coverage such as life and health insurance. Under qualified life and health insurance programs, the employee saves the income taxes that would have been paid if the funds had been paid to the employee as cash. Under qualified retirement programs, the tax is deferred until after the employee retires. For long deferral periods, such as 20 years, the value of the deferral can be significant.[3]

In exchange for the tax-favored treatment, the employer agrees to abide by the complex and ever-changing web of regulations applying to qualified plans. These regulations, particularly ones discouraging discrimination, create the possibility of some employees preferring cash to the benefit. In concept, a flexible benefits program offers design features that provide an escape route from this problem. Employees simply adjust the allocation of their accounts to achieve an ideal balance between different forms of compensation. The problem is that unused amounts cannot be rolled over into cash and near-cash (e.g., 401(k) plans) without jeopardizing the tax status of the benefits.

The Organization's Mission

In an organization, an expenditure of resources can be justified if it contributes toward achieving the organization's mission. The concept of an organization as a collection of agreements between resource suppliers and managers is helpful in understanding how the expenditure is justified. As explained in Chapter 11, the collection of agreements is directed toward the organization's mission. Individuals provide resources to organizations, whose managers assemble the resources and employ them to accomplish the mission. In return for these resources, the organization's managers make commitments to compensate the individuals who provide them. Benefits are but one form that the compensation can take.

One effect of a well-designed benefit program can be an improvement in employee morale. Morale is likely to be improved when the coverage meets the three earlier-noted requirements for an employee group to prefer a benefit in lieu of direct cash payments: nearly all members of the group individually face a substantial exposure to the risk; available methods for managing the risk are expensive, technically complicated, or inadequate; and the employer has relative advantage in securing coverage.

---

[3] At an 8 percent interest rate, a $1 deposit accumulates to $4.66 after 20 years. If a 30 percent tax rate applies to the total amount but deferred until the end of the 20 years, $3.26 remains after taxes. If interest earnings had been taxable currently, the 8 percent interest would have been reduced to 5.6 percent after taxes. If, in addition, the $1 deposit had been taxed when made, $0.70 would have remained as the initial after-tax deposit. The $0.70 deposit earning 5.6 percent interest after taxes would have accumulated to $2.08 after 20 years, as compared to $3.26 when taxes are deferred.

However, an improvement in morale is not necessarily a requirement for a benefit program to be successful. As explained earlier, one objective of a benefit program is to provide cost-effective compensation. Because cost-effective compensation packages are less expensive than inefficient ones, they increase resources available for accomplishing the organization's mission. Also, cost-effective compensation increases earnings available for distribution to the organization's owners, which is part of the mission of privately held firms.

In some instances, benefits may be tied directly to the organization's mission. An example in the public sector might be a local authority whose mission includes the maintenance of public health. Providing a health benefit program for employees directly serves this stated mission. The program also contributes indirectly to this mission by setting a standard for other employers in the community.

Benefit programs can contribute directly to the organization's mission in another way. Particularly in small or closely held business firms, the organization's mission may be tied closely to the owners' welfare. The close tie between owners' welfare and the organization's mission creates the possibility that benefit programs in these organizations may be created for the explicit purpose of benefiting owners or some other specially favored group. The supplemental executive retirement plan (SERP) described later in this chapter is one example of a plan designed for this purpose. Because these programs usually do not qualify for favorable tax treatment, they may appear inefficient if only tax-reduction motives are considered. However, constraints imposed by qualification requirements on the design of a program can be so strong that tax advantages of qualification cannot overcome costs of complying. This issue arises when demands for benefits (e.g., for retirement income) vary across categories of employees but regulations do not allow a qualified plan to accommodate the variation in demands.

BASIC DECISIONS IN GROUP BENEFIT PROGRAMS

The first issue encountered in designing a benefit program is the decision on whether to offer a given type of benefit. Next is the decision on the level or amount of the benefit to provide under the program. In the case of flexible benefits programs, the allocation to employee's individual accounts is determined. Although the design of a benefit program might appear complete at this point, in most cases, the the most complex issues are yet to be determined: eligibility requirements; financing and administration; and the design of information, reporting, and communication systems. This section discusses these issues as they affect the design of benefit programs.

Eligibility Requirements

The timing and extent to which employees become entitled to a given type of benefit are spelled out in a program's eligibility requirements. For some benefits, employees become entitled to the full amount immediately upon employment. For other benefits, employees may gradually acquire entitlement (e.g., gradual vesting in a pension plan), or the benefit may become available only after a waiting period. When employees have the right to switch between optional benefits within the same program (e.g., choosing between different medical plans) the freedom to choose may be restricted to an *open enrollment period* (e.g., the last two months of each calendar year). At the time the employee first enters employment, these same options may be offered; after that point, the option to switch becomes available only during the open enrollment period.

Because restrictions on eligibility can raise concerns about equity among employees, strong government regulations often apply to this aspect of a benefit program. The usual justifications for restricting eligibility are related to possible adverse selection and record-keeping costs. The discussion of dental benefit programs appearing earlier in this chapter illustrates how concern with adverse selection can affect plan design. Providing full and immediate access to dental benefits creates the possibility of heavy use during the first year of employment by individuals who have neglected dental care, increasing their compensation relative to other employee subgroups. Full and immediate access might even result in an individual accepting employment for only the period of time needed to have dental work performed. Perhaps ideally, a set of eligibility requirements that recognizes these problems might provide full and immediate access to routine cleaning and examinations (which are restricted in frequency for all covered persons), with eligibility for other procedures delayed for a period such as one year.

A defined benefit pension plan can illustrate how possible record-keeping costs affect the design of a benefit program. Particularly in a group of employees in which substantial turnover is expected in the first year or two of employment, record-keeping burdens for a defined benefit pension plan offering full and immediate vesting could be burdensome related to benefits actually delivered to the group. Cost savings that result from vesting delayed beyond the period of substantial turnover could be used to improve benefits actually provided to retired persons. When record-keeping burdens and adverse selection programs are small, however, full and immediate eligibility would not be expected to create any special problems. Group life insurance offers an example of a type of benefit in which adverse selection problems and record-keeping burdens would be expected to be minimal.

Financing and Administration

The responsibility for financing and administering a benefit program is allocated among three individuals or entities: group members, the plan sponsor, and the insurer or plan administrator. The financing decision determines the allocation of (1) financial burdens of the plan, and (2) the risk associated with the group's use of the benefit program. These two aspects of a benefit program are not necessarily the same. For example, an employee benefit program may require employees to pay part of the cost, with the employer shouldering the burdens of unexpected increases in benefit costs.

With respect to item 1, the financial burdens, a distinction between *contributory* and *noncontributory* plans is fundamental. Under contributory plans, group members pay part or all of the cost of coverage. Under noncontributory plans, the plan sponsor pays the full cost of coverage. Neither approach has a conclusive advantage over the other, and both are used widely. Noncontributory plans are popular with covered employee groups and often are simple to administer. Contributory plans create an awareness and possibly an appreciation among group members about the cost of the plan, but also may lead group members to want a voice in designing the plan when the plan sponsor would prefer that plan design be solely or primarily under its control.

With respect to item 2, the risk of the plan, the financial risk of the group's claims may be transferred to an insurer or it may be allocated between the plan sponsor and group members. Co-payments, deductibles, and participation required in medical benefit programs can be considered methods for allocating part of the financial risk to group members themselves.

At one extreme is a fully insured plan, in which the financial risk is borne by an insurer. Plans that are fully contributory (i.e., in which group members pay the full cost) often are fully insured. A manually rated life insurance plan on a small employee group offers a second illustration of a fully insured approach. At the other extreme is a plan in which an administrator provides only claim-adjustment and other services for a fee, with the administrator bearing none of the financial risk of the plan. Large group medical benefit programs (e.g., a plan covering 10,000 employees) often use this ASO approach. This approach also is common in defined benefit pension plans, in which plan administration is delegated to a trustee. A variety of options, such as experience rating, retrospective rating, minimum premium plans, and, in the case of pensions, deposit administration and separate account plans, lie between these extremes. With the exception of pension financing plans, these financing options are described in Chapter 10 of this text.

If an insured plan requires payment of premiums at the beginning of the period of coverage, a decision to self-fund a benefit program can have a favorable immediate effect on cash flow. In addition, self-funding may allow the plan sponsor to avoid other costs of insurance, such as the state tax on insurers' premium income. If benefit mandates applying to insurance do not apply to self-funded plans, greater freedom may be present in the design of self-funded plans. In exchange for these advantages, the plan sponsor directly bears the financial consequences of a self-funded plan, giving the sponsor a stake in the design and administration of the plan.

Although plan administration at first may appear unrelated to the method of financing, in fact the two decisions are related. When a plan is fully insured, for example, the insurer typically is responsible for claims administration. In this instance, the party bearing the financial risk also has control of activities affecting the financial burden. At the other extreme, an employer that self-insures a benefit program may assume full responsibility for claims administration, again resulting in the party bearing the financial burden having control over the evolution of the burden.

A variety of alternatives exist between these extremes. In some, the party bearing the financial burden delegates some or all of the administrative activities to another party. For example, employers commonly delegate claims administration in health benefit programs to an insurer or an organization that specializes in adjusting medical claims for a fee. Purchasing these services relieves the plan sponsor of problems associated with hiring and training the staff required for this activity. Most organizations would not be expected to possess any special skills in medical claims administration, skills that an organization specializing in the area would be more likely to develop. Specialists in medical claims administration that manage a large number of benefit plans also may offer data collection and analysis services that are beyond the capacity of even a large employer to provide. Such services may be useful in identifying cost-effective medical providers and procedures.

The use of a separate organization instead of the employer's own claims processing staff also can reduce the likelihood of employee resentment against the employer when the administrator enforces restrictive plan provisions. In addition, the purchase of health claims administration from health insurers may entitle the sponsor to discounted prices negotiated by the insurer with health care providers. Employers often continue to be responsible for administrative activities over which they have control and access to information: enrollment, disenrollment, and payroll deduction in contributory plans.

However, possible financial incentives can become an important issue when plan administration and financing are unbundled. If the party bearing the plan's financial burden delegates claims administration to a specialist, a natural incentive to administer claims in a cost-effective manner becomes weakened. Especially when the compensation to the claims administrator is positively related to claims activity, other controls such as claim audits or experience reports may be required. Such reports allow the plan's experience to be contrasted against benchmark data. The preparation and analysis of claims audits, experience reports, and data to identify cost-effective medical procedures and providers adds to the administrative burdens of the benefit program, of course.

Information and Communication Systems in Benefit Programs

Benefit programs can place heavy burdens on an organization's information systems. The information system used for the organization's payroll offers a foundation for the benefit information system because of the close connection between benefits and other forms of compensation. Typically, the benefit information system is more complex than the payroll system. Even when an organization purchases claims administration from a specialist, a large amount of data storage and processing may be required to determine individuals currently eligible for benefits (e.g., eligible dependents), levels of benefits if more than one plan is available, and contribution levels in contributory plans. Flexible benefits programs and flexible spending accounts impose especially heavy record-keeping burdens on benefit programs. Such programs would be impractical or impossible without modern data processing equipment and software dedicated to the task of benefit administration.

Additional data storage and processing capability is imposed by the COBRA requirements that an employer notify individuals who lose their eligibility for benefits of their right to continue coverage under an individual policy. For example, federal law requires an employer to contact a dependent who passes an age threshold at which eligibility is lost and offer the dependent an opportunity to continue health insurance coverage. Failing to meet this notification requirement is likely to result in the employer offering retroactive coverage (at the legally required 102 percent of the employer's average cost) when dependents file claims that are denied because the dependent is past the age of eligibility.

The design of an information system considers procedures for collecting, storing, and analyzing data; the equipment and software used to store and process the data; and materials used to communicate plan provisions to employees. The information collected and stored may include data on enrollment and disenrollment, eligible dependents, claims data to determine whether an employee has met deductible and other cost-sharing arrangements, employee choices in flexible benefit programs, employee contributions and expenditures if flexible spending accounts are available, and, if the plan is self-funded, cost data and other data used to evaluate plan performance. In self-funded health benefit programs especially, data allowing the identification of specific medical procedures and providers of medical services may be required for meaningful performance evaluation.

Cost data collected in a benefit program may be required for legally mandated disclosure to regulators and to tax authorities. Other uses include periodic reports to employees on plan performance and cost levels, setting of employer and employee contribution rates, the reporting of total costs of compensation in collective bargaining sessions, the preparation of reports to management on plan performance, and for comparison against benchmark data available from sources such as compensation and benefit surveys offered by benefit consulting firms. Particularly in plans providing medical benefits, performance evaluation often is based on a ratio, such as cost per employee-year or cost as a percentage of payroll. Cost data in this form also may be simple to interpret. Employees are more likely to appreciate a statement that the employer's share of health plan costs last year was $5500 for a typical head of family as contrasted with a report that health plan costs were $4,950,000.

A system for the collection, storage and analysis of data manages the *receipt* of information provided to a benefit program and the plan manager. Because the task of designing this part of the information system can be formidable, a plan manager may underestimate the importance of information *transmission* to persons affected by the plan, particularly employees to whom coverage is provided. The form of communication used to provide information to employees can have important effects on employee morale and on plan usage. The information should be written at a level that is understandable by covered persons, yet also be complete and accurate. If the benefit plan offers different options, the financial effects of choosing different options should be clearly communicated in documents provided to employees. In addition, important legal requirements apply to the timing, amount, clarity, and level of information offered to employees. McCaffery (1988, ch. 10) offers guidelines and illustrations useful in designing these communications with employees.

NONQUALIFIED DEFERRED COMPENSATION AND RETIREMENT PLANS

Most of Chapters 24 and 25 has been devoted to describing qualified benefit programs and explaining their rationale. Nonqualified plans also deserve brief attention because a risk manager may be consulted in the design of this type of plan. Nonqualified plans often are found in businesses that are privately or closely held. When these plans are designed to favor highly compensated individuals, they fail to meet regulations against discrimination applying to qualified plans. When the mission of a small or closely owned organization is tied closely to the welfare of its owners, regulations may not allow a qualified plan to fully meet this aspect of the organization's mission. Often, a nonqualified plan exists alongside a qualified plan applying to all employees in the same organization.

Regulations applying to qualified benefit programs are complex and ever-changing. Faced with the complex web of regulations, an employer may question whether a qualified benefit program is worth the effort. The widespread usage of qualified benefit programs suggests that the answer to this question is yes in many cases. In a few cases, however, regulations applying to qualified plans are too stringent. The relatively few cases in which the plan is not qualified are the subject of this section. Two types of nonqualified plans are discussed: deferred compensation plans and the supplemental executive retirement plan (SERP).

Because few if any regulations apply to nonqualified plans, their design tends to be simpler than comparable qualified plans. In designing a nonqualified plan, however, a risk manager may consider the possibility of future changes in regulation that may restrict or even prohibit the plan. One way to consider the possibility is to enumerate possible effects on covered persons and on the organization itself if the plan were to be modified in response to future changes in regulation. If life insurance is used to fund the plan, for example, the risk manager may enumerate the effects of surrendering or otherwise modifying the policy if new regulations were to make such changes necessary.

Deferred Compensation

Under a deferred compensation plan, an employee defers receipt of salary under a later time period, usually after retirement. Typically, the deferred salary payments are credited with interest to determine the ultimate payment. For the employee, the advantage of deferring salary is the deferral of tax payments on this salary. In addition, if the employee is in a lower tax bracket when the deferred salary is paid, the employee's ultimate tax burden is reduced. The typical deferred compensation plan is not qualified, in which case no funding requirements necessarily apply. The deferred compensation plan is simply a promise by the employer to pay future salary, and the source of the future payments simply might be expected future earnings. When the plan is funded, life insurance might be used as a funding mechanism.

In concept, deferred compensation is taxed like ordinary salary or wages: the compensation is taxable to the employee and deductible by employer in the year that it is paid to the employee. The doctrine of *constructive receipt* governs the timing of the deduction for the employer and the reporting by employee. The employee is deemed to be in constructive receipt of the compensation when he or she acquires an irrevocable right, even though the employee may not be paid in cash at that time.

For the employee to avoid reporting the employer's contribution as current taxable income, the employee must face a *substantial risk of forfeiture*. A substantial risk of forfeiture is present if assets used to fund the deferred compensation are subject to claims of the employer's creditors and payment of the compensation is contingent on the employee remaining with the employer. If the employer were to make premium payments to a whole life insurance policy owned by the employee, for example, the premium payments would be considered part of the employee's taxable income. If the life insurance is owned by the employer and not shielded from claims by the employer's creditors, the employee faces a substantial risk of forfeiture when payment of the deferred salary is contingent on the employee remaining with the employer. The latter condition allows deferred compensation to serve as a method for tying a talented executive to an employer.

Supplemental Executive Retirement Plan

A supplemental executive retirement plan (SERP) is a nonqualified pension plan designed to provide supplemental retirement income to a specific individual, possibly as a reward for long service to an employer. For example, a SERP could provide a $2000 monthly income to an executive payable over 10 years, with payments commencing on the date of the executive's retirement. The $2000 monthly income is a supplement, payable in addition to the benefit from the employer's qualified pension plan applying to all employees. Because the SERP discriminates in favor of a selected executive who is likely to be highly compensated in other ways, the SERP does not meet standards required for qualification.

In concept, a SERP closely resembles a deferred compensation agreement. Because a SERP is not qualified, it does not enjoy the same degree of legal protection and favorable tax treatment accorded a qualified plan. Three aspects of a nonqualified SERP are discussed in this section: (1) the tax treatment, (2) the funding mechanism, and (3) the degree of legal protection and security.

Tax Treatment. The tax treatment of a SERP closely resembles the tax treatment of deferred compensation plans. The employer is allowed to deduct contributions to the plan in the same year the employee reports them as taxable income. The timing of the deduction and reporting is determined by the principle of constructive receipt. The employee is not required to report employer contributions as long as a substantial risk of forfeiture is present. If life insurance or any other asset is used to fund the SERP, for example, the employee would be required to report employer contributions as current taxable income if the funding assets are shielded against possible action by the employer's creditors in bankruptcy proceedings.

The Funding Mechanism. Life insurance agents and financial planners may suggest life insurance as a funding vehicle. Typically, the employer is the owner and beneficiary of the life insurance policy. Because the employer is the owner of the policy, the policy's cash value appears as an asset on the employer's balance sheet. The costs of funding the SERP are accrued over the executive's years of active employment but are offset by increases in the policy's cash value in the employer's financial reports. Upon the executive's death, the employer receives the face amount of insurance, which offsets any accrued costs remaining on the ledger of the SERP.

The life insurance may be set aside in a trust agreement. If the trust is owned by the employer but the use of trust assets is restricted to the payment of promised retirement benefits during the executive's lifetime, the trust may be called a *rabbi trust,* so named after an agreement used to fund the retirement of a rabbi. If the trust is owned by the executive, it may be called a *secular trust.* Employer contributions to a secular trust usually would be considered taxable income to the employee. Employer contributions to a rabbi trust usually would not be taxable income if the employee faces a substantial risk of forfeiture.

Degree of Legal Protection and Security. The SERP is an agreement to provide a monthly income to the executive after retirement. Typically, the promise to provide retirement income is unsecured, so the executive is in the position of an unsecured creditor with respect to claiming benefits promised under the SERP. Because the plan is not qualified, no special regulations apply to the mechanism used to fund the SERP or even require that any funding be present. Funding of an SERP does not create the same type of assurance as funding of a qualified pension because the employee must face a substantial risk of forfeiture or else be taxed on the employer's contribution to the SERP. Funding the SERP in a manner that guarantees the future benefit to the employee almost certainly will create taxable current income to the employee.

The presence of a life insurance policy has little if any effect on this conclusion. If the employer owns the life insurance policy and becomes insolvent, the life insurance is merged with the employer's other assets used to satisfy claims of the employer's creditors. Also, the executive's claim for supplemental income is merged with other creditors' claims. The rabbi trust's restriction that trust assets be used only for payment of benefits to the retired executive offers some protection against arbitrary actions of future management who might decide to renege on the agreement. The restriction does not protect the executive against the employer's insolvency. Reducing the risk of forfeiture (e.g., transferring ownership of assets to a trust owned by the executive prior to retirement) is likely to create taxable income for the executive, even though the executive receives no cash.

The Use of Life Insurance. In concept, any type of asset could be used to fund a SERP, or the SERP could be unfunded. If life insurance owned by the employer in a rabbi trust is used to fund the SERP, the executive has some protection against arbitrary actions by future management. This protection, however, arises from the terms of the trust agreement, not any special characteristics of life insurance.

In one respect, life insurance receives favorable treatment as compared with other assets that might be used to fund a SERP: life insurance is a tax-favored investment. While the executive is alive, increases in the policy's cash value are not considered part of the owner's taxable income. Further, death benefits paid to the employer who owns the policy and designates itself as beneficiary usually would not be considered taxable income to the employer. However, these favorable tax consequences would arise in the absence of the SERP. In other words, the issue of whether life insurance is a good funding mechanism is resolved by asking whether the life insurance is a good investment, independent of its use as a funding mechanism for a SERP. When the untaxed rate of return on the life insurance policy exceeds the after-tax rate of return the employer could earn on alternative investments carrying the same degree of risk as the life insurance, the life insurance will compare favorably to other alternatives. If the employer would not hold the life insurance in the absence of a SERP, however, establishing the SERP creates no special reason to hold the policy.

Key Concepts

qualified plan   A benefit program meeting standards required for tax-favored treatment.

nonqualified plan   A benefit program that fails to meet one or more of the standards required for tax-favored treatment.

open enrollment period   A period of time during which employees have the right to switch between optional benefits plans within the same program (e.g., choosing between different medical plans). The open enrollment period usually occurs every year, and at the time an employee first enters employment.

contributory plan   A benefit plan in which group members pay part or all of the cost of coverage.

noncontributory plan   A benefit plan in which the plan sponsor (such as an employer) pays the full cost of coverage.

deferred compensation plan   A benefit plan providing for the deferral of salary or other compensation, usually for the purpose of deferring income taxes on the compensation.

SERP   Supplemental executive retirement plan. A benefit plan, usually nonqualified, that provides a supplemental

retirement income benefit to an executive or other favored employee.

constructive receipt   In nonqualified benefit plans, a legal doctrine governing the timing of an employer's deduction for compensation paid to an employee and the reporting of the compensation as part of taxable income by the employee. The employee is deemed to be in constructive receipt of the compensation when he or she acquires an irrevocable right to receive it.

substantial risk of forfeiture   In nonqualified benefit plans, a legal doctrine determining when an employee is deemed to be in constructive receipt of compensation. Constructive receipt does not occur if the employee faces a substantial risk of forfeiture.

rabbi trust   A trust agreement applying to funds held to finance a nonqualified retirement benefit to a favored employee. A rabbi trust is owned by the employer.

secular trust   A trust agreement applying to funds held to finance a nonqualified retirement benefit to a favored employee. A secular trust is owned by the employee.

Review Questions

1. An employee's total compensation can be segmented into three categories: (1) cash, (2) in-kind benefits, such as health care, and (3) promised future income. Explain how you would determine whether the allocation of an employee's total compensation among these three categories could be improved.

2. List three requirements that a human resource risk exposure should meet for employees to prefer coverage against the exposure in lieu of direct cash payments. Explain why each requirement is important.

3. Explain why many dental benefit programs delay eligibility for one year.

4. Explain how OASDI disability benefits can affect the design of a disability benefit program provided by an employer to employees.

5. Identify the legislative objectives reflected in the following regulations:
   a. ERISA funding standards
   b. The COBRA requirement that an employer offer continued coverage to an individual who loses eligibility under a health benefit plan
   c. ERISA vesting standards.

6. Describe the tax treatment of the following types of benefit programs, assuming that the program qualifies for tax-favored treatment:
   a. term life insurance
   b. group universal life insurance
   c. a retirement income program
   d. a disability income program.

7. What would be the advantages and disadvantages of using full and immediate vesting instead of one of the minimum vesting schedules required by ERISA?

8. Explain how an organization's mission can affect the design of an employee benefit program.

9. Explain how a one-year delay on employees' eligibility to participate in a pension plan can mutually benefit the employer and the group of employees.

10. List the items of data that an employer must store as a result of establishing a program of medical benefits for its employees.

11. Identify possible problems that may arise when the party bearing the financial burdens of a benefit program delegates the responsibility for claims administration to another party.

12. Explain how an employer should communicate to employees the terms and availability of a newly established program of flexible spending accounts.

13. List the advantages and disadvantages of self-funding an employee benefit program.

14. Explain why an employer may establish a nonqualified SERP or deferred compensation plan covering a few executives despite availability of tax-favored qualified pension plans.

References and Suggestions for Additional Reading

BEAM, BURTON G., Jr., and JOHN J. MCFADDEN: *Employee Benefits* (3rd ed., Chicago: Dearborn Financial Publishing, Inc., 1992).

MCCAFFERY, ROBERT M.: *Employee Benefit Programs: A Total Compensation Perspective* (Boston, Mass.: PWS-Kent Publishing Company, 1988).

PIACENTINI, JOSEPH S., and JILL D. FOLEY: *EBRI Databook on Employee Benefits* (Washington, D.C.: Employee Benefit Research Institute, 1992 [annual]).

THE WYATT COMPANY: *Comparison* (Washington, D.C.: The Wyatt Company, published periodically).

Indexes

Index of Authors and Sources

Subject Index